Resources
tre

DIGITAL AND MICROPROCESS
ENGINEERING
Second Edition

DIGITAL AND MICROPROCESSOR ENGINEERING
Second Edition

S. J. CAHILL
Department of Electrical and Electronic Engineering,
Faculty of Science and Technology,
University of Ulster

ELLIS HORWOOD
NEW YORK   LONDON   TORONTO   SYDNEY   TOKYO   SINGAPORE

First published in 1993 by
ELLIS HORWOOD LIMITED
Market Cross House, Cooper Street,
Chichester, West Sussex, PO19 1EB, England

A division of
Simon & Schuster International Group
A Paramount Communications Company

© Ellis Horwood Limited, 1993

Printed and bound in Great Britain
by Redwood Press, Melksham

British Library Cataloguing in Publication Data

A catalogue record for this book is available from the British Library

ISBN 0–13–217928–8   (Hardback)
ISBN 0–13–213398–9   (Paperback)

Library of Congress Cataloging-in-Publication Data

Available from the publisher

26.9.94

Contents

To my wife Noreen, who has made everything worthwhile.

Preface

000

Digital electronic techniques have been around since before the electron was discovered. Historically the first commercial electronic system (defining the term electronic as pertaining to information processing by electrical means) was the electric telegraph. This communications system was based on a digital code devised by Samuel Morse around 1830. It was the harbinger of the coming electronic revolution of the 20th century.

The relay and allied electromechanical switches remained the only significant electronic device for over 50 years. Thus the development of electromagnetic switching networks was of paramount importance; and indeed many ingenious mechanisms were patented in that period.

During the early 20th century, the development of digital systems was overshadowed by analog systems, such as the telephone and radio. Nevertheless, some important work was done in applying switching networks to automatic telephone exchanges, railway signalling and similar applications. However, the most significant development was in the field of electromechanical business machines, which led shortly after the second world war to the stored-program computer.

Under the impetus of the digital computer, digital electronics and computer science became subjects in their own right. The rediscovery of Boolean algebra helped provide systematic design techniques. Digital implementation rapidly developed from relays through thermionic tubes and diodes to transistors and integrated circuits. Together with the growth of electronic technologies came a subtle change in the role of the hardware designer. Up to the early 1960s, most design tasks involved the extensive use of discrete components, which were used to build elementary digital elements such as gates and bistables. In practice, this preoccupation with circuit design limited the complexity of the overall system.

With the use of transistors and the printed-circuit board, some progress was made towards the concept of systems engineering, where design concentrated on interconnecting functional modules — often bought-in. This approach was accelerated with the introduction of SSI (eg. gates and bistables); MSI (eg. registers and arithmetic units) and LSI (subsystems such as memories and counter-timer chains).

The logical outcome of this trend was the provision of a complete system on a single integrated circuit. Although fabrication technology made this possible by the early 1970s, the economics of the profitable production of VLSI circuits is such that a large number of identical devices must be produced. By inference, this requires a general-purpose system architecture. The interconnection pattern of a typical digital system shows little order, or correlation between systems. This random pattern makes the large-scale production of a general system IC difficult. To overcome this problem the semiconductor houses turned away from the essentially parallel operating random logic concept to the structured serially operating bus-oriented computer architecture. The integrated bus controller and processing unit, known as a microprocessor (MPU), fulfils the role of a general-purpose system. The personality of a MPU-based system is imparted by storing code patterns in memory (which is itself regularly organized). For dedicated MPU-based circuits, this was normally programmable read-only memory (PROM); i.e. a 'blank' VLSI device which could be cheaply mass produced and later personalized by the end user.

In essence the core Preface of the first edition in 1981 ended at this point. In the intervening decade there have been many developments; the more important of which are:

- A ten-fold increase in the fabrication density of VLSI circuits, at no greater cost. Circuits with more than 1 million gates are in normal commercial use; such as the 68040 MPU.

- A parallel growth in the concept of the PROM, with a variety of user programmable logic devices architectures replacing most of the SSI and MSI circuitry, popular in the preceding decade.

- A dramatic fall in the cost of computer coupled with a similar rise in the power of the personal computer has led to the general use of computer-aided engineering (CAE) in the design, documentation and production of electronic systems.

- The use of the ANSII/IEC symbology to represent complex logic devices.

This new edition has tried to reflect these changes, whilst remembering that new students still must begin at the beginning. The original quoted:

> ... in order to efficiently implement current logic systems, the digital designer must be conversant with random logic, programmable logic and software. The objective of this text is to cover these topics in a progressive and unified manner.

This is still the intention.

The book commences by distinguishing between analog and digital concepts, from which the reader is taken through arithmetic algorithms, Boolean algebra, combinational and sequential circuit design. The treatment progresses from tradition gate-based design, through MSI, LSI and programmable VLSI. The MPU is treated in a bottom-up fashion; as a VLSI-based extension to random logic design, rather than as a top-down approach from computer science. This form of treatment enables the reader to design MPU chips into their circuit as a component, i.e. just another IC. It is in this area of dedicated embedded logic that the majority of MPUs are utilized rather than in computers. The text ends with examples of the use of CAE in both the areas of programmable logic and in MPU-code production. IEC/ANSII symbology is used throughout the text and described as it usefully arises. Appendix A provides an overall summary, which can be used for reference purposes.

Some selectivity must be exercised in using real-world products to illustrate an introductory text. In choosing a range of hardware devices and software packages, I have kept two principles in mind. The first of these is the KIS (Keep It Simple) factor to avoid describing the latest tempting gismo. The second of these is the creeping featurism syndrome, which as applied to textbooks, is the temptation to include just one more indispensable chip — the net result being an encyclopaedia. Thus I make no apology in the omission of your favorite chip/package.

The book has been designed to cover material suitable for two semester courses in digital and microprocessor engineering in degree and diploma courses in electronic engineering, computer science and the physical sciences. It should also prove useful to the industrially-based engineer wishing to update or broaden his or her area of application.

If the reader uses this text it was written, the field of specialist literature will be open to him/her. If the same reader gains a fraction of what I have learned in the writing of this text, I will consider the book a success.

S.J. Cahill   University of Ulster at Jordanstown, October, 1992.

Chapter 1

001

Introduction

1.1 What is Digital Data?

In our everyday dealings with the world, we naturally use digital concepts and manipulations. The vast majority of our representations of quantities involve the use of digits, usually in the form of patterns of ten possible digit values known as the decimal system. To appreciate the role of digital techniques in electronic engineering, we need a basic understanding of the two types of electrical signal representation; that is analog and digital.

After reading this section you should:

- Appreciate the difference between analog and digital signals.

- Understand the digital system concepts of multiplexing, the sampling theorm, resolution, quantizing noise, analog/digital signal conversion.

- Understand the binary 8-4-2-1 radix number system and octal, hexadecimal and BCD equivalents.

- Be able to convert between radix numbers of different bases.

- Understand the formats, advantages and disadvantages of fixed- and floating-point numbers.

- Appreciate common codes, including unweighted examples such as 7-segment and ASCII.

- To be able to convert between Gray and 8-4-2-1 binary codes.

1.1.1 Digital Versus Analog Systems

This book is concerned primarily with the processing of electronic data represented in a digital form. The manipulation of data depends radically on whether it is in analog or digital form.

The IEEE Dictionary of Electrical and Electronic Terms [1] defines the adjective **digital** as pertaining to data in the form of digits, i.e. implying data expressed as digits.**Analog**, on the other hand, pertains to data in the form of continuously variable physical quantities. The information content of an analog signal lies in the value of some constituent parameter, such as its amplitude, frequency, or phase. Digital signals convey their information in the form of arrangements of discrete digits. Processing such signals essentially consists of pattern manipulation. The particular system output pattern existing at any one time depends on the input pattern past and/or present, in a defined way.

As an example illustrating these concepts, consider the problem of measuring the level of an opaque fluid in a transparent tank, and transmitting the information electrically. One solution is to position a number of photocells at various heights, as shown in Fig. 1.1(a). Each of the ten cells is connected to a transmission link, and two values only are transmitted, representing light or dark. The patterns of the received data indicates the height. If we represent light by 0 and dark by 1, then from the diagram the received pattern will be 0000011111, a height of five units. Thus a specific pattern of digits represents a pre-determined height. This particular digital system uses a **binary** notation. Binary means two, implying that only two digits are used, eg. 0 and 1. Having only two states means that each digit can be physically represented with an electrical switch; just about the simplest electronic device. Simplicity means high speed and low cost. Thus virtually all practical digital systems are binary, although other bases are possible.

There are several points of interest which can be illustrated here, concerning the particular **code** (list of patterns) used. The first point regards the possibility of errors occurring. One of the major advantages of the binary system is the reduction in the possibility of error, as the receiver only needs to distinguish between two values. However, even with an enhanced noise immunity, transmission errors can happen, and there is always the possibility of failures occurring in some of the photocells. Consider a received pattern 0010011111, which is clearly in error, as it is a non-allowed or illegal code. Not only can certain errors be detected, but on the assumption that only a single error has occurred, the data may be corrected to read 0000011111. This process is a specific example of digital data processing, known as error correction.

The second point concerns the concept of **resolution** in electrical measurements. In this example, the resolution, or minimum increment of discernment, is a tenth part of full scale. An increase in resolution using this technique is only possible by using more photocells, and hence transmission paths.

In fact the code used for transmission is highly redundant, as only four binary digits can represent up to 16 (2^4) different values. The table shown in Fig. 1.2(a) shows one of the many possibilities of transmitting the same data using only four lines. As ten levels have still to be detected, the same photocell array is required, but before transmission a stage of digital processing would be necessary to convert from one code to another, see Fig. 1.2(b). Irrespective of the code used, each transmitted pattern depends uniquely on the input, and not on the past history of inputs. Such processing is known as **combinational**. If the outputs of a circuit depend on the sequence of input codes presented in time, then the processing is **sequential**.

One disadvantage in using a more efficient code is the reduction or loss of the error detecting facility, as the ratio of illegal to legal combinations is much small-

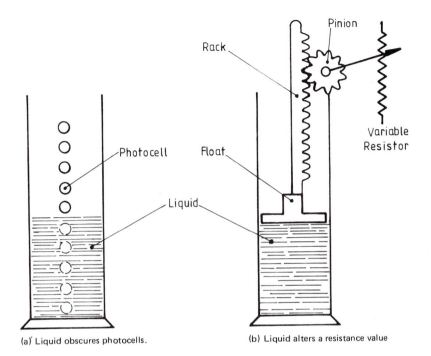

(a) Liquid obscures photocells.   (b) Liquid alters a resistance value

Figure 1.1: Two means of determining height of a liquid.

er. Often codes are deliberately reduced in efficiency to introduce error detection/correction. In such cases systematic processing techniques exist to obtain the highest degree of efficiency consistent with the specified error protection capability [2].

If binary representation is abandoned for a decimal form, then only one transmission line is needed to carry ten (0 to 9) levels. Two lines would suffice for a hundred, whilst the equivalent binary configuration would require seven ($2^7 = 128$) lines. However, this increase in efficiency must be costed against the receiver's need to now distinguish between ten levels and the consequent reduction in the ability to reject noise (parameter fluctuation) on the line; which consequently leads to greater error rates.

Finally, returning to the binary case, multiple transmission lines were used, each carrying one digit position. Such a transmission technique is known as **parallel**. As an alternative, each digit position could be sampled and transmitted in turn. Providing the two commutation switches are held in synchronization (see Fig. 1.3), the complete pattern will eventually be received. Each digit as it is received can be stored in a memory cell or **latch**, capable of holding either the values 0 or 1. This method of data transmission is known as **serial**. It has the disadvantage of slowness, especially when each code pattern or **word** contains a large number of digits. Although both the transmitter and receiver are more complex, the use of

10 – Line Code										4 – Line Code			
O	O	O	O	O	O	O	O	O	O	O	O	O	O
O	O	O	O	O	O	O	O	O	1	O	O	O	1
O	O	O	O	O	O	O	O	1	1	O	O	1	O
O	O	O	O	O	O	O	1	1	1	O	O	1	1
O	O	O	O	O	O	1	1	1	1	O	1	O	O
O	O	O	O	O	1	1	1	1	1	O	1	O	1
O	O	O	O	1	1	1	1	1	1	O	1	1	O
O	O	O	1	1	1	1	1	1	1	O	1	1	1
O	O	1	1	1	1	1	1	1	1	1	O	O	O
O	1	1	1	1	1	1	1	1	1	1	O	O	1
1	1	1	1	1	1	1	1	1	1	1	O	1	O

(a) A more efficient code using only four lines

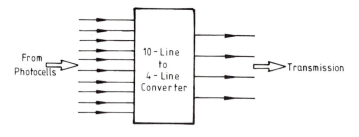

(b) A schematic of a code converter

Figure 1.2: Increasing transmission efficiency.

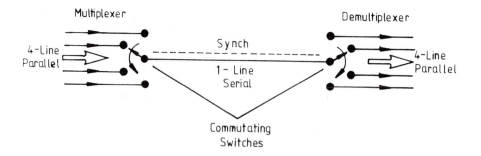

Figure 1.3: Showing how parallel data may be sent serially using time division multiplexing.

the serial system is economically justified where the transmission path is long. The method of sequential sampling is known as **time division multiplexing**.

Figure 1.1(b) shows an alternative analog height measurement scheme. A float operates a rack and pinion mechanism, which controls the value of a resistor. The change can be arranged to give a current proportional to height. Thus the transmitted current magnitude is an analog of the liquid height. The receiver could be a calibrated moving-coil meter. The relative simplicity compared to the digital e-quivalent is greater than is immediately apparent. This is because most physical quantities, such as height, pressure and speech, are naturally analog. Employing digital transmission in such instances would involve the use of an **analog to digital conversion** process at the transmitter, and perhaps **digital to analog conversion** at the receiver. An example of this is the sending of telephone speech data using digital techniques, known as **pulse code modulation** (PCM) [3]. Here the analog speech waveform is sampled at regular intervals, and the value of each sample is encoded to binary form and transmitted serially. At the receiving exchange, each binary word is stored and converted back to analog speech.

The conversion process between analog and digital representations is fairly complex [4]. Firstly, the analog signal is sampled at regular intervals, as depicted in Fig. 1.4(a). This sampling rate is important; too slow and information in the original signal will be missed; too fast and the number of samples will be expensive to handle. **Shannon's sampling theorem** states that this rate should be at least twice the highest frequency component in the analog signal [5]. In practice, a figure slightly higher than this is chosen to ease the filtering process, as illustrated in Fig. 1.4(d). Thus the PCM telephone system handling an analog bandwidth of 3.2 kHz, samples at an 8 kHz rate. The sampled analog value is compared to a series of quantum levels, each of which has an associated binary code. In Fig. 1.4(b), there are eight such levels, each represented as a 3-bit ($2^3 = 8$) binary code. This equivalent is then stored, transmitted or otherwise processed using only digital techniques.

The reverse process involves conversion of each code word to its analog equivalent, i.e. quantum level. Analog filtering then smooths out the sampled nature of this pulse amplitude modulated signal. The final signal shown in Fig. 1.4(d) is a close representation of the original. However, some differences can be seen, due to the quantizing approximations. This **quantizing noise** can be reduced by increasing the number of bits representing each sample. Our 3-bit example has a theoretical **signal to noise ratio** (S/N) of 20 dB [6]. PCM uses an 8-bit sample, giving $2^8 = 256$ quantum levels and a S/N ratio of 50 dB. Thus at 8000 samples per second, each digitized channel must carry $8000 \times 8 = 64,000$ bits per second, compared with an analog bandwidth of only 3400 cycles per second. From this numerical example, it can be seen that the noise immunity of a digital system is gained at the expense of a greater system bandwidth. Analog transmission by its nature is simple and cheap, has a theoretically infinite resolution and needs only a single line per message. Why then are more complex digital techniques used in the majority of electronic data processing systems? The answer to this lies in two disadvantages of analog representations.

A major transmission problem is the difficulty in providing an error protection capability. Consider our example of height measurement. If the analog signal is to be sent over a telephone line, then from time to time the characteristics of the path may change. If the attenuation should alter, then at the receiver it is

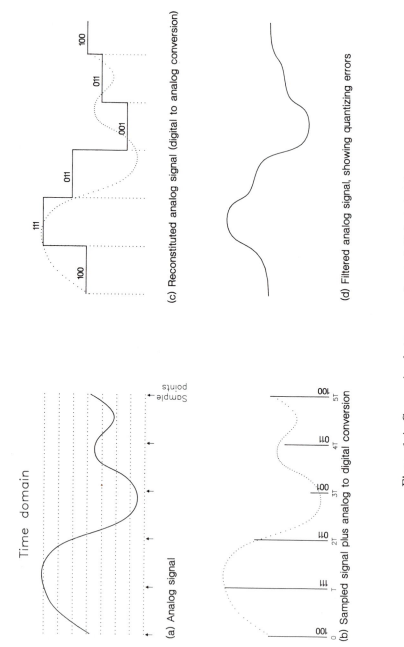

(a) Analog signal

Time domain

Sample points

(b) Sampled signal plus analog to digital conversion

(c) Reconstituted analog signal (digital to analog conversion)

(d) Filtered analog signal, showing quantizing errors

Figure 1.4: Conversion between analog and digital signals.

difficult to distinguish this from a height change. With an analog signal such noise is cumulative, i.e. cannot be removed. Using a binary representation requires only the detection of two possibilities for each digit, to give the full designed (albeit limited) resolution. Allied to the transmission problem is the deterioration of an analog signal at any processing stage. Any noise or distortion is passed on from one stage to the succeeding stage; which progressively impairs the quality of the signal.

The second major disadvantage of analog signal processing is limited **accuracy**, as opposed to resolution. The resolution of an analog signal is generally limited by the sensitivity of the receiving apparatus, such as the eye. With the aid of a magnifying glass, a moving-coil meter can be read to better than 0.1% of full scale. However, the accuracy of the reading may be only 3% full scale deflection. This is because analog processing demands a linear response for an infinite number of levels within the range, which is expensive and difficult to engineer. This sets an upper boundary to the accuracy of the reading. The only limit to the accuracy of a digital calculator, is that imposed by the number of digits used as the number representation.

	LP Long play (analog)	**CD** Compact disk (digital)
Size	30 cm (12″)	12 cm (5″)
Playing time	64 minutes (total both sides)	74 minutes (one side)
Frequency response	30 Hz–20 kHz ±3 dB	20 Hz–20 kHz ±0.5 dB
S/N ratio	60 dB	90 dB
Dynamic range	70 dB (at 1 kHz)	>90 dB
Distortion	1–2%	0.01%
Channel separation	25–30 dB	>90 dB
Wow and flutter	0.03%	Quartz crystal precision
Durability	Several tens of plays causes loss of high-frequency data. Dust, scratches and fingerprints cause noise.	Semi-permanent. Dust, scratches and finger-prints almost insignificant.

Table 1.1: A comparison of analog LP and digital CD parameters.

As a practical example, let us compare two techniques for storing audio signals. In the case of the analog process, a mechanical stylus tracks along a groove cut in vinyl plastic. The two walls of this groove are modulated with a direct analog of the original sound wave. The digital equivalent track contains bumps and pits. The original signal is sampled at 44.1 kHz, with each sample being converted to 16 bits (S/N ratio 98 dB). These bumps and pits affect the reflected light from a semi-conductor laser and hence operate a phototransistor switch. Between consecutive samples, two possibilities arise. Either the level (bump or pit) will be the same, or else there will be a change. These correspond to 0 and 1.

Figure 1.5 gives several dimensional statistics, with some performance data given in Table 1.1 [7]. Of course this is a little unfair, as we are comparing 1880's technology with 1980's. However, the latter has had over 100 years to perfect its act!

It is interesting to calculate how many bits are stored on a 12 cm audio CD.

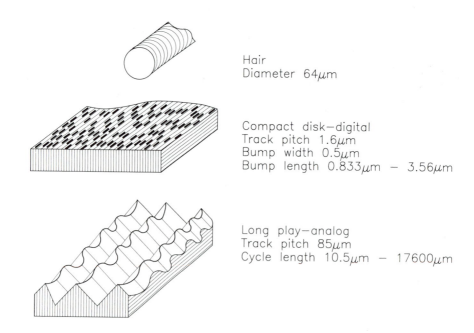

Hair
Diameter 64μm

Compact disk—digital
Track pitch 1.6μm
Bump width 0.5μm
Bump length 0.833μm — 3.56μm

Long play—analog
Track pitch 85μm
Cycle length 10.5μm — 17600μm

Figure 1.5: Digital vers analog audio.

A first approach multiplies 44.1×10^3 (sampling rate) by 16 (bits/sample) by 2 (number of channels); giving 1,411,200 bits/second. In practice extra bits are used to provide an error-correcting facility (bursts of 4000 bits — 2.5 mm/0.1″ on the disk — can be fully corrected!), track and other codes. Taking these into account, the actual capacity of a 74-minute CD is 8.6×10^9 bits! This gigantic storage capacity has led to the use of the CD-ROM (CD Read-Only Memory) for computers.

In summary, digital systems can be said to cover that class of data processing which represents quantities as patterns of digits. A further subdivision is based on the number of different digits used in the representation, with 2-digit (binary) schemes by far the most common. Digital processing has the advantages of noise immunity, in the broad sense including errors, and having a resolution which can easily be tailored to fit a particular requirement.

Processing in digital systems is mainly concerned with pattern recognition and conversion; whilst in the case of analog, amplification and frequency-response tailoring. Analog systems are inferior from the point of view of both noise immunity and accuracy, but are often cheaper to implement and maintain, if the specification is not too rigorous. Often it is possible to combine the advantages of both types in one system by using a mixture of both techniques, in so called hybrid circuits.

1.1.2 Number Systems

A considerable subset of digital systems deals with arithmetic operations. To understand the operation of this class of circuits, it is necessary to discuss the representation of numbers.

All modern number systems use the radix representation, which came to us from the Hindus via Arabia [8]. This format is based on the following ideas:

1. The position of a symbol within a number indicates the multiplication by a relevant power of the base.

2. A special symbol is used to represent nothing (zero).

3. The number of different symbols is restricted to the base quantity.

All these ideas are contained in the familiar **decimal** (or denary) system, which is base ten. For example, the decimal number 1908 is shorthand for 1×10^3 (1×1000) plus 9×10^2 (9×100) plus 0×10^1 (0×10) plus 8×10^0 (8×1). The ten symbols are 0,1,2,3,4,5,6,7,8 and 9. Each digit's value in moving leftwards is increased by a multiplicative factor of ten. Thus it is not only the values of the symbols which are used to represent a quantity, but also their position. Numbers may be extended to fractional values by signifying positions to the right of the unity column as having negative powers of the base. Thus the number 3.142 reads as 3×10^0 (3×1) plus 1×10^{-1} ($1 \times \frac{1}{10}$) plus 4×10^{-2} ($4 \times \frac{1}{100}$) plus 2×10^{-3} ($2 \times \frac{1}{1000}$). A (decimal) point is used to separate the integer (coefficients of the positive base powers) and fractional parts (coefficients of the negative powers) of the number. Any decimal number may be represented as:

$$N = \sum_{i=-\infty}^{\infty} K_i 10^i \tag{1.1}$$

where K_i is the coefficient of the ith power of ten.

We have already noted that digital systems are based on the use of switches. The condition of these 2-state devices are more easily described using base-2 numbers. The resulting **binary** notation is identical to decimal, but with each column signifying a power of two, and with only two symbols, i.e. 0 and 1. Thus any binary number can be represented as:

$$N = \sum_{i=-\infty}^{\infty} K_i 2^i \tag{1.2}$$

Binary numbers formatted in this way are often said to be in the **natural 8-4-2-1 code**, from the weighting of the first four positions; see Fig. 1.4(a).

Table 1.2 tabulates the first twenty integers in decimal, binary, **octal** and **hexadecimal** bases. Note that hexadecimal requires sixteen symbols, and these are

conventionally $0 - 9$ and $A - F$. The right-most digit of any number is known as
the **least significant digit** (LSD), and left-most is the **most significant digit**
(MSD).

0	00000	0	0
1	00001	1	1
2	00010	2	2
3	00011	3	3
4	00100	4	4
5	00101	5	5
6	00110	6	6
7	00111	7	7
8	01000	10	8
9	01001	11	9
10	01010	12	A
11	01011	13	B
12	01100	14	C
13	01101	15	D
14	01110	16	E
15	01111	17	F
16	10000	20	10
17	10001	21	11
18	10010	22	12
19	10011	23	13
20	10100	24	14
(a) Decimal (10)	(b) Binary (2)	(c) Octal (8)	(d) Hexadecimal (16)

Table 1.2: Some representations of numbers up to twenty.

Although digital machines exclusively use binary representations, most of us
prefer to work in decimal. Because of this, it is occasionally necessary to convert
between binary and decimal. Some procedures for doing this are outlined conveniently with the aid of examples.

Example 1.1

To convert from binary 11011101 to decimal.

Solution

The binary number can be written:

$$\begin{array}{cccccccc} 128 & 64 & 32 & 16 & 8 & 4 & 2 & 1 \\ 1 & 1 & 0 & 1 & 1 & 1 & 0 & 1 \end{array}$$

giving each column its decimal value or **weight**. The decimal equivalent is then
$128 + 64 + 16 + 8 + 4 + 1 = 221$. In cases where the base of a number is not obvious
from the context, the base may be indicated thus:

$$(11011101)_2 = (221)_{10}$$

or

$$11011101b = 221d$$

Example 1.2

To convert from binary 1101.11011 to decimal.

Solution

Remembering that powers of two to the right of the decimal point (strictly binary point) are negative, we have:

$$
\begin{array}{ccccccccc}
8 & 4 & 2 & 1 & \frac{1}{2} & \frac{1}{4} & \frac{1}{8} & \frac{1}{16} & \frac{1}{32} \\
1 & 1 & 0 & 1 & 1 & 1 & 0 & 1 & 1
\end{array}
$$

giving $8 + 4 + 1 + \frac{1}{2} + \frac{1}{4} + \frac{1}{16} + \frac{1}{32} = (13\frac{27}{32})_{10}$

It is possible to convert the integer and fractional portions of the binary number separately, as the binary fraction is never greater than 1 (2^0).

As an extension to this method, the conversion of decimal to binary can readily be accomplished by repetitively subtracting the highest possible power of two from the decimal number, until the remainder is zero.

Example 1.3

Convert from $(150)_{10}$ to binary.

Solution

Subtract 2^7 (128) i.e. $150 - 128 = 22$
Subtract 2^4 (16) i.e. $22 - 16 = 6$
Subtract 2^2 (4)   i.e. $6 - 4 = 2$
Subtract 2^1 (2)   i.e. $2 - 2 = 0$

$$
\begin{array}{cccccccc}
2^7 & 2^6 & 2^5 & 2^4 & 2^3 & 2^2 & 2^1 & 2^0 \\
1 & 0 & 0 & 1 & 0 & 1 & 1 & 0
\end{array}
$$

Answer: $1\ 0\ 0\ 1\ 0\ 1\ 1\ 0 = (10010110)_2$ Fractional decimals may be converted in a similar fashion.

Example 1.4

Convert $(0.565)_{10}$ to binary.

Solution

Subtract 2^{-1} (0.5)   i.e. $0.565 - 0.5$ $= 0.065$
Subtract 2^{-4} (0.0625)   i.e. $0.065 - 0.0625$ $= 0.0025$
Subtract 2^{-9} (0.001953125) i.e. $0.0025 - 0.001953125 = 0.000546875$ etc.

Answer: 0.100100001......... to the required accuracy.

It is possible to generalize the interbase conversion by simply repetitively dividing by the base. For example, 107 becomes 10.(7) becomes 1.(0) becomes 0.(1). Consider an expansion of Equations 1.1 and 1.2. Taking an integer number N_i first, we have for m digits and an arbitrary base b:

$$N_i = b(K_0 + b(K_1 + b(K_2 + b(K_3 + \cdots b(K_{m-1})) \cdots)) \tag{1.3}$$

Dividing across by b gives:

$$N_i/b = K_0 + b(K_1 + b(K_2 + b(K_3 + \cdots b(K_{m-1})) \cdots) \tag{1.4}$$

where K_0 is the remainder, and is the first and least significant digit.

Throwing away K_0 and dividing the residue by b gives:

$$K_1 + b(K_2 + b(K_3 + \cdots b(K_{m-1})) \cdots) \tag{1.5}$$

where the remainder K_1 is the second digit.

Continuing this process m times will produce a succession of remainders, which are the required coefficients.

Example 1.5

Using a successive division by the base, (a) convert decimal 150 to binary and (b) decimal 3509 to hexadecimal.

Solution

$$
\begin{array}{rcl}
150 \div 2 & = & 75 \text{ r } 0 \\
75 \div 2 & = & 37 \text{ r } 1 \\
37 \div 2 & = & 18 \text{ r } 1 \\
18 \div 2 & = & 9 \text{ r } 0 \\
9 \div 2 & = & 4 \text{ r } 0 \\
4 \div 2 & = & 2 \text{ r } 0 \\
2 \div 2 & = & 1 \text{ r } 0 \\
1 \div 2 & = & 0 \text{ r } 1 \\
\end{array}
$$

$$
\begin{array}{rcll}
3509 \div 16 & = & 219 \text{ r } 5 & \\
219 \div 16 & = & 13 \text{ r } B & \text{i.e. } (11)_{10} \\
13 \div 16 & = & 0 \text{ r } D & \text{i.e. } (13)_{10} \\
\end{array}
$$

(a) Answer: $(10000110)_2$ (b) Answer: $(DB5)_{16}$

Example 1.6

Convert $(5F06)_{16}$ (often designated as $5F06h$) to decimal by repeated division by ten.

$$
\begin{array}{rcl}
5F06 \div A & = & 980 \text{ r } 6 \\
980 \div A & = & F3 \text{ r } 2 \\
F3 \div A & = & 18 \text{ r } 3 \\
18 \div A & = & 2 \text{ r } 4 \\
2 \div A & = & 0 \text{ r } 2 \\
\end{array}
$$

Answer: $(5F06)_{16} = (24,326)_{10}$

This is a more difficult example; as the original number was in hexadecimal, the division is in base-16. A hexadecimal calculator is a definite asset for examples of this sort!

There is an analogous procedure where fractional numbers are concerned. This can be seen from the expansion of Equation 1.2:

$$N_f = b^{-1}(K_{-1} + b^{-1}(K_{-2} + b^{-1}(K_{-3} + \cdots b^{-1}(K_{n-m}))\cdots)) \qquad (1.6)$$

Multiplying across b gives:

$$b \times N_f = K_{-1} + b^{-1}(K_{-2} + b^{-1}(K_{-3} + \cdots b^{-1}(K_{-m}))\cdots) \qquad (1.7)$$

where K_{-1} is an integer and is the most significant fractional coefficient.

Continuing this process and rejecting the integers as they are produced after each multiplication, yields the required coefficients. An example will clarify.

Example 1.7

Convert the decimal fraction 0.1 to nine binary places accuracy.

Solution

$$
\begin{array}{rcll}
0.1 \times 2 & = & (0).2 & 0 \\
0.2 \times 2 & = & (0).4 & 0 \\
0.4 \times 2 & = & (0).8 & 0 \\
0.8 \times 2 & = & (1).6 & 1 \\
0.6 \times 2 & = & (1).2 & 1 \\
0.2 \times 2 & = & (0).4 & 0 \\
0.4 \times 2 & = & (0).8 & 0 \\
0.8 \times 2 & = & (1).6 & 1 \\
0.6 \times 2 & = & (1).2 & 1 \quad \text{etc.}
\end{array}
$$

Answer: $0.000110\dot{0}\dot{1}\dot{1}$

Notice that the pattern 0011 will repeat indefinitely (indicated thus: $\dot{0}0\dot{1}\dot{1}$), and so one tenth has no direct binary representation! The actual value given above is $2^{-4} + 2^{-5} + 2^{-8} + 2^{-9} = 0.099609375$; or around 0.39% too low.

In the case of binary, conversion by repeated multiplication or division by two is sometimes referred to as the **double-dabble** method.

The bases eight (octal) and sixteen (hexadecimal) are frequently used synonymously with binary, as they can very easily be interconverted.

Example 1.8

Represent (a) binary 1111000011001000 in a hexadecimal form, and (b) hexadecimal F69C as binary.

Solution

(a) Grouping the digits in blocks of four gives:
```
1111  0000  1100  1000
  F     0     C     8
```

(b) Expanding each hexadecimal digit into four binary digits gives:
```
  F     6     9     C
1111  0110  1001  1100
```

Octal is handled in the same way but in groupings of three binary digits.

Example 1.8 showed the economy in using a hexadecimal base rather than binary. This also considerably improves readability and reduces the scope for typing errors. However, digital machines deal with binary patterns only, and some hardware or software conversion will always be necessary as an interface.

Where **signed binary numbers** are to be represented, the MSD is conventionally used as the sign bit, with 0 for positive, $+$, and 1 for negative, $-$. Thus $+10110.1$ is represented as $0,10110.1$ (I have used a comma simply for emphasis); whilst -11001.1 is written $1,11001.1$. This type of format is known as **sign plus magnitude**, but in fact negative numbers are most often represented in an *inverted* form, i.e., $1 \rightarrow 0$ and $0 \rightarrow 1$. The reason for this will become apparent when subtraction is discussed in the next section.

One of major decisions to be made by the designer of a digital system, is the format and size of words which are to be processed. Figure 1.6 tabulates some typical word sizes in use together with their range.

All the number representations discussed up to this point are classified as fixed-point, as the number of integer and fractional digits are fixed. Where processing will involve a large dynamic range, say, between 2^{-128} and 2^{+128}, then fixed-point representations will require an inordinately large number of digits; 255 in this example. The lower two rows in Fig. 1.6 illustrate an alternative format known as **floating-point**. For example, decimal 186,000 can be written as 1.86×10^5 and 0.000000186 as 1.86×10^{-7}. The numerical value is called the **mantissa** or significand, and the power to which this is to be raised is the **exponent**. The mantiassa is usually **normalized** to lie between 1 and 10, and on this basis 186,000 may be written as 186E5 and 93,562,000 as 93562E7.

Example 1.9

Convert the following fixed-point numbers to their floating-point equivalents:

$$(-300,000)_{10}; \ (0.000000015)_{10}; \ (10110000)_2; \ (-0.00010111)_2.$$

Assume that the binary floating-point numbers have a **field** of five places each for the mantissa and exponent parts.

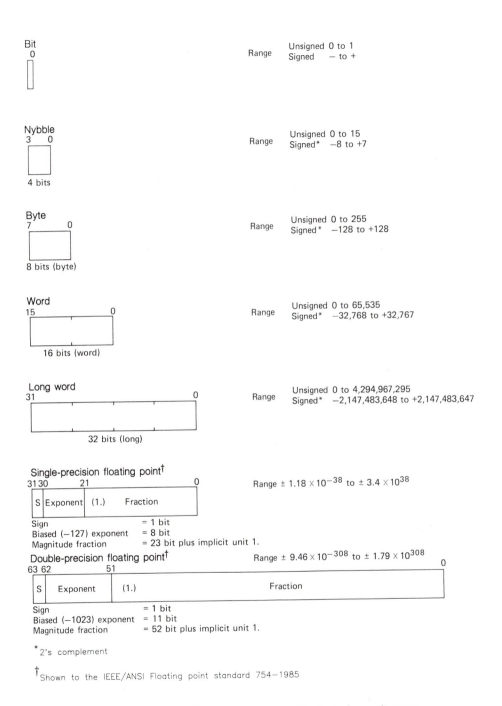

Figure 1.6: Some typical binary groupings, with their dynamic range.

Solution

(a) $-3E+5$	: Five places to the left	$= -3.0$	$\times$	10^5
(b) $+15E-8$	: Eight places to the right	$= +1.5$	$\times$	10^{-8}
(c) $0,1011E0,1000$	: Seven places to the left	$= +1.011$	$\times$	2^7
(d) $1,1011E1,0011$	: Four places to the right	$= -1.011$	$\times$	2^{-4}

The field of the mantissa basically defines the resolution, whilst the exponent field indicates the size, or dynamic range, of the number which can be represented. Digital machines must provide circuitry to store and process each bit, and thus the field size is limited by economic restraints. If a number occupies too large a field, it will either be truncated or (preferably) rounded off. This is what has happened to (d), where the true solution is $1,10111E1,100$ rather than the indicated $1,1011E1,100$; an error of around 1.4%.

The reader will be familiar with the scientific electronic calculator, which typically has a display field of eleven decimals for the mantissa and two for the exponent, both including sign digits. This gives outputs roughly between $\pm 9.9 \times 10^{99}$ and $\pm 0.1 \times 10^{-99}$.

Until recently the format of floating-point numbers was very much a matter for the designer of the hardware or software system. However, most designs from the beginning of the 1980s conform to IEEE/ANSI standard P754 [9, 10], some of which is outlined in Fig. 1.6. Taking the single-precision format as an example, the most significant bit (MSB) is the sign of the mantissa — 0 for positive and 1 for negative. The eight following bits represent the exponent plus $2^7 - 1$ (127); ranging from 0000 0000 (-127) through 0111 1111 (zero) up to 1111 1111 ($+128$). The 23-bit manitissa is normalized to (1.)fraction (see Example 1.9(c) & (d), but the leading one is assumed, not actually stored. Thus the mantissa has effectively a 25-bit (sign + virtual 1. + 23-bit fraction) resolution. Double-precision floating-point numbers are similar but with an 11-bit exponent biased by $2^{10} - 1$ (1023) and an effective 54-bit mantissa.

Example 1.10

Show how the following decimal numbers may be represented in ANSII standard single-precision floating-point format: (a) +1.0, (b) −0.1, (c) 53.2265625

Solution

(a) +1.0 is $(1.)0 \times 2^0$.

Fraction	is	00000000000000000000000	(23 bits)
Sign	is	0	(positive)
Exponent	is	01111111	(0 + 127 bias)

giving 0,01111111,00000000000000000000000
or   3F 80 00 00 in hexadecimal.

(b) From Example 1.7, $(-0.1)_{10}$ is: $-\boxed{1.}10011001100110011001100 \times 2^{-4}$.

Fraction	is	1001100110011001100	(23 bits)
Sign	is	1	(negative)
Exponent	is	01111011	(-4 + 127 bias)

giving 1,01111011,10011001100110011001100

or   BD CC CC CC in hexadecimal.

(c) $+53.2265625$ is $+110101.001101 = +(1.)10101001101 \times 2^5$.

Fraction	is	10101001101000000000000	(23 bits)
Sign	is	0	(positive)
Exponent	is	10000100	(+5 + 127 bias)

giving 0,10000100,10101001101000000000000

or   42 54 D0 00 in hexadecimal.

The ANSII standard reserves the exponent value of zero for the special case of very small numbers, where it is impossible to normalize the number without further decrementing the exponent down to zero (1.0×2^{-126} for the single format and 1.0×2^{-1022} for double). In such case the exponent is made zero and the implicit bit also zero. The fraction is then allowed to be denormalized. The limit to this is zero, which is represented by both fraction and exponent zero. Infinity is represented by a maximum exponent (all ones) with zero fraction.

One final format is **binary coded decimal** (BCD), which is extensively used at the input-output ports of a digital system. In this format, each decimal digit is represented by its binary equivalent. Thus $(906)_{10}$ is $(1001)(0000)(0110)$ in BCD. Using this hybrid system has many advantages; for example, in displaying decimal numbers in an electronic calculator; see Section 3.2.1.

Example 1.11

Represent the following decimal numbers in BCD, and compare with pure binary: 81; 1975.

Solution

$(8 \quad 1)_{10}$ $(1 \quad 9 \quad 7 \quad 5)_{10}$

$(1000 \quad 0001)_{BCD}$ $(0001 \quad 1001 \quad 0111 \quad 0101)_{BCD}$

$(1010001)_2$ $(11110110111)_2$

Example 1.12

Convert The following quantities from BCD to decimal:

$(00100110)_{BCD}$; $(011000110100)_{BCD}$; $(0001001000000111)_{BCD}$

Solution

$$(0010 \quad 0110)_{\mathrm{BCD}} \quad (0110 \quad 0011 \quad 0100)_{\mathrm{BCD}} \quad (0001 \quad 0010 \quad 0000 \quad 0111)_{\mathrm{BCD}}$$
$$(2 \qquad 6)_{10} \qquad (6 \qquad 3 \qquad 4)_{10} \qquad (1 \qquad 2 \qquad 0 \qquad 7)_{10}$$

Note that the digits 1010 to 1111 are illegal, and this may be used to give a limited degree of error detection. The code used in these examples is the natural 8-4-2-1 code, and strictly speaking the format should be termed 8-4-2-1 BCD. Other codes exist, for example see Table 1.3, but as these are comparatively rare, the unqualified term BCD may be taken to indicate this 8-4-2-1 code.

1.1.3   Codes

It is possible to represent quantities in a binary fashion without resorting to the use of 8-4-2-1 weightings [11]. As we have seen in Section 1.1.1, this can be useful from the point of view of error detection. Other advantages lie in reduction of electronic circuitry or ease of arithmetic computations. In addition to codes where the position of a bit carries a quantity significance, a large class of unweighted codes exist. In this case only the complete word pattern has any significance.

	2421	−2841		gfedcba
0	0000	0000	0011	1000000
1	0001	0001	0100	1111001
2	0010	1010	0101	0100100
3	0011	1011	0110	0110000
4	0100	0010	0111	0011001
5	1011	0011	1000	0010011
6	1100	1100	1001	0000011
7	1101	1101	1010	1111000
8	1110	0100	1011	0000000
9	1111	0101	1100	0011000

(a) Symmetrical   (b) −2-8-4-1   (c) Excess-3   (d) Active-Low
2-4-2-1   7-segment

Table 1.3: Some BCD codes

Table 1.3 gives a selection from the many possible BCD codes. Some of these codes have specific properties, such as the symmetrical 2-4-2-1 code. Inverting any digit expressed in this manner, gives the difference between that number and nine. Thus 7 is 1101 in 2-4-2-1 code and 0010 is 2, which is $9 - 7$. This property of 9's complementation can be useful when subtracting BCD-coded numbers, see Section 1.2.2. Table 1.3(b) shows a weighted code with digits in one column having negative value! Although the Excess-3 code of Table 1.3(c) is unweighted, close examination shows that is the normal code with an offset of plus three.

The 7-segment code of Table 1.3(d) is completely unweighted. This code pattern gives the segment configurations for the ubiquitous 7-segment readouts, used as

ASCII CHARACTER SET (7-BIT CODE)								
M.S. **CHAR** / **L.S.** **CHAR**	**0** 000	**1** 001	**2** 010	**3** 011	**4** 100	**5** 101	**6** 110	**7** 111
0 0000	NUL	DLE	SP	0	@	P	'	p
1 0001	SOH	DC1	!	1	A	Q	a	q
2 0010	STX	DC2	"	2	B	R	b	r
3 0011	ETX	DC3	#	3	C	S	c	s
4 0100	EOT	DC4	$	4	D	T	d	t
5 0101	ENQ	NAK	%	5	E	U	e	u
6 0110	ACK	SYN	&	6	F	V	f	v
7 0111	BEL	ETB	'	7	G	W	g	w
8 1000	BS	CAN	(	8	H	X	h	x
9 1001	HT	EM	)	9	I	Y	i	y
A 1010	LF	SUB	*	:	J	Z	j	z
B 1011	VT	ESC	+	;	K	[	k	{
C 1100	FF	FS	,	<	L	\	l	:
D 1101	CR	GS	−	=	M	]	m	}
E 1110	SO	RS	.	>	N	↑	n	~
F 1111	SI	VS	/	?	O	↓	o	DEL

Table 1.4: The 7-bit ASCII code (similar to ISO-7), including control and signalling commands.

decimal displays for calculators, clocks and the like. This is a simple example of an **alphanumeric code** used to represent letters and figures. In order to represent a full set of such characters, a more sophisticated code is required.

The **American Standard Code for Information Interchange (ASCII)** shown in Table 1.4, is the most commonly used alphanumeric code. The 7-bit code version shown here allows 128 possible symbol representations. As well as upper- and lower-case letters and the numerals, a selection of punctuation marks and mathematical symbols are included. The remaining combinations are used as control characters, which are decoded by terminals such as the teletypewriter (TTY) and visual display unit (VDU), but not printed. Examples of these are Carriage_Return ($< CR > = 000\ 1010$ or 0D in hexadecimal) and Line_Feed ($< LF > = 000\ 1010b$ or 0Ah).

When ASCII code is carried by byte-oriented (i.e. 8-bit) systems, the extra most significant bit is frequently used for error protection. Alternatively, this additional bit may signify an alternative character set. Some electronic readouts decode a 6-bit subset of the full code. Only upper-case letters can be displayed in this instance.

Another set of unweighted codes are the unit-distance codes; two of which are shown in Table 1.5. These codes all possess the property that any adjacent lines in the code table differ in only one digit; the top and bottom rows also being considered adjacent. Many codes with this property exist, but the Gray code of Table 1.5(a) is the most common. As can be seen, the portion of the table below the bisecting line is a reflection of the upper segment, with the exception of the most significant bit (MSB). This reflected binary code can be extended to five bits by continuing the table downwards, making the new fifth MSB 1 and reflecting all the lesser bits. The process is continued as required.

An application of unit-distance codes is shown with the coded disk of Fig. 1.7(b). These disks are commonly used attached to a rotating shaft, such as the lead screw

	DCBA	DCBA
0	0000	0000
1	0001	0001
2	0011	0011
3	0010	0010
4	0110	0110
5	0111	1110
6	0101	1111
7	0100	1101
8	1100	1100
9	1101	0100
10	1111	
11	1110	(b): A unit-distance BCD code
12	1010	
13	1011	
14	1001	
15	1000	(a) The 4-bit Gray code

Table 1.5: Two unit-distant codes.

of a numerical control machine. By using photocells, the pattern of light and dark areas gives an indication of the angular position of the shaft. Measurement of angles greater than 360° is possible by counting the number of complete revolutions, signalled by the reoccurrence of a specific pattern.

To see the advantage of unit-distance codes in this application, consider the binary-coded disk of Fig. 1.7(a). At one instant the position may be read as 0111. Because of misalignment of the heads, the advancement to 1000 may be read as 0111 ⇒ 0101 ⇒ 0000 ⇒ 1000. Although these errors may only be of short duration; this can be sufficient to store incorrect information in a memory circuit. As the Gray-coded disk has only one change between adjacent segments, this problem is unlikely to occur.

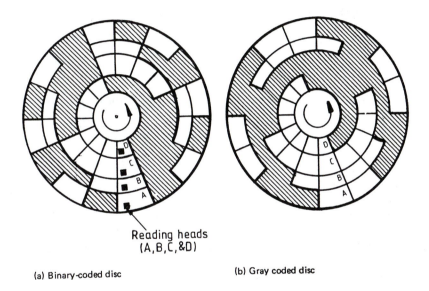

Reading heads
(A, B, C, &D)

(a) Binary-coded disc   (b) Gray coded disc

Figure 1.7: Shaft angle encoding disks

Arithmetic processing of the unweighted Gray code is difficult. Fortunately, conversion to and from normal binary code is simply accomplished. Suitable algorithms are outlined here, and by using techniques developed in later chapters, the reader will have little difficulty in designing hardware to implement these.

The most common technique used in conversion from Gray to natural binary code, is known as the **modulo-2** algorithm. This is illustrated in the following example.

Example 1.13

Convert from Gray 11011 to normal binary code.

Solution

1. The MSB Gray and binary are the same, i.e. :

$$
\begin{array}{cccccl}
1 & 1 & 0 & 1 & 1 & \text{Gray} \\
\downarrow & & & & & \\
1 & & & & & \text{binary}
\end{array}
$$

2. Compare the MSB binary with the second MSB Gray. If they are the same, the second MSB binary is 0 otherwise 1. This is known as the **modulo-2 operation**, the rules of which are $0 \leftrightarrow 0 \ \& \ 1 \leftrightarrow 1 = 0 : 0 \leftrightarrow 1 \ \& \ 1 \leftrightarrow 0 = 0$.

$$
\begin{array}{cccccl}
1 & 1 & 0 & 1 & 1 & \text{Gray} \\
& \nearrow \ \downarrow & & & & \\
1 & 0 & & & & \text{binary}
\end{array}
$$

3. Repeat with the second MSB binary and third Gray, i.e.:

$$
\begin{array}{cccccl}
1 & 1 & 0 & 1 & 1 & \text{Gray} \\
& & \nearrow \ \downarrow & & & \\
1 & 0 & 0 & & & \text{binary}
\end{array}
$$

4. Continue diagonal comparisons until both words are the same length.

$$
\begin{array}{cccccl}
1 & 1 & 0 & 1 & 1 & \text{Gray} \\
& & & \nearrow \ \downarrow \ \nearrow \ \downarrow & & \\
1 & 0 & 0 & 1 & 0 & \text{binary (Answer)}
\end{array}
$$

A hardware Gray-to-binary conversion circuit based on this algorithm is discussed in example SAE 2.3. An alternative technique, known as the **toggle algorithm**, is sometimes used. This equates the MSBs, with following bit values being determined by the corresponding Gray digits. If any Gray digit is 0, then the equivalent binary digit remains the same as that preceding it. If the Gray digit is 1, then it is opposite, i.e. toggles; see Example 4.25.

The modulo-2 function may also be used for conversion from normal binary to Gray code, as illustrated in the following example.

Example 1.14

Convert from binary 10111 to Gray code.

Solution

$$
\begin{array}{ccccccccc}
1 & \leftrightarrow & 0 & \leftrightarrow & 1 & \leftrightarrow & 1 & \leftrightarrow & 1 & \text{binary} \\
\downarrow & & \downarrow & & \downarrow & & \downarrow & & \downarrow & \\
1 & & 1 & & 1 & & 0 & & 0 & \text{Gray (Answer)}
\end{array}
$$

In this case each Gray bit is the modulo-2 comparison of the equivalent binary bit and next higher binary bit. The MSBs are the same. Example 2.41 shows a hardware implementation of this algorithm.

1.2 Binary Arithmetic

The four fundamental mathematical operations of addition, subtraction, multiplication and division are implemented in a base-independent manner. Binary-based numbers, because of their limited range of symbols, give rise to especially simple rules and manipulations.

After completing this section, you should:

- Be able to add and subtract binary numbers in fixed-point, BCD and floating-point formats.

- Know how to represent negative numbers in 2's complement form.

- Understand how to represent signed numbers and how to preserve the sign bit on extension.

- Appreciate the possibility of sign overflow when adding or subtracting signed numbers.

- Understand the difference between logic and arithmetic shift right.

- Be able to use subtraction to compare the magnitude of two quantities.

- Be able to multiply fixed- and floating-point numbers using the shift and add algorithm.

- Be able to divide fixed- and floating-point numbers using the shift and subtract algorithm.

1.2.1 Addition

The additive process is an algorithm based on the simpler scheme of counting. Counting is the means whereby a quantity is totalized by adding units one at a time. For example, if three is to be added to two, the counting solution is obtained as follows: $2 + 1 = 3$; $3 + 1 = 4$; $4 + 1 = 5$: answer. Electronic counters are a large and useful category of digital circuits and are discussed in Section 4.2.

Normal addition is a shorthand evolution of this technique. It is based on a number of rules which must be memorized. These rules give the result of all possible additions of two radix symbols. In decimal this covers all additions from $0 + 0 = 0$ to $9 + 9 = 18$. There are 45 decimal rules in all, assuming that order of addition is unimportant (the law of commutation).

Binary addition is covered by only three rules. These rules are:

$$0 + 0 \quad = \quad 0$$
$$\left. \begin{array}{l} 0 + 1 \\ 1 + 0 \end{array} \right\} \; = \; 1$$
$$1 + 1 \quad = 10 \quad \text{(0 carry 1)}$$

Based on these rules, binary addition follows the same procedure as for decimal, the LSB column being totalized first; passing a **carry** if necessary to the second LSB. The process ends with the MSB column; its carry being the new MSB of the sum.

Example 1.15

Add the following quantities:

$$\begin{array}{cccc}
(96) & (1011) & (111011) & (00101) \\
+\ (35)_{10} & +\ (0101)_2 & +\ (000111)_2 & +\ (10111)_2 \\
\hline
\text{(a)} & \text{(b)} & \text{(c)} & \text{(d)}
\end{array}$$

Solution

(a)
```
     96   Augend
    +35   Addend
    ----
     21
    +11   Carry
    ----
    131   Sum
```

(b)
```
    1011   Augend
   +0101   Addend
   -----
    1110
    +001   Carry
   -----
   10000   Sum
```

(c)
```
    111011   Augend
   +000111   Addend
   -------
    111100
    +00011   Carry
   -------
   1000010   Sum
```

(d)
```
    00101   Augend
   +10111   Addend
   ------
    10010
    +0101   Carry
   ------
    11100   Sum
```

Note that with some of the binary additions shown in this example, several carry rows are in fact needed, although for brevity only one is indicated. Normally separate carry rows are not shown, the carries being memorized (carried in your head!).

Floating-point addition requires a shifting operation before summation. Consider the two decimal numbers 0.356×10^6 and 0.105×10^5. Before these are added, the exponents must be equalized. This can be done by shifting the mantissa relative to the decimal point, i.e. $0.105 \times 10^5 = 0.0105 \times 10^6$. Totalization then follows by straight addition of the mantissas, the exponent remaining the same. Thus $(0.356 \times 10^6) + (0.105 \times 10^5) = (0.356 \times 10^6) + (0.0105 \times 10^6) = 0.3665 \times 10^6$.

Example 1.16

Add together the following floating-point quantities. Sign bits are not used.

$$\begin{array}{ccc}
(150E2) & (10110E001) & (10010E110) \\
+(963E3)_{10} & +(10100E010)_2 & +(10011E010)_2 \\
\hline
\text{(a)} & \text{(b)} & \text{(c)}
\end{array}$$

Solution

(a) Shifting the augend to exponent 3 gives:
```
    015E3
   +963E3
   ------
    978E3    Answer
```

(b) Shifting the augend to exponent 010 gives:

```
    01011E010
   +10100E010
    11111E010    Answer
```

(c) Shifting the addend to exponent 110 gives:
```
    10010E110
   +00001E110
    10011E110    Answer
```

Note the loss of accuracy in the final addition, due to the fixed field of the mantissa. It is because of the fixed mantissa field that the exponents are equalized to the largest of the two. If the mantissa should overflow its field due to the addition, it must be normalized by shifting, and the exponent adjusted. This is illustrated by the next example.

Example 1.17

Add the floating-point numbers 11101E01 and 11110E00 together, given a mantissa field of five, and exponent field of two places.

Solution

```
    11101E01
   +01111E01
    101100E01 = 10110E10        (Answer)
    overflow → normalized
```

If the augend and addend are in BCD form, then addition using the normal binary rules may give an incorrect result [12]. For example, 0101 + 0111 (5+7) gives 1100 after addition, but should give 1 0010 (12). Similarly, 1001 + 1001 (9+9) gives 1 0010 rather than 1 1000 (18). From these examples it can be seen that whenever the sum of two BCD decades exceeds nine, a correction must be made by adding six. This compensates for the six illegal BCD combinations (i.e. 1010 → 1111), which must be skipped. Thus **BCD addition** must follow the algorithm:

1. Commence with the least significant decades.

2. Add the two decades using normal addition.

3. If the result is greater than nine, then add six.

4. Repeat steps 2–4 until the most significant decade is reached, passing on any carry generated from steps 2 or 3.

Example 1.18

Evaluate the following BCD additions:

```
(a)        0001 0010 + 1001 0011 ( 12 + 93)
(b)    0001 0010 1001 + 1000 1001 (129 + 89)
```

Solution

(a)

1:	0010 + 0011 =	0101	; adding LS decades, no correction
2:	0001 + 1001 =	1010	; adding MS decades
3:	1010 + 0110 =	1 0000	; correcting by addition of six.

Answer   1 0000 0101 (105).

(b)

1:	1001 + 1001 =	1 0010	; adding LS decades
2:	1 0010 + 0110 =	1 1000	; correcting by addition of six
3:	1 + 0010 + 1000 =	1011	; adding second decades, plus carry
4:	1011 + 0110 =	1 0001	; correcting by addition of six
5:	1 + 0001 + 0000 =	0010	; adding MS decades, no correction.

Answer   0010 0001 1000 (218).

1.2.2   Subtraction

Just as addition implements an up count, subtraction corresponds to a down count, where units are removed from the total. Subtraction can be performed in the normal mode, in a similar manner to decimal; or in a **complement** mode more suited to arithmetic circuitry.

The normal mode of subtraction applies the subtraction rules, commencing with the LSB and working towards the MSB. When in a given column a larger quantity is to be subtracted from a smaller quantity, a borrow is taken from the next higher column and given back after the subtraction is completed. Based on the borrow principle, the subtraction rules are given by:

$$0 - 0 = 0$$
$${}^1 0 - 1 = 1 \quad \text{Borrowing 1 from the higher column}$$
$$1 - 0 = 1$$
$$1 - 1 = 0$$

Example 1.19

Using normal subtraction, totalize the following:

(a)	(b)	(c)	(d)
(63)	(1100)	(110011)	(0110)
$-(49)_{10}$	$-(0101)_2$	$-(011110)_2$	$-(1100)_2$

Solution

(a) Column 0 : $^1 3 - 9 = 4$ (borrow 1)
    Column 1 : $4 + 1 = 5$ (return borrow), $6 - 5 = 1$

    Answer   :   14

(b) Column 0 : $^1 0 - 1 =$ 1 (borrow 1)
    Column 1 : $0 + 1 =$ 1 (return borrow), $^1 0 - 1 = 1$
    Column 2 : $1 + 1 = 10$ (return borrow), $^1 1 - 10 = 1$
    Column 3 : $0 + 1 =$ 1 (return borrow), $1 - 1 = 0$

Answer   :   0111

(c) Column 0 : $1 - 0 =$ 1
    Column 1 : $1 - 1 =$ 0
    Column 2 : $^1 0 - 1 =$ 1 (borrow 1)
    Column 3 : $1 + 1 = 10$ (return borrow), $^1 0 - 10 = 0$
    Column 4 : $1 + 1 = 10$ (return borrow), $^1 1 - 10 = 1$
    Column 5 : $0 + 1 =$ 1 (return borrow), $1 - 1 = 0$

Answer   : 010101

(d) Interchanging minuend and subtrahend gives:

$$\begin{array}{r} 1100 \\ -0110 \\ \hline \end{array}$$

Column 0 : $0 - 0 =$ 0
Column 1 : $^1 0 - 1 =$ 1 (borrow 1)
Column 2 : $1 + 1 = 10$ (return borrow), $^1 1 - 10 = 1$
Column 3 : $0 + 1 =$ 1 (return borrow), $1 - 1 = 0$

Make difference negative, to compensate for our interchange.
Answer   : -0110

Subtraction can be regarded as the addition of a negative number; thus $A + (-B)$. If we can find a suitable representation for negative numbers, it may be possible to 'fool' our addition hardware into subtracting at little extra cost.

Consider the problem of subtracting decimal 45 from 73. The answer using the normal rules of subtraction, $73 - 45$, is of course 28. The alternative addition $73 + 55 = \cancel{1}\,28$ gives the same result if we ignore the hundreds overflow. Similarly $32 - 8 = 24$ or $32 + 92 = \cancel{1}\,24$. Clearly 55 and 92 relate in some way to -45 and -8. By inspection they are the difference from 100. In general the **10's complement** of a number B is $10^N - B$, where N is the number of digits of B. Mathematically we have:

$$A - B = A + (10^N - B) - 10^N = A + \overline{B} \qquad (1.8)$$

with any carry overflow being ignored.

An alternative way of creating the 10's complement is to first generate the 9's complement by inverting each of B's digits (defined as the difference from 9). This is effectively $(10^N - 1) - B$, as 10^N is always $99 \ldots 99$. Adding one then gives $10^N - B$, the 10's complement of B. Thus -062 becomes 937 (9's complement) + 1 (10's complement) $= 938$ (or $1000 - 062 = 938$).

Example 1.20

Using a 10's complement representation, perform the subtractions: $256 - 21$ and $98 - 306$.

Solution

1. The 9's complement of 021 is 978; add one to give the 10's complement 979; thus $256 + 979 = \not{1}\,235$.   (Answer 235).

2. The 9's complement of 306 is 693; add one to give the 10's complement 694, thus $098 + 694 = 792$.   (Answer? 792).

Solution 2 is interesting; 792 is indeed correct. The answer using normal subtraction is -208, but the 10's complement of 792 is 208. This implies negative answers will automatically be in the correct complement form.

Example 1.20 showed that complement arithmetic allows adding circuits to subtract. Furthermore no interchange when the minuend is greater than the subtrahend is required. Although conversion to this complement form is needed when data enters the system; it remains in the correct format throughout subsequent processing. If necessary, output data can be converted back to 'normal' sign plus magnitude by once again inversion plus one; as minus minus is plus.

In binary, the same rules hold. The **2's complement** of B is defined as $2^N - B$. Alternatively, find the difference between each digit and 1 to give the **1's complement** $(2^N - 1 = 1111 \dots 1111)$ and add one onto the result. This difference is simply obtained by inversion (i.e. $1 - \underline{0} = 1$; $1 - \underline{1} = 0$). Thus:

$$\text{2's complement} \iff \text{normal; invert and add one}$$

Binary inversion is the simplest of digital processes, whilst the addition of one is readily accomplished using the adder circuits. Furthermore, in binary numbers the sign bit can be treated in an identical way to the other bits. When this is done, the answer will always carry the correct sign bit. This is illustrated in Example 1.22.

Example 1.21

Form the 2's complement of the following numbers: (a) 10010; (b) 110110.

(a)	10010		Check; $N = 5$, $2^5 - B =$ 100000
	$\Downarrow$	Invert	-010010
	01101		$\overline{001110}$
	$+\quad 1$		
	$\overline{01110}$	(Answer)	
(b)	110110		Check; $N = 6$, $2^6 - B =$ 1000000
	$\Downarrow$	Invert	-0110110
	001001		$\overline{0001010}$
	$+\quad 1$		
	$\overline{001010}$	(Answer)	

Example 1.22

Carry out the following subtractions with the assumption that all numbers are signed (see page 14) and already in 2's complement form.

$$
\begin{array}{ll}
& 0{,}1100 \\
& 1{,}1011 \\
\hline
\text{(a)}
\end{array}
\qquad
\begin{array}{ll}
& 0{,}110011 \\
& 1{,}100010 \\
\hline
\text{(b)}
\end{array}
\qquad
\begin{array}{ll}
& 0{,}0110 \\
& 1{,}0100 \\
\hline
\text{(c)}
\end{array}
$$

Solution

When adding, the sign bits are treated as normal bits.

(a)
$$
\begin{array}{ll}
0{,}1100 & (+12) \\
1{,}1011 & (-5) \\
\hline
\mathit{1}\,0{,}0111 & (+7)
\end{array}
$$
(b)
$$
\begin{array}{ll}
0{,}110011 & (+51) \\
1{,}100010 & (-30) \\
\hline
\mathit{1}\,0{,}010101 & (+21)
\end{array}
$$
(c)
$$
\begin{array}{ll}
0{,}0110 & (+6) \\
1{,}0100 & (-12) \\
\hline
1{,}1010 & (-6)
\end{array}
$$

Note that the answer to (c) is in 2's complement form and needs no further processing. If it should be desired to convert to sign plus magnitude form; invert and add 1: e.g. $1010 \rightarrow 0101 + 1 = 0110$. Thus the answer in 'normal' notation is -0110. It must be again emphasized that this conversion is unnecessary if 2's complement is the normal machine representation. The reader should now compare this example with that of Example 1.19. The problems and answers are identical but using 2's complement notation means that no subtraction has had to be used. Furthermore, the use of this technique keeps track of the sign and obviates the minuend-subtrahend interchange for negative answers.

Example 1.23

The language **C** allows arithmetic to be performed on (amongst others) 8-bit bytes (chars) and 16-bit words (ints). Where these are mixed, the rules state that 8-bit bytes are promoted to 16-bit words before any arithmetic is performed. Show how both positive and negative bytes may be extended to their 16-bit equivalent.

Solution

Where the byte is positive there is no problem; for example:

$$
\begin{array}{cc}
0{,}0001100 & \\
+12 &
\end{array}
\implies
\begin{array}{cc}
0{,}0000000\ 00001100 \\
+12
\end{array}
$$

However, attempting the same process for a negative byte gives a ridiculous result:

$$
\begin{array}{cc}
1{,}1110100 & \\
-12 &
\end{array}
\implies
\begin{array}{cc}
0{,}0000000\ 11110100 \\
+244
\end{array}
$$

The correct approach is to insert 1s for a negative number, thus:

$$
\begin{array}{cc}
1{,}1110100 & \\
-12 &
\end{array}
\implies
\begin{array}{cc}
1{,}1111111\ 11110101 \\
-12
\end{array}
$$

This process of 2's complement promotion is known as **sign extension**, as additional higher order bits have the same value as the sign bit.

Floating-point subtraction is similar to addition, with the exponents being equalized to the largest of the two and the mantissa being shifted as appropriate (see Example 1.34(b)). However, note that the ANSII standard formats do not use 2's complement notation for either mantissa or exponent.

As well as producing the difference between two numbers, subtraction can be used to **compare** their magnitude. Assuming unsigned numbers, the subtraction $A - B$ will produce the following results:

    IF A HIGHER THAN B THEN no carry is produced
    IF A EQUAL TO B THEN the result is zero as well
    IF A LOWER THAN B THEN a carry is produced.

For example:

A	0110	(6)	A	0110	(6)	A	0011	(3)
B	$-$0011	(3)	B	$-$0110	(6)	B	$-$0110	(6)
	$\overline{0011}$			$\overline{0000}$			$\overline{(1)1101}$	

No carry	Zero	Carry
A is higher than B	A equals B	A is lower than B

For 2's complement numbers, the sign bit is examined rather than any carry:

    IF A GREATER THAN B THEN a positive difference is produced
    IF A EQUAL TO B THEN the result is zero as well
    IF A LESS THAN B THEN a negative difference is produced

For example:

A	0,0110	(+6)	A	0,1001	(+6)	A	1,1010	($-$6)
B	1,1101	($-$3)	B	0,0110	(+6)	B	1,1101	($-$3)
	$\cancel{1}\,0,1001$			$\overline{0,0000}$			$\cancel{1}\,1,0111$	

Positive answer	Zero	Negative answer
A greater than B	A equals B	A less than B

Note the subtle change in terminology, with higher/greater and lower/less being used for unsigned/signed comparisons respectively.

We have ignored the possibility of overflow. What if the sum should overflow into the sign position; eg. $-15 + -15$ gives $+2$! $(1,0001 + 1,0001 = \cancel{1}\,0,0010)$? Overflow will only occur when both operands have the same signs (otherwise the result is a difference), either positive or negative. Thus if the sign bits of both operands are the same and differ from the sum sign bit, then overflow has occurred see Example 2.40. Try example SAE 1.9 to develop a strategy to deal with this eventuality.

1.2.3   Multiplication and Division

Multiplication is an algorithm of use when a number is to be added to itself a given number of times. This is a slow process; although where speed is no problem, multiplication is sometimes implemented in this fashion. As was the case for counting/addition, the operation may be speeded up by using a set of rules — the familiar multiplication tables. As an example $3 + 3 + 3 + 3 = 12$ is memorized as $3 \times 4 = 12$. Because of the number of symbols, decimal multiplication tables are lengthy; however, **binary multiplication** is implemented with only three rules:

$$0 \times 0 \quad = 0$$
$$\left. \begin{array}{l} 0 \times 1 \\ 1 \times 0 \end{array} \right\} = 0$$
$$1 \times 1 \quad = 1$$

As a consequence of the radix number structure, multiplication by the base is easily achieved by shifting the number left relative to the point. Thus 526. becomes 5260. ($\times 10$) and 52600. ($\times 100$). Similarly in binary, 00110. becomes 01100. ($\times 2$) and 11000. ($\times 4$) ($6 \rightarrow 12 \rightarrow 24$). Using this shifting process together with our multiplication tables, enables us to multiply multi-digit numbers.

Example 1.24

Implement the following multiplications:

$$\text{(a)} \quad \begin{array}{r} (93) \\ \times \ (60)_{10} \\ \hline \end{array} \qquad \text{(b)} \quad \begin{array}{r} (1011) \\ \times \ (1001)_2 \\ \hline \end{array}$$

Solution

(a)
93	multiplicand
$\times 60$	multiplier
$\overline{00}$	1st partial product $(0 \times 93) \times 1$
$+558$	2nd partial product $(6 \times 93) \times 10$
$\overline{5580}$	product

(b)
1011	
$\times 1001$	
$\overline{1011}$	1st partial product $(1 \times 1011) \times 1$
0000	2nd partial product $(0 \times 1011) \times 2$
0000	3rd partial product $(0 \times 1011) \times 4$
$+1011$	4th partial product $(1 \times 1011) \times 8$
$\overline{1100011}$	product $(11 \times 9 = 99)$

As can be seen from (b), binary multiplication consists of the formation of partial products, which are the multiplicand successively shifted left and multiplied by either 0 or 1, as determined by successive multiplier digits. The final product is the addition of the partial products. Both shifting and adding are simple electronic processes, and hence this **shift and add** algorithm is normally used to implement binary multiplication. With this approach, Example 1.24(b) can be recast as the product $M \times 9 = M + M \ll 3$ or $M(\times 1 + \times 8)$; where M is the multiplicand and $\ll$ is the shift-left operator.

Where the multiplicand and/or multiplier is negative in 2's complement format, an alternative process known as Booth's algorithm [13, 14] may be used. However, it is often more convenient to convert any negative numbers to their positive equivalents and then apply the shift and add technique. If the answer is to be negative, the product is 2's complemented. The sign of the product is calculated according to the rules.

$$+ \times + = + \quad : \quad 0 \times 0 = 0$$
$$+ \times - = - \quad : \quad 0 \times 1 = 1$$
$$- \times + = - \quad : \quad 1 \times 0 = 1$$
$$- \times - = + \quad : \quad 1 \times 1 = 0$$

The reader may recognise that sign multiplication follows the modulo-2 rules used in Gray $\leftrightarrow$ binary conversion.

Division is an algorithm whereby the number of times a divisor can be subtracted from a dividend is evaluated. Although it may be implemented by repetitive subtraction, faster techniques exist, such as the familiar decimal long division.

In an analogous fashion to multiplication, division by powers of the base can be accomplished by shifting right. Thus $0,0110$ $(+6) \rightarrow 0,0011$ $(+3) \rightarrow 0,001.1$ $(+1.5)$. Where negative 2's complement numbers are involved, 1s shift in from the left. Thus $1,1010$ $(-6) \rightarrow 1,1101$ $(-3) \rightarrow 1,1110.1$ (-1.5). Shifting right with sign-bit propagation is known as **arithmetic shift right** as opposed to the normal **logic shift right** which always shifts in zeros. There is no difference between logic and arithmetic shift lefts.

Example 1.25

Evaluate the following divisions:

(a) $(4284 \div 14)_{10}$ and (b) $(101101 \div 101)_2$

Solution

(a)
```
               306     quotient
   divisor 14 |4284
              −42↓
               008     1st  remainder
              −000↓
                84     2nd  remainder
               −84
                00     3rd  remainder
```

(b)
```
                1001   quotient
   divisor 101 |101101
              −101↓
               0001     1st  remainder
              −0000↓
                 10     2nd  remainder
                −00↓
                101     3rd  remainder
               −101
                000     4th  remainder
```

The division of Example 1.25(b) can be characterized as a number of steps more suitable for machine implementation, known as the **shift and subtract** algorithm:

1. Align the MSBs of the divisor and dividend.

    101101   Dividend
    101000   Aligned divisor

    In this example, this involves shifting the divisor three places left, an effective multiplication by 2^3. It is the number of alignment shifts which determines the power of the most significant quotient digit. An alignment of N shifts gives the MSB as 2^N. In this case, the quotient MSB will be weighted as 2^3.

2. Evaluate the first remainder by subtracting the two. If the difference is positive (no borrow) then make $Q_N = 1$. Otherwise the remainder is just the dividend (no subtraction) and $Q_N = 0$.

    $$\begin{array}{r} 101101 \\ -101000 \\ \hline 101 \end{array}$$ 1st remainder (subtract), $Q_3 = 1$.

3. Shift the remainder once left (multiply by two).

    $101 \times 2 = 1010$.

4. Compare aligned divisor and shifted remainder. If the aligned divisor is smaller or equal to the shifted remainder then subtract to form the new remainder, and make the new quotient bit 1. Else, if the divisor is larger, do not subtract, giving the new remainder as the shifted last remainder and the new quotient bit is 0.

    $$\begin{array}{r} 1010 \\ -101000 \\ \hline 1010 \end{array}$$ 2nd remainder (no subtraction), $Q_2 = 0$.

5. Repeat steps 3 and 4 for as many places as necessary.

    $1010 \times 2 = 10100$

    $$\begin{array}{r} 10100 \\ -101000 \\ \hline 10100 \end{array}$$ 3rd remainder (no subtraction), $Q_1 = 0$

    $10100 \times 2 = 10100$

    $$\begin{array}{r} 101000 \\ -101000 \\ \hline 000000 \end{array}$$ 4th remainder (subtract), $Q_0 = 1$, etc.

Example 1.26

Using the shift and subtract division algorithm, divide 1010 by 11 $(10 \div 3)_{10}$, giving the quotient to two binary places.

Solution

i   1010
     1100   Align (two shifts, $N = 2$)

ii   1010
    $-$1100
     1010   1st remainder (no subtraction), $Q_2 = 0$

iii $1010 \times 2 = 101000$

     10100
    $-$ 1100
      1000   2nd remainder (subtract), $Q_1 = 1$

iv $1000 \times 2 = 10000$

     10000
    $-$ 1100
     0100   3rd remainder (subtract), $Q_0 = 1$

v $0100 \times 2 = 1000$

      1000
     $-$1100
      1000   4th remainder (subtract), $Q_{-1} = 0$

vi $1000 \times 2 = 10000$

     10000
    $-$ 1100
      0110   5th remainder (no subtraction), $Q_{-2} = 1$

Answer   011.01.

Notice that as the 3rd and 5th remainders are the same, the last two digits will repeat indefinately.

———————

Floating-point multiplication is implemented by adding the exponents and multiplying the mantissas. Thus $(2 \times 10^2) \times (6 \times 10^5) = 12 \times 10^7$. The exponents need not be aligned, but shifting may be necessary if the result overflows its field. **Floating-point division** is accomplished by subtracting the exponents and dividing the mantissas. Provided that the floating-point dividend and divisor are normalized, the initial alignment step of the shift and subtract algorithm is unnecessary.

Example 1.27

Multiply and divide the following single-precision ANSII format floating-point binary numbers.

0,01111111,10000000000000000000000   {0,(1)10ȯ E 01111111}   Decimal 1.5

0,10000000,00000000000000000000000   {0,(1)00ȯ E 10000000}   Decimal 2.0

Solution

(a) Multiplying mantissas and adding exponents gives:

$$
\begin{array}{ccc}
1.100 & 0 \Leftrightarrow 0 = 0 & 01111111 \\
\times 1.000 & & +10000000 \\
\overline{(1).100000} & & \overline{11111111}
\end{array}
$$

$$
\begin{array}{c}
-01111111 \;\; (-127 \text{ bias}) \\
\overline{10000000}
\end{array}
$$

Mantissas   Signs   Exponents

Answer: 0,(1)10ȯ E 10000000 {0,10000000,10000000000000000000000}
or   decimal 3

(b) Dividing mantissas and subtracting exponents gives:

$$
\begin{array}{ccc}
1.100 & 0 \Leftrightarrow 0 = 0 & 10000000 \;\; \text{Interchanging} \\
-1.000 & & -01111111 \;\; \text{minuend \& subtrahend} \\
\overline{0.100} \;\; Q_0 = (1) & & (-)\overline{00000001}
\end{array}
$$

$$
\begin{array}{cc}
1.000 & +01111111 \;\; \text{Add 127 bias} \\
-1.000 \;\; Q_{-1} = 1 & \overline{01111110} \\
\overline{0.000}
\end{array}
$$

Mantissas   Signs   Exponents

Answer: 0,(1)10ȯ E 01111110 {0,01111110,10000000000000000000000}
or   decimal $+1.5 \times 2^{-1} = 0.75$

Subtracting two excess-127 numbers gives a difference 127 too small. Thus 127 is added to the exponent difference to compensate.

Both solutions dealt with the exponents in their biased form, later correcting the resulting offset. Another approach is to convert the exponents to their 2's complement form, do the arithmetic and transform back. Example 1.34 adopts this technique.

1.3   Problems

1.3.1   Worked Examples

Example 1.28

A certain analog to digital converter transforms an analog voltage between 0 V and 15 V to 4-bit binary, as shown in Table 1.6 below. In order to accommodate bipolar input voltages, an offset bias of +8 V is added to the incoming analog signal. As shown, this gives an effective range from −8 V to +7 V. However, the resulting offset code is not in the 2's complement form required by the digital processor. How would you propose programming this processor to implement the conversion?

Analog input	Converter input	Converter output	2's complement
7V	15V	1111	0,111
6V	14V	1110	0,110
5V	13V	1101	0,101
4V	12V	1100	0,100
3V	11V	1011	0,011
2V	10V	1010	0,010
1V	9V	1001	0,001
0V	8V	1000	0,000
−1V	7V	0111	1,111
−2V	6V	0110	1,110
−3V	5V	0101	1,101
−4V	4V	0100	1,100
−5V	3V	0011	1,011
−6V	2V	0010	1,010
−7V	1V	0001	1,001
−8V	0V	0000	1,000
(+8V)	(actual)	(desired)	

Table 1.6: Offset to 2's complement code.

Solution

Comparing the 2's complement code with the converter's Offset code, clearly shows that inversion of the most significant digit will perform the conversion. Alternatively, subtracting $1000b$ (i.e. 8) from the offset code, and ignoring any final borrows, will give the same result. This can be thought of as compensating for the initial (surreptitious) addition of eight volts. As an aside, note that from this discussion, subtracting 1 from a binary digit is equivalent to toggling it, i.e. inversion.

    Using four bits as the digital word will give asymmetrical quantizing errors of up to −1 V; for example +2.0 to +2.99 V (biased) will be represented by +2 (1010/2 or

0,010/2 after conversion). Some improvement is obtained by using a bias of +7.5 V rather than +8 V. This leads to a symmetrical error of $\pm\frac{1}{2}$ V.

Example 1.29

Figure 1.8 gives a pictorial representation of the conversion process outlined in the last example. It is desired to convert the digitized signal to the modulus equivalent. Thus the sinusoid shown will effectively be full-wave rectified (shown dotted). Determine the conversion algorithm.

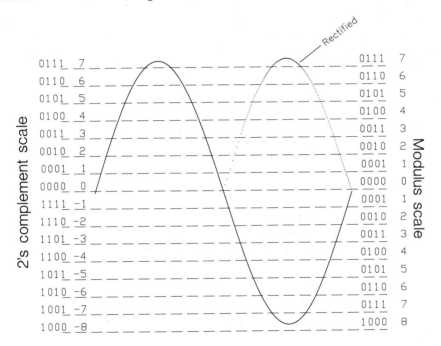

Figure 1.8: Digital rectification.

Solution

Signal levels above zero, i.e. 0000 to 0111, are left untouched. For negative levels of x we require the difference from zero, eg. $0000 - x$, which is just $-x$. Thus all values from 1111 down to 1000 are 2's complemented to obtain their negative equivalent. The resulting modulus scale is shown at the right of the diagram (see also Example SAE 5.3).

Example 1.30

Add the 2's complement binary numbers (a) +9 and +12 and (b) −9 and −12, and comment on your answers.

Solution

$$0,1001 \ (+ \ 9)$$
$$\underline{0,1100 \ (+12)}$$
$$1,0101 \ (-11)!$$

$$1,0111 \ (- \ 9)$$
$$\underline{1,0100 \ (-12)}$$
$$\cancel{1}0,1011 \ (+11)!$$

Careful examination of these two ridiculous answers shows that the problem lies in the **overflow** of the number into the sign space. This can only happen when two positive or two negative numbers are totalized. Most digital processors, such as microprocessors, set a semaphore (flag) to indicate the occurrence of overflow (i.e. $++ = -$ and $-- = +$). The action to be taken when the V flag is active is rather system dependent. In both cases above, the sum could be extended to a larger-sized word. Thus $1,0101b$ might become $0,001010b$, i.e. $+21$. Some computer languages do not signal overflow, which can lead to some unfortunate results!

Example 1.31

Determine the following differences using 2's complement arithmetic:

(1) $0,1101011$ and $0,1110$ {decimal $107 - 14$}
(2) $0,0.1010$ and $0,0.1101$ {decimal $\frac{10}{16} - \frac{13}{16}$}

Solution

1. In subtracting two numbers of unequal length, the sizes are first equalized. Thus the subtrahend is written as $0,0001110$; giving the 2's complement as $1,1110010$.

$$0,1101011$$
$$\underline{+1,1110010}$$
$$\cancel{1}0,1011101 \qquad \text{Answer: } 0,1011101 \qquad \{\text{decimal } +93\}$$

2. The 2's complement of 0.1101 is 1.0011.

$$0,0.1010$$
$$\underline{+1,1.0011}$$
$$1,1.1101 \qquad \text{Answer: } 1,1.1101 \qquad \{\text{decimal } -\frac{3}{16}\}$$

Example 1.32

Multiply $0,1011$ by $1,0110$ (decimal $+11$ by -10)

Solution

1. The positive equivalent of the multiplier is 1010.

2. Multiply the positive numbers, and evaluate the true sign.

$$
\begin{array}{r}
1011 \\
\times 1010 \\
\hline
0000 \\
1011 \\
0000 \\
+1011 \\
\hline
1101110
\end{array}
\qquad 0 \Leftrightarrow 1 = 1 \text{ sign (negative)}
$$

1101110   Product modulus

3. As the product is negative; 2's complement 1101110 to give the answer: *1*,0010010 (decimal −110).

Example 1.33

Show how the following decimal numbers will be represented in ANSII standard double-precision floating-point format: (a) +7.0, (b) −30.0, (c) 0.25.

Solution

(a) +7.0 is 1.75×2^2 or $(1).11 \times 2^2$

Fraction is   1100000000000000000000000000000000000000000000000000
Sign is   0
Exponent is 10000000001   (In excess 1023 format)

Answer: 0,10000000001,1100000000000000000000000000000000000000000000000000
or   40 1C 00 00 00 00 00 00   in hexadecimal

(b) −30.0 is -1.875×2^4 or $-(1).111 \times 2^4$

Fraction is   1110000000000000000000000000000000000000000000000000   (Magnitude)
Sign is   1
Exponent is 10000000011   (in excess 1023 format)

Answer: 1,10000000011,1110000000000000000000000000000000000000000000000000
or   C0 3E 00 00 00 00 00 00   in hexadecimal

(c) 0.25 is 1.0×2^{-2} or $(1).0 \times 2^{-2}$

Fraction is   0000000000000000000000000000000000000000000000000000
Sign is   0
Exponent is 01111111101   (in excess 1023 format)

Answer: 0,01111111101,0000000000000000000000000000000000000000000000000000
or   3F D0 00 00 00 00 00 00   in hexadecimal

Example 1.34

Add, subtract, multiply and divide +7.0 and −30.0, represented in double-precision ANSII floating-point format.

Solution

From Example 1.33 we have:

+7.0 $(+1.75 \times 2^2)$
2's complement mantissa   0,1.11000̇   (+1.75)
Debiased exponent (add 1023)   0,0000000010   (+2)

−30.0 (-1.875×2^4)
2's complement mantissa   1,0.00100̇   (−1.875)
Debiased exponent   0,0000000100   (+4)

(a) Addition: Shift addend right twice to equalize exponents.

Mantissa		Exponent
0,0.011100	(shifted right twice)	0,00000000100
+1,0.001000		0,00000000100

1,0.100100̇	(2's complement, $-1\frac{7}{16}$)	0,00000000100
1,1.011100̇	(sign + magnitude, $-1\frac{7}{16}$)	10000000011 (adding 1023)

Answer: 1,10000000011,0111000000000000000000000000000000000000000000000000000
or   C0 37 00 00 00 00 00 00 in hexadecimal
or $-1\frac{7}{16} \times 2^4 =$ decimal -23.

(b) Subtraction: Shift addend right twice to equalize exponents.

Mantissa		Exponents
0,0.011100̇	(shifted right twice)	0,00000000100
+0,1.111000̇		0,00000000100
0,10.0101000̇	(overflow)	0,00000000100
0,1.0010100̇	(normalized)	0,00000000101
0,1.0010100̇	(Sign + magnitude; $+1\frac{5}{32}$)	100000000100 (adding 1023)

Answer: 0,100000000100,0010100000000000000000000000000000000000000000000000000
or   40 21 40 00 00 00 00 00 in hexadecimal
or $+1\frac{5}{32} \times 2^5$ in decimal.

(c) Multiplication: Multiply mantissas and add exponents.

I Make multiplier positive, then multiply.

```
       1.1100
     ×1.1110
       00000
      11100
      11100
      11100
    +11100
   11 .01001000  (Number of places is sum of multiplier and multiplicand places)
```

II Add exponents.

```
  00000000010
+00000000100
 00000000110
```

```
+01111111111  (Add 1023 bias)
 10000000101
```

III Signs $0 \Leftrightarrow 1 = 1$ (Negative)

Giving: -11.010010 E 10000000101
Normalizing gives: -1.1010010 E 10000000110 $(1\frac{41}{64} \times 2^7)$

Answer: 1,10000000110,1010010000000000000000000000000000000000000000000000
or   C0 6A 40 00 00 00 00 00 in hexadecimal
or $-1\frac{41}{64} \times 2^7$ = decimal 210.

(d) Division: Divide mantissas and subtract exponents.

I Make divisor positive, then divide.

```
11110|11100
    −11110
     111000       1st remainder (no subtraction) ×2      Q₀ = 0
   − 11110
     110100       2nd remainder (subtract) ×2            Q₋₁ = 1
   − 11110
     101100       3rd remainder (subtract) ×2            Q₋₂ = 1
   − 11110
     011100       4th remainder (subtract) ×2            Q₋₃ = 1
   −  11110
     111000       5th remainder (same as 1st) ×2         Q₋₄ = 0
   −  11110
     110100       6th remainder (same as 2nd) ×2         Q₋₅ = 1
```

and repeat giving : $0.1110\dot{1}\dot{1}\dot{1}$

II Subtract exponents.

```
  00000000010  (+2)
+11111111100  (−4)
 11111111110  (−2)
```

```
 01111111111  (+1023 bias)
 01111111011
```

III Signs $0 \Leftrightarrow 1 = 1$ (Negative)

Giving: $-0.1110\dot{1}\dot{1}\dot{1}$ E 01111111011
Normalizing gives: $-1.110\dot{1}\dot{1}\dot{1}0$ E 01111111010

Answer: 1,01111111010,110111011110111011101110111011101110111101110111011101
or   BF AB BB BB BB BB BB BB in hexadecimal
or $\approx 1\frac{27}{32} \times 2^{-3} = 0.23$

1.3.2   Self Assessment Examples

SAE 1.1

A certain microprocessor port uses a 12-bit analog to digital converter to read an
input analog voltage ranging from 0 to 2.55V. How much is the least significant
digit worth? Can you see any practical considerations which may arise?

SAE 1.2

Implement the following base conversions:

(a)	$(11011101)_2$	to decimal and to BCD
(b)	$(1101.1101)_2$	to decimal and to BCD
(c)	$(150)_{10}$	to binary
(d)	$(0.565)_{10}$	to binary
(e)	$(53.2265625)_{10}$	to binary
(f)	$(1111000011001000)_2$	to hexadecimal
(g)	$(F69C)_{16}$	to binary and to decimal

SAE 1.3

Convert decimal +1.0, −0.1, 53.2265625 to ANSII single-precision floating-point
format.

SAE 1.4

Convert binary 10111 to Gray code.

SAE 1.5

Convert Gray code 1011 to binary.

SAE 1.6

The Bi-quinary BCD code is tabulated below. Determine the weight of each column.
Hint: column weights of zero are permitted. What property does this code have
and how could it be exploited for error detection purposes?

0	0100001	5	1000001
1	0100010	6	1000010
2	0100100	7	1000100
3	0101000	8	1001000
4	0110000	9	1010000

SAE 1.7

The **C** computer language represents strings (alphanumeric messages) as ASCII-coded characters terminated by NUL. Show how the string "**The Design of Small Digital Systems**" would be stored in memory. Give your answer in hexadecimal.

SAE 1.8

Build up a table using the Gray code from decimal 0 to 31, using the reflected construction of Table 1.5.

SAE 1.9

Based on the outcome of a signed 2's complement subtraction (see Section 1.2.2), determine the magnitude relationship between subrahend A and the minuend B by looking at the sign bit **N**, zero bit **Z** and overflow bit **V**. Hint: For each of greater-than and less-than there are two possibilities, see Example 1.31.

SAE 1.10

The exponents of ANSII single-precision floating-point numbers are coded as excess $(127)_{10}$ or $(01111111)_2$. Show that such numbers can be converted to 2's complement by simply toggling the most significant bit and adding one. Furthermore, in reverse the process is toggle MSB and subtract one. Hint: Compare toggling a bit to subtracting 1.

SAE 1.11

Add, subtract, multiply and divide the following binary numbers: $0{,}0101.11$ and $0{,}0010.001$. Check your answers by conversion to base ten and repeating the operations.

SAE 1.12

Add, subtract, multiply and divide the following 2's complement binary numbers: $0{,}0101.11$ and $1{,}1101.111$.

SAE 1.13

Divide the 2's complement number $(1,1000000)_2$ by $(0,10000)_2$ (i.e. $(64)_{10} \div (16)_{10}$).

SAE 1.14

Evaluate the following floating-point arithmetic operations, with the binary answer being in single-precision ANSII format.

(a): $(27 \times 2^{-5}) \ + \ (25 \times 2^0)$
(b): $(-12 \times 2^0) \ + \ (-6 \times 2^2)$
(c): $(31 \times 2^2) \ + \ (18 \times 2^3)$
(d): $(27 \times 2^5) \ + \ (16 \times 2^3)$.

References

[1] *IEEE Standard Dictionary of Electrical and Electronic Terms*, Wiley, 3rd ed., 1984.

[2] Rosie, A.M.; *Information and Communications Theory*, Van Nostrand Reinhold, 2nd ed., 1975, Section 6.

[3] Wakling, P.J.; *Pulse Code Modulation*, Mills and Boon, 1972.

[4] Clayton, G.B.; *Data Converters*, Macmillan, 1982, Section 5.

[5] Shannon, C.E.; Communication in the Presence of Noise, *Proc. IRE*, **37**, Jan. 1949, pp.10–21.

[6] Stark, H. et al.; *Modern commumications*, Prentice-Hall, 2nd ed., 1988, Section 4.6.

[7] Sony; *Digital Audio and Compact Disc Technology*, Heinemann, 1988.

[8] McLeish, J.; *Number*, Bloomsbury Publishing, 1991, Chapters 8 & 10.

[9] American National Standards Institute; *Standard for Binary Floating-Point Arithmetic*, 754-1985.

[10] Cody, W.J. et al.; Proposed Radix-and Word-Length Independent IEEE P854 Standard for Floating-Point Arithmetic, *Computer*, **17**, no.8, Aug. 1984, pp.37–51.

[11] Malvino, A.P. and Leach, D.P.; *Digital Principles and Applications*, McGraw-Hill, 1969, Section 3.

[12] Kostopoulos, G.K.; *Digital Engineering*, Wiley, 1975, Section 12.2.

[13] Booth, A.D.; A Signed Binary Multiplication Technique, *Quarterly J. of Mechanics and Applied Mathematics*, **4**, no. 2, 1951, pp.236–240.

[14] Kohenen, T.; *Digital Circuits and Devices*, Prentice-Hall, 1972, Section 4.4.2.

Chapter 2

010

Logic and Boolean Algebra

The design of efficient digital circuitry requires an ability by the engineer to manipulate binary system variables. The algebra governing these mathematical manipulations is known as **Boolean algebra**, and turns out to be that applicable to the laws of logic. The aim of this chapter is to investigate the structure of this algebra, and its relevance to digital design. The basis will be laid for the design algorithms outlined in succeeding chapters.

2.1 Logic

Logic may loosely be defined as the science of argument. Logical arguments or exercises involve ascertaining the validity of a series of interdependent propositions (clearly defined statements), which may be simple (containing only one proposition) or compound (comprizing a number of interconnected simple propositions). These systems of propositions lead 'logically' to the truth or falsity (non-truth) of certain assertions. Because a logic argument is normally true or false; such arguments may be represented by binary circuits. The outcome (output) of such a circuit is 2-valued, and may hence indicate the truth or non-truth of the argument as a function of its inputs; which in this case is the truth or falsity of the component propositions.

After completing this section you should:

- Appreciate the meaning and symbology of the Boolean operations of AND, OR, NOT, EOR and ENOR.

- Understand the role of 2-valued elements (switches) in synthesizing logic functions/networks.

- Be able to design a logic circuit directly from a defining truth table.

- Be familiar with the idea of using a symbol to represent a logic function.

- Be familiar with both the distinctive and uniform IEC/ANSII symbols for gates.

- Know the properties of AND, OR and EOR/ENOR gates and how to cascade them.

- Appreciate the use of dependency notation to signal the control relationships AND (**G**), OR (**V**), EOR-negate (**N**), even (**2K**) and odd (**2k+1**).

2.1.1 Logic Switching Operations

Although logic was a highly developed art in the Greek era, over 2000 years ago, it is only comparatively recently that serious attempts have been made to incorporate logic as a branch of mathematics [1]. In the mid-19th century, the mathematician George Boole (then professor of mathematics at Queen's College, Cork, Ireland [2]) popularized the algebra, now known as Boolean algebra; publishing in 1847 and 1854 his two major works [3, 4]. Boole derived his algebra by representing propositions (his logic variables) by symbols, and operating on them using symbolic representations of the connectives. In this way, once the imprecise statements of formal language, with its ambiguous connectives, are reduced to a set of precise equations, then this set may be solved according to the rules of this algebra.

The following riddle, reproduced by courtesy of *New Scientist* [5], is an example of a logic argument which may be solved using Boolean algebra:

> Chef D'oeuvres. The Gourmets' Gala is to end with a gastronomic symphony in four courses each created by a different chef. Only six chefs merit consideration but they are all men of temperament, making Maria Callas seem like a clergyman's niece.
>
> Thus M. Avocado would not contemplate accepting, unless M. Bernaise were included; and neither of them will prepare the soup. Only Herr Futtermeister could prevent hostilities between M. Bernaise and Mr. Cucumber and then only on condition that he (Futtermeister) took charge of the main course and Cucumber was kept off the fish. Diplomacy requires that M. Escargot (who refuses to prepare soup or fish) and M. Delice be not both excluded. And nothing in the world could prevent open war between M. Delice and Herr Futtermeister nor between M. Escargot and M. Avocado.
>
> That being so, who should be asked to do the pud?

Notice that this argument is made up of a number of propositions, giving an interconnecting whole. From each proposition a deduction can be made concerning the truth of the overall argument. For example, from the first proposition we may deduce that the choice of M. Avocado as a member of the set implies that M. Bernaise will also be a component of that set, i.e. A AND B is a possibility for inclusion in the set, but excludes A AND NOT B. The symbol A stands for the proposition that M. Avocado is a member of the set, and similarly B refers to M. Bernaise. Note the use of the connectives AND, AND NOT. By systematically setting out these conditions for either inclusion or exclusion, a consistent set of four members (one for each course) can be chosen. Although the problem will be solved analytically later in the chapter, it is a useful exercise for the reader to attempt to solve the argument intuitively. The actual problem lies not so much in determining who cooked the pud, but which four obstreperous cooks from the gaggle (the collective noun for a herd of cooks is obscure) were chosen to avoid a clash of temperament. Once this has been determined, the selection of dishes follows by a process of elimination.

It was Claud E. Shannon [6] who first recognized that the bi-valued Boolean algebra (there are a number of different Boolean algebras) used in the solution of logical problems, could also be used to analyze and synthesize switching networks. Switches are 2-valued elements, being either On or Off, corresponding to the true and false states of logic. This branch of Boolean algebra has since come to be known as **switching algebra**.

In common with any algebra, **Boolean algebra** consists of a system of mathematical operations on both variables, known as **literals**, and constants. In conventional algebra, variables can take on an infinity of values, and are operated on by, amongst others the $+, -, \times, \div, =$ operators. In switching algebra, variables can take on only two values, viz. logic 1 and logic 0; usually just written as 1 and 0.

In essence there are three Boolean operators or connectives, known as AND, OR, NOT. All logic functions may be described in terms of these three operators.

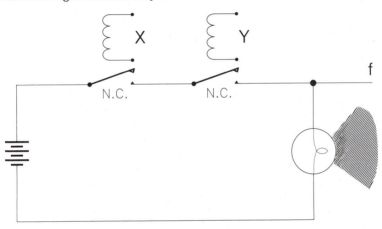

Figure 2.1: A relay AND circuit.

Consider the relay diagram in Fig. 2.1 [7]. In this circuit two normally-open (N.O.) relays are in series with a battery and bulb. The voltages at the inputs (relay coils) are designated X and Y, whilst the output (the state of the bulb) is labelled $\mathcal{F}$. If the presence or absence of a voltage at any point in the circuit (X, Y or $\mathcal{F}$) represents respectively true or false, then the response of the output for every possible combination of inputs can be tabulated. This is shown in Table 2.1(a). Only when both relays are energized, i.e. X AND Y are true, does the bulb light. We can represent this switching circuit by the Boolean function, $\mathcal{F} = \text{X·Y}$; the **AND operator** being represented by a multiplicative dot. Other symbols commonly used are noted in Table 2.1(c). The AND operation is often known as a logical product.

Tabulations of the response of a function to all possible input combinations, such as shown in Tables 2.1(a)&(b), are known as **truth tables**. Such tables define under what conditions the output is in the true state. Truth tables are the equivalent to the transfer functions of analog circuits, defining the relationship between input

X	Y	f
F	F	F
F	T	F
T	F	F
T	T	T

X	Y	f
0	0	0
0	1	0
1	0	0
1	1	1

(a) Truth table

(b) Using binary notation

$f = X \cdot Y$ Used in this text
$f = X \quad Y$ Commonly used
$f = X \,\&\, Y$ Used in computer aided software
$f = X * Y$ Used in computer aided software
$f = X \cap Y$ Used in mathematical texts
$f = X \wedge Y$ Used in mathematical texts

$0 \cdot 0 = \quad 0$
$0 \cdot 1 = \quad 0$
$1 \cdot 0 = \quad 0$
$1 \cdot 1 = \quad 1$

(c) AND symbols

(d) AND rules

Table 2.1: Definition of the AND operator for two variables.

and output. As will be seen, truth tables play a central role in the design of digital systems.

Multiple-input AND functions are possible, with N series switches giving an N-variable function. The truth table for such a function will show the response to the 2^N combinations. However, as the AND function is an 'all or nothing' operation, only the row for all inputs one will give a one output.

If a formal logic problem (i.e. an argument in language) is being considered, the connective AND may be substituted by other similar-meaning words to suit both grammar and style. Some of these are: BUT, ALTHOUGH, EVEN, THOUGH. More details of this aspect of logic are given in reference [8].

Switches in parallel implement the OR connective, as shown in Fig. 2.2(a), where the function $\mathcal{F} = X+Y$ is shown implemented. In general N-variable OR functions are implemented by N parallel switches. As the function is equivalent to the 'one or more' operation (i.e. ≥ 1), the resulting truth table will show a one output for all input combinations excepting all zeros. The **OR function** is often known as the logical sum.

The logic OR operator does not always directly translate into language. For example the statement:

At 7p.m. Aaron will go either to the cinema OR to the party.

implies that he will go either to the party or to the cinema, but not to both at the same time. Because of this variance, the logic OR operator is known as the **inclusive-OR** function, as it includes the case where more than one input is true. However, normally it is abbreviated to OR, and the less common **exclusive-OR (EOR)**, which excludes both events being true, is given its full title (see Example 2.2). EITHER...OR; EITHER...OR...OR BOTH; UNLESS are some common English translations of inclusive-OR.

The final elementary connective is the **NOT operator**. This is defined as inverting or reversing the truth value of the variable acted upon. The NOT truth

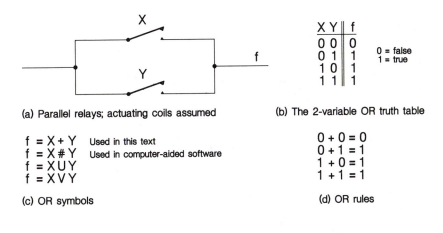

(a) Parallel relays; actuating coils assumed

(b) The 2-variable OR truth table

X	Y	f
0	0	0
0	1	1
1	0	1
1	1	1

0 = false
1 = true

f = X + Y   Used in this text
f = X # Y   Used in computer-aided software
f = X ∪ Y
f = X ∨ Y

(c) OR symbols

0 + 0 = 0
0 + 1 = 1
1 + 0 = 1
1 + 1 = 1

(d) OR rules

Figure 2.2: The OR operator and circuit.

table, together with a possible relay implementation, is shown in Fig. 2.3. When the input X is 0, the normally closed (N.C.) relay gives $\mathcal{F} = 1$, and conversely when X is 1 the relay is energized to open, giving $\mathcal{F} = 0$. Logic inversion is often known as **complementation** or **negation**.

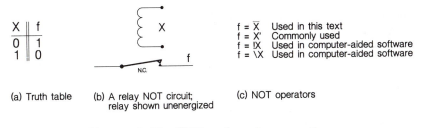

X	f
0	1
1	0

f = $\overline{X}$ Used in this text
f = X'   Commonly used
f = /X   Used in computer-aided software
f = \X   Used in computer-aided software

(a) Truth table

(b) A relay NOT circuit; relay shown unenergized

(c) NOT operators

Figure 2.3: The NOT, or inversion, operation.

In English, inversion is usually denoted by the prefix not, as in the sentence:

I will play golf IF it is NOT raining AND it is warm.

This can be written symbolically as $G = \overline{R} \cdot W$, where G is playing golf (by the unenthusiastic golfer!), R is rain and W is warmth. However, inversion is often signified by a change in word. Thus cold is equivalent to NOT warm.

Example 2.1

Design a relay circuit to implement the expression $\mathcal{F} = \overline{R} \cdot W$.

Solution

As shown in Fig. 2.4, two relays in series, implement AND. The R input is to a
N.C. relay, whilst the W input is to a N.O. relay.

Figure 2.4: Implementing the function $G = \overline{R} \cdot W$.

2.1.2   Switching Functions

Figure 2.4 is an example of a simple **switching function**. This function is combinational; defined as having an output which is solely dependent on the present state
of its inputs. We shall see in Section 4.1 that such networks can also implement
sequential functions (that is, having an output depending on the sequence of events
leading up to the current inputs). In general, a logic operation of any complexity
can be synthesized by means of a switching network. All that is necessary is to
determine a suitable contact topology.

Example 2.2

Deduce the logic function and the characteristic truth table for the relay circuit of
Fig. 2.5. Notice the new relay symbol.

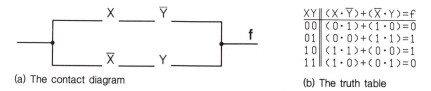

(a) The contact diagram   (b) The truth table

Figure 2.5: Relay logic. The complement sign indicates a N.C. relay, i.e. the variable
is complemented.

Solution

The top branch $(X \cdot \overline{Y})$ is in parallel with the lower branch $(\overline{X} \cdot Y)$, giving $\mathcal{F} = (X \cdot \overline{Y}) + (\overline{X} \cdot Y)$.

To determine the behavior of the circuit, a truth table showing the response to
all possible inputs should be derived. To do this, each combination of X and Y, i.e.
00, 01, 10, 11, is inserted into the logic function. The resulting response $\mathcal{F}$ is then
determined using the AND, OR, NOT rules. With a little practice the evaluation of
such functions for all combinations of inputs can easily be done by inspection. An

alternative, applicable to relay diagrams, is to determine for each input combination if a closed path exists across the network. If it does then $\mathcal{F} = 1$, otherwise $\mathcal{F} = 0$.

A close look at this truth table shows that the circuit implements the exclusive-OR function; the output being true if X or Y is true, but not if both are true. We have in fact already come across this operator in Section 1.1.3, where we used the modulo-2 operation for Gray $\leftrightarrow$ binary conversions. The exclusive-OR operator, although not basic in that it can be expressed in terms of AND, OR, NOT, finds sufficient use to be given its own symbol $\oplus$ (sometimes $\wedge$, $|+|$ or $\#\#$ in computer-aided engineering software) :

$$X \text{ EOR } Y = (X \text{ AND NOT } Y) \text{ OR } (\text{NOT } X \text{ AND } Y)$$
$$X \oplus Y = (X \cdot \overline{Y}) + (\overline{X} \cdot Y)$$

OR; EITHER... OR; EITHER... OR... BUT NOT BOTH; UNLESS are common English translations of exclusive-OR. For example:

At 9.00 p.m. I will read the paper UNLESS I watch television.

Comparing the truth table of Fig. 2.5(b) with the rules of addition detailed in Section 1.2.1, shows that the EOR operation actually implements the sum of two binary digits but ignoring the carry. This function is normally called **modulo-2 addition** (hence the name modulo-2 operator).

The EOR process is sometimes known as **logic differentiation**, as the result is true only if the inputs differ. Example 2.49 gives a practical use of this property.

Example 2.3

Determine the truth table for the network of Fig. 2.6.

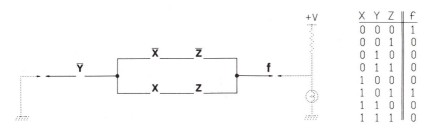

X	Y	Z	f
0	0	0	1
0	0	1	0
0	1	0	0
0	1	1	0
1	0	0	0
1	0	1	1
1	1	0	0
1	1	1	0

(a) Relay diagram showing alternative bulb connection dotted   (b) The truth table

Figure 2.6: A series-parallel switching network.

Solution

We have by inspection $X \cdot Z$ in parallel with $\overline{X} \cdot \overline{Z}$ all in series with $\overline{Y}$, giving $\mathcal{F} = \overline{Y} \cdot (\overline{X} \cdot \overline{Z} + X \cdot Z)$ and the truth table of Fig. 2.6(b). Thus there will be a transmission path across the network for the situation where X, Y and Z are all logic 0 and when both X and Z are logic 1 and Y is logic 0 (binary patterns 0 and 5).

If the purpose of the circuit is to light a bulb on these two patterns, then we must connect a battery to the left-hand side of the network, in the manner of Fig. 2.1.

The alternative connection, shown dotted in Fig. 2.6(a), lights the bulb when there is no transmission path (transmission diverts current away from the bulb). In terms of the truth table, this means that the bulb lights when there is a logic 0 at the output. Thus the active state (bulb lit) is logic 0, not the more intuitive logic 1 state. Such circuits are said to be **active-Low**. Now the bulb lights at binary states 1,2,3,4,6 & 7. In many cases, simpler circuitry results if the false output ($\mathcal{F} = 0$) is the active level, and in any case the function can always, if necessary, be inverted using a NOT stage. Thus in designing a combinational logic circuit, there is a minimum of two possible implementations; see also Example 2.32.

The last two examples have shown the analysis of switching networks. Let us now look at the opposite process where we design circuits from a specification.

Example 2.4

Design a switch network to implement the specification as given by the truth table of Fig. 2.7(a).

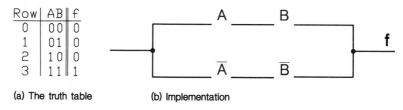

Row	AB	f
0	00	0
1	01	0
2	10	0
3	11	1

(a) The truth table   (b) Implementation

Figure 2.7: Designing logic circuits.

Solution

To implement this specification, we must develop some means of converting a truth table to a logic function. One means of doing this is to write down for each true row, the AND function of all input literals which gives a true output for that input combination. In this case, for row 0 we write $\overline{A}\cdot\overline{B}$ (as with $A\,B = 00$, $\overline{A}\cdot\overline{B} = 1$) and for row 3 we write $A\cdot B$ ($A\,B = 11$, $A\cdot B = 1$). Finally, as $\mathcal{F}$ is true for any of these rows, i.e. row 0 OR row 3; we OR the product terms together giving $\mathcal{F} = (\overline{A}\cdot\overline{B})+(A\cdot B)$, which leads to the relay diagram of Fig. 2.7(b). This function is true if $A\,B = 00$ or 11, otherwise false. Functions of this form are generally known as **sum of products (SOP)**, being a string of logic products logically summed together.

From this example we can deduce a simple algorithm which will give the SOP logic function directly from a truth table. This algorithm is as follows:

1. For each true row write down a product term containing all literals. In this expression each literal is uncomplemented if represented at the input by 1 and complemented for a 0 input.

2. Sum all product terms together.

The truth table of Fig. 2.7(a) shows that this network is the inverse of exclusive-OR. In this text this inverse is called the exclusive-NOT-OR or **exclusive-NOR**. Sometimes it is called COINCIDENCE, as the output is true if the inputs are the same, i.e. coincide. Symbolically the operation is represented as $\overline{A \oplus B}$ or $A \odot B$.

Example 2.5

Design a 3-input digital circuit which indicates when the majority of its inputs are logic 0.

Solution

From the truth table of Fig. 2.8(a) we have:

Row 0 (000) gives $\overline{C} \cdot \overline{B} \cdot \overline{A}$
Row 1 (001) gives $\overline{C} \cdot \overline{B} \cdot A$
Row 2 (010) gives $\overline{C} \cdot B \cdot \overline{A}$
Row 4 (100) gives $C \cdot \overline{B} \cdot \overline{A}$

Thus we can say that $\mathcal{F} = (\overline{C} \cdot \overline{B} \cdot \overline{A}) + (\overline{C} \cdot \overline{B} \cdot A) + (\overline{C} \cdot B \cdot \overline{A}) + (C \cdot \overline{B} \cdot \overline{A})$; which leads to the relay implementation of Fig. 2.8(b).

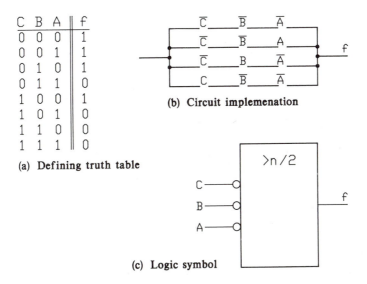

C	B	A	f
0	0	0	1
0	0	1	1
0	1	0	1
0	1	1	0
1	0	0	1
1	0	1	0
1	1	0	0
1	1	1	0

(a) Defining truth table

(b) Circuit implemenation

(c) Logic symbol

Figure 2.8: Three-input majority untrue design.

As an additional exercise, the reader should prove to his/her own satisfaction that the function $\mathcal{F} = (C \cdot \overline{B}) + (\overline{C} \cdot \overline{A}) + (\overline{B} \cdot \overline{A})$ is logically equivalent to the above function.

The early design stages are largely independent of the hardware which will eventually be used to implement the logic. Thus, the Boolean equations will not reflect whether transistor or pheumatic gates do the actual switching. As a consequence of this, it is necessary to symbolize the various logic processes in an implementation-independent manner. Such an abstract diagram will convey the logic of the system in a superior fashion to, say, a conventional circuit showing every transistor, resistor and capacitor.

An example of this is shown in Fig. 2.8(c). The internal function of the box is indicated by the general qualifying symbol $>$N/2 at the top center. This says that the output (right) is logic 1 when the inputs (left) have a majority of logic 1s. Our example specified a majority of 0s, which is indicated by the bubbles in series with the input lines C B A. These **inversion symbols** state that external 0s become internal (inside the box) 1s.

The overall function indicated by this logic symbol is (with a little practice) immediately apparent; which is certainly not the case for the circuit diagram of Fig. 2.8(b). Frequently, different interpretations of the logic is possible, and the logic symbol can be drawn to reflect this. For example, examination of the truth table shows that the circuit can be considered to be an active-Low detector of a majority of 1s. Using the inversion bubble symbol at the output line to indicate active-Low (external 0 is internal 1) draw the appropriate logic symbol. There are two other interpretations based on the $<$N/2 (minority) qualifier. Can you draw their logic symbol?

Example 2.6

Design a digital circuit to implement the logic of an automobile direction indicator and hazard warning system.

Solution

The output of car signalling schemes generally consist of two arrays of lights; one to the left (L_Lights) and one to the right (R_Lights) of the vehicle. Driver actuator inputs are the right indicator switch R, left indicator switch L and hazard warning switch H. Generally the L and R switches are interlocked so that both cannot be activated at the one time. A fourth input F is a nominal 0.5 Hz flasher unit, which is typically a thermal bi-metallic make-break switch.

The signalling protocol is outlined in the truth table of Fig. 2.9(b). Whenever a right-turn request is received, output R_Lights turns on whenever the flasher F is logic 1; thus giving a 0.5 Hz winking action. Similarly, the L_Lights wink for a left-turn request. An active hazard request overrides a right- or left-turn request, and causes both R_Lights and L_Lights to flash in unison. Not-possible combinations give a non-active (logic 0) outcome.

Using our rule to convert truth tables to a SOP expression gives the implementation shown in Fig. 2.9(c). Each output requires a total of 16 relay contacts, arranged as four serial contacts in four parallel branches. The total cost is then 32 contacts.

Although a working circuit, it seems a little complex for a rather simple operation. Abandoning the truth table approach and using a little intuition, we can condense the protocol to two statements:

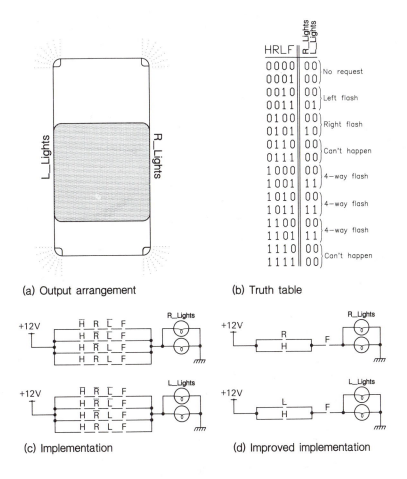

(a) Output arrangement

(b) Truth table

(c) Implementation

(d) Improved implementation

Figure 2.9: Direction and hazard-warning logic.

1. Activate the right indicator if a right-turn request or a hazard request is received and the flash input is active.

2. Activate the left indicator if a left-turn request or a hazard request is received and the flash input is active.

Mathematically this is expressed as:

$$R\_Lights = (R+H) \cdot F$$
$$L\_Lights = (L+H) \cdot F$$

Our new implementation is shown in Fig. 2.9(d). The cost is now six contacts, a reduction in price of over 500% between our systematic and intuitive outcomes!

Of course intuitive approaches are not always so easily come by or so productive as in this example. In any case, computers are not very good at intuitive reasoning, and computer-aided engineering software (CAE) is invariably used in logic design (see Section 6.1). Thus we need systematic procedures in minimizing the outcome of truth tables. We will develop some of these techniques in this chapter.

Can you redesign the logic so that the hazard warning flashes alternate sides in antiphase (probably illegally!).

Example 2.7

Using the techniques so far developed, determine who cooked the pud at the Gourmets' Gala; as described in page 46.

Solution

Initially it is best to concentrate on the problem of which of the four cooks actually are compatible, ignoring the various dishes. This is done by contriving a 6-variable truth table whose inputs are the six cooks labelled A, B, C, D, E, F (after M. Avocado, M. Bernaise etc.); the output being true if the selection of cooks for each row is compatible. The simplest way of obtaining the truth table is to frame the riddle as a logic equation. As the riddle actually lists exclusions, it is easiest to write the equation defining non-compatibility, $\overline{P}$.

1. "M. Avocado would not contemplate accepting, unless M. Bernaise were included". This gives exclusion for $A \cdot \overline{B}$.

2. "Only Herr Futtermeister could prevent hostilities between M. Bernaise and Mr. Cucumber". This excludes the case of $\overline{F}$ in conjunction with $B \cdot C$, i.e. $B \cdot C \cdot \overline{F}$.

3. "Diplomacy requires that M. Escargot and M. Delice be not both excluded". This means that $\overline{D} \cdot \overline{E}$ is not possible.

4. "Nothing in the world could prevent open war between M. Delice and Herr Futtermeister nor between M. Escargot and M. Avocado". This excludes $D \cdot F + A \cdot E$.

ORing these exclusion conditions together gives:

$$\overline{P} = (A \cdot \overline{B}) + (B \cdot C \cdot \overline{F}) + (\overline{D} \cdot \overline{E}) + (D \cdot F) + (A \cdot E)$$

By trying all possible inputs of six variables, we can now determine the truth table for $\overline{P}$ and thus P, as shown in Table 2.2(a). From this truth table we have all compatible groupings. However, only one grouping has four cooks, i.e. row $011011b$; M. Bernaise and Mr. Cucumber and M. Escargot and Herr Futtermeister.

We are now left with the problem of determining who cooked the pud. From the text, Table 2.2(a) is prepared. We know that M. Bernaise will not prepare the soup and that he presumably has no objections to preparing either meat, fish or pudding. This is indicated as ticks in his row under M, F and P. Mr. Cucumber is disallowed the fish as Herr Futtermeister is a member of the quartet. M. Escargot refuses to countenance the soup or fish, whilst Herr Futtermeister is going to do the meat. We thus have by elimination:

A	B	C	D	E	F	P̄	P	
0	0	0	0	0	0	1	0	
0	0	0	0	0	1	1	0	
0	0	0	0	1	0	0	1	E only
0	0	0	0	1	1	0	1	E & F only
0	0	0	1	0	0	0	1	D only
0	0	0	1	0	1	1	0	
0	0	0	1	1	0	0	1	D & E only
0	0	0	1	1	1	1	0	
0	0	1	0	0	0	1	0	
0	0	1	0	0	1	1	0	
0	0	1	0	1	0	0	1	C & E only
0	0	1	0	1	1	0	1	C & E & F only
0	0	1	1	0	0	0	1	C & D only
0	0	1	1	0	1	1	0	
0	0	1	1	1	0	0	1	C & D & E only
0	0	1	1	1	1	1	0	
0	1	0	0	0	0	1	0	
0	1	0	0	0	1	1	0	
0	1	0	0	1	0	0	1	B & E only
0	1	0	0	1	1	0	1	B & E & F only
0	1	0	1	0	0	0	1	B & D only
0	1	0	1	0	1	1	0	
0	1	0	1	1	0	0	1	B & D & E only
0	1	0	1	1	1	1	0	
0	1	1	0	0	0	1	0	
0	1	1	0	0	1	1	0	
0	1	1	0	1	1	0	1	B & C & E & F only √
0	1	1	1	0	0	1	0	
0	1	1	1	0	1	1	0	
0	1	1	1	1	0	1	0	
0	1	1	1	1	1	1	0	
1	0	0	0	0	0	1	0	
1	0	0	0	0	1	1	0	
1	0	0	0	1	0	1	0	
1	0	0	0	1	1	1	0	
1	0	0	1	0	0	1	0	
1	0	0	1	0	1	1	0	
1	0	0	1	1	0	1	0	
1	0	0	1	1	1	1	0	
1	0	1	0	0	0	1	0	
1	0	1	0	0	1	1	0	
1	0	1	0	1	0	1	0	
1	0	1	0	1	1	1	0	
1	0	1	1	0	0	1	0	
1	0	1	1	0	1	1	0	
1	0	1	1	1	0	1	0	
1	0	1	1	1	1	1	0	
1	1	0	0	0	0	1	0	
1	1	0	0	0	1	1	0	
1	1	0	0	1	0	1	0	
1	1	0	0	1	1	1	0	
1	1	0	1	0	0	0	1	A & B & D only
1	1	0	1	0	1	1	0	
1	1	0	1	1	0	1	0	
1	1	0	1	1	1	1	0	
1	1	1	0	0	0	1	0	
1	1	1	0	0	1	1	0	
1	1	1	0	1	0	1	0	
1	1	1	0	1	1	1	0	
1	1	1	1	0	0	1	0	
1	1	1	1	0	1	1	0	
1	1	1	1	1	0	1	0	
1	1	1	1	1	1	1	0	

(a) Compatibility, P

	S	M	F	P	← Dish
B		√	√	√	S = Soup
C	√	√		√	M = Meat
E		√		√	F = Fish
F		√			P = Pudding

↑
Cook

(b) Dish selection table

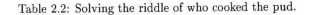

Table 2.2: Solving the riddle of who cooked the pud.

Herr Futtermeister	$\rightarrow$	meat	M. Bernaise	$\rightarrow$	fish
Mr Cucumber	$\rightarrow$	soup	*M. Escargot*	$\rightarrow$	*pudding*

2.1.3   Gates and Logic Diagrams

So far we have introduced the three fundamental logic operations of AND, OR, NOT in terms of networks of electro-mechanical switches. Present switching technology is now almost entirely based on solid-state techniques. Irrespective of the implementation technology, circuits which implement these basic functions are known as **gates**. We have already observed in Example 2.5 that it is desirable to use implementation-independent symbols to characterize logic functions. We will continue this line of argument by first looking at gate symbols.

Since the middle 1950s, several standards organizations have been working on formulating an international symbolic language, by which it is possible to determine the functional behaviour of a logic circuit with minimal reference to supporting documentation; such as data sheets. Several standards were published over a span of 20 years, cumulating in the International Electrotechnical Commission (IEC) Publication 617, Part 12 in 1983 [9]. Most countries with their own standards organizations have subsequently published national equivalents to this. Thus, in the U.K., the British Standards Institution (BSI) BS3939 Part 12 [10], and in the U.S.A., the American National Standards Institute/Institute of Electrical and Electronics Engineers, ANSI/IEEE standard 91-1984 [11]. Symbols used in this book are based on the latter standard and are referred to as the IEC/ANSII standard.

Two quite different sets of gate symbols are permitted by IEC/ANSII Standard 91-1984. The distinctive-shape symbols shown on the left of Fig. 2.10 are the older types. Although not preferred by IEC Pub 617, their use is so ingrained in existing (especially American and British) literature that custom and practice has ensured their continuing use. In the author's opinion they have many advantages over the uniform shapes; long used in European electronic literature. The former are more easily recognized in complex logic circuits, which have usually been reduced to a manageable size. Often qualifying symbols are indecipherable, especially where the reproduction is less than ideal.

The general qualifying symbol **&** (ampersand) for AND needs no further discussion. For OR, the ≥ 1 qualifier means output = 1 where one or more input is logic 1 (i.e. greater than or just one logic 1 input). The EOR qualifier $=1$ indicates a logic 1 output only if a single input is 1.

The distinctive $\triangleright$ shape denotes a buffer (input = output). Adding an inversion bubble at either input or output gives the NOT gate symbol. The uniform shape equivalents use the **1** qualifier to denote that an internal 1 is output for an internal 1 at the input.

Using these symbols, the logic of complete systems may be indicated, in a similar fashion to the previously depicted relay contact diagrams.

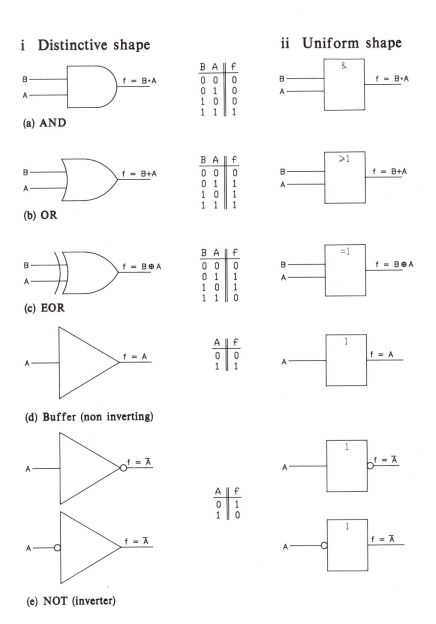

Figure 2.10: Gate symbols.

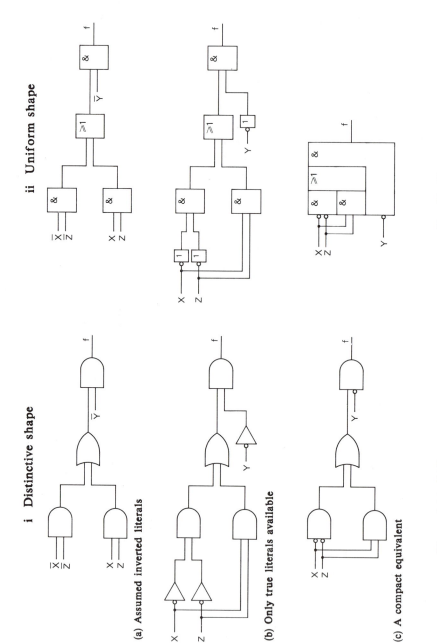

Figure 2.11: Different representations of the same function $\overline{Y} \cdot (\overline{X} \cdot \overline{Y} + X \cdot Y)$.

Example 2.8

Show how the logic of Fig. 2.6 can be represented using both distinctive and uniform gate symbols.

Solution

Like any other language, the language of logic is capable of many analogous expressions. In Fig. 2.11(a), I have assumed that both true and complement input variables (collectively known as **literals**) are simultaneously available from whatever circuit is driving our logic. This is often the case, and is assumed in most of the logic circuits in this book. If not, then explicit inverters are necessary, as shown in Fig. 2.11(b). In this case I have drawn the inversion bubbles at the input of the NOT gates to emphasize the fact that the input literal is being inverted, rather than place it at the more conventional output. Where two inverting stages follow each other, as in Fig. 2.16, inversion circles are frequently shown in adjacent pairs, to indicate cancellation (two inversions give the original input).

The alternative representation, shown in Fig. 2.11(c), is logically correct. However, it probably does not represent the actual hardware used to implement the functions. As such it is more a pure or abstract logic diagram. It will be shown in Section 2.2.4 that an inverted-input AND gate may be implemented using a NOR (OR-NOT) gate. The uniform logic representation of Fig. 2.11 embeds the various layers of gates into the single outline of the output AND gate. Signal flow is always assumed from left to right. This form of representation is even more abstract, but is very compact and often used to represent complex integrated circuits (see Fig. 3.40).

For yourself; can you replace part of the logic diagram with an EOR gate. Hint: See Fig. 2.5(b).

Example 2.9

Using both distinctive and compact uniform-shape representations, symbolize the logic of the car hazard and signalling system as designed in Example 2.6.

Solution

Scrutiny of the truth table of Fig. 2.9 shows that three of the product terms are common to both outputs. A considerable economy can be affected if each term is only generated once and shared between the two output OR gates. This **product-term sharing** is shown in Fig. 2.12(a)i by connections between each of the three common AND gates and the two OR gates. Commercial electronic gate circuits are designed to drive up to typically 20 gate inputs. This drive capability, known as **fan-out**, is discussed in Section 3.1.1. Replacing the distinctive by the equivalent uniform symbols is perfectly legitimate, but the compact version shown in Fig. 2.12(a)ii is the more usual representation. Here the double line drawn below the three relevant AND gates denote their commonality to all elements below.

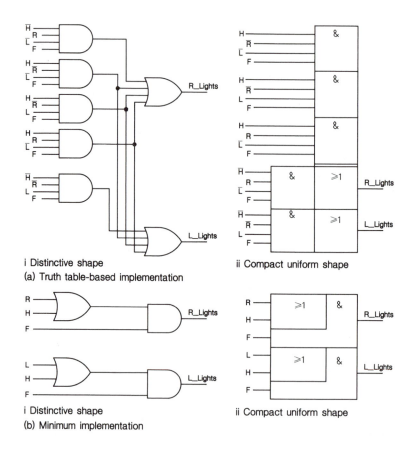

i Distinctive shape
(a) Truth table-based implementation

ii Compact uniform shape

i Distinctive shape
(b) Minimum implementation

ii Compact uniform shape

Figure 2.12: Logic diagrams for the hazard and direction warning system.

Product sharing, however depicted, reduces the number of required gate inputs (used as a convenient cost index) from 32 to 24. However, this does not compare with the minimized implementation of Fig. 2.12(b), which requires only six gate inputs; one quarter of the shared solution. This reinforces our statement that some effort must be made to minimize logic implementations.

As we have already stated, gates are the fundamental building blocks of more complex functions. But gates on their own have several useful properties. Looking first at AND gates; multiple-input circuits can easily be constructed by cascade, as shown in Fig. 2.13. Logically, both tree and linear cascade topology are the same. In practice, real gates do not act instantaneously, and the overall propagation delay of the tree topology will be less than the linear cascade (two delays as opposed to three in our example). Commercially available gates are normally available with up to eight inputs; so this example is somewhat trivial. However, the principle is the same for any number of input gates.

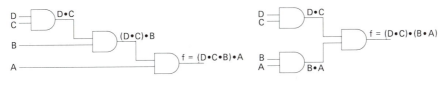

(a) Linear cascade   (b) Tree cascade

Figure 2.13: Building up AND networks.

The application shown in Fig. 2.14 is probably the origin of the term gate. A single data line is passed or gated through to $\mathcal{F}$ when the control line G is 1, otherwise it is 0 irrespective of data coming in. This follows as $\mathcal{F} = \text{D·G}$, and of G = 1 then we have $\mathcal{F} = \text{D·1} = \text{D}$. Thus an AND gate can be used to pass a signal through from one part of a circuit to another.

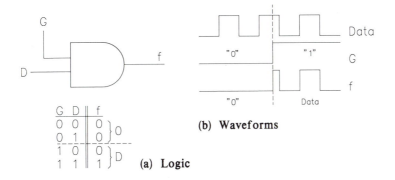

(b) **Waveforms**

(a) **Logic**

Figure 2.14: Controlling data flow using an AND gate.

The concept of two different groups of signals, namely **data** and **control**, is an important one. Although it must be stressed that this is conceptual only, in that the logic does not operate in a different manner just because we have categorized the signals. Indeed in this example, both signals are completely interchangeable. How control inputs affect data inputs and/or outputs and which data lines are affected, are of particular importance to the more complex logic circuits to be investigated in the succeeding chapters. Because of the complex relationship between these groups, the use of gate symbols will generally not clarify their interaction. The current logic symbology standards differ mainly from previous standards in their ability to describe the function of these control inputs. This is done by using **Dependency notation**.

Dependency notation is a large topic, as it is necessary to adequately cover a wide range of control/data interrelationships. Because of this, I have simply introduced the appropriate notations as they arise. However, I have reproduced a guide to the new standards, including dependency, as Appendix A. Further information is contained in the standards themselves and in reference [12].

A simple example of AND control, known as **G dependency** (for Gate; the

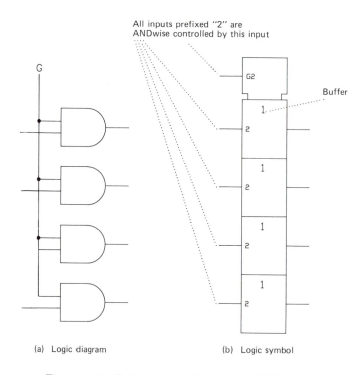

Figure 2.15: G dependency illustrating AND control.

A label is reserved for Address dependency), is shown in Fig. 2.15. Here, four data lines are controlled by a single line labelled **G**. When **G** is 0, all output data lines are 0. When **G** is 1, i.e. in its active state, all lines follow their corresponding input.

The logic symbol for this process, as shown in Fig. 2.15(b), uses a **control box** on top of an **array** of buffers. The two nibbles cut out of the bottom of the box signify control. The **G** label is followed by a number, here **G2**. The same dependency notation number also appears at the four inputs, showing that these are affected by **G** (there could be other inputs or outputs affected by additional control inputs, or not at all). Thus when **G** is active (that is, internally at 1) then all affected inputs are gated through to the innards of the logic (in this case the buffer) and are processed normally (here appearing at the output). If **G** is inactive (that is, internally at 0) then all affected inputs remain at 0. The dependency number used here has no significance; I did not use **1** to avoid confusion with the general qualifying symbol for a buffer.

In this simple example, we have introduced three new concepts. The control box, the array of identical logic elements and dependency notation. If it seems unnecessarily complex, then note that dependency is not designed to be used to replace gates in simple combinational logic, rather to describe the actions controlling data flow in more sophisticated circuits. The circuits being controlled here are only straight buffers!

Can you redraw the dependency showing the situation where data is to be passed through when the external control signal **G** is logic 0, otherwise inhibited?

Example 2.10

The logic diagram of one half of integrated circuit type 4555 is shown in Fig. 2.16 (there are two of these in the one chip). From the diagram determine the logic function of the circuit.

Solution

Consider the input labelled $\overline{EN}$ to be a single data line connected via an inverter to the four AND gates. Each gate is controlled by one of four combinations of inputs B & A, i.e. $Q_0 = (\overline{B} \cdot \overline{A}) \cdot EN$, $Q_1 = (\overline{B} \cdot A) \cdot EN$, $Q_2 = (B \cdot \overline{A}) \cdot EN$ and $Q_3 = (B \cdot A) \cdot EN$. For any given binary state n of B A, inverted data will be gated through gate n and appear at output Q_n. For example, if $BA = 01b$ then $Q_0 = 1 \cdot 0 \cdot EN = 0$; $Q_1 = 1 \cdot 1 \cdot EN = EN$; $Q_2 = 0 \cdot 0 \cdot EN = 0$ and $Q_3 = 0 \cdot 1 \cdot EN = 0$.

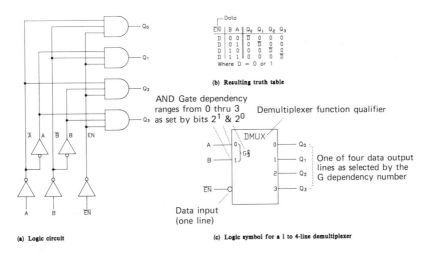

(a) Logic circuit

(b) Resulting truth table

(c) Logic symbol for a 1 to 4-line demultiplexer

Figure 2.16: Half of the 4555 integrated circuit.

The function of routing a single data line through to one of n output lines is shown on the left of Fig. 1.3, where it is labelled as a **demultiplexer**. This data could be n digitized telephone links sampled and time division multiplexed into the one channel. The demultiplexer must unscramble this to the individual subscribers.

The general qualifying symbol for a demultiplexer is **DX** or **DMUX**. As shown in Fig. 2.16(c), the outputs are labelled **0** to **3** corresponding to the range of the **G** dependency numbers, that is $\frac{0}{3}$. The **0** and **1** adjacent to the **G** inputs signifies the associated power of that line, i.e. 2^0 and 2^1. Inputs at these two lines target the output gate of corresponding number. Thus input 00 → gate 0, 01 → gate 1, 10 → gate 2 and 11 → gate 3. It is not necessary to use the control box symbol, as

only one element is affected; not an array of elements. We will return to the subject
of demultiplexers in Section 3.2.2.

An alternative way of looking at this circuit, is to consider $\overline{EN}$ as an enable
input. If logic 0, one of the four gates will go High, depending on the address B A.
Treated in this way, the circuit is said to be acting as a **decoder**. The symbol for
a decoder is given in Fig. 3.29.

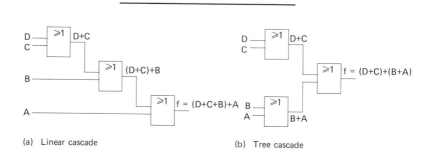

(a) Linear cascade   (b) Tree cascade

Figure 2.17: Building up OR networks.

OR gates can be networked in an identical manner to AND gates, and the same
comments apply. Indeed if I had used uniform symbols for Fig. 2.13, changing the **&**
to $\geq$ general qualifier symbols would give Fig. 2.17.

Again, the OR gate can be used as a controller element. From Fig. 2.18, we see
that this time the active control state of **V** is 0. When transmission is disabled, the
output goes to 1. Although logic 1 does not seem to be the obvious disable state,
on reflection there is no particular reason why logic 0 should be any better!

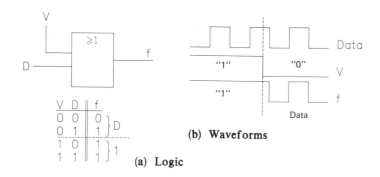

(b) **Waveforms**

(a) **Logic**

Figure 2.18: Controlling data flow using an OR gate.

The dependency symbol denoting OR control is **V** (**O** looks too like **0**; **V** is one
of the possible OR symbols shown in Fig. 2.2(c)). Where the internal state of a
V control input is 1, the affected lines are fixed at 1 also. When **V** is 0, the affected
lines take on their normally defined state.

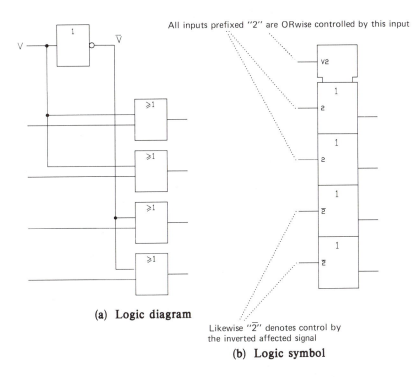

(a) Logic diagram

All inputs prefixed "2" are ORwise controlled by this input

Likewise "$\overline{2}$" denotes control by
the inverted affected signal

(b) Logic symbol

Figure 2.19: **V** dependency illustrating OR control.

The example I have given for **V** dependency in Fig. 2.19 is similar to Fig. 2.15, but I have arranged that for any value of **V**, only two outputs follow their respective inputs. Thus with **V** at 0, the top two lines follow the corresponding top two inputs, the bottom two staying at 1. With **V** at 1, the situation is reversed. The logic symbol shows this by overbarring the bottom two dependency numbers. This means that these inputs are qualified by the inverse of the **V** input, that is, enabled when **V** = 1.

Exclusive-OR gates can also be cascaded, as shown in Fig. 2.20(a), but the resulting function is not immediately obvious. In formal logic, the EOR function is defined as detecting when only one of n inputs is true. The truth table of Fig. 2.20(b) was built up by first evaluating $C \oplus B = \mathcal{F}_1$ and then $\mathcal{F}_1 \oplus A$. The resultant function $\mathcal{F}_2 = C \oplus B \oplus A$ certainly does not show this =1 property. Instead, close inspection indicates that patterns where the number of input 1s are odd are being detected. This feature can be proven by induction for any number of cascade inputs. If $\mathcal{F}_{n-1}$ represents the output of an EOR cascade, indicating $n-1$ inputs are odd, and this in turn is exclusively ORed with the nth input digit X_n; then we have: $\mathcal{F}_n = \mathcal{F}_{n-1} \oplus X_n$. Now we have the following relationship to comply with if $\mathcal{F}_n$ is to indicate the oddness of digits X_1 to X_{n-1} plus the extra digit X_n:

$\mathcal{F}_{n-1}$	X_n	$\mathcal{F}_n$
Even(0)	0	even(0)
Even(0)	1	odd (1)
Odd (1)	0	odd (1)
Odd (1)	1	even(0)

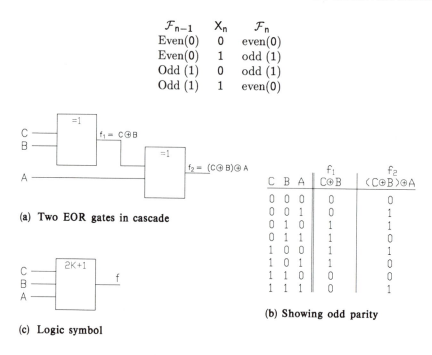

(a) Two EOR gates in cascade

(c) Logic symbol

C	B	A	f_1 $C \oplus B$	f_2 $(C \oplus B) \oplus A$
0	0	0	0	0
0	0	1	0	1
0	1	0	1	1
0	1	1	1	0
1	0	0	1	1
1	0	1	1	0
1	1	0	0	0
1	1	1	0	1

(b) Showing odd parity

Figure 2.20: Combining Exclusive-OR gates.

This is of course just the exclusive-OR relationship $\mathcal{F}_n = X_n \oplus \mathcal{F}_{n-1}$. Now if $\mathcal{F}_{n-1}$ indicates the oddness of the $n - 1$ data inputs, then so does $\mathcal{F}_n$ for the n inputs. As we have proved $\mathcal{F}_3$ indicates oddness, by induction so does $\mathcal{F}_n$.

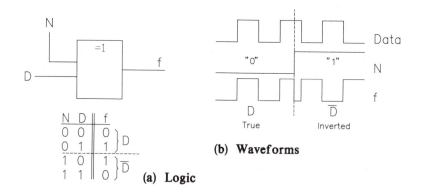

N	D	f
0	0	0
0	1	1
1	0	1
1	1	0

(a) Logic

(b) Waveforms

Figure 2.21: Controlling data flow using an EOR gate.

Even though cascading EOR gates does not produce a multiple-input $=1$ gate, the property of oddness detection is sufficiently important to have its own qualifying symbol **2K+1**, as shown in Fig. 2.20(c). At first sight this is a curious choice of symbol, but note that **2K+1** is always odd for any integer K. Similarly the symbol **2K** denotes an even-element detector. But really an odd-element detector can also be used as an even detector: if its not odd it must be even!

Used as a control function, the EOR gate has the property of **programmable inversion**. From the truth table of Fig. 2.21(a), we see that when N is 0, the output follows the logic state of the input. However, when N is 1, the logic state of the output is the opposite of the input. EOR gates are often integrated into programmable logic devices to provide the option of an active-Low or active-High output in the same integrated circuit. An example of this is shown in Fig.3.66. A signal affected in this manner is said to have **N** (for negative) dependency.

Example 2.11

The 4531 integrated circuit has the functional logic diagram shown in Fig. 2.22. Develop a Boolean expression for the output and determine the overall function. If input W is considered a control input, how will this affect the function and how could this be indicated using dependency notation.

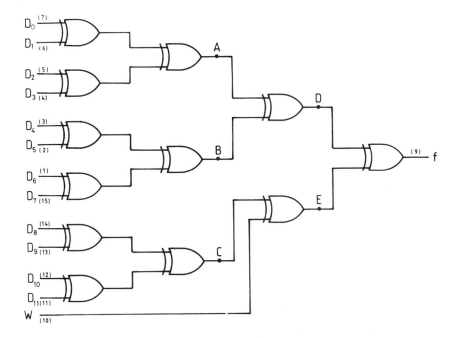

Figure 2.22: The 4531 parity tree. Figures in brackets indicate pin numbers.

Solution

At point **A** we have $(D_0 \oplus D_1) \oplus (D_2 \oplus D_3)$. At point **B** $(D_4 \oplus D_5) \oplus (D_6 \oplus D_7)$, and at point **C** $(D_8 \oplus D_9) \oplus (D_{10} \oplus D_{11})$. $(D_0 \oplus D_1 \oplus D_2 \oplus D_3) \oplus (D_4 \oplus D_5 \oplus D_6 \oplus D_7)$ is the function at point **D**, and point **E** is $(D_8 \oplus D_9 \oplus D_{10} \oplus D_{11}) \oplus W$. Finally:

$$\mathcal{F} = D_0 \oplus D_1 \oplus D_2 \oplus D_3 \oplus D_4 \oplus D_5 \oplus D_6 \oplus D_7 \oplus D_8 \oplus D_9 \oplus D_{10} \oplus D_{11} \oplus W$$

Thus overall $\mathcal{F}$ goes logic 1 wherever the 13 inputs have an odd number of 1s (or conversely goes logic 0 for an even number of 1s).

If we regard **W** as a control rather than data input, then it effectively acts as a programmable inverter on the output. Thus if **W** is 0 then $\mathcal{F}$ goes logic 1 for odd 1s on data inputs $D_0 \ldots D_{11}$. When **W** is 1, $\mathcal{F}$ is inverted and goes logic 0 for odd 1s. This is shown in the logic symbol of Fig. 2.23, which uses the **N** dependency. The **N** control is suffixed with the label **1**. It thus affects the output according to the Negate rules, as this has a prefix dependency number of **1**. The **2K+1** general qualifier label indicates odd detection of the data inputs. Can you redraw the symbol using the **2K** general qualifier?

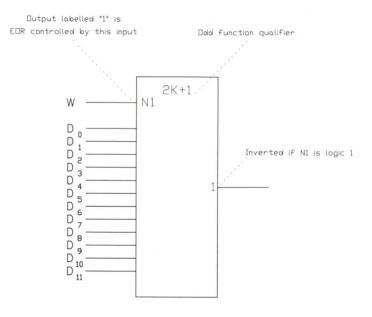

Figure 2.23: Logic symbol for the 4531 integrated circuit.

An alternative interpretation of **W**, is that it acts as an Odd/Even mode control. Thus $\mathcal{F}$ goes logic 1 if **W** is 0 and the data inputs have odd 1s, or if **W** is 1 and the data inputs have even 1s.

The 4531 is described in the catalogs as a **parity tree**. This term comes from its use in error detecting applications. One of the simplest error-detecting strategies is to add an extra bit to each transmitted word; which makes the total number of 1s always odd. This is known as **odd ones parity** (**even ones parity** is just as good, as is zeros parity). At the receiver the oddness of each word is checked. Both transmitter and receiver circuits use EOR gates as odd generators/detectors; hence the 4531's description as a parity circuit (see Example SAE 2.4). Simple parity can only detect if an odd number of errors in each word has occurred (why not an even number of errors?). However, most of the more complex algorithms, many of which can correct errors [13], are based on the parity function.

2.2 Boolean Algebra

Given that there are many different ways of expressing the same transfer function (truth table), it is necessary to develop the mathematical tools, based on the operators defined in the previous section, to simplify and structurally alter a given truth function. This is the aim of the section.

After completing this section you should be able to:

- Utilize the basic rules of Boolean algebra to manipulate a logic function.

- Convert between AND-OR logic to either all-NAND or all-NOR logic.

- Express a canonical sum of products function in the shorthand p-term notation.

- Use the Quine-McCluskey tabular method to reduce any sum of products function.

- Use the Karnaugh map as a graphical method to reduce an active-High or active-Low sum of products function of up to six variables.

- Use the duality theorm to convert between active-High and active-Low equivalent sum of products functions.

2.2.1 Boolean Function Manipulation

Boolean algebra is a comprehensive mathematical discipline, and only sufficient material will be covered here to enable the reader to follow the remainder of the text. References [14, 15] are useful for those interested in pursuing the subject further. The foundation of algebraic manipulation lies in a series of relationships or identities. Some of the relationships applicable to Boolean algebra are enumerated below.

I Basic Laws

(a)	$X \cdot 0 = 0$	(f)	$X + X = X$
(b)	$X + 0 = X$	(g)	$X \cdot \overline{X} = 0$
(c)	$X \cdot 1 = X$	(h)	$X + \overline{X} = 1$
(d)	$X + 1 = 1$	(i)	$\overline{\overline{X}} = X$
(e)	$X \cdot X = X$		

These theorems are self evident from the basic operator truth tables, but if proofs are required, then the equality can be tested by substitution of both values of X into the equation. For example proving (h): $X = 0$ then $0 + 1 = 1$; $X = 1$ then $1 + 0 = 1$. This approach is known as proof by perfect induction.

II Commutative Law

(a) $X \cdot Y = Y \cdot X$
(b) $X + Y = Y + X$

Proof

The definition of both AND (all or nothing) and OR (any or all) operations does not imply any ordering of variables. Thus, as in ordinary algebra, the order of either addition or of multiplication is irrelevant.

III Associative Law

(a) $(X + Y) + Z = X + (Y + Z) = X + Y + Z$
(b) $(X \cdot Y) \cdot Z = X \cdot (Y \cdot Z) = X \cdot Y \cdot Z$

Proof

The reader should verify this law using perfect induction, by constructing the appropriate truth tables. The associative law is similar to that of ordinary algebra.

IV De Morgan's Theorem

(a) $\overline{X \cdot Y} = \overline{X} + \overline{Y}$ →   (c) $X \cdot Y = \overline{\overline{X} + \overline{Y}}$
(b) $\overline{X + Y} = \overline{X} \cdot \overline{Y}$ →   (d) $X + Y = \overline{\overline{X} \cdot \overline{Y}}$

Proof

Table 2.3 shows the proof using a truth table for each side of equations (a) & (b).

X Y	$\overline{X \cdot Y}$	$\overline{X} + \overline{Y}$	$\overline{X + Y}$	$\overline{X} \cdot \overline{Y}$
0 0	$\overline{0 \cdot 0} = 1$	$1 + 1 = 1$	$\overline{0 + 0} = 1$	$1 \cdot 1 = 1$
0 1	$\overline{0 \cdot 1} = 1$	$1 + 0 = 1$	$\overline{0 + 1} = 0$	$1 \cdot 0 = 0$
1 0	$\overline{1 \cdot 0} = 1$	$0 + 1 = 1$	$\overline{1 + 0} = 0$	$0 \cdot 1 = 0$
1 1	$\overline{1 \cdot 1} = 0$	$0 + 0 = 0$	$\overline{1 + 1} = 0$	$0 \cdot 0 = 0$

Table 2.3: Proof by perfect induction of de Morgan's relationship.

De Morgan's theorem, sometimes known as duality, is useful in that it enables us to convert between AND and OR forms, see Fig. 2.26. It will be extensively used in the remainder of the book. The law is simply extended to n variables, i.e. :

$$\overline{X_1 \cdot X_2 \cdot X_3 \cdot \cdots \cdot X_n} = \overline{X}_1 + \overline{X}_2 + \overline{X}_3 + \cdots + \overline{X}_n$$
$$\overline{X_1 + X_2 + X_3 + \cdots + X_n} = \overline{X}_1 \cdot \overline{X}_2 \cdot \overline{X}_3 \cdot \cdots \cdot \overline{X}_n$$

V Distributive Law

$$\text{(a)} \quad X \cdot (Y+Z) = (X \cdot Y)+(X \cdot Z)$$
$$\text{(b)} \quad X+(Y \cdot Z) = (X+Y) \cdot (X+Z)$$

Proof

The proof of theorem V(a) using a truth table is left to the reader. Assuming its veracity, it is instructive to prove (b), using the previously formulated laws.

$$
\begin{aligned}
X+(Y \cdot Z) &= \overline{\overline{X} \cdot (\overline{Y \cdot Z})} && \text{De Morgan's Theorem, IV(d)} \\
&= \overline{\overline{X} \cdot (\overline{Y}+\overline{Z})} && \text{De Morgan's Theorem, IV(a)} \\
&= \overline{(\overline{X} \cdot \overline{Y})+(\overline{X} \cdot \overline{Z})} && \text{Distributive Law, V(a)} \\
&= \overline{(\overline{X} \cdot \overline{Y})} \cdot \overline{(\overline{X} \cdot \overline{Z})} && \text{De Morgan's Theorem, IV(b)} \\
&= (X+Y) \cdot (X+Z) && \text{De Morgan's Theorem, IV(a)}
\end{aligned}
$$

Note that although (a) is similar to ordinary algebra, this is not true of (b).

Example 2.12

Show that $\overline{A} \cdot \overline{C}+A \cdot \overline{B} \cdot \overline{C} = \overline{A} \cdot \overline{C}+\overline{B} \cdot \overline{C}$.

Solution

$$\overline{A} \cdot \overline{C}+A \cdot \overline{B} \cdot \overline{C} = \overline{C} \cdot \{\overline{A}+(A \cdot \overline{B})\} \quad \text{taking } \overline{C} \text{ outside brackets, V(a)}$$

$$
\begin{aligned}
&\overline{C} \cdot \{\overbrace{(\overline{A}+A)}^{1} \cdot (\overline{A}+\overline{B})\} && \text{Distributive Law, V(b)} \\
&\overline{C} \cdot \{1 \cdot (\overline{A}+\overline{B})\} && \text{Basic Law, I(h)} \\
&\overline{C} \cdot (\overline{A}+\overline{B}) && \text{Basic Law, I(c)} \\
&\overline{A} \cdot \overline{C}+\overline{B} \cdot \overline{C} && \text{Distributive Law V(a)/Commutative Law, II(a)}
\end{aligned}
$$

Several steps may be taken in the line, as in the line above, especially where the first three theorems (Basic, Commutative and Associative) are involved.

Example 2.13

The 6809 microprocessor generates three control signals; E (Enable_Clock), Q (Quadrature_Clock) and R/$\overline{\text{W}}$ (Read/Write). When the microprocessor reads data, its R/$\overline{\text{W}}$ line goes 1. In this situation, an enabling signal must be produced when either E or Q is 1. Conversely, during a write-data action, R/$\overline{\text{W}} = 0$ and an enable generated only when Q is 1. Simplify the resulting expression: $\{$ R/$\overline{\text{W}} \cdot (\text{E}+\text{Q})\}+(\overline{\text{R/}\overline{\text{W}}} \cdot \text{Q})$.

Solution

$$
\begin{aligned}
\mathcal{F} &= \{\text{R/}\overline{\text{W}} \cdot (\text{E}+\text{Q})\}+(\overline{\text{R/}\overline{\text{W}}} \cdot \text{Q}) && \text{1st term for read, 2nd for write} \\
\mathcal{F} &= (\text{R/}\overline{\text{W}} \cdot \text{E})+(\text{R/}\overline{\text{W}} \cdot \text{Q})+(\overline{\text{R/}\overline{\text{W}}} \cdot \text{Q}) && \text{Distributive Law, V(a)}
\end{aligned}
$$

$$
\begin{aligned}
\mathcal{F} &= (\text{R/}\overline{\text{W}} \cdot \text{E})+\text{Q} \cdot \overbrace{(\text{R/}\overline{\text{W}}+\overline{\text{R/}\overline{\text{W}}})}^{1} && \text{Taking Q outside, V(a)/Basic Law 1(h)} \\
\mathcal{F} &= (\text{R/}\overline{\text{W}}) \cdot \text{E}+\text{Q} && \text{Basic Law 1(c)}
\end{aligned}
$$

Example 2.14

Reduce $\mathcal{F} = \overline{\overline{X}\cdot(Y+\overline{Z})}\cdot(X+\overline{Y}+Z)\cdot\overline{(\overline{X}\cdot\overline{Y}\cdot\overline{Z})}$ to its simplest form:

Solution

$$\mathcal{F} = X+\overline{(Y+\overline{Z})}\cdot(X+\overline{Y}+Z)\cdot(X+Y+Z) \qquad \text{De Morgan's Theorem IV(a)}$$

$$\underset{0}{}$$

$$\mathcal{F} = \{X+(\overline{Y}\cdot Z)\}\cdot\{X+Z+(Y\cdot\overline{Y})\} \qquad \text{De Morgan's Theorem IV(b)/Rule I(g)}$$

$$\mathcal{F} = (X+\overline{Y})\cdot(X+Z)\cdot(X+Z) \qquad \text{Distributive Law V(b)}$$

$$\mathcal{F} = (X+\overline{Y})\cdot(X+Z) \qquad \text{Rule I(e)}$$

$$\mathcal{F} = X+(\overline{Y}\cdot Z) \qquad \text{Taking X outside, V(b)}$$

2.2.2 Inverting Gates

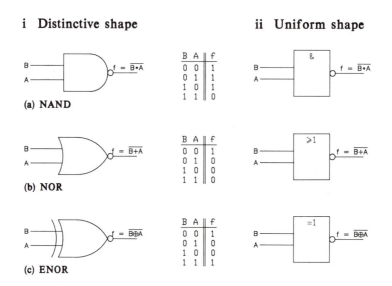

Figure 2.24: Inverted-output gate symbols.

Up to now we have used AND, OR and NOT gates to directly implement the primary logic operators. However, a glance through any semiconductor vendor's catalog shows that the majority of gates have inverted outputs, that is NOT-AND **(NAND)** and NOT-OR **(NOR)**. This is because of the inverting nature of a transistor switch (see Section 3.1.1). For example, an AND gate is actually phys-ically realized by following a NAND by an inverter gate (although the symbology of Fig. 2.24 would imply otherwise). As such gates cost more, use more power and are slower, it is clearly more efficient to use inverting gates. Furthermore, any logic

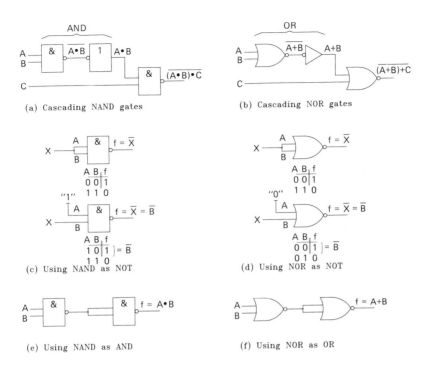

Figure 2.25: Some properties of inverted-output logic gates.

circuit may be implemented using only NAND or only NOR gates; as opposed to a mixture of AND, OR and NOT gates. This keeps the parts inventory to a minimum; with the additional bonus of bulk buying and consequent reduction in cost. The remainder of this section will be spent looking at this property in more detail.

Some properties of both NAND and NOR gates are illustrated in Fig. 2.25. Note especially the use of NAND, NOR gates as inverters. This can be extended to n-input gates by commoning the extra inputs, or connection to 1 or 0. Inverters are usually cheaper than gates, but depending on numbers involved, it may be more economical or convenient to utilize unused gates contained in a multiple-gate package. Also of note is the technique used to expand NAND or NOR gates. Simply cascading such gates does not produce the required function, as for the AND and OR cases.

De Morgan's theorem is extensively used in manipulating circuits to an NAND, NOR form. This theorem can be applied directly to the algebraic equations, but where a logic diagram is available, the pictorial transformations shown in Fig. 2.26 are often more effective. This shows that the type of gate, i.e. AND ↔ OR, may be changed by simply moving the inversion bubbles from output to inputs. For instance, NANDing A & B is equivalent to ORing $\overline{A}$ & $\overline{B}$. The following examples will illustrate the use of this technique.

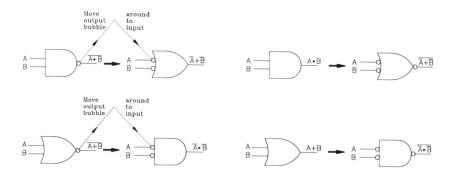

Figure 2.26: Genera transformations using de Morgan's theorm.

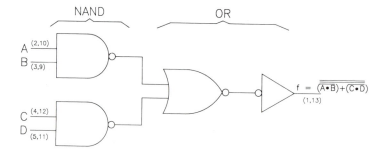

(a) Functional diagram for each of the two gates contained in the Motorola M-C14012B integrated circuit

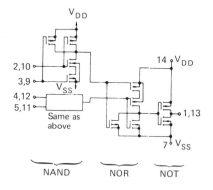

(b) The MC14012B CMOS gate. Courtesy of Motorola Ltd.

Figure 2.27: The Motorola MC14012B CMOS gate.

Example 2.15

The equivalent circuit of the IC type MC14012B is shown in Fig. 2.27. Determine the logic function of the device.

Solution

If we replace the NOR gate by an inverted-input NAND; this gives the equivalent circuit of Fig. 2.28(a); which is seen to be a 4-I/P NAND gate.

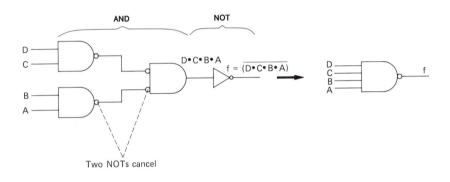

Figure 2.28: Showing that the MC 14012B is a 4-I/P NAND gate.

Example 2.16

Convert the 2-level AND-OR circuit of Fig. 2.29(a) to an NAND-only network.

Solution

. If double inversion circles are inserted between the first and second levels, we have the circuit of Fig. 2.29(b). Replacing the inverted-input OR by its AND equivalent gives the all-NAND circuit of Fig. 2.29(c). Sometimes the format of Fig. 2.29(b) is used in preference to 2.29(c), as it is indicative of the more easily appreciated AND-OR network.

Comparing Figs. 2.29(a) & (c) leads to the rule that a 2-level AND-OR circuit can be replaced with an all NAND network, by simply substituting NAND gates for all gate functions. This can be proven as follows:

$$\mathcal{F} \;=\; P_1 + P_2 + P_3 + \cdots + P_n$$

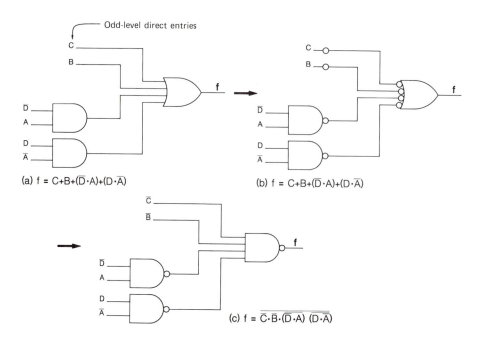

Figure 2.29: Odd-level entry conversion.

$$\mathcal{F} \;=\; \overline{\overline{P_1} \cdot \overline{P_2} \cdot \overline{P_3} \cdot \; \cdots \; \cdot \overline{P_n}}$$

where P_n represents the nth AND (i.e. product) term and $\overline{P_n}$ is the corresponding NAND term.

This rule can be extended to any number of levels as follows:

Any multi-level ... AND-OR-AND-OR network is logically unchanged if all gates are replaced by NAND; provided that all inputs directly entering at an odd level (taking the output OR as level-1) are inverted.

Example 2.17

Convert the three level OR-AND-OR network of Fig. 2.30(a) to an all NAND circuit.

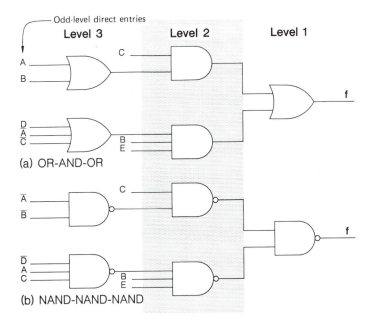

Figure 2.30: A 3-level conversion.

Solution

The first two levels of AND-OR can be replaced directly by NAND. Level-3 OR gates can be replaced by inverted-input NANDs, leading to Fig. 2.30(b). This obeys the rule which replaces all gates by NAND and complements the odd-level direct entries (level-3).

It should be noted that the rule developed here only applies if all gates of a given level are of the same type, and the variety alternates with adjacent levels. Other circuits may be partitioned to give this format where possible, or in any event de Morgan's theorem can always be applied irrespective of the network topology. However, the 2-level AND-OR arrangement, as has already been seen, follows naturally from the truth table, and will be extensively used here.

If it is desired to use all-NOR networks, then conversion from AND-OR is equally simple. The rule for conversion of ... OR-AND-OR to NOR-only states:

Any multi-level... OR-AND-OR network can be replaced by its NOR equivalent by replacing all gates by NOR; inverting all even-level direct entry inputs, and following the output by an inverter.

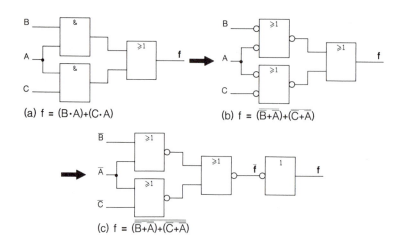

(a) f = (B·A)+(C·A)   (b) f = $\overline{(\overline{B}+\overline{A})+(\overline{C}+\overline{A})}$

(c) f = $\overline{\overline{(\overline{B}+\overline{A})+(\overline{C}+\overline{A})}}$

Figure 2.31: AND-OR to NOR-NOR-NOT.

Example 2.18

Convert the AND-OR circuit of Fig. 2.31(a) to an all-NOR version.

Solution

Replacing the input AND gates by inverted-input NORs gives Fig. 2.31(b). The
output OR can be replaced by a NOR followed by an inverter (remember that a
NOR can be used as a NOT). This gives the final circuit of Fig. 2.31(c).

Because of the necessity for the final inverter, all things being equal, it is better
to minimize the complement of the function, $\overline{\mathcal{F}}$, when a NOR implementation is
being contemplated. This means that, if the final NOT is omitted, the output
becomes $\mathcal{F}$ as required (see Example 2.46).

Most of our design algorithms will give AND-OR networks, and thus the following summary is worthwhile remembering:

1. An AND-OR to all-NAND transformation is obtained by substituting all gates
   by NAND, and inverting direct odd-level entries.

2. An AND-OR to all-NOR transformation is obtained by substituting all gates
   by NOR; inverting direct even-level entries and the output.

Although AND-OR networks are the most common, it is equally possible to
describe any given truth table in terms of an OR-AND type topology, i.e. product
of sums (see Example SAE 2.7). A similar approach is used to the one described

here, with the rules being the dual to those listed above. For example the OR-AND to all NOR transformation substitutes all gates by NOR, and inverts odd-level direct entries.

Advanced techniques for synthesizing networks directly in terms of NAND, NOR (often known as universal gates) exist, and the interested reader is directed to reference [16].

2.2.3 Tabular Minimization

The examples of Section 2.2.1 have shown the power of Boolean algebra in manipulating and simplifying truth functions. They have also shown that such processing of arbitrary functions is at best intuitive. Of greater interest to the engineer would be a systematic reduction algorithm which permits a routine processing of the class of functions most relevant to digital design. Most of these techniques are based on the Quine algorithm [17].

It was shown in Example 2.4 that an algebraic function could be derived from a truth table by ORing together all AND terms which give a true output. The resulting function was described as being in a **sum of primitive products** format (contains all input variables). Such sums of primitive products are known as **canonical** functions.

As this canonical **sum of product (SOP)** form appears frequently in the remainder of the text, it is expedient to use a shorthand notation for such functions. This notation represents each primitive product term (often known as **minterm**) by its equivalent natural binary number. The primitive product term (or **p-term**) number is calculated on the basis that each complemented input variable is replaced by 0 and uncomplemented variables are replaced by 1. Table 2.4 shows p-terms for both three and four variables.

Each p term has the property of being true only when its constituent variables take on the binary pattern defined by its subscript. Thus for example in a 4-variable case, p_{10} is true only when $DCBA = 1010b$. This means that if a 4-variable function is given as $\mathcal{F} = p_4 + p_8 + p_{11} + p_{15}$; then $\mathcal{F}$ is true when $DCBA = 0100$ OR 1000 OR 1011 OR $1111b$. Reading off a function from a truth table can now be done by rote; for example, the function defined by the truth table of Fig. 2.8 is given by:

$$\mathcal{F}_{CBA} = p_0 + p_1 + p_2 + p_4$$

This is commonly further shortened to read:

$$\mathcal{F}_{CBA} = \sum 0, 1, 2, 4$$

It should be noted here that p numbers are only a shorthand notation, which has by definition been defined on the basis of the 8-4-2-1 code. Thus p_{12} always refers to the pattern $1100b$, irrespective of the significance of each variable to the designer. The designer may be using a 2-4-2-1 code; but to the circuitry only the pattern of 1s and 0s is pertinent.

$p_0 = \overline{C}\cdot\overline{B}\cdot\overline{A}$ (pattern 000)
$p_1 = \overline{C}\cdot\overline{B}\cdot A$ (pattern 001)
$p_2 = \overline{C}\cdot B\cdot\overline{A}$ (pattern 010)
$p_3 = \overline{C}\cdot B\cdot A$ (pattern 011)
$p_4 = C\cdot\overline{B}\cdot\overline{A}$ (pattern 100)
$p_5 = C\cdot\overline{B}\cdot A$ (pattern 101)
$p_6 = C\cdot B\cdot\overline{A}$ (pattern 110)
$p_7 = C\cdot B\cdot A$ (pattern 111)

(a) 3-variable minterms

$p_0 = \overline{D}\cdot\overline{C}\cdot\overline{B}\cdot\overline{A}$ (pattern 0000)
$p_1 = \overline{D}\cdot\overline{C}\cdot\overline{B}\cdot A$ (pattern 0001)
$p_2 = \overline{D}\cdot\overline{C}\cdot B\cdot\overline{A}$ (pattern 0010)
$p_3 = \overline{D}\cdot\overline{C}\cdot B\cdot A$ (pattern 0011)
$p_4 = \overline{D}\cdot C\cdot\overline{B}\cdot\overline{A}$ (pattern 0100)
$p_5 = \overline{D}\cdot C\cdot\overline{B}\cdot A$ (pattern 0101)
$p_6 = \overline{D}\cdot C\cdot B\cdot\overline{A}$ (pattern 0110)
$p_7 = \overline{D}\cdot C\cdot B\cdot A$ (pattern 0111)
$p_8 = D\cdot\overline{C}\cdot\overline{B}\cdot\overline{A}$ (pattern 1000)
$p_9 = D\cdot\overline{C}\cdot\overline{B}\cdot A$ (pattern 1001)
$p_{10} = D\cdot\overline{C}\cdot B\cdot\overline{A}$ (pattern 1010)
$p_{11} = D\cdot\overline{C}\cdot B\cdot A$ (pattern 1011)
$p_{12} = D\cdot C\cdot\overline{B}\cdot\overline{A}$ (pattern 1100)
$p_{13} = D\cdot C\cdot\overline{B}\cdot A$ (pattern 1101)
$p_{14} = D\cdot C\cdot B\cdot\overline{A}$ (pattern 1110)
$p_{15} = D\cdot C\cdot B\cdot A$ (pattern 1111)

(b) 4-variable minterms

Table 2.4: A shorthand notation for primitive SOP terms.

Example 2.19

A certain function is logic 1 for input combinations greater than $1001b$ (see Example 2.21). Express the complement of the function both in p-term and expanded formats.

Solution

$$\overline{F}_{(DCBA)} = \sum 0, 1, 2, 3, 4, 5, 6, 7, 8, 9$$

$$\overline{F}_{(DCBA)} = \overset{0\ 0\ 0\ 0}{(\overline{D}\cdot\overline{C}\cdot\overline{B}\cdot\overline{A})}+\overset{0\ 0\ 0\ 1}{(\overline{D}\cdot\overline{C}\cdot\overline{B}\cdot A)}+\overset{0\ 0\ 1\ 0}{(\overline{D}\cdot\overline{C}\cdot B\cdot\overline{A})}+\overset{0\ 0\ 1\ 1}{(\overline{D}\cdot\overline{C}\cdot B\cdot A)}+\overset{0\ 1\ 0\ 0}{(\overline{D}\cdot C\cdot\overline{B}\cdot\overline{A})}+$$

$$\overset{0\ 1\ 0\ 1}{(\overline{D}\cdot C\cdot\overline{B}\cdot A)}+\overset{0\ 1\ 1\ 0}{(\overline{D}\cdot C\cdot B\cdot\overline{A})}+\overset{0\ 1\ 1\ 1}{(\overline{D}\cdot C\cdot B\cdot A)}+\overset{1\ 0\ 0\ 0}{(D\cdot\overline{C}\cdot\overline{B}\cdot\overline{A})}+\overset{1\ 0\ 0\ 1}{(D\cdot\overline{C}\cdot\overline{B}\cdot A)}$$

Example 2.20

Expand the following functions as SOP expressions:

(a) $\mathcal{F}_{(DCBA)} = \sum 5, 6, 7, 11, 12, 15$
(b) $\mathcal{F}_{(EDCBA)} = \sum 0, 6, 16, 23, 30$

Solution

(a) $\mathcal{F}_{(DCBA)} = \overset{0\,1\,0\,1}{(\overline{D}\cdot C\cdot\overline{B}\cdot A)} + \overset{0\,1\,1\,0}{(\overline{D}\cdot C\cdot B\cdot\overline{A})} + \overset{0\,1\,1\,1}{(\overline{D}\cdot C\cdot B\cdot A)} + \overset{1\,0\,1\,1}{(D\cdot\overline{C}\cdot B\cdot A)} + \overset{1\,1\,0\,0}{(D\cdot C\cdot\overline{B}\cdot\overline{A})} + \overset{1\,1\,1\,1}{(D\cdot C\cdot B\cdot A)}$

(b) $\mathcal{F}_{(EDCBA)} = \overset{0\,0\,0\,0\,0}{(\overline{E}\cdot\overline{D}\cdot\overline{C}\cdot\overline{B}\cdot A)} + \overset{0\,0\,1\,1\,0}{(\overline{E}\cdot\overline{D}\cdot C\cdot B\cdot\overline{A})} + \overset{1\,0\,0\,0\,0}{(E\cdot\overline{D}\cdot\overline{C}\cdot\overline{B}\cdot A)} + \overset{1\,0\,1\,1\,1}{(E\cdot\overline{D}\cdot C\cdot B\cdot A)} + \overset{1\,1\,1\,1\,0}{(E\cdot D\cdot C\cdot B\cdot\overline{A})}$

The **Quine algorithm** is based on a systematic search in SOP functions for unit-distance terms; for example:

$$(X_1 \cdot \overline{X}_2 \cdot X_3) + (\overline{X}_1 \cdot \overline{X}_2 \cdot X_3)$$

$$= (\overline{X}_2 \cdot X_3) \cdot \underbrace{(X_1 + \overline{X}_1)}_{1} \qquad\qquad \text{Distributive law V(a)/Basic Law I(h)}$$

$$= \overline{X}_2 \cdot X_3 \qquad\qquad\qquad \text{Eliminating } X_1$$

This removal can be written down by inspection between any two unit-distant terms in a function. If the product terms are non-primitive, they should be expanded to their canonical form before commencing the Quine elimination. Thus $(\overline{D}\cdot\overline{B}\cdot A)$ becomes $(\overline{D}\cdot\overline{B}\cdot A)\cdot(C+\overline{C}) = (\overline{D}\cdot C\cdot\overline{B}\cdot A) + (\overline{D}\cdot\overline{C}\cdot\overline{B}\cdot A)$. This allows comparison and elimination where an SOP function comprizes a mixture of both minterm and non-primitive product terms, i.e. non-canonical. Some examples will elucidate the principles involved.

Example 2.21

Design an illegal-combination detector for an 8-4-2-1 BCD signal.

Solution

A BCD code is a 4-bit representation of decimal $0 - 9$ (see Section 1.1.3). Four bits have 16 combinations, so six code patterns are not used; as shown in Fig. 2.32(a). Such an illegal-code detector would signal that some sort of error had occurred; perhaps in transmission.

The first step is to write down the SOP function from the truth table. Each true output gives one product to the sum. Thus:

$$\mathcal{F} = \overset{10\checkmark}{(D\cdot\overline{C}\cdot B\cdot\overline{A})} + \overset{11\checkmark}{(D\cdot\overline{C}\cdot B\cdot A)} + \overset{12\checkmark}{(D\cdot C\cdot\overline{B}\cdot\overline{A})} + \overset{13\checkmark}{(D\cdot C\cdot\overline{B}\cdot A)} + \overset{14\checkmark}{(D\cdot C\cdot B\cdot\overline{A})} + \overset{15\checkmark}{(D\cdot C\cdot B\cdot A)}$$

(First comparision $D\cdot\overline{C}\cdot B$)

Each bracketed term is then systematically compared to all other terms, looking for unit-distant expressions, i.e. compare $10 \to 11$; $10 \to 12$; $10 \to 13$; $10 \to 14$; $10 \to 15$. Now $p_{10} \leftrightarrow p_{11}$ are unit distant and give $(D\cdot\overline{C}\cdot B)$, as are $p_{10} \leftrightarrow p_{14}$ $(D\cdot B\cdot\overline{A})$. As each valid comparison is made, the reduced expression is written down, together with the p numbers used in that reduction. When a bracket is used

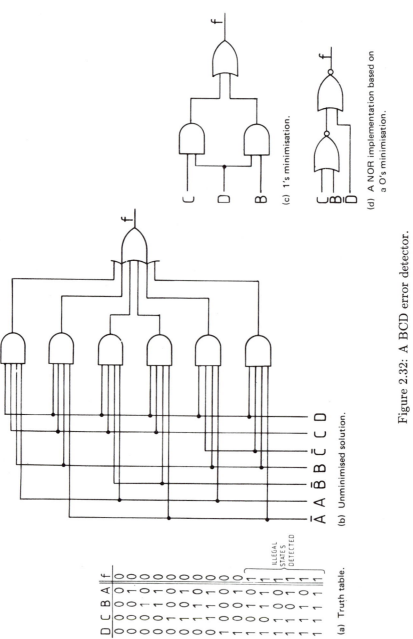

Figure 2.32: A BCD error detector.

in a successful comparison, it is ticked as shown. Ticking a bracket does not exclude its use for further comparisons. This follows from rule l(f):

$$(D \cdot \overline{C} \cdot B \cdot \overline{A}) = (D \cdot \overline{C} \cdot B \cdot \overline{A}) + (D \cdot \overline{C} \cdot B \cdot \overline{A}) + \cdots$$

Best results are obtained when a term is used for as many comparisons as possible.

The reduction process now continues by comparing the second bracket with all succeeding terms, i.e. $p_{11} \rightarrow p_{12}$; $p_{11} \rightarrow p_{13}$; $p_{11} \rightarrow p_{14}$; $p_{11} \rightarrow p_{15}$. This procedure goes on in a like manner with the remaining terms, and yields the expression:

$$\mathcal{F} = \underbrace{(D \cdot \overline{C} \cdot B)}_{10,11\checkmark} + \underbrace{(D \cdot B \cdot \overline{A})}_{10,14\checkmark} + \underbrace{(D \cdot B \cdot A)}_{11,15\checkmark} + \underbrace{(D \cdot C \cdot \overline{B})}_{12,13\checkmark} + \underbrace{(D \cdot C \cdot \overline{A})}_{12,14\checkmark} + \underbrace{(D \cdot C \cdot A)}_{13,15\checkmark} + \underbrace{(D \cdot C \cdot B)}_{14,15\checkmark}$$

The process is then repeated with the reduced function; once again ticking brackets used in successful unit-distant comparisons.

$$\mathcal{F} = \underbrace{(D \cdot B)}_{(10,11)(14,15)} + \underbrace{(D \cdot B)}_{(10,14)(11,15)} + \underbrace{(D \cdot C)}_{(12,13)(14,15)} + \underbrace{(D \cdot C)}_{(12,14)(13,15}$$
$$\text{Duplicate} \qquad\qquad\qquad \text{Duplicate}$$

In this example the reduction can go no further, and the result is given as:

$$\mathcal{F} = (D \cdot B) + (D \cdot C) \quad (\text{covering } 10,11,12,13,14,15)$$

with duplicated terms being removed. As a check to the accuracy of the process, the coverage of the reduced function (i.e. list of p numbers) should be compared to that of the original expression.

A comparison between Figs. 2.32(b) & (c) shows the power of the technique. One means of obtaining a quantitative measure of the goodness of the solution is to count the number of gate inputs required. Although gates cost very little, the associated expenses; such as the area of printed-circuit board or of silicon and power requirement, are nominally proportional to this measure. Assuming that inverted inputs are available from the driving circuit, the unminimized circuit requires 30 inputs, as against six for the minimized case. If inverters are necessary, the unminimized rating rises to 33, each inverter counting as one input. By this simple application of Boolean algebra, cost has been cut by 80%. A similar reduction results if an all-NAND or all-NOR implementation is used.

Example 2.22

Using the Quine algorithm, reduce the SOP function

$$\mathcal{F} = (\overline{D} \cdot \overline{C} \cdot A) + (\overline{D} \cdot C \cdot \overline{B} \cdot A) + (\overline{D} \cdot C \cdot B \cdot A) + (D \cdot C)$$

and estimate the savings in cost.

Solution

As the function is in a non-canonical form, we must firstly expand out the two non-primitive product terms thus:

$$(\overline{D}\cdot\overline{C}\cdot A) = (\overline{D}\cdot\overline{C}\cdot B\cdot A)+(\overline{D}\cdot\overline{C}\cdot\overline{B}\cdot A) \qquad\qquad \text{(Two minterms)}$$
$$(D\cdot C) \;\; = (D\cdot C\cdot\overline{B}\cdot\overline{A})+(D\cdot C\cdot\overline{B}\cdot A)+(D\cdot C\cdot B\cdot\overline{A})+(D\cdot C\cdot B\cdot A) \qquad \text{(Four minterms)}$$

giving:

i $\quad \mathcal{F} \;=\; \overbrace{(\overline{D}\cdot\overline{C}\cdot\overline{B}\cdot A)}^{1\checkmark}+\overbrace{(\overline{D}\cdot\overline{C}\cdot B\cdot A)}^{3\checkmark}+\overbrace{(\overline{D}\cdot C\cdot\overline{B}\cdot A)}^{5\checkmark}+\overbrace{(\overline{D}\cdot C\cdot B\cdot A)}^{7\checkmark}+$

$\qquad\qquad \overbrace{(D\cdot C\cdot\overline{B}\cdot\overline{A})}^{12\checkmark}+\overbrace{(D\cdot C\cdot\overline{B}\cdot A)}^{13\checkmark}+\overbrace{(D\cdot C\cdot B\cdot\overline{A})}^{14\checkmark}+\overbrace{(D\cdot C\cdot B\cdot A)}^{15\checkmark}$

ii $\quad \mathcal{F} \;=\; \overbrace{(\overline{D}\cdot\overline{C}\cdot A)}^{1,3\checkmark}+\overbrace{(\overline{D}\cdot\overline{B}\cdot A)}^{1,5\checkmark}+\overbrace{(\overline{D}\cdot B\cdot A)}^{3,7\checkmark}+\overbrace{(\overline{D}\cdot C\cdot A)}^{5,7\checkmark}+\overbrace{(C\cdot\overline{B}\cdot A)}^{5,13\checkmark}+$

$\qquad\qquad \overbrace{(C\cdot B\cdot A)}^{7,15\checkmark}+\overbrace{(D\cdot C\cdot\overline{B})}^{12,13\checkmark}+\overbrace{(D\cdot C\cdot\overline{A})}^{12,14\checkmark}+\overbrace{(D\cdot C\cdot A)}^{13,15\checkmark}+\overbrace{(D\cdot C\cdot B)}^{14,15\checkmark}$

iii $\quad \mathcal{F} \;=\; \underbrace{(\overline{D}\cdot A)}_{(1,3)(5,7)} \;+\; \underbrace{(\overline{D}\cdot A)}_{(1,5)(3,7)} \;+\; \overbrace{(C\cdot A)}^{(5,7)(13,15)} \;+\; \overbrace{(C\cdot A)}^{(5,13)(7,15)} \;+$

$\qquad\qquad\qquad\qquad\qquad \text{Duplicate} \qquad\qquad\qquad \text{Duplicate}$

$\qquad\qquad\qquad \overbrace{(D\cdot C)}^{(12,13)(14,15)} \;+\; \underbrace{(D\cdot C)}_{(12,14)(13,15)}$

$\qquad\qquad\qquad\qquad\qquad\qquad \text{Duplicate}$

iv $\quad \mathcal{F} \;=\; (\overline{D}\cdot A)+(C\cdot A)+(D\cdot C) \qquad\qquad$ covering 1,3,5,7,12,13,14,15.

In fact the solution of step iv is not a minimal answer, although it is a valid covering of all p numbers. The term $(\overline{D}\cdot A)$ is essential in that p_1 and p_3 are uniqely covered by that expression. Similarly $(D\cdot C)$ is an essential component of the solution for p_{12} and p_{14}. However, these two terms between them cover all the original function p numbers; therefore the final solution is:

$$\mathcal{F} = (\overline{D}\cdot A)+(D\cdot C) \qquad\qquad \text{covering 1,3,5,7,12,13,14,15.}$$

The final step of choosing a covering set of terms, known as **prime implicants, (PIs)**, should always be attempted; as it can result in a considerable reduction.

The cost of the original expression is 13 AND inputs plus four OR gate inputs; giving 19 inputs in total. The final solution reduces this to four AND inputs plus two OR inputs, giving six in total. This represents a saving of 70%. I have assumed inverted inputs are available without cost.

———

Although the Quine algorithm permits a systematic reduction of SOP functions, the number of comparisons grows exponentially with the size of function. It is possible to reduce the number of operations by noting that comparisons are fruitless between terms which differ in the number of complemented variables by more than one. Using this fact, in 1956 McCluskey published a tabular form of the Quine algorithm [18], which further systemized the procedure. The resulting process, known as the **Quine-McCluskey method**, is stated as follows:

1. List all primitive p terms in a column, labelling each with its p number. The terms should be listed in descending order of total of complemented literals. Groups containing the same number of such variables should be split into blocks.

2. Systematically compare each term with all terms in the block *below* only. Only adjacent blocks need be considered, as non-adjacent blocks cannot contain unit-distant terms. With each successful unit-distant comparison, tick-off the two terms involved and place the reduced term in column II, labelled with its constituent p numbers. Proceed with the comparison still using the original term, even though ticked off. Any such checked term in the lower block may also be used in succeeding comparisons. After each term has been checked, column II contains a listing of reduced terms already in the form of blocks.

3. Repeat the interblock comparisons for column II and succeeding columns until no further comparisons can be made. The function is then equated to all unchecked terms. These PI's may lie in different columns. The same terms will appear several times in columns succeeding column II; twice in column III, in triplicate in column IV etc. Duplicate terms should be eliminated.

4. From the prime implicant listing, choose a covering set.

Example 2.23

Repeat the design of Example 2.21, but this time minimizing the complement of the function. An all-NOR implementation should be used.

Solution

1. List the p terms comprizing the function (see Fig. 2.32(a)) in column I of Table 2.5, in descending order of the number of complemented variables. This column is then divided into blocks of equal-number complement variables.

2. The uppermost block (p_1) is then compared with each of the terms of the next lower block. The terms resulting from successful comparisons are listed in column II, together with their covering p numbers. Terms involved in these reductions are ticked, but their active role in unit-distance searches continues.

   The process is continued with every term of each block being compared with each term of the next lower block.

3. Column II splits up into blocks without any rearrangement. Adjacent interblock comparisons then proceed as before. However, note that all terms do not contain the same literals. This reduces the number of comparisons that must be made. For example, in column II ($\overline{C}\cdot\overline{B}\cdot\overline{A}$) cannot compare with any term in the lower block except ($\overline{C}\cdot\overline{B}\cdot A$).

   In columns III and IV, duplicates are reduced to a single term.

I	II	III	IV
0 $\bar{D}\cdot\bar{C}\cdot\bar{B}\cdot\bar{A}$ ✓	(0,1) $\bar{D}\cdot\bar{C}\cdot\bar{B}$ ✓	(0,1) (2,3) $\bar{D}\cdot\bar{C}$ ✓	(0,1) (2,3) (4,5) (6,7) $\bar{D}$
1 $\bar{D}\cdot\bar{C}\cdot\bar{B}\cdot A$ ✓	(0,2) $\bar{D}\cdot\bar{C}\cdot\bar{A}$ ✓	(0,1) (4,5) $\bar{D}\cdot\bar{B}$ ✓	~~(0,1) (4,5) (2,3) (6,7) $\bar{D}$~~
2 $\bar{D}\cdot\bar{C}\cdot B\cdot\bar{A}$ ✓	(0,4) $\bar{D}\cdot\bar{B}\cdot\bar{A}$ ✓	(0,1) (8,9) $\bar{C}\cdot\bar{B}$	~~(0,2) (4,6) (1,3) (5,7) $\bar{D}$~~
4 $\bar{D}\cdot C\cdot\bar{B}\cdot\bar{A}$ ✓	(0,8) $\bar{C}\cdot\bar{B}\cdot\bar{A}$ ✓	~~(0,2) (1,3) $\bar{D}\cdot\bar{C}$~~	
8 $D\cdot\bar{C}\cdot\bar{B}\cdot\bar{A}$ ✓	(1,3) $\bar{D}\cdot\bar{C}\cdot A$ ✓	(0,2) (4,6) $\bar{D}\cdot\bar{A}$ ✓	
3 $\bar{D}\cdot\bar{C}\cdot B\cdot A$ ✓	(1,5) $\bar{D}\cdot B̄... $		

$$\bar{f} = (\bar{C}\cdot\bar{B}) + \bar{D}, \quad \text{covering } 0;1;2;3;4;5;6;7;8;9$$

Table 2.5: Tabular reduction for an active-Low BCD error detector.

4. List the prime implicants; that is unticked terms. In this case these are $(\overline{C\cdot B})$ from column III, and $\bar{D}$ from column IV.

5. Ensure that all prime implicants (PIs) are essential. $(\overline{C\cdot B})$ is essential for p_8 and p_9, whilst $(\bar{D})$ essentially covers 2,3,4,5,6,7.

To implement the function using NOR gates, apply de Morgan's theorem:

$$\overline{\mathcal{F}} = (\bar{C}\cdot\bar{B})+\bar{D}$$
$$\overline{\mathcal{F}} = (\overline{C+B})+\bar{D}$$
$$\mathcal{F} = \overline{(\overline{C+B})+\bar{D}}$$

The circuit is shown in Fig. 2.32(d). This costs only three gate inputs, half the cost of the minimized AND-OR solution. This shows that minimizing the inverse of the function is a viable alternative, and sometimes can give a reduction in effort or produce better results.

Example 2.24

Reduce the function $\mathcal{F}_{(DCBA)} = \sum 0, 2, 3, 4, 6, 7, 11, 12, 14, 15$ to its least form.

Solution

The reduction of Table 2.6(a) follows in the manner discussed in the last example. However, this time the listing of PIs can be reduced further, whilst still retaining a

(a)

I	II	III
0 $\bar{D}\cdot\bar{C}\cdot\bar{B}\cdot\bar{A}$ ✓	(0,2) $\bar{D}\cdot\bar{C}\cdot\bar{A}$ ✓	(0,2)(4,6) $\bar{D}\cdot\bar{A}$
2 $\bar{D}\cdot\bar{C}\cdot B\cdot\bar{A}$ ✓	(0,4) $\bar{D}\cdot\bar{B}\cdot\bar{A}$ ✓	(0,4)(2,6) ~~$\bar{D}\cdot\bar{A}$~~
4 $\bar{D}\cdot C\cdot\bar{B}\cdot\bar{A}$ ✓	(2,3) $\bar{D}\cdot\bar{C}\cdot B$ ✓	(2,3)(6,7) $\bar{D}\cdot B$
3 $\bar{D}\cdot\bar{C}\cdot B\cdot A$ ✓	(2,6) $\bar{D}\cdot B\cdot\bar{A}$ ✓	(2,6)(3,7) ~~$\bar{D}\cdot B$~~
6 $\bar{D}\cdot C\cdot B\cdot\bar{A}$ ✓	(4,6) $\bar{D}\cdot C\cdot\bar{A}$ ✓	(4,6)(12,14) $C\cdot\bar{A}$
12 $D\cdot C\cdot\bar{B}\cdot\bar{A}$ ✓	(4,12) $C\cdot\bar{B}\cdot\bar{A}$ ✓	(4,12)(6,14) ~~$C\cdot\bar{A}$~~
7 $D\cdot C\cdot B\cdot A$ ✓	(3,7) $\bar{D}\cdot B\cdot A$ ✓	(3,7)(11,15) $B\cdot A$
11 $D\cdot\bar{C}\cdot B\cdot A$ ✓	(3,11) $\bar{C}\cdot B\cdot A$ ✓	(3,11)(7,15) ~~$B\cdot A$~~
14 $D\cdot C\cdot B\cdot\bar{A}$ ✓	(6,7) $\bar{D}\cdot C\cdot B$ ✓	(6,7)(14,15) $C\cdot B$
15 $D\cdot C\cdot B\cdot A$ ✓	(6,14) $C\cdot B\cdot\bar{A}$ ✓	(6,14)(7,15) ~~$C\cdot B$~~
	(12,14) $D\cdot C\cdot\bar{A}$ ✓	
	(7,15) $C\cdot B\cdot A$ ✓	
	(11,15) $D\cdot B\cdot A$ ✓	
	(14,15) $D\cdot C\cdot B$ ✓	

Prime implicants

$$
\underset{(\bar{D}\cdot\bar{A})}{[0,2][4,6]} + \underset{(\bar{D}\cdot B)}{[2,3][6,7]} + \underset{(C\cdot\bar{A})}{[4,6][12,14]} +
$$

$$
\underset{(B\cdot A)}{[3,7][11,15]} + \underset{(C\cdot B)}{[6,7][14,15]}
$$

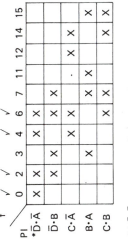

(b)

PI	0	2	3	4	6	7	11	12	14	15
f	✓	✓		✓	✓					
*$\bar{D}\cdot\bar{A}$	X	X		X	X					
$\bar{D}\cdot B$		X	X		X	X				
$C\cdot\bar{A}$				X	X		·	X	X	
$B\cdot A$			X			X	X			X
$C\cdot B$					X	X			X	X

(b) $\bar{D}\cdot\bar{A}$ is an essential PI, p_0; therefore p_0; p_2; p_4; p_6 are ticked off, and $\bar{D}\cdot\bar{A}$ is included in the final solution.

(c)

PI	0	2	3	4	6	7	11	12	14	15
f	✓	✓	✓	✓	✓	✓	✓	✓	✓	✓
*$\bar{D}\cdot\bar{A}$	X	X		X	X					
$\bar{D}\cdot B$		X	X		X	X				
*$C\cdot\bar{A}$				X	X			X	X	
*$B\cdot A$			X			X	X			X
$C\cdot B$					X	X			X	X

(c) Picking all essential PI's gives a full covering. The solution is thus: $f = (\bar{D}\cdot\bar{A}) + (C\cdot\bar{A}) + (B\cdot A)$.

Table 2.6: Reduction using a prime implicant table.

complete covering. Where the number of PIs is small, a selection may be taken by inspection. It is however better in most cases to use a **prime implicant table**, as shown in Table 2.6(b) & (c). Such a table is simply a horizontal list of the function p numbers, together with a vertical list of the PIs. Each PI covers a selection of p numbers, as indicated by crosses in that row. When the table has been completed it is searched for columns with only one cross. As such p numbers are only covered once, the covering PI is essential. For example, $\overline{D} \cdot \overline{A}$ is essential, as p_0 only appears in that term. $\overline{D} \cdot \overline{A}$ is starred to indicate that it is to be included in the final covering, and then each component p number of $\overline{D} \cdot \overline{A}$ is checked to show that they have been covered; in this case p_0; p_2; p_4; p_6 (Table 2.6(b)). In a similar manner, both $B \cdot A$ for p_{11} and $C \cdot \overline{A}$ for p_{12} are essential. There are no further essential PIs in the table. After all essential PIs have been chosen, the remaining unchecked p numbers are covered with a selection of the remaining non-essential PIs. In this case, all p numbers are covered by the essential PIs. In general this is not always the case.

In principle the Quine-McCluskey method may be extended to any number of variables. The amount of computation however tends to grow in an exponential manner. Computer programs [19, 20] exist based on this algorithm, but because of data storage limitations even they are limited to somewhere of the order of 12 variables. Other, less exacting algorithms are typically used for larger problems [21, 22]. The next example shows a particularly short 6-variable example, which nevertheless illustrates the growth tendency.

Example 2.25

A certain building has central heating controlled by six thermostats in various locations. Each thermostat has a logic 1 output for too low a temperature, and logic 0 for too high (thermostat cut off). Design a combination logic circuit which will indicate with a logic 1 when the majority of thermostats are cut off.

Solution

The truth table of Table 2.7(a) indicates when a majority of inputs are 0. From the truth table we have:

$$\mathcal{F} = \sum (0 \ldots 6), 8, 9, 10, 12, 16, 17, 20, 24, 32, 33, 34, 46, 40, 48.$$

The reduction of Table 2.7(b) leads to a listing of 15 PIs labelled; $a, b, \ldots n, o$ for convenience. Note that in general up to six columns are possible for the 6-variable function. This example only produced three columns. See Example 2.46 for an alternative technique used to solve this same problem. The PI table shows that all PIs are essential; each term's essential p number being bracketed alongside.

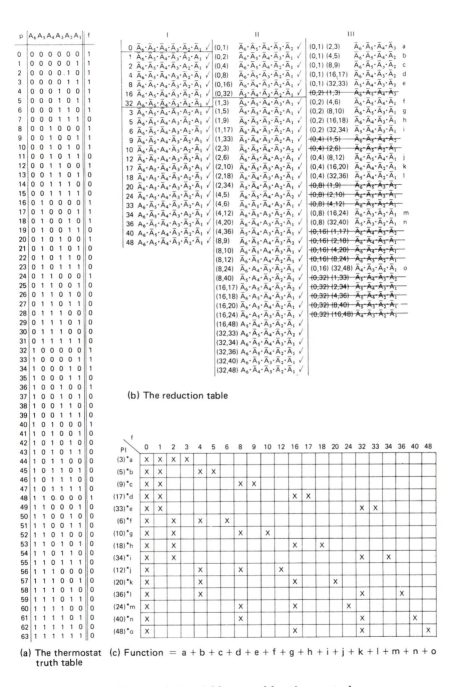

(b) The reduction table

(a) The thermostat truth table

(c) Function $= a + b + c + d + e + f + g + h + i + j + k + l + m + n + o$

Table 2.7: A 6-variable central heating control.

2.2.4   The Karnaugh Map

The Quine McCluskey technique is tedious and error prone, and thus is best left
to a moronic computer to solve. The alternative graphical representation of this
algorithm is better suited to the human facility of recognizing patterns and symmetries. The use of visual techniques in order to solve problems of logic goes back
at least to the 13th century, when the Spanish monk Ramon Lull used a circular
construction to demonstrate the various attributes of God. It was an original idea
for finding combinations of things, and the diagram had the added attraction that
it "perplexed disbelievers" [23].

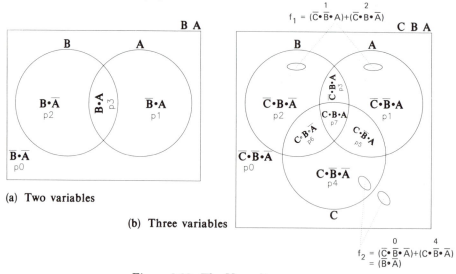

(a) Two variables

(b) Three variables

Figure 2.33: The Venn diagram.

As a direct descendent of the Lull map, the **Venn diagram** can be used to
map logic functions into space [24]. In the case of two variables, shown as circles
in Fig. 2.33(a), the set of objects B & A are considered bounded by the box. Any
point in space can be characterized as being inside or outside these two circles.
Thus the four areas are labelled $\overline{B}\cdot\overline{A}$, $\overline{B}\cdot A$, $B\cdot\overline{A}$, $B\cdot A$; that is, all possible product
terms. The 3-variable case, shown in Fig. 2.33(b) is similar, with eight minterms.
Here I have illustrated two sum of product expressions. Inside $\mathcal{F}_1$, the function is
either in $(\overline{C}\cdot\overline{B}\cdot A)$ or $(\overline{C}\cdot B\cdot\overline{A})$, whilst inside $\mathcal{F}_2$, we are either $(\overline{C}\cdot\overline{B}\cdot\overline{A})+(C\cdot\overline{B}\cdot\overline{A})$. In
this latter case we know that the function reduces to $\overline{B}\cdot\overline{A}$, as the two product terms
are unit distance.

A close inspection of these Venn diagrams shows that any areas which have a
common border, such as p_4 and p_5, are always unit distance. Thus functions which
straddle a border will reduce. Note that touching at a corner, for example p_2 and p_7,
does not constitute a border.

It is possible to construct Venn diagrams for four variables [24, 25], but the map
becomes rather irregular and difficult to use (try drawing a fourth area overlapping
each of the three circles of Fig. 2.33(b)). The following example shows a typical
application of a Venn diagram to solve a problem in logic.

Example 2.26

A certain university sports center enrols external members for evening classes in yoga, aerobics and swimming. Being thus enrolled as part-time students, these members of the center are entitled to certain privileges, such as the use of the student bar and library rights.

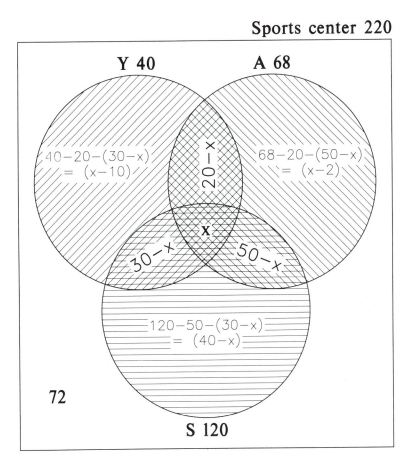

Figure 2.34: The university sports center.

Of the total enrolment of 220, a census of activities shows:

- 40 members take yoga classes
- 88 members do aerobic exercises
- 120 members swim
- 20 members do both yoga and aerobics
- 30 members swim and do yoga

- 50 members swim and do aerobics

- A startling 72 appear not to do anything (except exercise their stomach in the bar or mind in the library).

How many students do all three physical activities?

Solution

The Venn diagram for this problem is shown in Fig. 2.34. The universe (the sports center) comprizes a set of three objects; Y (Yoga), A (Aerobics) and S (Swimming). Bold lettering is used to label the diagram with the given information and unknown x. From this, the three remaining areas can be calculated. For example, the $45°$ hatched area (those doing only yoga) is 40 (inside the total Yoga circle) less 20 (those doing both Yoga and Aerobics) less $30 - x$ (those doing both Yoga and Swimming less x already assigned for in the Yoga plus Aerobics group); totalling $x - 10$. With all areas accounted, the total must equal 220; thus:

$$220 = (x - 10) + (20 - x) + (x - 2) + x + (30 - x) + (50 - x) + (40 + x) + 72$$

giving $x = 20$.

Incidentally, this result shows that nobody does both Yoga and Aerobics. Is there an antagonism between the two philosophies; or do their timetables just clash?

――――――――――――――

The **Karnaugh map (K-map)** can be thought of as a formalized Venn diagram, where each minterm appears in space as a box, with the boxes being arranged according to the common border topology [26, 27, 12]. Alternatively the K-map may be considered a 2-dimensional truth table. From Fig. 2.35, we see that the function variables are labelled around the periphery in the unit-distant Gray code. Each adjacent cell is thus also unit-distant, and corresponds to a truth table row; whose value may be read off from the surrounding code. Thus a K-map can altenatively be considered as a 2-dimensional truth table.

Figure 2.35 shows the correlation of the two properties of adjacency and unit-distance. Note that only cells sharing a common border, rather than at diagonal points, are unit-distant. Close inspection shows that cells that are not adjacent in the normal sense are seen to be unit-distant; for example, in Fig. 2.35(c), cells $0000b$ (p_0) and $0010b$ (p_2). In fact any cell at one of the four sides is unit-distant to its image on the opposite side. This can be reconciled with the adjacency rule if the K-map is thought of as being carried on the surface of a toroid (donut). With such a configuration, opposite sides are in fact logically adjacent.

The particular K-map format used here [27] facilitates the process of minimization. In this notation, lines are drawn at the sides of the map where the labelled variable is logic 1; thus all areas of the map to the right of the D line have $D = 1$. Likewise (for the 4-variable case) if a cell lies to the left of the C line, under the B line, or above the A line, then the respective variable appears uncomplemented; otherwise it is negated. For example, cell 9 is right of D ($= D$); not left of C ($= \overline{C}$); not under B ($= \overline{B}$) and above A ($= A$), i.e. $D \cdot \overline{C} \cdot \overline{B} \cdot A$.

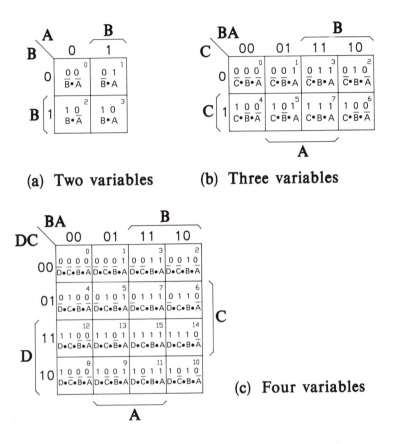

Figure 2.35: K-maps for two, three and four variables.

Normally each cell is labelled with its equivalent p number. It is not necessary to evaluate the p numbers each time a map is drawn; after a little practice the 'hop-skip' pattern of these numbers falls easily to memory. The hop always occurs after the second cell to the right, and the jump after the second row down; as a consequence of the Gray-code pattern.

Now that we have a map with adjacency equated to unit distance, we need to know how to use it as a minimization aid. The map algorithm can be summarized as follows:

1. Enter a 1 in each cell the function is true.

2. Cells which are adjacent are combined into one area; known as an elemental area or **loop**. The number of cells which may be contained within a loop is limited to 2^n, i.e. 1,2,4,8,16 etc. Such loops must be rectangular. The set of covering areas is known as a listing of prime implicants.

96   CHAPTER 2. LOGIC AND BOOLEAN ALGEBRA

3. Sufficient largest elemental areas are chosen to cover all cells marked with
   a 1 at least once; there being no limit on the number of times a cell may be
   covered. No blank cell may be included within a loop.

Some examples will illustrate the use of the K-map.

Example 2.27

Using K-maps, minimize the four functions defined as:

$$\mathcal{F}_{1(CBA)} = \sum 3,7 \qquad \mathcal{F}_{2(DCBA)} = \sum 4,5,6,7$$
$$\mathcal{F}_{3(DCBA)} = \sum 4,6,12,14 \qquad \mathcal{F}_{4(DCBA)} = \sum 0,2,8,10$$

Solution

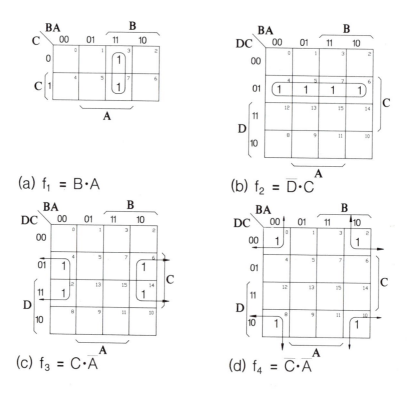

Figure 2.36: Using the K-map to minimize SOP functions.

1. In each case a 1 is entered into the specified p number cell. This is equivalent
   to inserting a 1 in each true table row. Normally, cells which are false are left
   blank, rather than inserting a zero.

2. In Fig. 2.36(a), cells 3 and 7 are looped together, giving a rectangular group
   of two. The reduced function is read off the map as follows: all the loop is

below the B line and above the A line, but with only a 50% coverage by the
C line ($C+\overline{C}$). Thus the solution is B·A.

3. Function $\mathcal{F}_2$ is similar, but with a grouping of four, which is all not to the
   right of D ($\overline{D}$); all to the left of C (C), but only 50% covered by both B and A.
   This gives $\mathcal{F}_2 = \overline{D}\cdot C$.

4. Function $\mathcal{F}_3$ illustrates adjacency on opposite sides of the K-map, with all the
   area covered by C and not covered by A, giving $C\cdot\overline{A}$.

5. In function $\mathcal{F}_4$, cells 10 and 8 are adjacent to each other, and taken as as
   a pair are adjacent to cells 2 and 0. All the resulting group of four corner
   cells are not covered by C or by A, giving $\overline{C}\cdot\overline{A}$. In a case where, say, cells 0
   and 10 were true, no adjacency would exist; in the same way as diagonal cells
   touching at only one point are not adjacent.

Notice that in all the cases covered by this example, the eliminated variable is
only covered by 50% of a loop; this is the case in general.

In these four cases, each function has been covered by only one elemental area,
but in most instances several loops are required for a complete covering. This is
illustrated by the following examples.

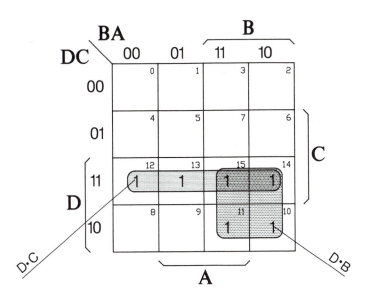

Figure 2.37: An illegal BCD detector.

Example 2.28

Repeat the illegal-BCD combination design of Example 2.21, but using a K-map
minimization.

Solution

Cells 12,13,14,15 combine to give D·C, leaving cells 10 and 11 uncovered. Whilst these could be combined to give a loop of two, a better solution is obtained by re-using cells 14 and 15 to give D·B. Unless there are special circumstances (see Section 2.3.2), loops should be as large as possible; doubling the size of an elemental area eliminates one variable.

In this example, more than one loop has been required to cover all the true outputs. Thus the function lies either in (D·B) or in (D·C) i.e. (D·B)+(D·C). It is instructive for the reader to compare the method of obtaining this solution with that of the Quine-McCluskey algorithm.

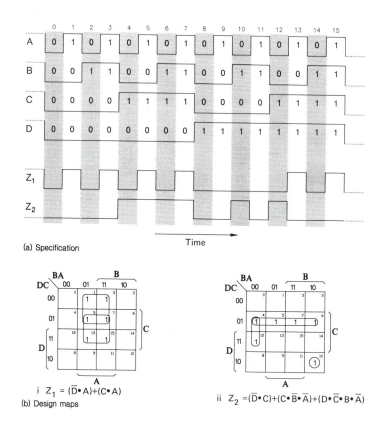

(a) Specification

(b) Design maps

i $Z_1 = (\overline{D} \cdot A) + (C \cdot A)$

ii $Z_2 = (\overline{D} \cdot C) + (C \cdot \overline{B} \cdot \overline{A}) + (D \cdot \overline{C} \cdot B \cdot \overline{A})$

Figure 2.38: Waveform generation.

Example 2.29

A frequency dividing circuit has four outputs ÷8, ÷4, ÷2, and ÷1, as shown in Fig. 2.38(a). With these four signals regarded as inputs D C B A respectively, design an appropriate circuit which will generate the waveforms, Z_1 and Z_2.

Examination of the divide waveforms shows that $DCBA$ represents a time sequence count of a 4-bit binary number. Binary counters are discussed in detail in Section 4.2, but it is sufficient for our purposes to note that $Z_1 = \sum 1, 3, 5, 7, 13, 15$ and $Z_2 = \sum 4, 5, 6, 7, 10, 12$. These are entered into K-maps in the normal way, and grouped together as shown in Fig. 2.38(b).

Notice the influence of loop size on the resulting product term in the Z_2 K-map. Cell 10 cannot be allied to any other cell and remains unminimized.

Example 2.30

Minimize the function defined as: $\mathcal{F}_{(DCBA)} = \sum 3, 7, 8, 9, 12, 13, 15$.

Solution

After the function has been entered into the K-map, the largest elemental areas are drawn. However, although there are four such groupings, a full covering may be obtained with only three loops; the two possibilities being shown in Figs. 2.39(a) & (b).

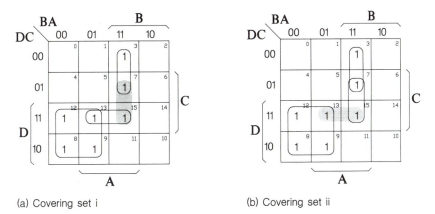

(a) Covering set i   (b) Covering set ii

Figure 2.39: Alternative covering sets.

In practice it is not necessary to fill in every possible elemental area (this is what the Quine-McCluskey method does), the process being stopped after all cells are covered. To obtain the best solution it is usually best to start with the smallest areas and work up in size until a full covering is obtained (try Example SAE 2.9). Thus single cells which cannot be paired, then double cells which cannot be made up to four, etc. With large complex maps it may be difficult to obtain the best result, and in such cases the map may be used to evaluate all possible elemental areas. A prime implicant table is then used to choose a covering; as explained in Section 2.2.3. However, if the designer has to resort to the use of these tables, probably the reduction is best done completely using a tabular method.

In cases, like this example, where there are several possible solutions, there may be other constraints which favor one solution over another, or even dictate a less minimized covering. This is discussed later.

It is possible to use the K-map to evaluate a covering of the function zeros. This may be interpreted as minimizing the complement of the function. Alternatively the function may be described as being **active-Low**, that is 'rings a bell' when its output is logic 0. Whichever interpretation is used, the minimization may be accomplished by simply looping all zeros together. A covering of zeros is sometimes called a **drop set**, a relic of relay terminology. Likewise a covering of ones is known as a **lift set**.

Example 2.31

Determine a minimal all-NOR implementation for the BCD error detector of Example 2.21.

Solution

As stated on page 80, the function complement frequently gives a better NOR implementation. To do this on the K-map, enter the zeros into the relevant cells, and group in exactly the same way as ones. The resulting covering is then the function

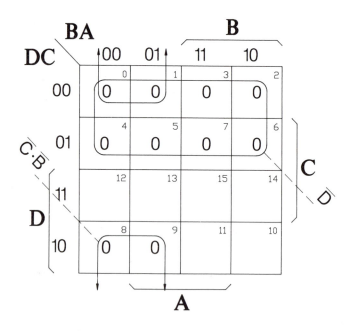

Figure 2.40: Mapping function zeros; drop sets . $\overline{\mathcal{F}} = \overline{D} + (\overline{C} \cdot \overline{B})$.

complement. Applying deMorgan's theorem:

$$\overline{\mathcal{F}} = \overline{D} + (\overline{C} \cdot \overline{B})$$
$$\overline{\mathcal{F}} = \overline{D} + (\overline{C+B})$$
$$\mathcal{F} = \overline{\overline{D} + (\overline{C+B})}$$

which is all NOR. The implementation is shown in Fig. 2.32(d).

Example 2.32

An electronic thermometer, designed for greenhouse use, has a 4-bit binary output
representing a temperature range from 0°C to 15°C (the range is in fact extended
to 31°C using a fifth bit, which we will initially ignore). A plug-in module is to
be designed to output a logic 1 when the temperature rises above 8°C. Design a
minimal circuit to implement this specification.

Solution

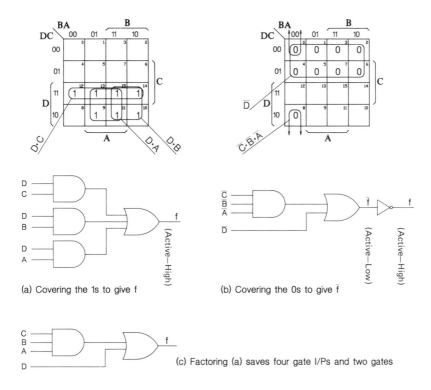

Figure 2.41: A digital thermostat.

The map of Fig. 2.41(a) directly gives the required active-High expression. If we
factorize this outcome thus:

$$\mathcal{F} = (D \cdot C) + (D \cdot B) + (D \cdot A) = D \cdot (C + B + A)$$

then we half the circuit cost, as shown in Fig. 2.41(c).

The map of Fig. 2.44(b) gives the alternative active-Low expression, $\overline{\mathcal{F}}$. As our specification requires an active-High outcome, then the circuit diagram shows an output inverter to give $\mathcal{F}$. Note the symmetry between the two circuits. In general, the **dual** of a circuit, i.e. active-High↔active-Low, can be obtained by reversing all gate types (AND↔OR) and inverting all variables. This is a consequence of the duality (de Morgan's) theorem.

In this text, most solutions will be left in the 2-level form derived directly from the map. However, any of the rules of Boolean algebra can be used to further minimize the network or to alter its topology. Although not in this case (see Example 2.33), factorizing usually leads to circuits of more than two levels, with a more complex interconnection pattern. This can lead to difficulties when characteristics, such as switching times or circuit layout, are taken into account.

Of course we cannot simply ignore the fifth bit (E); because, if we do, the thermostat will fail to indicate all temperatures from 16°C (*10000b*) to 24°C (*11000b*). The intuitive response would be to OR the active-High output with E. However, in most cases it is better to treat 5-variable problems using 5-variable maps.

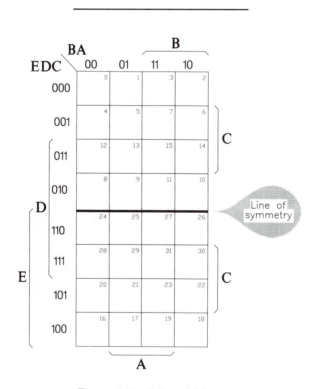

Figure 2.42: A 5-variable map.

Extension of the map to more than four variables is straightforward. However, the adjacency rules become progressively more difficult to use. Figure 2.42 shows the enlargement of the map to five variables. One side is simply doubled by using a 3-bit Gray code. This in essence gives two 4-variable maps joined by a line of symmetry. Notice that the pattern of p-terms is a mirror image about this line.

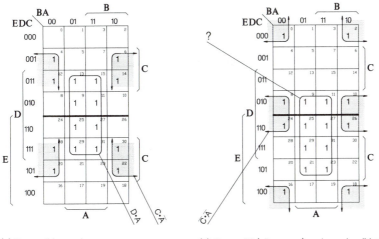

(a) Two valid groupings   (b) One valid (all corners) and one invalid grouping

Figure 2.43: Minimizing with a 5-variable K-map.

The normal rules of adjacency hold for each of the two constituent 4-variable maps (one E and one $\overline{E}$), and they may be used independently of each other. However, full reduction is only obtained by following an additional adjacency rule. This states that all elemental areas balanced about the line of symmetry are adjacent. Thus in Fig. 2.43(a), cells 13,15,9,11 can be combined with 29,31,25,27. Similarly 4,12,6,14 and 20,28,22,30. All eight 'corners' may also be grouped together, as shown in Fig. 2.43(b).

Beware of groups such as 9,11,25,27,29,31,21,23. This is a rectangular group of 8, but is not balanced about the line of symmetry. Instead two groups are required for a covering, viz. 9,11,25,27 and 21,23,29,31 ($D \cdot \overline{C} \cdot A$)+($E \cdot C \cdot A$).

Example 2.33

A certain computer memory uses the 8-6-4-2-1 BCD code of Table 2.8 as error protection. Design an active-High circuit which will indicate that a legal code group has been received. Only 2-I/P gates are available from the store.

Solution

The cells corresponding to the legal combinations of Table 2.8 are entered into the map and minimized in the normal way. The resulting function:

$$\mathcal{F} = (\overline{E \cdot D \cdot C}) + (\overline{D \cdot C \cdot B}) + (\overline{E \cdot D \cdot B}) + (\overline{E \cdot C \cdot B})$$

	8	6	4	2	1
p	E	D	C	B	A
0	0	0	0	0	0
1	0	0	0	0	1
2	0	0	0	1	0
3	0	0	0	1	1
4	0	0	1	0	0
5	0	0	1	0	1
8	0	1	0	0	0
9	0	1	0	0	1
16	1	0	0	0	0
17	1	0	0	0	1

Table 2.8: The 8-6-4-2-1 code.

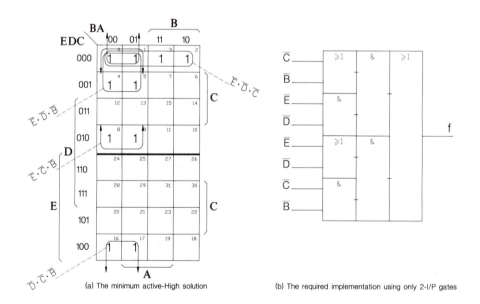

(a) The minimum active-High solution

(b) The required implementation using only 2-I/P gates

Figure 2.44: A 8-6-4-2-1 code detector.

requires both 3 and 4-input gates. Factorizing gives:

$$\mathcal{F} = \overline{E}\cdot\overline{D}\cdot(\overline{C}+\overline{B})+\overline{C}\cdot\overline{B}\cdot(\overline{E}+\overline{D})$$

giving the required circuit of Fig. 2.44(b). Can you determine the dual of this circuit for an active-Low output?

It is readily possible to extend the map to six variables, by folding the 5-variable map about a new line of symmetry. The process may be further repeated as many times as desired, but the increasing lines of symmetry make the map technique of doubtful utility (see Example SAE 2.13).

Example 2.34

A certain room thermometer has a 6-bit BCD output giving temperature readings between 0°C (00 0000) and 39°C (11 1001). Design a thermostat to detect all temperatures above 18°C (01 1001b).

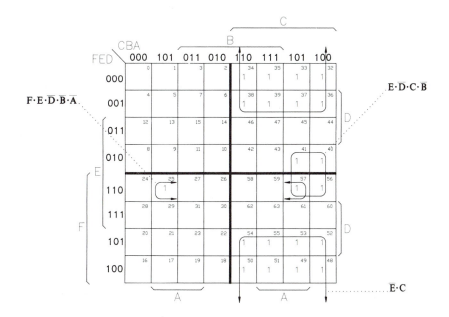

Figure 2.45: A 6-variable Karnaugh map.

Solution

The 6-variable K-map is shown in Fig. 2.45. Now there are two lines of symmetry, representing the two constituent 5-variable maps. Notice that the p-term 'hop-skip' pattern in the new section now runs from right to left; as dictated by the mirroring around the vertical symmetry line.

The specification requires the detection of temperatures $19°C$ ($01\ 1001b = p_{25}$); between 20 and $29°C$ ($10\ 0000b = p_{32}$ to $10\ 1001b = p_{41}$) and $30°-39°C$ ($11\ 0000 = p_{48}$ to $11\ 1001 = p_{57}$). Filling these cells gives two groups about the horizontal symmetry line, and one group of two about the vertical line.

The reader should not be misled by the simplicity of this example; most 6-variable problems are considerably more complex than this (try Example 2.47).

Before going on to the next section, can you verify that the alternative solution $\mathcal{F} = C + (F \cdot E \cdot A)$ costing five inputs (against 14) will also detect temperatures in the correct range? What assumption have I made in deriving this equation?

2.3   Combinational Design Techniques

We now have the basic tools with which we can design efficient combinational gate-based logic circuits. In this section, we extend these techniques to further improve the efficacy of this class of implementation.

After reading this section, the reader should be able to:

- Make use of don't care terms in minimizing functions using the K-maps technique.

- Make use of product-term sharing, if permitted by the circuit topology, when designing networks with common input variables and multiple outputs.

- Appreciate the origins of static, function and dynamic hazards.

- Find static hazards in a 2-level AND-OR network, and to be able to transform the circuit to a static hazard-free form.

2.3.1   Don't Care States

In many cases the response of a logic network is only defined for a subset of its possible input combinations. This may be because such **don't care states** will not occur in practice; or if they do, their outcome is irrelevant. We have already hinted at this in the last example, where the thermometer had a BCD output. In the K-map of Fig. 2.45, we ignored the illegal states $00\ 1010b$ to $00\ 1111b$ (p_{10}–p_{15}); $01\ 1010b$ to $01\ 1111b$ (p_{26}–p_{31}); $10\ 1010b$ to $10\ 1111b$ (p_{42}–p_{47}) and $11\ 1010b$ to $11\ 1111b$ (p_{58}–p_{63}). By appearing as blanks in the map, we are explicitly making their outcome in the truth table logic 0.

In general an over-specified system requires a more expensive implementation. Thus, there really is no need to make these states 0, as they should never occur. Instead, the response of a circuit to a don't care combination of input variables may be taken to be 1 or 0 as convenient. Such cells in a K-map, usually entered as X or ϕ, may be included inside a loop only where convenient.

Example 2.35

A digital clock is to display the month of the year. Because the length of the calendar months vary, it is necessary to reset the day display at differing points, depending on the month. The calendar month is to be internally present as a 4-bit number, i.e., January = 0001b, February = 0010b etc. As part of the resetting circuit, it is necessary to detect all months having 31 days. Design a minimal all-NAND circuit to implement this function.

Solution

The months to be detected are January (p_1); March (p_3); May (p_5); July (p_7); August (p_8); October (p_{10}) and December (p_{12}). Filling these in as a 1 in the K-map of Fig. 2.46(a) gives the function $(\overline{D}\cdot A)+(D\cdot\overline{B}\cdot\overline{A})+(D\cdot\overline{C}\cdot\overline{A})$ in the normal way.

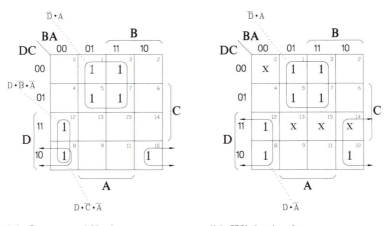

(a) Overspecified   (b) With don't care states

Figure 2.46: Incorporating don't cares into the K-map.

What about months 0,13,14 & 15? These are can't happen don't care states and should not be forced into a non-31-day mould. Instead, in Fig. 2.46(b) I have entered these as X. The map is minimized normally, with the following proviso:

> Don't care entries may be included inside a loop at the designer's discretion, if a better covering results.

It is not essential that all, or any, don't care cells be included in a covering. Any don't care term in a loop will be logic 1, whilst those outside are logic 0. Thus, by arbitrarily deeming month 14 to have 31 days the logic reduces to $(D\cdot\overline{A})+(\overline{D}\cdot A)$, and the cost drops from 11 inputs to six. As month 14 will never occur, there is no deterioration in circuit functionality. Non-existent months 0,13,15 do not have 31 days!

Example 2.36

Repeat Example 2.34, but this time making use of don't care states.

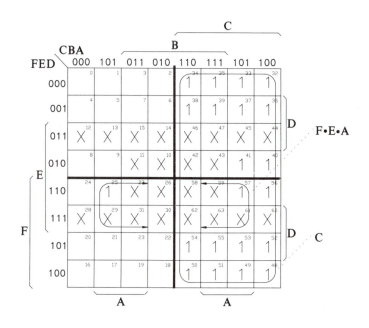

Figure 2.47: Don't cares for our BCD thermostat.

Solution

We have already listed the don't care inputs for this problem, i.e. all illegal BCD combinations. Entering these as X gives the K-map of Fig. 2.47. Here there is an even more dramatic drop in cost from 14 down to 5 inputs.

The reader should try minimizing the map for an active-Low output to give an outcome $\overline{\mathcal{F}} = \overline{C} \cdot (\overline{F} + \overline{E} + \overline{A})$, which is the dual of our active-High function.

Example 2.37

Use the K-map reduction technique to minimize the direction and hazard-warning logic of Example 2.6 and hence determine an all-NAND implementation.

Solution

Four entries in the truth table of Fig. 2.9 are can't happen, as both right and left indicator switches cannot be simultaneously applied. These are shown in the two K-maps of Fig. 2.48 as don't care entries in cells 6,7,14,15. The minimized outcome

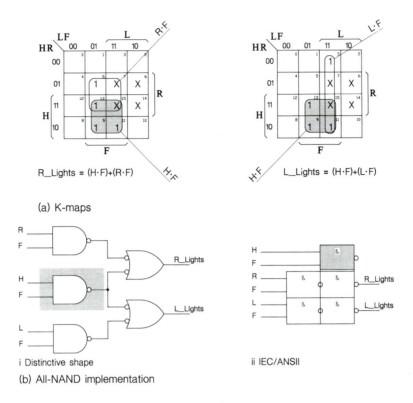

(a) K-maps

i Distinctive shape   ii IEC/ANSII

(b) All-NAND implementation

Figure 2.48: Minimizing the direction and hazard lighting logic.

is the same as that of the intuitive approach of Example 2.6 if F is factored out of
each equation. The circuit shown in Fig. 2.48(b) is a direct translation from the
AND-OR K-map equations. As the product term H·F appears in both maps, shown
shaded, the generating gate is shared between both the output circuits. Notice how
this sharing is depicted in IEC/ANSII symbology.

2.3.2   Multiple-Output Circuits

Most digital circuits have more than one output. Each output circuit may be
minimized separately as an independent stand-alone circuit, but sharing the same
inputs (see Example 2.29). However, this approach does not take into account the
possibility of sharing gates between circuits, such as shown in the previous example.
This is especially relevant where discrete gates are used to implement the circuit, in
programmable logic arrays, (see Section 3.3.4) and where custom integrated circuits
are being designed. However, some structures are organized so that product terms
cannot be shared. For example, the programmable array logic (PAL) architecture
(see Section 3.3.3) not only cannot share terms, but have a limited number of
AND gates for each output. In this case each output is minimized independently
and the number of AND terms (K-map loops) must also be minimized. However,

the product term size is irrelevant.

From this discussion, it can be seen that the approach to multiple-output circuits is dependent on the chosen circuit implementation. At this point, we will assume that gate sharing is possible.

Example 2.38

A circuit is to be designed to serially generate the constant π to 15 decimal places; i.e. 3.141 592 653 589 793. The input is to be driven by a 4-bit 8-4-2-1 coded counter, and the output is to be in the same code.

Solution

Once started, the counter presents each of the 16 binary numbers to the circuit in sequence. Every input state must be translated to give the required output, as defined by the truth table of Fig. 2.49(b). Four K-maps are required, one for each output, and they are shown each independently minimized according to the normal criterion. This gives the logic circuit of Fig. 2.49(d); needing 65 gate inputs, excluding inverters. However, an alternative covering for map Z is also shown, which at a first glance is decidedly inferior. Nevertheless, the resulting implementation of Z gives a saving of three inputs, due to sharing of gates. Replacing $D \cdot C$ by $D \cdot C \cdot A$ saves two inputs, as $D \cdot C \cdot A$ has already been generated for Y. Similarly, replacing $D \cdot \overline{A}$ by $D \cdot \overline{C} \cdot \overline{A} + D \cdot C \cdot \overline{A}$ saves inputs; however, because an extra loop is involved, the saving of two AND inputs is reduced by one extra OR input, giving a net saving of one. Every loop, irrespective of size, requires one OR input. Note that the former solution as applied to a PAL target (see Examples 3.25 & 6.2) is desirable, as the sole criterion here is the number of loops, and sharing is not possible.

———————————

Inter-map minimizing can be done by inspection, with a little practice. However, when many outputs are involved, it is difficult to produce a best result, and an algorithm specifically designed for multi-output systems may have to be applied. These normally use logic products of the maps to highlight common groups [29, 30]. In the last example, additional maps for $W \cdot X$, $W \cdot Y$, $W \cdot Z$, $X \cdot Y$, $X \cdot Z$, $W \cdot X \cdot Y$, $W \cdot X \cdot Z$, $W \cdot Y \cdot Z$, $X \cdot Y \cdot Z$, $W \cdot X \cdot Y \cdot Z$ are produced, and all 14 maps minimized. A modified prime implicant table is then used to pick a covering set for each output. This method destroys the main advantage of the map, namely speed; for example needing a possible 247 extra maps for an 8-output circuit, plus PI tables. For most practical cases, this is longer than the tabular equivalent procedure [31].

The author has found that the following map algorithm gives a satisfactory compromize, producing a fast and good solution.

1. Minimize each map separately, but where a choice of PI exists, an attempt should be made to common loops.

2. Note any p-numbers unique to the set of maps. Any PIs covering these can never be commoned. Enter these PIs into a fresh set of blank maps.

3. Enter all PIs covering half the map. Such PIs cost only one OR input, which is the minimum possible.

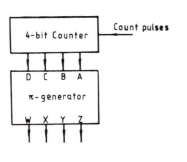

(a) Circuit schematic.

p	D C B A	W X Y Z	π
0	0 0 0 0	0 0 1 1	3
1	0 0 0 1	0 0 0 1	1
2	0 0 1 0	0 1 0 0	4
3	0 0 1 1	0 0 0 1	1
4	0 1 0 0	0 1 0 1	5
5	0 1 0 1	1 0 0 1	9
6	0 1 1 0	0 0 1 0	2
7	0 1 1 1	0 1 1 0	6
8	1 0 0 0	0 1 0 1	5
9	1 0 0 1	0 0 1 1	3
10	1 0 1 0	0 1 0 1	5
11	1 0 1 1	1 0 0 0	8
12	1 1 0 0	1 0 0 1	9
13	1 1 0 1	0 1 1 1	7
14	1 1 1 0	1 0 0 1	9
15	1 1 1 1	0 0 1 1	3

(with headers: Inputs — D C B A; Outputs — W X Y Z; π)

(b) The circuit truth table.

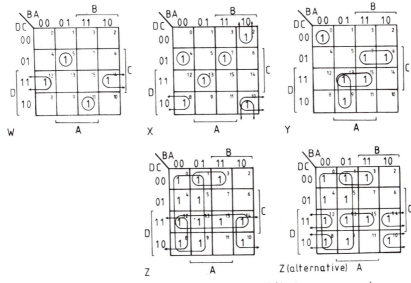

(c) K-maps for each output showing two alternatives for Z (*for key see next page*)

Figure 2.49: Designing a π generator (*continued next page*).

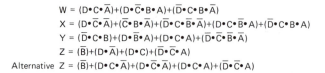

$W = (D \bullet C \bullet \overline{A}) + (D \bullet \overline{C} \bullet B \bullet A) + (\overline{D} \bullet C \bullet B \bullet \overline{A})$

$X = (D \bullet \overline{C} \bullet \overline{A}) + (\overline{C} \bullet B \bullet \overline{A}) + (\overline{D} \bullet C \bullet \overline{B} \bullet \overline{A}) + (D \bullet C \bullet \overline{B} \bullet A) + (\overline{D} \bullet C \bullet B \bullet A)$

$Y = (\overline{D} \bullet C \bullet B) + (D \bullet \overline{B} \bullet A) + (D \bullet C \bullet A) + (\overline{D} \bullet \overline{C} \bullet \overline{B} \bullet \overline{A})$

$Z = (\overline{B}) + (D \bullet \overline{A}) + (D \bullet C) + (\overline{D} \bullet \overline{C} \bullet A)$

Alternative $Z = (\overline{B}) + (D \bullet C \bullet \overline{A}) + (D \bullet \overline{C} \bullet \overline{A}) + (D \bullet C \bullet A) + (\overline{D} \bullet \overline{C} \bullet A)$

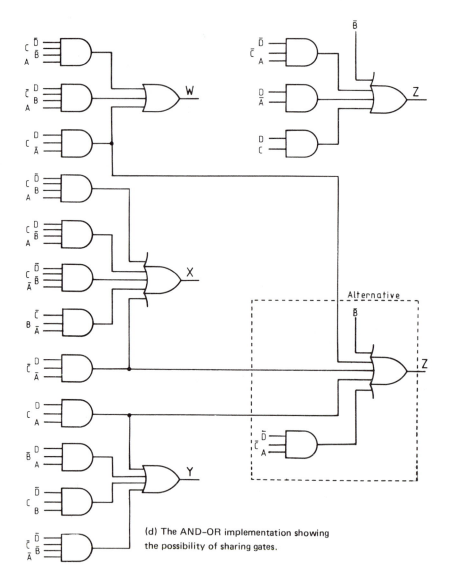

(d) The AND–OR implementation showing
the possibility of sharing gates.

Figure 2.49: (*continued*). Designing a π generator.

4. Of the remaining PIs, systematically starting with the largest and working down to the smallest loop of the set, note if they can be covered by other smaller PIs from other maps. If a saving results, these covering PIs are entered in place of the original PI, and also in the maps where they arise. When estimating costs, remember that each extra loop costs one OR input.

5. In a few cases it may be possible to further subdivide loops, giving groups which are not PIs of any map but which nevertheless give cost reductions. Such decompositions can be seen by inspection only.

Some examples will clarify.

Example 2.39

Design an AND-OR circuit to translate $0°$–$10°C$, expressed in the 8-4-2-1 code; to $°F$, correct to the nearest $\frac{1}{2}°F$, expressed in the 32-16-8-4-2-1-$\frac{1}{2}$ code.

Solution

Directly from the truth table we can say that $E = 1$. Don't care terms common to all outputs are p_{11} to p_{15} inclusive.

1. The six output maps, each separately minimized, are listed in Fig. 2.50(b).

2. p_9 uniquely appears in map F and is covered by loop 1. Similarly p_1 appears only in map I covered by loop 2. Both these prime implicants are transferred to the second set of maps, Fig. 2.50(c).

			32 16 8 4 2 1 ½	
p	°C	D C B A	E F G H I J K	°F
0	0	0 0 0 0	1 0 0 0 0 0 0	32
1	1	0 0 0 1	1 0 0 0 1 0 0	34
2	2	0 0 1 0	1 0 0 0 1 1 1	35½
3	3	0 0 1 1	1 0 0 1 0 1 1	37½
4	4	0 1 0 0	1 0 0 1 1 1 0	39
5	5	0 1 0 1	1 0 1 0 0 1 0	41
6	6	0 1 1 0	1 0 1 0 1 1 0	43
7	7	0 1 1 1	1 0 1 1 0 0 1	44½
8	8	1 0 0 0	1 0 1 1 1 0 1	46½
9	9	1 0 0 1	1 1 0 0 0 0 0	48
10	10	1 0 1 0	1 1 0 0 1 0 0	50

Common don't cares p_{11} to p_{15} inclusive

$E = 1$

(a) The truth table.

Figure 2.50: A $°C$ to $°F$ converter (*continued next page*).

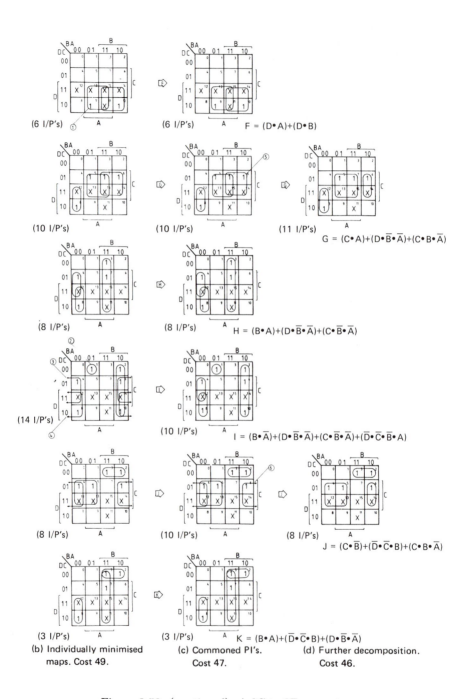

$F = (D \cdot A) + (D \cdot B)$

$G = (C \cdot A) + (D \cdot \overline{B} \cdot \overline{A}) + (C \cdot B \cdot \overline{A})$

$H = (B \cdot A) + (D \cdot \overline{B} \cdot \overline{A}) + (C \cdot \overline{B} \cdot \overline{A})$

$I = (B \cdot \overline{A}) + (D \cdot \overline{B} \cdot \overline{A}) + (C \cdot \overline{B} \cdot \overline{A}) + (\overline{D} \cdot \overline{C} \cdot \overline{B} \cdot A)$

$J = (C \cdot \overline{B}) + (\overline{D} \cdot \overline{C} \cdot B) + (C \cdot B \cdot \overline{A})$

$K = (B \cdot A) + (\overline{D} \cdot \overline{C} \cdot B) + (D \cdot \overline{B} \cdot \overline{A})$

(b) Individually minimised
maps. Cost 49.

(c) Commoned PI's.
Cost 47.

(d) Further decomposition.
Cost 46.

Figure 2.50: (*continued*). A °C to °F converter.

3. No PIs cover half of the map.

4. Starting with loops of four, each PI is transferred to the second set of maps if it cannot be covered by PIs from other maps. Loop 3 can be covered by $C \cdot \overline{B} \cdot \overline{A}$ from map H, in conjunction with $B \cdot \overline{A}$ in its own map. Thus $C \cdot \overline{B} \cdot \overline{A}$ and $B \cdot \overline{A}$ are entered into new maps I and H as applicable. Similarly loop 4 in the same map can be covered by $D \cdot \overline{B} \cdot \overline{A}$ from maps G, H & K; again in conjunction with $B \cdot \overline{A}$. Loop $D \cdot \overline{B} \cdot \overline{A}$ is entered into new maps I, G, H & K. No other loops can be decomposed.

5. By inspection it can be seen that both loops 5 & 6 can be covered by non-PI $C \cdot B \cdot \overline{A}$, saving one input.

The final equations show a saving of 6% over the separate minimization approach. An implementation using a programmable diode matrix is shown in Fig. 3.4. Here two product terms (horizontal rows) are saved out of 13; a saving of 15%, as the size of each such term is irrelevant.

Example 2.40

Determine a minimal set of Boolean equations, suitable for an all-NOR implementation, which will translate natural 8-4-2-1 BCD code to the 7-segment code of Table 1.3(d). The resulting decoder is to drive the active-Low display shown in Fig. 3.38.

Solution

We use a zeros covering to generate the complement of the function, as recommended for NOR implementations (see page 80).

1. The list of individually minimized drop set maps is given in Fig. 2.51(c).

2. Loop 1 is essential in covering unique p_0.

3. Loop 2 covers half of map e, and is transferred to the second column of maps.

4. Loop 4 may be replaced by $C \cdot \overline{B} \cdot \overline{A}$ of map d, which in conjunction with $C \cdot B \cdot \overline{A}$ of map b replaces loop 3. Loop 5 is replaced by $C \cdot B \cdot A$ of map d. Loop 6 is replaced by $\overline{C} \cdot B \cdot \overline{A}$ of map c.

5. No further decomposition is apparent.

A saving of 8% results in the use of the algorithm.

2.3.3 Hazards

In our discussions concerning Boolean relationships, it has been tacitly assumed that we are dealing with steady-state variables. In the real world, signal changes take a finite time to propagate through circuits. This is symbolized in Fig. 2.52(b) as t_{pd} (time, propagation delay). Thus for example, the function $A + \overline{A}$ is always 1 in steady state (Basic Boolean law I(h), page 71). However, in examining the practical

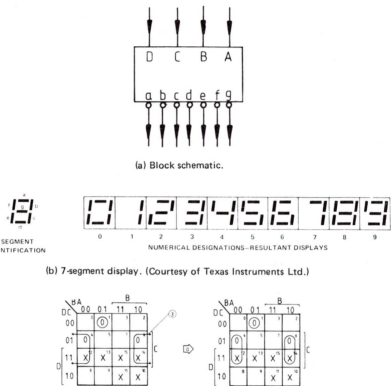

(a) Block schematic.

SEGMENT
IDENTIFICATION

0   1   2   3   4   5   6   7   8   9

NUMERICAL DESIGNATIONS–RESULTANT DISPLAYS

(b) 7-segment display. (Courtesy of Texas Instruments Ltd.)

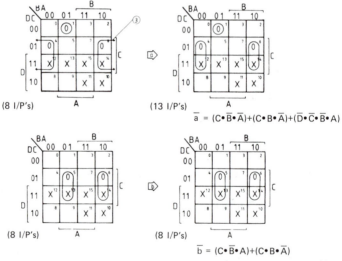

$$\overline{a} = (C \bullet \overline{B} \bullet \overline{A}) + (C \bullet B \bullet \overline{A}) + (\overline{D} \bullet \overline{C} \bullet \overline{B} \bullet A)$$

$$\overline{b} = (C \bullet \overline{B} \bullet A) + (C \bullet B \bullet \overline{A})$$

Figure 2.51: A drop set covering for an active-Low 7-segment decoder (*continued next page*).

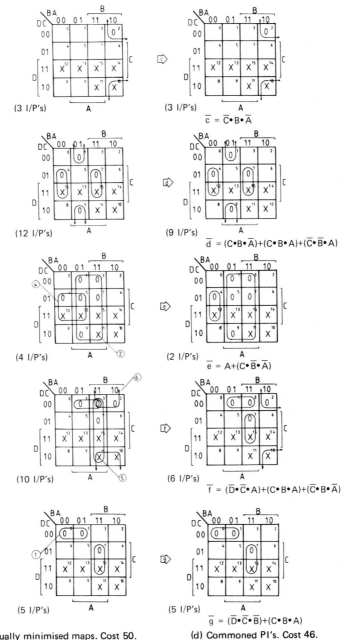

(c) Individually minimised maps. Cost 50.

(d) Commoned PI's. Cost 46.

Figure 2.51: (*continued*). A drop set covering for an active-Low 7-segment decoder.

realization of this function, as shown in Fig. 2.52(a), the delay through the inverter is such that when A goes $1 \rightarrow 0$, $\overline{A}$ will remain 0 for a short time. Of course two logic 0s into the OR gate will give a transient 0 output at $\mathcal{F}$. This 'glitch' occurring on a single variable changing and due to true/complement differential delays, is said to be caused by a **static 1-hazard**. Functions of the form $A \cdot \overline{A}$ (statically always 0) also exhibit similar glitches, this time on the rising edge of the input, known as a **static 0-hazard** [32].

The trace reproduced in in Fig. 2.52 was taken using a Hitachi VC-6025 digitizing oscilloscope with a 1 μs/div timebase. Although exaggerated by a slow inverterm the 100 ns hazard spike is significant. This is certainly long enough to trigger a memory circuit or cause a permanent malfunction, where feedback between output and input exists.

The effect described here may be deliberately courted. For example, the circuit in Fig. 2.52(a) may be used as a negative-edge detector. Replacing the OR by an AND gate gives a positive-edge detector. The delay in the inverting path can be deliberately increased (see Example 2.49), perhaps by cascading inverters, to give a longer output pulse.

We have assumed that the delay in the inverting path is longer than the non-inverting equivalent. This is not always the case; for example, in the decoder circuit in Fig. 2.16(a). In this situation, the reader should show that the glitch will occur on the opposite edge; for instance, the positive-going edge of Fig. 2.52(a).

In fact the decoder of Fig. 2.16(a) does not have a static hazard; as none of the four output equations contain terms like $A \cdot \overline{A}$ or $A + \overline{A}$. However, it is not immune from transient glitches where an input transition involves more than one bit change. Where this involves several bit changes, it is unlikely that these will be simultaneous. Thus a change in input C B A supposedly from 111*b* to 000*b* may actually go: $111 \rightarrow 101 \rightarrow 001 \rightarrow 000$. If the duration between intermediate states is greater than the propagation delay through the circuit, transient output states may occur. These are known as **function hazards** [33] because they are a consequence of the Boolean function rather than the implementation. In practice these often more of a problem than static hazards. If the delay paths of differing variables and their complements vary, hazards will occur even where all inputs do simultaneously occur.

Given that static hazards are a problem in a given situation, what can be done to eliminate them? Trying to equalize the true/negate path delays is unreliable, as propagation times differ considerable for various integrated circuits nominally of the same type. For example, the Texas Instruments SN74LS04 inverter has a maximum delay of 15 ns and is typically 10 ns at 25°C. There is no minimum given and figures also depend on temperature, power voltage, number of driven gates and even length of inter-connection path.

Where an attempt is made to equalize path delays, a complementary-output logic element should be used. A typical example of such a circuit is shown in Fig. 2.53. The SN74265 has a guaranteed maximum differential delay, or **skew**, of 3 ns, but typically skew between outputs is only 0.5 ns.

Static hazards can be reliably eliminated by including extra logic to cover the situation where a single variable change moves from one prime implicant to another. To show how this is done, consider the function described by the K-map of Fig. 2.54(a). Two prime implicants give a full covering, one of which contains D

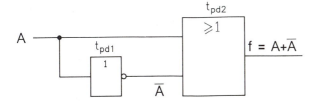

(a) An implementation of the function A + $\overline{A}$

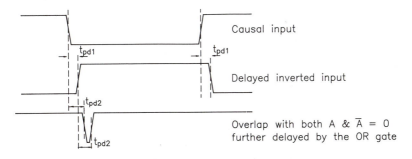

(b) Idealized waveforms, showing delays

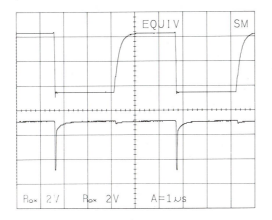

(c) Real waveforms using a 74L04 inverter and 74ALS32 OR gate

Figure 2.52: Illustrating a static 1-hazard.

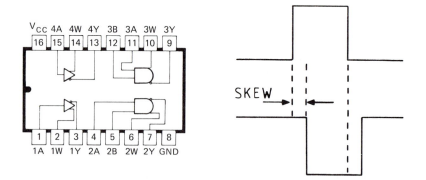

Figure 2.53: The SN74265 quad complementary output gate. Courtesy of Texas Instruments Ltd.

and the other $\overline{D}$. Now consider the circuit is in state cell 5, i.e. $DCBA = 0101b$, and moves to 13, $1101b$. During this move, variables CBA do not change, remaining at $101b$. Substituting into our function gives:

$$\mathcal{F} = (D{\cdot}A)+(\overline{D}{\cdot}\overline{B})$$
$$\mathcal{F} = (D{\cdot}1)+(\overline{D}{\cdot}1) = D+\overline{D} \qquad \ldots\ldots\text{Hazard!}$$

which we recognize as our hazard condition. Thus, when the circuit input changes from $DCBA = 1101b$ to $0101b$, the output may exhibit a narrow zero-going transient (assuming the $\overline{D}$ path is delayed from the D path; otherwise the transient will occur for the $0101b \rightarrow 1101b$ transition).

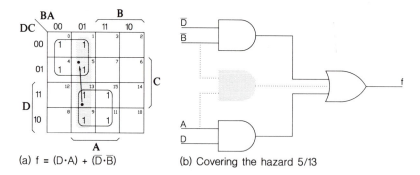

(a) $f = (D{\cdot}A) + (\overline{D}{\cdot}\overline{B})$ (b) Covering the hazard 5/13

Figure 2.54: Illustrating a static 1-hazard on a K-map.

The hazardous transition is shown on the K-map as a one-cell jump between adjacent loops sharing a common border. By virtue of the K-map construction, such loops always contain a variable affirmed in one case and false in the other. Other variables may either be in the same state (affirmed or negated) or only appear in one loop. Thus we can say that *the presence of a static hazard can be predicted on a K-map as occurring wherever loops share common boundaries.*

The common border property of static hazards leads to a preventive technique. This involves covering each jump by an additional loop, as shown shaded in the K-map. In such a case we are summing the original function with a loop which is independent of the changing variable, and thus remains High during the transition. The transition $5 \leftrightarrow 13$ now involves:

$$\mathcal{F} = (D{\cdot}A) + (\overline{D}{\cdot}\overline{B}) + (\overline{B}{\cdot}A)$$

which with $C\,B\,A = 101b$ becomes:

$$\mathcal{F} = (D{\cdot}1) + (\overline{D}{\cdot}1) + (1{\cdot}1) = D + \overline{D} + 1 = 1$$

irrespective of D.

The additional hazard-elimination gate is shown shaded in Fig. 2.54(b). Notice that it simply ANDs all variables from both adjoining loops excluding the literal which appears affirmed in one and negated in the other. This is generally the case. Adding extra gates obviously increases cost, and seems to indicate that minimization is incompatible with hazard-free circuits. Whilst this is true, it should be emphasized that such hazards are irrelevant in many cases. For example, a 30 ns spike at the output of a decoder driving a 7-segment readout is of no consequence. But care must be taken in certain sequential logic (i.e. containing memory) circuits.

Actually there is a second hazard which can be predicted from the K-map. Can you tell where it is? Fortunately it too is covered by $(\overline{B}{\cdot}A)$.

Example 2.41

For the circuit defined by the K-map of Fig. 2.55(a), design a hazard-free implementation for all defined transitions.

Solution

This is a more complex situation, as there are four hazardous transitions; namely $0 \leftrightarrow 1$, $2 \leftrightarrow 10$, $4 \leftrightarrow 5$ and $9 \leftrightarrow 11$. However, they are covered in the normal way, as shown in Fig. 2.52(b). Notice that the original cost of 10 inputs has increased to 21!

As the cost of making this network hazard free is significant, some analysis of whether hazards will actually occur should be made. For example, consider this circuit being driven by a counter sequentially incrementing from state 0 to state 15. In such cases neither transitions $9 \leftrightarrow 11$ nor $2 \leftrightarrow 10$ can occur. However, $0 \rightarrow 1$ and $4 \rightarrow 5$ will occur; with A going from logic 0 to logic 1 in both transitions. Now we have already observed that if the inverted line is delayed with respect to affirmed variables, then glitches only occur on zero-going edges (assuming a sum of product function). Thus no static hazard glitches will occur in this situation, even with a minimal covering. Note that this would not be the case if a down counter were used (i.e. decrementing $15 \rightarrow 0$). Of course the counter may be such that its outputs do not all change simultaneously. Coping with such function hazards is dealt with in Section 4.2.1.

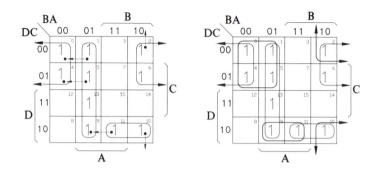

(a) Illustrating several potential hazards   (b) Covering the hazards

Figure 2.55: Static hazards.

In certain cases, **dynamic hazards** [34] may exist. These occur where there are several different-length time paths through the circuit. This may cause several output transitions until steady state is reached. Thus a predicted change of $1 \rightarrow 0$ appears as $1 \rightarrow 0 \rightarrow 1 \rightarrow 0$. Dynamic hazards only occur where the circuit is more than two levels deep.

In any case, irrespective of the name given to the hazard, it is unwise to trust an output for a short period after an input state change.

2.4   Problems

2.4.1   Worked Examples

Example 2.42

As part of a microprocessor-based system, the eight address lines are to be compared for equality with a preset 8-bit number $b_7 \ldots b_0$. Design a circuit, based on an array of ENOR gates, to detect $\mathbf{a} = \mathbf{b}$. The circuit should have provision for a cascade input, to permit expansion to more than 8-bits by another identical circuit. The

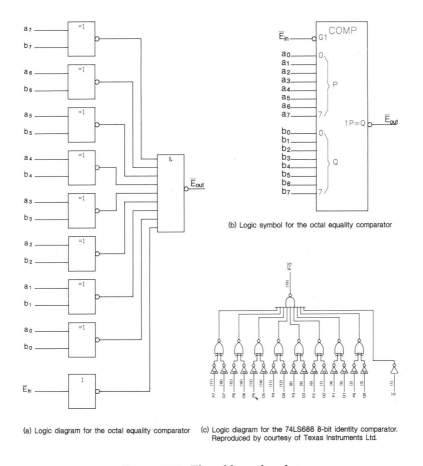

(a) Logic diagram for the octal equality comparator

(b) Logic symbol for the octal equality comparator

(c) Logic diagram for the 74LS688 8-bit identity comparator.
Reproduced by courtesy of Texas Instruments Ltd.

Figure 2.56: The address decoder.

output is to be active-Low.

Solution

The straightforward approach to this problem, which tabulates every combination of input variable, is hardly practicable. There are 16 variables involved here (65,536 combinations!); excluding the cascade input. Instead, the equality comparator is one of a class of circuits whose operation can be described as an **iterative** extension of an operation on a fundamental group of inputs; in this case the equality of two bits.

From Fig. 2.25(c), we see that the ENOR gate acts as a 2-bit equality detector. Based on this operation, we have for n-bit equality:

$$P \;=\; Q \text{ when } (P_0 = Q_0) \text{ AND } (P_1 = Q_1) \text{ AND } (P_2 = Q_2) \ldots \text{ AND } (P_{n-1} = Q_{n-1})$$

or $$\prod \overline{P_{n-1} \oplus Q_{n-1}}$$

This algorithm is implemented in Fig. 2.56 by eight ENOR gates feeding an output NAND, (considered as an active-Low output AND). Adding extra ENOR gates in this manner will increase the size of the comparison words to any desired value. However, if we treat the circuit as an indivisible entity, such as an integrated circuit, then this increase must be implemented by cascading in some manner. One possibility would be to combine the outputs of several circuits through inverters to an external front-end NAND. In essence this is the same as cascading NAND gates alone, as shown in Fig. 2.25(a). A better approach is to provide an extra input to the internal NAND; once again through an inverter ($\overline{E}_{in}$). In this case, the output of comparator N ($\overline{E}_{out}$) feeds the cascade input of the $(N + 1)$th comparator. The former tree cascade is faster for large numbers, whilst the latter sequential configuration is more economical; as no additional components are required.

The logic symbol for a comparator is shown in Fig. 2.56(b). Here the general qualifier symbol is **COMP**, and braces are used to delineate the two input groups. The expansion input is indicated as a **G** dependency acting on the output through dependency number **1**. Thus the output is active only if $\overline{E}_{in}$ is logic 0 (an external 0 gives an internal **G** of 1). If **G** is driven from the $\overline{E}_{out}$ from an identical circuit, then the output will be active only if both **P** = **Q** and all previous comparators register equality. If not used, the cascade input should be permanently connected to **0**. The **G** qualifier is sometimes replaced by the = symbol for a comparator.

Testing for equality is sufficiently useful to warrant specific integrated circuits implementing this function. One of these is shown in Fig. 2.56(c). The 74LS688 is identical to our circuit, except that each input is buffered by Schmitt trigger inverters. Schmitt inputs introduce hysteresis at the input, as described in Example 3.28, to enhance noise immunity. Inverting both input pairs has no effect on equality.

Our discussion has focused on using ENOR gates as the fundamental equality entity. Can you derive a similar arrangement using EOR gates?

Example 2.43

Arithmetic circuits store operational numbers in registers. Each register contains N storage cells (flip flops); one for each bit (see Section 4.3.1). The size of the number stored is obviously limited by the capacity of these storage registers. Where the MSB is being used as a sign bit (see Example SAE 1.10), an erroneous solution will occur when the sum of an adder is too large to fit the register, and overflows into the sign position.

Consider the two examples below, where 5-bit registers are used. Negative numbers are in 2's complement form:

A	0,0001	+ 1		0,1101	+13	
B	1,0001	−15		0,0101	+ 5	
C	$\overline{1,0010}$	−14		$\overline{1,0010}$	−14	overflow!!!!

Here the addition of two positive numbers in the right-hand sum, leads to an apparently negative answer. The design problem is then to implement a digital circuit which will accept the three sign bits involved and indicate when overflow has occurred.

Solution

Overflow can only occur when both sign bits A and B are the same. If they are not, then the result is a difference, and as such is smaller than the largest original number. If the sign bits are the same, but the sum sign bit C differs, i.e. $+ + \rightarrow -$; $- - \rightarrow +$, then overflow has occurred, as shown in Fig. 2.57(a). The resulting function $\mathcal{F}_1$ cannot be reduced.

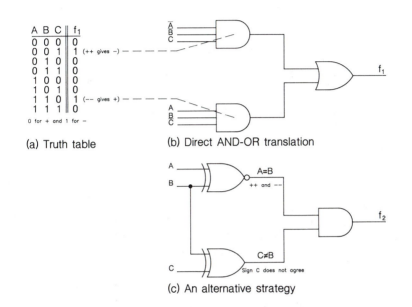

Figure 2.57: Overflow detection.

An alternative intuitive solution is possible. We require first to detect the coincidence A = B (i.e. $\overline{A \oplus B}$). With this condition, overflow occurs if $C \neq B$ (or $C \neq A$), i.e. $B \oplus C$. This gives as a solution the somewhat more expensive circuit of Fig. 2.57(c), with each EOR/ENOR gate-input costing approximately 40% more than a conventional input. The reader should prove for him/herself algebraically that the two functions $\mathcal{F}_1$ and $\mathcal{F}_2$ are equivalent.

Where numbers are represented in floating-point format, such an overflow signal may be used to shift the mantissa one place to the right, and to increment the exponent by one.

Example 2.44

Mirror image symmetry in a K-map indicates the presence of the EOR/NOR function. Consider the expression:

$$P = (\mathcal{F} \cdot Z) + (\overline{\mathcal{F}} \cdot \overline{Z}) = \overline{\mathcal{F} \oplus Z}$$
$$\overline{P} = (\mathcal{F} \cdot \overline{Z}) + (\overline{\mathcal{F}} \cdot Z) = \mathcal{F} \oplus Z$$

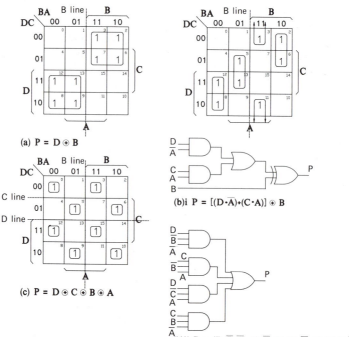

Figure 2.58: Exclusive-OR groupings in K-maps.

where $\mathcal{F}$ is a function of any complexity and Z is a single variable. In a K-map, this shows up as a mirror symmetry about the axis dividing Z from $\overline{Z}$. For example, in Fig. 2.58(a) the function $\mathcal{F}$, shown as the loop in the lower left-hand side, is reflected about the B-axis. Treating each half of the map as separate (one for B and one for $\overline{B}$), then the two functions must be complements, as each 1 in one map becomes a 0 in the other. In this case, the function in the $\overline{B}$ map is D and in the B map is $\overline{D}$. This gives the overall expression $P = (D \cdot \overline{B}) + (\overline{D} \cdot B)$, which is just $D \oplus B$.

This example is fairly trivial; however, consider the situation in Fig. 2.58(b). Here symmetry is still about the B-line. Calling the pattern in the $\overline{B}$ section $\mathcal{F}$, we have $\mathcal{F} = (D \cdot \overline{A}) + (C \cdot A)$. Thus by inspection we can say that $P = (\mathcal{F} \cdot \overline{B}) + (\overline{\mathcal{F}} \cdot B) = \mathcal{F} \oplus B = \{(D \cdot \overline{A}) + (C \cdot A)\} \oplus B$. This costs eight gate inputs as against 16 using AND-OR logic; although against this, EOR inputs cost around 40% more and there is an extra delay through this third level. Another way of looking at this, is to consider the EOR gate acting as a programmable inverter on $\mathcal{F}$ as controlled by B.

The final example is given in Fig. 2.58(c). This chequerboard pattern has many lines of symmetry. If we take the top left quarter, then we have by symmetry $\mathcal{F} = C \oplus A$. This in turn is reflected around the D-line, becoming $(C \oplus A) \oplus D$. As a group this is now reflected around the B-line, giving $(C \oplus A \oplus D) \oplus B$. The resulting

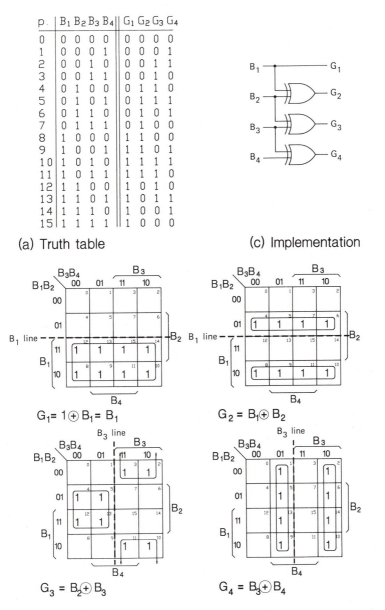

p.	B_1 B_2 B_3 B_4	G_1 G_2 G_3 G_4
0	0 0 0 0	0 0 0 0
1	0 0 0 1	0 0 0 1
2	0 0 1 0	0 0 1 1
3	0 0 1 1	0 0 1 0
4	0 1 0 0	0 1 1 0
5	0 1 0 1	0 1 1 1
6	0 1 1 0	0 1 0 1
7	0 1 1 1	0 1 0 0
8	1 0 0 0	1 1 0 0
9	1 0 0 1	1 1 0 1
10	1 0 1 0	1 1 1 1
11	1 0 1 1	1 1 1 0
12	1 1 0 0	1 0 1 0
13	1 1 0 1	1 0 1 1
14	1 1 1 0	1 0 0 1
15	1 1 1 1	1 0 0 0

(a) Truth table

(c) Implementation

$G_1 = 1 \oplus B_1 = B_1$

$G_2 = B_1 \oplus B_2$

$G_3 = B_2 \oplus B_3$

$G_4 = B_3 \oplus B_4$

(b) Mirror-image K-maps

Figure 2.59: Binary to Gray conversion.

function is just the parity tree of Fig. 2.23.

Finally, our example! Using K-maps, design a 4-bit binary to Gray code converter.

Solution

The truth table is shown in Fig. 2.59(a). The resulting four K-maps all show mirror image symmetry and the overall function can be written by inspection in EOR form.

We implemented this conversion as a 4-bit exercise. From the circuit diagram, or equations, we can see that this is another example of iterative design; where each binary bit n can be generated as $G_n \oplus B_{n-1}$. An examination of Example 1.14 shows that we have ended up implementing the modulo-2 conversion algorithm developed at that point.

Example 2.45

As part of a special purpose computer, a network is to be designed to indicate the occurrence of a prime number between 0 and 15; the prime number being represented by a 4-bit binary number. The circuit is to be implemented using only 2-I/P NAND gates.

Solution

Prime numbers are defined as being numbers with no factors other than themselves and one. For the purposes of this design, the trivial cases 0,1,2 will be included. Proper prime numbers are 3,5,7,11,13. The K-map of Fig. 2.60(a) yields a solution $\mathcal{F} = (\overline{W} \cdot \overline{X}) + (\overline{W} \cdot Z) + (X \cdot \overline{Y} \cdot Z) + (\overline{X} \cdot Y \cdot Z)$, which requires both 2- and 3-I/P gates. Multi-input gates can of course be synthesized with 2-I/P gates; but usually if the function can be factorized, the end solution is simpler. After factoring we have $\mathcal{F} = \overline{W} \cdot (\overline{X} + Z) + Z \cdot (X \cdot \overline{Y} + \overline{X} \cdot Y)$, which represents a solution implemented with only 2-I/P gates, and is shown in Fig. 2.60(b). Conversion to NAND can be made by using the AND-OR to NAND rule, i.e. replace all gates by NAND and invert odd-level entries; as shown in Fig. 2.60(c). Interestingly, both 2- and 4-level implementations cost 14 gate inputs; the latter of course has a longer propagation delay.

Example 2.46

Design a circuit which will detect natural binary 10 → 15 inclusive if a mode (control) input, labelled X, is Low; and 12 → 15 if $X = 1$. A zeros minimization is to be used, with a NOR implementation.

Solution

Mapping the zeros, as shown in Fig. 2.61(b), gives as a solution $\overline{\mathcal{F}} = \overline{D} + (\overline{C} \cdot \overline{B}) + (X \cdot \overline{C})$. The conversion from AND-OR to NOR entails the replacement of all gates by NOR; inverting even-level entries and placing an inverter in series with the output. Removing that inverter to implement $\mathcal{F}$ leaves the all-NOR circuit of Fig. 2.61(c).

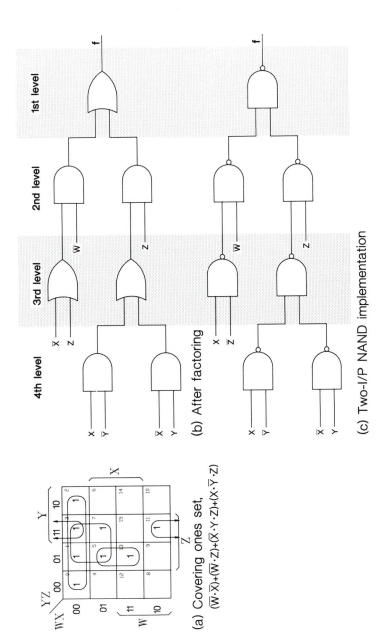

(a) Covering ones set,
$(\overline{W} \cdot \overline{X}) + (\overline{W} \cdot Z) + (\overline{X} \cdot Y \cdot Z) + (X \cdot \overline{Y} \cdot Z)$

(b) After factoring

(c) Two-I/P NAND implementation

Figure 2.60: A prime-number detector.

p	XDCBA	f
0	00000	0
1	00001	0
2	00010	0
3	00011	0
4	00100	0
5	00101	0
6	00110	0
7	00111	0
8	01000	0
9	01001	0
10	01010	1
11	01011	1
12	01100	1
13	01101	1
14	01110	1
15	01111	1
16	10000	0
17	10001	0
18	10010	0
19	10011	0
20	10100	0
21	10101	0
22	10110	0
23	10111	0
24	11000	0
25	11001	0
26	11010	0
27	11011	0
28	11100	1
29	11101	1
30	11110	1
31	11111	1

>9 if $X=0$

>11 if $X=1$

(a) Truth table

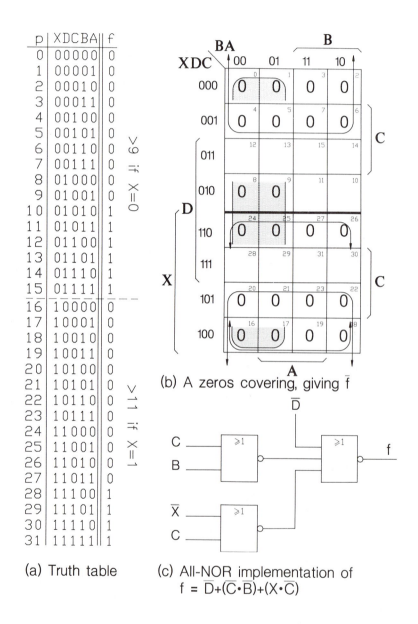

(b) A zeros covering, giving $\bar{f}$

(c) All-NOR implementation of
$f = \overline{D} + (\overline{C \cdot B}) + (X \cdot \overline{C})$

Figure 2.61: A programmable number detector.

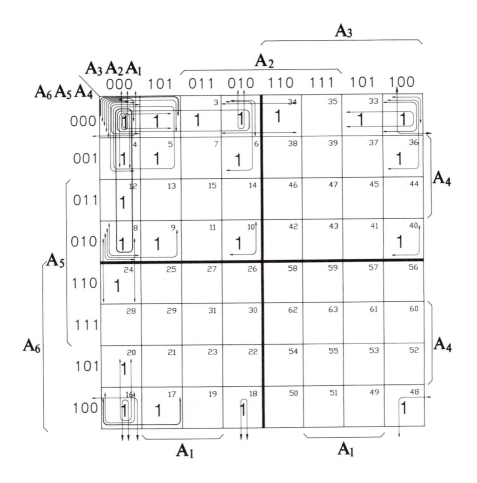

Figure 2.62: A 6-variable central heating controller using a K-map.

Example 2.47

In Example 2.25 we used the Quine-McCluskey method to determine a minimal 2-level implementation of a 6-thermostat central heating controller. Repeat this exercise but using a 6-variable K-map. Comment on the two solutions.

Solution

As expected, the outcome of both procedures are identical. This would be expected, as the K-map is simply a graphical version of the tabular technique. The K-map is a fairly nasty example of its type, as all prime implicants cover only four cells. In the Quine McCluskey version, this shows up in that only two columns of reduction are necessary. Hence this is one of the simplest of its kind. The effort in doing these examples was about the same. It does help in complex K-maps to use color; 16 were used in the original of Fig. 2.62! However, the complexity of locating symmetries does limit the practical use of K-maps to around seven variables (see Example SAE 2.13).

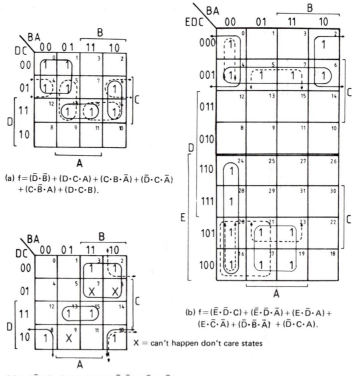

(a) $f = (\bar{D} \cdot \bar{B}) + (D \cdot C \cdot A) + (C \cdot B \cdot \bar{A}) + (\bar{D} \cdot C \cdot \bar{A}) + (C \cdot \bar{B} \cdot A) + (D \cdot C \cdot B).$

(b) $f = (\bar{E} \cdot \bar{D} \cdot C) + (\bar{E} \cdot \bar{D} \cdot \bar{A}) + (E \cdot \bar{D} \cdot A) + (E \cdot \bar{C} \cdot \bar{A}) + (\bar{D} \cdot \bar{B} \cdot \bar{A}) + (\bar{D} \cdot C \cdot A).$

X = can't happen don't care states

(c) $f = (\bar{D} \cdot B) + (D \cdot C \cdot A) + (D \cdot \bar{C} \cdot \bar{A}) + (\bar{C} \cdot B \cdot \bar{A}).$

Figure 2.63: Illustrating static hazards.

Example 2.48

Identify all possible hazardous transitions in the circuits defined by the solid line loops in the K-maps of Fig. 2.63. Modify the circuit to eliminate such hazards.

Solution

The map shown in Fig. 2.63(a) is uncomplicated, but the 5-variable map calls for some comment. The difficulty here is recognizing common borders. Thus p_{21}, p_{23} are adjacent to p_5, p_7, and therefore constitute a common border ($\overline{E}\cdot\overline{D}\cdot C : E\cdot\overline{D}\cdot A \rightarrow E+\overline{E}$). Similarly p_0, p_4 are adjacent to p_{16}, p_{20}, and must be covered by $\overline{D}\cdot\overline{B}\cdot\overline{A}$.

The map of Fig. 2.63(c) shows the hazard $p_2 \leftrightarrow p_{10}$ covered by $\overline{C}\cdot B\cdot\overline{A}$, but no cover is provided for $p_7 \leftrightarrow p_{15}$, as p_7 is a don't care state.

Example 2.49

Show that the circuit shown in Fig. 2.64 acts as an any-edge detector.

Solution

The two inputs to EOR G2 are statically complements, as G1 is connected as an inverter. However, any change in state at the input brings both G2 inputs to equality for a duration dependent on the propagation delay through G1 and the charge/discharge time of C. Gate G2 responds to equality at its inputs by going Low. Careful examination of the resulting waveform at Z shows that the circuit is acting as a frequency doubler. By a judicious selection of the time constants (CR), circuits may be cascaded giving frequency multiplication by any power of two.

In a practical situation, the width of the pulse will depend on the internal gate circuitry. Also, if the CR rise/fall (transition) times are too slow, the gate may oscillate as the slowly changing input enters the linear region between the two logic levels (see Fig. 3.14). Generally, time constants should be limited to no more than ten times a gate's propagation delay. Schmitt triggers may be used to sharpen up transition edges where long delays are required.

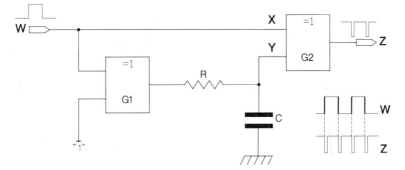

Figure 2.64: An any-edge detector using EOR gates.

The 4000 family of CMOS circuits (see Section 3.1.1) has a Low/High threshold of around 50% of supply voltage; zero input bias current and Low/High voltage levels of 0 V and the supply voltage. What CR time constant is required to give a 1 μs pulse? Well, the time delay to 50% is 0.69 CR (see Fig. 3.26). The 4030 EOR gate has an intrinsic maximum propagation delay of 175 ns (typical 85 ns) at a supply voltage of 5 V. Thus the CR delay must be $1000 - 175$ ns, i.e. $0.69\,CR = 825 \times 10^{-6}$s, giving $CR = 1.2$ μs (say R = 12 kΩ, C = 100 pF). However, such calculations are at best nominal, as gate propagation delay depends on the direction of input change (eg. 175 ns High to Low, 150 ns Low to High), rate of change of input edge (given here for transition times ≤ 20 ns), temperature (given for 25°C), load capacitance (given here for 50 pF) and power supply (at 15 V the typical delay falls from 175 ns to 55 ns maximum).

What function do you think the circuit would perform if EOR gate G1 where removed, with just the delay in situe, and what further change could be made to restore the initial function?

Example 2.50

Design a minimal all-NAND logic circuit to convert integer values of degrees Celsius in the range $0 - 10$°C, expressed in the 8-4-2-1 code, to degrees Fahrenheit expressed using two 8-4-2-1 BCD digits.

Solution

The truth table of Fig. 2.65(a) gives the correspondence between the two temperature scales. The don't care terms $p_{11} \rightarrow p_{15}$ inclusive are not shown, but are entered into the maps. Only seven K-maps are shown; as from the truth table we see that the 80's BCD digit (W_1) is always logic 0.

The map for X_1 uses the grouping $C \cdot B \cdot \overline{A}$, instead of $C \cdot B$, to common with the same group in Y_2. Other than this, no concession is made for common products. The logic diagram of Fig. 2.65(c) depicts shared terms with thicker lines. The all-NAND configuration was obtained by replacing the AND and OR gates with NANDs and inverting the direct entry into level 1 (i.e. $D \rightarrow \overline{D}$ for network X_1).

Example 2.51

A 4-function matrix-connected keyboard is shown in Fig. 2.66(a). If each row is sampled in turn; determine the logic that will indicate which of the 16 keys have been pressed. Hence design logic to encode these 16 key lines to the code shown in Fig. 2.66(b) and an 'anything-other-than-zeros' detector to be used as a Key_Pressed strobe.

Solution

The straightforward approach to a 16-input switch array would be to treat each switch as a separate input. Thus from the table we could write:

$$B_4 = (+) + (-) + (\div) + (\times) + (=) + (\cdot) \qquad \text{etc}$$

This arrangement requires 16 connections from the keyboard to the logic, whereas the 4×4 matrix connection shown reduces this to eight. The saving is more

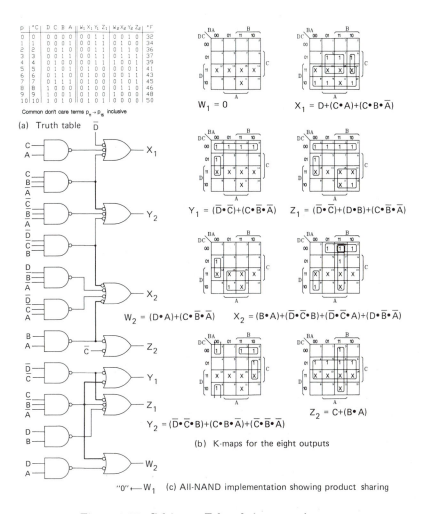

Figure 2.65: Celsius to Fahrenheit conversion.

apparent for larger keyboards; thus, for 64 switches the saving is 16 to 64. Each column is brought High for a short time and when the appropriate closed switch is found, the pattern on the X lines will change from $0000b$. This pattern plus the strobe line is sufficient to uniquely tell which switch has been pressed; thus:

$$0 = Y_0 \cdot X_3 \qquad 4 = Y_0 \cdot X_2 \qquad 8 = Y_0 \cdot X_1 \qquad = \; = Y_0 \cdot X_0$$
$$1 = Y_1 \cdot X_3 \qquad 5 = Y_1 \cdot X_2 \qquad 9 = Y_1 \cdot X_1 \qquad \times \; = Y_1 \cdot X_0$$
$$2 = Y_2 \cdot X_3 \qquad 6 = Y_2 \cdot X_2 \qquad + \; = Y_2 \cdot X_1 \qquad \div \; = Y_2 \cdot X_0$$
$$3 = Y_3 \cdot X_3 \qquad 7 = Y_3 \cdot X_2 \qquad - \; = Y_3 \cdot X_1 \qquad \cdot \; = Y_3 \cdot X_0$$

On the basis of these 16 key-identification signals, we have (just as if we had 16 straight switch connections):

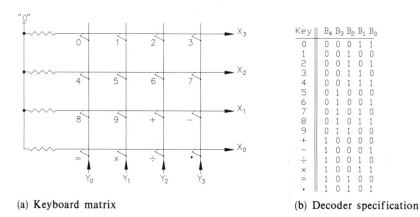

Key	B_4	B_3	B_2	B_1	B_0
0	0	0	0	1	1
1	0	0	1	0	0
2	0	0	1	0	1
3	0	0	1	1	0
4	0	0	1	1	1
5	0	1	0	0	0
6	0	1	0	0	1
7	0	1	0	1	0
8	0	1	0	1	1
9	0	1	1	0	0
+	1	0	0	0	0
−	1	0	0	0	1
÷	1	0	0	1	0
×	1	0	0	1	1
=	1	0	1	0	0
·	1	0	1	0	1

(a) Keyboard matrix   (b) Decoder specification

Figure 2.66: Decoding a calculator keyboard.

$$B_4 = (+) + (-) + (=) + (\times) + (\div) + (\cdot)$$
$$= (Y_2 \cdot X_1) + (Y_3 \cdot X_1) + (Y_0 \cdot X_0) + (Y_1 \cdot X_0) + (Y_2 \cdot X_0) + (Y_3 \cdot X_0)$$

$$B_3 = (5) + (6) + (7) + (8) + (9)$$
$$= (Y_1 \cdot X_2) + (Y_2 \cdot X_2) + (Y_3 \cdot X_2) + (Y_0 \cdot X_1) + (Y_1 \cdot X_1)$$

$$B_2 = (1) + (2) + (3) + (4) + (9) + (=) + (\cdot)$$
$$= (Y_1 \cdot X_3) + (Y_2 \cdot X_3) + (Y_3 \cdot X_3) + (Y_0 \cdot X_2) + (Y_1 \cdot X_1) + (Y_0 \cdot X_0) + (Y_3 \cdot X_0)$$

$$B_1 = (0) + (3) + (4) + (7) + (8) + (\times) + (\div)$$
$$= (Y_0 \cdot X_3) + (Y_3 \cdot X_3) + (Y_0 \cdot X_2) + (Y_3 \cdot X_2) + (Y_0 \cdot X_1) + (Y_1 \cdot X_0) + (Y_2 \cdot X_0)$$

$$B_0 = (0) + (2) + (4) + (6) + (8) + (-) + (\times) + (\cdot)$$
$$= (Y_0 \cdot X_3) + (Y_2 \cdot X_3) + (Y_0 \cdot X_2) + (Y_2 \cdot X_2) + (Y_0 \cdot X_1) + (Y_3 \cdot X_1) + (Y_1 \cdot X_0) + (Y_3 \cdot X_0)$$

$ST = X_3 + X_2 + X_1 + X_0$ i.e. = 1 on any non-zero row.

This extra logic is justified by the reduction in keyboard/circuit board connections.

2.4.2 Self Assessment Examples

SAE 2.1

A student goes to the stores and asks for an 8-I/P NAND gate IC (74LS30). All the storeman can supply is one 74LS00 quad 2-I/P NAND and one 74LS02 quad 2-I/P NOR circuit. How can the student connect up these two ICs to perform this function?

If the worst-case propagation delay of the 74LS00, 74LS02, 74LS30 gates are respectively 15 ns, 22 ns and 20 ns; how does the final configuration compare in its switching characteristic?

SAE 2.2

Show that all the logic symbols shown in Fig. 2.67 represent the same thing.

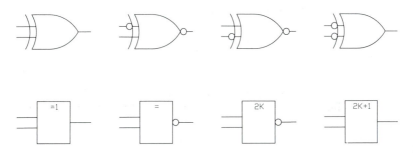

Figure 2.67: Equivalent logic symbols.

SAE 2.3

Using the modulo-2 algorithm presented in Example 1.13, design a circuit which will convert a 4-bit Gray-coded number $G_1G_2G_3G_4$ to binary $B_1B_2B_3B_4$.

SAE 2.4

A particular digital system is to transmit data in 8-bit bytes with an odd 1s parity bit added. Show how you would connect up the 4531 parity tree of Fig. 2.23 to generate this bit. How would another 4531 IC at the receiver be connected to active-Low detect an error.

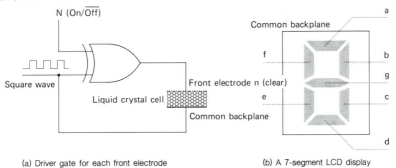

(a) Driver gate for each front electrode   (b) A 7-segment LCD display

Figure 2.68: The EOR gate used as a liquid crystal driver.

SAE 2.5

A certain class of materials exhibit the properties of a crystalline structure, whilst at the same time are fluid [35]. The application of an electric field will distort this structure and change the way the material absorbs or transmits light. However, the application of a d.c. voltage across a sandwich of electrodes and liquid crystal, such as shown in Fig. 2.68(a), will quickly cause deterioration, due to electrolytic action. Instead, as the field direction is irrelevant, it is usual to alternate the potential on a 50:50 basis, giving a zero average field. Discuss how the circuit of Fig. 2.68(a) operates as an on-off control on this basis.

SAE 2.6

The logic diagram shown in Fig. 2.69 shows part of a certain programmable logic array, with fuses integrated on the silicon die (see Fig. 3.5). Determine which of the fuses must be blown to implement the function developed in Example 2.13. You may assume that an open fuse results in a logic 1.

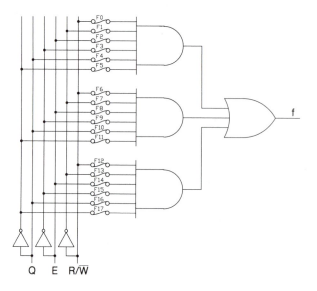

Figure 2.69: A fuse programmable logic array.

SAE 2.7

In Example 2.4 we developed a technique to read off a sum of products (SOP) function directly from a truth table. Show that there is a dual of this procedure, which directly generates a product of sum function [36]. Hint: Determine which combinations of input variables give 0 outputs.

Can you extend this approach to a kind of K-map in which loops represent sum terms, and the whole is ANDed together?

SAE 2.8

Using the Quine McCluskey algorithm with a PI table, show that there are two minimal outcomes which give a covering of the 5-variable function:

$$\mathcal{F} = \sum 0, 3, 4, 5, 7, 8, 11, 12, 13, 15, 16, 20, 24, 28.$$

SAE 2.9

Using a K-map, design a 2-level AND-OR implementation costing no more than 16 gate inputs, for the function $\mathcal{F} = \sum 1, 5, 6, 7, 11, 12, 13, 15$. How could you eliminate all static hazards for this function?

SAE 2.10

A voting system is to be designed for a company boardroom. There are four voters. The president has two votes and each of his three directors have one vote. The system logic is to indicate when a majority yes vote is registered. A yes input is logic 1. Aim for a logic implementation costing not more than ten inputs (you can factor the K-map outcome).

SAE 2.11

Design a circuit to compute the number of 1s in a 4-bit word. The 3-bit output is to be in natural code. How could you extend this function to, say, 8-bits, using the 4-bit 1s counter as a building block?

SAE 2.12

Design a circuit which detects when only one out of four inputs is logic 1. Although no K-map minimization is possible, show that it is feasible to implement this function with only seven 2-I/P gates of various types.

SAE 2.13

A certain calculator with a 7-segment display is to be used as the input to a digital system. Unfortunately the 4-bit BCD code used internally by the calculator chip is not available externally. You are to design a circuit to convert from 7-segment code (see Table 1.3(d)) to the 4-bit natural binary code which can be processed by the system.

This question requires four 7-variable K-maps; but do not despair, as only ten of the 128 p-terms are ever used, giving 118 don't care terms! See Example 3.23 for another approach.

SAE 2.14

A digital voltmeter having a 4-bit BCD output labelled D C B A in Fig. 2.70 is to be converted to Braille code W X Y Z. Braille is a system whereby a blind person can interpret alpha-numerics by recognizing a pattern of raised dots [37]. Use K-maps to design a minimal all-NAND implementation.

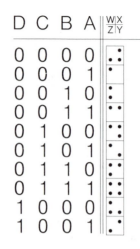

Figure 2.70: Four-bit Braille code.

SAE 2.15

Devise a gate implementation of a combinational logic code converter, which driven from an 8-4-2-1 BCD counter, will sequentially generate the constant

$$e = 2.718\ 281\ 828.$$

There are to be five outputs. W X Y Z represent the BCD digit and DP is used to drive the display's decimal point.

Can you rework the design with eight outputs to drive a 7-segment display directly (see Fig. 2.68(b))?

SAE 2.16

A minimal all-NAND network is to be designed to sequentially generate the telephone number 121-643 815 7 in 4-bit BCD code, when driven by an 8-4-2-1 BCD counter. Illustrate your answer with a logic diagram.

SAE 2.17

The square root of two, to nine decimal places, is given as $\sqrt{2} = 1.414\ 213\ 562.$ Design an all NOR implementation to sequentially generate the required digits when driven by an 8-4-2-1 coded BCD counter.

SAE 2.18

An electronic converter giving the imperial gallon equivalent of integer liters, over the range 0–9, is planned. Using the relationship 1 liter = 0.22 gallon, determine the appropriate gate configuration, giving an output to the nearest $\frac{1}{8}$ gallon. Use the natural binary code for your output.

SAE 2.19

A decimal digit N is to be converted to N^2. Both input and output are encoded in natural BCD. Design an appropriate minimal circuit.

SAE 2.20

The constant π, to 19 decimal places, is given as:

$$\pi = 3.141\ 592\ 653\ 589\ 793\ 238\ 4$$

Using four 5-variable K-maps, *or otherwise*, design an AND-OR network; which when driven by a modulo-20 naturally-coded counter, will sequentially generate these digits. See Example 6.4 for another approach.

References

[1] Logic, History of, entry *Encyclopaedia Britannica*, 15th ed., 1974.

[2] MacHale, D.; *George Boole: His Life and Work*, Boole Press, Dublin, 1985.

[3] Boole, G.; *Mathematical Analysis of Logic*, Blackwell, England, 1847 (reprinted in 1948).

[4] Boole, G; *An Investigation into the Laws of Thought*, 1854 (reprinted in 1954 by Dover Publications, New York).

[5] Hollis, M., Tantalizer no. 222 – Chef D'Oeuvers, Reproduced by courtesy of *New Scientist*, London. The weekly review of Science and Technology, **52**, no. 772, Dec. 2nd, 1971, pp.43.

[6] Shannon, C.E.; A Symbolic Analysis of Relay and Switched Circuits, *Trans. Am. Inst. Elect. Eng.*, **57**, 1938, pp.713–723.

[7] The implementation of operators with switches seems to have first been suggested in 1880 by C.S. Pierce in a letter to a student; reproduced in *A Computer Perspective*, C. and R. Eames, Harvard University Press, Massachusetts, USA, 1973.

[8] Walter, D.J., *Integrated Circuit Systems*, Iliffe, 1971, Section 3.9.

[9] IEC Publication 617; *Graphic Symbols for Diagrams. Part 12: Binary Logic Elements*, 1983. IEC, Bureau Central de la Varembé, Genève, Suisse and from ANSI, 1430 Broadway, New York, U.S.A., NY10018.

[10] BS3939; *Graphic Symbols for Electrical Power, Telecommunications and Electronics Diagrams: Part 12. Binary Logic Elements*, 1985. BSI, 2, Park Street, London W1A 2BS, U.K.

[11] ANSII/IEEE Std 91-1984; *IEEE Standard Graphic Symbols for Logic Functions*, 1984, 1430 Broadway, New York, U.S.A, NY10018.

[12] Kampel, I; *A Practical Introduction to the New Logic Symbols*, Butterworths, 2nd ed., 1986. (Also IEEE Press [SH10793-PBM].)

[13] Rosie, A.M.; *Information and Communication Theory*, Van Nostrand Reinhold, 2nd ed., 1975, Chapter 6.

[14] Mendleson, E.; *Boolean Algebra and Switching Circuits*, McGraw-Hill, Schaum's Outline Series, 1970.

[15] South, G.F.; *Boolean Algebra and its Uses*, Van Nostrand Reinhold Co. , 1970.

[16] Zissos, D.; *Logic Design Algorithms*, Oxford University Press, 1972, Chapter 2.

[17] Quine, W.V.; The Problem of Simplifying Truth Functions, *American Math Monthly*, **59**, Oct. 1952, pp.521–531.

[18] McCluskey, E.J.; Minimization of Boolean Functions, *Bell System Technical Journal*, **35**, Nov. 1956, pp.1417–1444.

[19] Shiva, S.G. and Nagle, H.T.; *Bypass Multi-variable Karnaugh Maps, Electronic Design*, **21**, no. 21, Oct. 11th, 1974, pp.86–91.

[20] Nagle, H.T. et al.; *An Introduction to Computer Logic*, Prentice-Hall, 1975, Chapter 4.

[21] Lewin, D.; *Computer-aided Design of Digital Systems*, E. Arnold/Crone Russak, 1977.

[22] Bolton, M.; *Digital Systems Design with Programmable Logic*, Addison-Wesley, 1990, Section 4.3.

[23] Darwood, N.; Logic Maps – From Lull to Karnaugh, *Wireless World*, **88**, no. 1563, Dec. 1982, pp.42–44.

[24] Venn, J.; On the Diagrammatic and Mechanical Representation of Propositions and Reasonings, *Philosophical Magazine and Journal of Science*, **9**, no. 59, July 1880, pp.1–18.

[25] Murphy, P. and Kempf, A.F.; *The New Mathematics Made Simple*, Doubleday & Co./W.H. Allen & Co., 1971, Chapter 1.

[26] Karnaugh, M.; The Map Method for Synthesis of Combinational Logic Circuits, *Trans. AIEEE*, **72**, Nov. 1953, pp.593–599.

[27] Biswas, N.N.; Veitch-Karnaugh Map (letter to the editor), *Control*, **79**, April 1965, pp.185.

[28] Dean, K.J.; An Extension of the use of Karnaugh Maps in the Minimization of Logic Functions, *The Radio and Electronic Engineer*, **34**, May 1968, pp.294–296.

[29] Hill, F.J. and Peterson, G.R.; *Switching theory and Logical Design*, Wiley, 2nd ed., 1974, Sections 7.4 & 7.5.

[30] Marcovitz, A.B.; *Switching System Design*, Wiley, 1971, Sections 4.6, 7.4 & 7.5.

[31] McCluskey, E.J.; *Logic Design Principles: with Emphasis on Testable Semiconductor Circuits*, Prentice-Hall, 1986, Section 6.8.

[32] McCluskey, E.J.; *Logic Design Principles: with Emphasis on Testable Semiconductor Circuits*, Prentice-Hall, 1986, Section 3.6.1.

[33] McCluskey, E.J.; *Logic Design Principles: with Emphasis on Testable Semiconductor Circuits*, Prentice-Hall, 1986, Section 3.6.2.

[34] Huffman, D.A.; The Design and Use of Hazard-Free Switching Networks, *J. Assoc. for Computing Machinery*, **4**, no. 1, 1957, pp.47–62.

[35] Wilson, J. and Hawkes, J.F.B.; *Optoelectronics: An Introduction*, Prentice-Hall, 1983, Section 4.9.

[36] Mano, M.M.; *Digital Design*, Prentice-Hall, 1984, Section 5.5

[37] 'Braille' entry *Encyclopaedia Britannica*, 15th ed., 1974.

Chapter 3

011

Logic Implementation

Now that we can design efficient networks of gates to implement combinational functions, as defined in the form of a truth table; we need to broaden our horizons.

In this chapter we will build on our foundations in two ways. Firstly; we have treated gates as abstract objects, having only properties describable in Boolean algebraic forms. In reality, gate networks must be physically realized using the appropriate hardware. Although the systems engineer does not require a detailed knowledge of the innards of the integrated circuits (ICs) which will be used, it is essential to clearly understand the gross terminal characteristics of such devices. Thus, although this is not a book on digital electronics, it is important to spend some time on this topic.

The second area of investigation concerns the architecture of the integrated circuits used to build the system. Except for relatively simple circuits, or when you are designing your own IC; discrete gates are rarely used as such. Instead, functional modules of various kinds are inter-connected and/or programmed in the appropriate manner. Discrete gates are usually found dotted around such circuits, helping in this process, and are often labelled **glue logic** for this reason.

Integrated circuits may be categorized in many ways. The most crude of these simply relates to the number of constituent gates. Thus **small scale integration (SSI)** describes IC's having up to a dozen gates. **Medium scale integration (MSI)** covers that category under 100 gates, **large scale integration (LSI)** for up to 1000 gates and **very large scale integration (VLSI)** for complexities above this.

A more sensible scheme is by function. Thus, we have glue logic, decoders, multiplexers, adders, read-only memories (ROMs), programmable array logic devices (PALs), application specific integrated circuits (ASICs) etc. In this chapter we will look at these functional categories; their properties, and how they implement combinational logic. In the following chapters we extend this to sequential logic.

143

3.1 Digital Electronics

One of the major decisions which must be made by the systems designer is the choice
of integrated circuit family. Considerable differences exist between families; for
example voltage levels, response to noise, speed of operation and power dissipation.
The designer's choice of family will in turn influence the system infrastructure, such
as power supplies and noise filtering. As these considerations frequently cost more
than the electronic components themselves, an intelligent choice is important. It
may be possible to optimize the system performance by mixing ICs from several
different families; thus power-hungry members where speed matters and low-power
devices where things happen slowly. This choice should be made early on in the
design process, as the availability of some logic functions varies between families.

In order to do all these things, the designer must be aware of the various relevant
parameters and how these relate to external performance. Thus knowledge of the
logic of a particular device is not enough; its terminal characteristics (i.e. input and
output) define how it will perform in the real world.

Although there are many thousands of logic ICs, fortunately their terminal characteristics run in families. A family is a line of ICs differing in logic function but
having similar terminal electrical properties. This standardization facilitates the
inter-connection of different elements within a family. Many logic families exist,
but the majority of these are related to the transistor-transistor logic (TTL) family, or at least have compatible parameters. This section will mainly concentrate on
this group of families and the 4000 series complementary metal-oxide semiconductor
(CMOS) line.

After reading this section, you should:

- Be able to configure diode arrays to implement 2-level AND-OR logic; both
  as discrete devices and as fusible-link ICs.

- Appreciate the use of transistors as switches and gates.

- Be able to distinguish between positive-logic, negative-logic and polarity-
  indicator conventions.

- Be able to follow the internal operation of basic TTL and MOS gate circuits.

- Appreciate the operation and utility of totem-pole open-collector/drain and
  3-state output structures.

- Know the meaning of the interface parameters; fan-in, fan-out, input and
  output voltage and current levels.

- Know the meaning of the performance parameters; noise margin, static and
  dynamic power dissipation, propagation delay and transition times.

3.1.1 Glue Logic

The diode was the first successful semiconductor device available in commercial
quantities. Compared to bulky and power-hungry thermionic tubes, resistor/diode

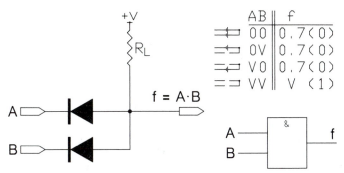

(a) A 2-input positive-logic AND gate.

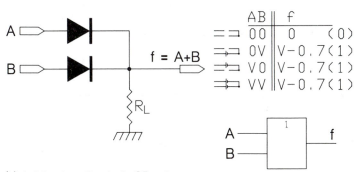

(b) A 2-input positive-logic OR gate.

Figure 3.1: Diode logic.

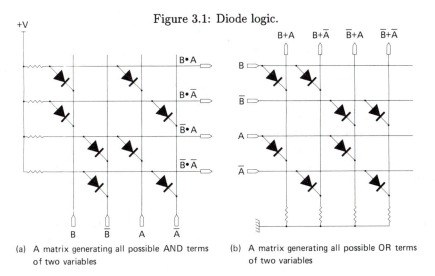

(a) A matrix generating all possible AND terms
   of two variables

(b) A matrix generating all possible OR terms
   of two variables

Figure 3.2: Diode logic arranged in the form of matrices.

networks were a popular alternative in the 1950s. Although these are largely obsolete, they still form the basis of many bipolar transistor integrated circuit logic.

Consider the circuit shown in Fig. 3.1(a). If any or both inputs are Low, then the relevant diodes conduct and the output is pulled Low. The voltage truth table is based on an ideal diode (infinite reverse and zero forward resistance), but with a (typical) silicon 0.7 V conduction offset. If we arbitrarily assign the more positive voltage level as logic 1, we have the AND function. The gate may be extended to n inputs by simply tying additional diodes to the output node.

A diode OR gate is shown in Fig. 3.1(b). Here if any input is brought High, that diode conducts and drags the output High.

Assigning the High voltage level to logic 1 (H = 1, L = 0) is known as **positive logic**. Can you repeat the analysis for **negative logic** (H = 0, L = 1)? We will return to this topic later.

Diode networks are frequently implemented in the form of an **AND-OR matrix**, especially where they appear in an integrated circuit. The topology of both an AND and OR XY matrix is shown in Fig. 3.2, where we assume positive logic.

Example 3.1

A certain integrated-circuit diode AND-OR matrix is shown in its virgin state in Fig. 3.3. Each diode is in series with a fusible link (see also Example SAE 2.7). These links may be selectively blown by the end user to implement the desired logic. Which fuses must be zapped to implement the circuit designed in Example 2.38?

Solution

As shown in Fig. 3.4, diodes are removed (fuses blown) in each horizontal AND row to create the eleven product terms of Fig. 2.50. The spare (top) row has all its diodes removed to give the logic 1 E output (in practice E would probably be connected directly to $+V$). Leaving all diodes in a row would give a logic 0. Each output is created by removing diodes connected to unwanted product terms. Thus F is $(D \cdot A) + (D \cdot B)$ is row 1 OR row 2. All other diodes in this column are removed.

If the matrix is built up from discrete devices, then the minimization criterion is that of fewest diodes. If, however, we use a programmable integrated circuit matrix, then the object is to squeeze the logic into the available configuration. Essentially this means reducing the number of product terms; in our example twelve p-terms is the maximum allowable. The size of such terms is irrelevant; in fact row 11 is easier to produce than row 0, as less fuses need be blown. Also the number of product terms ORed for an output is also logically irrelevant (although each term adds capacitance and thus slightly slows the response). From a K-map point of view; product term sharing is all important but the size of loops is not. Sharing manifests itself in the matrix by more than one OR diode hung on to a horizontal row (AND term). Thus diodes 9,8; 10,8 and 11,8 represent the sharing of the p-term $D \cdot \overline{B} \cdot \overline{A}$ for outputs G, H and I respectively.

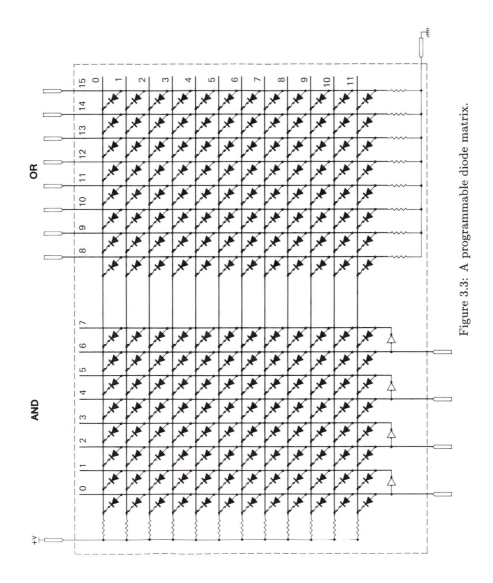

Figure 3.3: A programmable diode matrix.

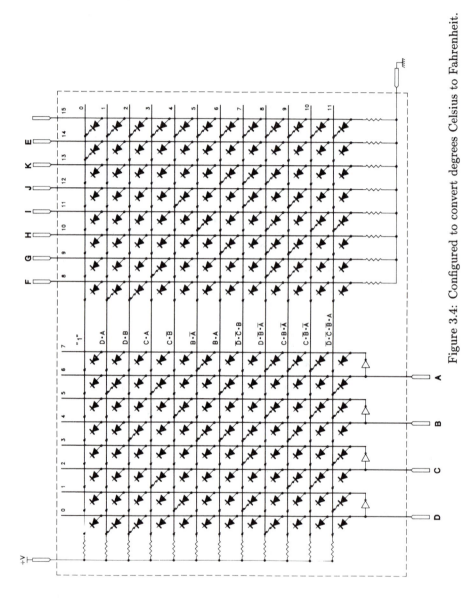

Figure 3.4: Configured to convert degrees Celsius to Fahrenheit.

Although diode matrices are rarely used as such, the principle of a programmable AND-OR matrix is extremely important. Section 3.3 looks at programmable arrays in more detail. Irrespective of the device used at each intersection, some means of creating the pattern of connections is required. If large quantities are involved, then it may be more economical to let the semiconductor manufacturer make the IC to your pattern. Where a standard base design is used, then the production of such devices is the same for all customers except for the one customized stage. This involves etching holes through the silicon dioxide insulation layer covering the active silicon. When the conducting tracks are laid, contact with the active device below is only made if a window has been etched in the appropriate position. Tooling-up charges for this customer-specified connection mask is expensive, but considerably less than making an IC which is original from bottom up. Whereas a semi-customized array might be economical in runs of 5000; a fully customized equivalent is likely to need a run of at least 50,000. However, not all designs lend themselves to implementation using standard architectures.

User (or field) programmable arrays give the flexibility necessary in prototyping and the ability to quickly make changes if bugs are discovered in the field. The absence of a large up-front tooling charge also makes this economical for small and medium production runs. Furthermore, the programming equipment (typically costing around $500 – $5000 (£300 – £3000) covers a large number of different devices.

As we have seen, user configurability is achieved by inserting a programmable link in series with each logic element. This is typically a conducting strip which is physically blown, or a switch. The most common implementation of the former uses a narrow metallic strip. As an example, Texas Instruments use a 0.15 μm (0.06 mil)-wide Titanium Tungsten strip (covered with Silicon Dioxide to prevent splutter) fusing in 1 – 10 ms at 10 – 60 mA. Nickel Chromium (Nichrome) is another common metallic material. Some manufacturers utilize polysilicon (silicon without a regular crystalline structure). Advanced Micro Devices use a 25 μm (0.1 mil) wide polysilicon strip, which fuses at currents between 20 and 80 mA for around 15 μs. As can be seen in the photograph of Fig. 3.5(b), a considerable gap (around 5 μm) occurs during this process. This is unlike metallic links, which have been known to grow back after a time!

An alternative approach uses **anti-fuses**. Here, the collector-emitter of an open-base transistor is connected across each matrix intersection. In the unprogrammed state this acts as an open circuit (actually two back to back diodes), as shown in Fig. 3.6(a). If a sufficiently high voltage is applied across the transistor, the now reverse-biased base-emitter breaks down due to avalanch induced migration. This leaves the PN base-collector junction intact, acting as (our old friend) a diode. This is the antithesis of the previous process, as initially there are no cross-point connections and diodes are programmed in rather than programmed out. These so called **vertical fuses** (as opposed to the horizontal geometry of a conventional lateral fuse) can be made very small and are thus useful in high-speed circuitry. It is also claimed that they are more reliable than metallic fuses [1].

None of these techniques are reversible; alterations can only be made by blowing additional fuses/transistors. Thus, such PLDs are often categorized as **one-time progammable (OTP)**. Where frequent changes are desirable, eg. during proto-typing, then reprogrammable links may be used. A simplified representation of

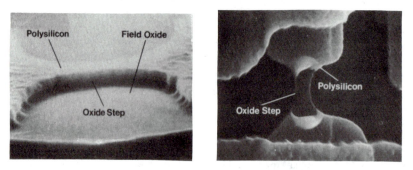

Intact polysilicon fuse   Blown polysilicon fuse

Figure 3.5: Blowing a polysilicon lateral fuse, viewed at 10,000×. Copyright Advanced Micro Devices, Inc. 1991. Reprinted with permission of copyright owner.

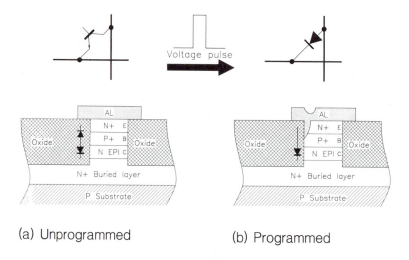

(a) Unprogrammed   (b) Programmed

Figure 3.6: Anatomy of a vertical fuse.

such a link is shown in Fig. 3.7(a). The cross-point device here is a metal-oxide enhancement n-channel field-effect transistor TR_1, rather than a diode, with its gate connected to the X line and source to the Y line. If its drain were connected to the positive supply and the X line is selected (positive), then the Y line too becomes positive (logic 1) as TR_1 is On. However, if TR_1 is disconnected from V_{DD} then it does not conduct (switch Off). Transistor TR_2 is in series with V_{DD} and thus acts as the programmable element. TR_2 has an extra unconnected gate which is buried in the silicon dioxide insulation layer. Normally there is no charge on this gate and TR_2 is Off. If the programming voltage V_{PP} is pulsed high to typically $20 - 25$ V, negative charges tunnel across the very thin insulation surrounding the buried gate [2]. This permanently turns TR_2 On and connects TR_1 to its supply.

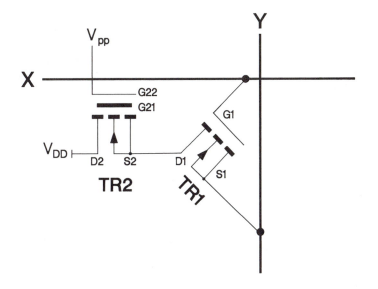

(a) Floating-gate MOS link.

(b) Quartz window into a reprogrammable logic array.

Figure 3.7: Reprogrammable logic.

This charge remains more or less permanently on the buried gate until it is exposed to ultra-violet (U.V.) light. The high-energy light photons knock electrons (negative charges) out of the buried (floating) gate (the Einstein effect), effectively discharging in around 20 minutes and wiping out all stored information. As an alternative to the overall U.V. wipeout technique, some devices allow selective erasing by pulsing the primary gate to a large negative voltage, which tunnels charges the other way. Programmable Read-Only Memories (PROMs) using this technique are known as EEPROMs (Electrical Erasable PROMs) or EAROMs (Electrical Alterable PROMs) [3].

Arrays in the form of U.V. erasable programmable read-only memories have been around since the mid 1970s. EPROMs (see Section 3.3.2) are slow (typically 450 – 150 ns access time) and are mainly used to store microprocessor programs. Generally, the much faster (and expensive) fusible link PROMs are used for general logic design, where they are called programmable logic elements (PLEs). Recently, high speed field effect transistor circuitry has been developed, and reprogrammable arrays, primarily designed for logic circuit implementation, are now available. These may either be U.V. or electrically erasable. The photograph of Fig. 3.7(b) shows the characteristic quartz window of the U.V. erasable Cypress 16L8-25WC programmable array logic (PAL) device. This has a programmable array of 64 32-input AND gates feeding eight 8-input NOR gates; an equivalent of 2048 diodes. Propagation delay is 25 ns maximum. PALs are discussed in Section 3.3.3.

The major problem encountered in diode logic is the potential drop across the conducting junction and the lack of isolation between input and output [4]. This especially causes problems when gates are cascaded. For example, in Fig. 3.4 the logic 1 output will not be $+V$ but $(+V - 2 \times V_{DON})R_1/(R_1 + R_2)$, where R_1 is the AND resistor and R_2 the OR resistor. Specifically, if $R_1 = 1$ KΩ, $R_2 = 10$ KΩ, $V_{DON} = 0.7$ V and $+V = 5$ V; then logic $1 = 3.27$ V. Making the OR resistor large reduces this potential divider effect, but leads to long time constants with a correspondingly slow response time (see Fig. 3.25). The problem is compounded if additional levels of logic are added.

These problems can be solved by using active switches. A bipolar junction transistor (BJT) switch is shown in Fig. 3.8(a). With a Low input voltage, V_{in}, there is no base and hence no collector current. The transistor is now Off. The output, V_{out}, is thus High, being V_{CC} through R_2. If now V_{in} is raised sufficiently positive, the resulting collector current will be such that V_{out} ($V_{CC} - I_C R_2$) falls close to ground potential. In this state, as the forward drop between base-emitter (V_{BE}) is around 0.7 V, the collector-base junction also becomes forward biased. The output is now a low resistance to the emitter. The two junction forward offsets are in opposing direction but do not quite cancel, leaving a small residual voltage of typically 0.2 V ($V_{CE(sat)}$). The transistor is said to be saturated, and the switch is On.

The collector current required to drop the output to nearly ground is V_{CC}/R_2, with a corresponding base current of $(V_{CC}/R_2)/h_{FE}$. This is the minimum base current which will saturate the transistor. Unfortunately h_{FE} (the current gain) of a BJT is a poorly defined parameter, and varies with operating and environmental conditions, such as temperature. For example, the 2N2222A type has a range between 100 and 300. This means that enough base current must be pumped in to

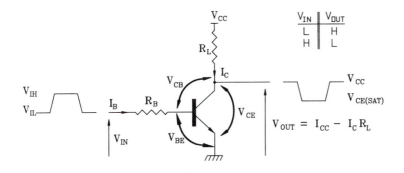

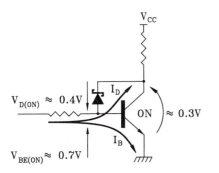

$$V_{OUT} = I_{CC} - I_C R_L$$

(a) A basic BJT switch

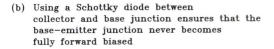

(b) Using a Schottky diode between collector and base junction ensures that the base–emitter junction never becomes fully forward biased

(c) Circuit symbol for Schottky transistor

Figure 3.8: A BJT switch-inverter.

cover the worst-case situation; typically giving a value several times greater than necessary. Thus if $V_{CC} = 5$ V and R_2 is 1 kΩ, a base current of 5 mA/100 = 50 μA must be supplied to cover the situation where h_{FE} is 100. If in a particular case h_{FE} were 250; then this represents a 250% overload. This has little effect on the output saturation voltage (Low state), but a large quantity of superfluous charge will be stored in the base. This charge must be withdrawn before the switch is turned Off, and clearly will affect the dynamic performance [5, 6].

In order to reduce the charge-storage induced delays, most high-speed BJT-based integrated circuitry use the modification shown in Fig. 3.8(b). This involves the addition of a low-offset 'catching' diode between base and collector. The object of this diode is to avoid the transistor going into hard saturation, by ensuring that the base collector junction is never fully forward biased. When the collector voltage drops below $V_{BE(On)} - V_{D(On)}$, the diode conducts and hence diverts excess current away from the base. The diode should exhibit a lower offset voltage than silicon and should have a fast switching action. A metal-semiconductor junction (Schottky diode) has these attributes and does not suffer from the stored charge phenomena [7]. The composite structure is usually known as a **Schottky transistor**.

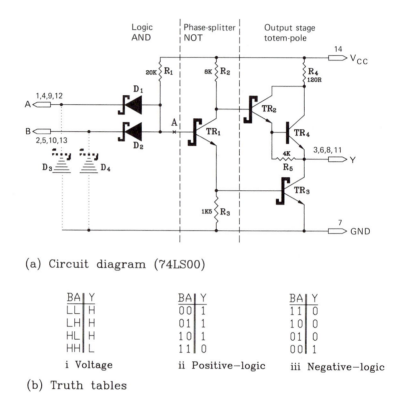

(a) Circuit diagram (74LS00)

B	A	Y
L	L	H
L	H	H
H	L	H
H	H	L

i Voltage

B	A	Y
0	0	1
0	1	1
1	0	1
1	1	0

ii Positive−logic

B	A	Y
1	1	0
1	0	0
0	1	0
0	0	1

iii Negative−logic

(b) Truth tables

Figure 3.9: A much simplified Low Power Schottky Transistor Transistor Logic (LSTTL) positive-NAND gate.

Combining diode logic with a transistor switch leads naturally to inverted-output logic, producing NAND and NOR gates. An example of such a structure is given in Fig. 3.9(a). Here diodes D_1 and D_2 are connected as for the AND gate of Fig. 3.1. When one or both inputs are Low, the conducting diode(s) hold node **A** Low (+0.4 V). This potential is insufficient to forward bias the base-emitter junctions of TR_1 and TR_3. Thus TR_3 is Off and TR_2/TR_4 are On, (biased through R_2). The output is then High. If both diodes are High (greater than ≈ 1 V), they do not conduct. Transistor TR_1 is now On (biased through R_1) as is TR_3. The transistor pair TR_2/TR_4 is now Off and the output is Low. Diodes D_3/D_4 do not conduct in either situation; they provide protection against the possibility of negative voltage transients at the input.

The positive-logic truth table of Fig. 3.9(b)ii shows that this structure implements the NAND function. It is in fact one of four identical 2-I/P NAND gates provided in the 74LS00 integrated circuit, see Fig. 3.11. A series of related families, known collectively as **transistor transistor logic (TTL)** is based on this type of implementation. The name comes from the original circuit (eg. the 7400) which used a multi-emitter transistor to implement the AND logic in place of the diodes [8]. The family types optimize parameters such as speed and power dissipation, but all have compatible voltage and current levels. Thus they can be mixed if desired. Some comparisons are given in Table 3.2.

Before looking at these parameters, it is instructive to examine the operation of the circuit in a little more detail. This will give us more feeling concerning the inter-relationship of the various voltage and current levels.

Consider input B of Fig. 3.10(a) is Low and A is High. Diode D_2 conducts and a current I_{IL} (Input Low) flows out of this node and into the driving circuit. If the input voltage V_{IL} (Input Low) is, say, 0.4 V and the supply $V_{CC} = 5$ V, then $I_{IL} \approx (5 - 0.4 - 0.4)/20 \approx 0.2$ mA. Input A is said to *source* 0.2 mA and the logic output providing the input must *sink* this current (the maximum I_{IL} is 0.4 mA for LSTTL). Conventionally in data sheets, source currents are indicated minus (outflow) and sink currents positive (inflow). Thus $I_{IL(max)} = -0.4$ mA. If the driver is connected to, say, 20 gate inputs in total, then it must be capable of sinking a maximum of 8 mA without its logic 0 voltage rising above the maximum permissible ($V_{OL(max)} = 0.4$ V for the TTL families).

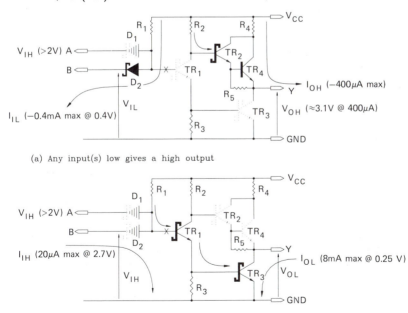

(a) Any input(s) low gives a high output

(b) Both inputs high gives a low output

Figure 3.10: Analyzing the Low-Power Schottky TTL positive-NAND gate.

The voltage at node **X** will be around 0.8 V if V_{IL} is 0.4 V, and this is insufficient to turn On TR_1 or TR_3. Transistors TR_2/TR_4 will conduct and provide current to any load (say another gate) connected to the output. For the LSTTL family, the maximum permitted source load is -400 μA ($I_{OH(max)}$, Output High) while maintaining a High output voltage of not less than 2.5 V ($V_{OH(min)}$, Output High). Now at 400 μA, the drop across R_4 is only 48 mV. With the Schottky transistor TR_2 conducting heavily and taking the minimum V_{CC} of 4.5 V; the base of TR_4 will be around $4.5 - 0.048 - 0.3 \approx 4.15$ V. The emitter, i.e. the output, will then be about 3.45 V.

Resistor R_4 provides current limiting if the output is short circuited to ground and during switching transients when the top TR_2/TR_4 pair are switching one way and TR_3 the other. Notice that TR_4 is a regular (non-Schottky) transistor. This is because its collector is always around 1 V above its emitter ($V_{BE(On)4} + V_{CE(On)2}$) and therefore it does not saturate.

If now the input at B is brought High, the voltage at **X** will rise until the base-emitter junctions of TR_1 and TR_3 both conduct; clamping this node to 1.4 V. This will occur with V_{IH} (Input High) at around 1 V. Thus any input voltage above this is treated as a High (actually 2 V is the recommended minimum value). With transistor TR_3 saturated, the output is Low, at around 0.3 V. This can sink up to 8 mA (twenty other LS loads) without rising above 0.4 V ($V_{OL(max)}$, Output Low). This contrasts with a $I_{OH(max)}$ of -400 μA. With TR_1 saturated, its collector will be around 1 V ($V_{BE(On)3} + V_{CE(On)1}$), and this is not sufficient to turn On the two base-emitters $V_{BE2} + V_{BE4}$ (1.4 V). This is the main reason for using a transistor pair at the top of the totem pole (the original TTL family used a diode in place of TR_2 to give this offset).

The data sheet reproduced in Fig. 3.11 applies to the 74-series advanced low-power Schottky (ALS) family. This is similar to the LS parts but around 40% faster and power efficient. Additional static parameters are the negative input voltage V_{IK} giving a source current of -18 mA (due to the protection diode conducting); the input leakage I_I if V_I is raised to $+7$ V; the output source short circuit current I_O (-70 mA max), and supply currents for both logic states, I_{CCH} and I_{CCL}. We will return to these parameters in the next section. Up to this point we have tacitly assigned the lower of the two bands of voltages as logic 0 and the higher voltages to logic 1. In abstract logic diagrams, only the logic states have any meaning; the actual physical parameters used to represent these are largely irrelevant. They could be current, light, pneumatic pressure etc. Most electronic logic circuits use voltage levels. Here the physical reality is described by the voltage truth table, such as in Fig. 3.9(b)i. This describes states in terms of Low (L), High (H) and (in Fig. 3.11) don't care (**X**). Where level L is assigned to logic 0 and H is assigned as logic 1 we have a **positive-logic** system. It is for this reason that the logic diagram in the data sheet is annotated "positive logic" and the catalog description as positive-NAND.

Of course there is no reason why we should make our assignment this way, and Fig. 3.9(b)ii shows the result of using a **negative-logic** assignment. Thus the 7400 family circuit could equally well be cataloged as a quad 2-input negative-NOR gate. To clarify the situation, each diagram showing real hardware should be annotated as "positive-logic" or "negative-logic". In practice the negative-logic convention is rarely used, and in the absence of any such qualifier, positive-logic is assumed by default. In the 74 series, this means that any circuit voltage above 2.0 V is taken as being logic 1 and below 0.8 V as logic 0. Between these values lies a no-man's

**SN54ALS00A, SN54AS00, SN74ALS00A, SN74AS00
QUADRUPLE 2-INPUT POSITIVE-NAND GATES**

D2661, APRIL 1982 – REVISED MAY 1986

- Package Options Include Plastic "Small Outline" Packages, Ceramic Chip Carriers, and Standard Plastic and Ceramic 300-mil DIPs
- Dependable Texas Instruments Quality and Reliability

description

These devices contain four independent 2-input NAND gates. They perform the Boolean functions $Y = \overline{A \cdot B}$ or $Y = \overline{A} + \overline{B}$ in positive logic.

The SN54ALS00A and SN54AS00 are characterized for operation over the full military temperature range of $-55\,°C$ to $125\,°C$. The SN74ALS00A and SN74AS00 are characterized for operation from $0\,°C$ to $70\,°C$.

FUNCTION TABLE (each gate)

INPUTS		OUTPUT
A	B	Y
H	H	L
L	X	H
X	L	H

logic symbol†

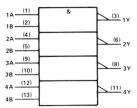

†This symbol is in accordance with ANSI/IEEE Std 91-1984 and IEC Publication 617-12.
Pin numbers shown are for D, J, and N packages.

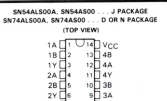

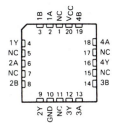

NC—No internal connection

logic diagram (positive logic)

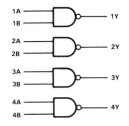

TEXAS INSTRUMENTS

Figure 3.11: Data sheet for the 54/74ALS00 TTL quad 2-input positive-NAND gate (*continued next page*).

TYPES SN54ALS00A, SN74ALS00A
QUADRUPLE 2-INPUT POSITIVE-NAND GATES

---

absolute maximum ratings over operating free-air temperature range (unless otherwise noted)

Supply voltage, V_{CC} . . . . 7 V
Input voltage . . . . 7 V
Operating free-air temperature range: SN54ALS00A . . . . $-55\,^\circ$C to $125\,^\circ$C
  SN74ALS00A . . . . 0 $^\circ$C to 70 $^\circ$C
Storage temperature range . . . . $-65\,^\circ$C to $150\,^\circ$C

recommended operating conditions

		SN54ALS00A			SN74ALS00A			UNIT
		MIN	NOM	MAX	MIN	NOM	MAX	
V_{CC}	Supply voltage	4.5	5	5.5	4.5	5	5.5	V
V_{IH}	High-level input voltage	2			2			V
V_{IL}	Low-level input voltage			0.8			0.8	V
I_{OH}	High-level output current			-0.4			-0.4	mA
I_{OL}	Low-level output current			4			8	mA
T_A	Operating free-air temperature	-55		125	0		70	$^\circ$C

electrical characteristics over recommended operating free-air temperature range (unless otherwise noted)

PARAMETER	TEST CONDITIONS		SN54ALS00A			SN74ALS00A			UNIT
			MIN	TYP†	MAX	MIN	TYP†	MAX	
V_{IK}	$V_{CC} = 4.5$ V,	$I_I = -18$ mA			-1.5			-1.5	V
V_{OH}	$V_{CC} = 4.5$ V to 5.5 V,	$I_{OH} = -0.4$ mA	$V_{CC}-2$			$V_{CC}-2$			V
V_{OL}	$V_{CC} = 4.5$ V,	$I_{OL} = 4$ mA		0.25	0.4		0.25	0.4	V
	$V_{CC} = 4.5$ V,	$I_{OL} = 8$ mA					0.35	0.5	
I_I	$V_{CC} = 5.5$ V,	$V_I = 7$ V			0.1			0.1	mA
I_{IH}	$V_{CC} = 5.5$ V,	$V_I = 2.7$ V			20			20	μA
I_{IL}	$V_{CC} = 5.5$ V,	$V_I = 0.4$ V			-0.1			-0.1	mA
I_O‡	$V_{CC} = 5.5$ V,	$V_O = 2.25$ V	-15		-70	-15		-70	mA
I_{CCH}	$V_{CC} = 5.5$ V,	$V_I = 0$ V		0.5	0.85		0.5	0.85	mA
I_{CCL}	$V_{CC} = 5.5$ V,	$V_I = 4.5$ V		1.5	3		1.5	3	mA

† All typical values are at $V_{CC} = 5$ V, $T_A = 25\,^\circ$C.
‡ The output conditions have been chosen to produce a current that closely approximates one half of the true short-circuit output current, I_{OS}.

switching characteristics (see Note 1)

PARAMETER	FROM (INPUT)	TO (OUTPUT)	$V_{CC} = 4.5$ V to 5.5 V, $C_L = 50$ pF, $R_L = 500\,\Omega$, T_A = MIN to MAX				UNIT
			SN54ALS00A		SN74ALS00A		
			MIN	MAX	MIN	MAX	
t_{PLH}	A or B	Y	3	14	3	11	ns
t_{PHL}	A or B	Y	2	10	2	8	ns

NOTE 1: For load circuit and voltage waveforms, see page 1-12.

TEXAS
INSTRUMENTS

Figure 3.11: (*continued*). Data sheet for the 54/74ALS00 TTL quad 2-input positive-NAND gate. Reproduced by courtesy of Texas Instruments Ltd.

land (see Fig. 3.13).

The IEC/ANSII logic symbol used in the data sheet uses an alternative **polarity-indicator convention** (sometimes called direct polarity indication). Here external (i.e. outside symbol boxes) voltage levels are depicted in the diagram. These become internal logic states according to the transformation L → 0 and H → 1. A half-arrow polarity symbol at the input of a symbol box denotes external levels H/L becoming internal logic 0/logic 1 states respectively. A polarity symbol at the output similarly means that an internal 0/1 appears externally as a H/L voltage level respectively. This is similar to positive-logic, with the inversion bubble replaced by the polarity half arrow. Generally it is used where the diagram denotes real hardware (catalog parts), such as in Fig. 3.29. Inversion bubbles are used in abstract (hardware independent) logic diagrams or inside an outline to indicate internal inversion (see Fig. 3.38). Do not mix conventions on the one diagram. The polarity-indicator convention is sometimes called the mixed-logic convention, as it subsumes both positive and negative conventions. This is because actual voltage levels are shown on the diagram as opposed to logic states.

Inversion may be equally well performed by replacing the bipolar junction transistor of Fig. 3.8(a) by an N-channel metal-oxide semiconductor transistor (MOST), as shown in Fig. 3.12(a). This type of transistor consists of a metal gate layer separated from the substrate semiconductor body by a thin oxide insulator. Application of a positive voltage between the gate and substrate, above a threshold potential of several volts, induces a layer of negative charge. This creates a conducting channel between source and drain [9]. In this manner the MOST acts as a voltage controlled switch (as opposed to the current controlled BJT).

From the above discussion we can analyse the MOST inverter of Fig. 3.12(a). With a Low voltage on the gate at less than the threshold (typically three volts), no conducting path exists between drain and source. The switch is Off, and the output is pulled High by R_L. Application of a High voltage to the gate induces a conducting channel of typically several hundred ohms. Provided that the load resistance is of an order of magnitude greater than the channel resistance, the resulting potential divider gives an output close to ground. Early MOST circuits used P-channel devices (PMOS). Current designs invariably use NMOS transistors. As electrons have a higher mobility than holes, NMOS devices feature lower channel On resistances. Nevertheless, the high resistance values inherent in MOST circuits leads to long time constants, and thus operating speeds which compare unfavourably with equivalent BJT implementations.

Despite the severe handicap of slow operation, most current LSI and VLSI circuits use MOST rather than BJT implementations. This is because the advantages of the MOST, i.e. simpler fabrication, higher packing density and lower power dissipation, are of over-riding importance in complex circuits. Although typically a MOST occupies only 5% of the area of a BJT, the large load resistor of the MOST inverter of Fig. 3.12(a) negates this advantage (each 50Ω of resistance requires the same area as a MOST). However, it is possible to replace the load with a gate-drain commoned MOST, as shown in Fig. 3.12(b).

By plotting the condition $V_{GS} = V_{DS}$ on the output characteristic of the load MOST, the resulting locus relates the voltage across the load to its current. This data may be used in turn to plot a non-linear load line on the TR_1 output characteristic, giving the precise relationship between the input and output inverter

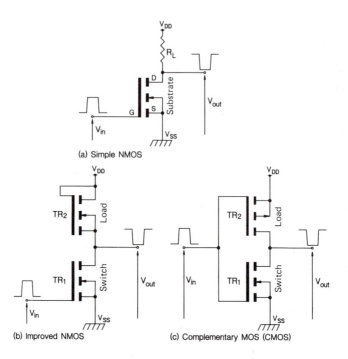

Figure 3.12: MOS inverter circuits.

voltages [9]. It is sufficient in this text to observe that with V_{in} High, TR_1 will be On, and the output will be Low. When V_{in} is Low, TR_1 will be Off. In this state only a small leakage current will flow through the load MOST. To support even this trickle of current, the voltage between the gate and substrate/source must be at the threshold potential, V_T. As the gate is commoned to the drain, the High-state output is $V_{DD} - V_T$; typically 9 V for a 12 V supply.

Multiple-input NMOS gates are implemented by using the same technique as the relay circuits of Figs. 2.1 and 2.2 Thus series transistors give NAND, and parallel transistors give NOR. In both cases all transistors share the same load.

The advantages of NMOS implementations are of relatively little importance for SSI and MSI circuits when set against the superior speed of BJT implementations. However, in the late 1960s, the Radio Corporation of America (RCA) introduced their 4000 series of MOST SSI and MSI functions, which used both N and P-channel transistors in a push-pull configuration. Consider the basic complimentary MOS (CMOS) inverter shown in Fig. 3.12(c). If V_{in} is Low, the lower transistor is Off, whilst the upper P-channel device is On (V_{GS2} negative). Thus the output is High and approximates to the supply voltage, V_{DD}. Conversely, with a High input, the lower transistor is On and the upper device is Off. The output is now Low, close to V_{SS}. Note that in CMOS logic the lower potential power pin is labelled V_{SS}; normally it is grounded, but other arrangements are possible provided that V_{DD} is more positive than V_{SS}, and that the difference does not exceed the maximum supply rating of the chip.

The inverting transfer characteristic, shown in Fig. 3.14, may be understood if both transistors are thought of as controlled resistors, R_N and R_P. As V_{in} goes High, R_P decreases as R_N increases. At the point where $R_N = R_P$, the output has fallen to midway between V_{DD} and V_{SS}. A further increase takes the output up to V_{SS}. The actual transition voltage is a function of the matching of TR_1/TR_2, but is $\pm 5\%$ of $(V_{DD} - V_{SS})/2$. Typically an On channel resistance lies between 250 and 1000 Ω, whilst in the Off state the channel is virtually an open circuit at 10^8 Ω.

The push-pull arrangement increases the speed of operation, although this is still tends to be lower than BJT equivalents. The major advantage of CMOS circuitry lies in their low standby power dissipation, which is typically measured in nanowatts (see Section 3.1.2). This is because at both ends of the transfer characteristic, one of the variable resistances is virtually open circuit, and thus there is no path from the supply to ground when either transistor conducts.

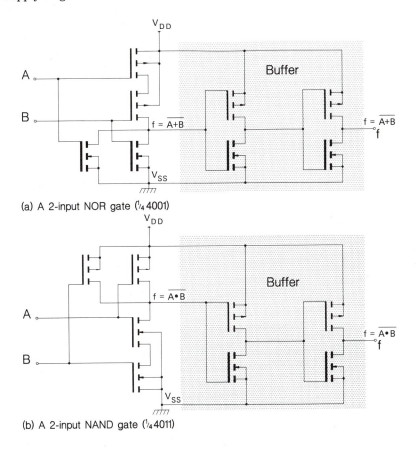

(a) A 2-input NOR gate ($\frac{1}{4}$ 4001)

(b) A 2-input NAND gate ($\frac{1}{4}$ 4011)

Figure 3.13: Two-input CMOS gates. Unbuffered 4000A series shown in solid line; buffered 74HC and 4000B series additional circuitry shown dotted.

Both NAND and NOR CMOS gates are equally feasible, and 2-I/P versions of both types are shown in Fig. 3.13. In the case of the NOR gate, both bottom MOSTs are paralleled, whilst the loads are in series. With both inputs Low, both bottom MOSTs are Off and both upper MOSTs are On; giving V_{out} High. If any input is High, the relevant bottom MOST conducts and the upper series chain is broken, pulling V_{out} Low. With the NAND configuration, all bottom series MOSTs must be On to give a Low output. If any input is Low, then the bottom chain is broken, and an upper On MOST brings the output High. Additional gate inputs can be accommodated by adding MOSTs in series or parallel as appropriate. However, there is a practical upper limit of four using this simple arrangement, owing to **pattern sensitivity**.

Pattern sensitivity arises because of the asymmetry of the upper and lower halves of a multi-input gate [10]. For example, if in the NOR gate one input is grounded and the other input is raised, the threshold occurs when the lower and upper resistances are equal. The same is true when both inputs are raised simultaneously. However, the bottom resistance is smaller in this case, because of paralleling, and the threshold is reached earlier. NAND gates similarly show a pattern sensitivity in their transfer characteristic, but in the opposite sense to NOR. In both cases, the variation of the transfer characteristic becomes worse as the number of gate inputs rises.

The basic 4000A series CMOS configurations also suffer from non-standard output resistances. For example the output resistance in the High state (R_{OH}) for the 2-I/P NOR gate is due to two series On MOSTs; whilst that of a 4-I/P NOR is due to four series MOSTs. This can be compensated for by increasing the size of the transistors, but this causes considerable differences between High- and Low-state resistance values. Using this technique, the 4002A 4-I/P NOR gate has a 400 Ω R_{OH}, but only a 60 Ω R_{OL}.

The addition of an output buffer, as shown dotted in Fig. 3.13, is used to give the 4000B series standard output resistances, with an enhanced current drive. In addition, the manufacturers took the opportunity of a redesign to alter the configuration of multi-input gates to reduce pattern sensitivity. In most current 4000-based designs, 4000B series is used in preference to 4000A parts.

In the 1980s, semiconductor fabrication technology improved the performance of MOS digital circuitry, by reducing the size of transistor and replacing the metal gate by polysilicon. The resulting increased speed and current drive made CMOS logic a serious competitor to the bipolar TTL 74-series families. Due to the popularity of the 74-series parts, these new families parallel their TTL cousins. Thus the 74HC00 (High-speed CMOS) and 74LS00 devices have the same function and pinouts. In this text I use the designation 74x to denote a generic part, for example 74x00.

These new families have similar circuitry to the 4000B series and share its low-power characteristics. The 74HC family has similar speed and drive characteristics to the bipolar 74LS parts whilst 74AC (Advanced CMOS) competes with 74ALS. Power supplies can range from 2 V to 6 V.

The transfer characteristics, (v_{out} vers v_{in}), of the various CMOS logic families are similar. The change-over from logic 0 to logic 1 is normally close to halfway between V_{DD} (the positive drain supply) and V_{SS} (the source voltage, normally 0 V). However, due to mismatch between upper and lower transistors and pattern sensitivity, a central band of around 40% is left to cover uncertainties. Thus the CMOS data sheet of Fig. 3.15 gives $V_{IL(max)}$ of 1.8 V with a V_{CC} (strictly V_{DD}) of 6 V and $V_{IH(min)}$ of 4.2 V.

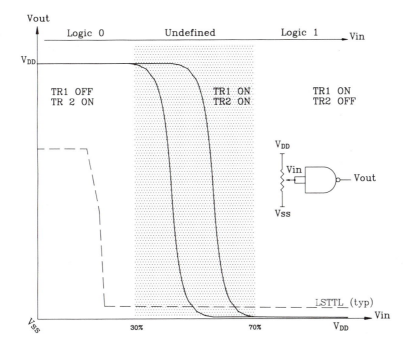

Figure 3.14: Showing production and environmental spreads of the transfer characteristics for 4000 and HCMOS series gates.

Output voltage levels are within 0.1 V of the supplies, provided little load current is taken (20 μA in the data sheet). Where a CMOS gate drives a TTL gate, several mA may have to be sunk or sourced. For example $V_{OL(max)}$ rises to 0.26 V @25°C for $I_{OL} = 5.2$ mA and $V_{CC} = 6$ V. However, little current is generally required when driving other CMOS logic, owing to the negligible input current $(\pm I_{I(max)})$ of 1 μA.

The high input impedance of CMOS circuits gives a large fan-out, as discussed in Section 3.1.2, but can lead to problems. Such inputs should never be left disconnected, because of noise pick-up. Even on unused gates, inputs should be grounded, as they may float up into the undefined region (Fig. 3.14) in which case both totem pole transistors may conduct. As a consequence of the large input impedance of MOS devices, electrostatically induced voltages may cause damage. A 10 μm gate-substrate oxide insulator layer will break down at 100 V. The human body walking on carpet can easily generate several tens of kilovolts, which when discharged from typically 300 pF body capacitance [11] can inject sufficient energy into the gate to destroy it. To help prevent this, all CMOS devices feature clamping input diode-resistor networks, such as shown in Fig. 3.15. However, care should still be exercised in the use of such circuits [12]. If the input to a system is driven from an external low-impedance signal source of greater voltage than the supply (this usually happens when power has not yet been switched on), sufficient current may flow through

HIGH-SPEED CMOS LOGIC

TYPES SN54HC02, SN74HC02
QUADRUPLE 2-INPUT POSITIVE-NOR GATES

D2684, DECEMBER 1982

- Package Options Include Both Plastic and Ceramic Chip Carriers in Addition to Plastic and Ceramic DIPs

- Dependable Texas Instruments Quality and Reliability

description

These devices contain four independent 2-input NOR gates. They perform the boolean functions $Y = \overline{A + B}$ or $Y = \overline{A} \cdot \overline{B}$ in positive logic.

The SN54HC02 is characterized for operation over the full military temperature range of –55°C to 125°C. The SN74HC02 is characterized for operation from –40°C to 85°C.

logic symbol

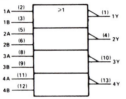

Pin numbers shown are for J and N packages.

SN54HC02 . . . J PACKAGE
SN74HC02 . . . J OR N PACKAGE
(TOP VIEW)

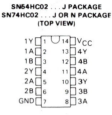

SN54HC02 . . . FH OR FK PACKAGE
SN74HC02 . . . FH OR FN PACKAGE
(TOP VIEW)

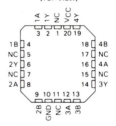

NC — No internal connection

FUNCTION TABLE (each gate)

INPUTS		OUTPUT
A	B	Y
H	X	L
X	H	L
L	L	H

switching characteristics over recommended operating free-air temperature range (unless otherwise noted)

PARAMETER	FROM	TO	CONDITIONS V_{CC}	$C_L = 50$ pF							UNIT
				$T_A = 25°C$			54HC02		74HC02		
				MIN	TYP	MAX	MIN	MAX	MIN	MAX	
t_{PLH}	A or B	Y	2.0V			100		150		125	ns
			4.5V			20		30		25	
			6.0V			17		25		21	
t_{PHL}			2.0V			100		150		125	
			4.5V			20		30		25	
			6.0V			17		25		21	
t_r		Y	2.0V			75		110		95	ns
			4.5V			15		22		19	
			6.0V			13		19		16	
t_f			2.0V			75		110		95	
			4.5V			15		22		19	
			6.0V			13		19		16	
C_{pd}	Power dissipation capacitance per gate at 25°C								22 typ		pF

TEXAS INSTRUMENTS

Figure 3.15: Data sheet for the 54/74HC02 CMOS quad 2-input positive-NOR gate (*continued next page*).

DC CHARACTERISTICS FOR 74HC

Voltages are referenced to GND (ground = 0 V)

SYMBOL	PARAMETER	T_{amb} (°C) 74HC +25 min.	typ.	max.	−40 to +85 min.	max.	−40 to +125 min.	max.	UNIT	V_{CC} V	V_I	OTHER
V_{IH}	HIGH level input voltage	1.5 3.15 4.2	1.2 2.4 3.2		1.5 3.15 4.2		1.5 3.15 4.2		V	2.0 4.5 6.0		
V_{IL}	LOW level input voltage		0.8 2.1 2.8	0.5 1.35 1.8		0.5 1.35 1.8		0.5 1.35 1.8	V	2.0 4.5 6.0		
V_{OH}	HIGH level output voltage all outputs	1.9 4.4 5.9	2.0 4.5 6.0		1.9 4.4 5.9		1.9 4.4 5.9		V	2.0 4.5 6.0	V_{IH} or V_{IL}	$-I_O = 20\,\mu A$ $-I_O = 20\,\mu A$ $-I_O = 20\,\mu A$
V_{OH}	HIGH level output voltage standard outputs	3.98 5.48	4.32 5.81		3.84 5.34		3.7 5.2		V	4.5 6.0	V_{IH} or V_{IL}	$-I_O = 4.0\,mA$ $-I_O = 5.2\,mA$
V_{OH}	HIGH level output voltage bus driver outputs	3.98 5.48	4.32 5.81		3.84 5.34		3.7 5.2		V	4.5 6.0	V_{IH} or V_{IL}	$-I_O = 6.0\,mA$ $-I_O = 7.8\,mA$
V_{OL}	LOW level output voltage all outputs		0 0 0	0.1 0.1 0.1	0.1 0.1 0.1		0.1 0.1 0.1		V	2.0 4.5 6.0	V_{IH} or V_{IL}	$I_O = 20\,\mu A$ $I_O = 20\,\mu A$ $I_O = 20\,\mu A$
V_{OL}	LOW level output voltage standard outputs		0.15 0.16	0.26 0.26	0.33 0.33		0.4 0.4		V	4.5 6.0	V_{IH} or V_{IL}	$I_O = 4.0\,mA$ $I_O = 5.2\,mA$
V_{OL}	LOW level output voltage bus driver outputs		0.15 0.16	0.26 0.26	0.33 0.33		0.4 0.4		V	4.5 6.0	V_{IH} or V_{IL}	$I_O = 6.0\,mA$ $I_O = 7.8\,mA$
$\pm I_I$	input leakage current		0.1		1.0		1.0		μA	6.0	V_{CC} or GND	
$\pm I_{OZ}$	3-state OFF-state current		0.5		5.0		10.0		μA	6.0	V_{IH} or V_{IL}	$V_O = V_{CC}$ or GND
I_{CC}	quiescent supply current SSI flip-flops MSI		2.0 4.0 8.0		20.0 40.0 80.0		40.0 80.0 160.0	μA μA μA		6.0 6.0 6.0	V_{CC} or GND	$I_O = 0$ $I_O = 0$ $I_O = 0$

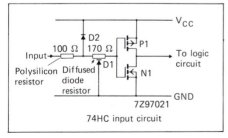

74HC input circuit

Figure 3.15: (*continued*). Data sheet for the 54/74HC02 CMOS quad 2-input positive-NOR gate. Reproduced by courtesy of Texas Instruments and Philips/Signetics Components Ltd.

the clamping diode network to cause damage. To overcome this, it is advisable to place a 10 kΩ resistor in series with such inputs.

Although 74-series TTL and CMOS parts are pin and speed compatible, logic voltage levels do not match, even with a CMOS supply corresponding to TTL's 5 V. This is particularly the case for the High state; which in CMOS covers the band 3.5 – 5.0 V and in TTL is 2.4 – 5.0 V. I have superimposed a typical LSTTL transfer characteristic on Fig. 3.14 to emphasize this. Thus a TTL gate with $V_{OH} = 3.0$ V driving a CMOS gate ($V_{IH(min)} = 3.5$ V) will probably fail to have its High state recognized as such. There are two ways round this. A resistor connecting the output of the TTL gate to V_{CC} will raise V_{OH} to close to +5 V, although the pull-up resistor will slightly degrade performance. Alternatively a 74HCT (High-speed CMOS TTL compatible) series is available with a lower cross-over voltage threshold which matches that of TTL. 74HCT is designed as a 'drop-in' replacement for LSTTL, with matching current, voltage and timing characteristics, but with CMOS's low power consumption advantage.

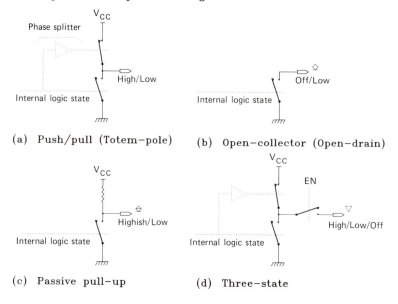

(a) Push/pull (Totem-pole)   (b) Open−collector (Open−drain)

(c) Passive pull−up   (d) Three−state

Figure 3.16: Standard logic output structures with their IEC/ANSII symbols. All shown in their High state.

Many aspects of the electrical behavior of logic circuits depend on their output structure. Historically the passive pull-up structure, shown in Figs. 3.8 and 3.12(a), is the oldest configuration, as discrete resistors are cheaper than transistors. Its main disadvantage is the relatively large output resistance when in the High-output state. Drive to other gates is limited, as an appreciable current lowers the voltage due to the ohmic drop across R_L. This large resistance leads to long propagation delays when driving into capacitive loads, as discussed in Section 3.1.2. Reducing the value of load resistance to improve these parameters, increases the power dissipated when the gate output is Low; as the transistor switch must carry the additional current ($\approx V_{CC}/R_L$).

With the advent of integrated circuitry, where transistors are much cheaper than resistors, the more complex push-pull (or **totem pole**) structure (see Figs. 3.9 and 3.12(c)) become the norm. Here both output levels are actively originated by a transistor, giving small resistances for the two logic states. Furthermore, as only one transistor conducts for any state, the steady-state power consumption is reduced.

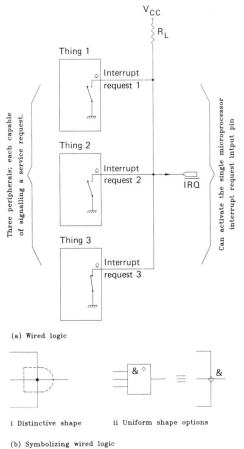

Figure 3.17: Showing how several open-collector drivers may drive the same line. Thing 3 is shown signalling an interrupt to the microprocessor.

Although push-pull outputs are the default structure, alternative forms are available, each with advantages and disadvantages. The most common of these is the **open-collector** (or open-drain), symbolized as ◇. Here the top transistor is missing and the user is free to provide either an external pull-up resistor or some other non-standard load, such as a lamp or relay.

A typical application of open-collector gates is shown in Fig. 3.17. Here three 'things' wish to signal a microprocessor for urgent attention. The microprocessor

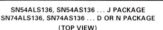

SN54ALS136, SN54AS136, SN74ALS136, SN74AS136
QUADRUPLE 2-INPUT EXCLUSIVE-OR GATES WITH OPEN-COLLECTOR OUTPUTS

D2837, MARCH 1984 – REVISED OCTOBER 1988

- Package Options Include Plastic "Small Outline" Packages, Ceramic Chip Carriers, and Standard Plastic and Ceramic 300-mil DIPs

- Dependable Texas Instruments Quality and Reliability

description

These devices contain for independent Exclusive-OR gates with open-collector outputs. They perform the Boolean functions $Y = A \oplus B = \bar{A}B + A\bar{B}$ in positive logic.

A common application is a true/complement element. If one of the inputs is low, the other input will be reproduced in true form at the output. If one of the inputs is high, the signal on the other input will be reproduced inverted at the output.

The SN54ALS136 and SN54AS136 are characterized for operation over the full military temperature range of −55°C to 125°C. The SN74ALS136 and SN74AS136 are characterized for operation from 0°C to 70°C.

logic symbol†

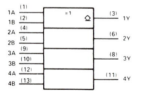

† This symbol is in accordance with ANSI/IEEE Std 91-1984 and IEC Publication 617-12.
Pin numbers shown are for D, J, and N packages.

SN54ALS136, SN54AS136 ... J PACKAGE
SN74ALS136, SN74AS136 ... D OR N PACKAGE
(TOP VIEW)

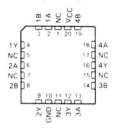

SN54ALS136, SN54AS136 ... FK PACKAGE
(TOP VIEW)

NC – No internal connection

FUNCTION TABLE
(each gate)

INPUTS		OUTPUT
A	B	Y
L	L	L
L	H	H
H	L	H
H	H	L

TEXAS
INSTRUMENTS

(a) Reproduced by courtesy of Texas Instruments Ltd.

Figure 3.18: Using open-collector EOR gates for multiple-bit equality comparisons (*continued next page*).

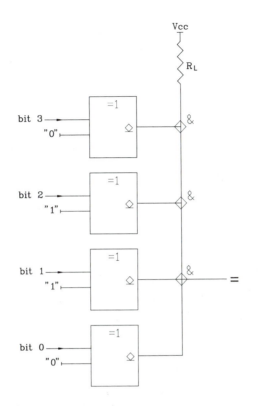

(b) Equal to 1001b (opposite to 0110b).

Figure 3.18: (*continued*). Using open-collector EOR gates for multiple-bit equality comparisons.

has only one interrupt pin. We wish to bring this Low if any request goes Low. This is the AND function. Assuming (as is usual) these 'things' have open-collector interrupt request outputs, then all that needs to be done is to tie all requests together to a common pull-up resistor. If all outputs are in their Off state (corresponding to High) then the composite output is pulled up to V_{CC}. If one or more outputs go Low, then the common point is pulled Low irrespective. Tying outputs together is not possible with push-pull outputs as some transistors would be pulling up to V_{CC} and some down to ground, giving an approximation to a short circuit!

The common resistor is frequently omitted from logic diagrams and replaced by a (phantom) gate symbol, known as wire-AND, as shown in Fig. 3.17(b). In the recommended uniform shape version, the diamond symbol denotes open collector/emitter. Gate families with open-emitter/source outputs give the wire-OR function.

Example 3.2

The logic diagram for the 74ALS136 quad 2-input EOR gate with open-collector
output is shown in Fig. 3.18(a). Show how it may be connected to detect whenever
the pattern 1001b appears. Calculate the value of the common resistor.

Solution

We know that the EOR gate will go to its logic 1 state (open circuit for this gate)
if both inputs differ, i.e. 10b or 01b. Based on this we need to detect when our
input differs in all four bits from the pattern 0110b. This is equivalent to equals
1001b. This all or nothing function is the AND operation, and can be obtained by
wire-ANDing the four outputs together, as shown in Fig. 3.18(b).

The minimum value of R_L is calculated assuming that only one bit comparison
is false. In this situation that gate will go Low and drag the output Low. For its
pains it must carry a worst-case current of $(V_{CC(max)} - V_{OL(min)})R_L$. From the data
sheet of Fig. 3.11, we see that this is 8 mA maximum. Taking $V_{CC(max)} = 5.5$ V
and $V_{OL(min)} = 0$ V, we have $R_{L(min)} = 5.5/8$ k$\Omega = 688$ Ω. The absolute maximum
R_L is dictated by the number of leakage currents taken by any driven circuits (I_{IH}),
plus the EOR Off leakages themselves (I_{OH}), which must not drop V_{OH} below the
74ALS normal of 2.5 V. A 20-gate load requires a total of $20 \times 20 + 4 \times 100 = 800$ μA,
and a worst-case V_{CC} of 4.5 V gives $(4.5 - 2.5)/800 = 0.005$ M$\Omega = 5$ kΩ. The greater
the resistance the lower is the power consumption; at a cost of a slower response
time.

Many open-collector outputs feature 'beefed-up' transistors giving enhanced
voltage or current handling abilities. Outputs which feature greater drive capabilities are said to be buffered. The amplifier symbol $\triangleright$ denotes this property.

Example 3.3

The 7406 is described in the catalog as a hex buffer/driver with open-collector
high-voltage outputs. It features six inverters; each with an output breakdown of
30 V and maximum sink current of 40 mA. It is proposed to use this IC to drive
an illuminated switch with an integral 14 V 80 mA filament lamp. A 20 V power
supply is available for this function. How could this be done?

Solution

There are two problems here. The lamp takes twice the buffer 40 mA rated current.
Thus in Fig. 3.19, two inverter buffers are paralleled (note the use of the $\triangleright$ symbol
after the **1** qualifier). The non matching of lamp rating and supply voltage is
overcome with a series resistor. At 80 mA this must drop 6 volts, i.e. $6/80 = 75$ Ω
and dissipate $V^2IR = 0.48$ W (use a 75 Ω $\frac{1}{2}$ W rating).

Power distribution lines exhibit inductance, and thus current surges induce voltages according to the relationship $V = L\frac{di}{dt}$. Buffers invariably switch rather large
currents and are particularly prone to cause noise of this kind. Decoupling capacitors (typically 1 nF disk ceramic) should be placed close to and across each buffers'

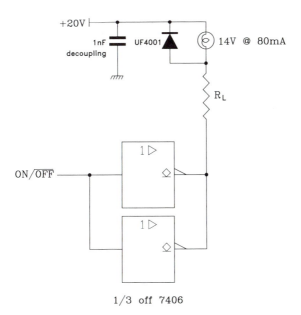

+20V

1nF UF4001 14V @ 80mA
decoupling

R_L

1▷

ON/$\overline{\text{OFF}}$

1▷

1/3 off 7406

Figure 3.19: Using an open-collector buffer to interface logic levels to a non-standard load.

supply pins to reduce this effect. Normally a decoupling capacitor each four or five SSI packages is sufficient.

A protection diode is placed across the load to prevent back emfs due to the load's inductance (also $L \frac{di}{dt}$) breaking down the output transistor. This is especially important when the load is a relay or motor.

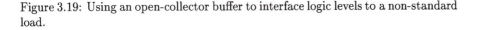

The **3-state output structure** is the most complex of the standard configurations. Conceptually a 3-state (or tristate) output may be considered to be a standard totem-pole in series with an enabling switch, as shown in Fig. 3.16(d). When enabled, the totem-pole is connected to the output pin, giving active-High and -Low states. When disabled, the output is effectively disconnected. This third state is usually referred as hi-Z, for high impedance; or in the data sheet of Fig. 3.20, just as Z. In practice, the 3-state enable turns off both totem-pole transistors, rather than a series switch. In this hi-Z state, only a small leakage current flows ($I_{OZ} = \pm 10 \ \mu A$ max, $\pm 0.5 \ \mu A$ typ for the 74HC125 of Fig. 3.20).

The IEC/ANSII symbol for 3-state is the down pointing triangle ∇ (i.e. three sides), which is normally placed adjacent to the output (as in Fig 3 of the data sheet Fig. 3.20). Most 3-state buffers have larger than normal current drive capabilities (± 6 mA for the 74HC125 as compared to ± 4 mA for standard HC series, see Fig. 3.15). This is indicated by the $\triangleright$ alongside the function qualifier **1**. Also shown in the IEC/ANSII symbol is the **EN dependency** (for ENable). When the

QUAD BUFFER/LINE DRIVER; 3-STATE

FEATURES

- Output capability: bus driver
- I_{CC} category: MSI

GENERAL DESCRIPTION

The 74HC/HCT125 are high-speed Si-gate CMOS devices and are pin compatible with low power Schottky TTL (LSTTL). They are specified in compliance with JEDEC standard no. 7A.

The 74HC/HCT125 are four non-inverting buffer/line drivers with 3-state outputs. The 3-state outputs (nY) are controlled by the output enable input (nOE). A HIGH at nOE causes the outputs to assume a HIGH impedance OFF-state.

The "125" is identical to the "126" but has active LOW enable inputs.

SYMBOL	PARAMETER	CONDITIONS	TYPICAL		UNIT
			HC	HCT	
t_{PHL}/ t_{PLH}	propagation delay nA to nY	C_L = 15 pF V_{CC} = 5 V	9	12	ns
C_I	input capacitance		3.5	3.5	pF
C_{PD}	power dissipation capacitance per buffer	notes 1 and 2	22	24	pF

GND = 0 V; T_{amb} = 25 °C; t_r = t_f = 6 ns

Notes

1. C_{PD} is used to determine the dynamic power dissipation (P_D in μW):

$$P_D = C_{PD} \times V_{CC}^2 \times f_i + \Sigma \ (C_L \times V_{CC}^2 \times f_o) \text{ where:}$$

f_i = input frequency in MHz C_L = output load capacitance in pF
f_o = output frequency in MHz V_{CC} = supply voltage in V
$\Sigma \ (C_L \times V_{CC}^2 \times f_o)$ = sum of outputs
2. For HC the condition is V_I = GND to V_{CC}
   For HCT the condition is V_I = GND to V_{CC} – 1.5 V

FUNCTION TABLE

INPUTS		OUTPUT
nOE	nA$_n$	nY$_n$
L	L	L
L	H	H
H	X	Z

H = HIGH voltage level
L = LOW voltage level
X = don't care
Z = high impedance OFF-state

ORDERING INFORMATION/PACKAGE OUTLINES

PC74HC/HCT125P: 14-lead DIL; plastic (SOT-27).
PC74HC/HCT125T: 14-lead mini-pack; plastic (SO-14; SOT-108A).

PIN DESCRIPTION

PIN NO.	SYMBOL	NAME AND FUNCTION
1, 4, 10, 13	1OE to 4OE	output enable inputs (active LOW)
2, 5, 9, 12	1A to 4A	data inputs
3, 6, 8, 11	1Y to 4Y	data outputs
7	GND	ground (0 V)
14	V_{CC}	positive supply voltage

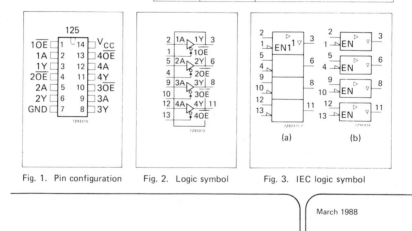

Fig. 1. Pin configuration   Fig. 2. Logic symbol   Fig. 3. IEC logic symbol

March 1988

Figure 3.20: The 74HC125 quad 3-state buffer. Reproduced by courtesy of Philips/Signetics Components Ltd.

internal **EN** signal is logic 0, the appropriate outputs are disabled (all of them if there is no dependency number). If these outputs are 3-state, this is the **Z** state; if open-collector the Off state; otherwise logic 0. When an internal **EN** input is logic 1, all designated outputs take up their normal condition, i.e. are enabled.

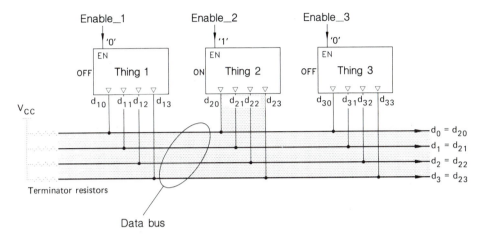

Figure 3.21: A 4-bit data highway using 3-state devices. Device 2 is shown being accessed.

One of the commonest uses of 3-state circuits is with bussing, an example of which is shown in Fig. 3.21. Here, three things are connected to a controller (typically a microprocessor, see Fig. 5.10), in parallel. To prevent interference, only *one* device must be connected to the bus at the time of reading. Such input circuits must have an enable function, which allows unselected data outputs to be taken off the bus. The requisite 3-state buffers are usually integral to devices, such as memories, designed to be used in a bus environment (for example, see Fig. 4.47). Alternatively, any readable entity can be connected to a bus using external 3-state buffers, such as the 74x125 (see Fig. 5.21).

As buses are normally physically fairly long, they act like transmission lines [13] and thus should preferably be terminated by matching resistors to reduce reflections. The characteristic impedance of these transmission lines are of the order of 100 Ω, and this presents a considerable loading on the driving circuits. It is for this reason that 3-state buffers normally have a boosted current drive capability.

Open-collector devices can also be used in the same way to drive buses. Here the terminator resistors act also as pull-up resistors. Open-collector buses are conventionally thought slower than their 3-state counterparts, but one school of thought considers them superior; provided proper termination is used [13].

One final example of the use of the 3-state structure is shown in Fig. 3.22(a). Here a programmable AND-OR matrix (eg. see Fig. 3.4) has four external inputs and four outputs. However, one output is labelled I/O (input/output), and is in series with a 3-state buffer whose enable is controlled with a fusible link.

If the link is intact, then the buffer is enabled and the internal state appears at the output. If the link is open, as shown in Fig. 3.22(b)ii, then this path is disconnected. Any signal applied to I/O3 is then connected to the internal input In4. This type of arrangement increases the flexibility of the programmable logic device; for it can be configured either as a 4-input/4-output or 5-input/3-output circuit by blowing the appropriate fuse. Increasing the flexibility of a given PLD means that more applications can be implemented. Thus the greater complexity and inherent cost is balanced by the economies of scale due to greater sales. The IC shown in Fig. 3.22(c) is a good example of this technique. There are ten dedicated inputs (labelled I) and two dedicated outputs (labelled O). Six outputs are programmable as either inputs or outputs (labelled I/O). The designation PAL16L8 (Programmable array logic 16 inputs and 8 active-Low outputs) is a bit of a misnomer, as you cannot have both 16 inputs and 8 outputs simultaneously. However, the flexibility is useful. The symbology used for the AND-OR matrix is discussed in Section 3.3.1.

Notice from Fig. 3.22(a) and (b), that the internal feedback input is functional even when a pin is programmed as an output. This means that, say, output O0 is not only a function of I0 – I3 but also O3 as well (although there will be a longer propagation delay from O3).

3.1.2   Logic Characteristics

Logic elements are characterized by a large number of electrical properties. Broadly, these deal with steady-state parameters (d.c. conditions), the transient response when changing state (a.c. conditions), and the reaction to small disturbances (noise conditions). Frequently these parameters are quoted on data sheets for both typical and **worst-case worst-case** situations. The latter figures refer to the worst allowable integrated circuit used in conjunction with the worst combination of other parameters, such as temperature and power supply voltage. Designs using these pessimistic values will be guaranteed to function under all combinations of conditions specified on the data sheet.

Before a logic circuit can operate correctly, it must be given a proper physical and electrical environment. Physical environment usually implies thermal consid-

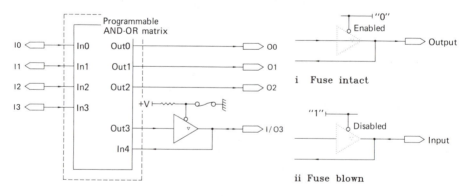

(a) Hypothetical programmable logic device   (b) Two possibilities for I/O3

Figure 3.22: Using a 3-state buffer to implement a programmable input/output (*continued next page*).

PAL16L8A, PAL16L8A-2
STANDARD HIGH-SPEED *PAL*® CIRCUITS

logic diagram

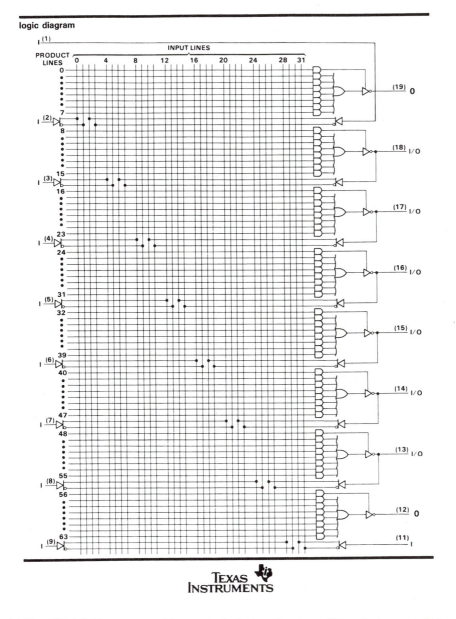

(c) The PAL 16L8A programmable array logic device. Courtesy of Texas Instruments Ltd.

Figure 3.22: (*continued*). Using a 3-state buffer to implement a programmable input/output.

erations. The normal industrial range is 0°C to 70°C free-air temperature, but
frequently an extended (military) operating range of −55°C to 125°C is available.
Data sheet parameters are not guaranteed outside these temperatures, but the circuit will not necessarily malfunction.

The supply voltage ratings are important, not only for their intrinsic worth but
for their effect on the power system costing. Logic families can differ considerably
in their requirements. For example the TTL family is rated for 5 ± 0.5 V; whilst
4000 series CMOS can operate over the range 3 – 18 V. However, in the latter case
the logic parameters, such as speed, differ considerably with supply value. Absolute
maximum values given ratings that will ensure survival, and do not imply correct
logical operation. Note that the maximum supply and input logic voltages are
not necessarily the same. For example, standard series 74 TTL has an absolute
V_{CC} of 7 V, but a maximum V_{in} of only 5.5 V. For this reason TTL inputs to be
permanently held to High should not be tied directly to V_{CC} (a series resistor of
nominal value 10 kΩ may be used for this purpose). However, newer TTL families
do not have this problem. Irrespective of family, input voltages should never exceed
the power supply.

Function	Designator	Family	Output type	Special features
Inverters				
Hex	7404/05/1005	74/LS/S/ALS/HC/HCT	TP/OC/OC	
	7406/16	74/LS	OC	High voltage outputs
	7414	74/LS/HC/HCT	TP	Schmitt trigger inputs
NAND gates				
Quad 2-input	7400	74/LS/S/ALS/AS/HC/HCT	TP	
	7438/39	74/LS/S/ALS	OC	'39 has hi-voltage O/P
	74132	74/LS/S/HC/HCT	TP	Schmitt trigger inputs
Triple 3-input	7410/**15**	74/**LS/S/ALS**/HC/HCT	TP/OC	
Dual 4-input	7420/22/40	74/LS/S/ALS/HC/HCT	TP/OC/TP	'40 has buffered O/Ps
	7413	74/LS/HC/HCT	TP	Schmitt trigger inputs
Single 8-input	7430	74/LS/S/ALS/AS/HC/HCT	TP	
Single 13-input	74133	S/ALS	TP	'134 is 12-I/P version
NOR gates				
Quad 2-input	7402	74/LS/S/ALS/AS/HC/HCT	TP	'ALS805 is hex version
Triple 3-input	7427	74/LS/S/ALS/AS/HC/HCT	TP	'ALS1011 is buffered
Dual 5-input	74260	LS/S	TP	'HC4002 is dual 4-I/P
Quad 8-input	4078	4000/HC	TP	
	74298/399	74/LS/AS	TP, active-High	with output storage
AND gates				
Quad 2-input	7408/**09**	74/**LS/S/ALS**/AS/HC/HCT	TP/OC	
Triple 3-input	7411	LS/S/ALS/HC/HCT	TP	
Dual 4-input	7421	LS/S/ALS/HC/HCT	TP	
OR gates				
Quad 2-input	7432	74/**LS/S/ALS**/AS/HC/HCT	TP	'832 hex buffer version
Triple 3-input	4075	4000/HC/HCT	TP	'AS802 TTL OR/NOR
EOR gates				
Quad 2-input	7486/136	74/LS/S/ALS/HC/HCT	TP/OC	
Quad 2-I/P ENOR	74**256**/811	**LS**/AS/ALS	TP/OC	
3-state buffers				
Quad	74125/126	74/LS/HC/HCT	3S, non-invert	Active Lo/Hi enable
Hex	74365/366	74/LS/ALS/HC/HCT	3S, active-Lo/Hi	NOR enable
Octal	74240/244	LS/S/ALS/AS/HC/HCT	3S, active-Lo/Hi	Line drivers
	74245	LS/S/ALS/LS	3S, non-invert	Bi-directional drivers

TP = Totem pole; OC = Open-collector; 3S = 3-state

Table 3.1: Some SSI integrated circuits.

We have already examined voltage and current levels in the various data sheets of the previous section. For reference they are defined below with values given for the 74LS, 74HC and 4000 family.

Power supply

V_{CC} The working positive supply voltage. (Series 74LS = 5 V±10%, 74HC = 2 – 6 V, 4000 = 3 – 18 V). Sometimes labelled V_{DD} for MOS circuits.

GND The common supply point, usually designated 0 V. Sometimes labelled V_{SS} for MOS circuits.

I_{CC} The unloaded quiescent supply current. (Value depends very much on the function. 74LS00 = 4.4 mA(max), 74HC00 = 0.004 mA(max)). Quiescent power dissipation is the product of V_{CC} and I_{CC}.

Logic levels, V

Voltage levels referring to the input are subscripted I, and output levels are subscripted O. Likewise H is the High level and L Low level. Based on this notation, we have the following definitions (see Fig. 3.10):

$V_{IH(min)}$ The lowest input voltage guaranteed to be accepted as a High level. (Series 74LS = 2 V, 74HC = $0.7V_{CC}$ = 3.5 V @ 5 V).

$V_{IL(max)}$ The highest input voltage guaranteed to be recognized as a Low level. (Series 74LS = 0.8 V, 74HC = $0.3V_{CC}$ = 1.5 V @ 5 V).

$V_{OH(min)}$ The guaranteed smallest High-level output voltage when delivering the maximum specified output (source) current. (Series 74LS = 2.7 V @ −400 μA, 74HC = V_{CC} − 0.1 V @ −20 μA).

$V_{OL(max)}$ The guaranteed largest Low-level output voltage when sinking the specified load current. (Series 74LS = 0.5 V @ 8 mA, 74HC = 0.1 V @ 20 μA).

Logic levels, I

Logic circuits can only supply (source, negative) a limited current when the output is High and accept (sink, positive) when the output is Low (see Fig. 3.10).

$I_{IH(max)}$ The maximum current flowing into an input at a specified input High voltage. (Series 74LS = 20 μA at 2.7 V, 74HC = 1 μA at V_{CC}).

$I_{IL(max)}$ The maximum current flowing out of an input at a specified Low input voltage. (Series 74LS = −0.4 mA at 0.4 V, 74HC = −1 μA at 0 V).

$I_{OH(max)}$ The maximum current an output can source at the High level without dropping below $V_{OH(min)}$. (Series 74LS = −400 μA at 2.7 V, 74HC = −20 μA at V_{CC} − 0.1 V and −4 mA at V_{CC} − 0.8 V).

$I_{OL(max)}$ The maximum current an output can sink at the Low level without rising above $V_{OL(max)}$. (Series 74LS = 8 mA at 0.5 V, 74HC = 20 μA at 0.1 V and 4 mA at 0.4 V).

Sometimes a short-circuit High-level output current is given. This is useful when determining the approximate current which can be driven directly into the base of a transistor or to charge up load capacitance. For 74LS, I_{OS} is given as ranging from -20 to -100 mA, with no more than one output shorted for a maximum of one second.

If all interconnecting logic functions are of the same family, then their voltage and current levels are compatible, and the designer need only follow simple loading rules. However, when non-standard interfacing is required, then more information than that given on a basic data sheet is required. In such cases family input, output and transfer characteristics must be used, as shown in the following example.

Example 3.4

A student has connected a signal generator with a 10 kΩ source resistance to a 74LS04 TTL inverter, as shown in Fig. 3.23(a). He/she finds that the output remains permanently Low. By using the series 74LS characteristic input voltage-current relationship of Fig. 3.23(b), show why this is so.

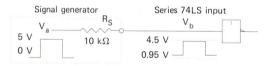

(a): Driving a series 74LS input from a high-resistance source

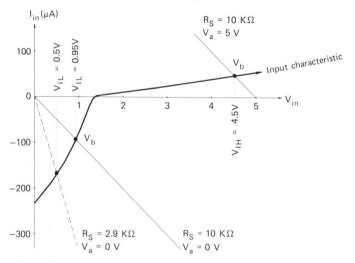

(b) Using load lines to determine the actual logic input V_b

Figure 3.23: Showing why high-resistance sources will not drive series 74LS TTL inputs.

Solution

The input characteristic shows that with a Low V_{in} the gate sources a considerable current, raising the signal generator's terminal voltage (V_b) above zero. The actual value of V_b when the internal source (V_a) is zero, is found by drawing a 10 kΩ load line from the origin, as shown in Fig. 3.23. This shows that V_b is 0.95 V, which is well above the maximum rated Low-level $V_{IL(max)}$ of 0.8 V. When V_a is 5 V, the terminal voltage is 4.5 V, due to the small gate sink current. Thus the input voltage is never low enough to reliably switch the inverter. The dashed locus shows that a 2.9 kΩ source resistance would give a gate input of 0.5 V, which is acceptable as an input Low level.

The characteristic of Fig. 3.23 only gives the typical source current and a reliable design should cope with all eventualities. A quick technique to determine the worst-case scenario is to use the relationship:

$$V_{IL(max)} = I_{IL(max)} \, R_{S(max)}$$

which for 74LS is:

$$-0.5 = 0.4(\text{mA})R_{S(max)}(\text{k}\Omega)$$

giving a maximum recommended source resistance of 1.25 kΩ.

This example has shown how an unwary designer can become unstuck. However, if remaining within a compatible family group, then simple driving rules based on the concept of **fan-in** and **fan-out** will be sufficient.

Fan-out

This is a number indicating the ability of an output to drive other standard inputs of the same or related families. It may be statically limited by the input current requirements of the driver inputs; or dynamically, by the ability to charge the driven gates' capacitance in the required time.

The static fan-out of a family can be easily calculated from the specification sheet. For example, for series 74LS driving series 74LS:

$$I_{OH} = -400 \; \mu A; \; I_{IH} = \;\; 20 \; \mu A \quad : \quad \text{High-state fan-out} = 20$$
$$I_{OL} = \;\;\; 8 \; mA; \quad I_{IL} = -0.4 \; mA \quad : \quad \text{Low-state fan-out} = 20$$

Series 74LS driving series 74S :

$$I_{OH} = -400 \; \mu A; \; I_{IH} = \;\; 50 \; \mu A \quad : \quad \text{High-state fan-out} = 8$$
$$I_{OL} = \;\;\; 8 \; mA; \quad I_{IL} = -2 \; mA \quad : \quad \text{Low-state fan-out} \; = 4$$

These figures are worst-case worst-case. If necessary, gates may be paralleled or special buffers used to boost fan-out.

Fan-in

This is a number indicating the number of static loads an input presents to a driver. Most inputs take one family load. Thus the fan-in of a 74LS00 is 1LS, and of a 74S00 is 5LS (or 1S). In the past, the expression fan-in has been used to describe the number of gate inputs.

We will look at dynamic fan-out later under the heading of propagation delay.

Static noise immunity, V_N

This is defined as the maximum perturbation of a level which will not cause the receiving circuit to act in an erroneous manner. Generally the range of voltages accepted by a logic circuit as a particular logic state, do not exactly coincide with the band of voltages output by that family for the same state. The slack between them is known as the static or d.c. noise immunity.

As an example, the noise immunity for 74ALS series TTL is illustrated in the band diagram of Fig. 3.24. With this series, the High-state output is guaranteed to be above 2.5 V, whilst any input above 2 V is regarded as High. Thus up to 500 mV of noise in the High state will not cause malfunction. Similarly the maximum Low-state output is 0.4 V, but all input voltages below 0.8 V are regarded as Low. Thus 74ALS series TTL features a worst-case worst-case noise immunity of around $\frac{1}{2}$ V in both states. In practice this figure is pessimistic, and noise immunities of one volt are typical [14].

In the case of the 4000 and 74HC CMOS families, logic levels are within 0.1 V of the supply values. As can be seen from Fig. 3.14, the output changes state when the input approaches $\frac{1}{2}V_{DD}$. To allow for worst-case worst-case variations and pattern sensitivity, a band of voltages centered at this point of $\pm20\%$ V_{DD} is undefined. Any input voltage below $0.3V_{DD}$ is acceptable as a Low level, whilst an input above $0.7V_{DD}$ is a valid High level. Thus noise immunity in each state is 30% of V_{DD}. This gives a 1.5 V worst-case worst-case immunity with a 5 V supply and 5.4 V for 4000 series operated at a 18 V supply.

Example 3.5

A series 74LS gate is to drive a 74HC input, both circuits powered by 5 V. Determine the noise immunities.

Solution

For CMOS running at a supply of 5 V, any voltage below 1.5 V will be regarded as Low. Thus the Low noise immunity is $V_{OL(min,74LS)} - V_{IL(max,74HC)}$ is $0.5 - 1.5 = 1$ V. However, CMOS requires a High level of 3.5 V, and as $V_{OH(min,74LS)}$ is 2.7 V, we have a negative High immunity of -0.8 V. Thus a 74LS High will not necessarily be recognized as such by 74HC.

The situation presented here is unduly gloomy, as the 74LS ratings are quoted for the worst-case worst-case situation when driving 20 LSTTL loads. As CMOS takes virtually no current, $V_{OH(74LS)}$ is likely to be higher than 2.7 V. To ensure a satisfactory interface, a pull-up resistor (to +5 V) of nominally 10 kΩ at the output of the LS gate will bring $V_{OH(74LS)}$ close to 5 V. This will give a noise immunity

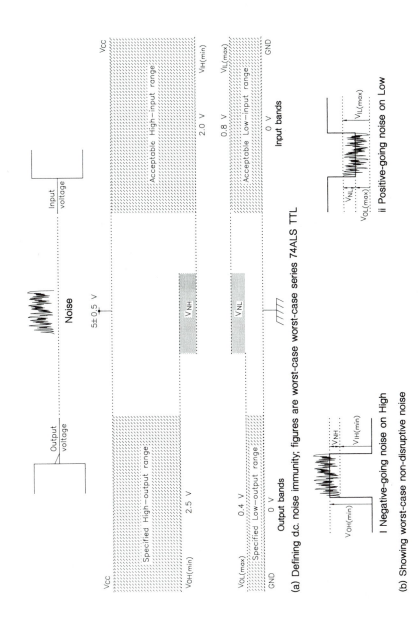

(a) Defining d.c. noise immunity; figures are worst-case worst-case series 74ALS TTL

(b) Showing worst-case non-disruptive noise

Figure 3.24: Noise considerations in a logic circuit.

V_{NH} close to 1.5 V. Alternatively, CMOS series 74HCT is specifically designed with a lower input threshold voltage to match that of the bipolar 74 series, obviating the need to use a pull-up resistor.

The static noise immunity figures only apply to signal inputs. Another source of noise is through the power lines. Predicting noise immunity to this variety of disturbance is somewhat complex. However, the signal line values give a good guide to immunity to this type of noise.

The parameters discussed up to this point have been concerned with static or at the most, slowly changing values. The response of circuits to high-frequency or transient changes is equally important. These are grouped together as dynamic parameters.

Propagation delay, t_{pd} and Transition times, t_{tr}

Propagation delay is the lag between reception of the signal and the correct response at the output. The oscillograph of Fig. 2.52(c) shows real signals, whilst the idealized waveforms of Fig. 3.25 illustrates how this parameter is measured. Normally this is from the 50% point of the input to the similar output point. The delays from High to Low (t_{PHL}) and Low to High (t_{PLH}) frequently differ; thus in Fig. 3.11, $t_{PLH(max)} = 11$ ns and $t_{PHL(max)} = 8$ ns for the 74ALS00 gate.

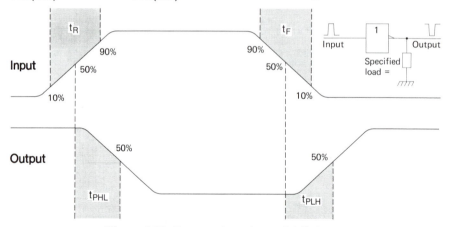

Figure 3.25: Propagation, rise and fall times.

Buffered CMOS families have balanced output drives, which in turn give similar symmetrical propagation delays; hence the t_{PHL} and t_{PLH} figures for the 74HC02 of Fig. 3.15 are identical. Families which have asymmetrical logic thresholds sometimes quote propagation delay figures from these points, rather than 50%. Thus t_{PD} for the 74HCT family are measured from the reference level of 1.3 V.

The **transition time** of a pulse waveform is measured as the delay in changing between 90% and 10% of the steady state values. The rise time is symbolized as t_r or t_{TLH} and fall time t_f or t_{THL}. As for propagation delay; buffered CMOS families have similar rise and fall times, whilst bipolar devices usually have shorter fall times.

Both transient parameters are greatly influenced by the load capacitance. In families which quote a maximum current-limited fan-out, switching times are normally given for this situation. For example, the times given in Fig. 3.11 for the 74ALS00 where for a load of 50 pF in parallel with a 500 Ω resistor. For CMOS families, where inputs take virtually no current, the load is normally given as a simple 50 pF capacitor. As a 74HC input presents a typical capacitance of 3.5 pF, this implies a loading of 14 gates. Of course this ignores wiring capacitance and (if applicable) the capacitance of the instrument's probe taking the measurement.

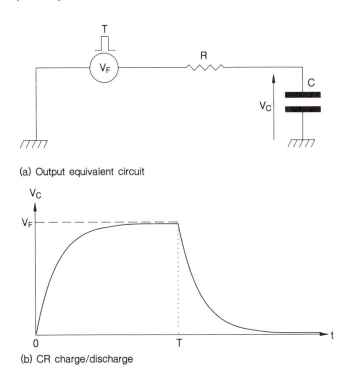

(a) Output equivalent circuit

(b) CR charge/discharge

Figure 3.26: Calculating propagation delays.

A simple model of a logic output is shown in Fig. 3.26(a). We have for a 1st order CR network:

$$V_C = V_F(1 - e^{-\frac{t}{\tau}})$$

where V_C = capacitor (output) voltage,
V_F = final (steady-state) capacitor voltage
and τ = time constant CR

The overall delay is equal to the intrinsic delay (due to internal charge storage and capacitance) plus the time to charge up the load capacitance to 50% of V_F.

$$V_F/2 = V_F(1 - e^{\frac{-t_{pd}}{\tau}})$$
$$e^{\frac{-t_{pd}}{\tau}} = 0.5$$
$$t_{pd} = -\tau \ln 0.5 = CR \ln 2 = 0.69CR$$

where t_{pd} is the charging delay or rise time (i.e. t_{PLH}). By symmetry the same delay results during discharge, to give t_{PHL}. In a similar manner the lag between the 10% and 90% points, i.e. the transition time, is given as:

$$t_{tr} = CR(\ln 10 - \ln \frac{10}{9}) = 2.2CR$$

Example 3.6

CMOS logic circuits have a negligible input current requirement, and therefore a theoretically large d.c. fan-out. In practice there is an upper limit due to the driven input and interconnection capacitances, which can be taken as nominally 5 pF each. Large fan-outs will hence give rise to long propagation delays and transition time.

A certain series 74HC output has a worst-case worst-case output resistance of 300 Ω at a supply of 4.5 V and an intrinsic propagation delay of 5 ns. Determine the maximum dynamic fan-out if the total delay is not to be more than 40 ns.

Solution

The additional delay is 35 ns:

$$0.69CR = 35 \times 10^{-9} \text{ seconds}$$
$$C = 170 \text{ pF}$$
$$\text{Dynamic fan-out} = \frac{170}{5} = 34$$

Example 3.7

A passive output has a pull-up resistor of 2 kΩ and a Low-level On resistance of 25 Ω. Determine the two propagation delays when feeding into a 100 pF capacitive load. The intrinsic propagation delay is 25 ns.

Solution

$$t_{PHL \text{ (switch On)}} = t_{PDI} + CR_1 \ln 2 \approx 27 \text{ ns} \quad (R_1 = 25 \text{ } \Omega)$$
$$t_{PLH \text{ (switch Off)}} = t_{PDI} + CR_2 \ln 2 \approx 160 \text{ ns} \quad (R_2 = 2 \text{ k}\Omega)$$

In practice the turn-On behavior of transistor switches is more complex than indicated here [15]. However, as a general rule the passive pull-up structure features a shorter turn-On delay as compared to turn-Off. We also see the potential superiority of a push-pull output with small output resistances in both levels.

The output resistance is rarely directly quoted by manufactures. Instead the maximum output current is sometimes given as a parameter which can be used to calculate capacitor charging time. Although our model is of limited practical use, it does predict that increasing capacitance raises transition times and propagation delays. This may be shown in data sheets as a graph, such as illustrated in

Fig. 3.27(a). Here 74HC maximum propagation delay is shown increasing approximately 1 ns for each additional 8 pF. Output transition times are given as typically 6.6 ns + 0.12 ns/δpF, where δpF is the excess over 50 pF load.

In families that have a range of supply values, propagation delay/transition times are dramatically affected by this parameter. Thus t_{pd} for 74HC is quoted as 125 ns max at $V_{CC} = 2$ V and 21 ns at 6 V (see Fig. 3.15). This is because the internal currents (the resistance in Fig. 3.28) are greater and capacitance charge/discharge times lower, for higher values of V_{CC}.

Dynamic Power Dissipation

We have already observed that the power dissipated can be calculated by multiplying the supply current by supply voltage, i.e. $I_{CC} \times V_{CC}$. For a series 74ALS gate, this is typically around 1.2 mW, and for the 74AS, around 8.5 mW. Generally faster bipolar TTL families have lower internal resistances which gives larger currents and hence higher power dissipation.

As the operating frequency rises, so does the power consumed by the circuit. TTL circuits have a relatively large quiescent power dissipation, so this dynamic component can be ignored below around 1 MHz. This is indicated by the flat portion of the 74LS00 curves of Fig. 3.27(c). However, the quiescent dissipation of CMOS logic families is virtually negligible, typically 2.5 nW for a series 74HC gate. In this case the actual dissipation is virtually proportional to frequency.

The most important mechanism leading to this phenomena, is the power lost in the output resistance when charging and discharging load capacitance. Consider the equivalent circuit of Fig. 3.28. When the capacitor is charged up to V volts (switch opens), $\frac{1}{2}CV^2$ Joules of energy is stored. Energy is dissipated in the load by this charging current as follows:

Initial charging current $(V_c = 0)$: $i_o = V/R_L$

Instantaneous current : $i_c = i_o e^{-\frac{t}{\tau}}$

Instantaneous power in R_L : $i_o^2 R_L e^{-2\frac{t}{\tau}} = V^2/R_L e^{-2\frac{t}{\tau}}$

Total energy dissipated in R_L : $E = V^2/R_L \int_0^\infty e^{-2\frac{t}{\tau}} dt$

$$= V^2/R_L \left| -\frac{\tau}{2} e^{-2\frac{t}{\tau}} \right|_0^\infty$$

$$= V^2/R_L (\frac{\tau}{2}) = \frac{1}{2}CV^2$$

Thus in going High, $\frac{1}{2}CV^2$ Joules are dissipated in the load resistance (irrespective of the value R_L!) and $\frac{1}{2}CV^2$ Joules is stored in the capacitor field. On discharge, this stored energy is dissipated in $R_S//R_L$ (once again irrespective of value). The energy dissipated in one switching cycle is then CV^2 Joules. The total power used by a function is this figure multiplied by the number of cycles per second ($CV^2 f$), plus any quiescent dissipation.

A logic function will exhibit a frequency dependent power dissipation, even if not driving a load. This is due to its intrinsic capacitance; denoted as C_{pd} in the data sheets of Fig. 3.15 and 3.20. Here a typical value of 22 pF per gate is given for the 74HC02/74HC125 (see also Note 1 on Fig. 3.20).

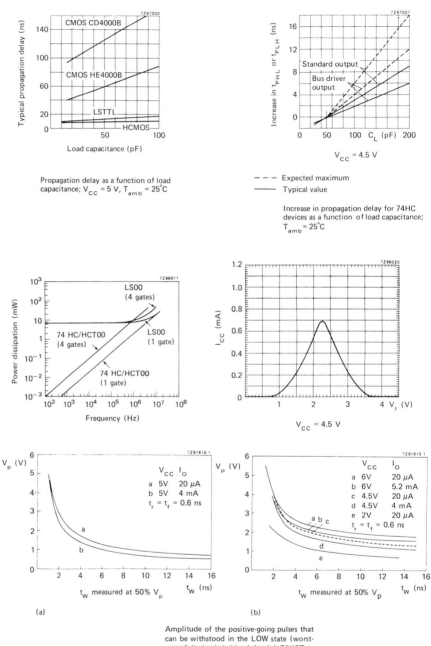

Figure 3.27:   Some   dynamic   characteristics.   Reproduced   by   courtesy   of
Philips/Signetics Components Ltd.

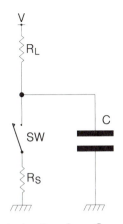

Figure 3.28: Equivalent output circuit, where C represents both intrinsic and external load capacitance.

Example 3.8

The maximum quiescent dissipation for a HCMOS gate is given as 10 μW at $V_{CC} =$ 5 V and a temperature of 25°C (the typical value is 2.5 nW) with a worst-case worst-case value of 30 μW. If such a gate is to be operated at 100 kHz with a fan-out of ten, determine the total dissipation.

Solution

If we take a typical unit HCMOS fan-in as 5 pF, including interconnection capacitance, we have a total capacitance of 22 pF (intrinsic) + 50 pF load. This gives:

$$P_{ac} = CV_{DD}^2 f = (72 \times 10^{-12}) \times 25 \times 10^5 = 180 \ \mu W$$

This is five times the worst-case worst-case quiescent dissipation and nearly 10^5 times the typical 25°C value.

It follows from the results of this example that quiescent dissipation figures given for CMOS functions are misleading, and are only useful as an indication of standby requirements. Above around 10 MHz, they tend to use more power than their TTL cousins. Nevertheless, typical CMOS-implemented systems tend to use an order of magnitude less power than a bipolar-based equivalent.

Push-pull output structures also dissipate energy due to transconductance or **overlap** power dissipation. This arises because of overlap of the two switches when changing state; during which time both switches may be conducting for a short period, eg. 7 ns for the standard 74 series TTL. This gives a transient path to ground. The resulting short current spikes can account for a significant portion of dynamic dissipation, as well as generating noise on the power supply lines.

Overlap dissipation considerably increases when the function is being driven by signals with long rise and fall times. This is due to the greater time spent in the

Comparison of CMOS and TTL technologies;
supply voltage V_{CC} = 5 V; ambient temperature T_{amb} = 25 °C; load capacitance C_L = 15 pF

parameters	family	HCMOS 74HC	metal gate CMOS 4000 CD	4000 HE	standard TTL 74	low-power Schottky TTL 74LS	Schottky TTL 74S	advanced low-power Schottky TTL 74ALS	advanced Schottky TTL 74AS	Fairchild advanced Schottky TTL 74F
Power dissipation, typ. (mW)										
Gate	static	0.0000025	0.001		10	2	19	1.2	8.5	5.5
Gate	dynamic @ 100 kHz	0.075	0.1		10	2	19	1.2	8.5	5.5
Counter	static	0.000005	0.001		300	100	500	60	–	190
Counter	dynamic @ 100 kHz	0.125	0.120		300	100	500	60	–	190
Propagation delay (ns)										
Gate	typical	8	94	40	10	9.5	3	4	1.5	3
Gate	maximum	14	190	80	20	15	5	7	2.5	4
Delay/power product (pJ)										
Gate	at 100 kHz	0.52	9	4	100	19	57	4.8	13	16.5
Maximum clock frequency (MHz)										
D-type flip-flop	typical	55	4	12	25	33	100	60	160	125
D-type flip-flop	minimum	30	2	6	15	25	75	40	–	100
Counter	typical	45	2	6	32	32	70	45	–	125
Counter	minimum	25	1	3	25	25	40	–	–	100
Output drive (mA)										
	standard outputs	4	0.51	0.8	16	8	20	8	20	20
	bus outputs	6	1.6		48	24	64	24	48	64
Fan-out (LS-loads)										
	standard outputs	10	1	2	40	20	50	20	50	50
	bus outputs	15	4		120	60	160	60	120	160

Table 3.2: Comparison of CMOS and TTL technologies. Reproduced by courtesy of Philips/Signetics Components Ltd.

linear region. As can be seen from Fig. 3.27(c), when the input is in the undefined band (see Fig. 3.14), a considerable supply current flows. If the input transition time is longer than the millisecond thermal time constant of the IC, then the peak (not average) power dissipation must be used in assessing the thermal safety of the chip. The allowable dissipation is typically about 200 mW, but it must be remembered that there may be several gates dissipating energy on the one chip.

Because of energy considerations and the danger of instability when gates are in their linear region, signals with slow transition times should always be avoided. A good rule of thumb is that transition times should not exceed ten times the worst-case t_{pd}. For sequential logic, where cascaded functions are clocked at the one time (such as a shift register; see Section 4.3.1), the transition times should not be longer than twice the propagation delay. Schmitt trigger gates are available to convert slow transition times to sharp edges, see Example 3.28.

Dynamic Noise Immunity

The figures previously given for static noise immunity hold until noise pulse widths approaching the propagation delay/transition time of the circuit. We see from Fig. 3.27(e) that short noise spikes tend to be ignored. Thus for example, at a 6 V supply, the HCMOS noise immunity rises from 1.8 V (30% V_{CC}) to around 5 V for a 2 ns wide spike. This rise is due to the finite time needed to charge and discharge internal capacitances. With this in mind, it is usually best to use a slow-speed family in a noisy environment, assuming speed of response is not critical.

The concept of voltage noise immunity is of only partial use in predicting the susceptibility of logic elements to externally induced noise. Of more relevance, but less well documented, is the **energy immunity**, E_N. This is the energy of a noise spike of duration τ which will just cause a malfunction. It is defined as:

$$E_N = \int_0^\tau V_N I_N \, dt$$

where I_N is the current which must be provided by the noise source for a time τ, in order to induce into the system sufficient noise voltage to overcome the voltage noise immunity, V_N.

Essentially the concept of energy noise immunity accounts not only for the noise voltage figure, but also for the input and output impedance levels of the family. Small values of impedances, as exhibited by totem-pole outputs, will require that the noise source supply comparatively higher currents to induce deleterious noise voltages. For fast logic, the characteristic impedance of interconnecting lines is of importance. The family speed characteristic is also accounted for, as V_N begins to increase at longer values of τ for slow as compared to fast families. Thus the noise source must provide more energy in the former case to cause disruption. More details are given in reference [11].

3.2 Combinational MSI Circuitry

Although gates are the fundamental building blocks of logic circuitry, some of the functions built up from gates are sufficiently general-purpose to be worth producing in the form of an integrated circuit. Such gate-based functions with a complexity of up to around 100 gates are known as **medium-scale integration (MSI)**.

Most current logic designs make considerable use of MSI catalog parts. Although the chip cost may be similar to an equivalent SSI gate implementation, there are many advantages in taking this approach. Reliability will be considerably enhanced due to the smaller number of external connections. The overall cost will be reduced due to the decrease in size of the PCB, power supply and testing complexity.

There are two approaches to an MSI system implementation. One of these is the traditional method of using a truth table to generate a series of logic equations. Certain MSI functions, such as decoders and multiplexers, are sufficiently flexible to be able to directly implement such equations. Thus the overall approach is the same as that adopted in Chapter 2.

An alternative course partitions the system into a series of interlinking functional blocks. If the partitioning is efficiently done, most of these functions can be directly implemented by standard catalog parts; such as adders, data selectors, shift registers and counters. It is rarely possible to partition a system as cleanly as this, and in practice a mixture of MSI functions glued together with SSI gates is used.

Traditionally, custom and semi-custom integrated circuit designs are based on a fundamental gate configuration (see Section 3.3.1) , the gates of course being implemented in an area of silicon as part of the overall chip. Whilst this is the most silicon-efficient approach, many computer-aided design packages in this area define MSI-level complexity circuits as macros. This approach is sometimes known as standard cell. So the design technique is not dissimilar to using discrete MSI. This considerably reduces the design complexity and enhances the possibility of getting it correct the first time! This is especially important, given the time involved in doing a software simulation and the cost of doing a trial fabrication.

Although a system functional partition has many advantages, this approach is heuristic and hence lacks the exactness of the mathematical method. For its efficient application, the designer must have an extensive knowledge of the characteristics of available devices. The objectives of this section is therefore to familiarize the reader with the various classifications of catalog combinational MSI functions, as well as illustrating the generalized mathematical techniques which are available. We will return to this theme in Chapter 4 where we examine sequential functions.

After reading this section, you should:

- Be aware of the function and symbology of natural and 7-segment decoders.

- Be able to create a natural decoder of any size using standard-parts.

- Understand the function and symbology of a priority encoder.

- Understand the function and symbology of multiplexers and decoders; in particular the correspondence between a decoder and demultiplexer.

- Be able to create any arbitrary combinational function using MSI parts.

- Know how to cascade 1-bit adders to n-bits using both ripple and parallel carry techniques.

- Appreciate the function and symbology of arithmetic logic units and comparators in generating combinational logic and arithmetic functions.

3.2.1 Decoders and Encoders

The category **decoder** (sometimes just coder) strictly encompasses any circuit converting from one code to another. This is not a very useful categorization, as it covers just about all combinational circuits. The largest subdivision of this class, is the **natural decoder**. These map each state of an X-bit input to a unique one of a set of Y output lines. Thus each input code combination, or state, addresses just one unary output state.

The logic of the binary to unary code converter is simple. Each defined code combination (2^X maximum) is detected as a product term. Thus in a 3-line (binary) to 8-line (unary) decoder there would be eight AND gates; one for each input state from 000 (gate $0 = \overline{A_2} \cdot \overline{A_1} \cdot \overline{A_0}$) to 111 (gate $7 = A_2 \cdot A_1 \cdot A_0$). A practical realization of a 3 to 8-line MSI decoder is shown Fig. 3.29. The 74x138 uses NAND gates to implement the decoding strategy, which gives active-Low outputs. An an example, in Fig. 3.29(a) we show line 5 (HLH) being activated, with all other outputs remaining in their inactive High state. This assumes that the internal Enable line (**EN**) is High; otherwise all outputs are inactive, irrespective of input code. In order to enable the decoder, the external Enable inputs E3 E2 $\overline{\text{E1}}$ must be High High Low respectively.

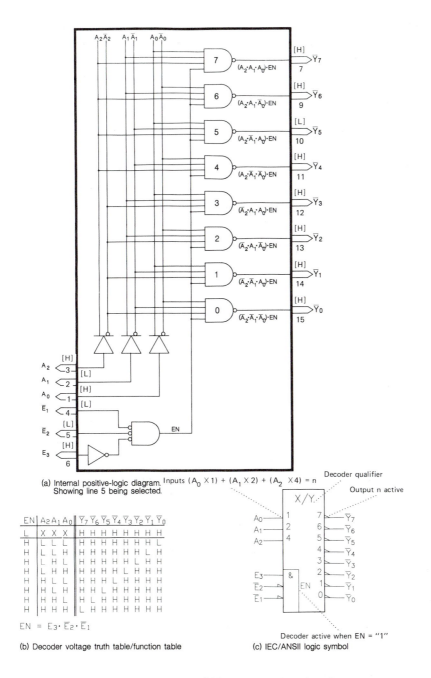

(a) Internal positive-logic diagram. Inputs $(A_0 \times 1) + (A_1 \times 2) + (A_2 \times 4) = n$
Showing line 5 being selected.

EN	$A_2 A_1 A_0$			$\bar{Y}_7 \bar{Y}_6 \bar{Y}_5 \bar{Y}_4 \bar{Y}_3 \bar{Y}_2 \bar{Y}_1 \bar{Y}_0$							
L	X	X	X	H	H	H	H	H	H	H	H
H	L	L	L	H	H	H	H	H	H	H	L
H	L	L	H	H	H	H	H	H	H	L	H
H	L	H	L	H	H	H	H	H	L	H	H
H	L	H	H	H	H	H	H	L	H	H	H
H	H	L	L	H	H	H	L	H	H	H	H
H	H	L	H	H	H	L	H	H	H	H	H
H	H	H	L	H	L	H	H	H	H	H	H
H	H	H	H	L	H	H	H	H	H	H	H

$EN = E_3 \cdot \bar{E}_2 \cdot \bar{E}_1$

(b) Decoder voltage truth table/function table

(c) IEC/ANSII logic symbol

Figure 3.29: The 74ALS/AS138 3 to 8-line decoder.

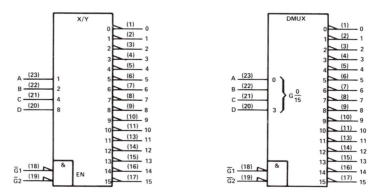

SN74ALS154
4-LINE TO 16-LINE DECODERS/DEMULTIPLEXERS

D2990, DECEMBER 1986

- Ideal for High-Performance Memory Decoding

- Decodes 4 Binary-Coded Inputs into One of 16 Mutually Exclusive Outputs

- Performs the Demultiplexing Function by Distributing Data from Two ANDed Input Lines to Any One of 16 Outputs

- Input-Clamping Diodes Simplify System Design

- High Fan-Out, Low-Impedance Totem-Pole Outputs

- Package Options Include Plastic "Small Outline" Packages and Standard Plastic 300-mil DIPs

DW OR NT PACKAGE
(TOP VIEW)

```
  0 [ 1   U 24 ] VCC
  1 [ 2     23 ] A
  2 [ 3     22 ] B
  3 [ 4     21 ] C
  4 [ 5     20 ] D
  5 [ 6     19 ] G2
  6 [ 7     18 ] G1
  7 [ 8     17 ] 15
  8 [ 9     16 ] 14
  9 [ 10    15 ] 13
 10 [ 11    14 ] 12
GND [ 12    13 ] 11
```

description

Each of these monolithic, 4-line-to-16-line decoders utilizes TTL circuitry to decode four binary-coded inputs into one of sixteen mutually exclusive outputs when both the strobe inputs, $\overline{G}1$ and $\overline{G}2$, are low. The demultiplexing function is performed by using the four input lines to address the output line, passing data from one of the strobe inputs with the other strobe input low. When either strobe input is high, all outputs are high. These demultiplexers are ideally suited for implementing high-performance memory decoders.

These circuits are fully compatible for use with most other TTL circuits. All inputs are buffered and input-clamping diodes are provided to minimize transmission-line effects and thereby simplify system design.

The SN74ALS154 is characterized for operation from 0°C to 70°C.

logic symbols † (alternatives)

†These symbols are in accordance with ANSI/IEEE Std 91-1984 and IEC Publication 617-12.

TEXAS INSTRUMENTS

Figure 3.30: The SN74ALS154 4 to 16-line decoder (*continued next page*).

logic diagram

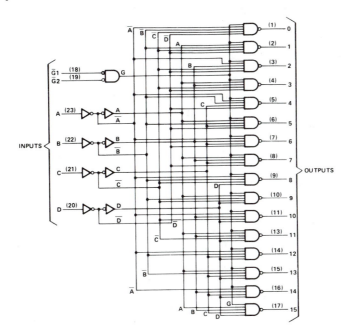

Pin numbers shown on logic notation are for J or N packages

switching characteristics

PARAMETER	FROM (INPUT)	TO (OUTPUT)	TEST CONDITIONS	$V_{CC} = 5$ V, $C_L = 50$ pF, $R_L = 500$ Ω, $T_A = 25$ °C		$V_{CC} = 4.5$ V to 5.5 V, $C_L = 50$ pF, $R_L = 500$ Ω, $T_A = $ MIN to MAX		UNIT
				TYP	MAX	MIN	MAX	
t_{PLH}	A, B, C, D	Any		7	11	3	12	ns
t_{PHL}			See Note 3	7	11	3	12	
t_{PLH}	Strobe	Any		7	11	3	12	ns
t_{PHL}				7	11	3	12	

Note 3: Load circuit and voltage waveforms are shown in Section 1.

Figure 3.30: (*continued*). The SN74ALS154 4 to 16-line decoder. Courtesy of Texas Instruments Ltd.

In the specific case of the ALS and AS versions of the x138 decoder; address variables are buffered by complementary-output gates. This decreases delay differences between true and complements of the same variables and hence reduces hazard glitches at the output. Notice the alternative symbology used for such gates, as compared to that shown in Fig. 2.53. All MSI circuits are buffered at their input to reduce loading on driver circuits. However, such complementary-output buffer gates are relatively rare. For example the sequential arrangement shown for the Texas Instruments SN74ALS154 in Fig. 3.30 is more usual; even the 74LS138 uses this approach.

The IEC/ANSI qualifier for a decoder is **X/Y**, signifying a conversion from code **X** to code **Y**. Sometimes the **X** and **Y** are substituted by code names. Thus the 74x138 is often labelled **BIN/OCT** (for binary to octal). Inputs are represented by numbers, normally the weightings of the code (4-2-1 in this case). If not weighted, these numbers can be arbitrary assigned. In a natural code, the input worth n (the internal state-number) resulting from an input pattern is transformed to the output line labelled with the same number **n**. For example; the input state $101b$ gives an internal number n of $4 + 1 = 5$. This in turn selects the output labelled **5**. In more complex cases, this internal number may refer to an accompanying truth table. An example of this is shown in Fig. 3.38.

Most decoders have one or more enabling inputs. We have already discussed the **EN** dependency in Section 2.2. In Fig. 3.29(c) it is shown as the output of an embedded AND gate, with two active-Low and one active-High inputs.

Catalog MSI decoders normally come in 2 to 4-line (dual), 3 to 8-line or 4 to 16-line varieties. An example of the former is shown in Fig. 2.16; although there it was called a demultiplexer and uses a different symbol (see Section 3.2.2). Part of the data sheet for the SN74ALS154 4 to 16-line (**BIN/HEX**) decoder is shown in Fig. 3.30. Here the internal **EN** is the AND function of two active-Low **Enable** inputs. Of the two IEC/ANSI logic symbols shown, the one with the **X/Y** qualifier is the one relevant to the use of this circuit as a decoder. Texas Instruments label their **Enable** inputs with **G**, as their function is really that of Gate dependency.

By using the enabling facility, decoder arrays of any size may be fabricated, as is shown in the following example.

Example 3.9

As part of a display system, one of 64 lines is to be selected from a microprocessor-based system, by sending out a naturally-coded binary line number. Show how this could be done using standard MSI decoder parts.

Solution

To provide 64 lines, four 4 to 16-line decoders are needed. These are shown in Fig. 3.31, addressed in parallel by the four least significant of the 6-bit input address. Which of these four are selected for any input is decided by a single 2 to 4-line pre-select decoder. Thus for any given 2-bit higher address F E, only one group of 16 lines is enabled. The one chosen within this group is decided by the lower address D C B A. The example shows address HL LHLH (10 0101b for positive logic),

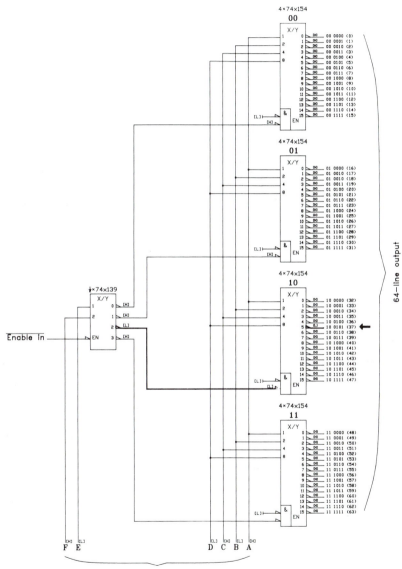

Figure 3.31: Expanding decoder circuits.

which selects output line 37. Now 37 is $32 + 5$. Thirty-two selects decoder $10b$ and five selects output $0101b$ of that group.

This 2-level topography can be extended to an 8 to 256-line capacity. Higher values are obtainable by in turn expanding the pre-select decoder. Can you draw a 10 to 1024 line decoder using 68 74x154 and $\frac{1}{2}$ 74x139 decoder chips! For large arrays like this a 2-dimensional XY crossover topography is preferred. What size of decoder would be needed to select one interstice of a square 32×32 matrix and what would have to lie at each crossover? See Fig. 4.44 for a simple example.

A decoder's enable input may be used to sample or strobe an output at specific instances of time. This avoids output glitches when an input change is skewed (not all inputs bit changing instantaneously). Even when there is no so called function hazard, narrow glitches can occur due to differing delays through internal logic paths. For example, the Texas SN74154 has differential delays up to 5 ns [16].

A natural decoder can be perceived as generating all primitive product terms of the input (i.e. select) variables. Thus any sum of products (SOP) function can be implemented by addressing the decoder with the input variables and ORing the relevant output lines. Thus the SOP function $\sum 0, 6, 7, 8$ is produced using a 3 to 8-line decoder and OR gate to give $\mathcal{F} = Y_0 + Y_6 + Y_7 + Y_8$. Some examples will clarify.

Example 3.10

Implement the π generator of Example 2.38 using a 74x154 4 to 16-line decoder together with appropriate gates.

Solution

As shown in Fig. 3.32, each output is simply the logic summation of the p-terms making up that function. As catalog decoders invariably have active-Low outputs, I have balanced this by using active-Low input OR gates, i.e. NAND gates (see Fig. 2.26), as the summers. Generating Z as the inverse of $\overline{Z}$ reduces the gate requirement from 12 to four input plus an inverter.

It is interesting to compare the implementations of Figs. 2.49(d) and 3.32 as regards cost. Using standard 74LS parts; a 74LS154 costs around four times a SSI gate package, such as a 74LS00. At the time of writing, the 100-off price of an SSI gate IC is around $0.18. On this basis the entirely SSI solution would cost $1.40; as would the MSI implementation. However, the real expense (taking factors such as the PCB, power supply, testing costs into account) is more nearly related to the number of ICs; irrespective of their price. On this basis, the MSI implementation costs five ICs against a 9-IC SSI cost — a saving of around 45%.

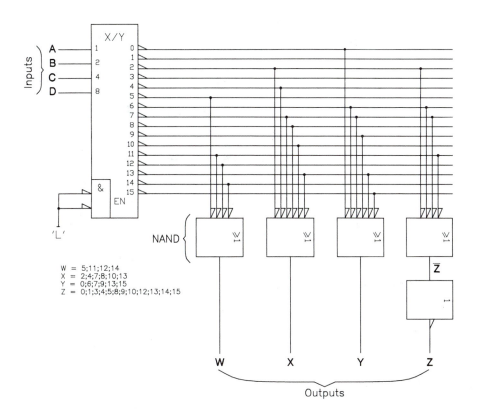

Figure 3.32: A decoder implementation of a π generator.

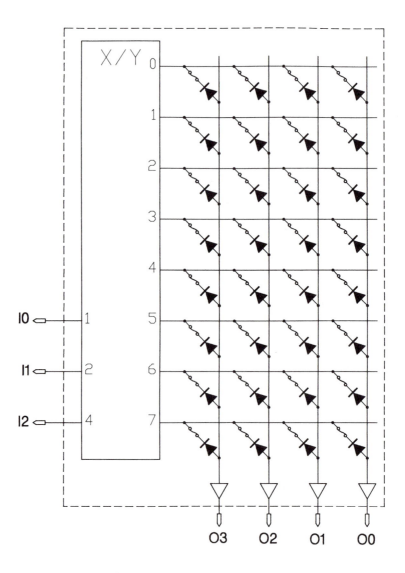

Figure 3.33: A hypothetical PLE, storing eight 4-bit words.

An interesting possibility arises from the use of a decoder/gate array to implement combinational logic. From the layout of Fig. 3.32, a truly universal logic circuit may be designed. Such a circuit could be implemented on a double-sided printed-circuit board. The decoder would drive the horizontal conductors on one side, whilst an array of multi-input OR gates would be fed using vertical conductors on the opposite side of the board. Each universal circuit could be programmed by the user with pins shorting the appropriate horizontal and vertical conductors. The pattern of such pins defines the personality of the circuit. In its silicon guise, such a configuration is known as a **Programmable logic element (PLE)**. The hypothetical PLE shown in Fig. 3.33 uses a diode OR-gate array, with a fusible link in series with each diode. Any four 3-variable combinational logic functions can be implemented, simply by blowing the appropriate fuses.

The structure presented in Fig. 3.33 is similar to the diode matrices of Figs. 3.3 and 3.4. In the former case both AND and OR arrays are programmable. In the PLE the AND array (decoder) is fixed, with only the OR array being configurable. Commercially, the smallest PLE stores 32 words of 8-bits each, and can therefore implement any eight 5-variable combinational functions in a single 16-pin package, see Fig. 3.58. Section 3.3.2 looks at PLEs and the analogous programmable read-only memories (PROMs) in some detail.

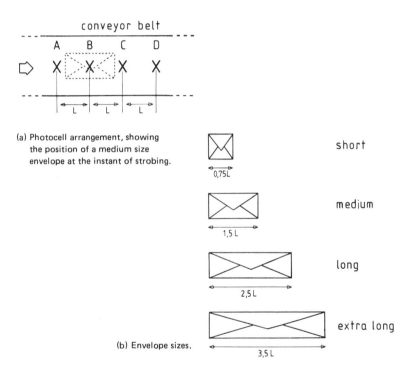

Figure 3.34: An automatic letter sorter.

Example 3.11

Envelopes of four lengths pass along a conveyer belt, as shown in Fig. 3.34(a). When the envelope passes over photocell **A**, a strobe pulse is generated. This causes the state of the photocells **B C D** to be stored in a 3-bit memory (register). Program the PLE shown in Fig. 3.33, to indicate which of the four sizes of envelopes has just passed **A**. You can assume that the envelopes are spaced at least 'extra-long' and that a covered photocell gives a logic 1 output.

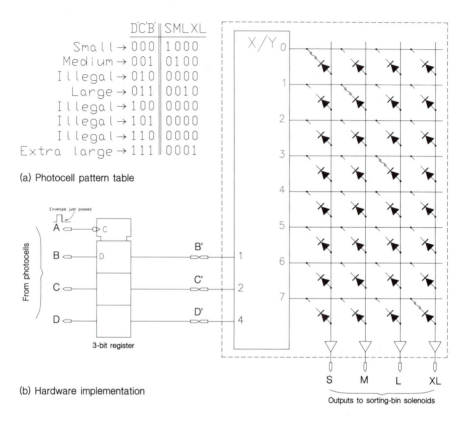

(a) Photocell pattern table

(b) Hardware implementation

Figure 3.35: Implementing the letter sorter.

The truth table of Fig. 3.35(a) shows the four legal patterns generated by the envelopes. These are the four legitimate patterns which should occur at the instant the back end of the envelope passes the **A** photocell. This pattern is held in the register (see Section 4.3.1) until the next event.

Each line in the truth table translates to the like-numbered line of diodes in the PLE (see also Fig. 3.58). A missing diode (fuse blown) can be assumed to give a Low output (pull-down resistor not shown) whilst an intact fuse gives a High output when selected. A comparison of the fuse pattern in Fig. 3.35(b) with the 1s and 0s of the truth table outputs, gives a direct correspondence. Thus a PLE is a truth table on silicon.

In a configuration like this, there is no such thing as a don't care state. All lines of a truth table appear in the fuse pattern. I have programmed the PLE so that an illegal state (which should not occur) would not activate any output. Another approach to this problem is given in Example 5.31.

These last two examples used a decoder/gate array to directly implement the combinational equations. The alternative approach of adopting a system partition of functional blocks is best illustrated by illustration.

Example 3.12

Light-controlled pedestrian crossings in the U.K. (Pelican crossings) obey the following mode of operation:

1. The sequence of lights is initiated when a Cross_Request signal has been received and a predetermined period has elapsed since the last cycle. Any request arriving during this guard period is stored and acted upon in due course.

2. After the request has been granted, the lights operate according to the sequence: green → amber → red → flashing amber → green.

It is required to implement this sequence using a natural 4 to 16-line decoder addressed by a 4-bit BCD counter (see Section 4.2). Timing periods are to be 3-second amber, 15-second red and 9-second flashing-amber. The minimum green period is to be nominally two minutes. Thus traffic has priority (green). Assume that a 1-bit memory cell is available to store cross-requests, as are edge-detectors and gates. A monostable is to be used to give a nominal 2-minute guard time between pedestrian cycles (see Example SAE 3.1).

Solution

A sequence truth table is shown in Fig. 3.36(a). As green is state 9, nine states remain for the pedestrian sequence. If the counting rate is 3 seconds, then the timing periods are correct.

The Cross_Request signal sets (S) the memory cell, which gates the 3-second period oscillator (a clock in digital terminology), through to the 10-state counter. Assuming that the counter is in state 9 (1001), then it will advance through states 0 back up again in 3-second duration steps. As it does so, the relevant decoder output is activated. These unary state outputs are ORed thus:

> Red   = states 1,2,3,4,5.
> Amber = state 0, or states 6,7,8 ANDed with the flashing clock.

When the counter reaches state 9 again, a 120 s-duration monostable is triggered. This both resets (R) the memory cell and also directly inhibits the 3 s counter clock. Any Cross_Request command received after this event sets the memory cell again, but this is locked out from the counter until the 120 s guard period has elapsed.

This example is a precursor for the sequential systems to be examined in subsequent chapters. It is sequential, in that events progress step by step. The 1-bit memory cell used here as a status flag is a typical sequential building block, as is the counter. Both are constructed with bistable elements known as latches or flip flops. Another approach to this problem is given in Examples 4.33 & SAE 5.12

It would be possible to enhance the system by using sensors aimed at the approaching cars (typically using the doppler effect). If no car has approached in the

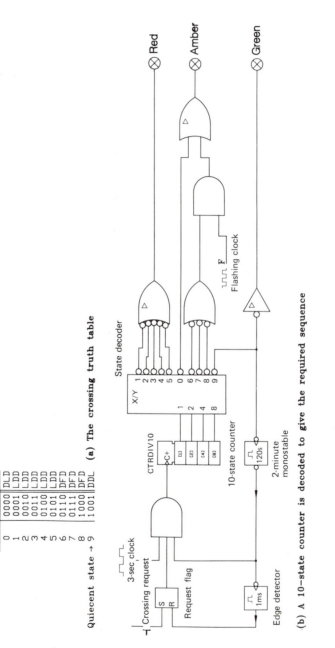

State	DCBA	RED AMBER GREEN
0	0000	D L D
1	0001	L D D
2	0010	L D D
3	0011	L D D
4	0100	L D D
5	0101	L D D
6	0110	D F D
7	0111	D F D
8	1000	D F D
9	1001	D D L

Quiecent state → 9   **(a) The crossing truth table**

(b) A 10–state counter is decoded to give the required sequence

Figure 3.36: A Pelican pedestrian crossing timing control circuit.

last 30 seconds, the 2-minute guardspace could be cancelled. This would remove the element of pedestrian frustration when the signals refuse to change when the road is empty. How could you implement this strategy?

Circuits which generate code patterns suitable for alphanumeric displays are known as **display decoders**. These are generally more complex than natural unary decoders, and frequently include buffer/drivers suitable for opto-display devices.

One of the simplest display format uses seven segments to build up the ten decimal digits. A 7-segment font is shown in Fig. 2.51(b). Commercial MSI 7-segment decoders usually have additional features to improve the aesthetics and testability of the resulting display. Thus all three decoders in Fig. 3.37 feature a blanking input. When $\overline{\text{BI}}$ is Low, all open-collector outputs go into their Off state. By switching $\overline{\text{BI}}$ with a variable mark:space (High:Low) waveform faster than the persistence of vision (around 50 Hz), the apparent brightness of the display can be altered.

Lamp_Test ($\overline{\text{LT}}$) is the opposite to $\overline{\text{BI}}$, in that all outputs go into their active-Low state; overriding any pattern which should be generated from binary input D C B A. This provides a quick diagnostic check of the integrity of all display segments. A careful examination of the logic diagram shows that $\overline{\text{LT}}$ overrides $\overline{\text{BI}}$.

Ripple_Blanking_Input ($\overline{\text{RBI}}$) and Ripple_Blanking_Output ($\overline{\text{RBO}}$) are concerned with the suppression of leading (or trailing) zeros in a multi-digit readout. Consider the 10-digit display:

$$00505.70100$$

Aesthetically, the alternative:

$$505.701$$

is more pleasing. Notice how only leading and trailing zeros are blanked, and not the zeros in the body of the number. To do this, each digit-decoder must make the following deduction:

1. Is my leading (or trailing) digit blanked?

2. Is my decoded digit zero?

In Fig. 3.38(b) I have shown a 5-digit leading-zero suppressed display. Each decoder generates a $\overline{\text{RBO}}$ output, which is passed on to the next right $\overline{\text{RBI}}$. $\overline{\text{RBO}}$ is based on the above relationship, i.e. :

$$\overline{\text{RBO}} = \overline{\text{RBI}} \cdot (\overline{\text{D} \cdot \text{C} \cdot \text{B} \cdot \text{A}})$$

As shown, it is usual to exclude the first digit left (or right) of the decimal point; thus **0.36** instead of **.36**. Trailing-edge suppression, to the right of the decimal point, is done by reversing the chain direction.

The IEC/ANSII logic symbol for the 7446/47 IC is shown in Fig. 3.38. This is the first really complex symbol we have met, and is rather daunting at a first (and second!) glance. However, it can be broken down into its various components fairly

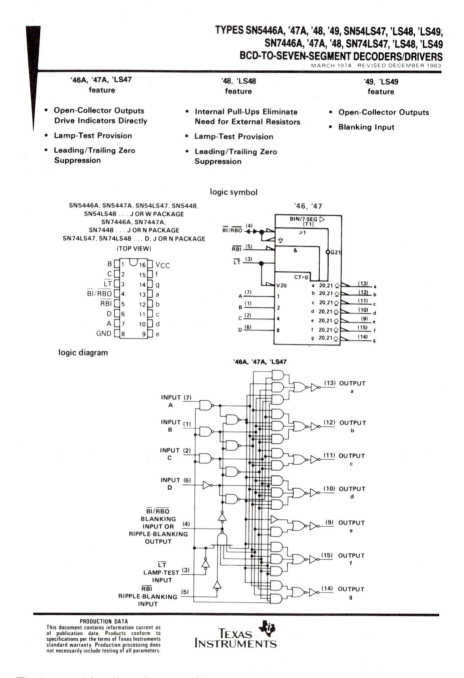

Figure 3.37: A collage from the SN7447 data sheet. Reproduced by courtesy of Texas Instruments Ltd.

readily. The qualifier is the normal decoder symbol, with the specific codes **BIN/7-SEG** replacing **X/Y**. The following ▷ buffer symbol indicates that the outputs have an enhanced drive capability — for example the 7447A can sink up to 40 mA and withstand a 15 V voltage, whilst the 7446A can withstand up to 30 V. All outputs are open-collector and active-Low. Under the decoder qualifier symbol the note **[T1]** refers to the code definition table, usually adjacent in the data sheet (see Table 1.3(d)). This table defines the relationship between inputs 8 4 2 1 and outputs g f e d c b a.

We must now account in the symbol for the control inputs $\overline{\text{LT}}$, $\overline{\text{RBI}}$ and $\overline{\text{BI}}/\overline{\text{RBO}}$. We note pin 4 can be used either as an input ($\overline{\text{BI}}$) or output ($\overline{\text{RBO}}$). This is shown as two separate lines coming together. $\overline{\text{RBO}}$ is open-collector but with an internal pull-up resistor (passive pull-up) to permit this dual function.

Besides its code letter designation, each output is qualified by two dependency numbers. Thus segment g is designated **g 20,21**. The comma indicates that *both* qualifiers are in series with **g**. An output will only 'do its own thing' if both qualifiers are in their enabling state. Qualifier **20** is an OR dependency of $\overline{\text{LT}}$. If $\overline{\text{LT}}$ is High, then **V20** is logic 0; which is the enabling state of the OR dependency (no lamp test). If $\overline{\text{LT}}$ is Low, then **V20** indicates that **20** is always logic 1 (the OR relationship). The logic of this is $(x+V20) \cdot G21$, i.e. segment x is the outcome of the internal logic for this segment ORed by **V20** followed by ANDing with **G21**.

Output qualifier **21** is a gate dependency generated by the blanking logic. When **G21** goes Low, its AND relationship is such that all internal outputs go Low (irrespective of **V20**, as ANDing with 0 always gives 0), and external outputs go Off. When $\overline{\text{LT}}$ is active, the blanking signal **G21** is simply the $\overline{\text{BI}}$ input. The zero suppression logic is thus disabled. Hence $\overline{\text{LT}}$ overrides the zero suppression function but is in turn overridden by $\overline{\text{BI}}$. We thus have for blanking:

$$(\overline{\text{RBI}} \text{ is Low AND (state} = 0000) \text{ AND } \overline{\text{LT}} \text{ is High)}$$

or else

$$\overline{\text{BI}} \text{ is externally Low, irrespective.}$$

This is generated as:

$$\overline{\text{RBI} \cdot \overline{\text{LT}} \cdot (\text{CT} = 0) + \text{BI}} = \text{G21}$$

where **CT = 0** indicates the internal state CoNtent (or count) is **0000**.

If $\overline{\text{LT}}$ is Low then **G21** is logic 0 only if $\overline{\text{BI}}$ is active. Otherwise the **21** qualifier is in its enabling state and gates through the logic 1 **V20** state. With all internal outputs logic 1, then all external outputs go Low and all segments light up.

In summary we have:

V20	G21	Internal O/P 20,21	Segment	State
0 (enable)	0 (disable)	0	Off	Blank I/P or zero suppress
0 (enable)	1 (enable)	Code	$\overline{\text{Code}}$	Display
1 (disable)	0 (disable)	0	Off	Blank I/P only
1 (disable)	1 (enable)	1	On	Lamp Test

The logic which defines **G21** is also that required for $\overline{\text{RBO}}$. It is shown in the diagram emerging from the OR gate on the left side, rather than the more traditional

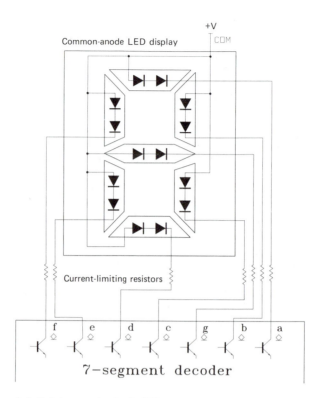

(a) Driving a typical LED display

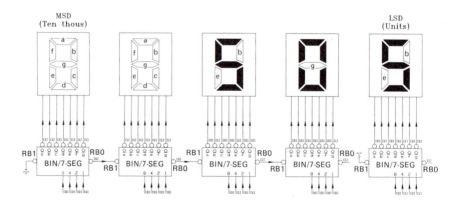

(b) A 5–decade leading–edge zero–supressed display. The LSD is not included
    in the supression chain, being presumed adjacent to the decimal point.

Figure 3.38: MSI 7-segment decoders

right side. This is done to more easily bring it together with the $\overline{\text{BI}}$ input. Its direction (right to left) is shown by the polarity symbol. If it were active-High and thus no polarity symbol used, an arrow-head should be used to indicate the non-standard signal direction (see Fig. 3.36(b)). Notice the two opposite arrow heads used to show bi-directionality at $\overline{\text{BI}}/\overline{\text{RBO}}$. The conventional signal flow directions are left to right and top to bottom.

The logic symbol described here is probably as complex a description as is useful. It does however illustrate that quite sophisticated functions can be successfully symbolized. More complex devices exist, but their representation is debatably of limited utility.

The last function covered in this section is known as a **priority encoder**. A priority encoder is a sort of natural decoder in reverse. Here n unary lines are decoded (or encoded) to its binary equivalent. In the case of a priority encoder, if more than one input line is active, then the highest of these is the one generating the binary equivalent code. For example, in Fig. 3.39, if lines 0 and 2 were simultaneously active, then the binary output would be $10b$. From the truth table we can deduce the logic relationships:

A_0 is active when line 3 is active or line 1 is active and neither line 2 or 3 is, i.e. $A_0 = 3 + 1 \cdot \overline{2} \cdot \overline{3}$.

A_1 is active when line 3 is active or line 2 is active and line 3 is not, i.e. $A_1 = 3 + \overline{3} \cdot 2$.

This gives the logic diagram of Fig. 3.39(b).

The IEC/ANSI logic symbol shown in Fig. 3.39(c) uses the normal decoder qualifying symbol, with **HPRI** indicating Highest PRIority. Input lines are labelled with their decimal significance, and outputs by their weights.

The same algorithm is used in the implementation of the SN74x148, as shown in the logic diagram of Fig. 3.40(a). Here there are eight unary lines being encoded to a 3-bit binary equivalent. Both inputs and outputs are active-Low, as shown by the polarity indicators in the IEC/ANSI logic symbols. The 74x147 encodes ten unary lines to their natural BCD equivalent, but does not have an input line 0 nor any provision for expansion.

Three control signals are provided in the 74x148 to give this expansion capability. These are $\overline{\text{Enable\_In}}$, $\overline{\text{Enable\_Out}}$ and $\overline{\text{Group\_Strobe}}$:

$\overline{\text{EI}}$ If High, all data and control outputs go to their inactive state (High).
$\overline{\text{EO}}$ Active when the 74x148 is enabled but *no* input line active.
$\overline{\text{GS}}$ Active when the 74x148 is enabled and *any* input lines active.

$\overline{\text{Group\_Strobe}}$ is normally the opposite of $\overline{\text{Enable\_Out}}$, but both are disabled when $\overline{\text{Enable\_In}}$ is High. This is shown in Fig. 3.40(b), where the **EN** dependency number α is shown for both $\overline{\text{EO}}$ and $\overline{\text{GS}}$ outputs. Dependency number β is shown as the result of ORing all input unary lines; i.e. β is logic 1 when *any* input lines are active. Thus output $\overline{\text{GS}}$ is active when the chip is enabled (α = enable) and any inputs are active (β = logic 1). $\overline{\text{EO}}$ is active when enabled (α = enable) and no inputs are active ($\overline{\beta}$ = logic 1). The α dependency number is also shown at each binary output. I have used α and β as dependency carriers rather than normal arabic numbers. This is to avoid confusion with the code input and output lines, which use number labels.

```
3 2 1 0 ‖ A₁ A₀
0 0 0 0 ‖ 0  0      ← No input active
0 0 0 1 ‖ 0  0      ← Input line 0 active
0 0 1 0 ‖ 0  1  ⎫
0 0 1 1 ‖ 0  1  ⎬   ← Input line 1 is highest active
0 1 0 0 ‖ 1  0  ⎫
0 1 0 1 ‖ 1  0  ⎪
0 1 1 0 ‖ 1  0  ⎬   ← Input line 2 is highest active
0 1 1 1 ‖ 1  0  ⎭
1 0 0 0 ‖ 1  1  ⎫
1 0 0 1 ‖ 1  1  ⎪
1 0 1 0 ‖ 1  1  ⎪
1 0 1 1 ‖ 1  1  ⎪
1 1 0 0 ‖ 1  1  ⎬   ← Input line 3 is highest active
1 1 0 1 ‖ 1  1  ⎪
1 1 1 0 ‖ 1  1  ⎪
1 1 1 1 ‖ 1  1  ⎭
```

(a) Truth table

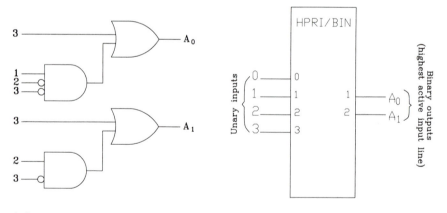

(b) Logic diagram   (c) IEC/ANSII logic symbol

Figure 3.39: The priority encoder.

TYPES SN54147, SN54148, SN54LS147, SN54LS148,
SN74147, SN74148 (TIM9907), SN74LS147, SN74LS148
10-LINE TO 4-LINE AND 8-LINE TO 3-LINE PRIORITY ENCODERS

logic diagram

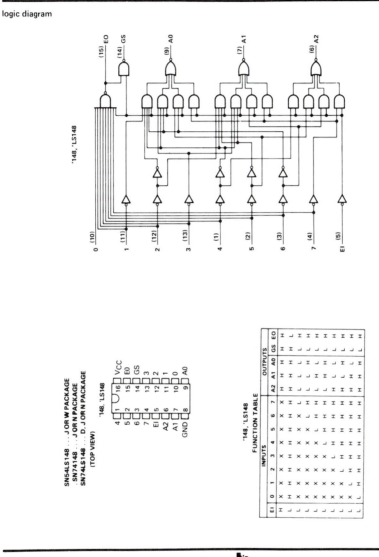

TEXAS
INSTRUMENTS

(a) Extract from the data sheet. Courtesy of Texas Instruments Ltd

Figure 3.40: The 74x147/148 priority encoders (*continued next page*).

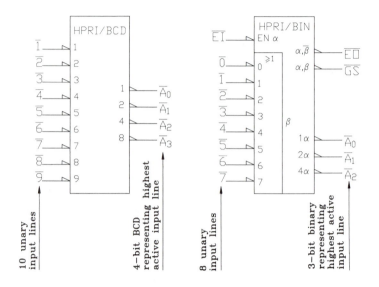

(b) IEC/ANSII symbols for MSI decoders

Figure 3.40: (*continued*). The 74x147/148 priority encoders.

Example 3.13

It is required to encode a hexadecimal keypad to active-High natural binary. As well as the data output, an active-Low control output is to indicate whenever any key is pressed.

Solution

The implementation shown in Fig. 3.41 is based on two 8 to 3-line 74x148 priority encoders. If any of the top eight keys (i.e. **8** to **F**) are pressed (go Low), then the upper encoder indicates both which one ($\overline{1A2}$ $\overline{1A1}$ $\overline{1A0}$) and brings its Enable_Out High. This feeds the lower encoder's Enable_In, and thus disables all bottom outputs. If no upper key is pressed, then the lower encoder is enabled and its binary outputs indicate the highest of the bottom keys which are pressed ($\overline{0A2}$ $\overline{0A1}$ $\overline{0A0}$).

As in any situation, only one priority encoder will have a non-zero binary output; these like bits are ORed together to give the bottom three binary outputs (remember that an active-Low input OR is an active-Low output AND, i.e. NAND). The upper and lower groups of keys can be distinguished by examining the state of $\overline{1EO}$. This is High for keys **8** ($1000b$) to **F** ($1111b$). Thus it directly generates the fourth binary bit B3.

If no key is closed, the output state B3 B2 B1 B0 is $0000b$. To distinguish between this and key **0** we need to generate a Key_Pressed indicator signal or strobe. One or both $\overline{GS}$ outputs will go Low if any key input is active. Thus we OR together $\overline{1GS}$

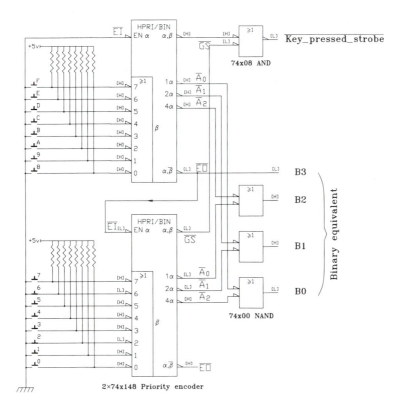

Figure 3.41: A simple hex keypad encoder. Showing key 6 pressed.

and $\overline{0\text{GS}}$ to give the requisite indicator. An AND gate is used, as both input and output signals are active-Low.

Although the logic of this circuit is impeccable, in a practical situation there will be problems. These are primarily due to switch bounce. When a metallic contact closes it will bounce for typically several ms. This will cause the strobe signal to similarly oscillate, as will the binary output lines. There are techniques for debouncing switches (see Fig. 4.62), but even with perfectly clean signals, the possibility exists of spurious outputs due to function hazards (i.e. due to differential delays).

The problem can be tackled using either software or hardware techniques. If the keypad encoder uses its strobe to interrupt a microprocessor, this can monitor the binary outputs and only accept them if, say, they are stable for 10 ms. In hardware this can be done by using two monostables. The strobe signal triggers, say, a 10 ms monostable which then triggers a second monostable only if the strobe signal is still active i.e. an AND function.

The function examined here is sufficiently common to warrant the production of specific keypad encoder ICs. The 74C922 is typical of these, accepting a 4×4 keyboard matrix and having a debounced 4-bit 3-state binary output and Data_Available flag (i.e. strobe). Inputs have integral pull-up resistors. If a key is pressed before another is released, the new value is output with strobe after the original key is released. This is known as 2-key roll-over. Outputs are held even when the key is released and only updated when new data is available. A scanning technique is used, as described in Example 2.50. The 74C922 is shown in Fig. 5.56.

3.2.2 Multiplexers and Demultiplexers

Two functions were shown in Fig. 1.3. These are multiplexing, where any one of n lines can be routed through to a single output line; and demultiplexing, where the one input line is routed through to any of n output lines. In this section we will look at MSI implementations of these functions.

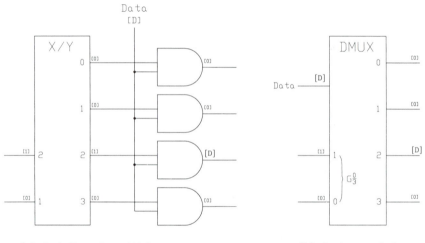

(a) A 4-line demultiplexer,   (b) Logic symbol

Figure 3.42: The demultiplexer. Channel 2 shown selected.

Consider the circuit shown in Fig. 3.42(a), consisting of a 2 to 4-line decoder addressing one of an array of AND gates. By this means, incoming data is routed to the selected output line. Now a decoder is really only a set of AND gates; so the two gate arrays can be subsumed into the one structure. This is clearly seen in Fig. 2.16(a), where the line labelled EN goes to all decoder gates and is the equivalent of our data line. In the case of the 74LS154, shown in Fig. 3.30, the two input enable lines combine to the common data line. Here one input can be used for the data input and the other as an overall inhibit.

The IEC/ANSI symbol for a **demultiplexer** is shown in Figs. 2.16(c) and 3.39(b). The general qualifier symbol is **DMUX** or **DX**. The select inputs are grouped together as a compound **G** dependency. Their range is indicated as a fraction, with the minimum value as numerator and maximum as denominator, i.e. $\frac{min}{max}$. The lines are labelled by the powers of two they represent in making up the internal dependency number. Thus $\mathsf{B\,A} = 11b$ signifies $\mathsf{G}(2^1 + 2^0) = \mathsf{G3}$. The output lines are labelled with their affected-by dependency number. Thus output **3** is chosen with the above select input pattern. Besides the select inputs, other inputs do not have a label; they are assumed to be the data input(s).

Looking at the 74LS154 data sheet, we see that two different IEC/ANSI symbols are given for the same physical device! One as a decoder and the other as a demultiplexer. This is not unreasonable, as they just reflect two ways of looking at the same thing. Virtually all commercial MSI decoders have at least one **Enable** input. This can be used either as a decoder enable or as a demultiplexer data input. As in all languages, the IEC/ANSI symbol should reflect the designer's intent as closely as possible.

Rather confusingly, inputs in the decoder symbol are labelled with their weights (**1**, **2**, **4**, **8** in this case), whilst in the demultiplexer they are in powers of two (**0**, **1**, **2**, **3**). This is because a decoder converts from one code to another (**X/Y**), and code X may not be natural binary. In a demultiplexer these corresponding inputs are always regarded as addressed in the natural binary code.

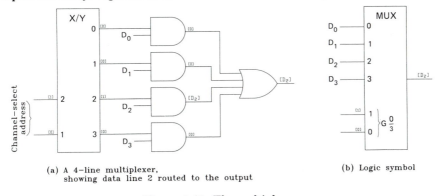

(a) A 4–line multiplexer, showing data line 2 routed to the output

(b) Logic symbol

Figure 3.43: The multiplexer.

Multiplexers (sometimes known as Data Selectors) perform the reverse operation of routing one of n lines through to a single output line [17]. The logic organization shown in Fig. 3.43(a) is similar to the multiplexer, but here each AND gate has a separate data input and an OR gate is used to transmit the selected line through to the output.

The IEC/ANSII symbol shown in Fig. 3.43(b) uses the general qualifier symbol **MUX** to indicate this function. The select inputs use **G** dependency to indicate that input n is ANDed through to the output. Select inputs are numbered according to their powers of two; as in the demultiplexer symbol.

The data sheet reproduced in Fig. 3.44 shows a commercial 8 to 1-line multiplexer (1 of 8 data selector). Here an overall **Enable** has been added to the basic

SN54ALS151, SN54AS151, SN74ALS151, SN74AS151
1 OF 8 DATA SELECTORS/MULTIPLEXERS

D2661, APRIL 1982 – REVISED MAY 1986

- **8-Line to 1-Line Multiplexers**
  Can Perform As:
   Boolean Function Generators
   Parallel-to-Serial Converters
   Data Source Selectors

- **Input Clamping Diodes Simplify System Design**

- **Package Options Include Plastic "Small Outline"**
  Packages, Ceramic Chip Carriers, and Standard
  Plastic and Ceramic 300-mil DIPs

- **Dependable Texas Instruments Quality and Reliability**

SN54ALS151, SN54AS151 . . . J PACKAGE
SN74ALS151, SN74AS151 . . . D OR N PACKAGE
(TOP VIEW)

```
        ___
D3 [ 1  U  16 ] V_CC
D2 [ 2     15 ] D4
D1 [ 3     14 ] D5
D0 [ 4     13 ] D6
 Y [ 5     12 ] D7
 W [ 6     11 ] A
 G [ 7     10 ] B
GND[ 8      9 ] C
```

description

These monolithic data selectors/multiplexers provide full binary decoding to select one of eight data sources. The strobe input ($\overline{G}$) must be at a low logic level to enable the inputs. A high level at the strobe terminal forces the W output high and the Y output low.

The SN54ALS151 and SN54AS151 are characterized for operation over the full military temperature range of $-55\,^{\circ}C$ to $125\,^{\circ}C$. The SN74ALS151 and SN74AS151 are characterized for operation from $0\,^{\circ}C$ to $70\,^{\circ}C$.

SN54ALS151, SN54AS151 . . . FK PACKAGE
(TOP VIEW)

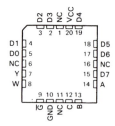

NC – No internal connection

FUNCTION TABLE

INPUTS				OUTPUTS	
SELECT			STROBE		
C	B	A	$\overline{G}$	Y	W
X	X	X	H	L	H
L	L	L	L	D0	$\overline{D0}$
L	L	H	L	D1	$\overline{D1}$
L	H	L	L	D2	$\overline{D2}$
L	H	H	L	D3	$\overline{D3}$
H	L	L	L	D4	$\overline{D4}$
H	L	H	L	D5	$\overline{D5}$
H	H	L	L	D6	$\overline{D6}$
H	H	H	L	D7	$\overline{D7}$

H = high level, L = low level, X = irrelevant
D0, D1 . . . D7 = the level of the D respective input

logic symbol [†]

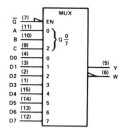

[†]This symbol is in accordance with ANSI/IEEE Std 91-1984 and IEC Publication 617-12.
Pin numbers shown are for D, J, and N packages.

TEXAS
INSTRUMENTS

Figure 3.44: The SN74AS/ALS151 multiplexer (*continued next page*).

SN54ALS151, SN54AS151, SN74ALS151, SN74AS151
1 OF 8 DATA SELECTORS/MULTIPLEXERS

logic diagram (positive logic)

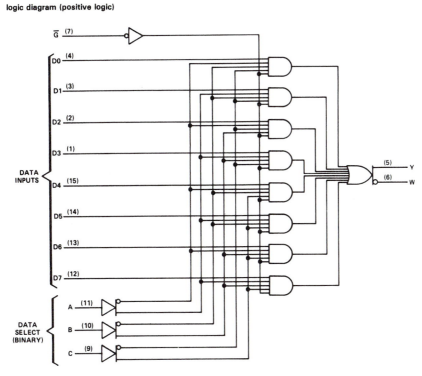

Pin numbers shown are for D, J, and N packages.

Figure 3.44: (*continued*). The SN74AS/ALS151 multiplexer. Reproduced by courtesy of Texas Instruments Ltd.

structure and both true and complement outputs are made available.

Expanding multiplexers is rather like decoder expansion, but in reverse. The m incoming lines are compressed by a series of front-end multiplexers, which are addressed by the least significant address bits. Their outputs are in turn compressed to one line using further multiplexers addressed by the higher address bits.

Example 3.14

A certain project has the requirement to route one of 32 digital lines through to a single output. Only 74x151 multiplexers are available from store. Show how five of these may be connected to perform this operation.

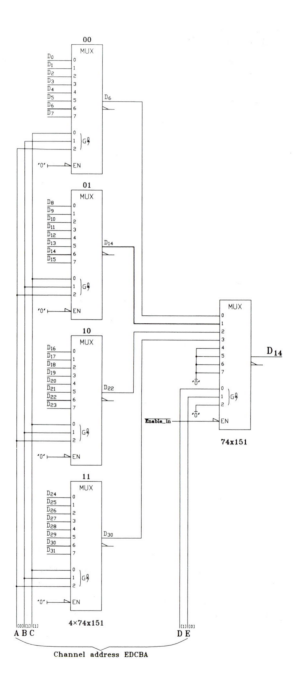

Figure 3.45: Expanding multiplexer circuits.

Solution

An array of four 8-line multiplexers form the front end; compressing 32 lines to four. Which one is routed to the output depends on the state of the top two address bits, using a back end multiplexer to make the choice.

The multiplexer is considerably more versatile than its use as a data selector suggests. Like the decoder, it may be used as a MSI universal logic module (ULM) [18], although this application has now been overshadowed with the advent of cheap LSI programmable logic elements (see Section 3.3). If the multiplexer address is driven by the truth table input variables, then the output for each address can be conditioned by placing the appropriate logic level on the corresponding data input. Thus a 5-variable function requires a 5-bit address, i.e. a 32 to 1-line multiplexer. It is possible to reduce the multiplexer size by transferring one or more variables from the address field to the data inputs, as is illustrated in the following examples.

Example 3.15

A 1-bit binary **full adder** is capable of summing two bits A and B, with a carry-in C_0, giving the sum Σ and a carry-out C_1. Show how this function can be implemented using (a), two 8 to 1-line multiplexers and (b), a dual 4 to 1-line multiplexer.

Solution

The full-adder truth tables of Fig. 3.46(a) are based on the rules of binary addition as given in Section 1.2.1. For example, line 7 shows that with $A\,B\,C_0 = 111$, A plus B plus C_0 gives a sum of 1 and carry-out of 1. As can be seen, each of the two outputs requires an 8 to 1-line multiplexer for its implementation. In each case, data input D_n is assigned the logic level appropriate to the nth output, as selected by address n.

We can half the multiplexer requirement by using only two of the input variables in the address field. The residue variable must then be applied in some fashion to the data inputs. With the method of **residues**, it is necessary to determine which function of these omitted variable(s) have to be applied to the data input lines. In this example we have used $A\,B$ to address one of four input lines. We can factor out the residue C_0 from the logic relationships as follows:

$$\begin{aligned}
\Sigma &= (\overline{A}\cdot\overline{B}\cdot C_0)+(\overline{A}\cdot B\cdot\overline{C_0})+(A\cdot\overline{B}\cdot\overline{C_0})+(A\cdot B\cdot C_0) \\
&= \overline{A}\cdot\overline{B}\cdot(C_0)+\overline{A}\cdot B\cdot(\overline{C_0})+A\cdot\overline{B}\cdot(\overline{C_0})+A\cdot B\cdot(C_0)
\end{aligned}$$

Thus when $A\,B = 00$ the function reduces to $1\cdot 1\cdot C_0 = C_0$. This must be applied to the D_0 input. Similarly $D_1 = \overline{C_0}$ ($A\,B = 01$), $D_2 = \overline{C_0}$ ($A\,B = 10$) and $D_3 = C_0$ ($A\,B = 11$).

Following the same procedure for output C_1, gives:

$$\begin{aligned}
C_1 &= (\overline{A}\cdot B\cdot C_0)+(A\cdot\overline{B}\cdot C_0)+(A\cdot B\cdot\overline{C_0})+(A\cdot B\cdot C_0) \\
&= \overline{A}\cdot B\cdot(C_0)+A\cdot\overline{B}\cdot(C_0)+A\cdot B\cdot(C_0+\overline{C_0})
\end{aligned}$$

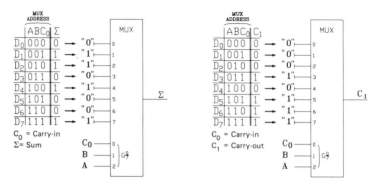

(a) Using two 8 to 1-line MUXs to implement a full adder

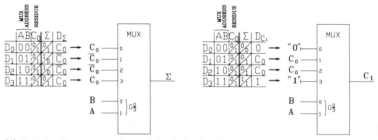

(b) Reducing the MUX requirement by 50% using the technique of residues

Figure 3.46: Logic design using multiplexers.

As $\overline{A}\cdot\overline{B}$ does not appear (i.e. $\overline{A}\cdot\overline{B}\cdot 0$), then $D_0 = 0$. $D_1 = C_0$ ($AB = 01$), $D_2 = C_0$ ($AB = 10$) and as $C_0 + \overline{C}_0 = 1$ then $D_3 = 1$ ($AB = 11$).

Data line conditioning can be deduced more conveniently by inspection from a modified truth table, as shown in Fig. 3.46(b). Essentially the truth table is rewritten in terms of the address variables only; in this case AB, giving four rows. For each such row, the two values of the residue ($C_0 = 0$ or 1) is indicated. The corresponding outputs are shown for each row of the compressed truth table. There are four outcomes for $C_0 = 0/1$; i.e. $\mathcal{F} = 0/1$ (then D_n must be C_0), $\mathcal{F} = 1/0$ (D_n must be $\overline{C}_0$), $\mathcal{F} = 0/0$ (D_n must be 0) and $\mathcal{F} = 1/1$ (D_n must be 1).

A minimized gate implementation costs 25 gate inputs, assuming inverted inputs are available. At the time of writing the 74LS153 dual 4 to 1-line multiplexer costs around 15 gate inputs. More importantly, the package count is reduced from three to one over the SSI equivalent.

For convenience the variables $A B$ were chosen in the last example as the address variables. Choosing the right hand variables as the residue eases the task of producing the compressed truth table, but any selection is possible. In some cases a judicious choice of partition may lead to a better solution, but trying all possible

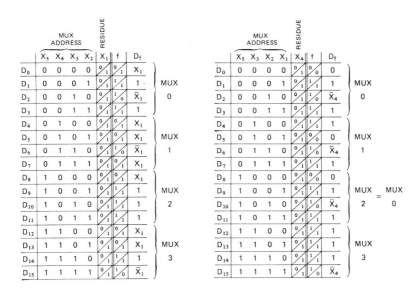

	X5	X4	X3	X2	X1 (RESIDUE)	f	Df	
D0	0	0	0	0			X1	
D1	0	0	0	1			1	MUX 0
D2	0	0	1	0			X̄1	
D3	0	0	1	1			1	
D4	0	1	0	0			X1	
D5	0	1	0	1			X1	MUX 1
D6	0	1	1	0			X̄1	
D7	0	1	1	1			X1	
D8	1	0	0	0			X1	
D9	1	0	0	1			1	MUX 2
D10	1	0	1	0			1	
D11	1	0	1	1			1	
D12	1	1	0	0			X1	
D13	1	1	0	1			X1	MUX 3
D14	1	1	1	0			1	
D15	1	1	1	1			X̄1	

(a) Address $X_5 X_4 X_3 X_2$.

	X5	X3	X2	X1	X4 (RESIDUE)	f	Df	
D0	0	0	0	0			0	
D1	0	0	0	1			1	MUX 0
D2	0	0	1	0			X̄4	
D3	0	0	1	1			1	
D4	0	1	0	0			1	
D5	0	1	0	1			0	MUX 1
D6	0	1	1	0			X̄4	
D7	0	1	1	1			1	
D8	1	0	0	0			0	
D9	1	0	0	1			1	MUX 2 = MUX 0
D10	1	0	1	0			X̄4	
D11	1	0	1	1			1	
D12	1	1	0	0			1	
D13	1	1	0	1			1	MUX 3
D14	1	1	1	0			1	
D15	1	1	1	1			X̄4	

(c) Address $X_5 X_3, X_2 X_1$.

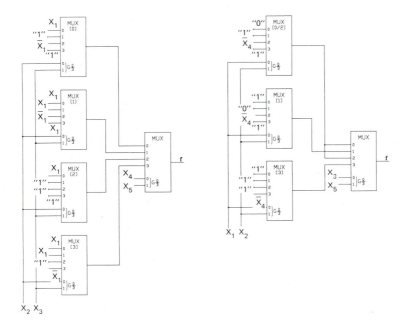

(b) A 4-channel MUX implementation

(d) Saving one MUX by repartitioning

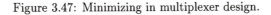

Figure 3.47: Minimizing in multiplexer design.

permutations of residue variables is a difficult task, even for small functions. Reference [19] discusses a technique which gives a good solution with less effort. No satisfactory algorithm exists to make this decision other than trial and error. The effect of differing partitions is illustrated in the following example.

Example 3.16

Using only 4 to 1-line multiplexers, implement the compressed truth tables of Fig. 3.47.

The implementation using $X_5 X_4 X_3 X_2$ as the address and X_1 as the residue, is shown in Fig. 3.47(b). With $X_5 X_4$ as the pre-select address, each front-end multiplexer implements a consecutive $\frac{1}{4}$ of the truth table.

An alternative partition using $X_5 X_3 X_2 X_1$ for the address is shown in Fig. 3.47(c). Here it can be seen that multiplexers 0 and 2 are identical and can be merged. The resulting circuit of Fig. 3.47(d) saves one 4 to 1-line multiplexer.

In general a good partition will maximize the number of identical stages in the tree; allowing merging, as in the above example. Also inverse cases can be implemented simply by using an inverter. Stages which have all data inputs the same, eg. all logic 1, can be replaced by the appropriate variable or logic level.

The process of partitioning the input variables may be extended to the case where more than one variable is omitted from the multiplexer address. In this situation, the data inputs will be logical functions of all the omitted variables.

Example 3.17

Implement the truth table of Fig. 3.47, this time using a single 8 to 1-line multiplexer together with any appropriate gates.

Solution

If we use variables $X_5 X_3 X_2$ to address the multiplexer, the data inputs will be functions of the residue variables $X_4 X_1$. For each multiplexer address there are four combinations of $X_4 X_1$, with four corresponding outputs. Each of these mini truth tables is shown as a 2-variable K-map; one for each major row in Fig. 3.48(a). For example, when address $X_5 X_3 X_2$ is 0 0 0, (major row D_0) then $X_4 X_1 = 00; 01; 10; 11 \rightarrow \mathcal{F} = 0; 1; 0; 1$. Minimizing the eight functions of $X_4 X_1$ gives the data inputs shown in Fig. 3.48(b).

It is useful to compare the cost of this implementation with that of the previous example. In this instance one 8 to 1-line multiplexer (eg. 74x151) and two OR gates (eg. $\frac{1}{2} \times$ 74x32) are required. A total cost of around 20 gate inputs. This compares with two dual 4 to 1-line multiplexers (eg. 74x153) costing around 30 gate inputs. I have assumed that variables are available in both true and complement forms.

As was the case previously, the choice of partition will influence the cost of implementation. It is left to the reader to try the residues $X_2 X_1$. The solution in this case requires six 2-I/P gates in addition to the multiplexer; a 50% increase in package count.

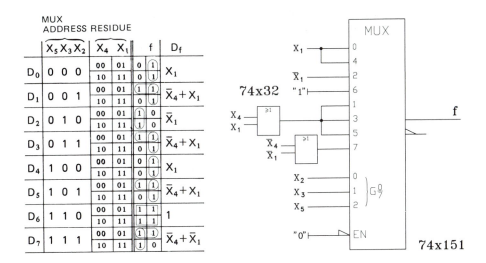

(a) Truth table (b) Implementation

Figure 3.48: Using two variables as the residue.

Function	Designator	Family	Output type	Special features
Decoders and encoders				
7-segment decoder:driver	7446/47/246/247	74,LS	OC, active-Low	High-voltage O/P
	4511	4000,HC,HCT	TP, active-High	4-bit input storage
	4543/4556	4000,HC,HCT	TP,pulsed High	Liquid xtal drivers
BCD to Decimal decoder:driver	7445/145/445	74,LS	OC,active-Low	30/15/7V outputs
	7442	74,LS,HC,HCT		
4 to 16-line decoder:DMUX	74154/159	74,HC,HCT	TP/OC, active-Low	
	4514/4515	4000,HC,HCT	TP, active-Low/High	4-bit input storage
3 to 8-line decoder:DMUX	74138	74,LS,S,ALS,AS,HC,HCT	TP, active-Low	
	74158	ALS	3s, active-Low	
	74131/137	ALS,AS,HC,HCT	3s, active Low	4-bit input storage
2 to 4-line decoder:DMUX	74139	74,LS,S,ALS,AS,HC,HCT	TP, active-Low	Dual circuits
	74155/156	74,LS	TP, active-Low	Common address
Priority encoder	74147	LS,HC,HCT	TP, active-Low	10-line
	74148/**348**	74,**LS**	TP/3S, active-Low	8-line
	74278	74	TP, active-High	Input 4-line storage
Multiplexers				
16 to 1-line	74150	74	TP, active-Low	
	74250	AS	3S, active-Low	
	74850/851	AS	TP/3S, active-Low	with input storage
8 to 1-line	74151	74,LS,S,ALS,AS,HC,HCT	TP, active-Low/High	True:negated O/Ps
	74251	74,LS,S,ALS,AS,HC,HCT	3S, active-Low/High	True:negated O/Ps
	74354/5/6	LS,HC,HCT	3S/OC/3S	with input storage
Dual 4 to 1-line	74153/253	LS,S,ALS,AS,HC,HCT	TP/3S, active-High	Common address
	74352/353	LS,ALS,AS	TP/3S, active-Low	Common address
Quad 2 to 1-line	74157/158	LS,S,ALS,AS,HC,HCT	TP, dual O/Ps	Common address
	74257/258	LS,S,ALS,AS,HC,HCT	3S, dual O/Ps	Common address
	74298/399	74,LS,AS	TP, active-High	with output storage
Octal 2 to 1-line	74606/7	LS	3S/TP, active-High	with input storage

TP = Totem pole; OC = Open-collector; 3S = 3-state

Table 3.3: Some MSI decoders, encoders and multiplexers.

3.2.3   Combinational Arithmetic Circuitry

Circuits dealing with the mathematical operations defined in Section 1.2, as well
as magnitude comparators and other EOR-based functions, are classified under the
heading of arithmetic circuits [20]. The basic arithmetic unit is the 1-bit **full adder**,
as defined in Example 3.13. Using this as a functional building block, additions of
two n-bit words in parallel is possible by utilizing a 1-bit adder for each column and
using the carry-out from the Mth adder as the carry-in to the $(M+1)$th adder.

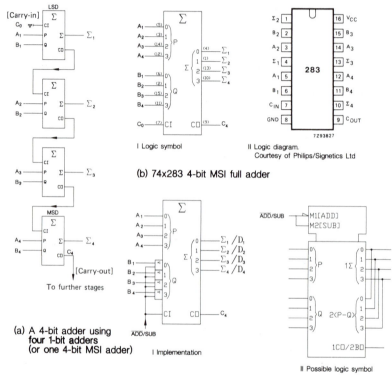

Figure 3.49: Addition and subtraction.

Figure 3.49(a) shows a 4-bit adder using this technique. The LSB does not
require a carry-in provision, as there is no previous column to generate such a
carry. If the adder circuits are being implemented using SSI gates, then the first
block can be a **half adder**. A half adder sums A and B only, giving a sum and
carry-out. However, MSI half adders are not available and the first carry-in is
connected to logic 0. If the augend and addend are unsigned; i.e. the MSB is not
used to indicate the sign of the word, then the final carry-out may be used as the
$(N+1)$th sum bit. As shown in Fig. 3.49(b), MSI adders are available as complete
4-bit modules. These may be cascaded in the same manner as described; thus a
32-bit adder may be implemented by eight 74x283 4-bit adders. Note the use of Σ
as the general qualifier symbol for addition, and **P** and **Q** to denote the addend and

augend respectively. **CI** and **CO** indicate Carry_In and Carry_Out respectively.

Adders may be utilized for subtraction by using the 2's complement of the augend. Remembering that the 2's complement of a number can be determined by inverting each bit and adding one leads to the dual-purpose adder/subtractor illustrated in Fig. 3.49(c)i. The $\overline{\text{Add}}$/Subtract mode control is directly connected to the LSB carry-in, thereby effectively adding one when in the subtract mode ($\overline{\text{Add}}$/Sub $= 1$). This control also drives an array of EOR gates, connected as programmable inverters, in series with the augend lines. This gives inversion if $\overline{\text{Add}}$/Sub is logic 1 and non-inversion for logic 0. Thus when $\overline{\text{Add}}$/Sub is logic 1 we have inversion plus one, otherwise non-inversion plus zero. If the numbers are signed, then the overflow detector of Example 2.42 may be used to determine if the sum has overflowed into the sign position.

The adder/subtractor function uses the same circuitry for two distinct operations. This is indicated using the IEC/ANSII dependency symbol **M** (for Mode). Thus in Fig. 3.49(c)ii, Mode 1 indicates addition, with the dependency number **1** qualifying the addition outputs, i.e. **1Σ**. Mode 2 indicates subtraction and qualifies the difference outputs, i.e. **2(P-Q)**. The symbol **P-Q** is also used as the general qualifier for a dedicated subtractor. Of course both sets of outputs are common, and this is shown by external connection. The cascade output functions as Carry_Out (**CO**) in Mode 1 or Borrow_Out (**BO**) for Mode 2. The compound label **1CO/2BO** indicates this, with the solidi (i.e. /) meaning as well as (cf. , for and).

Example 3.18

Describe how the circuit of Fig. 3.49(c) may be used to detect equality between two numbers.

Solution

If one of the numbers is 2's complemented, then with equality the sum bits will all be zero; i.e. $A - A = 0$. For example $A = 1101b$ and $B = 1101b$, gives $1011b$ plus $0011b = 10000b$. NORing the Σ outputs will give an active-High equality output, symbolized as **P=Q**.

Example 3.19

Show how a 4-bit full adder may be used to decrement a number A by one, i.e. $\Sigma \rightarrow A - 1$.

Solution

The 2's complement of one is $1111b$; thus A minus one is equivalent to $A + 1111b$. Hence if all B inputs are made logic 1, the sum output will be A decremented by one. For example if $A = 1101b$, then A plus $B = 1011b + 1111b = 11100b$.

The principle of the multi-function MSI arithmetic unit may be extended to the **Arithmetic logic Unit (ALU)**; an example of which is given in Fig. 3.50. As well as addition, the 74x181 is capable of subtraction and 14 extra arithmetic

SN54AS181A, SN54AS881A, SN74AS181A, SN74AS881A
ARITHMETIC LOGIC UNITS/FUNCTION GENERATORS

D2661, DECEMBER 1982 – REVISED MAY 1986

- Package Options Include the 'AS181A in Compact 300-mil or Standard 600-mil Packages. The 'AS881A is Offered in 300-mil Packages. Both Devices are Available in Both Plastic and Ceramic Chip Carriers.

- Full Look-Ahead for High-Speed Operations on Long Words

- Arithmetic Operating Modes:
  Addition
  Subtraction
  Shift Operand A One Position
  Magnitude Comparison
  Plus Twelve Other Arithmetic Operations

- Logic Function Modes
  Exclusive-OR
  Comparator
  AND, NAND, OR, NOR
  'AS881A Provides Status Register Checks
  Plus Ten Other Logic Operations

SN54AS181A . . . JT OR JW PACKAGE
SN54AS881A . . . JT PACKAGE
SN74AS181A . . . DW, NT OR NW PACKAGE
SN74AS881A . . . DW OR NT PACKAGE
(TOP VIEW)

$\bar{B}0$	1	24	V_{CC}
$\bar{A}0$	2	23	$\bar{A}1$
S3	3	22	$\bar{B}1$
S2	4	21	$\bar{A}2$
S1	5	20	$\bar{B}2$
S0	6	19	$\bar{A}3$
C_n	7	18	$\bar{B}3$
M	8	17	$\bar{G}$
$\bar{F}0$	9	16	C_{n+4}
$\bar{F}1$	10	15	$\bar{P}$
$\bar{F}2$	11	14	A = B
GND	12	13	$\bar{F}3$

logic symbol†

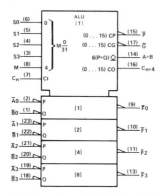

†This symbol is in accordance with ANSI/IEEE Std 91-1984 and IEC Publication 617-12.

TABLE 1

SELECTION				M = H	M = L, ARITHMETIC OPERATIONS	
					ACTIVE-LOW DATA	
S3	S2	S1	S0	LOGIC FUNCTIONS	C_n = L (no carry)	C_n = H (with carry)
L	L	L	L	F = $\bar{A}$	F = A MINUS 1	F = A
L	L	L	H	F = $\overline{AB}$	F = AB MINUS 1	F = AB
L	L	H	L	F = $\bar{A}$ + B	F = $A\bar{B}$ MINUS 1	F = $A\bar{B}$
L	L	H	H	F = 1	F = MINUS 1 (2's COMP)	F = ZERO
L	H	L	L	F = $\overline{A + B}$	F = A PLUS (A + $\bar{B}$)	F = A PLUS (A + $\bar{B}$) PLUS 1
L	H	L	H	F = $\bar{B}$	F = AB PLUS (A + $\bar{B}$)	F = AB PLUS (A + $\bar{B}$) PLUS 1
L	H	H	L	F = A $\oplus$ B	F = A MINUS B MINUS 1	F = A MINUS B
L	H	H	H	F = A + $\bar{B}$	F = A + $\bar{B}$	F = (A + $\bar{B}$) PLUS 1
H	L	L	L	F = $\bar{A}$B	F = A PLUS (A + B)	F = A PLUS (A + B) PLUS 1
H	L	L	H	F = A $\oplus$ B	F = A PLUS B	F = A PLUS B PLUS 1
H	L	H	L	F = B	F = $A\bar{B}$ PLUS (A + B)	F = $A\bar{B}$ PLUS (A + B) PLUS 1
H	L	H	H	F = A + B	F = (A + B)	F = (A + B) PLUS 1
H	H	L	L	F = 0	F = A PLUS A †	F = A PLUS A PLUS 1
H	H	L	H	F = $A\bar{B}$	F = AB PLUS A	F = AB PLUS A PLUS 1
H	H	H	L	F = AB	F = $A\bar{B}$ PLUS A	F = $A\bar{B}$ PLUS A PLUS 1
H	H	H	H	F = A	F = A	F = A PLUS 1

†Each bit is shifted to the next more significant position.

TYPICAL ADDITION TIMES (C_L = 15 pF, R_L = 280 Ω, T_A = 25°C)

NUMBER OF BITS	ADDITION TIMES			PACKAGE COUNT		CARRY METHOD BETWEEN ALUs
	USING 'AS881A AND'AS882	USING 'AS181A AND 'AS882	USING 'S181 AND 'S182	ARITHMETIC LOGIC UNITS	LOOK-AHEAD CARRY GENERATORS	
1 to 4	5 ns	5 ns	11 ns	1		NONE
5 to 8	10 ns	10 ns	18 ns	2		RIPPLE
9 to 16	14 ns	14 ns	19 ns	3 or 4	1	FULL LOOK-AHEAD
17 to 64	19 ns	19 ns	28 ns	5 to 16	2 to 5	FULL LOOK-AHEAD

TEXAS INSTRUMENTS

Figure 3.50: The 74AS181 4-bit ALU. Reproduced by courtesy of Texas Instruments Ltd.

operations; as selected with inputs $S_3 S_2 S_1 S_0$ and $M = 0$. Sixteen logic functions are implemented with $M = 1$. These operations are listed in Table 1 of Fig. 3.50 and are alluded to in the IEC/ANSII logic symbol by the **[T]** designator under the **ALU** general qualifying symbol. The Mode dependency inputs are shown as having a range of 0 through 31 ($\frac{0}{31}$), but in elements as complex as this, it is better to append a table rather than attempt to list all modes within the symbol. However, we can tell that Carry_Out, Carry_Generate and Carry_Propagate (**CO**, **CG**, **CP**) are only valid for Modes 0 through 15 (i.e. 0...15), and that the equality output is only operative in Mode 6. Mode 6 is the subtract mode, and we see from the table that this is subtract $A - B$ assuming a forced Carry_In (**CI** = H). An active Carry_In is necessary, as the 74x181 does its subtraction using 1's complement; with Carry_In = 1 we have invert $+ 1 = 2$'s complement. This requirement is not obvious from the logic symbol; it could have been added thus: **6(CI=1)(P−Q)**. Notice that this output is open-collector, to facilitate wire-ANDing several packages for larger equality comparisons. Output **CO** (or C_{n+4}) can be used in Mode 6 for comparisons $A{\geq}B$ (C_n = H, C_{n+4} = H), $A{<}B$ (C_n = H, C_{n+4} = L), $A{>}$ B (C_n = L, C_{n+4} = H) and $A{\leq}B$ (C_n = L, C_{n+4} = L) in the manner discussed in Section 1.2.2. These assume active-Low data designations. Similar deductions may be made for active-High inputs.

In the circuit shown in Fig. 3.49(a), a carry is propagated in the serial or ripple mode. For example, the addition $1111 + 1$ will be implemented as:

$$\begin{aligned}
&\textit{0}\ 1111 + \textit{0}001 \\
&\textit{0}\ 1110 \\
&\textit{0}\ 1100 \\
&\textit{0}\ 1000 \\
&\textit{0}\ 0000 \\
&\textit{1}\ 0000 = 0000\ \text{carry } 1.
\end{aligned}$$

This is particularly a problem with long words. Thus a 16-bit addition would give a delay of 16 times the single-stage carry propagation delay. Where this is unacceptable, a **carry-look-ahead** technique can be used to reduce carry delay [21]. The problem is not new; over 150 years ago, Babbage developed mechanisms to anticipate the carry over a number of stages of his mechanical adder stages proposed for the world's first computer [22].

In all cases the carry over n bits is a function of $A_1 \ldots A_N$; $B_1 \ldots B_N$ and C_0. Thus in a 4-bit adder, C_4 is a function of nine variables; A_1, A_2, A_3, A_4, B_1, B_2, B_3, B_4 and C_0. Rather than directly implementing this as a sum of products function, the alternative iterative technique shown here is the more effective and has the advantage of sharing logic with the sum circuitry.

The K-map of Fig. 3.51(a) shows the carry-out logic from the truth table of Fig. 3.46(a) to be:

$$C_1 = A_1{\cdot}B_1 + (A_1 + B_1){\cdot}C_0 \tag{3.1}$$

where C_1 is the carry-out and C_0 the carry-in to the first stage.

In general:

$$C_N = A_N{\cdot}B_N + (A_N + B_N){\cdot}C_{N-1} \tag{3.2}$$

If we replace $A_N{\cdot}B_N$ by G_N and $A_N{+}B_N$ by P_N in Equation 3.2, we have:

$$C_1 = G_1{+}P_1{\cdot}C_0 \tag{3.3}$$

and in the same manner:

$$C_2 = G_2{+}P_2{\cdot}C_1 \tag{3.4}$$

Substituting for C_1 in Equation 3.4, we have:

$$C_2 = G_2{+}P_2{\cdot}(G_1{+}P_1{\cdot}C_0) = G_2{+}G_1{\cdot}P_2{+}P_1{\cdot}P_2{\cdot}C_0 \tag{3.5}$$

Similarly:

$$
\begin{aligned}
C_3 = G_3{+}P_3{\cdot}C_2 &= G_3{+}P_3{\cdot}(G_2{+}G_1{\cdot}P_2{+}P_1{\cdot}P_2{\cdot}C_0) \\
&= G_3{+}G_2{\cdot}P_3{+}G_1{\cdot}P_2{\cdot}P_3{+}P_1{\cdot}P_2{\cdot}P_3{\cdot}C_0
\end{aligned}
\tag{3.6}
$$

$$
\begin{aligned}
C_4 = G_4{+}P_4{\cdot}C_3 &= G_4{+}P_4{\cdot}(G_3{+}G_2{\cdot}P_3{+}G_1{\cdot}P_2{\cdot}P_3{+}P_1{\cdot}P_2{\cdot}P_3{\cdot}C_0) \\
&= G_4{+}G_3{\cdot}P_4{+}G_2{\cdot}P_3{\cdot}P_4{+}G_1{\cdot}P_2{\cdot}P_3{\cdot}P_4{+}P_1{\cdot}P_2{\cdot}P_3{\cdot}P_4{\cdot}C_0
\end{aligned}
\tag{3.7}
$$

From Equation 3.7 we see that C_4 is generated directly as a function of $A_1\ldots A_4$, $B_1\ldots B_4$ & C_0; with no dependence on the intermediate carry terms C_1, C_2 & C_3.

The sum function of Example 3.15 does not minimize, but inspection of the truth table shows $\Sigma_N = A_N{\oplus}B_N{\oplus}C_N$ (see Fig. 2.20). Thus:

$$\Sigma_N = \overline{(\{A_N{\cdot}B_N\}{+}\{\overline{A_N}{\cdot}\overline{B_N}\})}{\oplus}C_{N-1} \; \{\text{as } (A_N{\cdot}B_N){+}(\overline{A_N}{\cdot}\overline{B_N}) = \overline{A_N{\oplus}B_N}\} \tag{3.8}$$

$$\Sigma_N = \overline{(\{A_N{\cdot}B_N\}{+}\overline{\{A_N{+}B_N\}})}{\oplus}C_{N-1} = \overline{(G_N{+}\overline{P_N})}{\oplus}C_{N-1} \tag{3.9}$$

This shows that if G_N and P_N are produced for the carry-look-ahead logic, then the sum outputs may be generated at relatively little expense.

Fig. 3.51(b) shows the implementation logic for these equations. G_N and P_N are produced for each bit pair and used as appropriate to generate each internal carry and sum output, together with the final carry-out. The effectiveness of this technique can be judged by the 74LS283's figures for carry-out, C_4, and sum delays, which are quoted as typically 11 and 16 ns respectively. Notice the correspondence between our implementation and that of the 74LS283 shown in Fig. 3.49(b)ii. Using four such adders in series to give a 16-bit module will produce an overall carry-out, C_{16}, in typically 44 ns.

If an even faster addition time is required, the carry-look-ahead concept can be extended to provide carries between each 4-bit module. Based on groups of 4-bit adders (or subtractors), the inter-module carry-look ahead equations have the same form:

$$
\begin{aligned}
C_4 &= G_4{+}G_3{\cdot}P_4{+}G_2{\cdot}P_3{\cdot}P_4{+}G_1{\cdot}P_2{\cdot}P_3{\cdot}P_4{+}P_1{\cdot}P_2{\cdot}P_3{\cdot}P_4{\cdot}C_0 \\
&= (G_4{+}G_3{\cdot}P_4{+}G_2{\cdot}P_3{\cdot}P_4{+}G_1{\cdot}P_2{\cdot}P_3{\cdot}P_4){+}(P_1{\cdot}P_2{\cdot}P_3{\cdot}P_4){\cdot}C_0 \\
&= G_1'{+}P_1'{\cdot}C_0
\end{aligned}
\tag{3.10}
$$

$$
\begin{aligned}
C_8 &= G_2'{+}P_2'{\cdot}C_4 = G_2'{+}P_2'{\cdot}(G_1'{+}P_1'{\cdot}C_0) \\
&= G_2'{+}G_1'{\cdot}P_2'{+}P_1'{\cdot}P_2'{\cdot}C_0
\end{aligned}
\tag{3.11}
$$

etc.

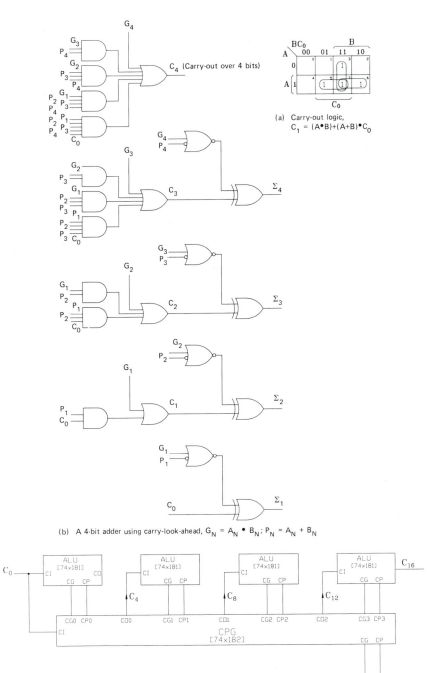

(a) Carry-out logic,
$C_1 = (A \cdot B) + (A + B) \cdot C_0$

(b) A 4-bit adder using carry-look-ahead, $G_N = A_N \cdot B_N$; $P_N = A_N + B_N$

(c) 16-bit ALU with 2-level carry-look-ahead. A,B,Σ lines not shown.

Figure 3.51: Illustrating Carry-Look-Ahead.

The G and P (i.e. **CG** and **CP**) outputs of the 74x181 ALU implement the $(G_4+G_3 \cdot P_4+G_2 \cdot P_3 \cdot P_4+G_1 \cdot P_2 \cdot P_3 \cdot P_4)$ and $(P_1 \cdot P_2 \cdot P_3 \cdot P_4)$ functions respectively. These may be fed into the 74x182 carry-look-ahead generator of Fig. 3.51(c), giving carries C_4, C_8, C_{12} and C_{16}. The internal logic of such look-ahead generators is exactly the same as that used to generate the carries in the 4-bit circuit of Fig. 3.49(b). Further G and P outputs are provided on the 74x182 to facilitate expansion to more than 16 bits, using a third level of look-ahead generators. The 74ALS882 is a 32-bit look-ahead generator, and using this device, the table at the bottom of Fig. 3.50 shows that a 64-bit addition can be accomplished in typically 19 ns. The general IEC/ANSII qualifier for these circuits is **CPG** (Carry Propagation Generator).

Where binary coded decimal (BCD) data is being processed, the designer has two options. The first of these is to convert from BCD to binary, perform the operation and then convert back to BCD. The second alternative is to design arithmetic circuitry to directly process such data according to the rules of BCD arithmetic. As an example, the addition of two valid natural (i.e. 8-4-2-1 code) BCD numbers can give non-valid results. Thus $1001b$ (9) plus $1001b$ (9) gives $100010b$ instead of $1\ 1000_{BCD}$ (18). To circumvent this problem, we need a circuit which will detect all numbers from $01010b$ to $10011b$ (ten to 19). To correct such outcomes, we add six to 'jump over' the six illegal BCD combinations $1010b$ to $1111b$. Note that 9 plus 9 plus 1 (carry-in) = 19, is the maximum output for valid BCD inputs.

Example 3.20

Design an active-High circuit to detect the numbers $01010b$ to $10011b$ inclusive. Using such a circuit in conjunction with two 4-bit binary full adders, show how a 4-bit BCD adder may be constructed.

Solution

The circuit design of the detector is shown in Fig. 3.52(a). Numbers 20...31 inclusive are treated as don't care. In Fig. 3.52(b), the primary adder sums the two BCD digits as if they are normal binary. If the sum is >9, the detector forces $0110b$ into the secondary adder, giving the corrected (+6) sum. The detector output also provides a carry-out for the next higher decade; indicating that the sum has overflowed.

The general qualifying symbol Σ applies also to BCD addition, but with the note **[BCD]** appended. The 74x583 is the MSI BCD equivalent to the 74x283 4-bit binary adder.

Our BCD adder may be modified to subtract. In this case the subtrahend is 2's complemented and added. If the sum is positive, i.e. A $\geq$ B, then no correction is needed, as the outcome must lie in the range 0...9. However, if the sum is negative, i.e. A < B, then ten has to be added to the result. This is equivalent to borrowing ten in normal subtraction. A negative sum is signalled by a logic 1 carry-out from the primary adder. From the K-map of Fig. 3.52(a) we see that the detector will go 1 when C_4 is 1. This can be used to force in ten (i.e. $1010b$) to the secondary adder, as well as providing the borrow-out for the next highest decade. Note that as $1010b$ is the 2's complement of $0110b$, an Add/Subtract control can automatically

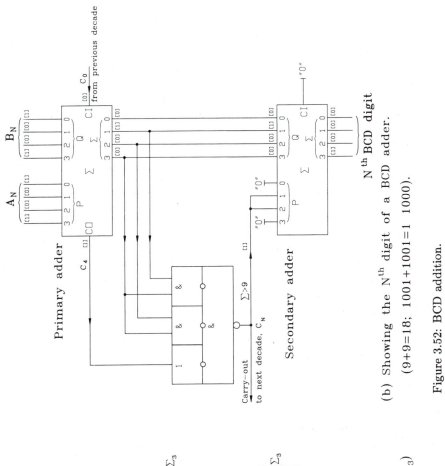

Primary adder

Secondary adder

(b) Showing the Nth digit of a BCD adder.
(9+9=18; 1001+1001=1 1000).

Figure 3.52: BCD addition.

(a) The >9 detector.
$f = C_4 + (\Sigma_4 \cdot \Sigma_2) + (\Sigma_4 \cdot \Sigma_3)$

enter +6 or +10 (i.e. −6) as appropriate, as well as changing the gender of the
primary adder.

Combinational implementations of multipliers are possible and give the fastest circuits, trading cost against speed. Several MSI multipliers are available in typically
4×2 and 4×4 formats. Such multipliers may be expanded in conjunction with
adders [23]. However, most designs are based on the shift and add principle outlined
in Section 1.2.3. As this technique involves the addition of the multiplicand several
times, as determined by the appropriate multiplier bit, a cascade of gated adders
will implement the algorithm. Shifting is accomplished by adding the appropriate
bits of each partial sum to the multiplicand in the Nth cascade adder [24].

If the operands are signed words, then the product sign is the EOR sum of
the two sign bits, as illustrated in Section 1.2.3. Signed words in 2's complement
form may either be converted to natural binary, or a direct signed procedure called
Booth's algorithm used, as outlined in reference [25].

We have noted that the 74x181 ALU may be used to compare the magnitude of
two unsigned numbers. The ALU is rather too sophisticated a circuit to be used
just for this application. A dedicated **digital comparator** will usually prove more
efficient for this purpose. In principle, it is possible to design a comparator using
standard truth table techniques; but such an approach is unwieldy. For example, a
4-bit comparator would require 8-variable K-maps or tables.

An alternative approach uses an iterative algorithm which is easily extended to
N bits. A 4-bit comparison is illustrated here, with magnitude information from
any lesser significant words presented as cascade inputs.

$A > B$ requires:

$A_N > B_N$ OR
$A_N = B_N$ AND $A_{N-1} > B_{N-1}$ OR
$A_N = B_N$ AND $A_{N-1} = B_{N-1}$ AND $A_{N-2} > B_{N-2}$ OR
$A_N = B_N$ AND $A_{N-1} = B_{N-1}$ AND $A_{N-2} = B_{N-2}$ AND $A_{N-3} > B_{N-3}$ OR
$A_N = B_N$ AND $A_{N-1} = B_{N-1}$ AND $A_{N-2} = B_{N-2}$ AND $A_{N-3} = B_{N-3}$
 AND all lesser digits $A > B$

$A = B$ requires:

$A_N = B_N$ AND $A_{N-1} = B_{N-1}$ AND $A_{N-2} = B_{N-2}$ AND $A_{N-3} = B_{N-3}$
AND all lesser digits $A = B$

$A < B$ is identical to $A > B$ with $>$ replaced by $<$.

From this algorithm we see that a comparison of N bits is a function only of
single-bit comparisons. Now $A = B$ is implemented by ANDing all ENORs (1-bit
equals) of each pair of input digits; as was done in Fig. 2.56(a). The condition
$A_x B_x = 10$ is the only case satisfying the relationship $A_x > B_x$ and is detected as
$A_x \cdot \overline{B_x}$. Similarly $A_x < B_x$ is $\overline{A_x} \cdot B_x$.

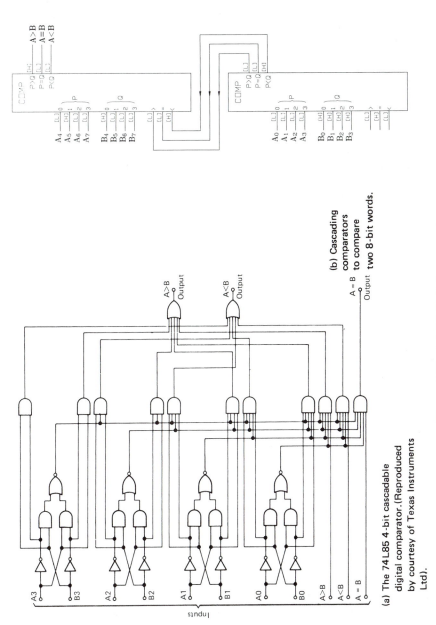

(a) The 74L85 4-bit cascadable digital comparator. (Reproduced by courtesy of Texas Instruments Ltd).

(b) Cascading comparators to compare two 8-bit words.

Figure 3.53: A MSI digital comparator

Figure 3.53(a) shows an MSI 4-bit magnitude comparator based on this algorithm. All four ENOR functions are produced as $\overline{A_x \cdot B_x + A_x \cdot \overline{B_x}}$, i.e. NOT ($A_x > B_x$ OR $A_x < B_x$). The outputs are generated as functions of the $A_x > B_x$, $A_x = B_x$, $A_x < B_x$ terms as indicated by the algorithm. In theory only two of the three magnitude parameters need be directly generated; the third following as a result of the absence of the other two. However, this adds one extra stage delay, and for this reason is not used in MSI implementations.

Figure 3.53(b) shows two 4-bit comparators cascaded to implement an 8-bit comparator. The cascade inputs of the LSD module are connected to imply that the lessor (phantom) digits are equal; which ensures that magnitude decisions are only based on digits actually present. Notice the use of the general qualifier symbol **COMP**, as explained in Fig. 2.56, as well as the $>$, $=$, $<$ symbol for the cascade inputs and **P<Q**, **P=Q** and **P>Q** for the outputs.

For high-speed applications, two levels of comparator may be used. The output comparator processes the **P>Q** and **P<Q** lines from the front-end comparators. Up to two 24-bit words may be compared with only six 74x85 4-bit comparators. The interconnection is left as an exercise for the reader.

Table 3.4 gives an indication of the availability of MSI arithmetic and allied circuitry.

Function	Designator	Family	Special features
Arithmetic			
4-bit full adder	7483	74,LS,S,HC,HCT	With integral carry-look-ahead
	74583	HC,HCT	BCD addition
4-bit ALU	74181	74,LS,S,AS,HC,HCT	32 functions
	74382	LS	8 functions
Serial adder/subtractor	74385	LS	Quad
Carry-look-ahead	74182	74,S,LS,AS,HC,HCT	16-bit
generator	74882	AS	32-bit
Multiplier	74261	LS	2 × 4 cascadable with adder circuits
	74285	74	4 × 4 cascadable with adder circuits
	74384	LS	8 × 1 2's complement
Comparators			
4-bit magnitude	7485	74,LS,S,HC,HCT	P = Q, P > Q, P < Q
8-bit equality	74**688**/689	LS,ALS,**HC,HCT**	**3S**/OC
16-bit equality	74526	ALS	Compares with internal fuse prog word
Parity generators/checkers			
9-bit	74280	LS,S,ALS,AS,HC,HCT	Odd/even
16-bit	747080	HC,HCT	Odd/even

OC = Open-collector; 3S = 3-state

Table 3.4: A selection of MSI combinational arithmetic functions.

3.3 LSI Programmable Logic

We have already observed that the main criterion for a successful design is to minimize the number of ICs, virtually regardless of type. Following this line of argument, the use of LSI and VLSI circuitry would seem to be a logical progression from implementations based on MSI and SSI technology.

This is not as straightforward as it would appear. LSI, and especially VLSI circuits, are really too complex to be general-purpose building blocks; in the manner of MSI multiplexers, decoders, adders etc. Most catalog LSI parts, such as micro-processors or memories are designed to be part of a programmable system whereby their operation is customized to fit the application.

In order to amortize the costs of designing and debugging an integrated circuit, the semiconductor vendor must produce large quantities. A typical example is a digital watch chip. This circuit hardly finds much application outside this restricted area, but its mass market means that it is economically feasible to commercially produce as a standard part.

The problem is then, how to use LSI/VLSI technology for production runs of less than several thousand per annum. At such levels the costs involved in designing an IC from scratch make this approach prohibitively expensive, except where the customer expects to pay a large premium for an ultra small and reliable product, such as military and some medical applications.

There are several approaches to this problem, all of which involve to some extent using a standard architecture with some user programmability capability. The former means that LSI/VLSI parts can be mass produced; the latter gives the means of tailoring to the specific application.

Of these, one of the earliest is the microprocessor. Here a VLSI computer central processor unit is configured to the application by means of a series of binary patterns (the software) stored in external memory. We will expand on this concept in Chapter 5.

An alternative method involves altering the hardware configuration of the chip itself. Most of the smaller devices are based on the principles of blowing fuses or charging floating-gate transistors in fixed AND-OR matrices, such as shown in Figs. 3.3 & 3.7.

A rather more ambitious scheme involves a general-purpose transistor or gate array, which is not in the form of a fixed AND-OR matrix. Most of these so-called semi-custom VLSI devices must be manufactured by a semiconductor fabrication house, known as a silicon foundary. These application specific integrated circuits (ASICs) make more efficient use of the silicon than the smaller user programmable logic devices (PLDs) but demand much more from the designer, as the internal layout of the integrated circuit is now his or her responsibility. The silicon foundary essentially just makes the device. This needs powerful computer-aided engineering (CAE) software and a similar level of expertize. A mistake on silicon means a large tooling-up and fabrication cost penalty plus the turn-around time delay.

In this section we mainly concentrate on the more popular PLD techniques, and place its use within the spectrum of solutions covered above. This is at the level of replacing up to around ten SSI/MSI catalog parts by a single device. Even at this level the cost savings are considerable. In Section 4.5 we look at sequential manifestations of the PLD architectures, and Section 6.1 looks at CAE aids in the design process.

After reading this section you will understand:

- The terms PLD, PLE, ROM, PAL, PLA, ASIC, custom and semi-custom and their application area.

- How to configure PAL, PLE and PLA devices to implement combinational functions.

- The symbology of representing large AND-OR arrays and fuse patterns.

- The differences in application areas between the three main PLD types.

- How to expand the size of a PLD.

- Address dependency and the symbology used to represent ROMs.

3.3.1   Introduction

LSI/VLSI logic spans a range covering a few hundred to some hundreds of thousand gate equivalents. The term **gate equivalent** is generally taken to be a measure of complexity in 2-I/P gate units. In spanning over three decades of circuit density many different architectures and processes are used, leading to a wide spectrum of technological and economic factors to consider.

In order to give an overview of these approaches, it is necessary to briefly review the process of actually fabricating integrated circuitry. Although there are a multitude of proprietary techniques, most of these are based on a series of steps whereby minute quantities of impurities are implanted in a silicon base to make up the pattern of P and N regions defining the various geometries of transistors, capacitors and resistors. The areas to be implanted are delineated by using a photographic technique involving a photoresist, mask and wash process. Photoresist is an organic material which polymerizes on exposure to ultra violet light. In that form, photoresist withstands attack by acids. Thus coating the silicon wafer, which has an oxidized surface (typically by heating in oxygen), with photoresist and exposing through a mask, leaves a pattern of acid resistant areas. Washing away the unexposed photoresist and then etching with hydrofluoric acid (HFl) leaves a pattern of holes through the glassy silicon dioxide. Through these windows the appropriate material is implanted. The photoresist is then removed, and sometimes the oxide islands; the wafer re-oxidized and the process repeated with a different mask.

Figure 3.54 shows a typical process, used to produce the HCMOS family of ICs. Beginning at the top left of the diagram, the virgin N type silicon has a layer of oxide and nitride grown on its surface and is covered with photoresist. After exposure, wells are etched through the surface material and into the silicon. This is followed by an oxidation process whereby the wells are filled with local oxidation (LOCOS in the diagram).

In all, eight oxidize, mask, etch and implant processes are shown. The last of these (bottom right) is the aluminium interconnection stage, whereby all the devices on the chip are electrically connected; the equivalent of copper tracks on a PCB. The interested reader should consult reference [26] for a detailed treatment.

Even from this brief description, it is obvious that producing an IC from scratch is a long and expensive proposition. The non-recurring engineering expenses (NRE), such as mask tooling, purchase and learning curve for the necessarily complex computer-aided engineering (CAE) tools, make the production of **custom integrated circuits** unrealistic, except where a total production of over 10,000 is planned. The period from design to actual devices in the hand is likely to be over a year, and much of the NRE money will have to be up front. If there is a bug in the design, not only will this time be considerably extended, but much of the NRE charges will reoccur. Nevertheless, customized implementations make

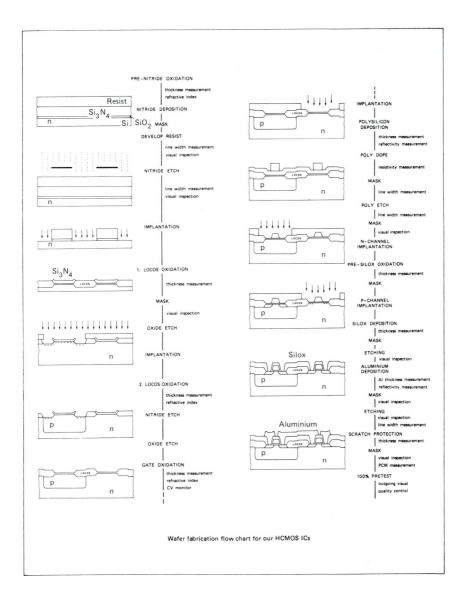

Figure 3.54: Manufacturing integrated circuits. Courtesy of Philips/Signetics Ltd.

the most efficient use of the silicon and there well may be situations where size is critical.

Closely related to full custom is **standard cell** devices. Once again a full set of masks and processing steps are involved, but the design stage is eased by the use of a standard cell library as part of the CAE software. Thus layouts for functional modules, such as decoders, multiplexers, counters etc. are available, and are placed and interconnected on silicon on the same manner as SSI and MSI catalog parts may be designed into a PCB. This approach still makes efficient use of the silicon and reduces the design time somewhat, but the NRE charges are still high, and standard cell ICs are thus mainly targeted to large production quantities.

Further down the complexity spectrum are **gate arrays**. A virgin gate array consists of a sea of gates (or sometimes groups of transistors) already formed on the die, with wide channels reserved for the customer specified interconnects. As only one mask is particularized to a design, this approach is known as **semi-custom**. Gate array designs cost considerably less than a full custom equivalent, although they will typically range from \$10,000 – \$50,000 [27]. The design to manufacture lead time is still measured in months, and NRE charges will recur if a bug fix is necessary. Arrays of over 50,000 gate-equivalents are available but, due to the problems of interconnection, in practice perhaps only 40% can be utilized in a real design, and thus silicon area efficiency is much less than a full custom equivalent. Gate arrays are typically used for medium/high production quantities, of over 5000 units.

By far the majority of designs using configurable LSI chips are described as **Programmable logic devices (PLDs)**. The difference between customization and programmability is that in the former the silicon foundary makes or customizes the chip to your specification, whilst in the latter the designer personalizes a standard part him/herself. Thus the LSI device now becomes a standard catalog part, but can be configured in the field to fit a specific situation. Devices manufactured by a silicon foundary to a specific customer specification are usually described as **Application specific integrated circuits (ASICs)**, although the term is sometimes used to categorize personalized ICs in general.

The first programmable ICs appeared in the 1960s in the form of diode matrices with aluminium fuses at the crosspoints, as shown in Fig. 3.3. This evolved into the structure illustrated in Fig. 3.33 in which a decoder generates all possible product terms of the input variable, and a programmable OR matrix provides the IC's personality. Such a structure is known as a **programmable read-only memory (PROM)**, as each combination of inputs can be regarded as addressing a unique word (pattern of diodes). PROMs are extensively used to store fixed programs for microprocessors (see Chapter 5), especially using floating-gate switches (see Fig. 3.5). The disadvantage of a PROM used to implement logic equations lies in its universality. As all possible 2^n p-terms are generated, each additional variable (input pin) doubles the size of the matrix. This approach degrades performancewhere there are large numbers of equation variables, due to the necessary size of the silicon chip . Many logic applications require detection of a relatively few combinations of many variables.

Regarded as an AND-OR array, as shown in Fig. 3.55(a), a PROM is a fixed AND array — the decoder — and a programmable OR matrix. The fixed connection is denoted by a • and an *intact* fuse by a **X**. The diagram shows the PROM programmed to the specification of Fig. 3.34.

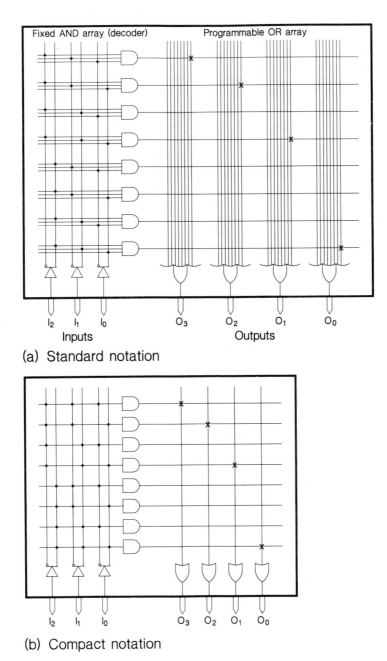

(a) Standard notation

(b) Compact notation

Figure 3.55: A PROM considered as an AND-OR array.

For larger arrays (the smallest commercial PROM is eight times this size, see Fig. 3.58) the traditional logic diagram becomes unwieldy. Normally the shorthand notation shown in Fig. 3.55(b) is used instead. Here multiple gate input lines are shown as a single composite line, with connections as appropriate with intersecting conductors. Although this notation seems rather abstract, in fact the actual X and Y lines of a diode matrix are being mimicked. An example of a complex array using this notation, was shown in Fig. 3.22(c). We will return to PROMs in Section 3.3.2.

The next development in PLD technology was the replacement of the fixed (decoder) AND matrix by a programmable array. This means that only the product terms required by the design need be generated. A device with a programmable AND array feeding a programmable OR array is known as a **programmable logic array (PLA)**. The basic PLA architecture is shown in Fig. 3.56.

The addition of a second fuse array makes this approach inherently more expensive and slower than a PROM equivalent, especially where less than around ten input variables are involved. Introduced in 1975 by Signetics Inc, PLAs took a long time to catch on, partly because of their cost (initially around $30) and the lack of any computer-aided software.

Technology	Gate price	NRE costs	Design time	Board space	CAE tools	Ease of design changes	Ease of pirating
Fixed function (SSI/MSI)	High	Very low	Short	Highest	Data books	Fair	High
Custom	Lowest	Highest	Very long	Lowest	Powerful software	Very difficult	Nearly impossible
Gate array	Low	High	Long	Low	Powerful software	Very difficult	Very Low
Programmable Logic Devices	Medium	Very low	Short	Medium	Good software	Good	Low

Table 3.5: Summary of configurable LSI.

Most small and medium-sized PLDs currently use the **programmable array logic (PAL)** architecture. This is the reverse of the PROM principle, having a programmable AND matrix feeding a series of fixed OR gates. PALs were introduced by Monolithic Memories Inc. (MMI) in 1978 [27]. The first PALs were available in skinny (0.3″, 7.6 mm) 20-pin DIL packages (as against the PLA fat (0.6″, 15.2 mm) 28-pin DIL equivalent) and were targeted at a $5 unit price (this was hard to achieve in practice due to problems with fuse yields). Learning from the PLA experience, good simple documentation was available from the start as was a low cost CAE package called PALASM (PAL ASeMbler) which turns Boolean equations into a fuse plot. This file in turn is downloaded to the PLD programmer which blows the appropriate fuses. This is discussed in Section 6.1.2.

Although other architectures are available, the three configurations (with extensions) outlined in Fig. 3.56 cover the vast majority of popular devices. Irrespective of the actual type, PLDs have the advantage of low NRE charges and turn-around times. They are ideal for small production runs and prototyping. Also many PLDs are standard devices and extensively second sourced (available from more than one supplier). The latter is especially helped by U.V. and electrically erasable technolo-

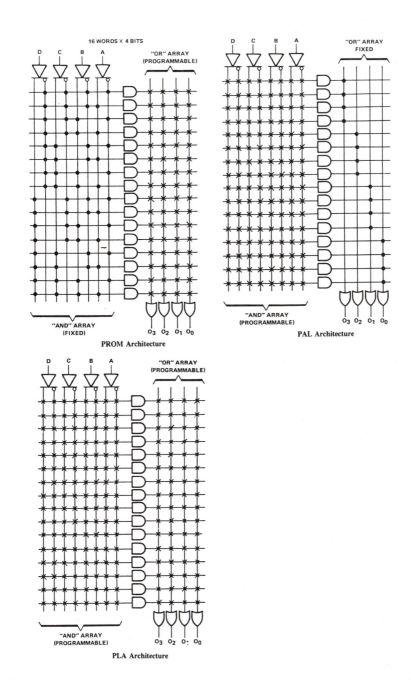

Figure 3.56: A comparison of the three basic PLD AND-OR architectures. Courtesy of Texas Instruments Ltd.

gies. However, they are still limited to around 20,000 gate equivalents per device
as opposed to 100,000+ for gate arrays. Where 10,000+ units of production are
envisaged, PLDs can be more expensive than gate arrays.

The following sections deal with the three standard architectures in turn, whilst
Section 4.5 looks at PLDs containing memory elements. The use of CAE in aiding
designing with these devices is the subject of Section 6.1

3.3.2   PROMs and PLEs

The structure whereby a 2^n-line natural decoder drives an array of programmable
OR gates,can be regarded as a memory. This is in the sense that each combination
of the n input variables accesses or addresses one of 2^n pattern words. Thus the
circuit in Fig. 3.55 stores eight 4-bit words, each with a unique address; i.e. a 32-bit
memory.

The first structures of this form were manufactured in the late 1960s as an
alternative to diode matrices to store fixed tables of conversion factors, such as
BCD/binary conversion. Thus the standard catalog part 74184 is actually a 32 × 8
read-only memory (ROM) patterned to give a 6-bit BCD (00 – 39) to binary
look-up table. Likewise the 74185 is the same memory but programmed to act as a
binary to BCD converter.

The term read-only memory refers to the property of the memory whereby it
can be read at any time but never altered by the circuit. This contrasts to the
read/write memories discussed in Section 4.3.2. The introduction of fusible links
in the OR array during the early 1970s gave the designer the ability to personalize
a 'blank' standard part **programmable read-only memory (PROM)** as a sort
of one-off write action. Thus it was possible to have the advantages of LSI without
the expenses of mass production. Within ten years a range of bipolar fusible-link
PROMs were available in sizes from 32 × 8 (256 bits) to 4096 × 8 (32 Kbyte).

The 82S147 512 × 8 device shown in Fig. 3.57 is a typical medium-complexity
PROM containing 4192 fusible links with a 9-bit address ($A_0 \ldots A_8$) selecting one
of 512 8-bit words. Outputs are via 3-state buffers enabled by $\overline{CE}$. Internally a 2-
dimensional decoding arrangement is used to access the target word. The upper six
address lines locate a single 64-bit word via a 6 to 64-line decoder. The lower three
address signals gate one of eight of these bits through to the output pins ($O_1 \ldots O_8$)
via an array of 8 to 1-line multiplexers. Two-dimensional decoding schemes are
normally used for larger memory arrays, as they considerably reduce the decoder
circuitry as compared to the simple linear scheme shown in Fig. 3.55. Another
example of this is shown in Fig. 4.45.

Initially PROMs were used for look-up tables and to hold programs and data for
microprocessors. The development of MOS-based erasable PROMs quickly sidelined
their faster but more expensive and power hungry bipolar fusible-link relatives.
However, where high speed is necessary, small and medium sized bipolar PROMs
are still useful as combinational logic replacements. Although it is difficult to give
cost comparisons that will stand the test of time, the 100-off price for the 74S472
512×8 PROM is £1.68 ($2.90) and that of the 82S123 32×8 PROM is £0.76 ($1.30).
It is probably more realistic to give prices as a multiple of the cost of a gate input,
based on a standard function, such as a 74LS00 quad 2-I/P NAND gate. This works
out at ≈ $0.02 a gate input. Using this normalized unit, a 74S472 PROM costs

Signetics

Bipolar Memory Products

82S147
82S147A
4K-Bit TTL Bipolar PROM

Product Specification

DESCRIPTION

The 82S147 and 82S147A are field-programmable, which means that custom patterns are immediately available by following the Signetics generic I fusing procedure. The standard devices are supplied with all outputs at logical Low. Outputs are programmed to a logic High level at any specified address by fusing the Ni-Cr link matrix.

The 82S147 and 82S147A includes on-chip decoding and one chip enable input for ease of memory expansion, and features Three-state outputs for optimization of word expansion in bused organizations.

Ordering information can be found on the following page.

The 82S147 and 82S147A devices are also processed to military requirements for operation over the military temperature range. For specifications and ordering information consult the Signetics Military Data Book.

FEATURES

- **Address access time:**
  - N82S147: 60ns max
  - N82S147A: 45ns max
- **Power dissipation: 625mW typ**
- **Input loading: $-100\mu A$ max**
- **One chip enable input**
- **On-chip address decoding**
- **No separate fusing pins**
- **Fully TTL compatible**
- **One chip enable input**
- **Outputs: Three-state**
- **Unprogrammed outputs are Low level**

APPLICATIONS

- **Prototyping/volume production**
- **Sequential controllers**
- **Microprogramming**
- **Hardwired algorithms**
- **Control store**
- **Random logic**
- **Code conversion**

PIN CONFIGURATION

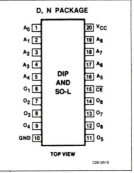

BLOCK DIAGRAM

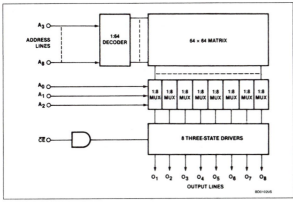

Figure 3.57: Data sheet for the 82S147/74S147 512×8 PROM. Courtesy of Philips/Signetics Ltd.

134 gate inputs and the 82S123 costs 60 such units. However, in evaluating overall price, remember that the former can replace *any* logic that can be described using eight 9-variable K-maps and the latter *any* eight 5-variable K-maps. Using our criterion that only package count is important, it is clear that using these devices will reduce the overall cost by at least a factor of ten for anything other than a trivial system.

To highlight the use of PROMs as general-purpose logic building blocks [28, 29, 30, 31, 32] the expression **programmable logic element (PLE)** is often used as an alternative to PROM. With this appellation, a standardized classification has been developed to characterize these devices. Thus the 32×8 and 512×8 PROMs previously discussed are known as PLE5P8 and PLE9P8, where the first digit is the number of inputs and the last the number of outputs. Unfortunately manufacturers seem reluctant to use this sensible scheme, and the same device often has nearly as many codes as it has manufacturers. Thus the PLE5P8 (AMD) is known as the 74S288 (National Semiconductors), 18S030 (Texas Instruments), N82S123 (Philips/Signetics) and HM7603-5 (Harris)!

Example 3.21

Show how a PLE5P8 PROM may be programmed to convert kilogrammes (kg) to pounds weight (lb), for the range 0–31 kg. The conversion factor is 1 kg = 2.205 lb. The input is to be in natural binary, and the output in 64-32-16-8-4-2-1-$\frac{1}{2}$ code.

Solution

The structure of a PLE5P8 is shown in Fig. 3.58. A linear 5 to 32-line decoder activates one of 32 horizontal AND lines as a function of the five inputs $I_0 \ldots I_4$. Each of the eight outputs $O_0 \ldots O_7$ is determined by a vertical 32-wide OR gate. The personality of the PROM is a function of the pattern of intact fuses in this OR matrix. Each output is driven through a 3-state buffer with a common enable line.

Generally the specification for a PLE is presented in the form of a truth table; sometimes called in this context a **personality table**. The personality table in this instance is shown in Table 3.6. However, in order to emphasize the relationship

PROM inputs					PROM outputs								
a_4	a_3	a_2	a_1	a_0	d_7	d_6	d_5	d_4	d_3	d_2	d_1	d_0	
E	D	C	B	A	P	Q	R	S	T	U	V	W	
0 kg 0	0	0	0	0	0	0	0	0	0	0	0	0	0.0 lbs
1 kg 0	0	0	0	1	0	0	0	0	0	1	0	0	2.0 lbs
2 kg 0	0	0	1	0	0	0	0	0	1	0	0	1	4.5 lbs
3 kg 0	0	0	1	1	0	0	0	0	1	1	0	1	6.5 lbs
⋮	⋮	⋮	⋮	⋮	⋮	⋮	⋮	⋮	⋮	⋮	⋮	⋮	⋮
31 kg 1	1	1	1	1	1	0	0	0	1	0	0	1	68.5 lbs

Table 3.6: Kilograms to pounds conversion.

between the truth table and silicon configuration, I have directly annotated the logic diagram with the input and output variable quantities. Comparing the table

PLE5P8/82S123

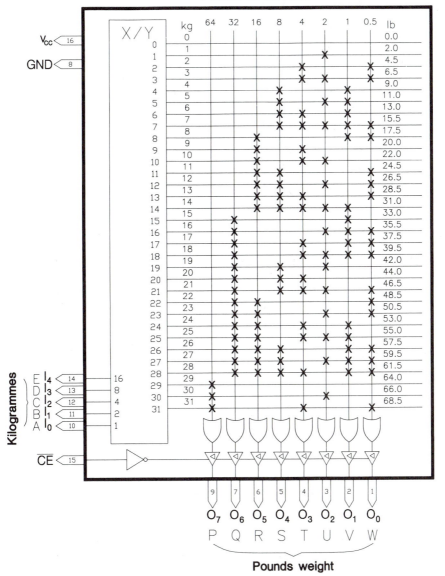

Figure 3.58: Programming a PLE5P8 as a kg to lb convertor.

to the OR matrix fuse pattern, we see that an intact fuse directly corresponds to an output 1 whilst the absence of a link is analogous to a 0. Thus a PROM/PLE is a truth table in silicon. *Any* truth table can be directly implemented without exception, by arranging the OR fuses appropriately. Thus this architecture is truly universal. Specifically the PLE5P8 can implement *any* combinational system that can be described by eight 5-variable truth tables. There is no minimization process necessary in using PROM/PLEs. In fact CAE software used to mechanize the design of systems using these devices, if fed by Boolean equations, simply reverse engineers them back into a truth table. See Example 6.4.

To end on a practical note. Although the pin-out of the PLE5P8 is fairly standardized, some varieties come with open-collector outputs. Thus the 82S23 is the open-collector counterpart of the 82S123 device. Some early devices used inverting open-collector buffer. The effect is the same, but the fuse pattern must be inverted to reverse this active-Low nature. Generally the PROM/PLE programmer should automatically take care of this problem. A last minute change has been made to the specification after the hardware has already been manufactured. It has been decided that the output is to be in 2-decade BCD to the nearest lb, rather than natural binary. Can you determine the new PROM/PLE's personality and will the printed circuit board have to be reformulated?

The very universality of the PROM/PLE structure is its achilles' heel. Thus in order to generate all possible elemental product terms of the input variables, the decoder (AND array) doubles in size with the addition of each new input variable. Thus coping with a large number of variables becomes expensive. The following examples look at ways around this problem.

Example 3.22

Determine the personality table for a PROM which will generate sin X. The PROM is to be addressed by the 7-bit binary equivalent to the angle in 1° steps. The output is to be in 10-bit natural binary.

Solution

Whilst not reproducing all ninety entries in the specifying table, the part reproduced below should give the reader the gist of the full solution. Implementing this table gives a resolution of 1° to a resolution of 1 part in 2^{10}, or around three decimal places. The PROM capacity for this table is $10 \times 2^7 = 1.25$ kbyte.

The principle is readily extended to any resolution and accuracy by increasing the address and output fields. Thus two 82S101 2048×8 PLE/PROMs in parallel would store the sine tables to a resolution of 0.05° with a 16-bit accuracy (better than four decimal places). The total capacity here is 32 kbytes.

Where a mathematical relationship exists, the use of an algorithm can reduce the required memory capacity, at the cost of additional arithmetic circuitry and speed [33]. As an example, for the sine function we could write:

$$\sin X = \sin(x + \Delta x) = \sin x \cos \Delta x + \cos x \sin \Delta x$$

	PROM address inputs							PROM data outputs										
	a_6	a_5	a_4	a_3	a_2	a_1	a_0	d_9	d_8	d_7	d_6	d_5	d_4	d_3	d_2	d_1	d_0	
Angle X°	A6	A5	A4	A3	A2	A1	A0	S9	S8	S7	S6	S5	S4	S3	S2	S1	S0	sin X
0	0	0	0	0	0	0	0	0	0	0	0	0	0	0	0	0	0	0.000
1	0	0	0	0	0	0	1	0	0	0	0	0	1	0	0	0	1	0.017
2	0	0	0	0	0	1	0	0	0	0	0	1	0	0	0	1	1	0.035
3	0	0	0	0	0	1	1	0	0	0	0	1	1	0	1	0	1	0.052
⋮	⋮	⋮	⋮	⋮	⋮	⋮	⋮	⋮	⋮	⋮	⋮	⋮	⋮	⋮	⋮	⋮	⋮	⋮
45	0	1	0	1	1	0	1	1	0	1	1	0	1	1	1	0	0	0.707
⋮	⋮	⋮	⋮	⋮	⋮	⋮	⋮	⋮	⋮	⋮	⋮	⋮	⋮	⋮	⋮	⋮	⋮	⋮
89	1	0	1	1	0	0	1	1	1	1	1	1	1	1	1	1	1	1.000
90	1	0	1	1	0	1	0	1	1	1	1	1	1	1	1	1	1	1.000

Table 3.7: Partial sine look-up table.

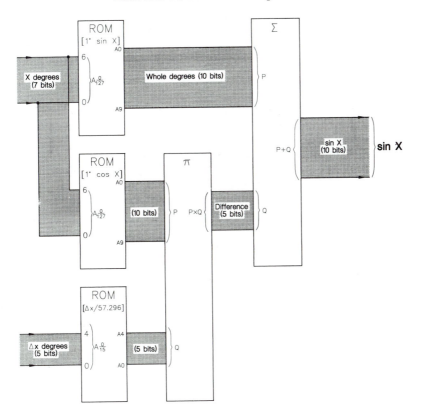

Figure 3.59: Using an algorithm to generate sin X.

where X is the angle, x is the nearest whole degree, and Δx is the difference. If Δx is small, then $\cos \Delta x \approx 1$ and $\sin \Delta x \approx \Delta x$ radians $= \Delta x / 57.296$ degrees:

$$\sin X \approx \sin x + (\Delta x / 57.296) \cos x$$

Figure 3.59 shows an arrangement using this algorithm, generating $\sin X$ in steps of $\frac{1}{32}^\circ$ to a 10-bit precision. Two 1° sin/cos ROMs are used together with a $\Delta x / 57.296$ ROM, giving a ≈ 1.5 kbyte capacity requirement. A straight lookup table would require a $10 \times 2^{11} = 20$ kbyte capacity, although this would give a $\frac{1}{22}^\circ$ resolution. As the largest value of $\Delta x / 57.296$ is $1/57.296$, only the five LSBs are needed for the $\Delta x / 57.296$ generation.

The IEC/ANSII symbol depicted in Fig. 3.59 uses the general qualifier symbol **ROM**. The symbol **PROM** denotes a field programmable equivalent. Inputs are grouped together using the **address dependency** symbol **A**. This indicates that the grouped inputs select or address a range of internal values depicted as $\frac{min}{max}$. Thus $\mathbf{A}_{127}^{0}$ indicates addresses ranging from 0 to 127. This is rather like the **G** range used for multiplexers and demultiplexers. Outputs have an **A** appended to show that they are the data accessed by the input address variables.

This symbol regards the device as a memory (see also Section 4.3.2) rather than a PLE. At present PLEs and other programmable devices have no specific IEC/ANSII symbolization. Sometimes the $\mathbf{\Phi}$ general qualifier symbol is used to indicate a device too complex to represent clearly.

The ROMs depicted in Fig. 3.59 required ten output lines. We see from Table 3.8 that commercial devices have only four and eight outputs. Implementing a larger data word is accomplished by paralleling ROMs/PROMs, as shown in Fig. 3.60(a). All devices are addressed in parallel, with each contributing lines to the output bus.

Increasing the word capacity is a little more complex. As this requires an increase in the number of horizontal AND lines, then in essence we have a problem of decoder expansion. Thus the use of a front-end decoder to select one of N ROMs is identical to the scheme previously shown in Fig. 3.31. The like outputs of the N ROMs are connected together to form the data bus. As ROMs invariably have open-collector or 3-state outputs and as only one device is enabled at any given time, then there is no interference between ROMs. Each ROM contributes 2^M words to the total $N \times 2^M$ word capacity.

Many functions having a large number of variables are sparse in nature. That is only a relatively few product terms need be decoded. In this situation it is possible to decrease the required ROM capacity by using reduction techniques [34].

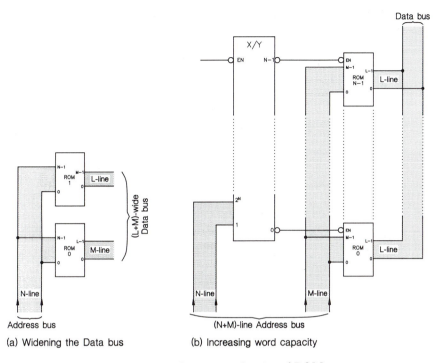

Figure 3.60: Increasing the size of ROM.

Example 3.23

Design an active-Low 7-segment to binary code convertor using a minimal PROM implementation.

Solution

A direct implementation of the table in Fig. 3.61(a) requires a $4 \times 2^7 = 512$-bit capacity. However partition $\mathbf{a\,b\,c\,d\,e}$ uses only seven out of a possible 32 combinations. ROM 0 of Fig. 3.61(d) is used to compress these five variables to three, i.e. $\mathbf{a\,b\,c\,d\,e} \rightarrow Y_2 Y_1 Y_0$. The 3-bit output of ROM 0 together with $\mathbf{f\,g}$, address ROM 1 which outputs the 4-bit binary equivalent $\mathbf{D\,C\,B\,A}$. The total requirement is now only 224 bits.

Actually this is not the best solution to this problem, as the partition $\mathbf{a\,b\,e\,f\,g}$ taken alone gives unique addresses for each of the ten outputs[1]. This reduces the requirement to $4 \times 2^5 = 128$ bits, which comfortably fits inside a PLE5P8 device. A more impressive example showing reduction by partition for a sparse function is given in reference [35].

---

[1]I am indebted to Professor R.E.B. Makinson of the School of Mathematics & Physics, Macquarie University, New South Wales, Australia, for this observation

a	b	c	d	e	f	g	D	C	B	A
0	0	0	0	0	0	1	0	0	0	0
1	0	0	1	1	1	1	0	0	0	1
0	0	1	0	0	1	0	0	0	1	0
0	0	0	0	1	1	0	0	0	1	1
1	0	0	1	1	0	0	0	1	0	0
0	1	0	0	1	0	0	0	1	0	1
1	1	0	0	0	0	0	0	1	1	0
0	0	0	1	1	1	1	0	1	1	1
0	0	0	0	0	0	0	1	0	0	0
0	0	0	1	1	0	0	0	1	1	0

(a) The partitioned 7-segment to binary truth table

a	b	c	d	e	Y_2	Y_1	Y_0
0	0	0	0	0	0	0	0
1	0	0	1	1	0	0	1
0	0	1	0	0	0	1	0
0	0	0	0	1	0	1	1
0	1	0	0	1	1	0	0
1	1	0	0	0	1	0	1
0	0	0	1	1	1	1	0

(b) Compressing five to three variables; ROM 0

Y_2	Y_1	Y_0	f	g	D	C	B	A
0	0	0	1	0	0	0	0	0
0	0	1	0	0	0	0	0	1
0	1	0	0	0	0	0	1	0
0	1	1	0	1	0	0	1	1
0	0	1	1	1	0	1	0	0
1	0	0	1	1	0	1	0	1
1	0	1	1	1	0	1	1	0
1	1	0	0	0	0	1	1	1
0	0	0	1	1	1	0	0	0
1	1	0	1	1	1	0	0	1

(c) The code convertor based on the recoded abcde partition with fg; ROM 1

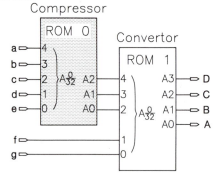

(d) The reduced 224-bit implementation

Figure 3.61: Partitioning a ROM to convert 7-segment to binary code.

The majority of PROMs are used as program/data stores in microprocessor-based circuits. The 27256 device shown in the data sheet of Fig. 3.62 is a U.V. erasable PROM (EPROM) typically used in this role. A 15-bit address accesses one of 32,768 (2^{15}) 8-bit words stored as described in Fig. 3.7. The chip is selected and output 3-state buffers enabled when both $\overline{\text{G}}$ and $\overline{\text{E}}$ are active. The $\overline{\text{G}}$ control line further acts to put the EPROM into a low-power standby mode, which more than halves its power consumption. This is shown in the IEC/ANSI logic symbol by the note **[PWR DWN]**. Programming is accomplished by bringing V_{PP} (pin 1) up to +12.5 V and V_{CC} to +6 V, with the appropriate address and data byte to be stored. The $\overline{\text{E}}$ pin is pulsed Low for 1 ms and then $\overline{\text{G}}$ pulsed Low to verify that the data has in fact been stored. This pulse-and-verify action can be repeated up to 15 times. When verification is successful a final 4 ms programming pulse is made to ensure correct operation. However, such details are invisible to the user, and are handled automatically by the programmer. Generally a file is downloaded to the programmer, as described in Chapter 6.

Most EPROMs and their electrically erasable counterparts have an access time

MOS
LSI

TMS27256
262,144-BIT ERASABLE PROGRAMMABLE READ-ONLY MEMORY

MAY 1985

- **32,768 X 8 Organization**
- **Single + 5-V Power Supply**
- **All Inputs and Outputs Are TTL Compatible**
- **Max Access/Min Cycle Time:**

TMS27256-20	200 ns
TMS27256-25	250 ns
TMS27256-35	350 ns

- **Low Active Current — 100 mA (Maximum)**
- **JEDEC Approved Pinout**
- **Fast Programming Algorithm**
- **Software Carrier Capability**
- **Two-line Control**
- **Silicon Signature**
- **Available in plastic package**

TMS27256 . . . JL PACKAGE
(TOP VIEW)

```
        +------\__/------+
 VPP  [ 1          28 ]  VCC
 A12  [ 2          27 ]  A14
  A7  [ 3          26 ]  A13
  A6  [ 4          25 ]  A8
  A5  [ 5          24 ]  A9
  A4  [ 6          23 ]  A11
  A3  [ 7          22 ]  Ḡ
  A2  [ 8          21 ]  A10
  A1  [ 9          20 ]  Ē
  A0  [ 10         19 ]  Q8
  Q1  [ 11         18 ]  Q7
  Q2  [ 12         17 ]  Q6
  Q3  [ 13         16 ]  Q5
 GND  [ 14         15 ]  Q4
        +---------------+
```

PIN NOMENCLATURE	
A0-A14	Addresses
Ē	Chip Enable/Power Down
Ḡ	Output Enable
GND	Ground
Q1-Q8	Outputs
VCC	+ 5-V Power Supply
VPP	+ 12.5-V Power Supply

description

The TMS27256 is an ultraviolet light-erasable, electrically programmable read-only memory. It has 262,144 bits organized as 32,768 words of 8-bit length. The TMS27256 only requires a single 5-volt power supply. The TMS27256-20 provides an access time of 200 ns, which is compatible with high-speed microprocessors.

The TMS27256 provides two output control lines: Output Enable ($\bar{G}$) and Chip Enable/Power Down ($\bar{E}$). This feature allows the $\bar{G}$ control line to eliminate bus contention in microprocessor systems. The TMS27256 has a standby mode that reduces the maximum power dissipation from 525 mW to 210 mW when the device is placed on standby.

FUNCTION (PINS)	MODE						
	Read	Output Disable	Power Down (Standby)	Fast Programming	Program Verification	Inhibit Programming	Silicon Signature
$\bar{E}$ (20)	V_{IL}	V_{IL}	V_{IH}	V_{IL}	V_{IH}	V_{IH}	V_{IL}
$\bar{G}$ (22)	V_{IL}	V_{IH}	X	V_{IH}	V_{IL}	V_{IH}	V_{IL}
A9 (24)	X	X	X	X	X	X	V_{PP}
V_{PP} (1)	V_{CC}	V_{CC}	V_{CC}	V_{PP}	V_{PP}	V_{PP}	V_{CC}
V_{CC} (28)	V_{CC}	V_{CC}	V_{CC}	V_{CC}	V_{CC}	V_{CC}	V_{CC}
Q1-Q8 (11 to 13, 15 to 19)	Q	HI-Z	HI-Z	D	Q	HI-Z	Q

X = V_{IL} or V_{IH}

Table 1

TEXAS
INSTRUMENTS

Figure 3.62:An abstract from the TMS27256 EPROM data sheet (*continued next page*).

TMS27256
262,144-BIT ERASABLE PROGRAMMABLE READ-ONLY MEMORY

operation

The seven modes of operation for the TMS27256 are listed in the table 1.

read

The dual control pins ($\overline{E}$ and $\overline{G}$) must have low-level TTL signals in order to provide data at the outputs. Chip enable ($\overline{E}$) should be used for device selection. Output enable ($\overline{G}$) should be used to gate data to the output pins.

power down

The power-down mode reduces the maximum active current from 100 mA to 40 mA. A TTL high-level signal applied to $\overline{E}$ selects the power-down mode. In this mode, the outputs assume a high-impedance state, indipendent of $\overline{G}$.

erasure

Before programming, the TMS27256 is erased by exposing the chip to shortwave ultraviolet light that has a wavelenght of 253.7 nanometers (2537 angstroms). The recommended minimum exposure dose (UV intensity X exposure time) is fifteen watt-seconds per square centimeter. A typical 12mW/cm2UV lamp will erase the device in approximately 20 minutes. The lamp should be located about 2.5 centimeters (1 inch) above the chip during erasure. After erasure, all bits are at a high level. It should be noted that normal ambient light contains the correct wavelength for erasure. Therefore, when using the TMS27256, the window should be covered with an opaque label.

fast programming

Note that application of a voltage in excess of 13 V to Vpp may damage the TMS27256.

After erasure, logic "O's" are programmed into the desired locations. Programming consists of the following sequence of events. With the level on Vpp equal to 12.5 V and E at TTL low, data to be programmed is applied in parallel to output pins Q8-Q1. The location to be programmed is addressed.

Programming uses two types of programming pulse: Prime and Final. The length of the Prime pulse is 1 millisecond; this pulse is applied X times. After each application the byte being programmed is verified. If the correct data is read, the Final programming pulse is then applied, if correct data is not read, a further 1 millisecond programming pulse is applied up to a maximum X of 15. The Final programming pulse is 4X milliseconds long. This sequence of programming pulses and byte verification is done at V_{CC} = 6.0 V and Vpp = 12.5 V. When the full fast programming routine is complete, all bits are verified with V_{CC} = Vpp = 5 V. A flowchart of the fast programming routine is shown in Figure 1.

logic symbol†

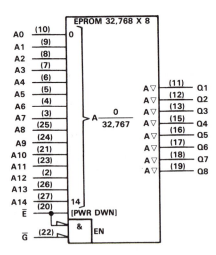

†This symbol is in accordance with ANSI/IEEE Std 91-1984 and IEC Publication 617-12.

Figure 3.62: (*continued*). An abstract from the TMS27256 EPROM data sheet. Courtesy of Texas Instruments Ltd.

Designation	Architecture	Size (bits)	Typical delay (ns)	Typical current (ma)
Fused bipolar				
74S288/82S123A/18S030/27S19	5P8	256	15–35	100
74S287/82S129A/24S10/27S21	8P4	1K	25–50	120
82S135A/38S22/27S13	8P8	2k	25–100	100–150
74S472/82S147A/28S42/27S33	9P8	4K	25–60	155
82S181A/B/C	10P8	8K	30–70	175
82S191A/C/38L165	11P8	16K	35–80	175
82HS321/A/B	12P8	32K	30–45	175
82HS641/A/B	13P8	64K	35–55	175
CMOS U.V. erasable PROM (EPROM)				
7C292	11P8	16K	35	90
27C32	12P8	32K	150–200	10/1[†]
7C261	13P8	64K	35	100/10[†]
27C64	13P8	64K	150–250	20/1[†]
7C251	14P8	128K	45–65	100/30[†]
27C128	14P8	128K	150–250	20/0.5[†]
7C271	15P8	256K	45–55	120/30[†]
27C256	15P8	256K	120–250	50/1[†]
27C512	16P8	512K	120–250	10/1[†]
27C010/101	17P8	1M	100–200	30/1[†]
27C1024/210	16P16	1M	85–200	50/1[†]
27C020/2001	18P8	2M	150–200	50/1[†]
27C040/4001	19P8	4M	80–150	50/1[†]
CMOS electrically erasable EPROM (EEPROM)				
28C16	11P8	16K	150–250	110/40[†]
28C64	13P8	64K	150–250	30/0.1[†]
28C256	15P8	256K	120–250	50/0.5[†]
28F512	16P8	512K	120–200	30/0.5[†]
28F010	17P8	1M	150–200	30/0.5[†]

[†] Standby current

Table 3.8: A selection of combinational PROM/PLE devices.

(time between address change and output of stable data) greater than 100 ns; typically 250 ns. This is considered rather slow for most logic replacement applications, but in reality this sort of speed is adequate for many situations. A few high-speed CMOS EPROMs are available (see Table 3.8) to suit fast microprocessors. Currently these are prohibitively priced compared to their bipolar equivalents, but this situation will undoubtedly change.

ROM-family devices are inherently prone to output glitches when their address (input data) is changed. To some extent this is because of static hazards. By their nature ROMs cannot be programmed to generate covering functions as depicted in Fig. 2.63, which are necessary to eliminate this problem. Glitches are also a consequence of the very large decoder circuits. If this is a problem, the output buffers should be disabled during an address change until after the access time. The outputs can then be sampled, based on the techniques outlined in Chapter 4.

3.3.3   PALs

The **programmable array logic (PAL)** architecture may be regarded as a mirror image of the PROM/PLE, with a programmable AND array feeding a fixed OR matrix — as shown in Fig. 3.56. Although this is technically correct, it is perhaps more productive to think of a PAL as a group of OR gates, each fed by several AND gates. Each AND gate can be connected to any set of the input literals. This can clearly be seen in Fig. 3.63 which shows the structure of a 12H6 device. This is an array of six OR gates, two of which are connected to four 24-input programmable AND gates and the rest each having two such AND gates. The twelve input variables and their complements are optionally connected to all 16 AND gates. The designation 12H6 means twelve inputs and six active-High outputs.

PALs were the brain child of John Birkner who persuaded a rather reluctant Monolithic Memories, Inc. (MMI were eventually taken over by Advanced Micro Devices, Inc., who now hold the rights to the trademark PAL) to manufacture and market them [27]. Although PALs were less powerful and flexible than the already existing PROM/PLE and PLA architectures, their very simplicity meant that manufacturing costs could be kept down. A new skinny DIP 20-pin package (0.3″ across) contrasted favourably with the rival PLA's 28-pin fat (0.6″ across) housing. The provision of good clear documentation and a computer-aided engineering (CAE) design package quickly popularized the PAL and it has remained in that position since its general introduction in 1978.

Example 3.24

Show how the PAL12H6 can be programmed to implement the car-indicator logic derived in Example 2.6.

Solution

The logic equations to be generated are:

$$R\_Light \;=\; (R{\cdot}F)+(H{\cdot}F)$$
$$L\_Light \;=\; (L{\cdot}F)+(H{\cdot}F)$$

This requires two output OR gates, each driven by two AND gates. In Fig. 3.63 I have arbitrarily chosen OR gate pin 17 for R_Light and that at pin 16 for L_Light. Connections between inputs (vertical lines) and AND gates (horizontal lines) are shown as **X** in the normal way. Thus the AND gate connected to line 128 generates H·F (symbolized as H&F), and **X**s are shown at the intersection of lines 128 and 4 (fuse 132) and 128:8 (fuse 136). In this manner the personalization of the PAL can be characterized simply by the fuse pattern list:

$$132, 136, 162, 168, 196, 200, 224, 232.$$

This is all the information needed by the programmer to 'blast' the appropriate fuses, leaving just the shown connections. In the case of vertical fuses (anti-fuses) and erasable technologies, the numbers indicate 'zapped' or charged transistors respectively. Although the characteristic numbers can be passed to the PAL programmer

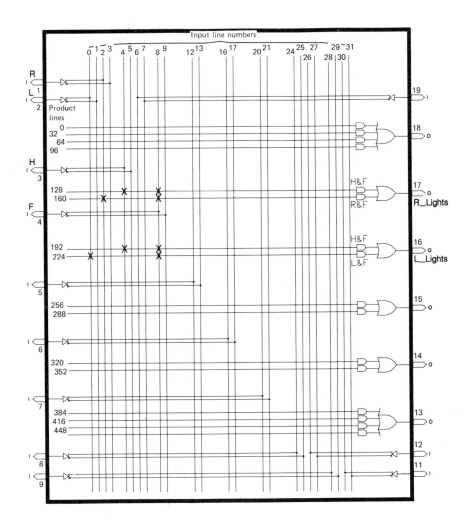

Figure 3.63: Indicator lights logic implemented in a PAL12H6.

by hand; normally the computer-aided engineering software generates a file with this information embedded, see Example 6.1. Thus the pictorial representation of Fig. 3.63 is for human documentation purposes only.

Note that the product term H&F has had to be generated twice. This is because there is no mechanism to share product terms in the standard PAL architecture.

The example presented here is a barely viable use of a PAL, as the logic may be implemented with five 2-I/P NAND gates, say, 2 × 74x00. The cost of a simple PAL is around ×7 that of a SSI package. Against this is the reduction in board space from 2 × 14 pins to a single 20-pin package.

The 12H6 has 512 fuses and only 16 AND gates, and thus is of limited utility. Small PALs, of which this is a representative example, were quickly followed by medium PALs, such as the 16L8 shown in Fig. 3.22(c). This has eight OR gates, each fed by seven 32-I/P AND gates, and eight 3-state buffered outputs, each separately enabled by a single 32-I/P AND gate. Thus there are 64 32-I/P AND gates, and a total of 2048 fuses. As is described in Fig. 3.22(a)&(b), the provision of individually enabled 3-state buffers with feedback returned into the AND matrix, permits outputs to be optionally used as inputs, by 'disconnecting' the relevant OR gate. On this basis, as six of the eight outputs have this configuration, we have a maximum of 16 inputs (10 dedicated always as inputs — labelled as I — and six which can be swapped over from outputs — labelled I/O). The designation 16L8 means a *maximum* of 16 inputs together with a *maximum* of eight active-Low outputs. A common mistake is to assume that the two numbers co-exist (they do with the small PAL range); thus if 16 input variables are needed, only two outputs (pins 19 and 12) are available.

Example 3.25

Determine the fuse plot for a PAL16L8 to implement the π-generator of Fig. 2.49.

Solution

As the PAL16L8 has active-Low outputs we require a zeros minimization to give an active-High implementation of the truth table of Fig. 2.49(b). This is shown in Fig. 3.64, who's K-maps are the inverse of those of Fig. 2.3(c).

In minimizing SOP equations to be implemented in a PAL, the major consideration is limiting the number of AND gates (K-map loops) to fit into the target architecture. The number of gate inputs, i.e. number of literals in each product term, is irrelevant. For example the term $\overline{D}\cdot\overline{C}\cdot\overline{B}\cdot A$ in the W K-map does not cost any more than the more obvious minimization $\overline{D}\cdot\overline{C}$. Thus only the number of loops in a K-map is of importance and not their size. I have used this criterion in generating the equations from the K-maps, which would be considered poor if targeted to a SSI gate implementation. If static hazards are of concern, then the function $\overline{D}\cdot\overline{C}$ is the loop of choice, as overlapping coverings prevent this type of hazard. Thus the SSI criterion of minimum loops of maximum size is still a good goal. Notice from the logic diagram that all input literals use complementary output buffers to provide time symmetrical true and complement variable signals; reducing the possibility of

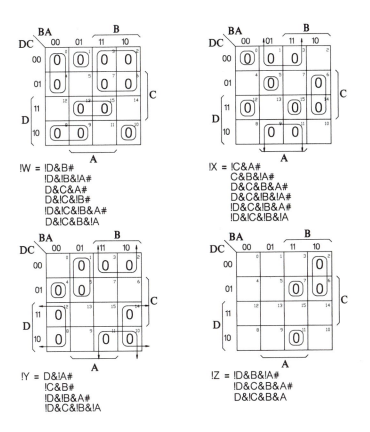

Figure 3.64: An active-Low minimization of the π-generator.

static hazards. The normal hazard prevention techniques can be used with PALs (see Section 2.3.3) [36].

In annotating the diagram of Fig. 3.65, I have used the symbology of the CAE software to be introduced in Section 6.1. Thus & symbolizes AND, # corresponds to OR and ! indicates inversion.

As before, an **X** indicates an intact lateral fuse, blown vertical fuse or charged FET. All other intersections show no connection (blown lateral fuse). Each OR gate is fed by seven AND gates. Where there are less than seven product terms required for an output, the left-over AND gates should generate a logic 0 into the OR gate. Remember that ORing a 0 does not alter the response of an OR gate to its other inputs. This is conveniently done by leaving all connections to the relevant AND gates intact, as denoted by showing an **X** inside the AND symbol itself. As the relationship $l \cdot \bar{l}$ always gives 0, and as this scheme will include both complement and uncomplemented versions of the same variables, then effectively this removes the AND gate's influence at the OR gate. Using all literals rather than just one reduces the chances of static hazard induced spikes at the output of the AND gate.

A gate input with no connection (eg. blown lateral fuse) floats to logic 1. Thus

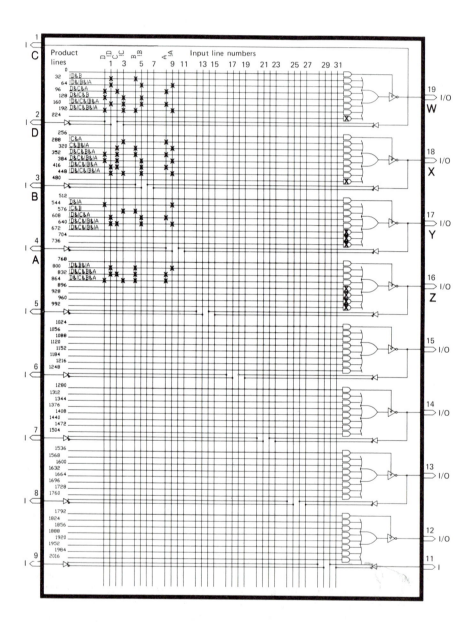

Figure 3.65: Using a PAL16L8 to implement a π-generator.

an AND gate with no input connections (i.e. no **X**s) gives a logic 1 output. This is the case for the AND gates driving the 3-state output buffers. As these are enabled on logic 1, I have left the driving AND gates unconnected.

Implementing the circuit of Fig. 2.49(d) takes nine SSI packages, at a cost of 80 gate inputs. The MSI equivalent of Fig. 3.32 requires five packages and costs 85 gate inputs. A PAL16L8 costs 60 gate inputs and requires one package. The alternative of using a PLE5P8 costs around the same, and has the advantage of having the capacity to generate up to 63 decimal places at no additional cost!

The tendency during the 1980s in PAL devices was to retain the AND fixed-OR architecture and provide additional flexibility at the output. The programmable 3-state outputs of the 16L8 is an example of this, allowing some pins to be used either as inputs or as outputs. The 18P8 device shown in Fig. 3.66 is an example of this tendency. Each output feeds a cell comprizing an ENOR gate driving a 3-state inverter. The ENOR gate acts as a programmable inverter. If its fused leg is intact (logic 0), then inversion occurs and the output is active-Low. An open fuse (logic 1) leads to an active-High output. Thus the P in 18P8 stands for polarity. As in the 16L8, the 18P8 has individually programmable AND gates enabling each 3-state buffer. This time all eight outputs have feedback from the 3-state buffers back into the AND matrix and therefore all outputs can be programmed as inputs, giving a potential maximum of 18 inputs. However, if this option is exercised, there would (rather uselessly) be no outputs! An additional enhancement is the increase from seven to eight AND gates driving each OR output. There are now 2600 fuses.

The extra flexibility means that the 18P8 can replace almost any 20-pin combinational PAL, as listed in the data sheet, as well as implementing logic that none of these older devices can cope with. The versatile PAL/generic PAL series (eg. 16V8) develop the sophistication of the output macro cell to optionally include memory elements. These are discussed in Section 4.5.

Example 3.26

Using a PAL20P8 design a bus-compatible 8-bit Gray to binary converter. The 3-state buffers are to be enabled when all four **Enable** inputs are in their active state; $\overline{\text{EN0}}$ and $\overline{\text{EN1}}$ are active-Low and EN2/EN3 are both active-High.

Solution

The modulo-2 conversion algorithm of Example 1.14 shows that any binary bit B_n can be generated as $G_n \oplus B_{n-1}$. Thus the outcome for bit n is dependent both on the current Gray bit and the outcome of the $(n-1)$th process. This iteration thus requires a feedback path which is illustrated in Fig. 3.67 with bold lines. Only six outputs have this internal 'buried' feedback path, but fortunately we can use the relationship $B_1 = G_1$ in generating output B_2; and the last output does not need to be passed back into the matrix. Buried feedback is especially useful where sequential circuits are implemented, as will be shown in Chapter 4. The alternative approach of making an external connection between output and input uses up input pins and has a longer propagation delay compared to an internal path. We have seen in

PLHS18P8A
PAL®-Type Device

Signetics Programmable Logic
Product Specification

Application Specific Products
● **Series 20**

DESCRIPTION

The PLHS18P8A is a two-level logic element consisting of 72 AND gates and 8 OR gates with fusible connections for programming I/O polarity and direction.

All AND gates are linked to 10 inputs (I) and 8 bidirectional I/O lines (B). These yield variable I/O gate configurations via 8 direction control gates, ranging from 18 inputs to 8 outputs.

On-chip T/C buffers couple either True (I, B) or Complement (Ī, B̄) input polarities to all AND gates. The 72 AND gates are separated into 8 groups of 9 each. Each group of 9 is associated with one bidirectional pin. In each group, eight of the AND terms are ORed together, while the ninth is used to establish I/O direction. All outputs are individually programmable via an Ex-OR gate to allow implementation of AND/OR or NAND/NOR logic functions.

In the virgin state, the AND array fuses are back-to-back CB-EB diode pairs which will act as open connections. Current is avalanched across individual diode pairs during fusing, which essentially short circuits the EB diode and provides the connection for the associated product term.

The PLHS18P8A is field-programmable, allowing the user to quickly generate custom pattern using standard programming equipment.

Order codes are listed in the Ordering Information Table.

FEATURES

● **100% functionally compatible with AmPAL18P8A and all 16L8, 16P8, 16H8, 16L2, 16H2, 14L4, 14H4, 12L6, 12H6, 10L8, 10H8, 16LD8 and 16HD8 PAL type products**
● **Field-Programmable**
● **10 inputs**
● **8 bidirectional I/O lines**
● **72 AND gates/product terms**
  – configured into eight groups of nine
● **Programmable output polarity (3-State output)**
● **I/O propagation delay: 20ns (max)**
● **Power dissipation: 500mW (typ)**
● **TTL compatible**
● **Security Fuse**

PIN CONFIGURATIONS

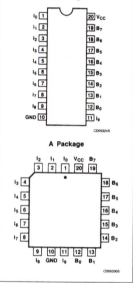

N Package

I₀ 1	20 V_CC
I₁ 2	19 B₇
I₂ 3	18 B₆
I₃ 4	17 B₅
I₄ 5	16 B₄
I₅ 6	15 B₃
I₆ 7	14 B₂
I₇ 8	13 B₁
I₈ 9	12 B₀
GND 10	11 I₉

CD05324S

A Package

CD05300S

APPLICATIONS

● **100% functional replacement for all 20-pin combinatorial PAL devices**
● **Random logic**
● **Code converters**
● **Fault detectors**
● **Function generators**
● **Address mapping**
● **Multiplexing**

FUNCTIONAL DIAGRAM

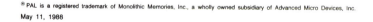

LD02583S

® PAL is a registered trademark of Monolithic Memories, Inc., a wholly owned subsidiary of Advanced Micro Devices, Inc.

May 11, 1988

Figure 3.66:   Extract from the PLHS18P8A data sheet.   Courtesy of Philips/Signetics Ltd.

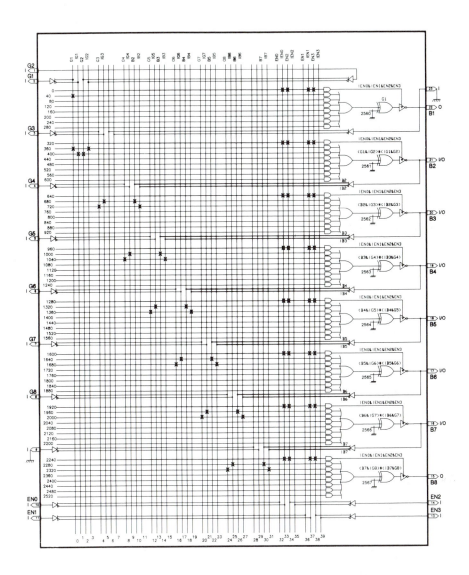

Figure 3.67: An 8-bit Gray code to binary converter with 3-state enable.

Fig. 3.21 that devices which can be read on a bus structure must be interposed with 3-state output buffers. All outputs on the 20P8 are 3-state buffered, and in keeping with our specification, is shown enabled by the function $\overline{EN0}\cdot\overline{EN1}\cdot EN2\cdot EN3$. Notice that this product term needs to be generated eight times, as there is no sharing provision.

As we require active-High outputs, fuses 2560–2567 are opened. The resulting logic 1 configures the EOR gates to give active-High outputs.

Implementing this function using SSI/MSI devices would require up to five devices; two quad EOR packages, see Fig. 2.59, one octal 3-state buffer, one 4-I/P NAND and one hex inverter device. Although the cost of the ICs is virtually the same in both cases; in reality the LSI solution represents a massive saving.

3.3.4   PLAs

An obvious extension of the PAL is to provide programmability of both AND and OR arrays [37]. In fact the resulting structure, known as the **programmable logic array (PLA)** preceded the simpler architecture by several years. Initial devices where masked programmed, just like the ROM predated the PROM. The first **field programmable logic array (FPLA)** device, the 82S100 (now called the PLS100) was introduced by Napoleone Cavlan of the Signetics Corporation in 1975 [27]. The PLS100 has a fully programmable array of 48 AND gates which drive a second configurable array of eight OR gates; each with a series EOR gate, acting as a programmable inverter. There are 16 dedicated inputs and eight fixed outputs, with a total of 1928 fuses.

The 82S100/PLS100 (PLS stands for Programmable Logic from Signetics) FPLA was ahead of its time. The two levels of lateral fuses made the device slow, the die size large (expensive) and there was no software support. All these problems were to be eventually overcome, especially as the success of PALs showed that the PLD market was important.

The PLUS153 FPLA of Fig. 3.68 is a typical small footprint (20-pin) device. Any 32 product terms of up to 18 input variables can be generated, and any selection of these OR'ed together by eight OR gates (labelled X9...X0). Each of these OR gates is in series with a programmable inverter (S9...S0) and a 3-state buffer. These output buffers are controlled by an additional ten programmable AND gates, operating on the same input variables, labelled D9...D0. As in the case of the PALs discussed at the end of the previous section, outputs (labelled B9...B0) are fed back into the AND matrix. This means that any output can be programmed as an input. Thus the description of the PLUS153 as a $18 \times 42 \times 10$ device means a maximum of 18 inputs, 42 product terms and a maximum of ten outputs. For example, if eight outputs are required, only ten input variables are permitted. Furthermore, ten AND gates are used to control the 3-state buffers, thus only 32 product terms can be used to generate output equations. The PLUS173 FPLA is a $22 \times 42 \times 10$ 24-pin version of the PLUS153, having twelve dedicated inputs instead of eight, but is otherwise identical.

The similarity of the FPLA and PAL architectures can be gauged by comparing the logic diagrams of Fig. 3.68 and Fig. 3.65. However, careful scrutiny of the two architectures shows the major advantage of the PLA. Any combination of logic product terms (vertical lines) can be ORed without restriction and irrespective

Philips Components

Document No.	853–1508
ECN No.	00750
Date of Issue	October 18, 1990
Status	Product Status
Programmable Logic Devices	

PLUS153–10
Programmable logic array
(18 × 42 × 10)

DESCRIPTION

The PLUS153–10 PLD is a high speed, combinatorial Programmable Logic Array. The Signetics state-of-the-art Oxide Isolated Bipolar fabrication process is employed to produce maximum propagation delays of 10ns or less.

The 20-pin PLUS153 device has a programmable AND array and a programmable OR array. Unlike PAL® devices, 100% product term sharing is supported. Any of the 32 logic product terms can be connected to any or all of the 10 output OR gates. Most PAL ICs are limited to 7 AND terms per OR function; the PLUS153–10 can support up to 32 input wide OR functions.

The polarity of each output is user-programmable as either Active-High or Active-Low, thus allowing AND-OR or AND-NOR logic implementation. This feature adds an element of design flexibility, particularly when implementing complex decoding functions.

The PLUS153–10 device is user-programmable using one of several commercially available, industry standard PLD programmers.

NOTES:
1. This is the initial unprogrammed state of all links.
2. Any gate P_n will be unconditioanlly inhibited if both the True and Complement of an input (either I or B) are left intact.

FEATURES

- I/O propagation delays (worst case)
  - PLUS153–10 – 10ns max.
- Functional superset of 16L8 and most other 20-pin combinatorial PAL devices
- Two programmable arrays
  - Supports 32 input wide OR functions
- 8 inputs
- 10 bi-directional I/O
- 42 AND gates
  - 32 logic product terms
  - 10 direction control terms
- Programmable output polarity
  - Active-High or Active-Low
- Security fuse
- 3-State outputs
- Power dissipation: 750mW (typ.)
- TTL Compatible

APPLICATIONS
- Random logic
- Code converters
- Fault detectors

PIN CONFIGURATIONS

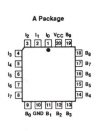

N Package

I_0	1	20 V_{CC}
I_1	2	19 B_9
I_2	3	18 B_8
I_3	4	17 B_7
I_4	5	16 B_6
I_5	6	15 B_5
I_6	7	14 B_4
I_7	8	13 B_3
B_0	9	12 B_2
GND	10	11 B_1

N = Plastic DIP (300mil-wide)

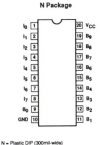

A Package

A = Plastic Leaded Chip Carrier

VIRGIN STATE
A factory shipped virgin device contains all fusible links intact, such that:
1. All outputs are at "H" polarity.
2. All P_n terms are disabled.
3. All P_n terms are active on all outputs.

OR ARRAY – (B)

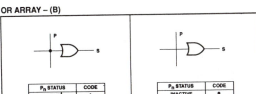

P_n STATUS	CODE
ACTIVE[1]	A

P_n STATUS	CODE
INACTIVE	•

AND ARRAY – (I, B)

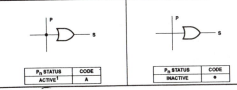

STATE	CODE
INACTIVE[1,2]	0

STATE	CODE
I, B	H

STATE	CODE
I, B̄	L

STATE	CODE
DON'T CARE	–

Figure 3.68: The PLUS153 FPLA (*continued next page*).

Philips Components Programmable Logic Devices   Product Specification

Programmable logic array (18 × 42 × 10)   PLUS153–10

LOGIC DIAGRAM

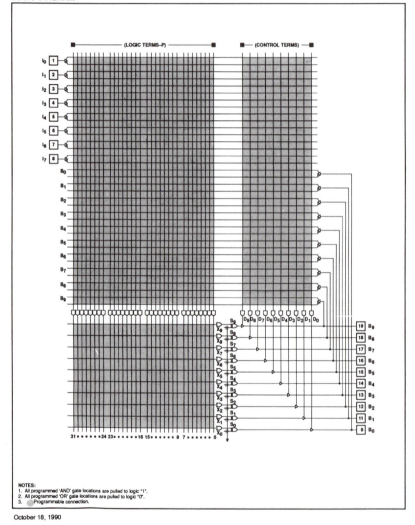

NOTES:
1. All programmed 'AND' gate locations are pulled to logic "1".
2. All programmed 'OR' gate locations are pulled to logic "0".
3. Programmable connection.

October 18, 1990

Figure 3.68: (*continued*). The PLUS153 FPLA. Courtesy of Philips/Signetics Ltd.

of its previous use by any other OR gates (horizontal lines). This means that unlike PALs, a minimization strategy that aims to share product terms (loops in K-maps) is relevant to the PLA architecture. Unlike the similar strategy used in Section 2.4.2, the size of the product terms is irrelevant; in a similar manner to PAL product terms. Thus the overall goal is not a minimum gate input count but simply the minimum number of overall product terms of any size. Sometimes it may be better to simply use the elementary p-terms (minterms) without reduction. This is because conventional reduction techniques, whilst considerably reducing the size of the requisite AND gates (of no relevance to PLAs), increase their number. For example, a direct PLA implementation of Fig. 2.51 would require ten AND gates, as opposed to using (and sharing) eight minterms. In a PLA, the grouping A costs the same as the grouping $\overline{D}\cdot\overline{B}\cdot A$! This is the approach taken in the following example.

Example 3.27

Using a PLUS153 PLA, design a converter from 8-bit ASCII $'0' \ldots '9'$, $'A' \ldots 'F'$ and $'a' \ldots 'f'$ to their 4-bit binary equivalent. The alpha characters have their usual hexadecimal meaning.

Solution

Eight-bit ASCII codes for the alphanumeric characters are as listed in Table 1.4, but with bit 7 logic 0. This gives ASCII codes 0011 0000 – 0011 1001b, 0100 0001 – 0100 0110b and 0110 0001 – 0110 0110b respectively for the three ranges. These are to translate to the corresponding binary patterns 0000 – 1001b, 1010 – 1111b and 1010 – 1111b.

Rather than illustrate the solution by placing **X**s on Fig. 3.68, I have entered the appropriate data in the Program table of Fig. 3.68. This shows the 32 AND gates top left feeding the ten OR gates at top right. A $\boxed{L}$ in the AND matrix indicates a connection to that variable complemented, whilst a true connection is symbolized as $\boxed{H}$. A $\boxed{-}$ means no connection to that variable and $\boxed{0}$ requests a connection to both true and complement (see also Fig. 3.68). This latter (which is the unprogrammed state) effectively removes the AND gate from the OR matrix, as its output is always logic 0. Input variables are the dedicated inputs, I[7...0] and ten input/outputs, B(I)[9...0].

Each of the product terms 0...31 can be connected to any OR gate as indicated by $\boxed{A}$ (for AND). Non-connection is symbolized by $\boxed{\cdot}$. Notice that most of the active product terms are shared with more than one output; for example, term 21 is shared between all four OR gates (B(O)[3...0]).

The ten 3-state buffers are controlled by the product terms D[9...0]. These are shown as $\boxed{-}$, which with no connected variables causes the AND gate to float to logic 1 and hence enabling the relevant 3-state buffer. The top polarity box has $\boxed{H}$ entries indicating an intact fuse. From Fig. 3.69 we see that such a connection gives a logic 0 and the relevant EOR gate does not invert. A blown fuse, symbolized as $\boxed{L}$, inverts, giving active-Low outputs.

Only 22 input combinations out of a possible 2^8 are used in this conversion. In general, like PALs, PLAs are useful for sparse functions of many variables. De-

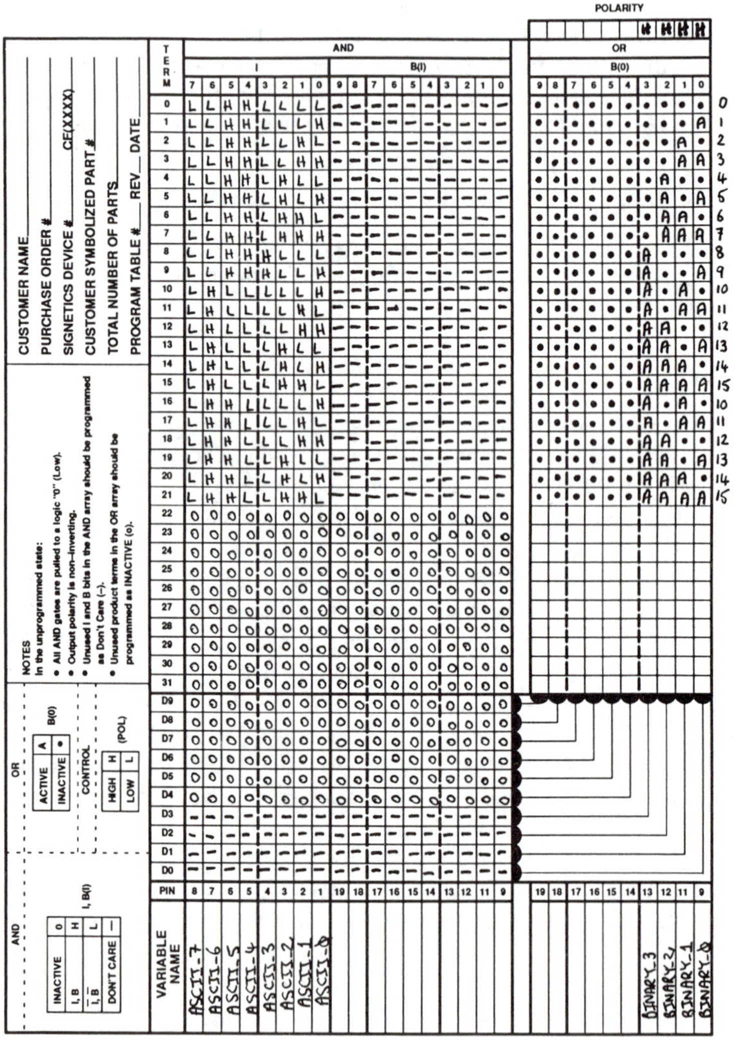

Philips Components Programmable Logic Devices — Product Specification

Programmable logic arrays (18 × 42× 10) — PLUS153

PROGRAM TABLE

CUSTOMER NAME
PURCHASE ORDER #
SIGNETICS DEVICE # CF(XXXX)
CUSTOMER SYMBOLIZED PART #
TOTAL NUMBER OF PARTS
PROGRAM TABLE # REV DATE

NOTES
In the unprogrammed state:
- All AND gates are pulled to a logic "0" (Low).
- Output polarity is non-inverting.
- Unused I and B bits in the AND array should be programmed as Don't Care (-).
- Unused product terms in the OR array should be programmed as INACTIVE (o).

AND: INACTIVE 0; I, B H; $\bar{I}, \bar{B}$ L; DON'T CARE — (I, B(I))

OR: ACTIVE A; INACTIVE • (B(0)); CONTROL: HIGH H, LOW L (POL)

POLARITY: B(0) 9–4 blank; B(0) 3, 2, 1, 0: H H H H

TERM	I 7	I 6	I 5	I 4	I 3	I 2	I 1	I 0	B(I) 9	B(I) 8	B(I) 7	B(I) 6	B(I) 5	B(I) 4	B(I) 3	B(I) 2	B(I) 1	B(I) 0	B(0) 9	B(0) 8	B(0) 7	B(0) 6	B(0) 5	B(0) 4	B(0) 3	B(0) 2	B(0) 1	B(0) 0	
0	L	L	H	H	L	L	L	L	–	–	–	–	–	–	–	–	–	–	•	•	•	•	•	•	•	•	•	•	0
1	L	L	H	H	L	L	L	H	–	–	–	–	–	–	–	–	–	–	•	•	•	•	•	•	•	•	•	A	1
2	L	L	H	H	L	L	H	L	–	–	–	–	–	–	–	–	–	–	•	•	•	•	•	•	•	•	A	•	2
3	L	L	H	H	L	L	H	H	–	–	–	–	–	–	–	–	–	–	•	•	•	•	•	•	•	•	A	A	3
4	L	L	H	H	L	H	L	L	–	–	–	–	–	–	–	–	–	–	•	•	•	•	•	•	•	A	•	•	4
5	L	L	H	H	L	H	L	H	–	–	–	–	–	–	–	–	–	–	•	•	•	•	•	•	•	A	•	A	5
6	L	L	H	H	L	H	H	L	–	–	–	–	–	–	–	–	–	–	•	•	•	•	•	•	•	A	A	•	6
7	L	L	H	H	L	H	H	H	–	–	–	–	–	–	–	–	–	–	•	•	•	•	•	•	•	A	A	A	7
8	L	L	H	H	H	L	L	L	–	–	–	–	–	–	–	–	–	–	•	•	•	•	•	•	A	•	•	•	8
9	L	L	H	H	H	L	L	H	–	–	–	–	–	–	–	–	–	–	•	•	•	•	•	•	A	•	•	A	9
10	L	H	L	L	L	L	L	H	–	–	–	–	–	–	–	–	–	–	•	•	•	•	•	•	A	•	A	•	10
11	L	H	L	L	L	L	H	L	–	–	–	–	–	–	–	–	–	–	•	•	•	•	•	•	A	•	A	A	11
12	L	H	L	L	L	L	H	H	–	–	–	–	–	–	–	–	–	–	•	•	•	•	•	•	A	A	•	•	12
13	L	H	L	L	L	H	L	L	–	–	–	–	–	–	–	–	–	–	•	•	•	•	•	•	A	A	•	A	13
14	L	H	L	L	L	H	L	H	–	–	–	–	–	–	–	–	–	–	•	•	•	•	•	•	A	A	A	•	14
15	L	H	L	L	L	H	H	L	–	–	–	–	–	–	–	–	–	–	•	•	•	•	•	•	A	A	A	A	15
16	L	H	H	L	L	L	L	H	–	–	–	–	–	–	–	–	–	–	•	•	•	•	•	•	A	•	A	•	10
17	L	H	H	L	L	L	H	L	–	–	–	–	–	–	–	–	–	–	•	•	•	•	•	•	A	•	A	A	11
18	L	H	H	L	L	L	H	H	–	–	–	–	–	–	–	–	–	–	•	•	•	•	•	•	A	A	•	•	12
19	L	H	H	L	L	H	L	L	–	–	–	–	–	–	–	–	–	–	•	•	•	•	•	•	A	A	•	A	13
20	L	H	H	L	L	H	L	H	–	–	–	–	–	–	–	–	–	–	•	•	•	•	•	•	A	A	A	•	14
21	L	H	H	L	L	H	H	L	–	–	–	–	–	–	–	–	–	–	•	•	•	•	•	•	A	A	A	A	15
22	0	0	0	0	0	0	0	0	0	0	0	0	0	0	0	0	0	0											
23	0	0	0	0	0	0	0	0	0	0	0	0	0	0	0	0	0	0											
24	0	0	0	0	0	0	0	0	0	0	0	0	0	0	0	0	0	0											
25	0	0	0	0	0	0	0	0	0	0	0	0	0	0	0	0	0	0											
26	0	0	0	0	0	0	0	0	0	0	0	0	0	0	0	0	0	0											
27	0	0	0	0	0	0	0	0	0	0	0	0	0	0	0	0	0	0											
28	0	0	0	0	0	0	0	0	0	0	0	0	0	0	0	0	0	0											
29	0	0	0	0	0	0	0	0	0	0	0	0	0	0	0	0	0	0											
30	0	0	0	0	0	0	0	0	0	0	0	0	0	0	0	0	0	0											
31	0	0	0	0	0	0	0	0	0	0	0	0	0	0	0	0	0	0											
D9	0	0	0	0	0	0	0	0	0	0	0	0	0	0	0	0	0	0											
D8	0	0	0	0	0	0	0	0	0	0	0	0	0	0	0	0	0	0											
D7	0	0	0	0	0	0	0	0	0	0	0	0	0	0	0	0	0	0											
D6	0	0	0	0	0	0	0	0	0	0	0	0	0	0	0	0	0	0											
D5	0	0	0	0	0	0	0	0	0	0	0	0	0	0	0	0	0	0											
D4	0	0	0	0	0	0	0	0	0	0	0	0	0	0	0	0	0	0											
D3	–	–	–	–	–	–	–	–	–	–	–	–	–	–	–	–	–	–											
D2	–	–	–	–	–	–	–	–	–	–	–	–	–	–	–	–	–	–											
D1	–	–	–	–	–	–	–	–	–	–	–	–	–	–	–	–	–	–											
D0	–	–	–	–	–	–	–	–	–	–	–	–	–	–	–	–	–	–											
PIN	8	7	6	5	4	3	2	1	19	18	17	16	15	14	13	12	11	9	19	18	17	16	15	14	13	12	11	9	
VARIABLE NAME	ASCII_7	ASCII_6	ASCII_5	ASCII_4	ASCII_3	ASCII_2	ASCII_1	ASCII_0																	BINARY_3	BINARY_2	BINARY_1	BINARY_0	

October 18, 1990

Figure 3.69: ASCII to hexadecimal binary. Courtesy of Philips/Signetics Ltd.

pending on the outcome of a logic minimization, it is unlikely that a PAL could implement this example, due to the limitation of eight product terms for each OR gate; although there are some PALs which incorporate limited sharing facilities. The PLUS153 PLA costs around twice the price of a general purposes PAL, such as the 16L8, but as we see is rather more flexible. A PLE8P4 would be suitable for this conversion and costs around 60% of the PLA equivalent. However, the PLA is capable of implementing 4-output functions with up to twelve inputs (which would require a PLE12P4), always provided that 32 product terms will suffice. It is possible to expand PLAs, increasing both product terms and outputs [38], but this is unlikely to be cost effective against a single PLE equivalent.

One of the advantages of the FPLA over the PLE/PROM, is the possibility of editing out minor mistakes. If a product term has either been generated incorrectly, or mistakenly, ORed to an output, it can be removed by blowing the fuses connecting the AND gate to the various OR lines. With vertical fuses the procedure is to insert links in the AND line to a variable and its complement, giving a logic 0 outcome. In either case a corrected term may be reinserted at any convenient unused location. Of course electrically erasable FPLAs do not require this flexibility.

Designation	Dedicated inputs	Dedicated outputs	Input/ Output	Delay typ(ns)	Current typ(ma)	Notes
Programmable array logic devices (PAL)[1]						
10H8/10L8	10	8	–	25–45	30–55	
16C1/20C1	16/20	1/$\bar{1}$	–	25–45	30–55	Complementary O/Ps
16L8	10	2	6	5–55	75–140[2]	
20L8	14	2	6	5–25	75–160	
20P8	14	2	6	15	140	Prog active-level O/Ps
20L10	12	2	8	15–50	120	
22P10	12	–	10	15–25	105–210	Prog active-level O/Ps
22XP10	12	–	10	20–45	90–210	AND-OR-EOR array
Programmable logic array devices (PLA)						
PLS153	8	–	10	10–40	130–150	32+10 p-terms
PLS173	12	–	10	10–30	150–165	32+10 p-terms
PLS100	16	8	–	50	120	48 p-terms
16N8	10	2	6	5–7	115–120	8 prog AND gates only

1: Largely replaced by the 16V8 and 20V8 versatile devices (see Table 4.5.)
2: CMOS version frequency dependent, typically ranging from (0.1+2/MHz) ma to (25+3.5/MHz) ma.

Table 3.9: A selection of combinational PAL and PLA devices.

3.4   Problems

3.4.1   Worked Examples

Example 3.28

The normal logic output exhibits a quasi-linear response to input changes, as exemplified by the transfer characteristic of Fig. 3.14. The High and Low states are characterized by regions of very low gain, where the output is saturated. In contrast the crossover area has a very large gain. An input changing state should not linger in this area, as the high gain may cause instability, a raised sensitivity to noise and a huge increase in power dissipation (see Fig. 3.27(d)).

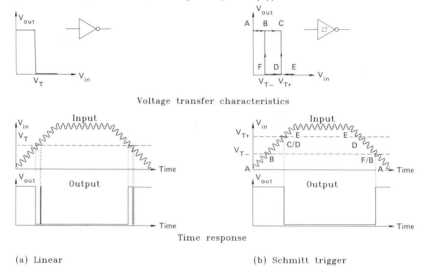

Figure 3.70: Schmitt trigger characteristics.

Normally these problems can be circumvented by ensuring that input signal transition times are no more than around ten times the worst-case family gate propagation delay; say, around 200 ns for the 74LS and 74HC families. It is not always possible to keep within this bound, especially where signals are derived from non-logic sources. Thus feeding in a mains-derived 50/60 Hz sinusoid to drive a clock circuit is not recommended! A common problem exhibited by noisy signals is shown in Fig. 3.70(a). Here noise riding on the legitimate rising and falling edge of a pulse gives spurious output spikes, where the threshold is exceeded more than once when the input is close to V_T. Even where fast input transition times are achieved, high-frequency noise can cause the same problem.

Gate circuits which feed back a fraction of their output to aid input changes have interesting properties which can be used to advantage where slow transition times and/or noisy conditions pertain. Positive feedback gives rise to hysteresis in the transfer characteristic, i.e. the threshold on the rising edge, V_{T+}, is higher than the threshold on the falling edge, V_{T-}. This is shown at the top of Fig. 3.70(b), where the path **A B C D E** going from an input Low to High is very different from the

EDFBA High to Low path. As a consequence of this, a slowly changing input has a snap action on the output, as the transition point is shifted away from the input level. The effect of the two thresholds is clearly seen at the bottom of Fig. 3.70(b), which gives a clean output from the rather dubious input.

Inputs with positive feedback are said to be **Schmitt** inputs. A typical example was shown in Fig. 2.56(c), where all 74LS688 inputs are symbolized with the hysteresis symbol. A small range of gates are also available with a Schmitt action, sometimes known as Schmitt trigger gates; see Table 3.1. Typical of these is the 74HC132, which is a quad 2-I/P NAND Schmitt trigger, which is pin compatible with the 74x00 standard NAND package. At a V_{CC} of 4.5 V, $V_{T-(typ)}$ is 1.67 V and $V_{T+(typ)}$ is 2.38 V.

Now to the question! The circuit shown in Fig. 3.71 is claimed to be a relaxation oscillator. Describe how it operates and show that its cycle period is given as:

$$t = CR \ln \frac{V_{T+}(V_{CC} - V_{T-})}{V_{T-}(V_{CC} - V_{T+})}$$

and hence determine the value of R which will give a 10 Hz frequency with $C = 0.47\mu F$.

Solution

Consider the capacitor discharging down towards V_{T-}. When V_A drops below this point, the output V_B goes to V_{CC} and the capacitor proceeds to charge up toward V_{T+}. When V_A exceeds this point, the output goes down to ground and the cycle repeats. Thus the total time for one cycle is the time to charge towards V_{CC} from V_{T-} to V_{T+} and the time to discharge back towards 0 V from V_{T+} to V_{T-}.

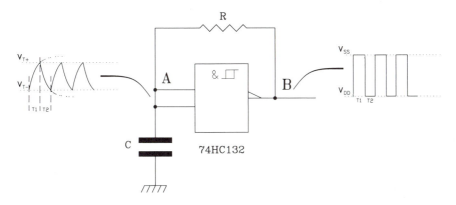

Figure 3.71: A Schmitt trigger oscillator.

The generalized first-order CR equation is:

$$v_C = V_F + \delta V e^{\frac{-t}{\tau}}$$

where v_C is the capacitor voltage at time t, V_F is the fixed final target voltage and δV the fixed difference between final and initial values. Thus period 1 is characterized by $V_F = V_{CC}$ and δV by $V_{CC} - V_{T-}$. Thus at time $t = T1$ when v_C reaches V_{T+} we have:

$$V_{T+} = V_{CC} - (V_{CC} - V_{T-})e^{-\frac{T1}{\tau}}$$

or

$$\frac{V_{CC} - V_{T+}}{V_{CC} - V_{T-}} = e^{-\frac{T1}{\tau}}$$

Thus

$$-\frac{T1}{\tau} = \ln \frac{V_{CC} - V_{T+}}{V_{CC} - V_{T-}}$$

and

$$T1 = \tau \ln \frac{V_{CC} - V_{T-}}{V_{CC} - V_{T+}} = CR \ln \frac{V_{CC} - V_{T-}}{V_{CC} - V_{T+}}$$

For period 2, when the capacitor is discharging, $V_F = V_{T+}$ and $\delta V = 0 - V_{T+}$. Thus at time $t = T2$ when v_C reaches V_{T+}, we have:

$$V_{T-} = 0 - (0 - V_{T+})e^{-\frac{T2}{\tau}}$$

or

$$\frac{V_{T-}}{V_{T+}} = e^{-\frac{T2}{\tau}}$$

Thus

$$-\frac{T2}{\tau} = \ln \frac{V_{T-}}{V_{T+}}$$

and

$$T2 = -\tau \ln \frac{V_{T-}}{V_{T+}} = -CR \ln \frac{V_{T-}}{V_{T+}}$$

Adding gives

$$T = T1 + T2 = CR \left(\ln \frac{V_{CC} - V_{T-}}{V_{CC} - V_{T+}} + \ln \frac{V_{T+}}{V_{T-}} \right)$$

$$T = CR \ln \frac{V_{T+}(V_{CC} - V_{T-})}{V_{T-}(V_{CC} - V_{T+})}$$

Taking the numerical situation and substituting gives:

$$0.1 = 0.47 \times 10^{-6}R \ln \frac{2.38(4.5 - 1.67)}{1.67(4.5 - 2.38)} = 330 \text{ k}\Omega$$

In using oscillators like this, you should note that frequency values are rather nominal and somewhat temperature and supply-dependent. For example, over a range $-40°C$ to $+85°C$, $V_{T+(max)}$ can be as high as 3.15 V and $V_{T-(min)}$ as low as 0.9 V. Substituting these values into the above equation gives a frequency of 2.9 Hz! Can you determine a formula for the mark:space ratio of the circuit and modify it giving a long mark (High) and short space (Low)? Hint: you will have to use an extra resistor and two diodes. How could you modify the circuit to give an oscillator which can be gated by an external control input?

Example 3.29

A burglar alarm is to automatically dial the telephone number 011-44-232-365-131 on detecting an intruder. The number generator is to consist of a 74x154 decoder with appropriate gates, sequentially accessed with a modulo-14 counter.

The output of this network is to be passed to a dialler whose characteristics are such that loading in a number n produces $n - 1$ pulses into the telephone network.

p	DCBA	WXYZ	N
0	0000	1011	0
1	0001	0010	1
2	0010	0010	1
3	0011	0101	4
4	0100	0101	4
5	0101	0011	2
6	0110	0100	3
7	0111	0011	2
8	1000	0100	3
9	1001	0111	6
10	1010	0110	5
11	1011	0010	1
12	1100	0100	3
13	1101	0010	1

(a) Truth table

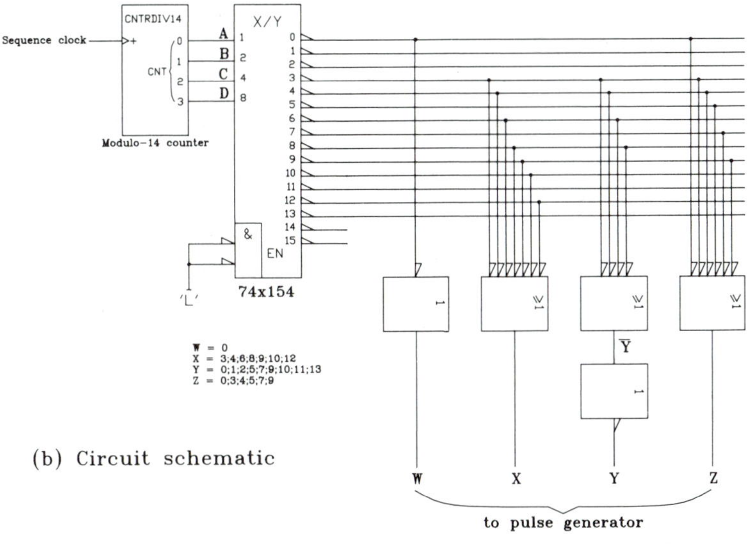

$W = 0$
$X = 3;4;6;8;9;10;12$
$Y = 0;1;2;5;7;9;10;11;13$
$Z = 0;3;4;5;7;9$

(b) Circuit schematic

to pulse generator

Figure 3.72: A telephone-number generator.

Solution

The truth table of Fig. 3.72(a) shows each digit coded as $n + 1$, with the exception of digit 0 which generates ten pulses. On this basis, NAND gates OR the relevant lines (p terms) to give the 4-bit output corresponding to each input state. Output Y is generated from its inverse, to reduce the gate size.

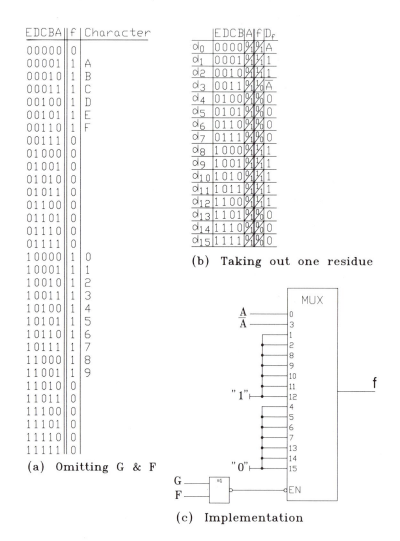

(a) Omitting G & F

(b) Taking out one residue

(c) Implementation

Figure 3.73: ASCII hex character detector.

Example 3.30

A certain keyboard interface circuit is required to detect the ASCII-coded characters '0'...'9' and 'A'...'F'. It is proposed to use a single 16 to 1-line multiplexer, together with appropriate gates, to effect this detection. Show how this could be done.

Solution

From Table 1.4 we see that the relevant code (G F E D C B A) ranges from 011 0000 through 011 1001 and 100 0001 through 100 0110. As each code group comprises seven digits, the conventional approach would use three variables as residues. However, if we note that omitting bits G and F leaves us with a 5-bit unique set, then we can use the function G$\oplus$F to enable the multiplexer (i.e. G F = 01 or 10) and, say, A as a residue.

Implementation follows in normally from the truth tables in Fig. 3.73(a) & (b). The simplicity of the resulting circuits illustrates that it is worth examining code tables with many don't care states, i.e. sparse functions, for such redundancies (see also Example 3.23).

Example 3.31

Show how the central-heating controller of Example 2.25 can be implemented using two 74LS151 8 to 1-line multiplexers, together with any appropriate gates. Do a cost comparison with MSI and LSI implementations.

Solution

Rearranging the truth table of Table 2.6(a) using two residues leads to the implementation of Fig. 3.74(b). Two 74LS151 multiplexers are expanded using a 74LS00 quad NAND-gate package as a 2 to 1-line multiplexer. Another 74LS00 package generates the residue functions, assuming $\overline{A_2}$ and $\overline{A_1}$ are already available. The 74LS151 costs around 15 gate inputs, giving a total cost of 46 inputs and a package count of four. The package count would be reduced to two if a 74150 16 to 1-line multiplexer were used in the implementation. Unfortunately this device is hard to obtain, other than in the original, nearly obsolete, 74 series, and is expensive.

The SSI implementation of Table 2.6(c) requires fifteen 4-I/P NAND gates plus a 15-I/P NAND gate, giving a cost of 75 gate inputs. More important by far, the chip count would be ten packages.

As there are 15 product terms in the equation the cheapest LSI implementation would use a PLE8P4 costing around 80 gate inputs. However, with a chip count of one, this is by far the cheapest outcome.

Example 3.32

Design a decoder-based implementation of a 2×2 binary multiplier, implementing the function:

$$(A_2 A_1 \times B_2 B_1) = P_4 P_3 P_2 P_1$$

How could this basic building block be used with adders to implement a 4×4 multiplication?

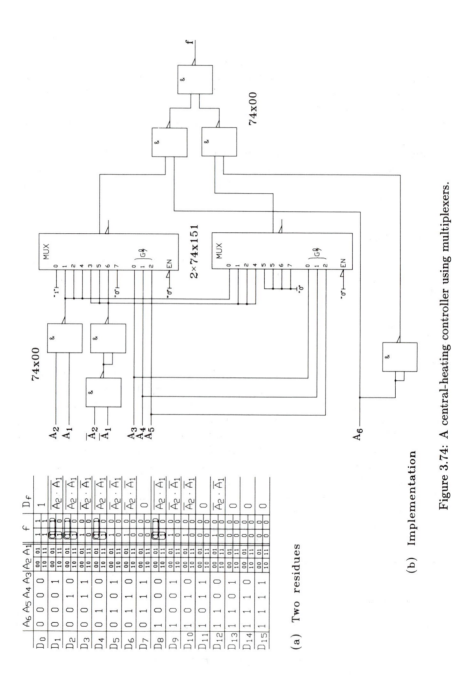

(a) Two residues

(b) Implementation

Figure 3.74: A central-heating controller using multiplexers.

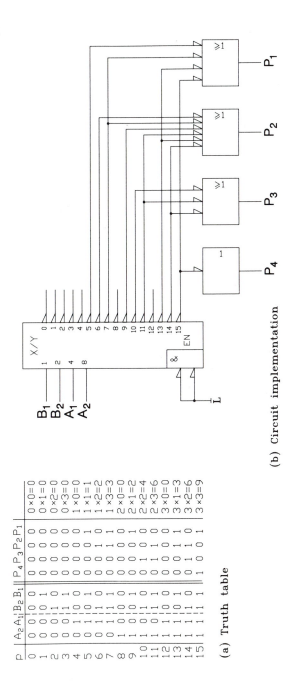

(a) Truth table

(b) Circuit implementation

Figure 3.75: Combinational multiplication.

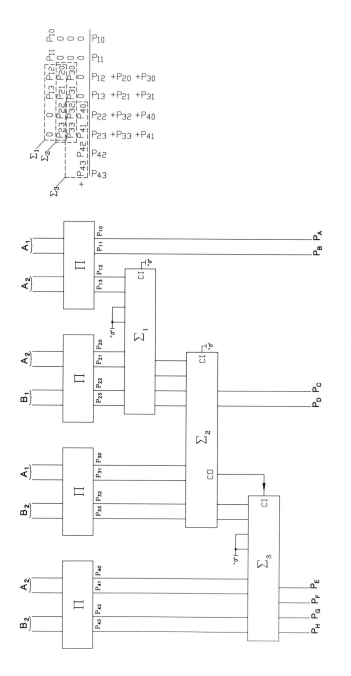

Figure 3.76: 4×4 multiplication using 2×2 multipliers.

Solution

The truth table of Fig. 3.75(a) simply enumerates the rules of binary multiplication from $0 \times 0 = 0$ to $3 \times 3 = 9$, and this gives the implementation of Fig. 3.75(b) in the normal way.

The second part of this question is the more difficult. Four 2×2 multiplications summed together give a 4×4 product thus:

$$
\begin{array}{r}
A_2A_1 \\
\times\ B_2B_1 \\
\hline
A_1B_1 \\
A_2B_1\ 0\ \ 0 \\
A_1B_2\ 0\ \ 0 \\
+\ A_2B_2\ 0\ \ 0\ \ 0\ \ 0 \\
\hline
\text{Final product}
\end{array}
\qquad
\begin{array}{l}
\text{1st partial product, } P_1 \\
\text{2nd partial product, } P_2 \\
\text{3rd partial product, } P_3 \\
\text{4th partial product, } P_4
\end{array}
$$

The implementation of Fig. 3.76 uses four 2×2 multipliers to generate the four partial products. Three 4-bit adders sum these together to give the 8-bit final product. The shift-left action is hard wired into the adder connections. Notice the use of the general qualifier symbol $\prod$ to denote the multiplication function.

Large multipliers can be implemented using LSI techniques. For example a 4×4 multiplication can be stored as a look-up table in a standard PLE8P8 PROM, such as the 82S135, in the manner of Example 3.21. The limits here are approximately 8×8, which would require two $64\text{K} \times 16$ PROMs. Of course, larger capacities can be achieved using techniques similar to that demonstrated in this example.

Example 3.33

Using a 4-bit MSI adder, demonstrate how you could construct both a 5-bit BCD to binary and binary to BCD converter.

Solution

As can be seen from the combo truth table of Fig. 3.77(a), conversion from BCD to binary requires the subtraction of six for $\text{BCD} > 9$. This corrects for the six unused states. In all cases, the LSB of both codes are identical and therefore the adder (used as a 2's complement subtractor) need operate on the four MSBs only, as shown in Fig. 3.77(b). The 2's complement of 00110 is 11010, and this is forced into the adder when D_5 is logic 1 (i.e. $\text{BCD} > 9$). The conversion algorithm can be stated as:

> If the LSB of the higher BCD digit is logic 1, then subtract six to give the binary equivalent.

The conversion may be extended to additional bits by adding the appropriate factors. For example, with 6-bit conversion, the second 10's decade bit requires the subtraction of 12 ($2^6 - 20$).

The conversion from binary to BCD uses a similar algorithm:

> If the binary equivalent is > 9, then add six to give the BCD equivalent.

BCD ↔ Binary

Decimal	D_5	D_4	D_3	D_2	D_1	B_5	B_4	B_3	B_2	B_1
0	0	0	0	0	0	0	0	0	0	0
1	0	0	0	0	1	0	0	0	0	1
2	0	0	0	1	0	0	0	0	1	0
3	0	0	0	1	1	0	0	0	1	1
4	0	0	1	0	0	0	0	1	0	0
5	0	0	1	0	1	0	0	1	0	1
6	0	0	1	1	0	0	0	1	1	0
7	0	0	1	1	1	0	0	1	1	1
8	0	1	0	0	0	0	1	0	0	0
9	0	1	0	0	1	0	1	0	0	1
10	1	0	0	0	0	0	1	0	1	0
11	1	0	0	0	1	0	1	0	1	1
12	1	0	0	1	0	0	1	1	0	0
13	1	0	0	1	1	0	1	1	0	1
14	1	0	1	0	0	0	1	1	1	0
15	1	0	1	0	1	0	1	1	1	1
16	1	0	1	1	0	1	0	0	0	0
17	1	0	1	1	1	1	0	0	0	1
18	1	1	0	0	0	1	0	0	1	0
19	1	1	0	0	1	1	0	0	1	1

(a) 5-bit BCD/binary and binary/BCD conversion.

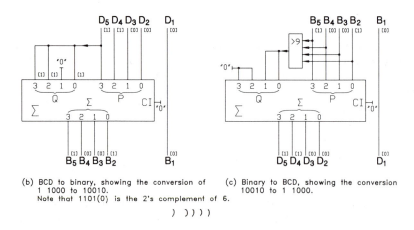

(b) BCD to binary, showing the conversion of
1 1000 to 10010.
Note that 1101(0) is the 2's complement of 6.

(c) Binary to BCD, showing the conversion
10010 to 1 1000.

Figure 3.77: Using adders in BCD ↔ binary conversion.

The circuit designed in Fig. 3.48(a) for the BCD adder will function as a > 9 circuit, and using this gives the conversion of Fig. 3.77(c). The process can be extended to 6-bit BCD by adding 12 for binary $> 19 < 30$; 18 if $> 29 < 40$.

Both BCD to binary and binary to BCD conversion can be implemented using a PLE/PROM as a look-up table in the same manner as the previous multiplier. The function is sufficiently common to be commercially available as a mask-programmed ROM. The 74184 converts 6-bit BCD (00 – 39) to binary, and the 74185 translates 6-bit binary (00 – 63) to BCD. These devices can be cascaded to achieve conversions of any desired size.

Example 3.34

An 8-bit counter continually cycles, generating an ascending number from 0 to 255, feeding one set of adder inputs. The other set n originates from an external circuit, typically a bank of switches or from a microprocessor. A repetitive pulse is observed at the adder's carry-out. How does the mark:space ratio of this signal depend on the programmable input n?

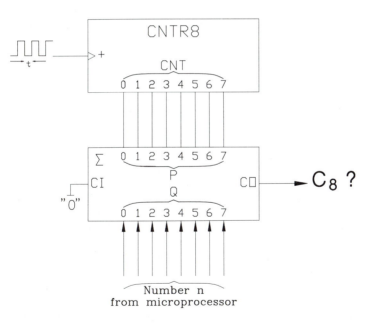

Figure 3.78: Pulse-width modulation.

Solution

The carry-out will go to logic 1 whenever the sum of the counter state (CNT) and n exceeds 255 (11111111b). The higher is n the earlier in the cycle will this occur. Thus whenever n is 0, the carry-out will always be logic 0; up to $n = 255$, when the carry-out will be logic 0 only for the first count state and logic 1 for the remaining 255 clock pulses. The waveform will repeat continuously as the counter cycles through its states.

Formally C_O is 1 whenever

$$(\text{CNT})t + nt \geq 256t$$

where t is the duration of the counter's input clock,

$$\text{CNT} \geq 256 - n$$

The time when the change over occurs is when CNT reaches $256 - n$, which gives the space duration. As the total duration is 256, then the mark duration is directly proportional to n and the mark:space ratio is $n : 256 - n$.

Consider a heater connected (via a power switch) to the carry-out. Provided that the thermal time constant is much less than the cycle time, we have a simple way of regulating power output as a direct function of a number n. This is a form of digital to analog conversion, known as **pulse width modulation**. It is frequently used where power circuits are involved, as heavy-current switching is much more efficient and cost effective as compared to using linear power amplifiers.

Example 3.35

Determine the personality table for a PLE5P8 PROM that is to add two 2-bit binary numbers $A_1 A_0$ and $B_1 B_0$ together with a carry input C_0. The output is to be a 2-bit sum $\Sigma_1 \Sigma_0$ with a carry output C_2. The output should also give the comparision outcomes $A = B$, $A > B$ and $A < B$.

Solution

Table 3.10 gives all possible combinations from $00 + 00 + 0 = 00$ carry 0 $(0 + 0 + 0 = 0)$ to $11 + 11 + 1 = 11$ carry 1 $(3 + 3 + 1 = 7)$. The PROM/PLE outputs $d_0 d_1 d_2$ are utilized to indicate the three relationships $A_1 A_0 < B_1 B_0$, $A_1 A_0 > B_1 B_0$ and $A_1 A_0 = B_1 B_0$ respectively. The input carry, C_0, is ignored in the derivation of these relationships. Only six of the eight PLE data outputs are utilized and $d_7 d_6$ are shown as always 0. In fact their state is irrelevant and they are normally left at their unprogrammed value.

Implementing addition as a look-up table in this manner has the advantage that the overall carry output is generated without any additional delay. Extending the concept to a 4-bit addition $A_3 A_2 A_1 A_0 + B_3 B_2 B_1 B_0 + C_0$ giving $\Sigma_3 \Sigma_2 \Sigma_1 \Sigma_0 + C_4$ means that no carry-look-ahead circuitry is required. The complete addition and three relational outcomes will fit in a single PLE9P8 device.

PROM inputs					PROM outputs							
a4	a3	a2	a1	a0	d7	d6	d5	d4	d3	d2	d1	d0
A1	A0	B1	B0	C0			C2	Σ1	Σ0	A=B	A>B	A<B
0	0	0	0	0	0	0	0	0	0	1	0	0
0	0	0	0	1	0	0	0	0	1	1	0	0
0	0	0	1	0	0	0	0	0	1	0	0	1
0	0	0	1	1	0	0	0	1	0	0	0	1
0	0	1	0	0	0	0	0	1	0	0	0	1
0	0	1	0	1	0	0	0	1	1	0	0	1
0	0	1	1	0	0	0	0	1	1	0	0	1
0	0	1	1	1	0	0	1	0	0	0	0	1
0	1	0	0	0	0	0	0	0	1	0	1	0
0	1	0	0	1	0	0	0	1	0	0	1	0
0	1	0	1	0	0	0	0	1	0	1	0	0
0	1	0	1	1	0	0	0	1	1	1	0	0
0	1	1	0	0	0	0	0	1	1	0	0	1
0	1	1	0	1	0	0	1	0	0	0	0	1
0	1	1	1	0	0	0	1	0	0	0	0	1
0	1	1	1	1	0	0	1	0	1	0	0	1
1	0	0	0	0	0	0	0	1	0	0	1	0
1	0	0	0	1	0	0	0	1	1	0	1	0
1	0	0	1	0	0	0	0	1	1	0	1	0
1	0	0	1	1	0	0	1	0	0	0	1	0
1	0	1	0	0	0	0	1	0	0	1	0	0
1	0	1	0	1	0	0	1	0	1	1	0	0
1	0	1	1	0	0	0	1	0	1	0	0	1
1	0	1	1	1	0	0	1	1	0	0	0	1
1	1	0	0	0	0	0	0	1	1	0	1	0
1	1	0	0	1	0	0	1	0	0	0	1	0
1	1	0	1	0	0	0	1	0	0	0	1	0
1	1	0	1	1	0	0	1	0	1	0	1	0
1	1	1	0	0	0	0	1	0	1	0	1	0
1	1	1	0	1	0	0	1	1	0	0	1	0
1	1	1	1	0	0	0	1	1	0	1	0	0
1	1	1	1	1	0	0	1	1	1	1	0	0

Table 3.10: PLE5P8 personality table for 2-bit full addition and magnitude comparision.

Example 3.36

Two 8-bit signed 2's complement numbers are to be compared for $A > B$. It has been decided to base the design on the 8-bit unsigned comparator circuit of Fig. 3.53, but add circuitry to compensate for the 2's complement nature of the operands. Design such a converter [39].

Solution

Consider the binary numbers $A = 0,0001111b$ and $B = 1,0000001b$. Clearly A is greater than B as the former is positive ($+15$) and the latter negative (-127). However, feeding these patterns into an 8-bit comparator based on unsigned magnitudes only, would register $A < B$ ($15 < 129$)! Clearly, any conversion circuit must examine both sign (A_S and B_S) and magnitude bits separately. Assuming that the magnitude bits feed the comparator in the normal way, then we can modify the $P>Q$ (unsigned) output using the sign bits, according to the truth table in Fig. 3.79(a).

The only surprising relationship is the situation where both operands are negative. Here the table states that the straight magnitude comparison functions correctly. This is confirmed by examining the table to the left of Fig. 1.8. For example, $(1)010b$ (-6) is greater than $(1)000b$ (-8).

Using these four statements, the K-map of Fig. 3.79(b) gives us a function in terms of A_S B_S and $P>Q$. This function defines A GT B for the signed 2's complement numbers, as defined in Fig. 3.79(a).

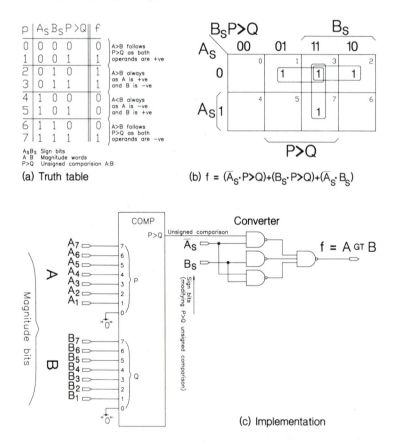

p	A_S	B_S	$P>Q$	f	
0	0	0	0	0	A>B follows P>Q as both operands are +ve
1	0	0	1	1	
2	0	1	0	1	A>B always as A is +ve and B is −ve
3	0	1	1	1	
4	1	0	0	0	A<B always as A is −ve and B is +ve
5	1	0	1	0	
6	1	1	0	0	A>B follows P>Q as both operands are −ve
7	1	1	1	1	

$A_S B_S$ Sign bits
A B   Magnitude words
$P>Q$ Unsigned comparision A:B

(a) Truth table

(b) $f = (\overline{A_S} \cdot P>Q) + (B_S \cdot P>Q) + (\overline{A_S} \cdot B_S)$

(c) Implementation

Figure 3.79: An 8-bit 2's complement greater-than comparator.

Example 3.37

Using a 16L8 PAL, design a 4-bit combinational logic shift-right circuit. There are to be four data inputs $D_3 D_2 D_1 D_0$, two shift control signals $S_1 S_0$ and eight data outputs $Q_7 Q_6 Q_5 Q_4 Q_3 Q_2 Q_1 Q_0$. The output is to be a replica of the input 4-bit word 'slid' across the output field, left aligned with a shift index of $S_1 S_0 = 00$.

Solution

Following the specification, the four possible transforms are:

D_3	D_2	D_2	D_0	0	0	0	0
↓	↓	↓	↓	↓	↓	↓	↓
Q_7	Q_6	Q_5	Q_4	Q_3	Q_2	Q_1	Q_0

$S_1 S_0 = 00$ (Shift zero places)

0	D_3	D_2	D_2	D_0	0	0	0
↓	↓	↓	↓	↓	↓	↓	↓
Q_7	Q_6	Q_5	Q_4	Q_3	Q_2	Q_1	Q_0

$S_1 S_0 = 01$ (Shift one place)

0	0	D_3	D_2	D_2	D_0	0	0
↓	↓	↓	↓	↓	↓	↓	↓
Q_7	Q_6	Q_5	Q_4	Q_3	Q_2	Q_1	Q_0

$S_1 S_0 = 10$ (Shift two places)

0	0	0	D_3	D_2	D_2	D_0	0
↓	↓	↓	↓	↓	↓	↓	↓
Q_7	Q_6	Q_5	Q_4	Q_3	Q_2	Q_1	Q_0

$S_1 S_0 = 11$ (Shift three places)

The resulting equations for the eight outputs are:

$$Q_7 = (\overline{S_1} \cdot \overline{S_0}) \cdot D_3$$
$$Q_6 = (\overline{S_1} \cdot \overline{S_0}) \cdot D_2 + (\overline{S_1} \cdot S_0) \cdot D_3$$
$$Q_5 = (\overline{S_1} \cdot \overline{S_0}) \cdot D_1 + (\overline{S_1} \cdot S_0) \cdot D_2 + (S_1 \cdot \overline{S_0}) \cdot D_3$$
$$Q_4 = (\overline{S_1} \cdot \overline{S_0}) \cdot D_0 + (\overline{S_1} \cdot S_0) \cdot D_1 + (S_1 \cdot \overline{S_0}) \cdot D_2 + (S_1 \cdot S_0) \cdot D_3$$
$$Q_3 = \qquad\qquad + (\overline{S_1} \cdot S_0) \cdot D_0 + (S_1 \cdot \overline{S_0}) \cdot D_1 + (S_1 \cdot S_0) \cdot D_2$$
$$Q_2 = \qquad\qquad\qquad\qquad (S_1 \cdot \overline{S_0}) \cdot D_0 + (S_1 \cdot S_0) \cdot D_1$$
$$Q_1 = \qquad\qquad\qquad\qquad\qquad\qquad (S_1 \cdot S_0) \cdot D_0$$

with Q_0 always logic 0.

In order to compensate for the active-Low PAL16L8 outputs, D_n has been replaced by $\overline{D}_n$ in the fuse plot shown in Fig. 3.80. Other than this substitution, the implemented equations are identical to those above. Output Q_0 is shown for convenience as an output from the PAL, but as it is always logic 0 this is a needless extravagance.

The basic specification for the shifter can be augmented; for example, an extra input can be used as a bidirectional control, with the unshifted word being aligned in the middle of the output field. However, the maximum number of product terms is then eight, which is beyond the maximum of seven provided by standard PALs

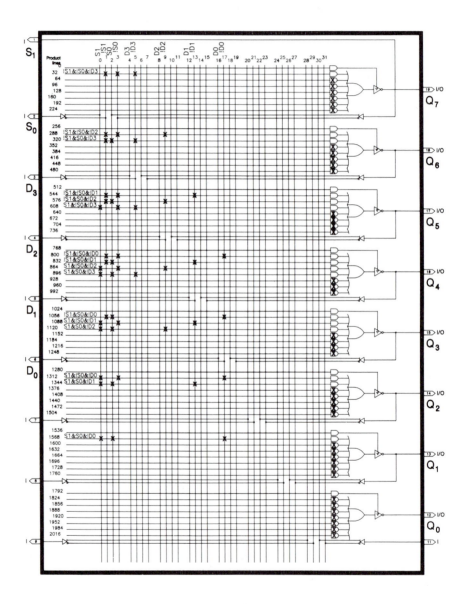

Figure 3.80: A PAL-based hard-wired logic shift-right circuit.

such as the 16L8 and 20L8. In this case the 18P8 PAL of Fig. 3.66 could be used. Equations of this type do not exhibit common product terms and thus using a PLA-based implementation will not help in overcoming the problem of overabundant AND gates as the specification is extended. An 8-bit hard-wired unidirectional shifter requires 8+3 inputs and eight outputs also with a maximum of eight product terms. This can be implemented by a 20V8 PAL. We will discuss the versatile PAL range in Section 4.5. The 22V10 PAL of Fig. 4.58 with a maximum product-term count of 16 could be used to implement a bidirectional 8-bit shifter.

Example 3.38

Show how a $18 \times 42 \times 10$ PLA could be programmed to implement the 10-line unary code to 4-bit natural binary conversion outlined in Fig. 1.2(a). As well as the 4-bit code, an active-High status output indicating an erroneous code, eg. caused by a defective photocell, is to be generated.

Solution

From the truth table we see that that there are eleven legal code combinations, each one of which is implemented in Fig. 3.81 as an AND gate, Terms $0 \ldots 10$. As the PLA153 has only eight dedicated inputs, input/outputs 8 & 9 are programmed as inputs $B(I)_9$ and $B(I)_8$. This is shown in rows D9 and D8, which represent the AND gates controlling the 3-state buffers in series with output EOR gates S_9 and S_8 in Fig. 3.68. By entering $\boxed{0}$ in these rows, the resulting logic disables these buffers.

The five output OR gates are connected to the appropriate product terms as indicated by $\boxed{A}$. The status output at $B(O)_4$, labelled Illegal, needs some explanation. An illegal code is defined as any code pattern not listed in the truth table. By ORing together all legal combinations and programming EOR gate S_4 as an inverter, we generate an active-High illegal-code detector (i.e. not legal).

An entirely SSI-based designed would require a minimum of eight chips at about the same price as the PLA, but taking up around six times the board space. As an alternative, a 74x147 BCD priority encoder (see Fig. 3.40) will provide the basic code conversion, but the illegal-code detection would require four additional SSI chips.

The same PLA153 20-pin device could deal with 13-line code at no extra expense. The PLA173 24-pin equivalent could translate 16-line code to 5-bit binary and also generate the illegal-code detection. Larger codes would have to be generated by cascading PLAs, which would have to provide for an All_Ones carry-out and carry-in programming.

FPLA PROGRAM TABLE

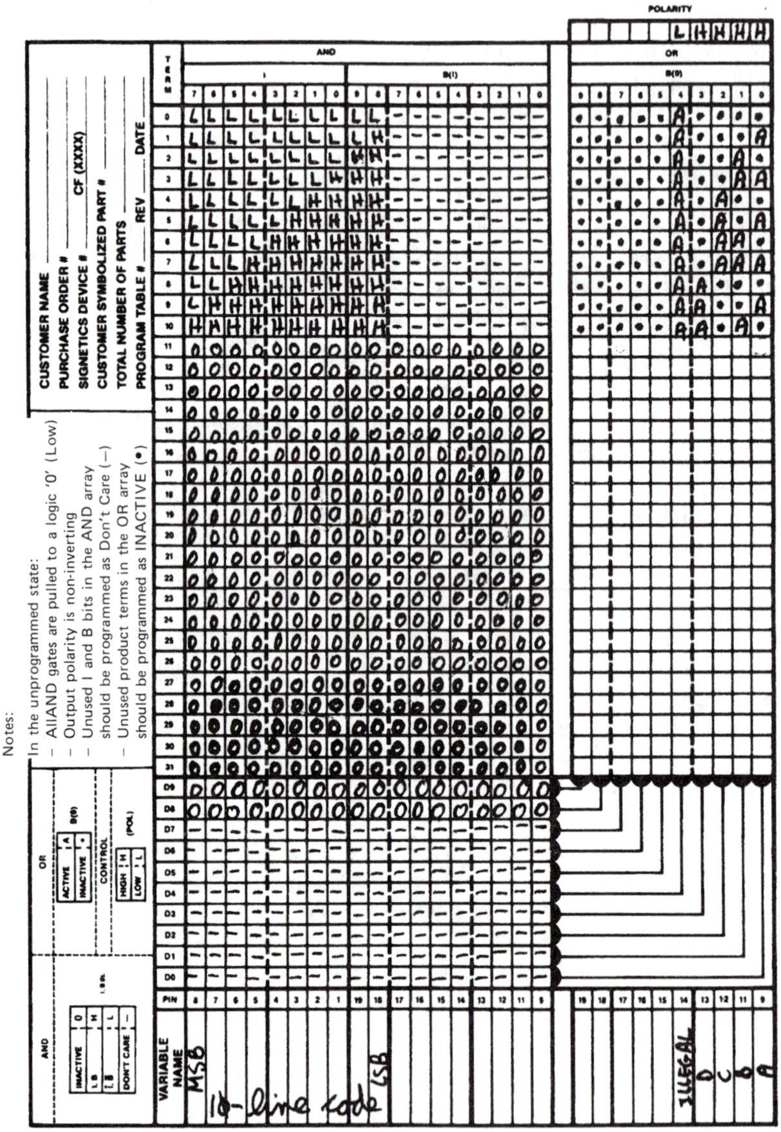

Figure 3.81: A PLA-based 10-line unary to 4-bit natural binary converter. Courtesy of Philips/Signetics Components Ltd.

3.4.2   Self Assessment Examples

SAE 3.1

A circuit which when triggered gives a single pulse output of a predetermined length
is often called a **monostable** or one shot. The circuit shown in Fig. 3.82 is claimed
to be a negative-edge triggered monostable, designed to interface a narrow pulse to
an electromechanical pulse counter needing activation of not less than 100 ms duration. Assuming CMOS family inverters (i.e. no input current and a logic threshold
at $V_{DD}/2$), verify the claim by describing the circuit operation and show that a
nominal pulse duration of 0.15 s duration would be produced.

Further show that the circuit is not retriggerable, in that a further trigger input
before the monostable has relaxed will not extend the output by a further 150 ms.
The **1** alongside the pulse in the IEC/ANSII symbol indicates this property, i.e.
trigger once only. The absence of this qualifier means that the monostable period
is reset if triggering occurs during this active phase.

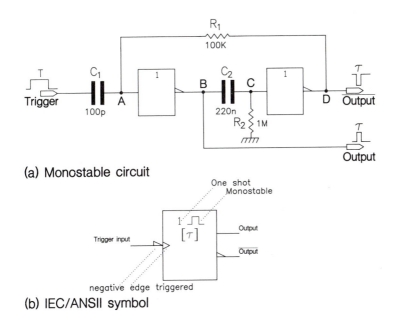

Figure 3.82: A CMOS monostable circuit.

SAE 3.2

Determine the worst-case worst-case input resistance which will give the full Low-
state noise margin for the 74AS family. This family has a worst-case worst-case I_{IL}
of −0.5 mA and V_{IL} of 0.4 V.

SAE 3.3

Logic buffer circuits designed to boost the current drive into a bus structure, such as shown in Fig. 3.21, can only operate when data flow is in one direction. Micro-processors normally both send and receive data along the same bus. Show how two 3-state buffers could be connected to give bi-directional buffering. The micropro-cessor provides a control line $R/\overline{W}$ which is High when it reads data (incoming) and Low when it writes data (outgoing).

SAE 3.4

Fig. 3.83 shows four alternative logic symbols for the to 74ALS156 device. Justify Texas Instruments description above each symbol.

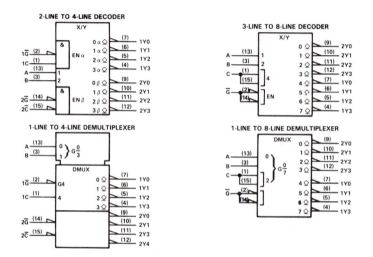

Figure 3.83: Alternative symbols for the SN74ALS156. Reproduced by courtesy of Texas Instruments Ltd.

SAE 3.5

The 74x138, shown in Fig. 3.29, has two active-Low and one active-High **Enable**. Using this feature, describe how three 74x138 decoders can be used without *any* additional circuitry to give a 5 to 24-line decoder. Further, show how four such decoders plus *one* gate may be connected to give a 5 to 32-line decoder.

SAE 3.6

It is desired to decode 4-bit Gray code (See Fig. 1.7) to unary one of 16 lines. How would a 74x154 decoder (see Fig. 3.30) be used to perform this function?

SAE 3.7

Efficient recording techniques used for storing digital data on floppy disks, require that no more than two successive zeros be presented to the write amplifier. One solution to this problem is to preprocess incoming data in groups of four bits to give a 5-bit code possessing this property; as shown:

Incoming data	Outgoing data to disk	Incoming data	Outgoing data to disk
0000	11001	1000	11010
0001	11011	1001	01001
0010	10010	1010	01010
0011	10011	1011	01011
0100	11101	1100	11100
0101	10101	1101	01101
0110	10110	1110	01110
0111	10111	1111	01111

Using an active-Low 4 to 16-line decoder, together with any appropriate gates, design a minimal code converter to this specification.

SAE 3.8

An electronic die is to be implemented by decoding the output of a 6-state counter, to directly drive the seven active-Low LED lamps arranged in the characteristic form shown in Fig. 3.84.

Design the die decoder using a 3 to 8-line decoder and appropriate gates. Hint: Look carefully at your truth table for redundancies.

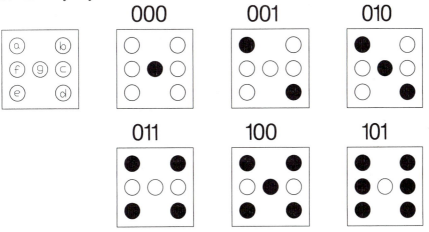

Figure 3.84: Die patterns.

SAE 3.9

The 7-segment format of Fig. 3.33(a) is capable of displaying all 16 hexadecimal characters, including A b C d E F. Using a 4 to 16-line decoder and any appropriate gates, design an active-Low open-collector hexadecimal to 7-segment decoder.

Repeat the exercise using a PLE5P8 open-collector PROM (eg. 74S188, 82S23A, TBP18SA030) and compare the costs.

SAE 3.10

A certain hospital drip pump assembly uses 7-segment readouts to display a number of status and diagnostic messages, such as **bat** (for battery low). These are given in Fig. 3.85. Use a 4 to 16-line decoder/gate array to implement a suitable code conversion. Assume outputs are active-Low open-collector.

How could you combine the circuit of Example SAE 3.9 together with this, to allow a 5-bit code to display all ten numbers plus status letters?

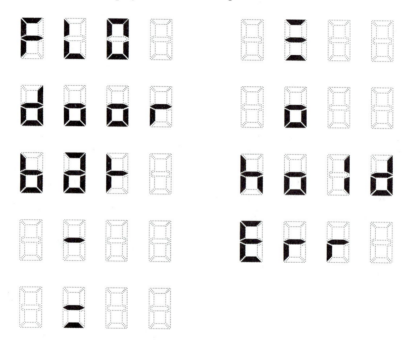

Figure 3.85: Message repertoiré.

SAE 3.11

Figure 3.35 showed how a PLE could be programmed as an envelope-size sorter. Repeat the design exercise targeted to an SSI, decoder/gate array and multiplexer implementations. Compare all three outcomes.

SAE 3.12

Show how you could implement a 64 to 6-line priority encoder circuit using nine 74x148 ICs plus any necessary gates.

SAE 3.13

Using any MSI technique, design an active-High thermostat to detect temperatures greater than $16°C$. The temperature is represented in a 6-bit 2-decade BCD format, i.e. F E D C B A.

SAE 3.14

Using a decoder/gate array, implement a 1-bit full adder summing three binary digits X Y Z plus a carry-in; giving a 2-bit sum $\Sigma_2 \Sigma_1$ and a carry-out. Compare the cost with a MSI adder implementation.

SAE 3.15

Determine the personality table for a PLE8P8 to convert an 8-bit signed byte to its negative equivalent. Cost this solution with an equivalent SSI/MSI solution.

SAE 3.16

Program a PLE5P8 to convert from 8-4-2-1 naturally-coded binary to active-Low 7-segment code, to display all hexadecimal digits. As well as the code inputs, there is a $\overline{\text{Blank\_Input}}$, and a $\overline{\text{Blank\_Output}}$ is to be generated.

SAE 3.17

The control unit for a computer must generate 64 control signals according to a 14-bit input pattern (see Fig 5.5). Calculate the necessary capacity if a single ROM is used and how many output patterns are possible if no assumptions about the circuits to be controlled are made. If it is known that only 256 actual output patterns are actually needed, show that the storage capacity is reduced to about 14% of the original value if a 2-tier memory configuration is used — as in Fig. 3.61.

SAE 3.18

Show how a PLE12P8 could be programmed as an ALU to add, subtract, bitwize AND and bitwize OR two 5-bit numbers P and Q. Two input lines specify the mode; $00b$ (Add), $01b$ (Sub), $10b$ (AND) and $11b$ (OR). The data inputs are to be treated as signed 2's complement numbers for the arithmetic operations. No carry-in/borrow-in is required, but there should be a carry-out/borrow-out if adding/subtracting.

SAE 3.19

Show how you would program a PAL16L8 to implement a 4-bit rotary shifter (also known as a **barrel shifter**). A barrel shifter takes the set data signals and 'rotates' them by a variable all at one go. The shifter is entirely combinational, unlike the sequential shift registers of Section 4.3.1. This specification requires four input and four output data signals with two input controls:

$$D_3\, D_2\, D_2\, D_1\, D_0 \qquad \text{Input data}$$
$$Q_3\, Q_2\, Q_2\, Q_1\, Q_0 \qquad \text{Output data}$$
$$S_1\, S_0 \qquad\qquad\quad \text{Shift amount}$$

If the shift amount is zero ($S_1 S_0 = 00$) then $Q_n = D_n$. If ($S_1 S_0 = 01$) then $Q_n = D_{n-1}$, where the index $n-1$ wraps around modulo-4, i.e. $Q_3 = D_2$, $Q_2 = D_1$, $Q_1 = D_0$, $Q_0 = D_3$. In the same manner $Q_n = D_{n-2}$ for $S_1 S_0 = 10$ and $Q_n = D_{n-3}$ for $S_1 S_0 = 11$

SAE 3.20

The 68008 microprocessor has twenty address lines from a_{19} thru a_0, a strobe which goes Low whenever the address is stable and valid ($\overline{\text{Address\_Strobe}}$, $\overline{\text{AS}}$) and a $\text{Read}/\overline{\text{Write}}$ line. Show how you would program a PAL20L8 to generate the following active-Low outputs:

SYSROM	Range: 00000–07FFF*h* and $R/\overline{W}$ High
USERPORT	Range: 08000–08FFF*h*
IO	Range: 09000–09FFF*h*
RAM	Range: 0A000–0FFFF*h*
USERMEM	Range: 10000–1FFFF*h*
DTACK	All but range 08000–09FFF*h*
NOTRW	$R/\overline{W}$

Only a sufficient number of address lines require processing in order of distinguish between the various address ranges.

SAE 3.21

A certain calculator has an active-Low BCD 7-segment output. Design a suitable active-High Braille (see Fig. 2.70) converter using a PLA153.

References

[1] Kamdar, J.; Vertical Fuse Technology for Programmable Logic Devices or PLDs, *National Anthem* (National Semiconductor), no. 1, 1990, pp.7&10.

[2] Frohman-Bentchkowsky, D; A Fully-decoded 2048-bit Electrically Programmable FAMOS Read-Only Memory, *Journal of Solid-State Circuits*, **SC-6**, no. 5, Oct.1971, pp.301–306.

[3] Johnstone, W.S et al.; 16-K EE-PROM Relies on Tunnelling for Byte-Erasable Program Storage, *Electronics International*, **53**, no. 5, Feb.28, 1980, pp.113–117.

[4] Strong, P.F.; Rectifiers as Elements of Switching Circuits, *Proc. Assocn. Computing Machinery*, May 1952, pp.281–286.

[5] Millman, J. and Taub, H.; *Pulse, Digital and Switching Waveforms*, McGraw-Hill, 1965, Chapter 20.

[6] Sparkes, J.J.; *Transistor Switching and Sequential Circuits*, Pergamon Press, 1969, Chapter 1.

[7] Mauro, R.; *Engineering Electronics*, Prentice-Hall, 1989, Section 1.11.

[8] Ruegg, H.W.; Transistor Transistor Logic Circuits, *Electronics*, **36**, no. 12, March 22nd, 1963, pp.54–57.

[9] Millman, J. and Halkias, C.C.; *Integrated Electronics*, McGraw-Hill, 1972, Chapter 10.

[10] Mauro, R.; *Engineering Electronics*, Prentice-Hall, 1989, Section 10.5.

[11] Cergel, L.; *McMOS Handbook*, Motorola Semiconductors Inc, Revised edition, 1974, Section 3.

[12] Painter, R.R.; *Gate-Oxide Protection in RCA COS/MOS Digital Integrated Circuits*, RCA Solid State Division Application Note ICAN-6218.

[13] Catt, I. et al.; *Digital Hardware Design*, MacMillan, 1979, Chapter 4.

[14] Morris, R.L. and Miller, J.R.; *Designing with TTL Integrated Circuits*, McGraw-Hill, 1971, Section 8.12.

[15] Millman, J. and Taub, H.; *Pulse, Digital and Switching Waveforms*, McGraw-Hill, 1965, Section 8.12.

[16] Douce, A.; Decoders/Demultiplexers, *Semiconductor Circuit Design*, **II**, ed., Norris, B., Texas Instruments Ltd, Bedford, U.K., 1973, Chapter IX.

[17] Wolff, S.; Data Selectors, *Semiconductor Circuit Design*, **II**, ed., Norris, B., Texas Instruments Ltd, Bedford, 1973, Section VIII.

[18] Anderson, J.L.; Multiplexers Double as Logic Circuits, *Electronics*, **42**, no. 22, Oct. 27th, 1969, pp.100–105.

[19] Almaini, A.E.A.; *Electronic Logic Systems*, Prentice-Hall, 1986, Section 7.4.

[20] Kostopoulos, G.K.; *Digital Engineering*, Wiley, 1975, Part 2.

[21] Mowle, F.J.; *A Systemic Approach to Digital Logic Design*, Addison-Wesley, 1976, Section 6.5.

[22] Hyman, A.; *Charles Babbage: Pioneer of the Computer*, Princeton University Press, 1982, Chapter 12.

[23] Wallace, C.D.; A Suggestion for a Fast Multiplier, *IEEE Trans. on Electron. Computers*, **EC13**, no. 1, Feb. 1964, pp.14–17.

[24] Cavanaugh, G.; Fast Multipliers, *Semiconductor Circuit Design*, **II**, ed., Norris, B., Texas Instruments Ltd, Bedford, U.K., 1973, Chapter XII.

[25] Booth, A.D.; A Signed Binary Multiplication Technique, *Quart. J. of Mechanics and Applied Maths*, **4**, no. 2, 1951, pp.236–240.

[26] Sze, S.M. (ed.); *LSI Technology*, McGraw-Hill, 2nd ed., 1988.

[27] Alford, R.C.; *Programmable Logic Designer's Guide*, H.W. Sams, 1989, Chapter 1.

[28] Nichols, J.L.; A Logical Next Step for Read-Only Memories, *Electronics*, **40**, no. 12, June 12th, 1967, pp.111–113.

[29] Fletcher, W.I. and Despain, A.M.; Simplify Combinational Logic Circuits, *Electronic Design*, **13**, no. 13, June 24th, 1971, pp.72–73.

[30] McDowell, J.; Large Bipolar ROMs amd p/ROMs Revolutionize Logic Design, *Computer Design*, **13**, June 1974, pp.100–104.

[31] Percival, R.; ROMs are Versatile in Digital Systems, *Electronic Design*, **12**, no. 12, June 8th, 1972, pp.66–71.

[32] Wyland, D.C.; Using p/ROMs as Logic Elements, *Computer Design*, **13**, Sept. 1974, pp.98–100.

[33] Hemel, A.; Making Small ROMs do Maths Quickly, Cheaply and Easily, *Electronics*, **43**, no. 10, May 11th, 1970, pp.104–119.

[34] Kavamme, F.; Standard Read Only Memories Simplify Complex Logic Design, *Electronics*, **43**, no. 1, Jan. 5th, 1970, pp.88–95.

[35] Cahill S.J.; Digital and Microprocessor Engineering, Ellis Horwood, 1st ed., 1982, Example 3.21.

[36] Bolton, M.; *Digital Systems Design with Programmable Logic*, Addison-Wesley, 1990, Section 5.7.2.

[37] Maundy, B.; Designing with Programmable Logic Arrays, *Microprocessors and Microsystems*, **11**, no. 9, Nov. 1987, pp.475–486.

[38] Lala, P.K.; *Digital System Design using Programmable Logic Devices*, Prentice-Hall, 1990, Section 3.3.

[39] Bergman, G.D.; 8-bit Highest-wins Store, *Electronic Engineering*, **62**, no. 759, March 1990, pp.29&30.

Chapter 4

100

Random Sequential Logic

Previous chapters have dealt with networks of gates, essentially designed to convert binary patterns according to a specified transform table of i.e. the truth table. In steady state, the outputs of such networks are independent of the sequence of input states which lead up to the present input. Thus the output of a 7-segment decoder for an input $0111b$ may be $1111000b$ irrespective of whether the previous input was, say, $0000b$ or $1001b$. By definition, circuits whose response is independent of history, are known as **combinational networks**.

Most digital networks require an action progressing sequentially through a number of states. The elementary building blocks of such circuits must possess memory, in order to recall the past sequence of events. A simple example is a bell push versus a light switch. The former has no memory of past events; for as soon as you remove your finger, the switch reverts back to its rest state. The latter has two stable states, On and Off. On pushing such a switch the light turns On (sets) and remains On, even when your finger is taken away; that is, it remembers your last command. Similarly with the Reset command, which turns the light Off.

The remainder of this book will examine the basic sequential elements and some of the design techniques which are available to the designer of **sequential networks**. Specifically, implementations where the hardware is hard-wired to perform the specified tasks are reviewed here. As opposed to such **random logic** implementations, sequential circuits in which a standard hardware architecture is configured using software, is the topic of the following chapter.

4.1 The Basic Building Blocks

The application of feedback to combinational networks can endow these circuits with the property of memory, and hence sequential action. Using this approach, two basic sequential bistable elements; the latch and the flip flop, may be constructed. Although in reality these units consist of gates, it is convenient to treat them as fundamental building blocks; just as gates themselves in turn consist of transistor switching elements.

After reading this section, you should:

293

- Be able to analyze a gate circuit with feedback using a Y-map.

- Be able to recognize a critical race situation.

- Understand the operation of simple $R\,S$, $\overline{R}\,\overline{S}$ and D latch circuits.

- Understand the meaning of the **R, S, D, C, J, K** and **T** dependencies.

- Be aware of the nature and problems incurred by metastable states in latches and flip flops.

- Appreciate the difference between a flip flop and a latch.

- Understand the operation of D, T and J K flip flops.

- Appreciate the difference between edge-triggered, master-slave and data-lockout flip flops types.

4.1.1   Logic Feedback

Consider the gate network of Fig. 4.1(a). With this circuit the output is not only a function of the inputs $X_1\,X_2$, but of the outputs themselves, $Y_1\,Y_2$; fed back via the two cross-coupled paths. Investigating the response of even this simple network to changes in the inputs causes problems, because the output state must be assumed à priori, in order to deduce that output state. This is a common problem in linear amplifier feedback circuits, and the approach normally taken is to analyze the open-loop circuit; i.e. with the feedback removed. The closed-loop response (feedback in place) is deduced by constraining this open-loop response by the requirements of the feedback network. A similar approach is taken in digital feedback networks.

The open-loop circuit is shown in Fig. 4.1(b). The inputs originating from the outputs are disconnected and treated as separate inputs, $y_1\,y_2$; known as **feedback inputs** (or secondaries, from relay terminology). The original inputs $X_1\,X_2$ are the **programmable inputs**, or primaries. This resulting circuit is a simple 2-output, 4-input combinational network, obeying the relationship $Y_1 = \overline{X_1 + y_2}$; $Y_2 = \overline{X_2 + y_1}$. It is thus possible to derive the truth table showing the output state for each input combination. This is usually shown in the form of a map, with all the relevant outputs inserted in each cell; Fig. 4.1(c). This map is known as a **Y-map**, and summarizes the open-loop transfer characteristic of the circuit.

It now remains to constrain the Y-map according to the dictates of the feedback connections. The restriction here, is that in steady state we have the relationship $y_1 = Y_1$ and $y_2 = Y_2$, by direct connection. In Fig. 4.2(a), this is indicated on the Y-map by circling cells which obey this criterion. For example, cell 6 states that with $y_1\,y_2 = 01$ and $X_1\,X_2 = 10$, then $Y_1\,Y_2 = 01$; which is a stable condition. This annotated Y-map, showing all stable states, gives the closed-loop response.

By considering all possible programmable inputs and transitions, it is possible to determine how the closed-loop circuit reacts. Thus if $X_1\,X_2 = 01$, then $Y_1\,Y_2 = 10$; state 9 being the only stable state for that input. Similarly $X_1\,X_2 = 11$ gives $Y_1\,Y_2 = 00$ (state 3), and $X_1\,X_2 = 10$ gives $Y_1\,Y_2 = 01$ (state 6). However, a problem arises when $X_1\,X_2 = 00$, where two stable states are indicated. In such cases the change to $X_1\,X_2 = 00$ from each of the other input combinations

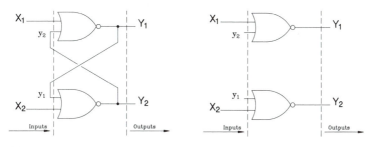

(a) The closed-loop circuit   (b) The open-loop circuit

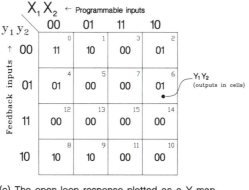

(c) The open-loop response plotted as a Y-map.
    $Y_1 = X_1 + y_2$; $Y_2 = X_2 + y_1$.

Figure 4.1: A simple example of logic feedback.

must be considered. When the input changes, there will be a time lag before the
output responds; due to gate delays. Figure 4.2(b) shows the cross-coupled NOR
circuit; assuming instantaneously responding gates and lumped delays. Notice the
IEC/ANSI symbol for a delay. Using this model, a change of input $(X_1 X_2)$ alters
the ideal gate outputs $(Y_1 Y_2)$ immediately, followed later by the feedback inputs,
$y_1 y_2$. Points $Y_1 Y_2$ cannot of course be accessed in reality. Thus, during transients
the entries in the Y-map can be thought of as indicating the next state, in response
to the total input $X_1 X_2 y_1 y_2$. If this is a stable state, the transient terminates. If
unstable, then after the characteristic delay the outputs are fed back to the input;
forcing the circuit to yet another state. This will continue until a stable state is
reached.

    With the circuit under investigation, three transitions are possible, as shown in
Fig. 4.2(c). If $X_1 X_2 = 01 \rightarrow 00$, then $Y_1 Y_2$ is $10 \rightarrow 10$ (stable); i.e. the transition
is horizontal (X changes give a horizontal movement) from stable state 9 to stable
state 8. The net result at the output is no change. Similarly $X_1 X_2 = 10 \rightarrow 00$
gives a horizontal movement from cell 6 to cell 4 (stable). This also gives no change
at the output. The transition $X_1 X_2 = 11 \rightarrow 00$ is more complex. Initially when

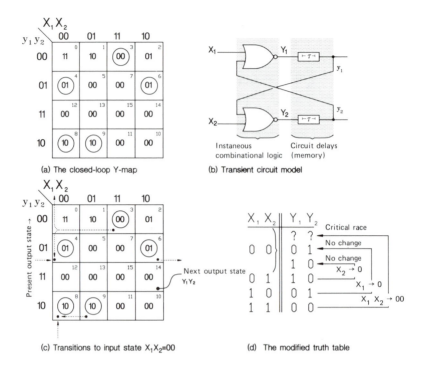

(a) The closed-loop Y-map

(b) Transient circuit model

(c) Transitions to input state $X_1X_2=00$

(d) The modified truth table

Figure 4.2: Determining the closed-loop response.

X changes, the circuit moves horizontally to cell 0. Cell 0 is unstable and directs the output to change to 11; i.e. with $X_1 X_2 y_1 y_2 = 0000$, $Y_1 Y_2 = 11$. However, the delays are extremely unlikely to be equal; so although both y_1 and y_2 are changing $0 \rightarrow 1$, one of the feedback inputs will 'win the race'. If y_2 wins, i.e. $y_1 y_2 = 01$, then the vertical movement (change in y) takes the circuit to stable state 4, with $y_1 y_2 = Y_1 Y_2 = 01$. On the other hand, if y_1 wins, the circuit ends up in stable cell 8, with $y_1 y_2 = Y_1 Y_2 = 10$. This situation, where the outcome of a change in input depends on relative delays, is called a **critical race**. Non-critical race conditions can exist, where the transient path can differ but the outcome is the same.

In the unlikely situation where the delays are the same, the map predicts an oscillation between cells 0 and 12. In this event, random noise fluctuations would knock the circuit one way or the other, but in reality it is virtually impossible to change both inputs simultaneously. Should the circuit oscillate in this manner, the underlying analog nature of the gates predominate. The system can then enter an unpredictable metastable state, as shown in Fig. 4.12.

The two non-simultaneous possibilities are $X_1 X_2 = 11 \rightarrow 01 \rightarrow 00$, giving the transition $\boxed{3} \rightarrow 1 \rightarrow \boxed{9} \rightarrow \boxed{8}$, and $X_1 X_2 = 11 \rightarrow 10 \rightarrow 00$ giving $\boxed{3} \rightarrow 2 \rightarrow \boxed{6} \rightarrow \boxed{4}$. Thus in this case the critical race situation will not occur. Because the circuit gives a different output, depending on which input alters first, it can be used to detect and memorize the order of input changes (see Example 4.26). The truth table of Fig. 4.2(d) summarizes the closed-loop transfer characteristic.

The analysis of a feedback logic circuit can be summarized as follows:

1. Redraw the circuit in an open-loop mode.

2. Determine the open-loop Y-map.

3. Indicate the stable states according to the criterion $Y = y$.

4. By considering all X inputs, draw up a truth table. If more than one stable state exists for a given programmable input, all transitions to that input must be considered, to determine race conditions. If no stable state exists, the circuit is unstable for that input.

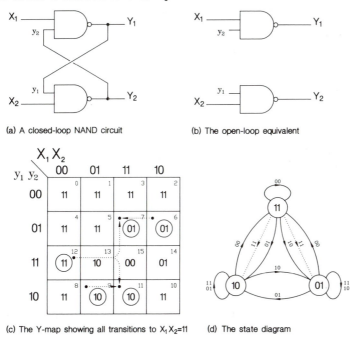

(a) A closed-loop NAND circuit   (b) The open-loop equivalent

(c) The Y-map showing all transitions to $X_1 X_2 = 11$ (d) The state diagram

Figure 4.3: The closed-loop response of a cross-coupled NAND circuit.

Example 4.1

Determine the closed-loop response of the cross-coupled NAND circuit of Fig.4.3(a).

Solution

Figures 4.3(b) & (c) show the open-loop circuit and resulting Y-map. Constraining the Y-map to $Y = y$ gives the stable states shown ringed. For inputs $X_1 X_2 = 00, 01, 10$ only one stable state exists; $12, 9, 6$ respectively. Input $X_1 X_2 = 11$ has two stable states, and this gives rise to a critical race in going from $X_1 X_2 = 00$, as shown by the transition path. This is summarized in Fig. 4.3(d). As in the previous case, the circuit may be used to determine the order of arrival of the signals $X_1 X_2$. $X_1 \rightarrow 1$ first, leads from state $\boxed{12}$ to $\boxed{6}/\boxed{7}$, whilst $X_2 \rightarrow 1$ first gives states $\boxed{9}/\boxed{11}$.

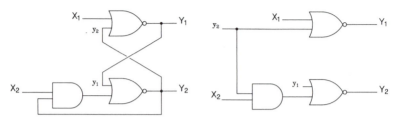

(a) The closed-loop circuit   (b) The open-loop equivalent

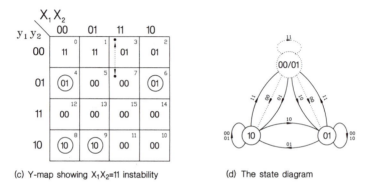

(c) Y-map showing $X_1 X_2$=11 instability   (d) The state diagram

Figure 4.4: Oscillation in a feedback circuit.

Example 4.2

Deduce the reaction of the closed-loop circuit of Fig. 4.4(a), to the input $X_1 X_2$.

Solution

The resulting Y-map of Fig. 4.4(c) shows no stable state for $X_1 X_2 = 11$. Thus, for this input the circuit is unstable and oscillates. Consider the circuit resident in one of the unstable states 7,11 or 15. The output will be forced to $Y_1 Y_2 = 00$; leading to $y_1 y_2 = 00$ (state 3) after the circuit delay. In state 3 the output is directed to $y_1 y_2 = 01$, state 7. Thus the circuit will oscillate between states 3 and 7 as long as the input $X_1 X_2$ is 11. The response to all other inputs, as summarized in Fig. 4.4(d), is the same as the cross-coupled NOR circuit.

In practice this analysis is rather simplistic; as (see Section 3.1.1) digital circuits operating in this manner behave as high-gain analog amplifiers. However, the general outcome remains the same; although when the input alters towards a stable règime, there will be an unpredictable, but usually short, delay whilst the circuit recovers its digital composure. This type of behavior is known as metastability, and is discussed in more detail on page 305.

4.1.2 Latches

The majority of sequential circuits use bistables of various kinds as a fundamental building block. A bistable circuit is really a 1-bit memory cell, which can be moved into one of two stable states, where it remains indefinitely until pushed out. The **reset-set latch** defined in Fig. 4.5(a) has this property. Making S logic 1 Sets the output (usually labelled Q) to logic 1. When the stimulation is removed, the latch remains in the Set state. Similarly, activating the R input resets the output to logic 0. The latch remains Reset until the next Set command. Attempting to both set and reset a latch at the same time is not part of the latch definition. What actually happens is a function of the hardware used to implement the latch.

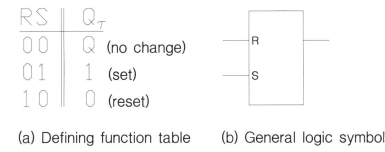

(a) Defining function table   (b) General logic symbol

Figure 4.5: Definition of a R S latch.

Replacing X_1 by R, X_2 by S and Y_1 by Q in Fig. 4.2(d), shows that the cross-coupled NOR circuit acts as an R S latch. In the simplified analysis of Fig. 4.6(a)i, bringing S to logic 1 forces $\overline{Q}$ to logic 0 irrespective. After this, both inputs to the top gate are 0 and Q then goes to 1. The latch is now Set. If subsequently S goes back to 0, then there is still a logic 1 presented to the lower gate (from Q) and its output remains unchanged. By symmetry, the resetting action occurs in the same way, as shown in Fig. 4.6(a)ii.

The R S definition table of Fig. 4.5(a) is seen to be a subset of the function table of Fig. 4.6(b). During steady state, the Y_2 circuit output can be used as a complement latch output. This of course is not true when both Set and Reset inputs are simultaneously applied.

The logic symbol of Fig. 4.6(c) makes use of the **R** and **S** **dependencies** to show how the circuit reacts to simultaneous Set and Reset [1]. The upper output (i.e. Q) is seen to be dependent on the R input via the dependency **1**. This means that this output will Reset (i.e. go to 0) irrespective of the S input (see Fig. 4.6(a)ii). Similarly the lower output, labelled **2**, will go to 1 (externally $\overline{Q}$ to 0) when S2 is 1; irrespective. However, the use of the S and R dependencies is rather limited, in that it cannot depict latch circuits in which the outputs oscillate (such as in Fig. 4.4) or do nothing (see Example SAE 4.3) when R and S are both applied.

As might be expected, the cross-coupled NAND circuit of Fig. 4.3 also acts as a latch. This can be deduced from the state diagram or by an analysis such as in Fig. 4.6. This is left as an exercise for the reader. In this case both Set and Reset

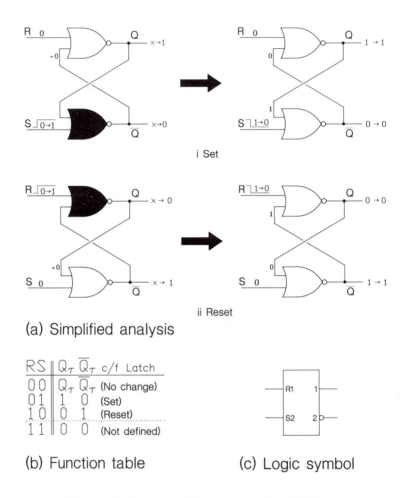

Figure 4.6: Analysis of the cross-coupled NOR latch.

inputs are active on logic 0, i.e. a $\overline{R}\,\overline{S}$ latch. Also the Set input is into the top gate (Q output) and Reset drives the bottom gate ($\overline{Q}$ output).

Example 4.3

Show how you could configure a PAL16L8 (see Fig. 3.22(c)) to implement a R S latch.

Solution

We could of course directly implement the cross-coupled NOR circuit as it stands, but this would require two of the precious eight output NOR gates. Instead, in Fig. 4.7(a) we have converted the bottom NOR to an AND gate using De Morgan's

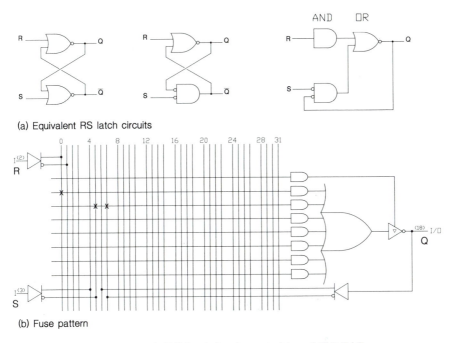

(a) Equivalent RS latch circuits

(b) Fuse pattern

Figure 4.7: A RS latch implemented in a 16L8 PAL.

duality relationship (see Fig. 2.26). The resulting implementation clearly shows how PAL internal feedback paths can be used to implement sequential functions.

It is possible to use multiple-input gates to implement latches with several **Reset** and/or **Set** inputs [1]. In the example of Fig. 4.8(a), the **Set** NOR gate has two external inputs. Now a 3-I/P NOR gate is logically a 2-I/P OR gate feeding a 2-I/P NOR (see Fig. 2.25(b)). Thus we have $\overline{Q} = \overline{S+Q} = \overline{(S_1+S_2)+Q}$. Hence if S_1 OR S_2 are activated, the latch is set. Similarly the 3-I/P NAND gate can be decomposed to a 2-I/P AND feeding a 2-I/P NAND. In this case $\overline{S}$ goes to 0 if $\overline{S_1}$ OR $\overline{S_2}$ go to logic 0. To emphasize this, I have drawn this AND gate in its NOR form for the IEC/ANSII symbol in Fig. 4.8(b).

Most integrated circuit latches are of the D variety; the 74279 IC shown in Fig. 4.8(c) being the only common exception. The **Data latch** stores one bit of information, as controlled by the input C. When C is logic 1, the latch output simply follows the data input D. When C goes to logic 0, this data is locked out and the latch freezes, maintaining this last state until the Control line again goes to 1. This relationship is shown in the logic symbol of Fig. 4.9(b) using the **C dependency** (**C** for Control). The data input **1D** is seen to be dependent on **C1**. Control signals in this context are usually known as **clock signals**.

Although D latches can be implemented by converting RS latches (see Fig. 4.12(c)), it is instructive at this stage to design a suitable circuit using the analysis procedure outlined in the last section, but in reverse. First drawing the state diagram of

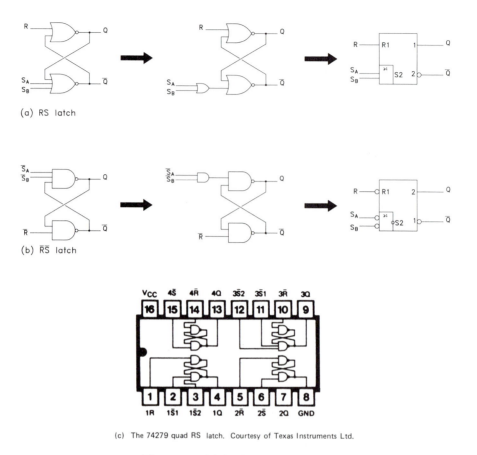

(a) RS latch

(b) $\overline{RS}$ latch

(c) The 74279 quad RS latch. Courtesy of Texas Instruments Ltd.

Figure 4.8: Multiple-input latches.

Fig. 4.9(c) which then leads to the Y-map.

In this elementary case, the Y-map of Fig. 4.9(d) can directly be used as a K-map to determine the logic function for the output (normally a further step is necessary to unscramble the Y-map). The resulting circuit is particularly simple, but inspection of the K-map shows a static hazard going between cell 7 (output Q = 1, D = 1 and C = 1) and cell 5 (C → 0). The reduced equation of $\overline{C}+C$ will produce a logic 0 glitch at the output Q if the $\overline{C}$ delay path is longer than that of C. Could this hazard cause the latch to assume an erroneous state? In practice this will only occur if the delay through G1 plus G3 is longer than that through the inverter. In this case the glitch Q → 0 will arrive at the G2 gate before $\overline{C}$ → 1, and the output will then remain latched at logic 0! Although this is unlikely to occur in practice, some IC manufacturers take the precaution of eliminating the hazard [2]. How would you do this, and how could you adapt the resulting circuit to be implemented using a PAL16L8, which remember effectively has a NOR output gate?

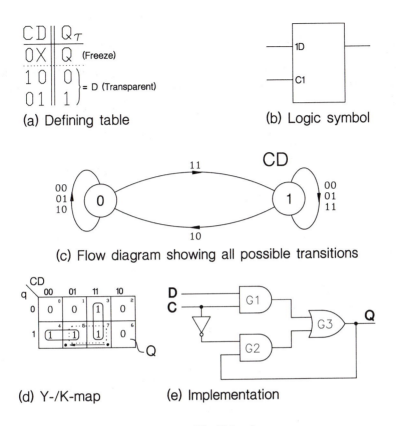

(a) Defining table

(b) Logic symbol

(c) Flow diagram showing all possible transitions

(d) Y-/K-map

(e) Implementation

Figure 4.9: The D latch.

Fig. 4.10 shows an extract from the data sheet for the Texas Instruments 74x75 and 74x77 quad D latch IC. Here it can be seen that the implementation is that of our design outcome. Four independent latches are supplied in this package, but they are clocked in pairs.

The dynamic characteristics of any sequential device must be carefully considered. The data sheet for the SN74LS77 quotes the following figures; some of which are shown in Fig. 4.11:

t_{PLH} from D to Q   11 ns typ,   19 ns max
t_{PHL} from D to Q   9 ns typ,   17 ns max

These characterize the delay in the output reflecting changes of data input during the time the latch is transparent $(C = 1)$.

t_{PLH} from C to Q   10 ns typ,   18 ns max
t_{PLH} from C to Q   10 ns typ,   18 ns max

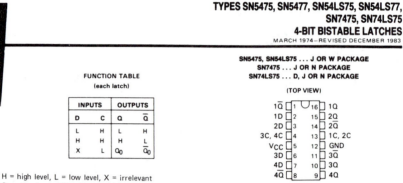

TYPES SN5475, SN5477, SN54LS75, SN54LS77, SN7475, SN74LS75
4-BIT BISTABLE LATCHES
MARCH 1974—REVISED DECEMBER 1983

FUNCTION TABLE
(each latch)

INPUTS		OUTPUTS	
D	C	Q	$\bar{Q}$
L	H	L	H
H	H	H	L
X	L	Q_0	$\bar{Q}_0$

H = high level, L = low level, X = irrelevant
Q_0 = the level of Q before the high-to-low transition of G

SN5475, SN54LS75 ... J OR W PACKAGE
SN7475 ... J OR N PACKAGE
SN74LS75 ... D, J OR N PACKAGE

(TOP VIEW)

1$\bar{Q}$	1 16	1Q
1D	2 15	2Q
2D	3 14	2$\bar{Q}$
3C, 4C	4 13	1C, 2C
V_{CC}	5 12	GND
3D	6 11	3$\bar{Q}$
4D	7 10	3Q
4$\bar{Q}$	8 9	4Q

SN5477, SN54LS77 ... W PACKAGE

(TOP VIEW)

1D	1 14	1Q
2D	2 13	2Q
3C, 4C	3 12	1C, 2C
V_{CC}	4 11	GND
3D	5 10	NC
4D	6 9	3Q
NC	7 8	4Q

NC — No internal connection

description

These latches are ideally suited for use as temporary storage for binary information between processing units and input/output or indicator units. Information present at a data (D) input is transferred to the Q output when the enable (C) is high and the Q output will follow the data input as long as the enable remains high. When the enable goes low, the information (that was present at the data input at the time the transition occurred) is retained at the Q output until the enable is permitted to go high.

logic diagram (each latch)   'LS75

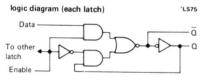

logic symbol

1D (2)	1D	(16) 1Q
1C,2C (13)	C1	(1) 1$\bar{Q}$
	C2	(15) 2Q
2D (3)	2D	(14) 2$\bar{Q}$
3D (6)	3D	(10) 3Q
3C,4C (4)	C3	(11) 3$\bar{Q}$
	C4	(9) 4Q
4D (7)	4D	(8) 4$\bar{Q}$

Pin numbers shown are for J and N packages

Figure 4.10: The SN74x75/74x77 quad D latch. Reproduced by courtesy of Texas Instruments Ltd.

These indicate the delay in the output following the data input after C goes to logic 1, the latch changing from the freeze to the transparent mode.

t_w, width of enabling pulse   20 ns min.

The minimum width of the clock pulse guaranteed to catch and store the new value of D.

t_{su}, setup time   20 ns min

The time the data must be in steady state before the clock falls below 1.5 V, in order to guarantee that the data is caught.

t_h, hold time   5 ns min

The time the data must remain after the clock edge has fallen below 1.5 V to guarantee that it will be held.

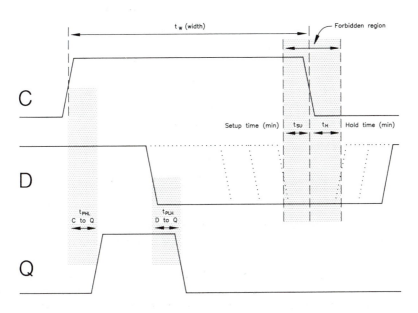

Figure 4.11: Some timing waveforms for a D latch.

What would happen if the data changed during the forbidden region $-t_{su} + t_h$ around the falling clock edge? This is an example of more than one input changing at the same time, and as we saw in the last section, this can lead to unpredictable results. The problem is not so much whether the change will be caught or missed, but there is a finite chance that the circuit will go into a **metastable state** [3, 4].

A metastable situation usually occurs when a signal does not fully force a logic circuit into its saturated High or Low state. As we observed in Fig. 3.14, a logic gate has an analog region of operation. As sequential circuits have feedback paths, this can cause the entire circuit to act as a high-gain analog feedback amplifier.

As a very simple example, consider the D latch circuit of Fig. 4.12(a). This converts an R S to D latch by gating D through to S and $\overline{D}$ to R. Thus when C is logic 1 and D is 1 then S = 1, R = 0 and Q = 1 (i.e. D). Conversely with D = 0 then S = 0, R = 1 and Q = 0 (i.e. D). When C is logic 0 both R and S are 0 and the latch is frozen.

Now consider D is rising just at the time C is falling. Depending on the characteristics of the AND gates, a small 'runt' pulse may occur at the S input. If this is barely enough to drive the R S latch into saturation, a quasi-analog metastable

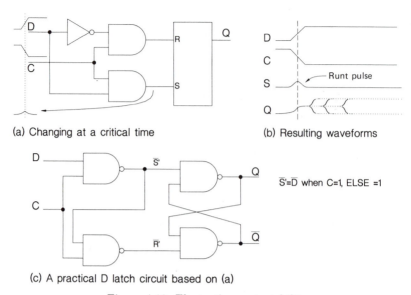

(a) Changing at a critical time   (b) Resulting waveforms

(c) A practical D latch circuit based on (a)

Figure 4.12: Illustrating metastability.

state may occur. Although this can theoretically persist indefinitely; normally the system will revert to one of the stable logic states in a maximum of a few μs, and typically much less [5].

In a typical system sampling a randomly changing data line at, say, a 1000 times each second and with a forbidden region of 25 ns, a metastable situation will occur on average once each four seconds. The characteristics of a metastable state depend very much on the circuitry (one manufacturer's IC may well react differently to another's of the same kind, and from batch to batch) and environmental considerations (such as power supply and loading).

When a metastable state occurs, at the very least the timing parameters (eg. propagation delays) are violated. Its effect depends very much on the driven circuits, which if possible should not rely on data at the active edge of the clock.

To complete this section, let us look at an example of a practical application of D latches.

Example 4.4

A certain microprocessor (MPU)-based system sends data to the outside world over an 8-bit bus, much as depicted in Fig.3.21. An 8-bit output port (a port is a point of entry or exit into a system) is to be designed which can grab data off the bus when pulsed by the MPU.

It has been suggested that a 74ALS373 array of eight D latches be used for this purpose, part of whose data sheet is reproduced in Fig. 4.13. What would be the logic symbol for this chip and how could the 74ALS373 be used as an input port?

TYPES SN54ALS373, SN54AS373, SN74ALS373, SN74AS373
OCTAL D-TYPE TRANSPARENT LATCHES WITH 3-STATE OUTPUTS

D2661, APRIL 1982—REVISED DECEMBER 1983

- 8 Latches in a Single Package
- 3-State Bus-Driving True Outputs
- Full Parallel Access for Loading
- Buffered Control Inputs
- P-N-P Inputs Reduce D-C Loading on Data Lines
- Package Options Include Both Plastic and Ceramic Chip Carriers in Addition to Plastic and Ceramic DIPs
- Dependable Texas Instruments Quality and Reliability

description

These 8-bit latches feature three-state outputs designed specifically for driving highly capacitive or relatively low-impedance loads. They are particularly suitable for implementing buffer registers, I/O ports, bidirectional bus drivers, and working registers.

The eight latches of the 'ALS373 and 'AS373 are transparent D-type latches. While the enable (C) is high the Q outputs will follow the data (D) inputs. When the enable is taken low, the Q outputs will be latched at the levels that were set up at the D inputs.

A buffered output-control input ($\overline{OC}$) can be used to place the eight outputs in either a normal logic state (high or low logic levels) or a high-impedance state. In the high-impedance state the outputs neither load nor drive the bus lines significantly. The high-impedance third state and increased drive provide the capability to drive the bus lines in a bus-organized system without need for interface or pull-up components.

The output control $\overline{OC}$ does not affect the internal operations of the latches. Old data can be retained or new data can be entered while the outputs are off.

The SN54ALS373 and SN54AS373 are characterized for operation over the full military temperature range of $-55\,°C$ to $125\,°C$. The SN74ALS373 and SN74AS373 are characterized for operation from $0\,°C$ to $70\,°C$.

FUNCTION TABLE (EACH LATCH)

INPUTS			OUTPUT
$\overline{OC}$	ENABLE C	D	Q
L	H	H	H
L	H	L	L
L	L	X	Q_0
H	X	X	Z

SN54ALS373, SN54AS373 . . . J PACKAGE
SN74ALS373, SN74AS373 . . . N PACKAGE
(TOP VIEW)

```
        ┌──┐ ┌──┐
  OC  ❏ 1   20 ❏ Vcc
  1Q  ❏ 2   19 ❏ 8Q
  1D  ❏ 3   18 ❏ 8D
  2D  ❏ 4   17 ❏ 7D
  2Q  ❏ 5   16 ❏ 7Q
  3Q  ❏ 6   15 ❏ 6Q
  3D  ❏ 7   14 ❏ 6D
  4D  ❏ 8   13 ❏ 5D
  4Q  ❏ 9   12 ❏ 5Q
  GND ❏ 10  11 ❏ C
```

SN54ALS373, SN54AS373 . . . FH PACKAGE
SN74ALS373, SN74AS373 . . . FN PACKAGE
(TOP VIEW)

logic diagram (positive logic)

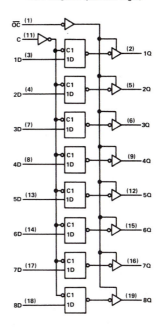

Figure 4.13: The SN74ALS373 octal D latch. Reproduced by courtesy of Texas Instruments Ltd.

Solution

We see from the logic in Fig. 4.13 that all latch outputs are fed through a 3-state buffer enabled in common by input $\overline{OC}$ ($\overline{Output\ Control}$). All latches are also clocked in common by the control signal C. This suggests the use of a common control box on top of an array of D latch cells as the logic symbol, as shown in Fig. 4.14. Only the top cell is annotated; the lower seven are assumed to be replicas.

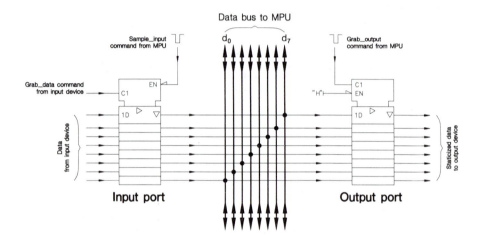

Figure 4.14: How the 74x373 can be used both as an input and output port to a bus structured system.

Used as an output port, each D input is connected to a Data-bus line. When the system controller wants to send out data, it need only bring **C1** High. Output data then follows the bus data until **C1** goes back Low. This data then remains static, independent of any further transactions on the bus. The 3-state outputs are usually permanently enabled in this application.

In Fig.3.21, we saw that ingress into a bus must be made using 3-state (or open-collector) buffers. Utilizing a latch array with integral 3-state buffers allows the input peripheral device to load the input port any time it has data available. Such latched data can be subsequently placed on the bus by the MPU pulsing the 3-state **EN** control in the manner described in Fig.3.21.

To facilitate the use of the 74x373 as an input port, its outputs are capable of supplying more current than normal. For example the 74ALS373 can source at least 30 ma into a bus line while keeping V_{OH} at 2.25 V. A large current drive reduces switching transients on the bus. This capability is indicated by the $\triangleright$ buffer symbol in the top array cell of the logic symbol.

Arrays of latches clocked in parallel are often known as **registers**. A register can be defined as a memory structure holding one word of data. In this case the structure is parallel-in parallel-out; indicating how the data is entered and taken out. We look at registers in some detail in Section 4.3.1.

4.1.3 Flip Flops

D latches are transparent for the duration that the **C** control is logic 1, in that the output follows the input. Many applications require data to be caught on a transition of the clock, and for the memory cell to be opaque at all other times. Latches which have this edge-triggered property, are known as **flip flops**. Sometimes the term opaque latch is used as an alternative.

Figure 4.15 shows an extract from the data sheet for the SN74x74 dual **D flip flop**. Each flip flop has complement outputs and direct entry $\overline{\text{Preset}}$ ($\overline{\text{PRE}}$) and $\overline{\text{Clear}}$ ($\overline{\text{CLR}}$) inputs. These inputs respectively Set and Reset the flip flop, irrespective of and overriding the **Clock** (**CLK**) input. As they are not synchronized by the **Clock**, they are classified as asynchronous data inputs. In contrast, the **D** input is synchronized by the **Clock**, and this is indicated by the dependency number in the logic symbol; i.e. **C1 → 1D**. The control input is shown with a triangular dynamic symbol, to indicate operation on an external rising (or positive-going)-edge (internally logic 0 to logic 1). A negative-edge trigger is symbolized with an external polarity symbol in addition to the internal dynamic qualifier, as shown in Fig. 4.19.

The only real difference between the logic symbol for a D latch and a D flip flop, is the dynamic indicator at the Control input. To clarify the difference, consider the following example.

Example 4.5

A data line (say, a bus line in Fig. 4.14) is sampled by both a D latch and a D flip flop. Given the waveforms of Fig. 4.16(a), determine the waveforms at both memory cells' output.

Solution

The D latch is transparent during times where the sampling clock is logic 1. This following action is clearly shown in the shaded portions of Fig. 4.16(b). Notice how the noise spike comes through during one of these periods.

In contrast, the flip flop only grabs data at the rising edge of the clock and misses the noise pulse. Examining Fig. 4.16(c) shows a waveform which is a clone of the input but synchronized to the clock and quantized to the sampling period. Provided that the sampling rate is greater than the period of the input waveform, no transitions are lost. Shorter events (eg. the noise spike) may be missed.

If the sampling rate is many times this minimum, then the output will be virtually identical to the incoming waveform, but synchronized to the clock. Synchronizing an arbitrary external waveform to a system clock is one of the standard applications of D flip flops. However, care must be taken, as by its nature input transitions may well occur during the forbidden region of $t_{su} + t_h$ of Fig. 4.11. The setup and hold times from Fig. 4.15 are given as 20 and 5 ns respectively for the 74LS74. If this violation occurs, then the flip flop may enter a metastable state, as described in Fig. 4.13.

The logic implementation of the 74x74 D flip flop, as shown in Fig. 4.15, comprizes three cross-coupled NAND latches [6]. In order to analyze its operation, I

**TYPES SN5474, SN54LS74A, SN54S74
SN7474, SN74LS74A, SN74S74
DUAL D-TYPE POSITIVE-EDGE-TRIGGERED FLIP-FLOPS WITH PRESET AND CLEAR**

REVISED DECEMBER 1983

- Package Options Include Both Plastic and Ceramic Chip Carriers in Addition to Plastic and Ceramic DIPs

- Dependable Texas Instruments Quality and Reliability

description

These devices contain two independent D-type positive-edge-triggered flip-flops. A low level at the preset or clear inputs sets or resets the outputs regardless of the levels of the other inputs. When preset and clear are inactive (high), data at the D input meeting the setup time requirements are transferred to the outputs on the positive-going edge of the clock pulse. Clock triggering occurs at a voltage level and is not directly related to the rise time of the clock pulse. Following the hold time interval, data at the D input may be changed without affecting the levels at the outputs.

The SN54' family is characterized for operation over the full military temperature range of $-55\,°C$ to $125\,°C$. The SN74' family is characterized for operation from $0\,°C$ to $70\,°C$.

SN5474 . . . J PACKAGE
SN54LS74A, SN54S74 . . . J OR W PACKAGE
SN7474 . . . J OR N PACKAGE
SN74LS74A, SN74S74 . . . D, J OR N PACKAGE
(TOP VIEW)

```
1CLR  [1    14]  VCC
1D    [2    13]  2CLR
1CLK  [3    12]  2D
1PRE  [4    11]  2CLK
1Q    [5    10]  2PRE
1Q    [6     9]  2Q
GND   [7     8]  2Q
```

logic symbol

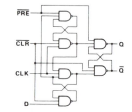

Pin numbers shown are for J and N packages.

logic diagram

FUNCTION TABLE

INPUTS				OUTPUTS	
PRESET	CLEAR	CLOCK	D	Q	Q̄
L	H	X	X	H	L
H	L	X	X	L	H
L	L	X	X	H*	H*
H	H	↑	H	H	L
H	H	↑	L	L	H
H	H	L	X	Q_0	$\overline{Q}_0$

*The output levels in this configuration are not guaranteed to meet the minimum levels for V_{OH} if the lows at Preset and Clear are near V_{IL} maximum. Furthermore, this configuration is nonstable; that is, it will not persist when either Preset or Clear returns to its inactive (high) level.

recommended operating conditions

			SN54LS74A			SN74LS74A			UNIT
			MIN	NOM	MAX	MIN	NOM	MAX	
t_w	Pulse duration	CLK high	30			30			
		CLK low	37			37			ns
		PRE or CLR low	30			30			
t_{su}	Input setup time before CLK ↑		20			20			ns
t_h	Input hold time-data after CLK ↑		5			5			ns
T_A	Operating free-air temperature		-55		125	0		70	°C

TEXAS
INSTRUMENTS

Figure 4.15: The SN74x74 dual D flip flop. Reproduced by courtesy of Texas Instruments Ltd.

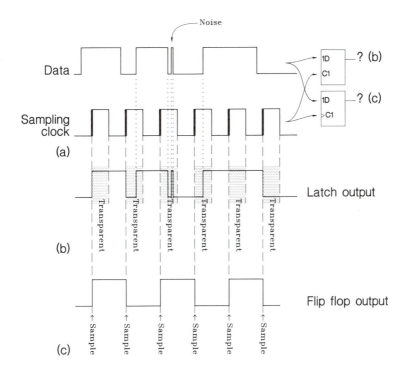

Figure 4.16: Staticizing an arbitrary waveform.

have redrawn the circuit in Fig. 4.17(a) with the direct entry $\overline{\text{Preset}}$ and $\overline{\text{Clear}}$ inputs removed, and the output characterized as a $\overline{R}\,\overline{S}$ block. This reduces the open-loop equivalent and resulting Y-map to manageable proportions, with four feedback and two programmable inputs.

The Y-map of Fig. 4.17(c) shows six stable states. When the Clock is logic 0, the system is either in cell 24 (D = 0) or cell 62 (D = 1). When C goes to logic 1 ($\_\!/\!\overline{}$) the system either moves 24 → 21 (D = 0) or 62 → 47 (D = 1). Any subsequent change in D simply moves the system 21 ↔ 23 (D = 0 at C $\_\!/\!\overline{}$) or 47 ↔ 41 (D = 1 at C $\_\!/\!\overline{}$). In the former case Y_2Y_3 (i.e. $\overline{S}\,\overline{R}$) is 10 and the output remains Reset irrespective of any further gyrations of D. Similarly, states 41 & 47 both have $Y_2Y_3 = 01$ and the output remains at Set irrespective. When C later goes back to logic 0, then both cells 24 & 62 have $Y_2Y_3 = 11$, which is the no-change input for the front end $\overline{R}\,\overline{S}$ latch.

The D flip flop circuit can be used as the basis of a series of flip flop types, most of which are based on the toggle function. This is shown in Fig. 4.18(a), where a D flip flop is shown with its D input permanently connected to its $\overline{Q}$ output. In

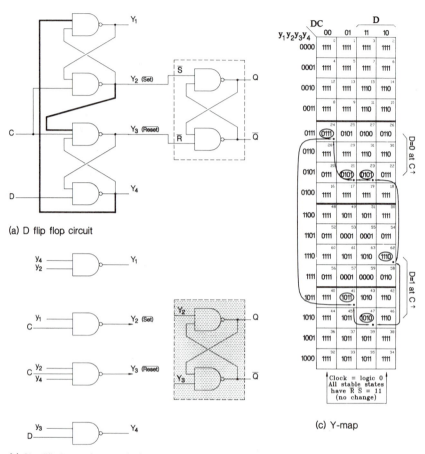

(a) D flip flop circuit

(b) Simplified open-loop equivalent

(c) Y-map

Figure 4.17: Analysis of the 74x74 flip flop circuit.

this situation, D is always opposite to Q at the instant of C = ___/‾. Thus the flip flop state changes over at each sampling instant, i.e. toggles. Can you deduce the relationship between input and output waveforms?

The traditional **T flip flop** has a T Control input in place of D. When this is logic 0, the flip flop state is held on the sample edge. When T is logic 1, the output toggles on the active Clock edge. The EOR gate in Fig. 4.18(b) acts as a programmable inverter controlled by T. When T = 0, D = Q (no change on C = ___/‾). When T = 1, D = $\overline{Q}$ (toggle on C = ___/‾).

The most versatile of the commercially available bistables is the **J K flip flop** [7]. This allows synchronous Set and Reset (i.e. a R S flip flop) together with Toggle. As can be seen from the defining function table of Fig. 4.18(c), J is analogous to S

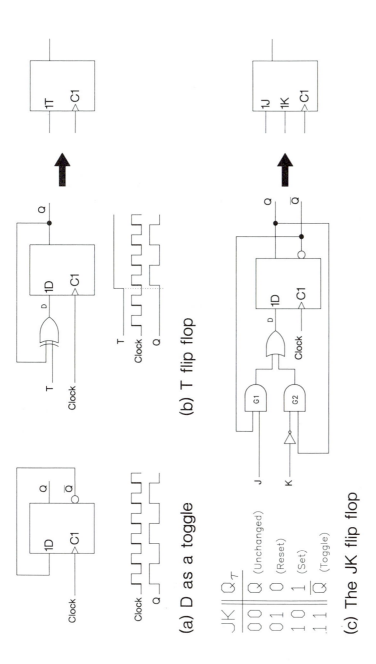

(a) D as a toggle

(b) T flip flop

(c) The JK flip flop

Figure 4.18: Flip flops with a toggling action.

(aide-mémoire, Jet Set) and K to R, but when both J and K are logic 1, then the flip flop toggles.

The logic network converting a D flip flop to J K in Fig. 4.18(c) was designed from the relationships:

$$
\begin{aligned}
&\text{IF } \mathsf{J\,K} = 00 \text{ THEN make } \mathsf{D} = \mathsf{Q} && \text{(Hold)}\\
&\text{ELSE IF } \mathsf{J\,K} = 01 \text{ THEN make } \mathsf{D} = 0 && \text{(Reset)}\\
&\text{ELSE IF } \mathsf{J\,K} = 10 \text{ THEN make } \mathsf{D} = 1 && \text{(Set)}\\
&\text{ELSE IF } \mathsf{J\,K} = 11 \text{ THEN make } \mathsf{D} = \overline{\mathsf{Q}} && \text{(Toggle)}
\end{aligned}
$$

A similar (but simpler) relationship is used to convert a D to R S flip flop. Can you draw the resulting diagram. Think about the situation $\mathsf{R\,S} = 11$!

Commercial IC J K flip flops are sometimes based on D flip flop circuitry, but more usually have a unique implementation, such as shown in the data sheet of Fig. 4.19. This can be analyzed in the same manner as in Fig. 4.17, but (without $\overline{\mathsf{PRE}}$) has three programmable inputs and only two feedback variables. The elongated circle shapes are pre-IEC/ANSII delay symbols.

The 74ALS113A package contains two J K flip flops, each with a double-rail output (i.e. Q and $\overline{\mathsf{Q}}$). Each flip flop has an overriding asychronous $\overline{\mathsf{Preset}}$ ($\overline{\mathsf{PRE}}$) input and is clocked on a falling edge (as symbolized by the polarity arrow abutting the dynamic qualifier at **C1**). The 74x112 is similar, but with an added $\overline{\mathsf{Clear}}$ ($\overline{\mathsf{CLR}}$) asynchronous input. Timing characteristics shown are the minimum Clock and $\overline{\mathsf{Preset}}$ durations, setup and hold times (the latter being zero). The propagation delay times are given from the active Clock edge, which, unlike the waveforms of Fig. 4.11, are from the same reference point as the setup and hold times.

Historically, before integrated circuits, toggling flip flops were implemented with transparent latches as the memory cell. Now if a D latch was used in place of the D flip flop in Fig. 4.8(a), then the circuit would continue to toggle as long as the clock was a logic 1! Capacitor-resistor networks were used to both shorten this clock input and delay the feedback signal [8]. The idea was to produce a sample pulse of shorter duration than the propagation delay back to the input, so that only one toggle was allowed to occur.

As it is not feasible to reproduce this technique in integrated circuitry, most early ICs, such as the 7476 dual J K flip flop, used the the **master-slave** configuration. As shown in Fig. 4.20, this comprizes two cascaded gated latches, operated in antiphase. During one clock cycle, several phases of operation occur:

1. When C is logic 0, the master latch is cut off from outside data and its unchanging state is gated through to the slave latch.

2. When C rises, the slave is disconnected from the master and the former enabled. Outside data can now activate the master, but this is not reflected at the slave's output.

3. When C falls again, the master is cut off, but its state is gated through to the slave and appears at the flip flop output.

Although the master-slave technique permits only one toggle per clock pulse, it is not truly edge-triggered, in that it takes both edges to go through one cycle. This is defined as pulse triggering. The logic symbol for such a J K flip flop, as shown

SN54ALS113A, SN74ALS113A
DUAL J-K NEGATIVE-EDGE-TRIGGERED FLIP-FLOPS WITH PRESET

D2261, APRIL 1982–REVISED MAY 1986

- Fully Buffered to Offer Maximum Isolation from External Disturbance

- Package Options Include Plastic "Small Outline" Packages, Ceramic Chip Carriers, and Standard Plastic and Ceramic 300-mil DIPs

- Dependable Texas Instruments Quality and Reliability

TYPE	TYPICAL MAXIMUM CLOCK FREQUENCY	TYPICAL POWER DISSIPATION PER FLIP-FLOP
'ALS113A	40 MHz (C_L = 15 pF)	6 mW

description

These devices contain two independent J-K negative-edge-triggered flip-flops. A low level at the Preset input sets the outputs regardless of the levels of the other inputs. When Preset ($\overline{PRE}$) is inactive (high), data at the J and K inputs meeting the setup time requirements are transferred to the outputs on the negative-going edge of the clock pulse. Clock triggering occurs at a voltage level and is not directly related to the fall time of the clock pulse. Following the hold time interval, data at the J and K inputs may be changed without affecting the levels at the outputs. These versatile flip-flops can perform as toggle flip-flops by tying J and K high.

The SN54ALS113A is characterized for operation over the full military temperature range of −55°C to 125°C. The SN74ALS113A is characterized for operation from 0°C to 70°C.

SN54ALS113A . . . J PACKAGE
SN74ALS113A . . . D OR N PACKAGE
(TOP VIEW)

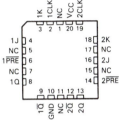

SN54ALS113A . . . FK PACKAGE
(TOP VIEW)

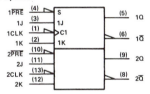

NC—No internal connection

logic symbol†

†This symbol is in accordance with ANSI/IEEE Std 91-1984 and IEC Publication 617-12.

Pin numbers shown are for D, J, and N packages.

FUNCTION TABLE

INPUTS				OUTPUTS	
PRE	CLK	J	K	Q	$\overline{Q}$
L	X	X	X	H	L
H	↓	L	L	Q_0	$\overline{Q}_0$
H	↓	H	L	H	L
H	↓	L	H	L	H
H	↓	H	H	TOGGLE	
H	H	X	X	Q_0	$\overline{Q}_0$

TEXAS INSTRUMENTS

Figure 4.19: The SN74ALS113A dual JK flip flop (*continued next page*).

SN54ALS113A, SN74ALS113A
DUAL J-K NEGATIVE-EDGE-TRIGGERED FLIP-FLOPS WITH PRESET

logic diagram (positive logic)

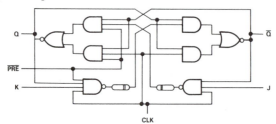

absolute maximum ratings over operating free-air temperature range (unless otherwise noted)

Supply voltage, V_{CC} . . . . 7 V
Input voltage . . . . 7 V
Operating free-air temperature range: SN54ALS113A . . . . −55 °C to 125 °C
                                       SN74ALS113A . . . . 0 °C to 70 °C
Storage temperature range . . . . −65 °C to 150 °C

recommended operating conditions

			SN54ALS113A			SN74ALS113A			UNIT
			MIN	NOM	MAX	MIN	NOM	MAX	
V_{CC}	Supply voltage		4.5	5	5.5	4.5	5	5.5	V
V_{IH}	High-level input voltage		2			2			V
V_{IL}	Low-level input voltage				0.7			0.8	V
I_{OH}	High-level output current				−0.4			−0.4	mA
I_{OL}	Low-level output current				4			8	mA
f_{clock}	Clock frequency		0		25	0		30	MHz
t_w	Pulse duration	$\overline{PRE}$ low	20			10			ns
		CLK high	20			16.5			
		CLK low	20			16.5			
t_{su}	Setup time	Data	25			22			ns
	before CLK↓	$\overline{PRE}$ inactive	25			20			
t_h	Hold time, data after CLK↓		0			0			ns
T_A	Operating free-air temperature		−55		125	0		70	°C

switching characteristics

PARAMETER	FROM (INPUT)	TO (OUTPUT)	V_{CC} = 4.5 V to 5.5 V, C_L = 50 pF, R_L = 500 Ω, T_A = MIN to MAX				UNIT
			SN54ALS113A		SN74ALS113A		
			MIN	MAX	MIN	MAX	
f_{max}			25		30		MHz
t_{PLH}	$\overline{PRE}$	Q or $\overline{Q}$	3	23	3	14	ns
t_{PHL}			4	26	4	16	
t_{PLH}	CLK	Q or $\overline{Q}$	3	22	3	15	ns
t_{PHL}			5	23	5	19	

TEXAS
INSTRUMENTS

Figure 4.19: (*continued*). The SN74ALS113A dual JK flip flop. Reproduced by courtesy of Texas Instruments Ltd.

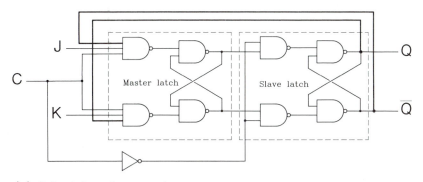

(a) Principle of operation

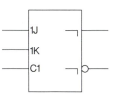

(b) Logic symbol

Figure 4.20: The master-slave JK flip flop.

Function	Designator	t_{setup}(ns)	t_{hold}(ns)	t_{width}(ns)	f_{max}(MHz)
Flip flops					
Dual ↑D	LS/ALS/AS/HC74	20/15/5/8	5/0/0/3	25/15/6/24	25/34/105/20
Hex ↑D	LS/ALS/AS/HC174	25/10/4/18	5/0/1/3	20/10/6/24	25/50/100/20
Octal ↑D	LS/ALS/AS/HC374	20/10/2/18	5/0/2/5	15/14/4/24	35/35/125/20
Dual ↓JK	LS/ALS/S/HC112/3/4	25/20/7/24	0/0/0/0	25/17/8/24	30/30/80/20
Quad ↓JK	74276	3	10	15	35
Latches					t_{pd}(ns)
Quad $\overline{R}\,\overline{S}$	74LS279	–	–	27	27
Quad D	74LS/HC75	20/18	5/3	20/24	27/38
Octal D	LS/ALS/AS/HC373	5/7/2/13	20/10/3/5	15/10/5/24	30/23/12/38

Table 4.1: A selection of 74-series flip flops and latches, with worst-case worst-case parameters.

in Fig. 4.20(b), denotes this by using the prosponed edge symbol ¬ at the outputs. This, together with the lack of a dynamic symbol at the Control input, indicates master-slave.

One major problem with the master-slave configuration, is that the master can be changed several times if the J and K inputs vary whilst the Clock is logic 1. This makes the flip flop susceptible to noise-induced malfunction. A **data lockout** flip flop modifies the basic master-slave circuit to enable the master for only a short time. This is symbolized by using a dynamic qualifier at C together with the prosponed symbol at the output.

Devices introduced since the early 1970s inevitably use pure edge-triggered designs. However, early designs are still available. Care should be taken, as subfamily members with the same postfix may use different trigger techniques. Thus the 7476 is a dual master-slave J K device, whilst the 74LS76 is a dual negative-edge triggered equivalent.

4.2   Counters

Arrays of flip flops which have the property of incrementing or decrementing when pulsed are known as counter registers, or just **counters**. Counters cover a vast field, with complete texts devoted to them [9], and all we can do in the allocated space is to indicate some of the commonest techniques.

Normally each bit of the binary code is stored in a flip flop, with N flip flops giving up to 2^N states (code groups). Essentially there are two kinds of counters. Synchronous counters have all flip flops simultaneously clocked by the count pulse. In asynchronous circuits, normally only the first flip flop is directly clocked; this change then propagating through the remaining logic.

The remainder of this section looks at the properties, symbology and design techniques for both kinds of counter. Also covered are typical MSI counter circuits.

After completing this section you should:

- Appreciate the difference and properties of ripple and synchronous counters.

- Recognize that transient states produced by ripple action can cause decoding spikes and limit the counting rate.

- Be able to design reliable ripple counters to any base.

- Understand the meaning of the general qualifying symbols **CNT** and **RCNT**, and the symbols **CT**, **+**, **−**.

- Be able to design synchronous counters at the flip flop level.

- Be able to analyze the response of a synchronous counter to illegal states.

- Be aware of the range of MSI counters and how to use them.

4.2.1 Ripple Counters

In Fig. 4.18(a) we saw that a toggling flip flop will divide an input pulse frequency by two. Cascading several such circuits gives waveforms of $\div 2$, $\div 4$, $\div 8$, $\div 16$ etc. These waveforms taken as a group are seen in Fig. 4.21(b) to represent the natural 8-4-2-1 code. This particular counter configuration is described as asynchronous or **ripple**, because changes propagate through the chain from LSB to MSB.

Several IEC/ANSII symbols are in common use for ripple counters. The rather complex symbol shown at in Fig. 4.21(c)i is the recommended depiction. This symbol makes use of **Z** dependency, which denotes interconnection; i.e. the existence of internal logic connections. Thus in cell **[32]**, **Z6** shows a connection to **6T** in cell **[64]**. The general qualifying symbol **CTR12** indicates a counter with 12 stages. Finally the **CT=0** common control input is a master Reset, returning the contents (**CT**) of the counter to state 0 (i.e. $000000000000b$). A **R** symbol could be used instead, but **CT** is preferred, as counters can often be reset to other non-zero states. The cell weight notes, eg. **[2048]**, are optional; the normal sequence is LSB at the top, working down.

Although this symbol clearly shows the internal structure of a ripple counter, it is unnecessarily complex and cannot easily be adapted to show more sophisticated configurations. The ripple action is depicted in Fig. 4.21(c)ii by the general qualifying symbol **RCTR**. This symbol has not been fully approved by IEC, but is under discussion [10]. The common control box also shows the count input, which is symbolized as **+** for up count (**–** for down count).

A simpler symbol is shown in Fig. 4.21(c)iii. This is commonly used in manufacturer's data books, especially for counters which do not have a parallel load facility.

Example 4.6

A student has by mistake constructed the counter of Fig. 4.21(a), but with the $\overline{Q}$ outputs driving to the succeeding Clock input. If this individual still monitors the count on the Q outputs, describe the counting action.

Solution

So far as the counter is concerned, the basic operation is the same; with the $\overline{Q}$ outputs replacing Q. Thus the $\overline{Q}$ count is $0000b \rightarrow 0001b \rightarrow 0010b \rightarrow 0011b$ $\ldots 1110b \rightarrow 1111b$. The Q outputs are respectively then $1111b \rightarrow 1110b \rightarrow 1101b \rightarrow$ $1100b \ldots 0001b \rightarrow 0000b$. Thus the student has inadvertently produced a **down counter** (the required action being an up count). This would be symbolized by replacing **+** by **–** in Fig. 4.20(c)ii & iii and (rather obscurely) in (c)i by overbarring the **T** prefixes; eg. $\overline{8T}$ for cell **[256]**. Can you prove that replacing the flip flops by $\_\!\!\!\int\overline{}$ -triggered devices also gives a down count?

The result of the last example enables us to design an **up/down counter** (sometimes called bi-directional). A control input M determines the mode. With $M = 0$, Q_n is connected to C_{n+1} **[UP]** and with $M = 1$, $\overline{Q}_n$ connects to C_{n+1} **[DOWN]**. This

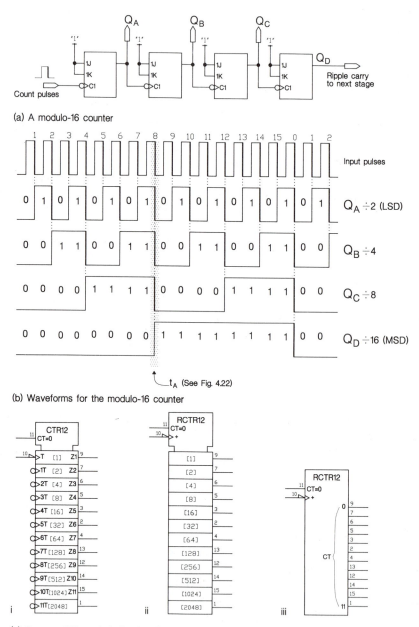

(a) A modulo-16 counter

(b) Waveforms for the modulo-16 counter

(c) Common IEC symbols for the 4040 12-stage ripple counter

Figure 4.21: The basic ripple counter.

change-over is simply accomplished using EOR gates as programmable inverters between each $Q_n \rightarrow C_{n+1}$ connection and controlled by M. A disadvantage of this simple approach, is that changing M may cause false triggering, as some clock inputs will likely change from $1 \rightarrow 0$.

Can you redraw the symbol of Fig. 4.21(c)ii or iii to depict such a circuit? Hint: see Fig. 4.40(a).

The main advantage of ripple counters is their relative simplicity. However, their asynchronous nature gives problems in some situations. Because of cumulative delays as changes propagate along the chain, some alterations of state occur in a staggered manner. Consider the counter in state $0111b$ when clocked, as shown shaded in Fig. 4.21(b). Initially Q_A goes to logic 0, then Q_B also goes down as then does Q_C and finally Q_D goes to logic 1. Taking worst-case worst-case Clock to Q propagation times for the SN74ALS113A from the data sheet of Fig. 4.19, we have:

$$3 \times t_{PHL} + 1 \times t_{PLH} = 3 \times 19 + 1 \times 15 = 72 \text{ ns}$$

For the situation going from state $1111b$ to $0000b$, we have $4 \times t_{PHL} = 76$ ns worst-case worst-case. This is known as the **resolution time** of the counter, and indicates the maximum frequency ($\frac{1}{76}$ ns $= 13.2$ MHz) beyond which some states may not appear at the output. At frequencies greater than this, the first flip flop may be changing towards state $n + 1$ before the last flip flop has received information regarding its change to state n.

The problem is compounded with longer counters. For example the 12-stage 74HCT4040, symbolized in Fig. 4.20(c), has a worst-case worst-case t_{PHL} & t_{PLH} of 30 ns for internal $Q \rightarrow C$ connections and 60 ns for the external count input. Hence the resolution time is 390 ns, giving $f_{max} = 2.6$ MHz. It should be emphasized that the ability of a ripple chain to act as a frequency divider, as opposed to a counter, is only limited to the maximum speed of an individual flip flop. The figure given for this device is 20 MHz worst-case worst-case, and 72 MHz typically at 25°C. But there will be a noticeable phase shift between input and output transitions.

Another more insidious problem arises due to the staggered change of counter states, known as **decoding spikes**. Consider a circuit which is supposed to detect counter state $1000b$, i.e. $\overline{D} \cdot \overline{C} \cdot \overline{B} \cdot \overline{A}$ in Fig. 4.22(c). Although state $1000b$ is correctly detected, the transient occurrences of $1000b$ when changing from 9 to 10, $11 \rightarrow 12$ and $15 \rightarrow 0$ may also be sufficiently long to change the decoder gate's output. These glitches are very short, but if fed into memory circuits can lead to false triggering or a runt pulse (see Fig. 4.12) possibly leading to a metastable state. The all-zero's detector used to reset a latch in Fig. 3.36 is a prime instance of where trouble can occur.

Example 4.7

Example 2.29 used a counter to generate a waveform Z_2. On examination with an oscilloscope, additional short spikes were seen to occur. Can you predict their position?

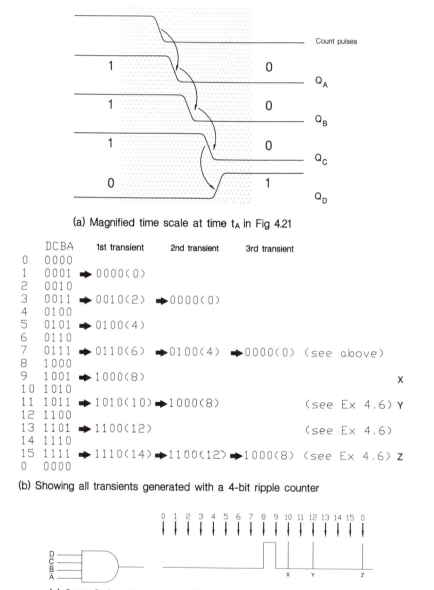

(a) Magnified time scale at time t_A in Fig 4.21

```
       DCBA    1st transient   2nd transient   3rd transient
 0     0000
 1     0001 ➡ 0000(0)
 2     0010
 3     0011 ➡ 0010(2) ➡0000(0)
 4     0100
 5     0101 ➡ 0100(4)
 6     0110
 7     0111 ➡ 0110(6) ➡0100(4) ➡0000(0) (see above)
 8     1000
 9     1001 ➡ 1000(8)                                       X
10     1010
11     1011 ➡ 1010(10)➡1000(8)          (see Ex 4.6) Y
12     1100
13     1101 ➡ 1100(12)                  (see Ex 4.6)
14     1110
15     1111 ➡ 1110(14)➡1100(12) ➡1000(8) (see Ex 4.6) Z
 0     0000
```

(b) Showing all transients generated with a 4-bit ripple counter

(c) State-8 decoding spikes at X, Y and Z

Figure 4.22: Transient behavior of ripple counters.

Solution

The function Z_2 is $\sum 4, 5, 6, 7, 10, 12$. When the counter goes from state 11 ($Z_2 = 0$) to state 12 ($Z_2 = 1$) it passes through state 10 ($Z_2 = 1$) to 8 ($Z_2 = 0$) to 12 ($Z_2 = 1$), giving the transient shown at α in Fig. 4.23(a). Spikes also occur at points $13 \rightarrow 14$ (β) and $15 \rightarrow 0$ (τ). Some functions are naturally clear of decoding spikes. Thus Z_1 from the same example covers $\sum 1, 3, 5, 7, 13, 15$; none of which appear in the transient table of Fig. 4.22(b).

The duration of decoder spikes only depends on the propagation delay of the flip flops and not the clock frequency. Thus examining a waveform, such as Z_2, on an oscilloscope may not show up any glitches. If the clock frequency were 1 kHz, then the duration of the counter cycle would be 16 ms, and would be typically viewed with a 2 ms/div timebase. In this situation, a 20 ns glitch would represent only 10^{-5} of a division!

Where glitch-free signals are necessary, strobing may be used to clean up the waveforms. Either a simple gate may be utilized to examine the decoder output well after the counter has reached steady state, or a D flip flop used as the sampling device. The former is simpler, but as can be seen from Fig. 4.23(a), will serrate long pulses. In the latter case the cleaned-up signal is phase shifted from the original. Typically for a ⌐_-triggered counter, the logic 1 phase of the clock can be used as the strobe.

A typical application of a counter requiring clean-up techniques is shown in Fig. 4.23(b). Here serialized 8-bit data transmitted along a communications link is to be gathered together as 8-bit parallel bytes. The basic technique uses a modulo-8 counter (i.e. eight states) addressing a 3 to 8-line demultiplexer which sequentially routes through the serial bits to eight RS latches. These latches are cleared at the beginning of the process and each cell's **Set** input is strobed in turn, effectively by the appropriate serial bit; either logic 1 (latch Set) or logic 0 (latch remains Reset). The demultiplexer is gated by the counter's clock, which only permits this routing half a clock cycle after the ⌐_ Count_Clock. This also eliminates internal function hazards in the demultiplexer itself.

After the complete 8-bit byte has been built up, internal counter logic detecting state 7 (eg. $Q_C \cdot Q_B \cdot Q_A$) clocks a D flip flop on its trailing edge (**CNT=7** $\rightarrow$ 0) to signal the end of conversion ($\overline{EOC}$). This then dumps the data into an 8-bit D flip flop array, which holds the data static until the next byte is built up. $\overline{EOC}$ also sets a D flip flop, which generates a $\overline{Data\_AVailable}$ status signal ($\overline{DAV}$) to inform the outside world that new data is available. The system outside responds by reading the data and then pulsing its $\overline{Data\_ACcepted}$ ($\overline{DAC}$) line Low to cancel the transaction. This $\overline{DAV}/\overline{DAC}$ ritual is known as **handshaking**. See also Section 5.3.4.

The length of a counter's sequence can be increased to 2^N by using N flip flops. However, in many cases a count base R other than 2^N is desired. The most common of these is the decade counter, counting in tens. These can be used in conjunction with display decoders to give a decimal count. A simple design procedure in such cases is to commence with a counter of N bits, such that $2^N \geq R$, and use feedback to eliminate the redundant states. Usually a gate is used to detect the first illegal state of the sequence; which then resets the counter.

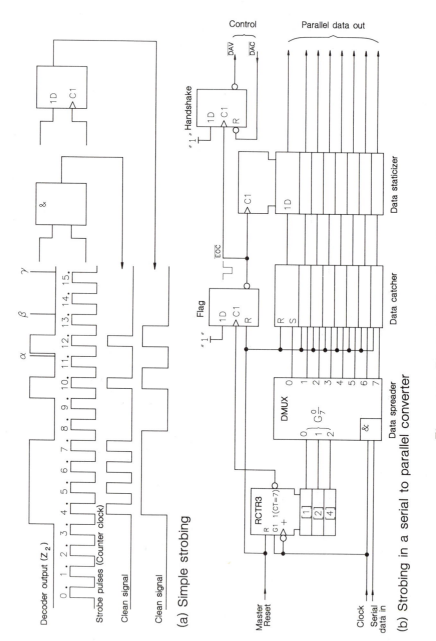

Figure 4.23: Eliminating decoding spikes.

Example 4.8

Design a BCD ripple counter, using the 8-4-2-1 code, to count up from $0000b$ to $1001b$. Use ⌐__-triggered D flip flops to implement the counter.

Solution

The basic counter is shown in Fig. 4.24(a). D flip flops are connected as toggles by connecting $\overline{Q_n}$ to D_n (see Fig. 4.18(a)) and Q_n drives D_{n+1}.

Now for a 10-state counter we wish to eliminate states $1010b \ldots 1111b$. Assuming active-Low direct Clear inputs, a NAND gate $D \cdot \overline{C} \cdot B \cdot \overline{A}$ goes Low at state $1010b$. Using states $1011b \ldots 1111b$ as don't care combinations, reduces the feedback decoder logic to $\overline{D \cdot B}$. It is a general rule that the decoder gate need only detect stages which are logic 1 in the first illegal state.

The resetting signal is used to clear flip flops which are logic 1, i.e. D & B. However, clearing flip flop B will generate a ⌐__ edge into flip flop C which will then toggle to logic 1! Thus flip flop C also has to be reset.

This resetting signal only lasts for the duration of the propagation delay of the gate and clearing delay of the flip flop. Taking as an example the 74LS74/74LS00 D flip flop/NAND combination would produce a typical resetting signal of $25 + 9 = 34$ ns duration. However, the clearing time for a flip flop will have a considerable spread of values; the maximum is quoted as 40 ns with no minimum given. Thus it may well happen that the Reset pulse disappears before one or more laggard flip flops clear, and if so they may not clear at all! Even when all the flip flops are matched, eg. all on the one chip, the problem persists. This is because propagation delay, depends on loading, and one flip flop may be driving 20 gates, whilst another has no load.

To avoid this hazardous race situation, the resetting pulse must be lengthened. One approach to this problem is shown in Fig. 4.24(b), where a $\overline{R}\,\overline{S}$ latch is set by the decoder gate. The $\overline{Q}$ latch output is then used to clear the count. The latch will remain Set even after the decoder pulse is removed. By using the inverted counter clock to reset this latch, the counter clearing signal lasts for the duration this clock is Low. This is illustrated in Fig. 4.24(c).

The IEC/ANSII symbol for the decade counter is shown in Fig. 4.24(d). The same outline is used but with the general qualifying symbol **RCNTRDIV10** indicating a divide by ten count. The **DIVr** extension is generally used for a counter of any arbitrary base, other than a straight 2^N.

We used the 74LS74 as an example of a D flip flop when calculating propagation delay. This device is actually a __/‾-triggered flip flop. How would you modify the circuit to use this IC?

On the basis of this example we can summarize the design procedure for a reliable modulo-R counter:

1. Determine the number of flip flops needed, N, such that $2^N \geq R$.

2. Use a NAND (AND for active-High Clear) gate to detect flip flops which are logic 1 in the first illegal state.

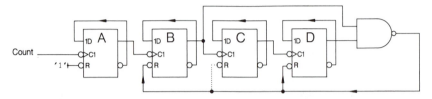

(a) A decade counter. Note that the dotted link must be present for correct operation

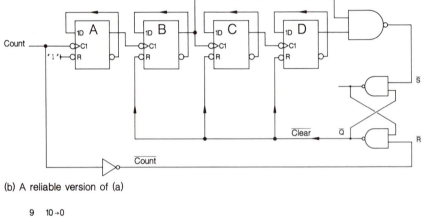

(b) A reliable version of (a)

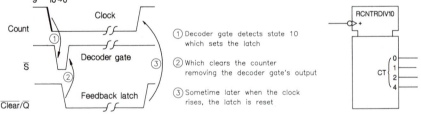

① Decoder gate detects state 10
   which sets the latch

② Which clears the counter
   removing the decoder gate's output

③ Sometime later when the clock
   rises, the latch is reset

(c) Timing waveforms for the resetting mechanism   (d) IEC symbol for this counter

Figure 4.24: Using feedback to reduce the count length.

3. Use the illegal-state pulse of 2 to set a latch, which is connected to clear all flip flops which are logic 1 in the illegal state and any flip flops immediately following.

4. Use the inverse of the count clock to reset this latch.

Example 4.9

A certain pea-canning emporium is to install an automatic packaging machine to box batches of 2-dozen tins. Assuming the cans are detected as they pass along a conveyer belt, giving the count pulse; design a ripple counter giving an indication every 24 cans.

Solution

Five flip flops must be used to represent 24 states, 0 to 23. The illegal-state decoder detects $EDCBA = 11000b$ (24), i.e. $\overline{E \cdot D}$. This sets the $\overline{R} \, \overline{S}$ feedback latch which clears D and E. This signal can also be used as the indicator.

If the count had been in BCD, then $\overline{F \cdot C}$ will detect the first illegal state $10\ 0100b$ and should clear F, C and D. This counter could consist of a decade module (D C B A), with the final stage Q_D clocking a 2-bit counter F E. In general, ripple counters are cascaded by connecting the last stage of the mth counter to the $(m + 1)$th clock.

Example 4.10

Design a BCD counter using the Excess-3 code of Table 1.3.

Solution

The first illegal state is $1101b$, detected as $\overline{D \cdot C \cdot A}$. The counter must now be returned to $0011b$. This can be done by clearing D and C and presetting B.

Several MSI ripple counters are available. The 4040 12-stage counter with asynchronous **Reset** was shown in Fig. 4.21(c). The 4020 is similar, with 14 flip flops. Fig. 4.25 shows two of the early TTL ripple counters, both of which are still popular [11]. The 74x93 (top right) comprises a ripple-connected array of three flip flops, with an additional uncommitted flip flop. Normally Q_A is connected to flip flop B's **Clock** (pin 12 to 1) to give a modulo-16 counter, as in Fig. 4.21(a). Counters may be cascaded by using Q_D to clock the following counter. The NANDed **Reset** inputs can be used for feedback applications, as described in Example 4.8. If the Reset facility is not used, the **Reset** pins ($R_{0(1)}$ and $R_{0(2)}$) should be held Low. The 74x293 is functionally identical, but with the supply pins at the corner, whilst the 74x393 contains two of these counters in the one chip.

The 74x90/74x290 are the decade versions of the 74x93/74x293. As in the latter case, a flip flop array of three plus one is provided. The 3-bit array is configured as a modulo-5 counter, which follows the natural 4-2-1 code shown in Fig. 4.25(b)I. Can you prove this? If the A flip flop is used as the LSB feeding this modulo-5 counter (pins 12 to 1), the 8-4-2-1 BCD code of Fig. 4.25(b)II results. However, if A is used

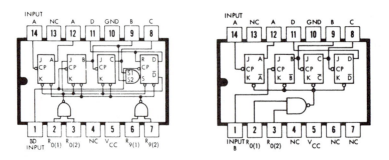

(a) Two integrated ripple counters, f_{max} = 32 MHz, typical.

Courtesy of Texas Instruments Ltd.

4	2	1
D	C	B
0	0	0
0	0	1
0	1	0
0	1	1
1	0	0

I

8	4	2	1
D	C	B	A
0	0	0	0
0	0	0	1
0	0	1	0
0	0	1	1
0	1	0	0
0	1	0	1
0	1	1	0
0	1	1	1
1	0	0	0
1	0	0	1

II

5	4	2	1
A	D	C	B
0	0	0	0
0	0	0	1
0	0	1	0
0	0	1	1
0	1	0	0
1	0	0	0
1	0	0	1
1	0	1	0
1	0	1	1
1	1	0	0

III

(b) Three counting modes of the 7490.

Figure 4.25: Integrated ripple counters.

as the MSB by feeding Q_D to CP_A (pins 11 to 14), then the 5-4-2-1 BCD code of Fig. 4.25(b)III results. This can be useful where a symmetrical $\div 10$ frequency is required. Compare the MSB columns of Figs.4.25(b)II and III. In addition to the 2-I/P NAND Reset (**CT=0**) a similar Preset to $1001b$ (**CT=9**) is provided for some specialized applications. If these inputs are not used, they should be held Low. Also available in this series is the 74x390 dual decade counter and 74x92 duo-decimal counter, which consists of a modulo-6 counter with an additional free flip flop, for symmetrical $\div 12$ frequency applications.

Most ripple counter designs are based on MSI devices, rather than using individual flip flops. The next example illustrates this technique.

Example 4.11

Using the 74x93 IC counter, design a modulo-12 **dead-end** counter.

Solution

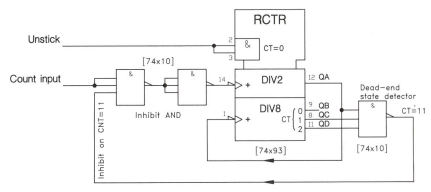

Figure 4.26: A modulo-12 dead-end counter using a 74x93 plus 74x10 ICs.

A dead-end counter increments to its last state and stops; it does not keep on recycling as did our previous counters. However, the design is similar. In this case the last legal state is detected, i.e. $1011 = \overline{\text{D}} \cdot \text{B} \cdot \text{A}$. This is ANDed with the incoming clock; which is then inhibited. The counter may be 'unstuck' by using its Reset (**CT=0**) inputs. If desired, this may be synchronized with the count clock by using a D flip flop to sample the Unstick command.

Notice how the IEC/ANSII symbol for the 74x93 handles the dual (i.e. ÷8 plus ÷2) nature of this device. The common reset action is shown in the control box which sits astride two separate counters with a modulo-2 and modulo-8 count.

4.2.2 Synchronous Counters

Most of the problems exhibited with ripple counters can be ameliorated by clocking each flip flop at the same time. A simple example of such a structure is shown in Fig. 4.27. If we assume that both flip flops are initially cleared, then we have the following sequence of events:

CK	Q_A	Q_B	J_A	K_A	J_B	K_B	
	0	0	1	1	0	1	(on next clock, A will toggle, B will clear)
↑	1	0	1	1	1	0	(on next clock, A will toggle, B will set)
↑	0	1	0	1	0	1	(on next clock, A will clear, B will clear)
↑	0	0	1	1	0	1	(repeat)

i.e. $00 \rightarrow 10 \rightarrow 01 \rightarrow 00$; which is a modulo-3 count. Can you add an extra flip flop in the middle to give a modulo-5 count?

Each state of the counter, sets up the J and K inputs ready for the next clock event. As every flip flop is clocked at the same time, flip flop N can be treated in isolation from what is just about to happen to neighbours $N-1$ and $N+1$. Correct operation relies explicitly on *simultaneous* clocking. If this clock is skewed between two devices by more than the propagation delay less setup time of the flip flop, then changes will propagate down the chain, and our isolationist analysis is invalid.

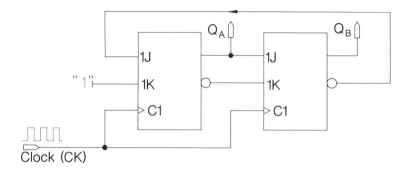

Figure 4.27: A modulo-3 synchronous counter.

The counter in Fig. 4.27 is a very simple example of a **synchronous counter** [12]. The general structure of such a counter is shown in Fig. 4.28. An array of simultaneously clocked flip flops feeds a combinational logic block, which in turn drives the flip flop inputs. In essence, the combinational logic sets up the condition for the $(n+1)$th state based on the nth counter state at its input. The diagram illustrates the situation where the counter is about to change from state $0111b$ to $1000b$.

To ensure this, flip flops D, C and B must change from $0 \rightarrow 1$. This can be accomplished by toggling $(J_n K_n = 11)$ or by setting $(J_n K_n = 10)$. Thus $J_D K_D$ & $J_C K_C$ & $J_B K_B$ must be $1X$ at this time. The opposite situation $(1 \rightarrow 0)$ is required for flip flop A; i.e. $J_A K_A = X1$.

If we tabulate the outputs for each counter state input, then this is the defining truth table. The combinational logic can then be implemented using any suitable technology. This technique works with any kind of flip flop.

Example 4.12

To design a 4-bit natural-coded synchronous counter based on J K flip flops.

Solution

We observe from Table 1.2, that natural 8-4-2-1 code has the property that column n toggles whenever all $n-1$ lower bits are logic 1. Thus $0111b \rightarrow 1000b \cdots \rightarrow 1111b \rightarrow 0000b$. A J K flip flop will toggle if $J K = 11$, and will remain unaltered when clocked with $J K = 00$.

With this in mind we can deduce the logic equations as:

$$J_A K_A = 1 \qquad \qquad \text{(Always toggles)}$$
$$J_B K_B = Q_A \qquad \qquad \text{(Toggles when A = 1)}$$
$$J_C K_C = Q_B {\cdot} Q_A \qquad \qquad \text{(Toggles when BA = 11)}$$
$$J_D K_D = Q_C {\cdot} Q_B {\cdot} Q_A \qquad \qquad \text{(Toggles when CBA = 111)}$$

In general for a counter of any length, we have $J_n K_n = Q_{n-1} {\cdot} Q_{n-2} \ldots Q_1 {\cdot} Q_0$.

The structure of this counter is shown in Fig. 4.29(a) and follows directly from the equations above. As an alternative, each flip flop could be driven from a 2-

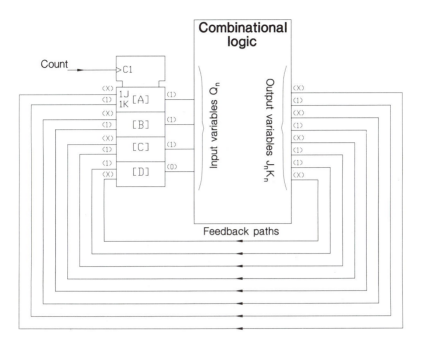

Figure 4.28: A 4-bit skeleton synchronous counter showing conditions prior to the change $0111b \rightarrow 1000b$.

I/P AND gate taking as its input the output of the prior flip flop and AND gate, i.e.

$$J_n\,K_n = Q_{n-1}{\cdot}(Q_{n-2}{\cdot}(Q_{n-3}{\cdot}(\cdots{\cdot}(Q_1{\cdot}(Q_0)))\ldots)$$

as AND gates are cascadable. As the clocking rate must not exceed the propagation delay through the flip flop/combinational logic, cascading AND gates will reduce the maximum counting rate.

The alternative implementation shown in Fig. 4.29(b) has been designed as a general-purpose 4-bit module with provision for expansion. Here a carry-out signal (Ripple_Carry_Out, RCO) detects when the counter is in state $1111b$ (**CT=15**) and the module is enabled (**EN** = 1). This is the signal necessary to tell the subsequent module that it must increment on the next clock event. All the module's flip flops are gated by the Enable_In line (sometimes called Carry_In), which when logic 0 forces all J and K inputs to 00 (no change).

The 74x160 series of 4-bit synchronous counters uses a variation of this theme. Two enable inputs are provided; ENT (ENable_Trickle) and ENP (ENable_Parallel). Ripple_Carry_Output (RCO) is now Counter-Full·ENT, but the counter itself is enabled by the product of the two enables.

To explain how this operates, consider Fig. 4.30, which shows how a 16-bit synchronous counter can be implemented with 4-bit modules. The simplest method simply cascades Carry_Out from the Nth module to the Count_Enable input of the

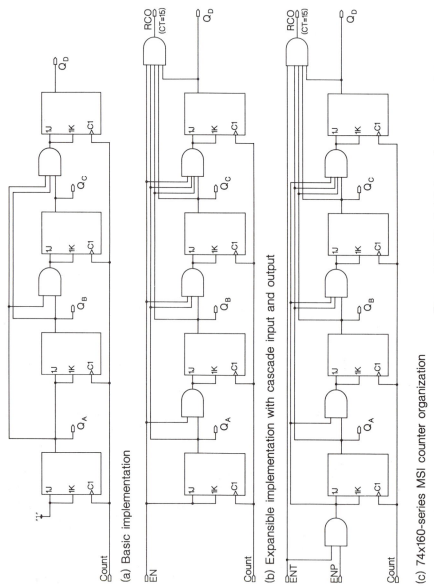

(a) Basic implementation

(b) Expansible implementation with cascade input and output

(c) 74x160-series MSI counter organization

Figure 4.29: The 8-4-2-1 synchronous counter.

$(N + 1)$th module. Each additional stage adds one propagation delay through the (**CT=15**) AND gate to the total combinational logic delay; as effectively these gates are cascaded. For the 74ALS160 series (see Fig. 4.32), this can be as long as 13 ns. For example, when the counter changes from 1111 1111 1111 1110b to 1111 1111 1111 1111b, the intelligence of this change now ripples through the four modules. The dust must have settled on this process before the next clock event, remembering that all flip flops are simultaneously clocked.

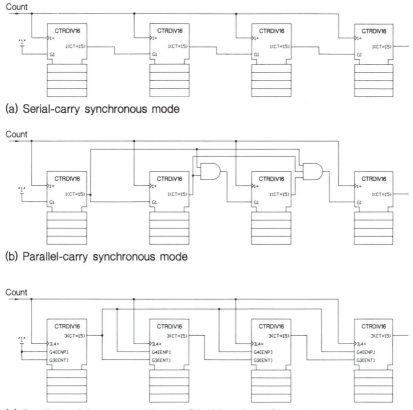

(a) Serial-carry synchronous mode

(b) Parallel-carry synchronous mode

(c) Parallel/serial-carry used by the 74x160-series MSI counter

Figure 4.30: A 16-bit counter cascading 4-bit modules.

Where high speed is important, the parallel-carry arrangement of Fig. 4.30(b) can be used. Here each Nth module is enabled by an external AND gate detecting when all $(N - 1)$ modules are full. Thus only one AND propagate time is added, irrespective of the length of the counter.

The 2-part cascade scheme of Fig. 4.30(c) allows full-speed operation with no external logic. Here the first stage feeds the succeeding (**CT=15**) gates directly (through **ENT**) and also enables the three subsequent modules, which are connected

in a serial cascade chain. If the counter is in state 1111 1111 1111 0000b, then all
the RCOs of these latter counters go to logic 1, and have plenty of time to do so;
right up to when the counter reaches 1111 1111 1111 1111b. The intelligence that
the LSD counter is full is communicated directly to subsequent modules in parallel
via ENP. Thus when the next clock event occurs, all these modules will be enabled
(ENP·ENT) and will change accordingly. The counter can be thought of as being a
slow counter (going at $\frac{1}{16}$ rate) driven by a 1-stage faster counter.

Most MSI synchronous counters provide a **parallel loading** facility whereby
data can be entered directly into the flip flops at any time. The simplest way of
doing this is to use the asynchronous flip flop Preset and Clear (S and R) inputs, as
shown in Fig. 4.31(a). Parallel data is forced into the counter as long as Load goes
to logic 0, overriding Clock.

Synchronous loading schemes are more common. Here the Load control switches
between the normal counting logic and the parallel data. Thus when Load is logic 0,
the data $\sum D_n$ is only loaded into the counter on the following clock event. Although
Fig. 4.31(b) shows a D flip flop, the principle is the same for any kind of flip flop.

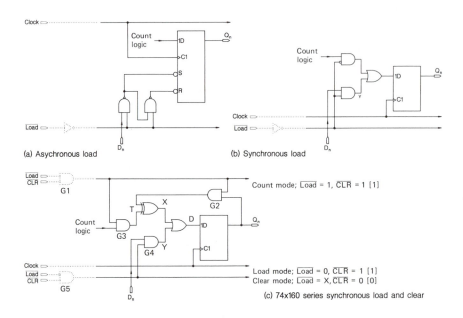

Figure 4.31: Parallel loading.

The final diagram shows the arrangement used by the 74ALS162/163 MSI counters (see also Fig. 4.32). Here matters are more complex, as a synchronous clearing
facility is also provided. Normally both CLR and Load are logic 1 and thus gate
G1 is High. This enables the feedback loop through G2 to the EOR gate, which
converts the D to a T flip flop (see Fig. 4.18(b)), and gates the count logic to the
T input through G3. This is the normal count mode. If either or both CLR and
Load are active, then point X is forced to logic 0 and the state of gate G4 determines

the input to the flip flop. If $\overline{\text{CLR}}$ is 0, then irrespective of the state of $\overline{\text{Load}}$, G5 and hence G4 are also 0. On the next clock event, $D = 0$ is synchronously moved into the flip flop. This is the Clear mode. If $\overline{\text{CLR}}$ is 1 and $\overline{\text{Load}}$ is 0 then G5 is logic 1. This gates D_n through G4 to D, which is synchronously moved into the flip flop on the next clock event. This is the Load mode.

Synchronous Load, Clear and Enable transitions are subject in the normal way to setup and hold time restrictions. Setup time for the SN74ALS160 family is between 10 and 15 ns with a zero hold time.

An extract from this series data sheet is shown in Fig. 4.32. The 74x161 and 74x163 are 4-bit 8-4-2-1 coded synchronous counters with 2-part enabling and with a synchronous loading facility. The former has an asynchronous $\overline{\text{Clear}}$ whilst the latter a synchronous equivalent. The logic symbols are identical except that the 74x163 shows this $\overline{\text{Clear}}$ input qualified by the Control (i.e. CLK) input. Thus 5(CT=0) is affected by C5. The absence of this qualifier in the 74x161 symbol shows that clearing is asynchronous, i.e. independent of any other input.

These counters have two operating modes, M1 ($\overline{\text{Load}}$ Low) and M2 ($\overline{\text{Load}}$ High). The former is the parallel loading mode and affects the D inputs as denoted by 1,5D (i.e. Data loaded on Mode M1 and Clock C5). The latter is the Count mode, as denoted by 2,3,4+. This indicates incrementation when in M2 (Mode 2) and both G3 (ENT) and G4 (ENP) inputs are active. The total annotation is thus C5/2,3,4+ where the / denotes the dual function of the input (as a clock for loading or clearing and as a count input). In both modes RCO indicates a count of 15 when G3 (ENT) is active, i.e. 3CT=15.

The 74x160/162 mirror the 74x161/163, except that they are 8-4-2-1 BCD counters. The logic symbols are also the same, with **CTRDIV16** replaced by **CTRDIV10** and **CT=9** instead of **CT=15**. Of course the internal count logic is somewhat different.

Designing a synchronous counter to follow the natural 8-4-2-1 BCD code can be done in the same manner as our previous design; that is by looking for patterns in the count sequence $0000b \dots 1001b$ [13]. Following this approach we have:

1. Bit A toggles on each clock, so $\qquad\qquad\qquad\qquad\qquad\qquad J_A = K_B = 11$

2. Bit B toggles whenever $Q_A = 1$ and $Q_D = 0$, so $\qquad\qquad J_B = K_B = Q_A \cdot \overline{Q_D}$

3. Bit C toggles whenever $Q_A = 1$ and $Q_B = 1$, so $\qquad\qquad J_C = K_C = Q_A \cdot Q_B$

4. Bit D toggles whenever $Q_A = 1$ and $Q_B = 1$ and $Q_C = 1$ (7)

   or when $Q_A = 1$ and $Q_D = 1$ (9), so $\qquad J_D = K_D = (Q_A \cdot Q_B \cdot Q_C) + (Q_A \cdot Q_D)$

Although this approach is legitimate, it becomes more awkward for the more difficult examples; particularly so for the more generalized sequential machines. Instead we can adopt a more systematic procedure; which is analogous to the fundamental asynchronous design technique of Fig. 4.9. An example will clarify.

Example 4.13

From basic principles, design a synchronous 8-4-2-1 BCD counter based on J K flip flops.

SN54ALS160B THRU SN54ALS163B, SN54AS160 THRU SN54AS163
SN74ALS160B THRU SN74ALS163B, SN74AS160 THRU SN74AS163
SYNCHRONOUS 4-BIT DECADE AND BINARY COUNTERS

D2661, APRIL 1982 – REVISED MAY 1986

- Internal Look-Ahead for Fast Counting
- Carry Output for n-Bit Cascading
- Synchronous Counting
- Synchronously Programmable
- Package Options Include Plastic "Small Outline" Packages, Ceramic Chip Carriers, and Standard Plastic and Ceramic 300-mil DIPs
- Dependable Texas Instruments Quality and Reliability

SN54ALS', SN54AS' . . . J PACKAGE
SN74ALS', SN74AS' . . . D OR N PACKAGE
(TOP VIEW)

```
        _____
$\overline{CLR}$ [ 1  U 16 ] V_CC
 CLK [ 2    15 ] RCO
   A [ 3    14 ] Q_A
   B [ 4    13 ] Q_B
   C [ 5    12 ] Q_C
   D [ 6    11 ] Q_D
 ENP [ 7    10 ] ENT
 GND [ 8     9 ] $\overline{LOAD}$
```

description

These synchronous, presettable counters feature an internal carry look-ahead for application in high-speed counting designs. The 'ALS160B, 'ALS162B, 'AS160, and 'AS162 are decade counters, and the 'ALS161B, 'ALS163B, 'AS161, and 'AS163 are 4-bit binary counters. Synchronous operation is provided by having all flip-flops clocked simultaneously so that the outputs change coincident with each other when so instructed by the count-enable inputs and internal gating. This mode of operation eliminates the output counting spikes that are normally associated with asynchronous (ripple clock) counters. A buffered clock input triggers the four flip-flops on the rising (positive-going) edge of the clock input waveform.

These counters are fully programmable; that is, they may be preset to any number between 0 and 9, or 15. As presetting is synchronous, setting up a low level at the load input disables the counter and causes the outputs to agree with the setup data after the next clock pulse regardless of the levels of the enable inputs.

SN54ALS', SN54AS' . . . FK PACKAGE
(TOP VIEW)

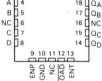

NC – No internal connection

The clear function for the 'ALS160B, 'ALS161B, 'AS160, and 'AS161 is asynchronous and a low level at the clear input sets all four of the flip-flop outputs low regardless of the levels of the clock, load, or enable inputs.

The clear function for the 'ALS162B, 'ALS163B, 'AS162, and 'AS163 is synchronous and a low level at the clear input sets all four of the flip-flop outputs low after the next clock pulse regardless of the levels of the enable inputs. This synchronous clear allows the count length to be modified easily by decoding the Q outputs for the maximum count desired. The active-low output of the gate used for decoding is connected to the clear input to synchronously clear the counter to 0000 (LLLL).

The carry look-ahead circuitry provides for cascading counters for n-bit synchronous applications without additional gating. Instrumental in accomplishing this function are two count-enable inputs and a ripple carry output. Both count-enable inputs (ENP and ENT) must be high to count, and ENT is fed forward to enable the ripple carry output. The ripple carry output (RCO) thus enabled will produce a high-level pulse while the count is maximum (9 or 15 with Q_A high). This high-level overflow ripple carry pulse can be used to enable successive cascaded stages. Transitions at the ENP or ENT are allowed regardless of the level of the clock input.

These counters feature a fully independent clock circuit. Changes at control inputs (ENP, ENT, or $\overline{LOAD}$) that will modify the operating mode have no effect on the contents of the counter until clocking occurs. The function of the counter (whether enabled, disabled, loading, or counting) will be dictated solely by the conditions meeting the stable setup and hold times.

The SN54ALS160B through SN54ALS163B and SN54AS160 through SN54AS163 are characterized for operation over the full military temperature range of −55°C to 125°C. The SN74ALS160B through SN74ALS163B and SN74AS160 through SN74AS163 are characterized for operation from 0°C to 70°C.

TEXAS
INSTRUMENTS

Figure 4.32: The SN74ALS/AS160 series of synchronous counters (*continued next page*).

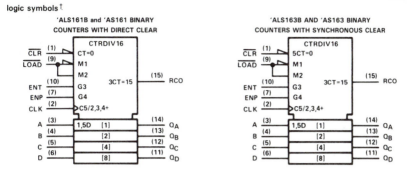

SN54ALS161B, SN54ALS163B, SN54AS161, SN54AS163
SN74ALS161B, SN74ALS163B, SN74AS161, SN74AS163
SYNCHRONOUS 4-BIT BINARY COUNTERS

logic symbols†

'ALS161B and 'AS161 BINARY
COUNTERS WITH DIRECT CLEAR

'ALS163B AND 'AS163 BINARY
COUNTERS WITH SYNCHRONOUS CLEAR

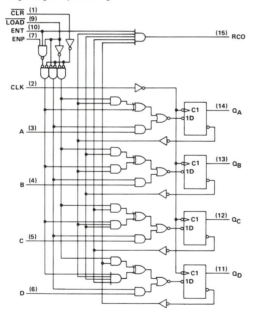

'ALS163B and 'AS163 logic diagram (positive logic)

†These symbols are in accordance with ANSI/IEEE Std 91-1984 and IEC Publication 617-12.

Pin numbers shown are for D, J, and N packages.

'ALS161B and 'AS161 synchronous binary counters are similar; however the clear is asynchronous as shown for the 'ALS160B and 'AS160 decade counters.

TEXAS
INSTRUMENTS

Figure 4.32: (*continued*). The SN74ALS/AS160 series of synchronous counters. Reproduced by courtesy of Texas Instruments Ltd.

Solution

The specification for a counter is its counting sequence, shown diagrammatically by the **flow diagram** of Fig. 4.33(a). This shows the counter repetitively cycling through ten states. This is tabularized in the **state table**, which simply lists the next state for each present state. In this instance, the table could easily be derived without using a flow diagram, but in more complex situations the latter is an excellent visualization aid.

Each state is represented by a binary pattern, which is listed in the **state assignment table**. Here it is just the 8-4-2-1 code. Replacing each of the states in the state table by its binary representation leads to the **Y-map**. This Y-map is similar to those of Section 4.1.1, but the requirement that y = Y does not hold. This is because the feedback paths are only closed at the instant of the clock event. The Y-map holds all the required information to design the combinational logic.

Up to this moment, the design has been independent of which kind of flip flops form the basis of the counter. Each type of flip flop will need a specific set of inputs to force a given change on the active clock edge. For example, to setup a change $0 \rightarrow 1$, we have for a JK flip flop $JK = 10$ or 11; a RS flip flop, $RS = 10$; a T flip flop, $T = 1$ and a D flip flop, $D = 1$. The **transition table** in Fig. 4.33 shows the JK inputs necessary to force all four possible changes.

From both the Y-map, which tabulates the transitions for each state, and the appropriate flip flop transition table, we can evaluate the **setting equations** (sometimes known as the **excitation equations**). For example, if the counter is in state $0000b$, the requisite transitions are: $0 \rightarrow 0$; $0 \rightarrow 0$; $0 \rightarrow 0$; and $0 \rightarrow 1$ to move to the next state $0001b$. Thus with $0000b$ as input, we need $J_D K_D$ to be $0X$; $J_C K_C = 0X$; $J_B K_B = 0X$; $J_A K_A = 1X$. When in state $0001b$ the transitions $0 \rightarrow 0$; $0 \rightarrow 0$; $0 \rightarrow 1$; $1 \rightarrow 0$ will move the system to state $0010b$, requiring $J_D K_D = 0X$; $J_C K_C = 0X$; $J_B K_B = 1X$; $J_A K_A = X1$. In this manner a truth table having $Q_D Q_C Q_B Q_A$ as inputs and $J_D K_D J_C K_C J_B K_B J_A K_A$ as outputs can be constructed. Once the truth table has been found, any logical procedure can be used to derive the required combinational logic. In the case of this example we are using K-maps and I have entered the data directly into each of the eight maps. Each Y-map cell number (based on $Q_D Q_C Q_B Q_A$) translates to the like-numbered K-map cell. Thus in cell 0, the maps for $J_D K_D J_C K_C J_B K_B J_A K_A$ are loaded with $0X0X0X1X$ as required for the move to state $0001b$, etc.

The question now arises regarding the handling of illegal states; in this case the counts $1010b$ to $1111b$. These have been entered in the K-map cells 10 to 15 as dashes. If we treat them as don't care situations, to further minimize the logic, then seemingly no problem should arise as such states can't happen. However, this is not robust design, because the possibility does exist that owing to noise or power switch on, an illegal state will be entered. We must ensure that in the event of this occurring, the illegal count will eventually lead back to the correct cycle.

In the K-map minimizations of Fig. 4.33(a), we have treated these so-called 'can't-happen don't cares' in the same manner as the 'can-happen don't cares'; that is, they have been included inside loops where appropriate. By doing this we have effectively dictated the illegal count. With the setting equations evaluated, we can reverse engineer the counter to inspect its response when in each illegal state. For example, when in illegal state $1010b$, the K-maps (cell 10) give $J_D K_D = 00$

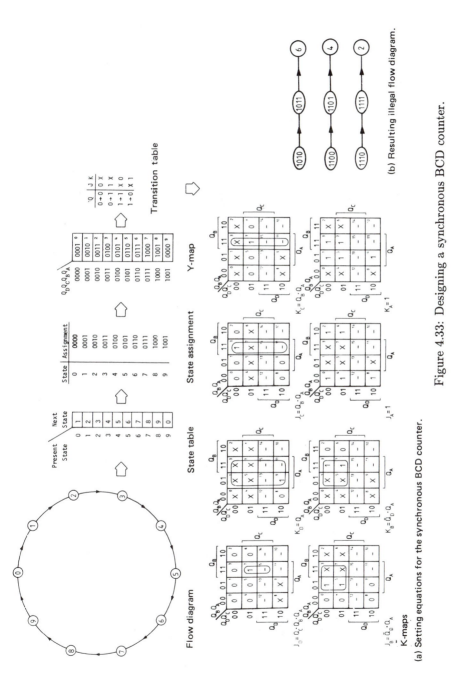

Figure 4.33: Designing a synchronous BCD counter.

($Q_D = 1 \rightarrow 1$); $J_C K_C = 00$ ($Q_C = 0 \rightarrow 0$); $J_B K_B = 00$ ($Q_B = 1 \rightarrow 1$); $J_A K_A = 11$ ($Q_A = 0 \rightarrow 1$). Thus, if in illegal state 1010b, the counter will advance to illegal state 1011b. Repeating the process from K-map cell 11, we have $J_D K_D = 0X$ (clear); $J_C K_C = 11$ (toggle); $J_B K_B = 00$ (unchanged); $J_A K_A = 11$ (toggle) giving 1011$b \rightarrow$ 0110b, i.e. legal state 6. The illegal-state flow diagram of Fig. 4.33(b) shows all possible unspecified transitions and indicates that the legal cycle will always be re-entered after one or two clock events.

The illegal-state behavior radically depends on the chosen minimization. If, say, all can't-happen don't care states were omitted from the coverage, then a disastrous situation would occur if the counter should enter an illegal state. As these states lie outside of all loops, the setting equations give all Js and Ks as logic 0; i.e. no change! Thus the counter would stick permanently in that state. If the specification calls for a return to a legal state in not more than one clock event, then this can be accommodated on the state table/Y-map by listing all illegal states together with a legal next sate. However, increasing the rigidity of the specification will often lead to extra complexity, and generally all that is required is the back check outlined above. If the number of illegal states is much less than the legal states, then problems rarely arise in practice. Later we will look at an example which does exhibit this problem.

Notice that the logic deduced by this procedure gives a slightly better implementation than our previous attempt. This is because we did not constrain the flip flops to only act as a toggle (i.e. $J_n K_n = 00$ or 11). Can you deduce the illegal-state response if the first set of equations has been used?

Unless designing your own IC from fundamental principles, it is unlikely that one would implement a decade counter using discrete SSI parts. We see from Fig. 4.32 and Table 4.2, that decade counters are standard MSI catalog items. Frequently more complex counters can be implemented using MSI counters as the building blocks; as the next two examples show.

Example 4.14

Using the 74x163 binary counter (a), design a modulo-12 counter and (b) a modulo-12 dead-end counter.

Solution

The simplest approach is shown in Fig. 4.34(a). When the counter is in state 1111b, Carry_Out causes 0100b to be parallel loaded on the next leading clock edge. Thus the count is from 0100b to 1111b; twelve states.

If a natural binary count is desired, the structure shown in Fig. 4.34(b) can be used. The last legal state is detected (1011$b \rightarrow \overline{Q_D \cdot Q_B \cdot Q_A}$) and used to drive $\overline{\text{Clear}}$. The next clock event then resets the count to 0000b. If the 74x161 were used in place of the 74x163, then its asynchronous $\overline{\text{Clear}}$ would require the detection of the first illegal state, in the manner of Fig. 4.24(a). A better solution here, which avoids this transient situation, would be to use the synchronous $\overline{\text{Load}}$ instead and set the parallel data inputs to 0000b.

Replacing the parallel data of Fig. 4.34(a) by 1011b, results in a modulo-12 dead-end counter, as state 11 is repetitively loaded into the counter at this point. The

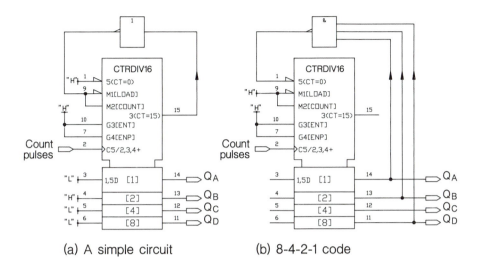

(a) A simple circuit   (b) 8-4-2-1 code

Figure 4.34: Modulo-12 counters.

locked counter could be restarted by clearing. Could you draw the flow diagram specifying this dead-end sequence, as necessary for a fundamental design for a dead-end count?

Example 4.15

A digital stop clock is to be constructed to measure the period of an event in tenths of seconds, up to a maximum of 99.9 s. Should the period exceed this, the count should stop and indicate overflow.

Solution

Figure 4.35 shows the schematic of a digital stop clock based on three cascaded 74x160 decade counters. The count in BCD is directly proportional to the number of 10 Hz (0.1 s) Clock pulses allowed through by the Gate event. To give a dead-end facility, the carry-out from the last state ($\overline{\text{MAX\_999}}$), which goes Low whenever the count is in state 99.9, drives all stages' Load inputs. Any succeeding Clock pulses then repeatedly load 99.9 into the counter, effectively dead-ending the count. The overflow D flip flop inserts one Clock pulse delay between the carry-out and the Overflow LED. This distinguishes between the legitimate 99.9 state and overflow.

The counter cascade must be cleared before reuse. This could automatically be done by generating a narrow pulse at the beginning of the event pulse (see Fig.2.52(a)). As the 74x160 has an asynchronous $\overline{\text{Clear}}$, this will immediately reset the count. Why would this not work with a 74x162 implementation? A better solution would be to staticize the counter at the end of the event pulse (the falling edge) and at the same time feeding this signal to the counters' asynchronous $\overline{\text{Clear}}$

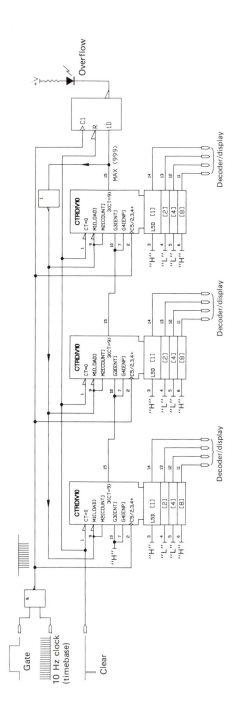

Figure 4.35: A 3-decade stop clock.

inputs. In this way the circuit displays will not continually show the count. This is necessary if the circuit were to be used to measure the duration of repetitive events; for example as a high-speed frequency meter.

Although most counters may be implemented using MSI parts; ASIC-based and the more esoteric functions require the more fundamental approach outlined back in Example 4.13. This is also the technique used in Section 4.5.

Solution

Example 4.16

Using D flip flops, design a 4-bit counter to fill up with ones from the left and then zeros.

The state assignment of Fig. 4.36(a) defines the so called **Johnston**, walking or **twisted-ring** code. Substituting this code into the state table gives the Y-map in the normal way. Notice how the cells are numbered in this instance. This time the D flip flop transition table is used; the D input simply taking on the value of the next condition, i.e. $Q \to 0$ then $D = 0$, $Q \to 1$ then $D = 1$. Thus the entries in the Y-map are loaded without change into the appropriate K-maps' cells. For example, Y-map cell 7 gives the next state as $0011b$. The four corresponding K-map cell 7 entries are $D_D D_C D_B D_A = 0011$. With the illegal states entered as can't happen don't care, the K-maps give the simple implementation of Fig. 4.36(b)I. As a J K flip flop can be used as a D flip flop by making $J = \overline{K} = D$ ($D = 0$, $J = 0$, $K = 1 \to$ Reset; $D = 1$, $J = 1$, $K = 0 \to$ Set), this gives the equivalent implementation of Fig. 4.36(b)II [14].

Checking the response of these circuits to the undefined states, gives the illegal-state flow diagram of Fig. 4.36(c). This is a closed ring, and thus if entered will never return to the specified sequence. If the counter is extended by using extra flip flops in the same chain structure, the ratio of legal to illegal states increases, compounding the problem. Thus for eight flip flops, the legal:illegal ratio is 16:240! The K-maps could of course be altered to ensure illegal states always lead back to the one true path, but the counter then loses its advantage of simplicity.

A simple error-correcting scheme for J K flip flop implementations is shown in Fig. 4.36(d) [14, 15]. This is based on the fact that the Johnston code of any length n is divided into only two blocks of ones and zeros. More than two blocks means an illegal code, with at least one block $\leq \frac{n}{3}$. With the modification shown, the K feedback line is the product of the $\frac{n}{3}$ final counter bits. Blocks of ones $< \frac{n}{3}$ are ignored by the AND gate, keeping $\overline{K}$ logic 0. In this situation, if the nth flip flop is 0, then $J_0 K_0 = 10$, which feeds a logic 1 into the left side of the counter on the next Clock. The converse gives $J_0 K_0 = 00$; no change. In this manner, the number of ones in the counter increases until only two blocks remain. The reader should confirm that the modified feedback does not affect the normal count by looking at the four legal situations in the final $\frac{1}{3}$ of the chain in Fig. 4.36(d). As an example showing the correction of an illegal code, we have: $10100011 \to 11010001 \to 11101000 \to 11110100 \to 11111010 \to 11111101 \to 11111110$ (legal) $\to 11111111 \to 0111111 \to 00111111 \to 00011111 \to 00001111 \to 00000111 \to 00000011 \to 00000001 \to 00000000 \to 10000000b$ etc.

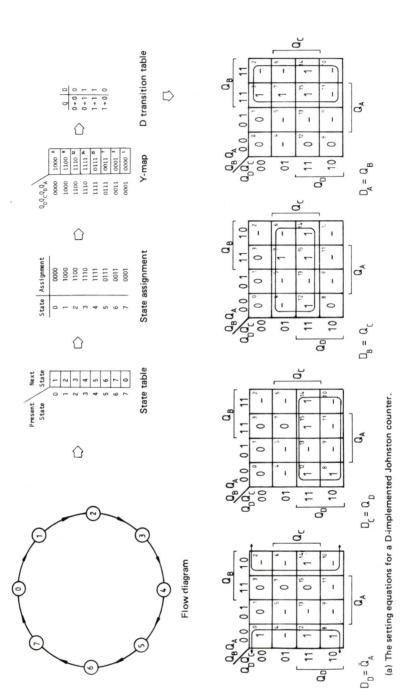

Figure 4.36: The Johnston counter (*continued next page*).

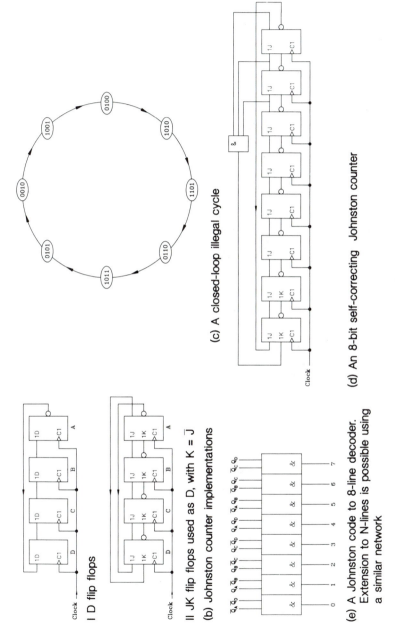

(c) A closed-loop illegal cycle

(d) An 8-bit self-correcting Johnston counter

I D flip flops

II JK flip flops used as D, with K = $\overline{J}$

(b) Johnston counter implementations

(e) A Johnston code to 8-line decoder.
Extension to N-lines is possible using
a similar network

Figure 4.36: *continued*. The Johnston counter.

Besides the advantage of simplicity, another bonus of this type of counter lies in the simple decoding to 2^n lines using only 2-I/P AND gates, as shown in Fig. 4.36(e). Because only one code bit alters at any change, decoders fed with a Johnston counter are virtually immune to decoding spikes and hazards. Despite simultaneous clocking, ordinary synchronous counters cannot be absolutely guaranteed immune to this problem, due to the spread of flip flop propagation delays; although in practice this rarely causes problems. The 4022 CMOS counter uses a 4-bit Johnston counter with error correction and decoding, giving guaranteed clean outputs [16].

Example 4.17

Design a symmetrical 2-4-2-1-coded BCD counter which will be implemented on an ASIC which uses NOR gates and D flip flops as its basic building blocks.

Solution

The flow diagram for this counter is shown in Fig. 4.33(a). In deriving the relevant Y-map, the only difference from Example 4.13 is the 2-4-2-1-assignment. The implementation in this case targets D flip flops; thus the Y-map is simply directly split into the four K-maps, one for each of the D inputs. I have used a zeros minimization to suit a all-NOR implementation, as discussed in page 80. The resulting logic diagram is shown in Fig. 4.37(c).

There are six illegal states, as defined by cells 5–10 in the K-maps. From the covering shown, we have for the illegal state response:

cell 5 → 1110 state 8
cell 6 → 0100 state 4
cell 7 → 0000 state 0
cell 8 → 1001 (cell 9) → 1010 (cell 10) → 1111 state 9
cell 9 → 1010 (cell 10) → 1111 state 9
cell 10 → 1111 state 9

One major category of MSI counter remains; the **up/down counter**. We have previously observed that toggling any bit n when all previous $n - 1$ bits are one gives an up count. In the same manner, a down count results when a toggle occurs when all previous $n - 1$ bits are zero. Figure 4.38(a) shows the nth stage of an up synchronous counter based on a T flip flop (see also Fig. 4.18(b)). Changing the stage counter logic from $\sum Q_n$ to $\sum \overline{Q}_n$ gives the corresponding down count.

In Fig. 4.38(b), the two counter logic gates are combined; giving effectively a toggle flip flop with two T inputs. The active toggle input is selected via a $\mathsf{Down}/\overline{\mathsf{Up}}$ $(\mathsf{D}/\overline{\mathsf{U}})$ control; with the Up logic selected if $\mathsf{D}/\overline{\mathsf{U}}$ is logic 0 and the Down mode if $\mathsf{D}/\overline{\mathsf{U}}$ is logic 1.

The alternative approach of Fig. 4.38(c) uses two count inputs, Up_Clock and Down_Clock. These are internally converted to an Up and Down line, which operate on the changeover logic in the same manner as Fig. 4.38(b). This conversion latch

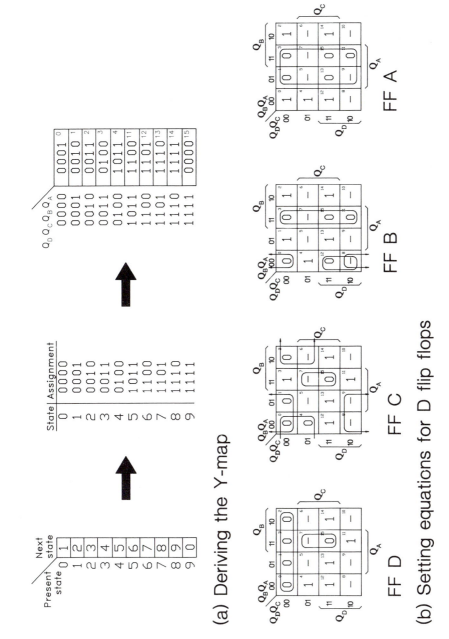

(a) Deriving the Y-map

(b) Setting equations for D flip flops

Figure 4.37: A symmetrical 2-4-2-1 synchronous counter (*continued next page*).

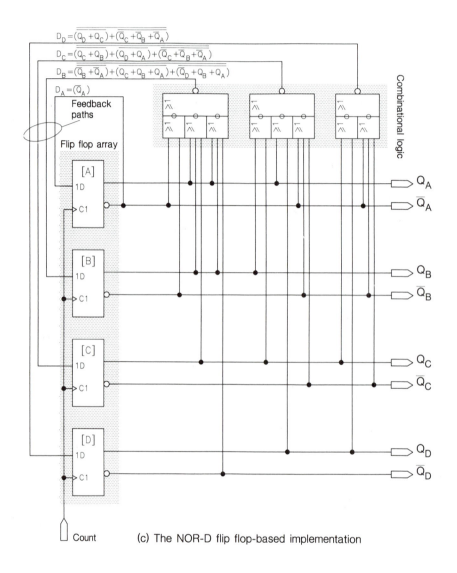

$$D_D = \overline{(Q_D + Q_C) + (\overline{Q_C + \overline{Q}_B + \overline{Q}_A})}$$

$$D_C = \overline{(Q_C + Q_B) + (Q_D + Q_A) + (\overline{Q_C + \overline{Q}_B + \overline{Q}_A})}$$

$$D_B = \overline{(\overline{Q}_B + \overline{Q}_A) + (Q_C + Q_B + Q_A) + (\overline{Q}_D + Q_B + Q_A)}$$

$$D_A = \overline{(\overline{Q}_A)}$$

Feedback paths

Flip flop array

[A]

1D

C1

[B]

1D

C1

[C]

1D

C1

[D]

1D

C1

Count

Combinational logic

Q_A

$\overline{Q}_A$

Q_B

$\overline{Q}_B$

Q_C

$\overline{Q}_C$

Q_D

$\overline{Q}_D$

(c) The NOR-D flip flop-based implementation

Figure 4.37: (*continued*). A symmetrical 2-4-2-1 synchronous counter.

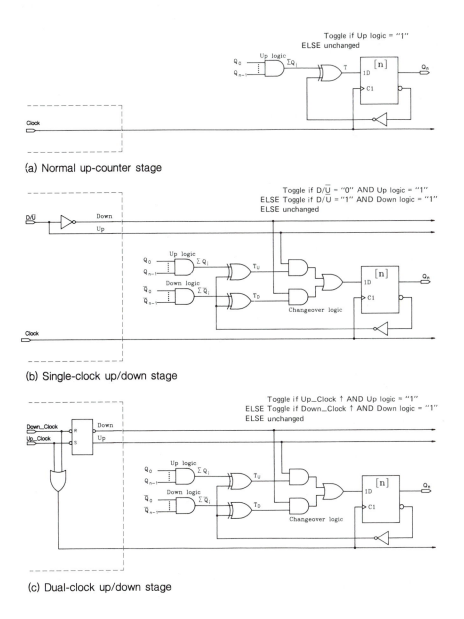

(a) Normal up-counter stage

(b) Single-clock up/down stage

(c) Dual-clock up/down stage

Figure 4.38: The up/down synchronous counter.

SN54ALS190, SN54ALS191, SN74ALS190, SN74ALS191
SYNCHRONOUS 4-BIT UP/DOWN DECADE AND BINARY COUNTERS

D2661, DECEMBER 1982 – REVISED MAY 1986

- Single Down/Up Count Control Line

- Look-Ahead Circuitry Enhances Speed of Cascaded Counters

- Fully Synchronous in Count Modes

- Asynchronously Presettable with Load Control

- Package Options Include Plastic "Small Outline" Packages, Ceramic Chip Carriers, and Standard Plastic and Ceramic 300-mil DIPs

- Dependable Texas Instruments Quality and Reliability

SN54ALS190, SN54ALS191 . . . J PACKAGE
SN74ALS190, SN74ALS191 . . . D OR N PACKAGE
(TOP VIEW)

```
        B  [ 1   U  16 ]  VCC
       QB  [ 2      15 ]  A
       QA  [ 3      14 ]  CLK
     CTEN  [ 4      13 ]  RCO
      D/U  [ 5      12 ]  MAX/MIN
       QC  [ 6      11 ]  LOAD
       QD  [ 7      10 ]  C
      GND  [ 8       9 ]  D
```

descriptions

The 'ALS190 and 'ALS191 are synchronous, reversible up/down counters. The 'ALS190 is a 4-bit decade counter and the 'ALS191 is a 4-bit binary counter. Synchronous counting operation is provided by having all flip-flops clocked simultaneously so that the outputs change coincident with each other when so instructed by the steering logic. This mode of operation eliminates the output counting spikes normally associated with asynchronous (ripple clock) counters.

The outputs of the four flip-flops are triggered on a low-to-high-level transition of the clock input if the enable input (CTEN) is low. A high at CTEN inhibits counting. The direction of the count is determined by the level of the down/up (D/U) input. When D/U is low, the counter counts up and when D/U is high, it counts down.

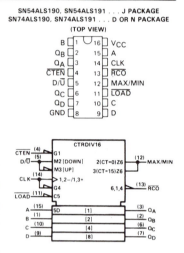

'ALS191 logic symbol

These counters feature a fully independent clock circuit. Changes at the control inputs (CTEN and D/U) that will modify the operating mode have no effect on the contents of the counter until clocking occurs. The function of the counter will be dictated solely by the condition meeting the stable setup and hold times.

These counters are fully programmable; that is, the outputs may each be preset to either level by placing a low on the load input and entering the desired data at the data inputs. The output will change to agree with the data inputs independently of the level of the clock input. This feature allows the counters to be used as modulo-N dividers by simply modifying the count length with the preset inputs.

The CLK, D/U, and LOAD inputs are buffered to lower the drive requirement, which significantly reduces the loading on, or current required by, clock drivers, etc., for long parallel words.

Two outputs have been made available to perform the cascading function: ripple clock and maximum/minimum count. The latter output produces a high-level output pulse with a duration approximately equal to one complete cycle of the clock while the count is zero (all outputs low) counting down or maximum (9 or 15) counting up. The ripple clock output produces a low-level output pulse under those same conditions but only while the clock input is low. The counters can be easily cascaded by feeding the ripple clock output to the enable input of the succeeding counter if parallel clocking is used, or to the clock input if parallel enabling is used. The maximum/minimum count output can be used to accomplish look-ahead for high-speed operation.

The SN54ALS190 and SN54ALS191 are characterized for operation over the full military temperature range of −55 °C to 125 °C. The SN74ALS190 and SN74ALS191 are characterized for operation from 0 °C to 70 °C.

TEXAS
INSTRUMENTS

Figure 4.39: The 74x190 series of up/down counters (*continued next page*).

SN54ALS192, SN54ALS193, SN74ALS192, SN74ALS193
SYNCHRONOUS 4-BIT UP/DOWN COUNTERS (DUAL CLOCK WITH CLEAR)

D2661, DECEMBER 1982 – REVISED MAY 1986

- Look-Ahead Circuitry Enhances Cascaded Counters
- Fully Synchronous in Count Modes
- Parallel Asynchronous Load for Modulo-N Count Lengths
- Asynchronous Clear
- Package Options Include Plastic "Small Outline" Packages, Ceramic Chip Carriers, and Standard Plastic and Ceramic 300-mil DIPs
- Dependable Texas Instruments Quality and Reliability

SN54ALS192, SN54AS193 . . . J PACKAGE
SN74ALS192, SN74ALS193 . . . D OR N PACKAGE
(TOP VIEW)

description

The 'ALS192 and 'ALS193 are synchronous, reversible up/down counters. The 'ALS192 is a 4-bit decade counter and the 'ALS193 is a 4-bit binary counter. Synchronous operation is provided by having all flip-flops clocked simultaneously so that the outputs change coincidently with each other when so instructed by the steering logic. This mode of operation eliminates the output counting spikes normally associated with asynchronous (ripple clock) counters.

The outputs of the four flip-flops are triggered by a low-to-high-level transition of either count (clock) input (Up or Down). The direction of counting is determined by which count input is pulsed while the other count input is high.

All four counters are fully programmable; that is, each output may be preset to either level by placing a low on the load input and entering the desired data at the data inputs. The output will change to agree with the data inputs independently of the count pulses. This feature allows the counters to be used as modulo-N dividers by simply modifying the count length with the preset inputs.

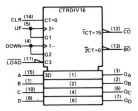

'ALS193 logic symbol

A clear input has been provided that forces all outputs to the low level when a high level is applied. The clear function is independent of the count and the load inputs. The clock, count, and load inputs are buffered to lower the drive requirements. This significantly reduces the loading on clock drivers, etc., for long parallel words.

These counters were designed to be cascaded without the need for external circuitry. The borrow output (BO) produces a low-level pulse while the count is zero (all outputs low) and the count-down input is low. Similarly, the carry output ($\overline{CO}$) produces a low-level pulse while the count is maximum (9 or 15) and the count-up input is low. The counters can then be easily cascaded by feeding the borrow and carry outputs to the count-down and count-up inputs, respectively, of the succeeding counter.

The SN54ALS192 and SN54ALS193 are characterized for operation over the full military temperature range of −55 °C to 125 °C. The SN74ALS192 and SN74ALS193 are characterized for operation from 0 °C to 70 °C.

TEXAS
INSTRUMENTS

Figure 4.39: (*continued*). The 74x190 series of up/down counters. Reproduced by courtesy of Texas Instruments Ltd.

is such that the unused Clock must be held at logic 1 (the inactive state) to allow proper operation.

Figure 4.39 shows an extract from the data sheets for the SN74ALS190 series of 4-bit up/down synchronous counters [17]. The 74x190/191 are single-clock circuits based on the architecture of Fig. 4.38(b). The logic symbol characterizes the Down/$\overline{\text{Up}}$ control as two modes. **M2** = logic 1 for the Down mode (D/$\overline{\text{U}}$ = H) and **M3** = logic 1 in the Up mode (D/$\overline{\text{U}}$ = L). The single Clock input is symbolized as **1,2-/1,3+** which means decrement (–) when **M2** is active (D/$\overline{\text{U}}$ = High) and the Counter_Enable input **G1** is active ($\overline{\text{CTEN}}$ = Low) or else increment (+) if **M3** is active (D/$\overline{\text{U}}$ = Low) and input **G1** is active ($\overline{\text{CTEN}}$ = Low).

Two Carry outputs are provided for cascade purposes. MAX/MIN indicates when the counter is in state 15 (state 9 for BCD) and an Up count is in progress (**3(CT=15)**) or else state 0 in the Down count mode (**2(CT=0)**). Ripple_Carry_Output ($\overline{\text{RCO}}$) is a function of MAX/MIN and both the Counter_Enable imput ($\overline{\text{CTEN}}$) (**G1**) and CLK (**G4**), as symbolized **6,1,4**. The dependency number **6** comes from the trailing **Z6** interconnection symbol describing MAX/MIN, **2(CT=0)Z6/3(CT=15)Z6**. This shows that $\overline{\text{RCO}}$ depends (amongst other things) on MAX/MIN being logic 1.

Like the 74x160 series, parallel loading of all four flip flops is provided. This control input, **C5** ($\overline{\text{Load}}$), is not prefixed by a qualifier from the Clock input, therefore it operates asynchronously.

The 74x192/3 shows two separate rising-edge triggered clocks. Up_Clock is dependent on Down_Clock being High and vice versa. Thus the former is symbolized as **2+** with **2** coming from Down_Clock's connection to **G2**. Similarly, Down_Clock is symbolized as **1-**, with **1** coming from Up_Clock's connection to **G1**. Two cascade outputs are provided. Carry_Out ($\overline{\text{CO}}$) is active when Up_Clock is Low and the count is 15 (or 9), whilst Borrow_Out ($\overline{\text{BO}}$) is active when Down_Clock is Low and the count is zero. Counters are cascaded by connection of $\overline{\text{CO}}_{n-1}$ and $\overline{\text{BO}}_{n-1}$ to Up$_n$ and Down$_n$ respectively.

Example 4.18

Based on the 74x190 series of MSI counters, design an up/down counter that can neither overflow or underflow.

Solution

Figure 4.40(a) shows the 1-line solution. MAX/MIN inhibits any further counting by bringing Counter_Enable ($\overline{\text{CTEN}}$) Low whenever either the counter is full and in Mode 3 (Up) or else when the counter is empty and in Mode 2 (Down). Changing the Down/$\overline{\text{Up}}$ control when in a stuck state removes the MAX/MIN output and allows counting in the reverse direction, away from the end stop.

The 2-line solution of Fig. 4.40(b) uses $\overline{\text{BO}}$ to clear the counter when on the down count (end stop 0000b) and $\overline{\text{CO}}$ to load the maximum state when on the up count (1111b, or 1001b for the 74x192).

Both circuits may be adapted to end stops other than full and empty by using external detection logic, in the manner of Fig. 4.34(b).

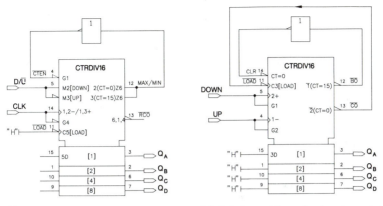

(a) A 1-line up/down dead-end counter   (b) A 2-line up/down dead-end counter

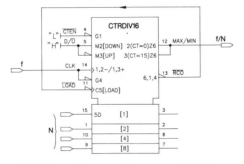

(c) Using a down counter as a rate divider

Figure 4.40: Some applications of up/down counters.

Example 4.19

Using a 74x190/191 down counter, design a programmable $\div N$ counter.

Solution

The counter of Fig. 4.40(c) is permanently connected as a down counter ($\mathrm{D}/\overline{\mathrm{U}} =$ High) with $\overline{\mathrm{RCO}}$ driving $\overline{\mathrm{Load}}$. When the counter enters the empty state $0000b$ on the rising edge of CLK, nothing untoward happens, as $\overline{\mathrm{RCO}}$ is only activated when CLK is Low. When this later occurs, the counter then assumes state n, as $\overline{\mathrm{Load}}$ is asynchronous. This deactivates $\overline{\mathrm{RCO}}$, and the counter is free again to decrement down to state $0000b$. This means that the division ratio is n and not $n + 1$ (n plus state 0); thus the output frequency (conveniently taken from MAX/MIN) is $\frac{f}{n}$, where f is the clock frequency. This circuit is often known as a **rate divider**. A similar arrangement can be used for the 2-line counter. The CMOS 4522/26 is an integrated down counter especially configured for this mode of operation.

Function	Designator	Clock	Clear	Load	Additional features
Ripple					
BCD/4-bit binary	7490/93	↓	Asy L	–	74393/390 dual versions
BCD/4-bit binary	74196/197	↓	Asy L	Asy L	
12-bit binary	4040	↓	Asy H	–	All **Q** O/Ps accessible
14-bit binary	4060	*	Asy H	–	Ten **Q** O/Ps accessible
Synchronous					
BCD/4-bit binary	74160/161	↑	Asy L	Sy L	
BCD/4-bit binary	74162/163	↑	Sy L	Sy L	
Dual BCD/4-bit binary	4518/20	↓ or ↑	Asy H	–	
BCD/4-bit binary	74190/191	↑	–	Asy L	Up/Down single clock
BCD/4-bit binary	74168/169	↑	–	Sy L	Up/Down single clock
BCD/4-bit binary	74668/669	↑	–	Sy L	Improved '168/169
BCD/4-bit binary	74568/569	↑	Sy/Asy L	Sy L	As above; 3-s O/Ps
BCD/4-bit binary	4510/16	↑	Asy H	Asy H	Up/Down single clock
BCD/4-bit binary	74192/193	↑	Asy L	Asy L	Up/Down dual clock
8-bit up/down	74867	↑	Asy L	Sy L	74869 has Sy Clear
Octal/decade Johnston	4022/17	↓ or ↑	Asy H	–	Fully decoded
Miscellaneous					
2-decade BCD/8-bit bin	40102/103	Down counter used as a rate divider			
8-bit binary	74591	with 3-s output register; 74590 has OC O/Ps			
8-bit binary	74592	with parallel input register and single carry O/P			
3-decade BCD	4553	Internal multiplexer scans the counter			
5-decade BCD	4554	using built-in oscillator			
BCD	TIL306	Counter; latch; 7-segment decoder; display			

* Built-in oscillator. Asy = asynchronous; Sy = synchronous; 3-s = 3-state; OC = open-collector.

Table 4.2: A selection of MSI counters.

4.3   Registers and Read/Write Memories

Latches and flip flops can be regarded as 1-bit memory cells. In this section we will examine several ways of organizing such elements as arrays, giving storage of larger quantities of data.

After reading this section, you should:

- Recognize the four basic register structures, SISO (shift register), SIPO, PISO and PIPO. Also the term universal register.

- Understand the meaning of the general qualifying symbols **SRG** and **RAM**, and the symbols **A**, →, ←.

- Be aware of clock skew.

- Be able to distinguish between dynamic and static shift registers and RAMs.

- Be able to use RAM chips to implement read/write arrays of any given capacity and word width.

4.3.1 Registers

Small arrays of flip flops which are simultaneously clocked are usually categorized as **registers**. We have already met several instances of registers, although we may not have used this term. The output port in Fig. 4.14 comprized eight D flip flops organized to grab the parallel data from the bus and present it to the outside world as an 8-bit parallel word. This **parallel-in parallel-out (PIPO)** register structure was also used as an input port to grab data from a peripheral and hold it steady, awaiting the pleasure of the microprocessor unit. The same PIPO register was used in Fig. 4.23(b) to sample the data whenever the serial to parallel conversion has been completed. Besides storage, many registers are capable of shifting data within their structures; such circuits being known as **shift registers**.

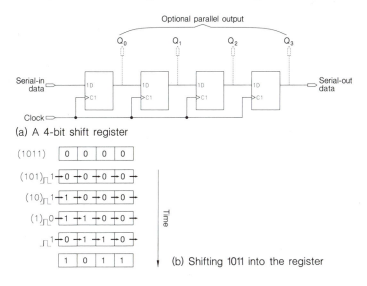

(a) A 4-bit shift register

(b) Shifting 1011 into the register

Figure 4.41: The shift register.

Figure 4.41(a) shows the basic shift register configuration using a D flip flop implementation. In this structure, the data held in the nth flip flop is presented to the input of the $(n + 1)$th stage. On receipt of a clock pulse (shift pulse in this context), this data moves into this $(n + 1)$th flip flop, i.e. effectively moving from stage n to stage $n + 1$. As all flip flops are clocked simultaneously, the entire word moves once right on each shift pulse. External data is fed into the left-most stage in synchronization with the clock. If we have an m-bit register, then after m shift pulses the serial m-bit word is held in the register. To get it out again, m further shifts moves the word bit by bit out of the right-most flip flop. The shift register is the digital equivalent to an analog delay line, with Q_{m-1} being a replica of the input m clock periods past.

From the point of view of integrated circuitry, this **serial-in serial-out (SISO)** circuit is economical to fabricate, as only one pin is needed for input and one for output, irrespective of the register length; be it 4 or 1024 bits. If the individual flip flop outputs are accessible, then we have the **serial-in parallel-out (SIPO)** architecture. This can be used for serial to parallel data conversion, as a simpler alternative to Fig. 4.23. It also permits the register to act as a tapped delay line.

Shift registers may have provision for parallel loading, in exactly the same way as provided for synchronous counters. Indeed counters are specialized registers having the ability to increment; as an example, the Johnston counter of Fig. 4.36 is actually a shift register with feedback. This leads to the structure **parallel-in serial-out (PISO)**.

As an example of a MSI register, the SN74AS95 illustrated in the data sheet of Fig. 4.42, is capable of assuming all four of the register structures. It is based on four R S flip flops, each connected with $S = \overline{R}$; which is effectively a D flip flop. Each D input is connected either to the previous stage (Shift mode) or to an external data line (Load mode), in the manner illustrated in Fig. 4.31(b).

This synchronous loading facility is controlled by the Mode input, which is Low for Shift and High for Load. Rather idiosyncratically, Mode also switches one of two input clock input lines through to the flip flop array. Thus when Mode is Low (i.e. Shift), then Clock_1 is the source of shifting pulses, whilst Clock_2 is the source for the parallel loading action when Mode is High. Normally they are just connected together, but it is possible to use them as a shift-right clock (Clock_1) and a shift-left clock (Clock_2). When in the Load mode, if data line D_n is connected to flip flop output Q_{n+1} (i.e. C to Q_D, B to Q_C, A to Q_B) then the data fed in at D will appear to be shifted left, eventually appearing at Q_A. Thus we have the ability to shift left or right with separate clocks (if required). However, this bidirectionality is obtained at the expense of the parallel-load facility. When changing modes, there are short delays before one clock is inhibited and the other enabled. These are the figures t_{en} and t_{in} given in the data sheet. The next example exploits this mode of operation.

The IEC/ANSI logic symbol of Fig. 4.42 uses the general qualifier **SRGn** for a shift register with n stages. Registers with no shifting action, are simply depicted as an array of flip flops, such as shown in Fig. 4.14. As in the synchronous counter-registers, the Mode dependency is used to depict the two modes. The shifting clock is qualified as **1C3/1→** , where the 1→ indicates a shift right action dependent on Mode 1 (The ← symbol is similarly used to depict a shift-left operation.). Also **1C3** is the control for the serial input **3D**, and is also qualified by Mode 1. The parallel-load clock **2C4** is qualified by Mode 2 and qualifies the parallel data inputs **4D**.

Registers like this are often known as **universal**, as they have a serial input (SI), serial output (SO), parallel inputs (PI) and parallel outputs (PO).

Longer registers may be implemented by cascading MSI register chips, with SI_n connected to SO_{n-1}. However, as the shifting mechanism depends on simultaneously clocking each stage, care must be taken to avoid **clock skew**. If there is a delay in the active clock edge between flip flop n and $n+1$ which is greater than the propagation delay of n less the setup time of $n+1$ (around 8 ns for the SN74AS95) then Q_n may have changed before flip flop $n+1$ is ready to grab its data. This delay may be because a buffer has been used between stages to boost the fan-out of the clock line or even because different paths have been utilized to carry this signal (propagation speed is around 1 ns per 30 cm/10″). The same problem can occur in synchronous counter-registers.

SN54AS95, SN74AS95A
4-BIT PARALLEL-ACCESS SHIFT REGISTER

D2661, DECEMBER 1983 – REVISED JULY 1988

- Serial-to-Parallel Conversions
- Parallel Synchronous Loading
- Right or Left Shifts
- Package Options Include Plastic "Small Outline" Packages, Ceramic Chip Carriers, and Standard Plastic and Ceramic 300-mil DIPs
- Dependable Texas Instruments Quality and Reliability

```
           SN54AS95 ... J PACKAGE
        SN74AS95A ... D OR N PACKAGE
                 (TOP VIEW)

        SER IN [ 1      14 ] VCC
           A   [ 2      13 ] QA
           B   [ 3      12 ] QB
           C   [ 4      11 ] QC
           D   [ 5      10 ] QD
        MODE   [ 6       9 ] CLK 1
        GND    [ 7       8 ] CLK 2
```

```
        SN54AS95 ... FK PACKAGE
                 (TOP VIEW)

                 A  SER IN  NC  VCC  QA
                 3   2   1  20  19

          B  [ 4                18 ] QB
         NC  [ 5                17 ] NC
          C  [ 6                16 ] QC
         NC  [ 7                15 ] NC
          D  [ 8                14 ] QD

                 9  10  11  12  13
              MODE GND  NC CLK 1 CLK 2
```

NC – No internal connection

description

These four-bit registers feature parallel and serial inputs, parallel outputs, mode control, and two clock inputs. The registers have three modes of operation:

Parallel (broadside) load
Shift right (the direction Q_A toward Q_D)
Shift left (the direction Q_D toward Q_A)

Parallel loading is accomblished by applying the four bits and taking the mode control input high. The data is loaded into the associated flip-flops and appears at the outputs after the high-to-low transition of the Clock-2 input. During loading, the entry of serial data is inhibited.

Shift right is accomplished on the high-to-low transition of Clock 1 when the mode control is low; shift left is accomplished on the high-to-low transition of Clock 2 when the mode control is high by connecting the output of each flip-flop to the parallel input of the previous flip-flop (Q_D to input C, etc.); and serial data is entered at input D. The clock input may be applied commonly to Clock 1 and Clock 2 if both modes can be clocked from the same source. Changes at the mode control input should normally be made while both clock inputs are low. However, conditions described in the last three lines of the function table will also ensure that the register contents are protected.

The SN54AS95 is characterized for operation over the full military temperature range of −55 °C to 125 °C. The SN74AS95A is characterized for operation from 0 °C to 70 °C.

logic symbol[†]

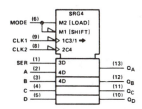

[†] This symbol is in accordance with ANSI/IEEE Std 91-1984 and IEC Publication 617-12.
Pin numbers shown are for D, J, and N packages.

TEXAS
INSTRUMENTS

Figure 4.42: The SN74AS95 4-bit universal register (*continued next page*).

TYPES SN54AS95, SN74AS95
4-BIT PARALLEL-ACCESS SHIFT REGISTER

FUNCTION TABLE

MODE CONTROL	CLOCKS 2 (L)	CLOCKS 1 (R)	SERIAL	PARALLEL A	PARALLEL B	PARALLEL C	PARALLEL D	Q_A	Q_B	Q_C	Q_D
H	H	X	X	X	X	X	X	Q_{A0}	Q_{B0}	Q_{C0}	Q_{D0}
H	↓	X	X	a	b	c	d	a	b	c	d
H	↓	X	X	$Q_B\uparrow$	$Q_C\uparrow$	$Q_D\uparrow$	d	Q_{Bn}	Q_{Cn}	Q_{Dn}	d
L	L	H	X	X	X	X	X	Q_{A0}	Q_{B0}	Q_{C0}	Q_{D0}
L	X	↓	H	X	X	X	X	H	Q_{An}	Q_{Bn}	Q_{Cn}
L	X	↓	L	X	X	X	X	L	Q_{An}	Q_{Bn}	Q_{Cn}
↑	L	L	X	X	X	X	X	Q_{A0}	Q_{B0}	Q_{C0}	Q_{D0}
↓	L	L	X	X	X	X	X	Q_{A0}	Q_{B0}	Q_{C0}	Q_{D0}
↓	L	H	X	X	X	X	X	Q_{A0}	Q_{B0}	Q_{C0}	Q_{D0}
↑	H	L	X	X	X	X	X	Q_{A0}	Q_{B0}	Q_{C0}	Q_{D0}
↑	H	H	X	X	X	X	X	Q_{A0}	Q_{B0}	Q_{C0}	Q_{D0}

Column headers (upper): INPUTS | OUTPUTS; MODE CONTROL | CLOCKS | SERIAL | PARALLEL | Q_A Q_B Q_C Q_D

†Shifting left requires external connection of Q_B to A, Q_C to B, and Q_D to C. Serial data is entered at input D.
H = high level (steady state), L = low level (steady state), X = irrelevant (any input, including transitions).
↓ = transition from high to low level, ↑ = transition from low to high level.
a, b, c, d = the level of steady-state input at inputs A, B, C, or D, respectively.
Q_{A0}, Q_{B0}, Q_{C0}, Q_{D0} = the level of Q_A, Q_B, Q_C, or Q_D, respectively, before the indicated steady-state input conditions were established.
Q_{An}, Q_{Bn}, Q_{Cn}, Q_{Dn} = the level of Q_A, Q_B, Q_C, or Q_D, respectively, before the most-recent ↓ transition of the clock.

recommended operating conditions		SN54AS95 MIN	NOM	MAX	SN74AS95A MIN	NOM	MAX	UNIT
f_{clock}	Clock frequency	0		80	0		100	MHz
t_w	Pulse duration, CLK high or low	6.5			5			ns
t_{su}	Setup time, data before CLK↓	2.5			2			ns
t_h	Hold time after CLK↓ — Data	2.5			2.5			ns
	CLK 1 to Mode	3.5			3			
	CLK 2 to Mode	1			0			
t_{en}	Clock enable time — CLK 1	13			12			ns
	CLK 2	13			12			
t_{in}	Clock inhibit time — CLK 1	3			2.5			ns
	CLK 2	1			0			
T_A	Operating free-air temperature	−55		125	0		70	°C

logic diagram (positive logic)

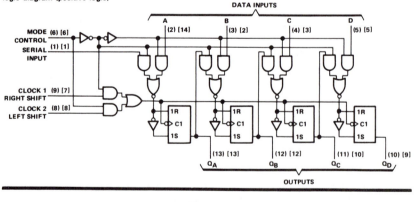

DATA INPUTS

MODE CONTROL (6) [6]
SERIAL INPUT (1) [1]

A (2) [14]   B (3) [2]   C (4) [3]   D (5) [5]

CLOCK 1 (9) [7] RIGHT SHIFT
CLOCK 2 (8) [8] LEFT SHIFT

1R C1 1S (×4)

(13) [13] Q_A (12) [12] Q_B (11) [10] Q_C (10) [9] Q_D

OUTPUTS

TEXAS INSTRUMENTS

Figure 4.42: (*continued*). The SN74AS95 4-bit universal register. Reproduced by courtesy of Texas Instruments Ltd.

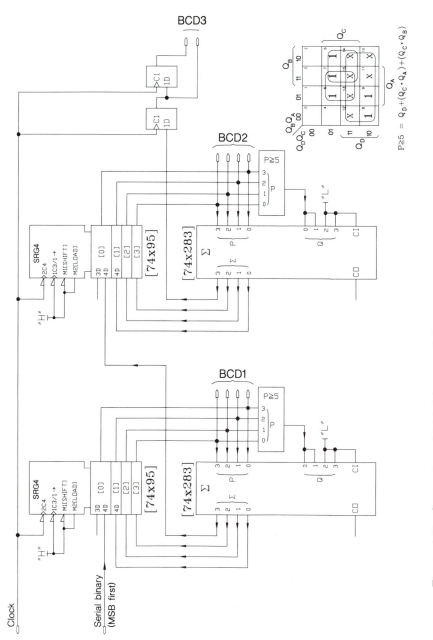

Figure 4.43: Conversion of 8-bit binary to BCD using the shift and correct algorithm.

Example 4.20

To implement a 8-bit binary to 3-digit BCD converter using the shift and correct algorithm [18, 19]:

> Repetitively shift each decade left, one place at a time. If after each shift the resulting 5-bit binary number is between 10 and 19, then add six.

Solution

The algorithm as stated can be modified slightly so that each decade is examined *before* the shift for a number between 5 and 9 inclusive (10 to 15 never occurs if the correction has previously been applied) and three added if affirmative. As each shift multiplies by two, this is an equivalent procedure.

The implementation of Fig. 4.43 is based on this modified algorithm. Essentially the synchronous parallel load facility is used to shift in a filtered version of the previous data. The filter is a 4-bit 74x283 adder which either sums $0000b$ or $0011b$ (zero or three) to state n, depending on the outcome of the relation $n > 5$, and presents this as state $n + 1$, but one place over to the left. Thus bit Q_n is connected to the $(n + 1)$th stage's parallel-in through the adder. Hence there is an effective shift left one place on each clock pulse, adding three if the decade was greater than five. Thus a number K held in a 4-bit register becomes $2(K + F \times 3) = 2K + F \times 6$, where $F = 1$ if $K > 5$, otherwise 0. After eight clock pulses the BCD equivalent is held in the registers. Note that ten register places are needed for 8-bit binary ($11111111b \rightarrow 10\ 0101\ 0101b = 255$). As the maximum contents of register 3 will be $0010b$, no correction is needed, and we have used a simple 2-bit shift register for this stage. The circuit may be extended adding the appropriate number of registers and adders. Thus a 16-bit binary to BCD conversion requires four 4-bit register/adders with the 5th decade being a simple 3-bit shift register. The conversion would take 16 clock periods.

All the previously described registers, are known as **static**. Many registers are **dynamic**, having the property of a minimum shifting rate as well as the more familiar maximum [20].

Figure 4.44(a) shows the schematic of a 2-phase dynamic register cell. Data is stored as a charge on the parasitic (stray) capacitance at the MOS-based inverter's gate. As this charge will leak away in a few ms, the voltage levels must be regenerated and shifted at a minimum rate. Figure 4.44(b) gives the 2-step cycle, based on two switches ($\overline{TG}_1$ and TG_2) working in antiphase. A 2-phase clock with the timing shown, is necessary to correctly sequence the cycle. Figure 4.44(c) shows a NMOS 2-phase cell implementation. Note that when a TG switch is Off, the adjacent drain load FET is also Off; e.g. if TR_3 is Off, so is TR_2. This reduces the power dissipation, as the inverter drain current only flows during part of the cycle.

Low power dissipation is important, as it allows a high packing density. Thus long (typically 1024-stage and up) registers are typically dynamic, as are the internal registers in VLSI devices such as microprocessors. Such long dynamic shift registers

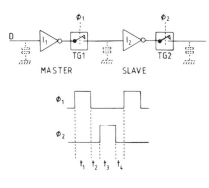

MASTER SLAVE

(a) A dynamic shifting cell,
showing the 2-phase clock.

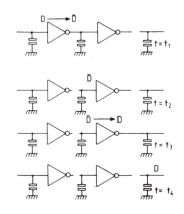

(c) An NMOS 2-phase cell.

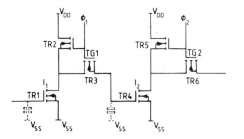

(b) Shifting data one place.

Figure 4.44: Dynamic shift registers.

Organization	Designator	Bits	Shifting rate typ MHz	Additional features
SISO	74LS91	8	18	Gated serial input
SISO	4031B	64	5–20	2 data I/Ps, comp. O/P
SISO	4557B	64	5–20	Variable length
SIPO	74LS/ALS164	8	36/75	Asy $\overline{\text{Clear}}$
PISO	74LS/ALS165	8	35/45	
PISO	74LS674	16	20	Recirculating memory
PIPO	74LS396	8	30	4+4 bank
Universal	74LS/AS195	4	39/70	Asy $\overline{\text{Clear}}$, Sy $\overline{\text{Load}}$
Universal	74LS/ALS299	8	25/30	3-S data I/O, bidirectional
Universal	74198/199	8	30	'198 is bidirectional

Asy = asynchronous; Sy = synchronous; 3-s = 3-state

Table 4.3: A selection of MSI registers.

are commonly used as **sequential access memories**. Data held in the register will circulate indefinitely if the last stage is connected to the input. Stored data is read serially from the last stage. The contents can be altered by disconnecting the feedback and injecting new data directly into the first stage. This structure is often called a **first-in first-out (FIFO) memory**. This is ideal for such applications as a visual display unit memory, where the CRO display is continually refreshed by the circulating data [21]. However, most current systems are based on random-access memories, which are the subject of the next section.

4.3.2   Random Access Read/Write Memories

Although registers may be organized to hold several words, generally **random access read/write memory** ICs are used where larger quantities of data must be stored. These LSI and VLSI devices are normally known as RAMs, although strictly the ROM of Section 3.3.2 is also random access. The term random access just means that any data cell may be 'got at' without sequencing through previous locations.

A **static RAM** typically comprizes an array of simple latches, each implemented by two cross-coupled inverters, as shown in Fig. 4.45(a). This latch may be forced into one of its bistable states by closing switch SW_W, when the output will be the inverse of d_{in}. If SW_W is now opened, the latch will remain in this stable state ($Q = d_{in}$, $\overline{Q} = \overline{d_{in}}$). This process is known as writing. The inverse reading action is accomplished by closing switch SW_R. The state of the latch can then be monitored at d_{out}, without affecting the state of the latch.

RAM ICs are normally internally organized as a 2-dimensional array; one possibility being shown in Fig. 4.45(b). Here, only one cell is activated for a given address input $A_3 A_2 A_1 A_0$, for example cell 2-1 for address $1001b$. The common d_{in} and d_{out} lines are usually combined into a single input/output line, which appears at the outside world. This reduces the number of IC pins and suits a common bus connection, through which data may flow in either direction (see Fig. 4.14). An external direction control signal labelled Read/Write (R/W) (or sometimes just Write or Write_Enable ($\overline{W}$ or $\overline{WE}$)) is used to activate the appropriate 3-state buffer.

A more detailed look at one of these 2-dimensional cells is given in Fig. 4.45(c) [22]. The latch itself comprizes two cross-coupled NMOS transistor switches, as detailed in Fig. 3.12(a). Both d_{in} and d_{out} are connected through two series switches, which are driven by the $X_m Y_n$ lines, giving an AND gate.

The user's view of the RAM, is of Address, Data and Control buses. Fig. 4.46 shows an extract of the MCM6264D CMOS static RAM data sheet. This device stores 65,536 (64K) bits, organized as 8192 (8K) bytes of eight bits each. To address this, we require a 13-bit address, which is labelled $A_{12} \ldots A_0$. The eight data lines are $DQ_7 \ldots DQ_0$ (D for latch input, Q for latch output). The RAM is enabled when $\overline{E1}$ is Low and E2 is High. The output 3-state buffers have their own enable $\overline{G}$, which is active-Low. The $\overline{W}$ input enables a writing action (gates data into the addressed latch). Internally the 65,536 cells are arranged as eight 256×32 2-dimensional arrays, each array contributing one D/Q line.

In order to read a byte stored at an address m, the following sequence of operations must occur:

1. Put the 13-bit address m on the address lines.

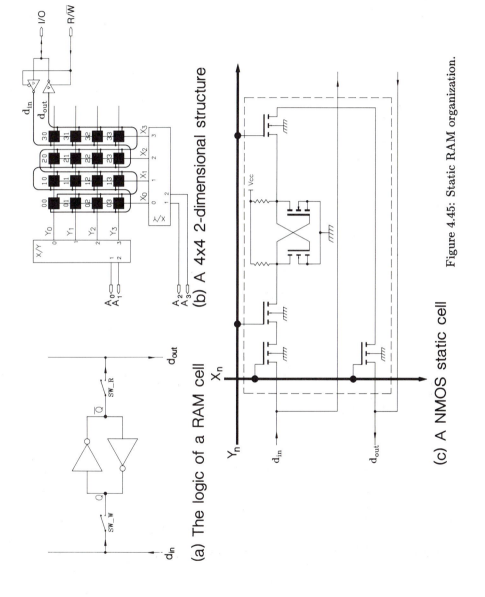

(a) The logic of a RAM cell

(b) A 4x4 2-dimensional structure

(c) A NMOS static cell

Figure 4.45: Static RAM organization.

MOTOROLA
SEMICONDUCTOR
TECHNICAL DATA

Order this data sheet
by MCM6264D/D

8K × 8 Bit Fast Static RAM

The MCM6264D is a 65,536 bit static random access memory organized as 8,192 words of 8 bits, fabricated using high-performance silicon-gate CMOS technology. Static design eliminates the need for external clocks or timing strobes, while CMOS circuitry reduces power consumption and provides for greater reliability.

Chip enables ($\overline{E1}$ and E2) control the power-down feature. They are not clocks but rather chip controls that affect power consumption. In less than a cycle time after $\overline{E1}$ goes high (and E2 goes low), the part automatically reduces it power requirements and remains in this low-power standby mode as long as $\overline{E1}$ remains high and (E2 remains low). This feature provides significant system-level power savings.

The MCM6264D is available in a 300 mil, 28 lead plastic dual-in-line package or a 300 mil, 28 lead plastic SOJ package with the JEDEC standard pinout.

- Single 5 V ± 10% Power Supply
- Fast Access Time: 20, 25, 35, 45 ns
- Chip Controls:
  Chip Enables ($\overline{E1}$ and E2) for Reduced-Power Standby Mode
  Output Enable ($\overline{G}$) Feature for Increased System Flexibility and to Eliminate Bus Contention Problems
- Three-State Outputs
- Fully TTL Compatible
- Power Operation: 120, 100, 90, 80 mA (Maximum)
- High Board Density SOJ Package Available
- Also Available in Industrial Temperature Range as MCM6264D-C

MCM6264D

P PACKAGE
300 MIL PLASTIC
CASE 710B

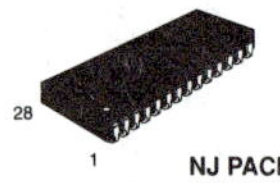

NJ PACKAGE
300 MIL SOJ
CASE 810B

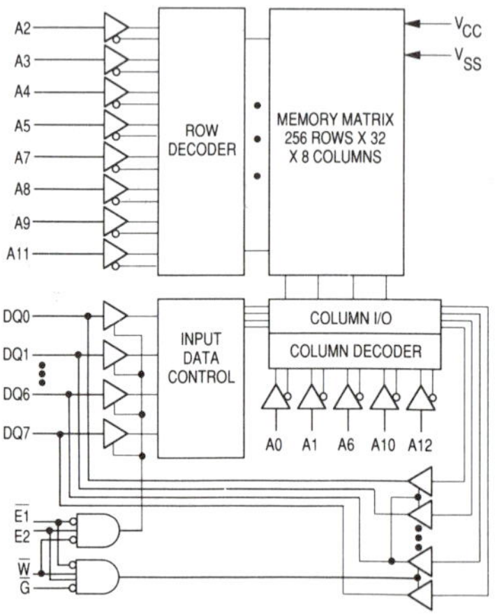

PIN ASSIGNMENT

NC	1 ●	28	V_{CC}
A12	2	27	$\overline{W}$
A7	3	26	E2
A6	4	25	A8
A5	5	24	A9
A4	6	23	A11
A3	7	22	$\overline{G}$
A2	8	21	A10
A1	9	20	$\overline{E1}$
A0	10	19	DQ7
DQ0	11	18	DQ6
DQ1	12	17	DQ5
DQ2	13	16	DQ4
V_{SS}	14	15	DQ3

BLOCK DIAGRAM

PIN NAMES

A0–A12	Address Inputs
$\overline{W}$	Write Enable
$\overline{G}$	Output Enable
$\overline{E1}$, E2	Chip Enable
DQ0–DQ7	Data Input/Output
V_{CC}	+ 5 V Power Supply
V_{SS}	Ground
NC	No Connection

All power supply and ground pins must be connected for proper operation of the device.

Ⓜ **MOTOROLA**

Replaces DS9925R1 and NP484R

Figure 4.46: The MCM6264D static RAM (*continued next page*).

WRITE CYCLE 2 ($\overline{\text{E}}$ Controlled, See Note 1)

Parameter	Symbol Std.	Alt.	MCM6264D -25 Min	Max	MCM6264D -35 Min	Max	MCM6264D -45 Min	Max	MCM6264D -55 Min	Max	Unit	Notes
Write Cycle Time	t_{AVAV}	t_{WC}	25	—	35	—	45	—	55	—	ns	
Address Setup Time	t_{AVEL}	t_{AS}	0	—	0	—	0	—	0	—	ns	2, 5
Address Valid to End of Write	t_{AVEH}	t_{AW}	20	—	25	—	35	—	45	—	ns	2, 5
Enable to End of Write	t_{ELEH}	t_{CW}	20	—	25	—	35	—	45	—	ns	2, 3, 5
Data Valid to End of Write	t_{DVEH}	t_{DW}	10	—	15	—	20	—	25	—	ns	2, 5
Data Hold Time	t_{EHDX}	t_{DH}	0	—	0	—	0	—	0	—	ns	2, 4, 5
Write Recover Time	t_{EHAX}	t_{WR}	0	—	0	—	0	—	0	—	ns	2, 5

NOTES:
1. A write cycle starts at the latest transition of a low $\overline{\text{E1}}$, low $\overline{\text{W}}$, or high E2. A write cycle ends at the earliest transition of a high $\overline{\text{E1}}$, high $\overline{\text{W}}$, or low E2.
2. $\overline{\text{E1}}$ and E2 timings are identical when E2 signals are inverted.
3. If $\overline{\text{W}}$ goes low coincident with or prior to $\overline{\text{E1}}$ low or E2 high then the outputs will remain in a high impedance state.
4. During this time the output pins maybe in the output stage. Signals of opposite phase to the outputs must not be applied at this time.
5. $\overline{\text{E1}}$ and E2 are both represented by $\overline{\text{E}}$ in this data sheet. E2 is of opposite polarity to $\overline{\text{E1}}$.

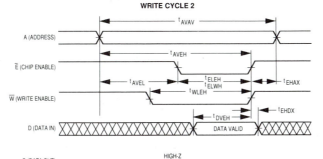

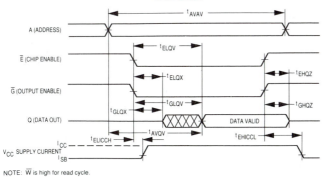

Figure 4.46: (*continued*). The MCM6264D static RAM. Reproduced by courtesy of Motorola Semiconductor Products Ltd.

2. Enable the device ($\overline{\mathsf{E1}}$ E2 = LH).

3. Put data to be written in onto the Data lines.

4. Bring $\overline{\mathsf{W}}$ Low.

5. Deactivate the Chip_Enable and $\overline{\mathsf{W}}$ lines.

6. Remove address and data.

The timing diagram appropriate to this sequence is shown in the data sheet. Taking the MCM6264D-25 as an example, the minimum time to do a write (the write cycle time, t_{AVAV} takes 25 ns. Data must be set up no more than 10 ns before the end of the write pulse (t_{DVWH}) and the hold time (t_{EHDX}) is zero.

It is possible to enable the chip and then subsequently pulse $\overline{\mathsf{W}}$ Low; this is described in the data sheet as WRITE CYCLE 1 but is not shown in Fig. 4.46. When this happens, data will appear at the D/Q pins when $\overline{\mathsf{W}}$ returns High, unless the Enable ($\overline{\mathsf{G}}$) is High, to deactivate the output buffers.

Reading from memory is very similar to writing, but this time $\overline{\mathsf{W}}$ is kept High and $\overline{\mathsf{G}}$ must be Low. The Read Access time is also 25 ns from a valid address. Data is guaranteed to be valid by the end of this cycle, i.e. $t_{\mathsf{AVQV}} \leq 25$ ns.

As semiconductor RAMs are **volatile** (i.e. loose their data when the supply is removed), battery backup is required if data is to be retained in this situation. Some devices have a sleep state which facilitates battery backup. For example, the 32K × 8 MCM60L256 can retain data at a reduced V_{CC} of 2 V and only 2 µA maximum current @ 25°C. A few RAMs even come with an integral lithium cell for this purpose.

The logic symbol for the 6264 RAM is shown in Fig. 4.47, which shows two devices hung on the one Data bus. The general qualifier symbol **RAM** needs no elaboration. The Address dependency symbol is used to indicate an array of elements from 0 to 8191, as in the case of a ROM (see Fig. 3.59). The prefix **A** qualifying the eight cells indicates that only the addressed cell actually contributes to the input and output latch lines. The $\overline{\mathsf{W}}$ control is shown split into a **[READ]** and a **[WRITE]** action, both of which are dependent on $\overline{\mathsf{E1}}$ and E2. Writing is indicated as a control action on the D input, in the same manner as a latch. Reading qualifies the output, which is disabled when $\overline{\mathsf{W}}$ is Low ($\overline{4}$) and is shown to the right of the latch box as $\mathsf{A,3,\overline{4}Z5}$. This is internally commoned to the input pin, and $\mathsf{Z5}$ is used to show this internal connection across the cell. The output is 3-state. Note again that both input and output lines are prefixed by **A**, which indicates that the actual cell data appearing here is a function of the address inputs.

RAMS (and indeed ROMs) may be expanded in both word size (width) and the number of words. Width can be increased by simply using RAM chips in parallel, all addressed and enabled together. Thus four paralleled 6264 8K × 8 devices would give an 8K × 32 capacity.

Increasing the number of words requires that the outputs of several RAM chips be commoned, as shown in Fig. 4.47. Each RAM chip is addressed in parallel, with the additional higher-order address bits being used to select only one out of the n devices for any given address. During a read action, all disabled devices are Off (3-state or open collector), with only the one enabled device contributing its

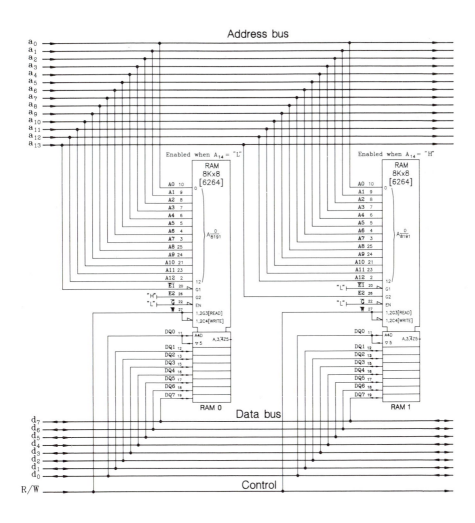

Figure 4.47: Expanding word size.

data. Similarly, during a write action, only the enabled RAM grabs the data off
the bus. Typically these upper address bits use a decoder to select one of n RAM
chips. In the example of Fig. 4.47, we make use of the one active-High and the
one active-Low Enable on the 6264 RAM IC. When a_{13} is Low then RAM_0 is
active and contributes data at addresses $00\ 0000\ 0000\ 0000$ to $01\ 1111\ 1111\ 1111b$
($0000 - 1FFFh$). Conversely when a_{13} is High, then RAM_1 is active and responds
to addresses $10\ 0000\ 0000\ 0000$ through $11\ 1111\ 1111\ 1111b$ ($2000 - 3FFFh$); a total
of 16K cells, each of eight bits.

Like dynamic shift registers, random access memories can use capacitance to
store data. Each cell simply comprises a storage capacitance which can be switched
through to a column by the X-decoder line. The charge level on each column is
detected and regenerated by a sense amplifier, and the appropriate column gated
through to the outside world via the Y-decoder [23].

The problem here is that the very low value of cell capacitance (typically a
fraction of a picofarad) is less than the capacitance of the column line, and the
ratio depends on the position of the cell. The sense amplifier typically comprises a
cross-coupled NOT latch. Initially both outputs have equal voltage SW_1 closed).
When SW_1 is opened and SW_X closed, the bistable will latch into one of two states
depending on the relative magnitude of the dummy capacitor's charge and the cell
plus column line charge. This regenerative action brings the column line to either
logic 0 or logic 1, and hence refreshes the charge on the cell; which of course will
have partly leaked away since the last read.

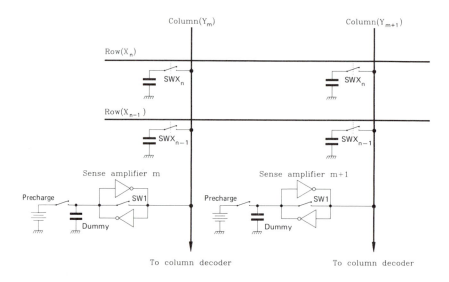

Figure 4.48: The dynamic RAM.

Although the sense amplifier is relatively complex, there is only one per column,
and overall the complete memory uses perhaps only 25% of the silicon area compared
to an equivalent static RAM (SRAM). Thus typically **dynamic RAMs (DRAMs)**
are available at four times the size. At the time of writing (1992) 16 Mbyte (1M =

$10^{20} = 1,048,576$) DRAMS are just becoming available, and prototype 64 Mbyte devices are in the research laboratory. The MCM514400 is a typical 1M × 4 CMOS DRAM, featuring a 80 ns access time and a 105 mA operating current (1 mA during standby, i.e. if deselected).

The downside of DRAMs is the need to periodically refresh the charge on each bit capacitor. For example, the MCM514400 requires a refresh every 16 ms. Refreshing is accomplished a column at a time; each X address selecting one row. Each column sense amplifier then regenerates the charge. The MCM514400 has 1024 row addresses, which implies a refresh (i.e. a dummy read) every 15.6 μs. Generally DRAMs multiplex their pins between the column and row addresses; with each being presented to the chip in sequence and being latched in using the CAS (Column_Address_Strobe) and RAS (Row_Address_Strobe) control lines. A refresh is accomplished by sequencing through the row addresses without bothering with the column addresses.

The overhead of arranging this refresh is such that DRAMs are used where large memory arrays are required, typically a computer. Some microprocessors have specific provision for refresh, typically during idling cycles; for example the Z80 device.

Organization	Designator	Access time typ ns	Power (ma) active/standby	Additional features
Static				
256 × 8	48T02B-25	250	70	Integral 10-year battery
2K × 8	6116AE3	120	100/1 μA	Low power
16K × 8	6267-35	35	100/20 μA	High-speed
8K × 8	6264-12	120	80/1	Low power
16K × 8	7C128-45	45	120/20	High-speed
32K × 8	43256-10	100	70/0.1	
128K × 8	51008-12	120	100/2	
Dynamic				
64K × 1	4164-15	150	39/5	16-pin DIL package
64K × 4	4416-15	150	39/5	18-pin DIL package
256K × 1	4256-10	100	70/4.5	18-pin DIL package
64K × 4	50464-12	120	83/10	18-pin DIL package
1M × 1	511000-10	100	60/2	18-pin DIL package
256K × 4	4256C-80	80	70	20-pin DIL package
4M × 1	44100L-8	80	95/2	CMOS 20-ZIP package
1M × 4	44400L-8	80	95/2	CMOS 20-ZIP package

DIL = Dual in-line; ZIP = Zig Zag in-line. All memories have 3-state outputs.

Table 4.4: A selection of memory devices.

4.4 Sequential Arithmetic Circuitry

In Section 3.2.3 we discussed the use of combinational logic in implementing arithmetic functions. However, many of these algorithms are inherently sequential in nature and can be implemented in a more cost effective way using sequential circuitry, albeit at the expense of speed. The binary to BCD conversion process illustrated in Fig. 4.43 is a good example of this approach.

Two n-bit words can be **sequentially added** by summing each column in turn, from the least significant bit upwards, and storing the sum in a shift register. The carry, C_n, must be stored between adds, ready for the $(n + 1)$th addition. This is the approach shown in Fig. 4.49. Here a parallel loading shift register holds the 4-bit addend, which serially feeds a 1-bit full adder. This shift register's input is symbolized as $C2/ \rightarrow$, which means that it controls the input **2D** (the serial input) as well as the shifting action. A second shift register both feeds this adder and also accepts the Σ output as its input. A D flip flop holds the adder's Carry_Out, which is the new Carry_In after the clock pulse. To add two 4-bit words X_0 and X_1, the following sequence of events occurs:

1. Clear the Augend/sum register by pulsing $\overline{\text{Initiate}}$ Low (zeros the sum).

2. Parallel load X_0 into the addend register and clear the carry flip flop by pulsing Add Low ($C_0 = 0$).

3. Clock the system eight times. The number X_0 will now lie in the top four bits of the Augend/sum register.

4. Parallel load X_1 into the Addend register.

5. Clock the system eight times. The number $X_0 + X_1$ is now located at the top of the Augend/sum register.

The Augend/sum register has been deliberately made larger than the Addend register so that several additions may be accumulated. In this implementation, the worst-case situation is where X_n is $1111b$ (15) which gives $11111111b$ (255) after 17 additions. The circuit is therefore known as an **accumulator adder**. A subtraction can be performed by inverting the addend and setting the initial carry state to logic 1 ($C_0 = 1$). This gives inversion plus one, ie. the 2's complement of the addend.

An alternative faster (but more expensive) parallel scheme is shown in Fig. 4.50(a). An 8-bit adder is being used to add the contents of an 8-bit PIPO register (an array of D flip flops) to an incoming 4-bit word. If we initially assume that the $\overline{\text{Add}}$/Sub line is logic 0, then the addend can be considered extended to eight bits, with its four upper bits permanently 0. The Σ outputs of the adders at any time n is simply the sum of the 4-bit input X_n and the 8-bit register contents, R_n. When the register is clocked, the contents are updated to this sum; thus $R_{n+1} = R_n + X_n$. If the input is now changed to X_{n+1}, the outputs of the adders become $R_{n+1} + X_{n+1} = R_n + X_n + X_{n+1}$. This in turn is loaded into the register at the $(n + 1)$th clock pulse.

To add three 4-bit words X_0, X_1 and X_2, we must:

1. Clear the register by pulsing $\overline{\text{Initiate}}$ Low; $R_0 = 0$.

2. Present X_0 to the adder.

3. Pulse the register clock Add. This moves the adder outputs into the register, $R_1 = X_0$.

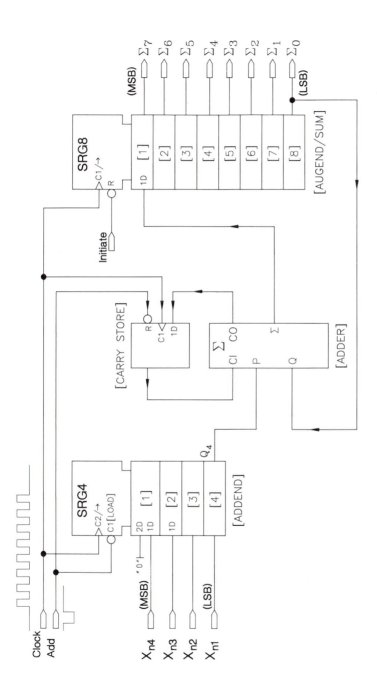

Figure 4.49: A serial adder/accumulator.

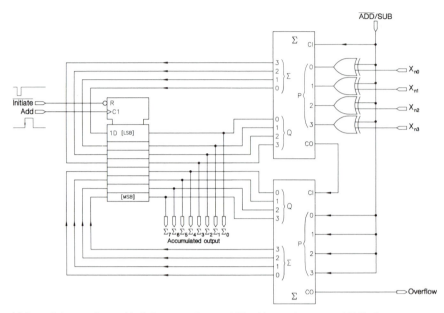

(a) A parallel accumulator adder/subtractor using two 4-bit adders and an array of D flip flops

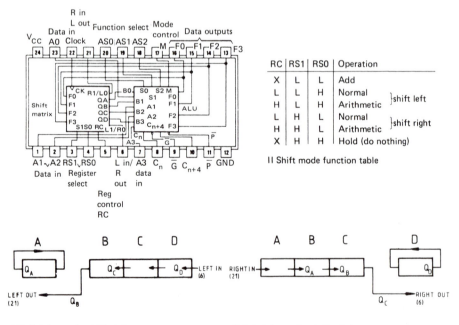

III Arithmetic shift left   IV Arithmetic shift right

(b)

Figure 4.50: A parallel accumulator adder/subtractor.

4. Present X_1 to the adder.

5. Pulse the register clock. This moves the adder outputs to the register, giving $R_1 = R_0 + X_1 = X_0 + X_1$.

6. Present X_2 to the adder.

7. Pulse the register clock, giving $R_2 = R_1 + X_2 = (X_0 + X_1) + X_2$.

As in the serial circuit, the number of additions is limited by the target register size. A larger capacity may be obtained by using a bigger register, but the adder capacity must in all cases match that of the register. This is because the register contents will be larger than the (cut down) addend; the most significant adder bits being simply used to add the carry from the lower bits.

As in Fig. 3.49(c), subtraction is accomplished by using EOR gates as programmable inverters and forcing a logic 1 into the carry input. The 'phantom' addend upper bits are also made logic 1 to give an overall 8-bit 2's complement.

Example 4.21

Show how you could use the accumulator adder/subtractor as an up/down counter.

Solution

If the input $X_3 X_2 X_1 X_0$ is held at $0001b$, then the contents of the accumulator will be incremented or decremented on each clock pulse according to the state of the $\overline{\text{Add}}/\text{Sub}$ control; which could then be labelled $\overline{\text{Up}}/\text{Down}$. X_0 may be used as an $\overline{\text{Add}}/\text{Sub}$ inhibit control; for if X_0 is brought to $0000b$, the counter will repetitively add zero, i.e. stop.

An interesting possibility arises using this circuit as a counter with a non-unity increment. Thus using the input as a 'speed control', the counter may be made to count in twos or any number up to 15 (symbolized as +n or −n, where n is the step size). The larger the input X the sooner is the cycle completed; thus the frequency of the most significant register stage is directly proportional to X. If the clock frequency is F, then the output frequency is $\frac{F}{256}$X. Used in this way, the circuit is known as a **rate multiplier** [24].

Replacing the adder/subtractor by an arithmetic logic unit (ALU) gives a versatile accumulator function unit, capable of addition, subtraction and any of the functions outlined in Fig. 3.50. In the next chapter we will see that a microprocessor is in essence an accumulator function unit, whose operation (i.e. mode) is controlled by a sequence of instructions brought down from memory and decoded by a control unit: the program.

The 74S281 shown in Fig. 4.50(b) is an example of an integrated 4-bit accumulator 'slice', cascadable to any length, using an integral 74S181 type ALU. The parallel loading register (shift matrix), besides loading, can be inhibited (do nothing) or shifted right/left: it is controlled by Register_Select and Register_Control (RS1; RS0; RC, pins 3,4,5), as detailed in Fig. 4.50(b)II. An arithmetic shift (RC = H) differs from a normal shift, in that the MSB (Q_A for left shift and Q_D for right shift; Fig. 4.50(b)III) remains unchanged and propagates down the chain. This is useful in signed 2's complement arithmetic, as outlined in Section 1.2.3. The shift registers are cascaded by connecting the bidirectional port Right_In/Left_Out (RI/LO) to Left_In/Right_Out (LI/RO) of the next unit. The ALU is cascaded as detailed in Section 3.2.3.

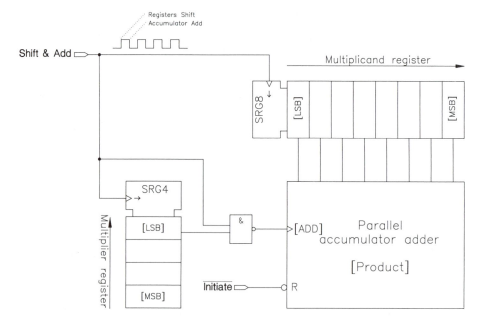

Figure 4.51: A 8 × 4-bit multiplier using the shift and add principle. Assume registers are initially parallel loaded with data.

The **shift and add multiplication** algorithm of Section 1.2.3 lends itself to a sequential implementation, as shown in Fig. 4.51. The multiplicand is repetitively shifted left and conditionally added to the contents of the accumulator. At the Kth addition, either the shifted multiplicand or zero is added to the subtotal, depending on the state of the Kth multiplier bit; i.e. add if multiplier bit = 1 or else do nothing. With an n-bit multiplicand and m-bit multiplier, the product register requires an $(m + n)$-bit capacity and the multiplication takes m shifts. In Fig. 4.51, we require a 12-bit accumulator adder, and multiplication takes four shift pulses.

A similar approach can be used to implement division, according to the **shift and subtract algorithm** of Section 1.2.3. Basically, the dividend will be parallel loaded into an accumulator subtractor and the divisor conditionally subtracted as it is shifted right for the appropriate number of times. The results of each condition (can or cannot subtract) are shifted into a quotient register.

4.5 Programmable Sequential LSI

The general structure of a synchronous counter was shown back in Fig. 4.28. Here an array of flip flops holds the current state of the counter which feeds a combinational logic stage. This generates the conditions that will cause the flip flop array to change to the next state on receipt of the next clock pulse. As this clock signal is common to all flip flops, any change occurs simultaneously, subject to the spread of the flip flop propagation delays. To ensure reliable operation, the times between clock pulses must be greater than the sum of the worst-case propagation time through the combinational logic, and the setup and hold times of the flip flops.

The basic counter structure may be extended by connecting control inputs directly into the combinational logic block, in addition to the feedback inputs. These programmable inputs can be used to change the counter mode, giving facilities such as count-up, count-down, dead-end, synchronous load etc.

The combinational logic block could of course be any of the LSI circuits discussed in Section 3.3. However the architecture outlined in Fig. 4.28 is sufficiently general to warrant the production of programmable LSI devices with integral flip flops and feedback paths.

A typical registered PAL device is shown in the data sheet extract of Fig. 4.52. The PAL16R4 comprises a classical PAL AND-OR matrix, identical to the combinational PAL16L8 of Fig. 3.65, but with four D flip flops interposed between the OR gates and 3-state buffer outputs. We see from Fig. 4.54 that these outputs are fed back into the AND matrix, in the same way as the four remaining combinational outputs are. The 16R6 & 16R8 devices are similar but with more flip flops at the expense of the purely combinational outputs. The 20R series of PALs are the 24-pin analog of the 20-pin 16R series. The R symbol of course denotes Registered.

As registered PALs are the most popular sequential PLD, we will restrict our coverage to this architecture in this section. Examples of sequential machines based on PLEs and PLAs are given in the following section. ASIC implementations are simply integrated versions of the random logic circuits previously designed. Flip flops of the appropriate kinds are implemented from the basic gate or transistor building blocks. Normally appropriate circuits are available as library parts in the CAE software used as the design tool.

Example 4.22

Using a PAL16R4 show how you would implement the 2-4-2-1 BCD counter of Example 4.17. Additional facilities will include a synchronous $\overline{\text{Clear}}$ and $\overline{\text{Load}}$ input, and an output to indicate when the counter is in state 9.

Solution

Directly implementing the equations of page 346 will lead to an active-Low count sequence, due to the PAL16R4's inverting output buffers. We can cancel this inverting action by noting that evaluating the functions $\overline{D}_n$, by using a zero's covering, effectively interchanges the flip flop outputs Q_n & $\overline{Q}_n$. As Q_n has now become $\overline{Q}_n$, then the inverting buffer gives the external value of Q_n, the actual active-High state values. This allows us to use these equations; and the fuse plot of Fig. 4.53 takes

TIBPAL16L8-15M, TIBPAL16R4-15M, TIBPAL16R6-15M, TIBPAL16R8-15M
TIBPAL16L8-12C, TIBPAL16R4-12C, TIBPAL16R6-12C, TIBPAL16R8-12C
HIGH-PERFORMANCE *IMPACT ™PAL*® CIRCUITS

JANUARY 1986–REVISED DECEMBER 1987

- **High-Performance Operation**
  Propagation Delay
    M Suffix . . . 12 ns Max
    C Suffix . . . 15 ns Max

- **Functionally Equivalent, but Faster than**
  PAL16L8B, PAL16R4B, PAL16R6B, and
  PAL16R8B

- **Power-Up Clear on Registered Devices**
  (All Registered Outputs are Set Low)

- **Package Options Include Both Plastic and**
  Ceramic Chip Carriers in Addition to Plastic
  and Ceramic DIPs

- **Dependable Texas Instruments Quality and**
  Reliability

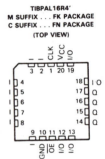

DEVICE	INPUTS	3-STATE O OUTPUTS	REGISTERED Q OUTPUTS	I/O PORTS
PAL16L8	10	2	0	6
PAL16R4	8	0	4 (3-state)	4
PAL16R6	8	0	6 (3-state)	2
PAL16R8	8	0	8 (3-state)	0

description

These programmable array logic devices feature high speed and functional equivalency when compared with currently available devices. These IMPACT™ circuits combine the latest Advanced Low-Power Schottky[†] technology with proven titanium-tungsten fuses to provide reliable, high-performance substitutes for conventional TTL logic. Their easy programmability allows for quick design of "custom" functions and typically results in a more compact circuit board.

Pin assignments in operating mode

switching characteristics over recommended supply voltage and operating free-air temperature ranges (unless otherwise noted)

PARAMETER	FROM	TO	TEST CONDITIONS	-12M			-10C			UNIT
				MIN	TYP[†]	MAX	MIN	TYP[†]	MAX	
f_{max}[‡]	With Feedback			48	80		55.5	80		MHz
	Without Feedback			56	85		62.5	85		
t_{pd}	I, I/O	O, I/O	R1 = 200 Ω,	3	7	12	3	7	10	ns
t_{pd}	CLK↑	Q	R₂ = 390 Ω,	2	5	10	2	5	8	ns
t_{en}	OE↓	Q	See Figure 1	1	4	10	1	4	10	ns
t_{dis}	OE↑	Q		1	4	10	1	4	10	ns
t_{en}	I, I/O	O, I/O		3	8	12	3	8	10	ns
t_{dis}	I, I/O	O, I/O		3	8	12	3	8	10	ns

[†] All typical values are at V_{CC} = 5 V, T_A = 25°C.

[‡] f_{max} (with feedback) = $\dfrac{1}{t_{su} + t_{pd} \text{ (CLK to Q)}}$, f_{max} (without feedback) = $\dfrac{1}{t_w \text{ high} + t_w \text{ low}}$

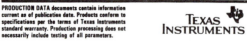

Figure 4.52: The PAL16R4/6/8 registered PALs. Courtesy of Texas Instruments Ltd.

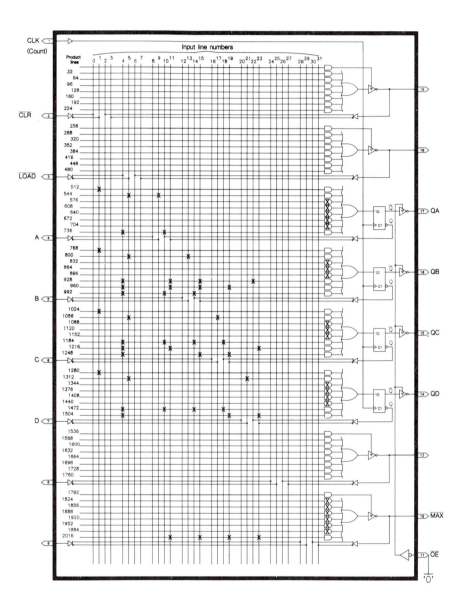

Figure 4.53: Using a PAL16R4 to implement a 2-4-2-1 counter.

this interchange into account. An equivalent technique is to assign the state codes as active-Low in the first place, i.e. $1111b \rightarrow 0000b$, and minimize on the basis of a 1s covering.

Providing a parallel load is simply a matter of using four inputs for the data and a fifth input as the $\overline{\text{Load}}$ control. This gives us:

$$
\begin{aligned}
\overline{D}_A &= (\text{Load} \cdot (Q_A)) + (\overline{\text{Load}} \cdot \overline{A}) \\
\overline{D}_B &= (\text{Load} \cdot (Q_B \cdot Q_A) + (\overline{Q}_C \cdot \overline{Q}_B \cdot \overline{Q}_A) + Q_D \cdot \overline{Q}_B \cdot \overline{Q}_A)) + (\overline{\text{Load}} \cdot \overline{B}) \\
\overline{D}_C &= (\text{Load} \cdot ((\overline{Q}_C \cdot \overline{Q}_B) + (\overline{Q}_D \cdot \overline{Q}_A))) + (\overline{\text{Load}} \cdot \overline{C}) \\
\overline{D}_D &= (\text{Load} \cdot ((\overline{Q}_D \cdot \overline{Q}_C) + (Q_C \cdot Q_B \cdot Q_A))) + (\overline{\text{Load}} \cdot \overline{D})
\end{aligned}
$$

where $\overline{\text{Load}}$ is used to switch between setting equation n and the appropriate parallel data line D_n thus:

$$
\overline{D}_n = (\text{Load} \cdot \text{equation } n) + (\overline{\text{Load}} \cdot \overline{n})
$$

The complement of the parallel input line n is used to compensate for the inverted output.

Finally, a sixth input is used for $\overline{\text{Clear}}$. By ORing the inverse of this input to all four equations above, i.e. $+\text{Clear}$, then all outcomes will go to logic 1 whenever $\overline{\text{Clear}}$ is Low. Thus on the next clock event all flip flop true outputs will also go High. Because of the series inverting buffers, external output signals go Low; that is clear. These are the equations directly implemented by the fuse plot of Fig. 4.53 in the manner shown in Section 3.3.3, where the **X**s indicate intact fuses. Notice that the outputs of all four flip flops are fed back in true and complement form into the AND matrix, in the same manner as the combinational outputs. Of course, this feedback is vital for sequential implementations. If this had to be done externally, valuable input resources would be used. The four feedback terms Q_D, Q_C, Q_B and Q_A are shown ANDed together to generate the state 9 ($1111b$) detector at the lower combinational output. Note again the interchange of Q_n & $\overline{Q}_n$ to give an active-High output.

Registered outputs cannot be used as alternative inputs in the manner of combinational equivalents, by disabling the 3-state buffer; thus all flip flop buffers are simply enabled in parallel from an external signal at pin 11.

The Texas Instruments registered PAL family feature a power-up clear facility, with all outputs going Low (all flip flops going High). However, this is not a universal feature and thus a machine's response to an illegal state must be checked. From Example 4.17 we see that all such states lead back to the legal sequence. Remember that illegal states can be entered due to noise or to race hazards as well as a consequence of power-up. For example, if $\overline{\text{Clear}}$ becomes inactive during the setup-hold time window around the active clock edge, some flip flops may respond, some may not and others may go metastable [25]

Example 4.23

As part of an electric game a double die of the format shown in Fig. 3.84, are to be 'rolled' when a switch is pushed [26]. Using a registered PAL, design a counter to give the appropriate 36 states, as shown in Fig. 4.54(a).

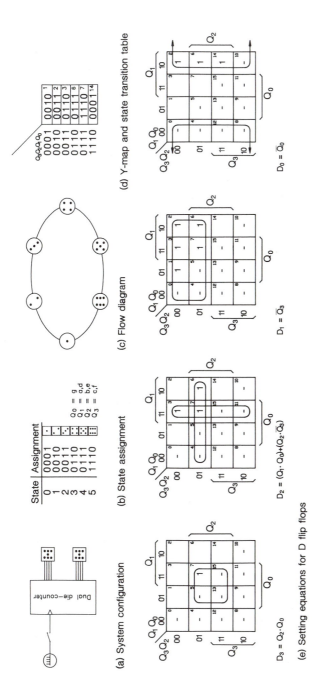

Figure 4.54: Design equations for a die counter.

Solution

Both halves of the die counter will be following the same sequence, so we begin our design by determining the setting equations for a single 6-state count.

We could implement a normal 6-state counter and design a combinational decoder to convert from natural binary to die code. However, this would use up scarce registered and combinational PAL outputs, and will thus require several packages in the implementation. Instead we will design the counter sequence to directly follow the die patterns. This approach does not require combinational-only PAL outputs, and thus a single PAL16R8 should be capable of driving the seven LED outputs. We can further reduce the logic by observing that there are really only four independent outputs as d always follows a, b = e and c = f. Thus the design has now been reduced to a 4-bit counter following the state assignment of Fig 4.54(b).

The flow diagram of Fig. 4.54(c) follows a classical counter's circular path leading directly to the Y-map of Fig. 4.54(d). Splitting this into its four components gives the K-maps and setting equations for the D flip flops:

$$\begin{aligned}
D_0 &= \overline{Q}_0 \\
D_1 &= \overline{Q}_3 \\
D_2 &= (Q_1 \cdot Q_0) + (Q_2 \cdot \overline{Q}_3) \\
D_3 &= Q_2 \cdot Q_0
\end{aligned}$$

As the PAL16R8 has eight flip flops, we should be able to incorporate both die counters in the one chip. To do this we must figure out how to cascade the counters, as the second counter should only advance once for each complete sequence of the first; but the clock is common to both counters. We can use the Q_3 output of the first counter as a carry-out, to enable the second group of setting equations; as conveniently Q_3 is only 1 once per cycle. Whenever Q_3 is 0, each of the counter's flip flops should be in a no-change or hold condition ($D_n = Q_n$). This gives:

$$\begin{aligned}
D_4 &= \overline{Q}_3 \cdot \{Q_4\} + Q_3 \cdot \{\overline{Q}_4\} \\
D_5 &= \overline{Q}_3 \cdot \{Q_5\} + Q_3 \cdot \{\overline{Q}_7\} \\
D_6 &= \overline{Q}_3 \cdot \{Q_6\} + Q_3 \cdot \{(Q_5 \cdot Q_4) + (Q_6 \cdot \overline{Q}_7)\} \\
D_7 &= \overline{Q}_3 \cdot \{Q_7\} + Q_3 \cdot \{Q_6 \cdot Q_4\}
\end{aligned}$$

The first component of each equation is the hold term. If Q_3 is 0 then we have $D_n = Q_n$, which defines a no change situation. Where Q_3 is 1 then the hold component is 0 and we have D_n = setting equation n. These setting equations are the same as the first set, but with the subscripts advanced by four, eg. $Q_0 \rightarrow Q_4$

The final implementation is shown in Fig. 4.55. As a practical consideration the oscillator should be around 50 kHz to ensure a proper 'throw'. The series switch, which should have a pull-up, will add to the uncertainty with a component of bounce.

The minimization shown in Fig. 4.54(e) is based on a ones covering. I have assumed that the die LEDs light on a Low, as generated by the inverting buffers. A zeros covering should be used for an active-High LED arrangement, interchanging Q_n & $\overline{Q}_n$.

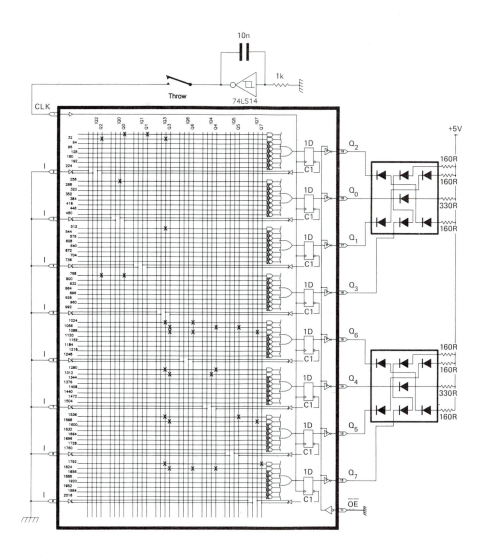

Figure 4.55: A PAL16R8-based double-die counter.

A zeros covering should be used for an active-High LED arrangement, interchanging Q_n & $\overline{Q}_n$.

The reader should confirm that our implementation will always return to the correct sequence if the machine should find itself in one of the ten illegal states.

Example 4.24

Design a PAL-based sequential circuit to act as a serial magnitude comparator. The two programmable inputs $X_1 X_0$ are to be fed with words 1 and 2 respectively, MSB first, in synchronism with the clock. There are to be three active-High outputs, $Z_1 Z_2 Z_3$ respectively, indicating equality (word 1 = word 2), greater than (word 1 > word 2) and less than (word 1 < word 2).

Solution

Unlike all our previous examples, this sequential machine is definitely not a counter. However, if we consider a programmable counter a special case of a machine, the sequence of which can be controlled by external signals, then we can use the same techniques for the solution of this problem.

Our first task is to draw the flow diagram of Fig. 4.56(b). We can assume that there are three states, **Equal**, **Greater** and **Less**. As long as $X_1 = X_2$ the circuit remains in the **Equal** state. If at any time X_1 is 1 and X_2 is 0 then the next active edge moves the circuit to the **Greater** state. This is a dead-end state, as once entered the lesser word bits cannot alter the decision $W_1 > W_2$. If the pattern $X_1 X_2 = 01$ should occur *first*, then the dead-end **Less** state is entered instead, indicating the condition $W_1 < W_2$. Each of the three states are labelled with the state number/outputs. Thus 2/001 means state 2 with output $Z_1 Z_2 Z_3 = 001$, that is $Z_3 = 1$ for <. A machine where the outputs only depend on the state (i.e. independent of the programmable inputs) is called a **Moore machine** [28]. Where the outputs are dependent on both state and inputs, for example in Fig. 4.67, is known as a **Mealy machine** [27].

If we assign the normal binary code to the three states, then the resulting Y-map of Fig. 4.56(b) can be split into the two K-maps in the normal way. In minimizing the logic, I have not included the four can't-happen don't-care states. Thus, for example, we have $D_B = Q_B \cdot \overline{Q}_A + (\overline{Q}_A \cdot \overline{X}_1 \cdot X_2)$ instead of $D_B = Q_B + (\overline{Q}_A \cdot \overline{X}_1 \cdot X_2)$. If the 'best' solution were picked, then entry to illegal state $11b$ would mean that both $D_B D_A$ are $11b$ and the system would stick in this state. The equations used ensure that if the machine strays off the beaten path, it will always return to state $00b$.

We should now proceed to minimize the logic for the three output variables, the so-called Z logic. However, there are only two state variables involved, so by inspection we can write:

$$\overline{Z}_1 = Q_A + Q_B \quad \text{Equal}$$
$$\overline{Z}_2 = \overline{Q}_A \quad\quad\quad \text{Greater}$$
$$\overline{Z}_3 = \overline{Q}_B \quad\quad\quad \text{Less}$$

where I have generated complements to cancel the inverting output buffers. More complex output situations can use K-maps in the normal way, although these are

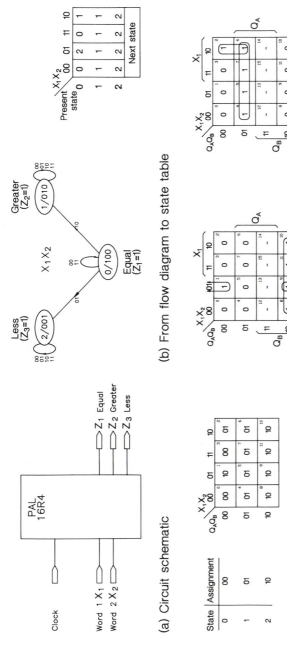

(a) Circuit schematic

(b) From flow diagram to state table

(c) From Y-map to the setting equations

Figure 4.56: A serial magnitude comparator.

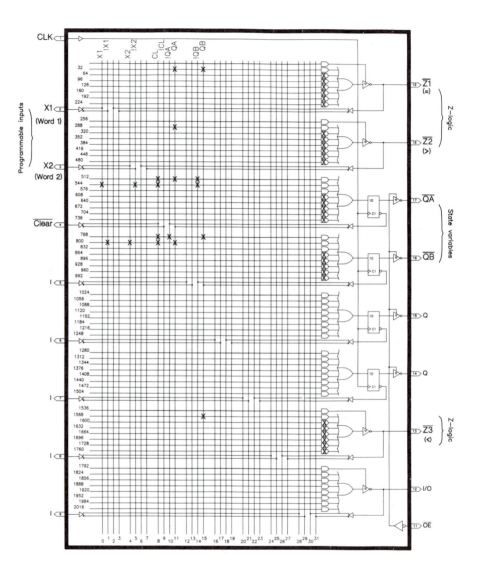

Figure 4.57: A PAL16R4-based serial magnitude comparator.

often called Z-maps. Machines where the outputs are a function of both state variables and programmable inputs (i.e. Mealy machines) demand more of the Z logic.

The implementation of Fig. 4.57 incorporates a synchronous clearing facility, which operates by ORing each flip flop's setting equation with CLR. This is identical to that provided for the counter of Example 4.22. Obviously some such facility is necessary, as both final states are dead-end! A synchronous clear by definition requires an extra clock pulse, which may not be convenient in practice. It is in areas like this, for example a lack of polarity programming, fixed sequential and combinational logic outputs, where simple registered PALs begin to show their limitations.

There have been many developments since medium architecture PALs (i.e. 16x8 and 20x8 families) were introduced. The first of these new-generation devices was the PAL22V10, shown in Fig 4.47 [29]. From the logic diagram we see that the familiar programmable AND fixed OR matrix structure has been retained. There are ten OR gates fed by a variable number of product terms, ranging from 8 to sixteen. Most design equations do not require the same complexity across the range, and this variable distribution efficiently supports this situation. There are a total of 5388 fuses in this package and a complexity of around 500–800 gates.

A feature common to all the versatile PAL family (VPAL) is the **output logic macro cell, OLMC**. This is a development of the single-fuse polarity selection cell used in combinational PALs, such as the PAL18P8 of Fig. 3.66. In the OLMC used in the PAL22V10, there are two selection fuses, labelled S0 and sf S1 in Fig. 4.59. These fuses give four independent optional configurations for each output as follows:

Cell Select S1 S0	Feedback and output configuration		
0 0	Register feedback	Registered	Active Low
0 1	Register feedback	Registered	Active High
1 0	I/O feedback	Combinational	Active Low
1 1	I/O feedback	Combinational	Active High

We see from the table and Fig. 4.59 that fuse S1 essentially selects between a combinational or sequential output. This is done by using a multiplexer to feed through the OR gate directly or the output of the D flip flop. S1 simultaneous gates through the combinational or flip flop output back into the AND matrix as appropriate to the combinational/sequential mode. In the former case an output can be assigned as an input variable by programming the 3-state buffer as Off, as described in Fig. 3.22. Fuse S0 acts as a polarity selector in either combinational or sequential mode.

From the logic diagram we see that the clock input CLK is dual purpose, acting as a normal combinational input I into the AND matrix. In some more advanced PALs, such as the PAL20RA10, each clock is driven asynchronously from its own local AND gate. This would have been useful in Example 4.23 where the output of the first stage could have been used to generate the clock for the second.

TICPAL22V10M, TICPAL22V10C
EPIC™ CMOS PROGRAMMABLE ARRAY LOGIC

D3089, DECEMBER 1987

- 24-Pin Advanced CMOS PAL
- Virtually Zero Standby Power
- Propagation Delay Time . . . 20 ns Typ
- Variable Product Term Distribution Allows More Complex Functions to be Implemented
- Each Output is User-Programmable for Registered or Combinatorial Operation, Polarity, and Output Enable Control
- Extra Terms Provide Logical Synchronous Set and Asynchronous Reset Capability
- Preload Capability on All Registered Outputs Allow for Improved Device Testing
- Power-Up Clear on Registered Outputs
- UV Light Erasable Cell Technology Allows for:
  Reconfigurable Logic
  Reprogrammable Cells
  Full Factory Testing for
  Guaranteed 100% Yields
- Programmable Design Security Bit Prevents Copying of Logic Stored in Device
- Package Options Include Plastic and Ceramic Dual-In-Line Packages and Chip Carriers

JL PACKAGE
(TOP VIEW)

```
          ┌──┬──┐
CLK/I  [ 1   24 ]  Vcc
   I   [ 2   23 ]  I/O/Q
   I   [ 3   22 ]  I/O/Q
   I   [ 4   21 ]  I/O/Q
   I   [ 5   20 ]  I/O/Q
   I   [ 6   19 ]  I/O/Q
   I   [ 7   18 ]  I/O/Q
   I   [ 8   17 ]  I/O/Q
   I   [ 9   16 ]  I/O/Q
   I   [10   15 ]  I/O/Q
   I   [11   14 ]  I/O/Q
 GND   [12   13 ]  I
          └─────┘
```

description

This PAL device features high-speed performance, increased and variable product terms, flexible outputs, and virtually zero standby power. It combines TI's EPIC™ (Enhanced Processed Implanted CMOS) process with ultraviolet-light-erasable EPROM technology. Each output has an OLM (Output Logic Macrocell) configuration allowing for user definition of the output type. This PAL provides reliable, low-power substitutes for numerous high-performance TTL PALs with gate complexities between 300 and 800 gates.

The 'PAL22V10 has 12 dedicated inputs and ten user-definable outputs. Individual outputs can be programmed as registered or combinational and inverting or noninverting as shown in the Output Logic Macrocell (OLM) diagram. These ten outputs are enabled through the use of individual product terms.

The variable product-term distribution on this device removes rigid limitation to a maximum of eight product terms per output. This technique allocates from 8 to 16 logical product terms to each output for an average of 12 product terms per output. The variable allocation of product terms allows for far more complex functions to be implemented in this device than in previously available devices.

With features such as the programmable OLMs and the variable product-term distribution, the TICPAL22V10-25 offers quick design and development of custom LSI functions. Since each of the ten output pins may be individually configured as inputs on either a temporary or permanent basis, functions requiring up to 21 inputs and a single output or down to 12 inputs and 10 outputs can be implemented with this device.

EPIC is a trademark of Texas Instruments Incorporated.

Figure 4.58: Extract from the PAL 22V10 data sheet (*continued next page*).

logic diagram (positive logic)

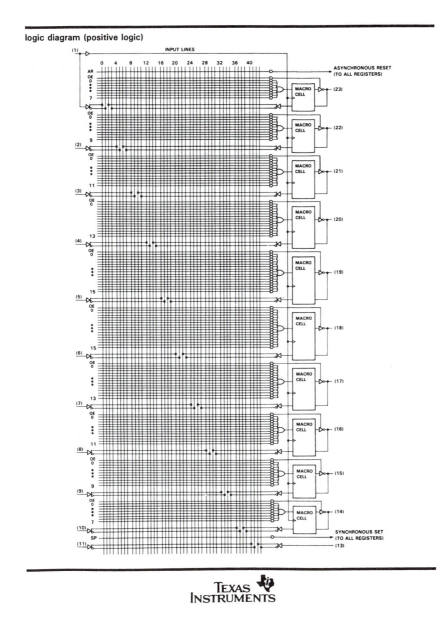

Figure 4.58: (*continued*). Extract from the PAL22V10 data sheet. Courtesy of Texas Instruments Ltd.

output logic macrocell diagram

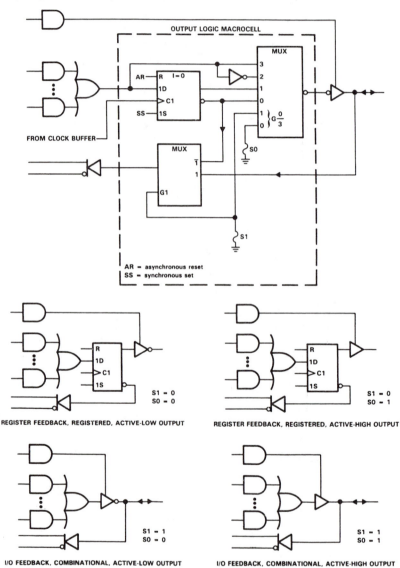

Figure 4.59: The PAL 22V10 output logic macro cell. Courtesy of Texas Instruments Ltd.

All ten flip flops in the PAL22V10 may be asynchronously reset as an AND function of the input variables, see top right of Fig. 4.57. Similarly a single AND gate (bottom right) drives each flip flop's synchronous set input. All flip flops are automatically reset on power-up.

Most higher-complexity PALs have a special test mode which enables each flip flop to be individually preset at any arbitrary state. In the PAL22V10 this is typically accomplished by raising pin 13 to 10.5 V, applying the state pattern to the outputs and clocking the device. Removing the impressed output voltages and lowering pin 13 to its normal input logic level enables the PAL to progress normally from this state.

Designation	Dedicated inputs	Registered feedback lines	Combinational input/output	Flip flops	Frequency min (MHz)
Programmable array logic devices (PAL)					
16R4	8	4	4	4D	16–115
16R6	8	6	2	6D	16–115
16R8	8	8	0	8D	16–115
20R4	12	4	4	4D	15–115
20R6	12	6	2	6D	16–115
20R8	12	8	0	8D	16–115
16V8	8	8^1	8^1	8D	13–55
20V8	12	8^1	8^1	8D	13–55
22V10	11	10^1	10^1	10D	16–87
39V18	10	18^1	10^1	10D	14
Programmable logic sequencers (PLS)					
105	16	6^2	8^3	14RS	$14–55^4$
167	14	8^2	4^3	12RS	$14–50^4$
168	12	10^2	4^3	14RS	$14–20^4$
155	4	4	8	$4JK^5$	14
157	4	4	6	$6JK^5$	14
179	8	8	4	$8JK^5$	18

1: Outputs are programmable either as combinational or registered.
2: Some or all are buried
3: Through a register
4: Slower if complement array used
5: Can be programmed as JK, D or T types

Table 4.5: A selection of registered PALs and PLSs.

Despite the introduction of more sophisticated PALs, the 16x8 and 20x8 families remain the most popular and economical. They are the first to be implemented in new techniques, such as 5 ns parts. In an attempt to capitalize on this, the Lattice Semiconductor Corp. introduced its **generic array logic (GAL)** family in 1985 [30, 31]. The 16V8 and 20V8 devices were designed to replace all the 16, 18 and 20L, H and P PALs and also most of the earlier small PALs, such as the 12H6 of Fig. 3.63.

The core of these devices is the standard PAL matrix with eight programmable AND gates feeding eight fixed output OR gates. Each output is driven via a

In this manner each output can be configured as active-High or -Low, registered or combinational and feed back into the matrix or not. Certain combinations allow the 'output' to be used as an input in the usual manner. Like the PAL22V10, the GAL family support a special preload test mode.

The GAL family use electrically erasable CMOS technologies and thus are reusable. They can be quickly erased without exposure to U.V. radiation and have the typical CMOS low standby power consumption. Programmable logic devices (PLDs) using this technology are generically known as EEPLDs, as opposed to U.V. erasable types (see Fig. 3.7) which are classified as EPLDs.

4.6   Problems

4.6.1   Worked Examples

Example 4.25

The circuit shown in Fig. 4.25(a) is described as a 3-state flip flop in reference [32]. Use a Y-map to justify this description.

Solution

The open-loop equivalent is shown in Fig. 4.60(b). The corresponding Y-map shows in the normal way, the state of the three outputs $Y_1 Y_2 Y_3$ as a function of the six input variables $X_1 X_2 X_3$ and $y_1 y_2 y_3$. Applying the constraints $y = Y$ then gives ten stable states.

From the Y-map of Fig. 4.60(c) we see that if *only* one input is active, i.e. logic 0, then one output will also go to logic 0. Thus, when $X_1 = 0$ then $Y_3 \rightarrow 0$. If the active X input now returns to logic 1, the set output remains unchanged; as shown by the transitions on the map. Should more than one input be activated, all outputs go to logic 1. If the inputs are then removed, the system will end up in one of three stable end states in the column $X_1 X_2 X_3 = 111$; depending on the sequence of changes of X, propagation delays or the outcome of a metastable condition.

In summary, there are three outputs, each of which can be reset by one of three inputs. A new set condition cancels the previous state. The circuit is then a 3-state latch (the term flip flop being a misnomer).

Example 4.26

We have seen that the cross-coupled NOR circuit of Fig. 4.2 can detect which of its two inputs $X_1 X_2$ goes to logic 0 initially in going from $11 \rightarrow 00$. Using three of these 'queuing' circuits, with additional logic, design a circuit to drive the indicator matrix of Fig. 4.61(a). This indicator records the sequence of the arrival of three active-Low signals A, B and C; eg. requests for access to a printer from three computers. If, say, request C arrives first, followed by A, then B; lamps C1, A2, B3 should light.

Solution

From the Y-map of Fig. 4.2, we see that no request ($X_1 X_2 = 11$) gives both outputs $Y_1 Y_2 = 00$. If X_1 goes to 0 first then Y_1 goes to 1 ($X_1 X_2 = 11 \rightarrow 01 \rightarrow 00$,

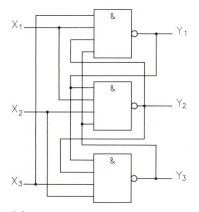

(a) Flip flop circuit

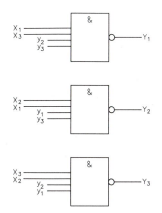

(b) Open-loop equivalent

$y_1 y_2 y_3$ \ $X_1 X_2 X_3$	000	001	011	010	110	111	101	100
000	111	111	111	111	111	111	111	111
001	111	111	111	111	111	111	111	111
011	111	111	111	111	111	(011)	(011)	111
010	111	111	111	111	111	111	111	111
110	111	111	(110)	111	111	(110)	111	111
111	(111)	(111)	110	(111)	101	000	011	(111)
101	111	111	111	111	(101)	(101)	111	111
100	111	111	111	111	111	111	111	111

IF X_1 alone goes to 0 THEN output $Y_3 = 0$
IF X_1 now returns to 1 THEN output remains unchanged.
IF X_2 alone goes to 0 THEN output $Y_1 = 0$
IF X_2 now returns to 1 THEN output remains unchanged.
IF X_3 alone goes to 0 THEN output $Y_1 = 0$
IF X_3 now returns to 1 THEN output remains unchanged.

(c) Y-map

Figure 4.60: Analysis of the 3-state flip flop.

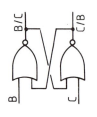

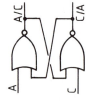

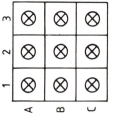

(a) Indicator matrix.

(b) Queuing elements.

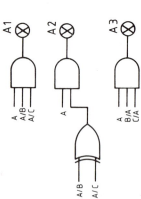

(c) Indicator bulb decoders.

Figure 4.61: A 3-terminal priority circuit.

Solution

From the Y-map of Fig. 4.2, we see that no request ($X_1 X_2 = 11$) gives both outputs $Y_1 Y_2 = 00$. If X_1 goes to 0 first then Y_1 goes to 1 ($X_1 X_2 = 11 \rightarrow 01 \rightarrow 00$, cell $\boxed{3} \rightarrow \boxed{9} \rightarrow \boxed{8}$). Similarly, the arrival of X_2 first sends Y_2 to 1 ($X_1 X_2 = 11 \rightarrow 10 \rightarrow 00$, cells $\boxed{3} \rightarrow \boxed{6} \rightarrow \boxed{4}$). Thus, in this context Y_1 can be labelled X_1/X_2 (X_1 before X_2) and $Y_2 = X_2/X_1$. Using three of these circuits labelled as shown in Fig. 4.61(b) gives all the queuing information needed.

The decoding relationships for the nine indicators are deduced as follows. For the A lights we have: A1 lit if A is present AND A before B AND A before C, i.e. $A \cdot (A/B) \cdot (A/C)$. A2 lights if A is present AND A arrives before B OR A arrives before C but not both, i.e. $A \cdot (A/B \oplus A/C)$. Also A3 is true where A is present and A arrives after both B AND C; giving $A \cdot (B/C) \cdot (C/A)$. Similarly for the other indicators we have:

$$B1 = B \cdot (B/C) \cdot (B/C) \qquad B2 = B \cdot (B/A \oplus B/C) \qquad B3 = B \cdot (A/B) \cdot (C/B)$$
$$C1 = C \cdot (C/A) \cdot (C/B) \qquad C2 = C \cdot (C/A \oplus C/B) \qquad C3 = C \cdot (A/C) \cdot (B/C)$$

Two points arise from this solution. If a request is removed (i.e. because a computer has completed its print run), the indicator matrix will adjust accordingly. A new request from the same source will be placed last in the queue. Secondly, a similar implementation can be made by using cross-coupled NANDs. The requests will then be active-High, with active-Low outputs.

Example 4.27

Mechanical switches are frequently used as inputs to logic circuits. However, most metallic contacts will exhibit the property of bounce. This occurs when the switch blade traverses from one contact to another, bouncing off the destination contact many times before setting [33]. Thus, for up to around 30 ms a series of rapid makes and breaks will occur. Although mechanically rapid, to electronic logic circuits these spurious pulses are of long duration and may cause erroneous behavior. Hence, for example, using a mechanical switch to clock a counter will give entirely unpredictable results.

One proposal to 'clean up' a mechanical switch is shown in Fig. 4.62(a). The switch is a single-pole double-throw (SPDT) device which breaks before make, and is guaranteed not to bounce all the way back to the broken-from contact. How does it work?

Solution

When the switch is up, contact A is Low ($\overline{S} = L$) and contact B High ($\overline{R} = H$). Thus the output is set High. When the switch is thrown down, it first breaks with contact A, as shown in the diagram. Now the both contacts are pulled High through the resistors, giving $\overline{R}\,\overline{S} = 11$, which is the no-change situation. Eventually the switch will make contact with B giving $\overline{R}\,\overline{S} = 01$ and the output will reset Low. If the switch now bounces off, then $\overline{R}\,\overline{S}$ will take the no-change state $= 11$ and the output remains Low, no matter how many bounces happen. By symmetry, the same process occurs when the switch is lifted to contact A.

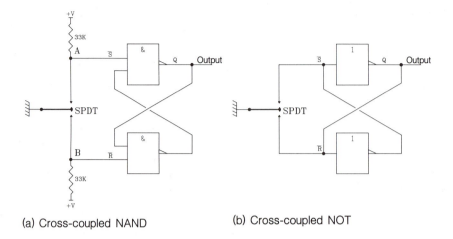

(a) Cross-coupled NAND   (b) Cross-coupled NOT

Figure 4.62: A proposed switch debouncer.

A similar arrangement is shown in Fig. 4.62(b), using inverters and not requiring pull-up resistors. Can you analyze this circuit?

Both circuits shown require change-over switches. Single-pole single-throw (SPST) switches have only two contacts and cannot be debounced using latches. References [34, 35] gives some techniques suitable for this type of switch.

Example 4.28

The toggle algorithm used to convert Gray code to natural binary was discussed as part of Example 1.13. A slightly modified version is given below:

1. Make the MSB of the binary equivalent provisionally logic 0.

2. If the MSB of the Gray-coded word is logic 1 then toggle the binary equivalent, else leave unchanged.

3. For each following Gray bit, generate the correct binary bit by toggling the previous outcome if $G_n = 1$, else leave unchanged.

Can you design a synchronous circuit, accepting a serial Gray-coded input MSB first and outputting the binary equivalent in series?

Solution

Figure 4.18 shows a D flip flop used to implement a T flip flop. If the input is logic 1 whenever the D flip flop is clocked, then the output will toggle, otherwise no change will occur. If we clear the flip flop before the conversion begins, then we have a direct implementation of the toggle algorithm.

Typically the n-bit Gray word will be parallel loaded into a shift register, at the same time clearing the T flip flop. The shift register clock and flip flop clocks are common. The binary output is also stored in a shift register, which may be the same register as held the original Gray number. A dead-end counter is used to count the n clock pulses to end of conversion. The final configuration is then that of the serial adder of Fig. 4.49, but with the 1-bit adder/carry flip flop replaced by the toggle-connected D flip flop.

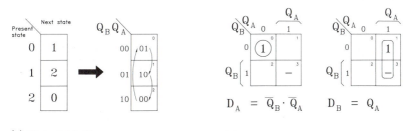

(a) State table/Y-map   (b) Setting equations

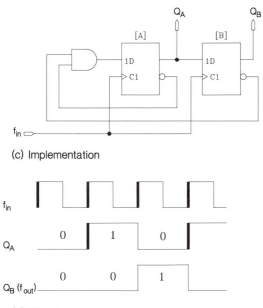

(c) Implementation

(d) Waveforms

Figure 4.63: A synchronous modulo-3 counter.

Example 4.29

Part of the front end of an ASIC-based frequency divider is to be a $\div 3$ stage. Design a suitable implementation based on D flip flops; sketch the output waveform from this stage, and determine the response of the circuit if an illegal state is entered on power-up.

Solution

This is a simple circular count specification, giving the Y-map of Fig. 4.63(a) with the three states assigned the natural binary code. As I am using D flip flops, the K-maps follow directly by splitting the Y-map in two.

The waveform diagram is generated by showing the three states advancing as synchronized by the rising edge of the clock. Notice that the frequency of Q_B is $\frac{1}{3}$ that of the clock input.

Should the counter enter illegal state $11b$, then cell 3 in the K-maps point to $D_B D_A = 10$ (state 2) on the next active clock edge. Thus the counter is self correcting.

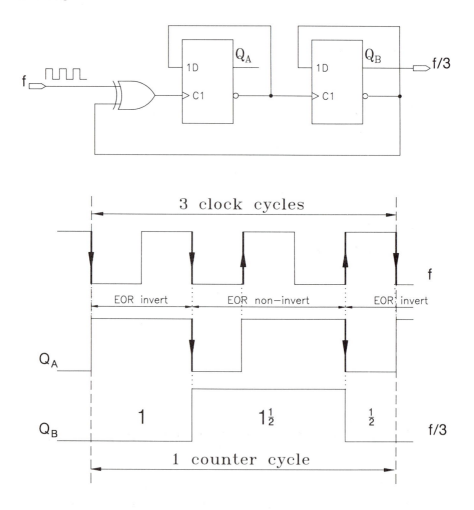

Figure 4.64: A symmetrical ÷3 frequency divider.

Example 4.30

Although the counter in the last example divided the incoming frequency by three, the mark:space ratio was 1:2 (see Fig. 4.63(d)). The circuit shown in Fig. 4.64(a) claims to be a $\div 3$ circuit which gives a square waveform, i.e. 1:1 mark:space ratio [36]. Analyze the circuit and show that this is so.

Solution

This is actually a 2-bit ripple counter implemented using toggling D flip flops. Its novelty lies in the EOR gate which effectively controls the active clock edge of flip flop A. If Q_B is logic 0, the EOR gate will act to invert the count input, giving a ‾__ -edge trigger for flip flop A. Conversely, with Q_B at logic 1, the EOR gate does not invert, giving a __/‾ -edge trigger for A.

On the basis of this, we derive the sequence table of Fig. 4.64(b), which shows all four binary codes. The corresponding waveform diagram was generated by toggling A on two ‾__ clock edges followed by two __/‾ clock edges. Flip flop B always triggers on Q_A ‾__ , giving the final output, which on inspection is seen to be square. However, the author of this circuit has made a fundamental assumption in advertising the circuit as having a mark:space ratio of 1:1. Can you determine what it is?

Every time the phase of the incoming frequency is altered, the counter loses $\frac{1}{2}$ a clock cycle. Thus the inherently 4-state ripple counter becomes $4 - \frac{1}{2} - \frac{1}{2} = 3$-state. As the loss occurs equally when Q_B goes $0 \to 1$ and $1 \to 0$, the inherently 2:2 output waveform becomes $1\frac{1}{2} : 1\frac{1}{2}$. Can you generalize this to give a symmetrical $\div k$ counter, where k is $2^n - 1$; for example, a $\div 7$ divider.

Example 4.31

Using a PLE/ROM in conjunction with a D flip flop array, design a 4-bit programmable synchronous counter which will count in natural binary when X is zero and in Gray code when X is one.

Solution

With each state coded in natural binary, the resulting flow diagram is shown in Fig. 4.65(a). This leads in the normal way to the Y-map, which when unrolled gives the personality table for the PLE/ROM. The implementation is shown in Table 4.6.

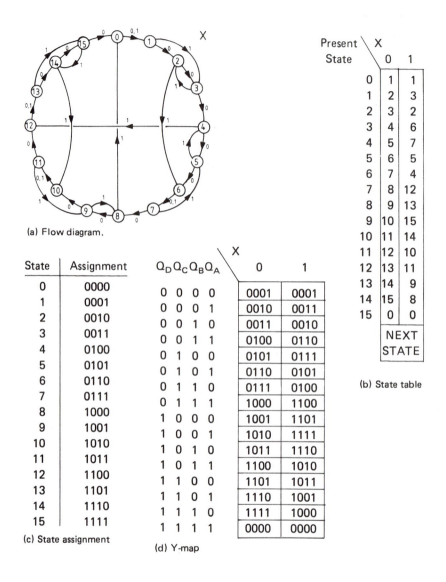

(a) Flow diagram.

State	Assignment
0	0000
1	0001
2	0010
3	0011
4	0100
5	0101
6	0110
7	0111
8	1000
9	1001
10	1010
11	1011
12	1100
13	1101
14	1110
15	1111

(c) State assignment

Present State	X 0	1
0	1	1
1	2	3
2	3	2
3	4	6
4	5	7
5	6	5
6	7	4
7	8	12
8	9	13
9	10	15
10	11	14
11	12	10
12	13	11
13	14	9
14	15	8
15	0	0
	NEXT	STATE

(b) State table

$Q_D Q_C Q_B Q_A$	X 0	1
0 0 0 0	0001	0001
0 0 0 1	0010	0011
0 0 1 0	0011	0010
0 0 1 1	0100	0110
0 1 0 0	0101	0111
0 1 0 1	0110	0101
0 1 1 0	0111	0100
0 1 1 1	1000	1100
1 0 0 0	1001	1101
1 0 0 1	1010	1111
1 0 1 0	1011	1110
1 0 1 1	1100	1010
1 1 0 0	1101	1011
1 1 0 1	1110	1001
1 1 1 0	1111	1000
1 1 1 1	0000	0000

(d) Y-map

Figure 4.65: A programmable binary/Gray-coded counter.

ROM Address					ROM Data			
Q_D	Q_C	Q_B	Q_A	X	D_3	D_2	D_1	D_0
a_4	a_3	a_2	a_1	a_0	d_3	d_2	d_1	d_0
0	0	0	0	0	0	0	0	1
0	0	0	0	1	0	0	0	1
0	0	0	1	0	0	0	1	0
0	0	0	1	1	0	0	1	1
0	0	1	0	0	0	0	1	1
0	0	1	0	1	0	0	1	0
0	0	1	1	0	0	1	0	0
0	0	1	1	1	0	1	1	0
0	1	0	0	0	0	1	0	1
0	1	0	0	1	0	1	1	1
0	1	0	1	0	0	1	1	0
0	1	0	1	1	0	1	0	1
0	1	1	0	0	0	1	1	1
0	1	1	0	1	0	1	0	0
0	1	1	1	0	1	0	0	0
0	1	1	1	1	1	1	0	0
1	0	0	0	0	1	0	0	1
1	0	0	0	1	1	1	0	1
1	0	0	1	0	1	0	1	0
1	0	0	1	1	1	1	1	1
1	0	1	0	0	1	0	1	1
1	0	1	0	1	1	1	1	0
1	0	1	1	0	1	1	0	0
1	0	1	1	1	1	0	1	0
1	1	0	0	0	1	1	0	1
1	1	0	0	1	1	0	1	1
1	1	0	1	0	1	1	1	0
1	1	0	1	1	1	0	0	1
1	1	1	0	0	1	1	1	1
1	1	1	0	1	1	0	0	0
1	1	1	1	0	0	0	0	0
1	1	1	1	1	0	0	0	0

Table 4.6: PLE/ROM personality table for a programmable binary/Gray counter.

Example 4.32

Using J K flip flops and gates (see also Example 6.6), design a synchronous sequential machine which will detect in which direction a car is passing along a constricted roadway into a car park. Two light beams are placed across the path of the car, spaced at less than one car length. These sensors, labelled $X_1 X_2$ in Fig. 4.66(a), give logic 0 when unbroken and logic 1 when the beam is cut, and provide the programmable inputs to the system. It is assumed that owing to the narrowness of the path, cars can pass in only one direction at a time past the sensors.

Two outputs are to be provided. Z_1 goes to logic 1 if the car is going into the car park and conversely Z_2 indicates an outgoing car.

Solution

As always, the first task is to draw the flow diagram, which is shown in Fig. 4.66(b). We define three states; a rest condition (state 0), an ingoing situation (state 1) and an outgoing situation (state 2).

Let us take an incoming car first. The initial action of such a car is to break beam X_1, which is shown as a transition from state 0 to state 1. As long as this situation persists, the circuit remains in state 1, as shown by the sling 10/00 ($X_1 X_2 = 10$ giving $Z_1 Z_2 = 00$). Z_1 remains logic 0, as it is possible that the beam has been broken by a pedestrian walking by. In this latter case, the beam becomes unbroken and the flow diagram shows a transition back to the rest state, hence ignoring the false alarm. However, in the normal course of events, the second beam will be interrupted after a short duration. This event ($X_1 X_2 = 11$) when in state 1 brings Z_1 to logic 1 — the car is definitely going in (sling 11/10). As the car proceeds further, the first beam is re-established. The circuit remains in state 1 when this happens, but Z_1 drops back to logic 0 (sling 01/00). The system finally returns to the rest state when both beams are unbroken. Repeating this process of deduction for an outgoing car completes the flow diagram. This type of notation $X_1 X_2/Z_1 Z_2$ is indicative of a Mealy model [27], where the output depends not only on the present state, but also on the value of programmable input. Contrast this with a Moore machine [28] (e.g. see Example 4.24), where the output is only dependent on the present state, irrespective of the value of the X inputs.

With the flow diagram as the starting point, we progress from the state table, state assignment to the Y-map, as shown in Fig. 4.66(c). Using the J K transition table gives the K-maps defining the four setting equations for the two flip flops. Notice that the situation where X_1 and X_2 are simultaneously broken when in the rest state is not specified; cell 3 in the Y-map. Examining the corresponding cell 3 in the K-maps shows that the circuit will return to the rest state when both beams are reinstated.

The final step is to determine the decoding equations for $Z_1 Z_2$. The Z-map of Fig. 4.66(e) shows these outputs as a function of inputs $X_1 X_2 Q_A Q_B$ (the system's total state). Splitting the Z-maps into two K-maps yields the requisite equations, which gives the implementation of Fig. 4.66(f). Note that the sampling rate, i.e. clock frequency, must be such that no change in the car position will be missed. In the unlikely event of a simultaneous breaking of both beams, our use of can't happen don't care states to minimize the Z logic means that spurious outputs will occur.

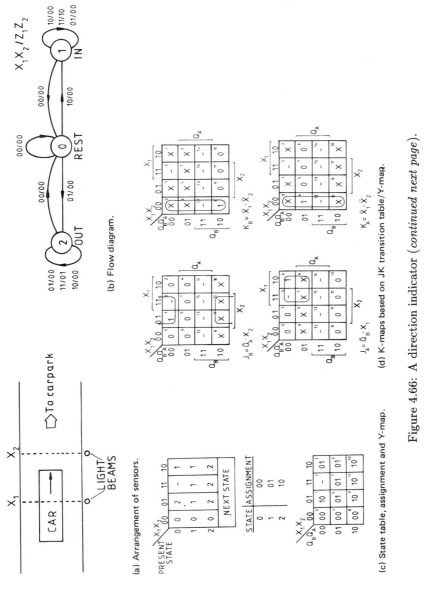

(a) Arrangement of sensors.

(b) Flow diagram.

(c) State table, assignment and Y-map.

(d) K-maps based on JK transition table/Y-map.

Figure 4.66: A direction indicator (*continued next page*).

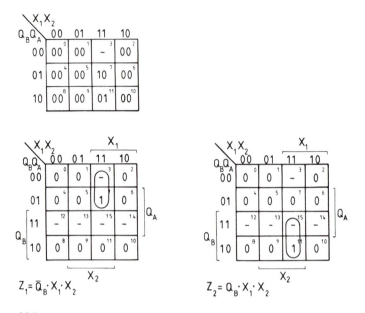

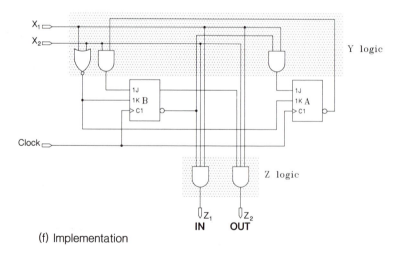

(e) Z-map showing the decoder outputs for each total state of the circuit; and resulting K-maps for Z_1 and Z_2.

(f) Implementation

Figure 4.66: (*continued*). A direction indicator.

This can be avoided by excluding these states from the grouping sets.

Example 4.33

Integrate as much as possible of the logic of the pedestrian controlled crossing light system, specified in Example 3.12, into a single PLS168 sequential PLA.

Solution

First we need to discuss the architecture of the PLS168 device, as shown in Fig. 4.67 (ignore the programming **X**s) [37, 38, 39]. Like the sequential PALs discussed in Section 4.5, a classical AND-OR matrix is integrated with an array of flip flops. This time both AND and OR gates are programmable, and thus the circuit is a sequential PLA. This architecture is usually given the acronym **PLS** for **programmable logic sequencer**. The OR-gates drive an array of 14 $\_\_\overline{}$ -triggered RS flip flops. These can be divided into two groups. Flip flops $P_9 \ldots P_0$ hold the present P state, and feed back into the AND-OR matrix in the classical sequential configuration (see Fig. 4.28). The four flip flops $F_3 \ldots F_0$ do not have any feedback connections and are used for the output function F. There is no provision for a direct combinational output, instead the F OR gates can be considered as performing this role (the Z logic), but with the output appearing delayed by one clock period. State flip flops $P_3 \ldots P_0$ are accessible to the outside world (pins 16... 13), and can if necessary be used to give additional outputs, typically at the expense of state variables. $P_9 \ldots P_4$ are known as buried flip flops as they are not accessible and therefore do not use any output resources. All flip flops are preset to 1 during power turn-on. They may optionally be asynchronously preset from pin 17, which alternatively acts (by default) as an enable for the output 3-state buffers.

The AND matrix generates 48 product terms of twelve external inputs $I_{11} \ldots I_0$, together with feedback from the ten state flip flops. Twenty eight OR gates drive the 14 R and S flip flop inputs. These sum any combination of the 48 AND terms, any of which may be shared in the normal PLA way. One extra OR gate, labelled C in the diagram, feeds the complement of a single su, of any of the product terms back into the AND matrix. Its function is discussed later. The total circuit complexity is 3361 fuses.

From the sequence table of Fig. 3.36 we require a 10-state machine with four active-Low outputs; $\overline{G}$ for the green traffic light, $\overline{A}$ for amber, $\overline{R}$ for red and $\overline{F}$ for flashing amber. If we assume that the machine is clocked at 3 s intervals to give the required timing, then an additional 30 null states can be used to give a total cycle time of 40×3 s, thus obviating the use of the external 2 minute monostable. This still leaves the request flag (latch) and flashing amber/amber combinational logic. The following example uses a PAL for this purpose and also to divide down the 0.5 Hz flashing clock to give the 3 s PLS drive. The flow diagram of Fig. 4.68 shows the 40 machine states, with delay states 10–39 lumped together. Each individual state shows the path taken for both values of the Crossing_Request signal Req. in the case of state 0, the sling indicates no change as long as Req = 0, and a move to state 1 on the first occurrence of Req = 1. Thereafter the progression through the cycle is independent of this variable. We will use the Flashing_Amber signal; F to cancel the request latch in the next example.

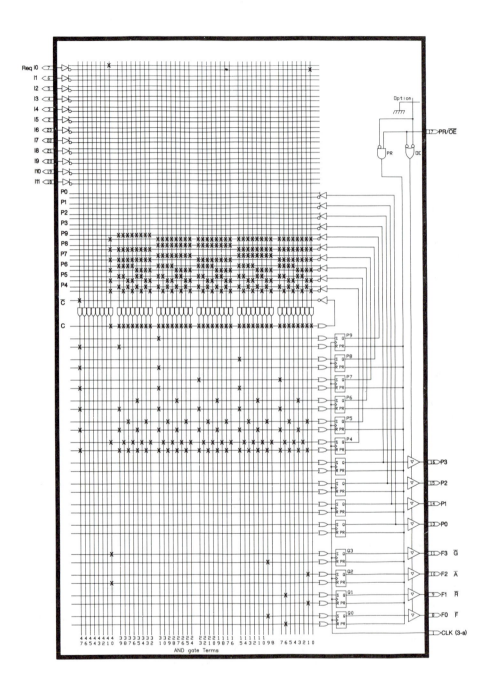

Figure 4.67: Logic diagram of the PLS168.

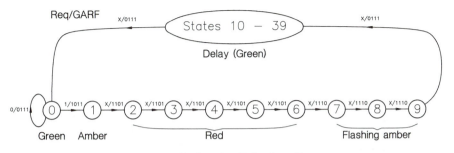

Figure 4.68: Pedestrian-light flow diagram.

Shown alongside each transition is the value that the four outputs $\overline{G}\,\overline{A}\,R\,\overline{F}$ will assume when the *next* active clock edge arrives. For example, the annotation 1/1011 between states $0 \rightarrow 1$ means that if the machine is in state 0 and **Req** = 1 on the active clock edge, then the machine is to shift to state 1 and the outputs are to go to 1011, i.e. the amber light is to be activated. The annotation **Req**/GARF always shows the *next* output, as combinational outputs are delayed one clock pulse through an array of flip flops. Machines where the outputs are a function of both the state and programmable input are known as Mealy machines [27]. The modified form where the outputs are passed through a register and hence do not respond immediately to changes in the programmable inputs, is sometimes called the synchronous Mealy configuration [37].

The state table of Table 4.7 uses a natural binary state assignment from state 0 $000000b$ to state 39 $100111b$. For each present state, the next state is shown for all values of programmable input **Req**. In most cases, this column is X to show that the transition is irrespective of the condition of the variable **Req**, i.e. don't care.

For each present state, the AND-OR logic must present the appropriate values to the R and S inputs of the six state flip flops $P_9 \ldots P_4$. These setting values are shown for all 41 possible transitions. To explain these entries, we must first examine the transition requirements of the $R\,S$ flip flop. Where the flip flop is *changing* to 0, then the R input must be assigned to 1. Conversely, a *change* to 1 requires the S input to be set at 1. The no-change transitions $0 \rightarrow 1$ and $1 \rightarrow 0$ do not require any active input to hold their state. This is summerized in the $R\,S$ transition table:

Q	R	S	
$0 \rightarrow 0$	0	0	(Hold)
$0 \rightarrow 1$	0	1	(Set)
$1 \rightarrow 0$	1	0	(Reset)
$1 \rightarrow 1$	0	0	(Hold)

On the basis of this transition table, the state setting values column of Table 4.7 is determined. The advantage of using $R\,S$ flip flops over D flip flops is that the number of 1 entries is much smaller, and such entries translates to AND gates (listed in the leftmost column). Some PLS devices use $J\,K$ flip flops, which require even less terms. On the basis of this table, we can say:

$$R_9 \;=\; T_{39}$$

	T	Req	Present state P9 ... P4	Next state p9 ... p4	RS9	RS8	RS7	RS6	RS5	RS4	$\overline{G}\,\overline{A}\,R\,F$	RS3	RS2	RS1	RS0
0	0		000000	000000	00	00	00	00	00	00	0111	00	00	00	00
40	1		000000	000001	00	00	00	00	00	01	1011	01	10	00	00
1	X		000001	000010	00	00	00	00	01	10	1101	00	01	10	00
2	X		000010	000011	00	00	00	00	00	01	1101	00	00	00	00
3	X		000011	000100	00	00	00	01	10	10	1101	00	00	00	00
4	X		000100	000101	00	00	00	00	00	01	1101	00	00	00	00
5	X		000101	000110	00	00	00	00	01	10	1101	00	00	00	00
6	X		000110	000111	00	00	00	00	00	01	1110	00	00	01	10
7	X		000111	001000	00	00	00	10	10	10	1110	00	00	00	00
8	X		001000	001001	00	00	00	00	00	01	1110	00	00	00	00
9	X		001001	001010	00	00	00	00	01	10	0111	10	00	00	01
10	X		001010	001011	00	00	00	00	00	01	0111	00	00	00	00
11	X		001011	001100	00	00	00	01	10	10	0111	00	00	00	00
12	X		001100	001101	00	00	00	00	00	01	0111	00	00	00	00
13	X		001101	001110	00	00	00	01	01	10	0111	00	00	00	00
14	X		001110	001111	00	00	00	00	00	01	0111	00	00	00	00
15	X		001111	010000	00	01	10	10	10	10	0111	00	00	00	00
16	X		010000	010001	00	00	00	00	00	01	0111	00	00	00	00
17	X		010001	010010	00	00	00	00	01	10	0111	00	00	00	00
18	X		010010	010011	00	00	00	00	00	01	0111	00	00	00	00
19	X		010011	010100	00	00	00	01	10	10	0111	00	00	00	00
20	X		010100	010101	00	00	00	00	00	01	0111	00	00	00	00
21	X		010101	010100	00	00	00	00	01	10	0111	00	00	00	00
22	X		010110	010111	00	00	00	00	00	01	0111	00	00	00	00
23	X		010111	011000	00	00	01	10	10	10	0111	00	00	00	00
24	X		011000	011001	00	00	00	00	00	01	0111	00	00	00	00
25	X		011001	011010	00	00	00	00	01	10	0111	00	00	00	00
26	X		011010	011011	00	00	00	00	00	01	0111	00	00	00	00
27	X		011011	011100	00	00	00	01	10	10	0111	00	00	00	00
28	X		011100	011101	00	00	00	00	00	01	0111	00	00	00	00
29	X		011101	011110	00	00	00	00	01	10	0111	00	00	00	00
30	X		011110	011111	00	00	00	00	00	01	0111	00	00	00	00
31	X		011111	100000	01	10	10	10	10	10	0111	00	00	00	00
32	X		100000	100001	00	00	00	00	00	01	0111	00	00	00	00
33	X		100001	100010	00	00	00	00	01	10	0111	00	00	00	00
34	X		100010	100011	00	00	00	00	00	01	0111	00	00	00	00
35	X		100011	100100	00	00	00	01	10	10	0111	00	00	00	00
36	X		100100	100101	00	00	00	00	00	01	0111	00	00	00	00
37	X		100101	100110	00	00	00	00	01	10	0111	00	00	00	00
38	X		100110	100111	00	00	00	00	00	01	0111	00	00	00	00
39	X		101111	000000	10	00	00	10	10	10	0111	00	00	00	00

Table 4.7: State table for the pedestrian-light controller.

$$S_9 = T_{31}$$
$$R_8 = T_{31}$$
$$S_8 = T_{15}$$
$$R_7 = T_{15}+T_{31}$$
$$S_7 = T_{23}$$
$$R_6 = T_7+T_{15}+T_{23}+T_{31}+T_{39}$$
$$S_6 = T_3+T_{11}+T_{19}+T_{27}+T_{35}$$
$$R_5 = T\sum 3,7,11,15,19,23,27,31,35,39$$
$$S_5 = T\sum 1,5,9,13,17,21,25,29,33,37$$
$$R_4 = T\sum 1,5,7,9,11,13,15,17,19,21,23,25,27,29,31,33,35,37,39$$
$$S_4 = T\sum 2,4,6,8,10,12,14,16,18,20,22,24,26,28,30,32,34,36,38,40$$

where T_n indicates AND term n, i.e. AND gate n.

The right table column shows the values to be output when the transition is completed, i.e. *next* output pattern. The appropriate setting values are calculated in the same manner as for the state flip flops, but based on the change from the output of the line above, which is the previous set (treating the table as circular). This gives the equations:

$$R_3 = T_9$$
$$S_3 = T_{40}$$
$$R_2 = T_{40}$$
$$S_2 = T_1$$
$$R_1 = T_1$$
$$S_1 = T_6$$
$$R_0 = T_6$$
$$S_0 = T_9$$

Finally we must analyze the the reaction of the machine to an illegal state, which are all the unused combination state bits ($11000 - 11111b$) together with programmable input **Req**. If for any reason the machine lands in any of these states, no AND term will be active, and all R and S inputs will be at logic 0. This is the no change condition and the machine will remain stuck in this illegal condition forever more! We could of course generate all illegal terms and OR them together to the R flip flop inputs to reset the machine to state 0. However, this would require another 24 AND gates; far more than is available. Instead, in Fig. 4.67 I have connected the Complement OR gate **C** to all legal AND terms $T_0 \ldots T_{40}$. If the machine is *not* in a defined state, no term will be active and the C OR gate will go to 0. As its complement $\overline{C}$ is connected back around into the AND matrix, a single unused AND gate (T_{48} in the fuse plot) can be connected to all state flip flop R inputs; giving an automatic reset action. This is a very efficient technique.

The so called Complement array has more uses than indicated here. In machines where there are many programmable inputs, only a few combinations are typically

specified at transitions out of states. All other combinations may be lumped together as an ELSE path. Thus we may have the statement "IF $X_2X_1X_0$ is 000 THEN
state k OR IF $X_2X_1X_0$ is 010 THEN state l **ELSE** state m". The ELSE transition
can be forced by using the C gate to detect *all* jumps explicitly defined in the flow
diagram, and ANDing this state n. Thus if in state n and *not* in an explicit jump,
then set up flip flops to go to state m. The one Complement gate, together with
the appropriate number of AND gates can perform this ELSE exception for several
states. More details are given in [39, 40].

There is of course an extra delay, and thus a reduced maximum operating frequency, in using this technique as two passes through the AND array are required
before product terms with the Complement gate input can settle. For example, the
PLS168A is rated at 20 MHz without the use of the Complement gate and 12.5 MHz
with.

The fuse plot shown in Fig. 4.67 follows the same convention to those of Section 4.5 for PALs, with an **X** used to indicate a connection (intact horizontal fuse).
Normally PLS devices are documented using a programming table in a similar manner as those used for PLAs (see Fig. 3.69). A PLS table shows the same information
as Table 4.7, but in a more stylized form.

Example 4.34

Although the core of the pedestrian light controller has been implemented by
the PLS168 of the previous example, there still remain three functions to complete
the system.

1. To divide down the system 0.5 Hz flashing clock to give the 3 s clock used to
   time the main machine.

2. To latch the pedestrian's Cross_Request switch, giving Req.

3. To amalgamate the $\overline{\text{Amber}}$ and $\overline{\text{Flashing\_Amber}}$ outputs of the PLS168 to drive
   the amber traffic lamp.

Using a PAL16R4, implement the required logic.

Solution

The pedestrian Cross_Request signal originates from a normal mechanical switch. A
request must be latched as the PLS168-based sampling rate is only once per three
seconds. The latch can be conveniently reset again by the $\overline{\text{Flashing\_Amber}}$ output
signal, which occurs near the end of the active light sequence cycle. The fuse pattern
for an is shown in Fig. 4.7(b). From this we deduce equation:

$$\text{Req} = \overline{\text{F}} + \overline{(\text{Cross\_Request} \cdot \text{Req})}$$

where $\overline{\text{F}}$ replaces R, Cross_Request for S and the Q output is Req.

Combining the $\overline{\text{Flashing\_Amber}}$ and $\overline{\text{Amber}}$ signals follows the relationship:

$$\text{Amber\_Signal} = \text{Flashing\_Amber} \cdot \text{Flashing\_Clock} + \text{Amber}$$

This is the logic shown in Fig. 3.36.

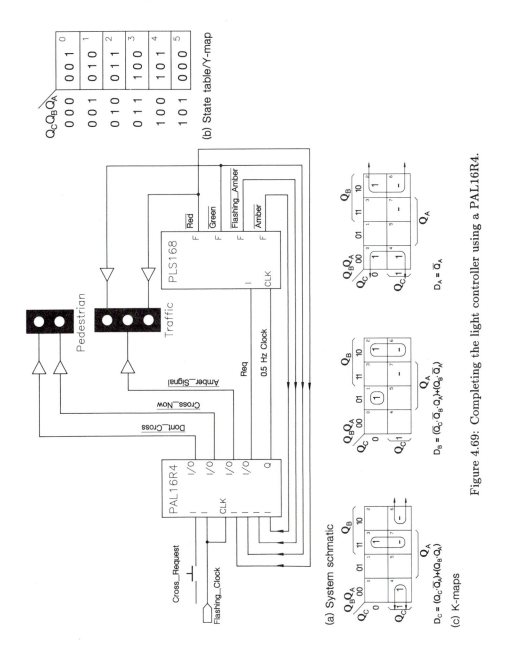

(b) State table/Y-map

(a) System schmatic

(c) K-maps

$D_A = \overline{Q}_A$

$D_B = (\overline{Q}_C \cdot \overline{Q}_B \cdot Q_A) + (Q_B \cdot \overline{Q}_A)$

$D_C = (Q_C \cdot \overline{Q}_A) + (Q_B \cdot Q_A)$

Figure 4.69: Completing the light controller using a PAL16R4.

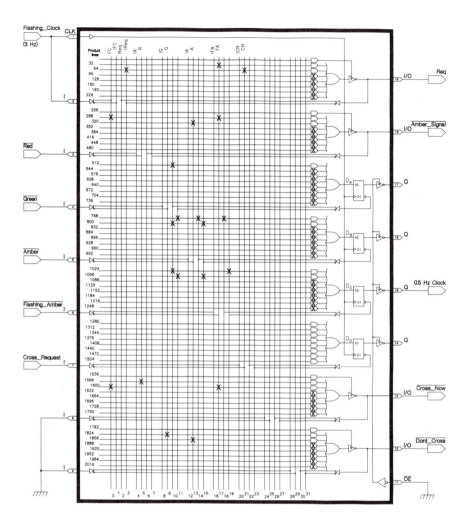

Figure 4.70: Fuse plot for the auxiliary PAL.

Dividing down the 0.5 Hz flashing rate to the 3 s system clock is simply a matter of implementing a modulo-6 counter using Flashing_Clock to clock the flip flops. The Y-map based on a circular flow diagram and naturally coded 4-2-1 state assignment is shown in Fig. 4.69(b). Splitting this into three k-maps gives the setting equations. The MSB output Q_C gives the required 3 s clock. Actually the 3-line counter output will be active-Low, but this is irrelevant to this application. Only the C flip flop is actually required, the B and A devices could have been buried if this PAL had such resources, and would release valuable output pins.

There are two combinational outputs left over. We could utilize them to activate the two pedestrian status lights, Cross_Now and Dont_Cross. The Red, Green and Amber lights already implemented are for the vehicular traffic. The relationships are:

$$
\begin{aligned}
\text{Dont\_Cross} &= \text{Vehicle Green or Amber} \\
\text{Cross\_Now} &= \text{Vehicle Red} \\
\text{Flashing Cross\_Now} &= \text{Vehicle Flashing Amber}
\end{aligned}
$$

This gives us the equations:

$$
\begin{aligned}
\text{Cross\_Now} &= \text{Red} + (\text{Flashing\_Clock} \cdot \text{Flashing\_Amber}) \\
\text{Dont\_Cross} &= \text{Green} + \text{Amber}
\end{aligned}
$$

These equations are shown in the fuse plot.

Example 4.35

Determine the count sequence of the **feedback shift register** shown in Fig. 4.71(a).

Solution

The serial input to the shift register 1D is given as $Q_C \oplus Q_D$. Thus, every state of the register will generate an input for shifting in at the next clock. For example, if the register is in state 1000b, then 1D $= 0$, giving 0100b after the first shift. 1D remains 0, giving 0010b as the next state. 1D now becomes 1 and the succeeding state is 1001b. The table shown in Fig. 4.71(b) shows the complete cycle of 15 states. Note that state 0000b does not appear. If the register should be reset, then 1D $= 0$ and the register sticks in this illegal state. If an ENOR feedback gate is used, state 1111b is the sticking state. How could you modify the feedback to eliminate this problem?

The shift register counter shown in the diagram is only one of a large class of such counters employing EOR feedback. The table of Fig. 4.71(c) gives a listing of the appropriate feedback for up to 18 stages [41]. EOR feedback other than those tabulated may give shorter cycles [14].

Shift register counter codes have the property that they are random; that is, succeeding states are non-related. Because of this property, they are often known as **pseudo-random number generators (PRNGs)**. If the number of stages is sufficiently large, the repetitive nature of the generator is not apparent over the period of interest. If all bits are analog summed together, as shown in Fig. 4.71(d), then a random fluctuating voltage is produced with a flat spectrum (i.e. white noise) up to the clocking rate ÷ number of stages. Thus, a 16-stage register clocked at

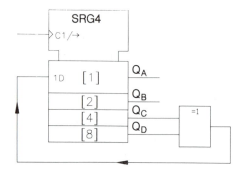

(a) A shift-register counter

ABCD	Number of stages	EOR/ENOR feedback inputs
1000		
0100	3	B,C
0010	4	C,D
1001	5	C,E
1100	6	E,F
0110	7	F,G *
1011	8	D,E,F,H
0101	9	E,I
1010	10	H,J
1101	11	I,K
1110	12	F,H,K,L
1111	13	A,C,D,M
0111	14	A,F,J,N
0011	15	A,□
0001	16	A,C,L,P
	17	C,Q
	18	G,R

(b) The counting code for (a)

(c) Showing feedback connections for up to 18-stages

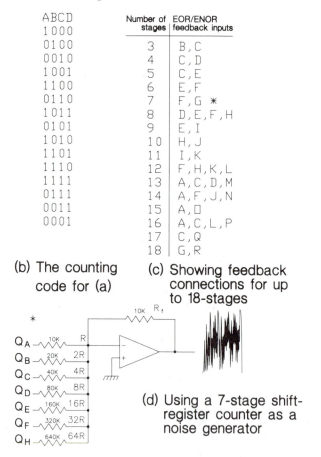

(d) Using a 7-stage shift-register counter as a noise generator

Figure 4.71: Pseudo-random binary number generators.

100 Hz, recycles after 10.9 minutes and acts as a white-noise generator of 6.25 Hz bandwidth. PRNGs are extensively discussed in both control and logic literature and references [42, 43] are useful for further reading.

Example 4.36

Using an accumulator subtractor with a counter and comparator, show how division could be implemented by repetitive subtraction.

Solution

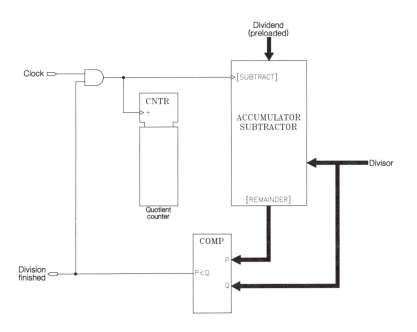

Figure 4.72: Division by the repetitive subtraction of the divisor from the preloaded dividend.

A possible scheme is shown in Fig. 4.72. The dividend is directly loaded into the accumulator register. The divisor is then continuously subtracted until the remainder is less than the divisor. The number of subtractions necessary for this is equal to the quotient, as recorded by an up counter. The accumulator holds the remainder. What would happen if the divisor were zero?

An accumulator/counter arrangement can also be configured as a multiplier. The multiplier is loaded into a down counter which decrements each time the multiplicand is added to the accumulator. When the counter reaches zero, the accumulator holds the product.

Example 4.37

An alternative to the invert-and-add 2's complement algorithm, is to copy down the uncorrected word from LSB to the first logic 1. Thereafter, the remaining bits are complemented. Thus, 110*100* becomes 001*100*. The process is reversible. Assuming the *n*-bit word is in a shift register, use an EOR gate as a programmable inverter and J K flip flop as a ones detector, to implement the conversion.

Solution

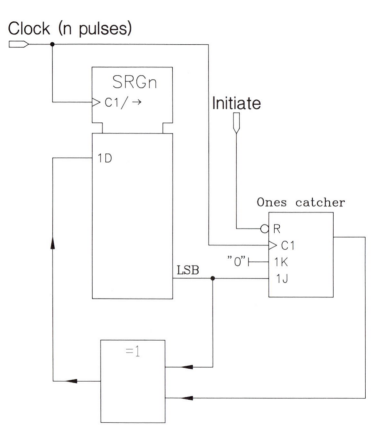

Figure 4.73: A serial 2's complementer.

The outline of the circuit is shown in Fig. 4.73. The *n*-stage shift register is loaded (not shown) with the *n*-bit word positioned LSB at the top (shifted out first). The J K flip flop is initially cleared, which configures the EOR gate as a non-inverter. Thus the data is clocked out and around to the top of the register (or another register) unchanged. This remains the case as long as these bits are zero ($J = 0$, $K = 0$), up to the first logic 1. This initial one is shifted around whilst at the same time the J K flip flop is set (J = 1, K = 0). Thereafter, all bits are inverted by the EOR gate, as the J K flip flop cannot be synchronously reset (K is always 0). The J K flip flop thus acts as a ones catcher.

4.6.2   Self Assessment Examples

SAE 4.1

Analyze the fundamental mode feedback circuit of Fig. 4.74 and predict its behavior when X cycles through the sequence $0 \rightarrow 1 \rightarrow 0 \rightarrow 1$.

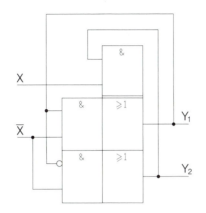

Figure 4.74: Analysis of a feedback circuit.

SAE 4.2

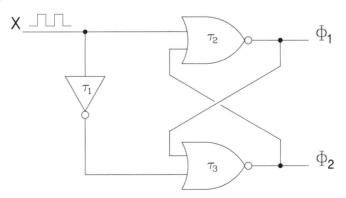

Figure 4.75: A 2-phase non-overlapping clock splitter.

The circuit shown in Fig. 4.74 has been described as a 2-phase non-overlapping clock generator [44]. The outputs ϕ_1 and ϕ_2 are normally orthogonal (180° out of phase) but are guaranteed never both High at the same time. With the help of the Y-map of Fig. 4.2, show that this is so. For convenience you can assume that the propagation delay of the inverter and NOR gates are the same.

SAE 4.3

Two cross-coupled NOR R S latches are cascaded with Q_1 feeding R_2 and $\overline{Q}_1$ feeding S_2 [45]. What will be the overall action?

SAE 4.4

A simple phase meter is to be constructed by squaring two same-frequency sine inputs. The phase is measured by determining the percentage of overlap between the two square waves. Complete overlap is $0°$ and no overlap is $180°$. Using an EOR gate will give a maximum output for $180°$ and zero for $0°$. However, it is also necessary to determine whether A leads or lags the reference B. Show how you would use a flip flop to generate a lead/lag indicator.

SAE 4.5

The circuit shown in Fig. 4.76 is a flip flop of some kind. What does it do and can you depict its operation by drawing an IEC/ANSII symbol?

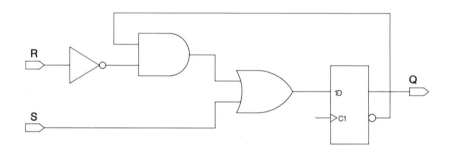

Figure 4.76: A flip flop of unknown operation.

SAE 4.6

Most digital watches are timed using a 32.768 kHz crystal. In designing a watch ASIC, how could you produce one pulse each second?

SAE 4.7

Show how you would modify the T flip flop of Fig. 4.18(b) to introduce a synchronous Reset facility.

SAE 4.8

Using J K ‾_ -triggered flip flops, design a modulo-11 ripple counter and suitable decoder giving a 1:1 mark:space ratio ÷11 output. Assume that the clock pulse is square and can be used in the decoder design.

SAE 4.9

It is required to design a modulo-3 dead-end synchronous counter using J K flip flops. The counter is to be decoded in such a manner as to give an output of exactly one clock cycle duration each time the counter is initiated by resetting. Determine the response of the counter to its one illegal state.

SAE 4.10

An ASIC is to be designed as the intelligence behind a digital clock. The timing waveform is to be derived from the mains frequency, but because there is an anticipated world-wide market, the ASIC must be capable of accepting 50 or 60 Hz pulses. It is proposed to implement this by using a programmable counter as a front end prescaler, giving a ÷5 or ÷6 function. One of the ASIC pins is to be utilized as the control input X, giving ÷5 when Low and ÷6 when High. The resulting 10 Hz output then drives the counting chain. Design this prescaler based on D flip flops.

SAE 4.11

Somebody has had the bright idea of marketing a combo synchronous counter which will offer four codes, as determined by the two programmable inputs $X_1 X_0$. The codes are:

$$X_1 X_0 = 00 : \qquad \text{8-4-2-1 natural binary up.}$$
$$X_1 X_0 = 01 : \qquad \text{8-4-2-1 natural BCD down.}$$
$$X_1 X_0 = 10 : \qquad \text{2-4-2-1 symmetrical BCD up.}$$
$$X_1 X_0 = 11 : \qquad \text{4-bit Gray up.}$$

The implementation is to be based on a PLE6P4/D flip flop array. Can you determine the relevant personality table?

SAE 4.12

Using a parallel loading BCD down counter in conjunction with a binary up counter, show how you could convert from BCD to binary. Both counters are of an appropriate length.

SAE 4.13

The IEC/ANSII symbol for the SN74LS697 IC is shown in Fig. 4.77. How does it differ from the SN74LS699 and what are they?

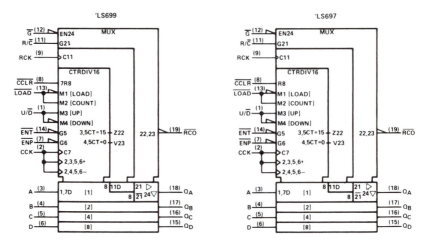

Figure 4.77: The SN 74LS697/699 ICs. Courtesy of Texas Instruments Ltd.

SAE 4.14

A 4-bit naturally-coded 8-4-2-1 counter supplies a continuously cycling word P to a 4-bit adder chip. Determine the relationship between the signal monitored at Carry_Out and the magnitude of word Q. How would you use this circuit as a digital to analog converter?

SAE 4.15

Using the table of Fig. 4.71(c), determine the 7-bit pseudo binary random number sequence, and plot the analog equivalent assuming that the normal binary weights are applied (see Fig. 4.71(d)). Assume that the code begins at $0000001b$.

SAE 4.16

Show how a combinational AND-OR PAL section can be connected to implement an active-High clocked R S latch.

SAE 4.17

Use a PAL16R4 to generate the constant π to 15 decimal places, in the manner of Example 2.38, but including the counter.

SAE 4.18

Design a direction decoder that can be used to generate an up clock (clockwise) or down clock (counter-clockwise) that will activate a dual clock up/down counter (such as the 74x190 series). Use a PAL16R4, and assume that this is clocked at a rate greater than $4 \times n \times r$, where n is the number of pulses produced by one revolution of the shaft and r is the maximum shaft revolution rate. The up/down counter's $\overline{\text{Reset}}$ is also to clear your direction encoder.

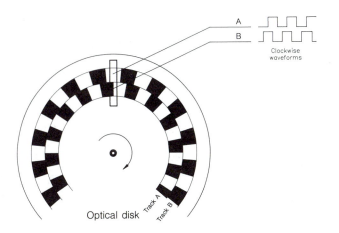

Figure 4.78: A 2-channel shaft encoder.

SAE 4.19

The intelligence for a coin in the slot vending machine is to be based on a PLD. This vending machine can accept coins of 5, 10 or 20 unit denomination, and can dispense drinks of tea, coffee or hot chocolate, costing a minimum of 20, 25 or 30 units respectively. Each coin is guided by size into three channels, activating one of three debounced microswitches $X_2X_1X_0$ as appropriate to 20, 10, 5 denomination coins.

There are to be three system outputs $Z_2Z_1Z_0$. These will be ANDed with the three customer selection buttons, labelled **Tea**, **Coffee** and **Hot Chocolate**, ensuring that enough money has been inserted before the appropriate solenoids are activated. You may assume that after a drink has been dispensed, that a reset signals generated. You may further assume that the passage of *any* coin generates a single pulse that can be used to clock your machine.

SAE 4.20

A certain communications system can send only seven messages. These are of variable length, self synchronizing and are coded in binary as follows:

$$A = 00 \quad B = 01 \quad C = 10 \quad D = 110 \quad E = 1110 \quad F = 11110 \quad G = 11111$$

Data is transmitted in series, MSB first, with a clock being provided in the middle of each signal bit. There are to be seven outputs, one for each message. Design a suitable PLD-based receiver.

Why do you think that in variable-length coding systems, the lengths are allocated inversely to the probability of occurrence of the message?

References

[1] McCluskey, E.J.; *Logic Design Principles: with Emphasis on Testable Semiconductor Circuits*, Prentice-Hall, 1986, Section 7.2.1.

[2] McCluskey, E.J.; *Logic Design Principles: with Emphasis on Testable Semiconductor Circuits*, Prentice-Hall, 1986, Section 7.2.2.

[3] Pěchouček, M.; Anomalous Response Times of Input Synchronizers, *IEEE Trans. Comput.*, **C-25**, no. 2, Feb. 1976, pp.133–139.

[4] Chaney, T.J. et al.; Beware the Synchronizer, *Digest paper 6th Ann. IEEE Comp. Soc. Int. Conf.*, Sept. 1972, pp.317–319.

[5] Chaney, T.J.; Measured Flip-Flop Responses to Marginal Triggering, *IEEE Trans. Comput.*, **C-32**, no. 12, Dec. 1983, pp.1207–1209.

[6] Breeding, K.J.; *Digital Design Fundamentals*, Prentice-Hall, 1989, Section 6.3.

[7] Phister, M, Jr.; *Logical Design of Digital Computers*, J.Wiley, 1958, Chapter 5.

[8] Millman, J and Taub, H.; *Pulse, Digital and Switching Waveforms*, McGraw-Hill, 1965, Chapter 10.

[9] Oberman, R.M.M.; *Electronic Counters*, MacMillan, 1973.

[10] Kampel, I.; *A Practical Introduction to the New Logic Symbols*, 2nd ed., Butterworths, 1986, Section 11.7.

[11] Erdmann, D.R.; TTL Counters and Registers, *Semiconductor Circuit Design*, **II**, ed. Norris, B., Texas Instruments Ltd., Bedford, 1973, Chapter XIV.

[12] Dean, K.J.; The Design of Parallel Counters using the Map Method, *The Radio and Electronic Engineer*, **32**, no. 3, Sept. 1966, pp.159–162.

[13] Floyd, T,; *Digital Fundamentals*, Merrill, 4th ed., 1990, Section 8.2.

[14] Morris, R.L. and Miller, J.R.; *Designing with TTL Integrated Circuits*, McGraw-Hill, 1971, Section 11.2.

[15] Bleickhardt, W.; Multimoding and its Suppression in Twisted Ring Counters, *Bell Syst. Tech. J*, **47**, no. 9, Nov. 1968, pp.2029–2050.

[16] Heuner, R. et al.; *COS/MOS MSI Counter and Register Design and Applications*, RCA Applications note ICAN-6166.

[17] Parsons, B.; Reversible Counters, *Semiconductor Circuit Design*, **II**, ed. Norris, B., Texas Instruments Ltd, Bedford, 1973, Chapter VI.

[18] Morris, R.L. and Miller, J.R.; *Designing with TTL Integrated Circuits*, McGraw-Hill, 1971, Section 9.8.

[19] Couleur, J.K.; BIDEC–A Binary-to-Decimal or Decimal-to-Binary Converter, *IRE Trans. on Electronic Computers*, **EC7**, Dec. 1958, pp.313–316.

[20] Chirlian, P.M.; *Analysis and Design of Integrated Circuits: Volume 2, Digital Electronics*, Harper & Row, 1982, Section 11.9.

[21] Millman, J. and Halkias, C.C.; *Integrated Electronics*, McGraw-Hill, 1971, Section 17.21.

[22] Mauro, R.; *Engineering Electronics*, Prentice-Hall, 1989, Section 11.6.

[23] Mauro, R.; *Engineering Electronics*, Prentice-Hall, 1989, Section 11.7.

[24] Elliot, A.R.; A High-Speed Binary Rate Multiplier, *Proc. IEEE*, **59**, Aug. 1971, pp.1256–1257.

[25] Bolton, M.; *Digital Systems Design with Programmable Logic*, Addison-Wesley, 1990, Section 6.7.

[26] Monolithics Memory, PAL Handbook; *Electronic Dice Game*, 3rd ed., 1983, Chapter 6, pp.57–63.

[27] Mealy, G.H.; A Method for Synthesizing Sequential Circuits, *Bell System Technical Journal*, Sept. 1955, pp.1045–1079.

[28] Moore, E.F.; Gedanken Experiments on Sequential Machines, *Automata Studies*, Princeton University Press, **34**, 1955, pp.129–153.

[29] Alford, R.C.; *Programmable Logic Designer's Guide*, Howard W. Sams, Chapter 3, 1989.

[30] Alford, R.C.; *Programmable Logic Designer's Guide*, Howard W. Sams, Chapter 1, 1989.

[31] Gembris, D.; Generic Array Logic, *Elecktor Electronics*, **18**, no. 199., April 1992, pp.24–27.

[32] Greenfield, J.D.; *Practical Digital Design Using ICs*, J.Wiley, 2nd Ed., 1983, Section 6.6.

[33] Greenfield, J.D.; *Practical Digital Design Using ICs*, J.Wiley, 2nd Ed., 1983, Section 7.8.

[34] Mauro, R.; *Engineering Electronics*, Prentice-Hall, 1989, Section 11.3.

[35] Boukadoum, M.; Debouncer for SPST Switches Uses Few Parts, *EDN*, 29 Oct. 1987, pp.252.

[36] Babbra, M.S.; Divide-by-Three with 1:1 M/S Ratio, *Electronics World + Wireless World*, **97**, no. 1660, Feb. 1991, pp.116.

[37] Bolton, M.; *Digital Systems Design with Programmable Logic*, Addison-Wesley, 1990, Section 6.2.

[38] Lala, P.K.; *Digital System Design using Programmable Logic Devices*, Prentice-Hall, 1990, Chapter 4.

[39] Philips/Signetics application note AN23, *PLS168/168A Primer*, 1988.

[40] Bolton, M.; *Digital Systems Design with Programmable Logic*, Addison-Wesley, 1990, Section 6.10.2.

[41] Mann, R.; Programmable Synchronous Frequency Counter, *Semiconductor Circuit Design*, **II**, ed. Norris B., Texas Instruments Ltd., Bedford, 1973, Section VII.

[42] Chow, P.E.K. and Davis, A.C.; The Synthesis of Cyclic Code Generators, *Electronic Engineering*, **36**, no. 4, Apr. 1964, pp.253–259.

[43] Kramer, C.; A Low-Frequency Pseudo-Random Noise Generator, *Electronic Design*, **26**, no. 14, 5th July 1978, pp.106.

[44] McCluskey, E.J.; *Logic Design Principles: with Emphasis on Testable Semiconductor Circuits*, Prentice-Hall, 1986, Section 7.9.

[45] Cahill, S.J.; Resynchronize Staggered Signals with Cascaded Flip Flops, *Electronic Design*, **26**, no. 14, 5th July 1978, pp.106.

Chapter 5

101

Microprocessors

In the early 1970s, LSI was a technology looking for a use. LSI was expensive to design and tool up for production, and needed the economics of mass production to pay for these costs. Paradoxically, the more successful the technology the more complex and hence specialized the end product, the smaller was the potential applications the chip could be sold for. There were exceptions, where a single-product market was large enough to support such designs, such as the calculator chip.

To give LSI technology the impetus to develop further, a complex but general-purpose architecture had to be found which would target as wide a market as possible.

One of the earliest, and certainly the most successful of these designs, was the **microprocessor**, introduced in 1971 by the Intel corporation [1, 2]. At that time, Intel was a startup company making semiconductor memories and doing LSI consultancy. One of their assignments was a LSI calculator chip for a Japanese company called Beecom. As part of this project, it was decided to see if a simple computer-like central processing unit (CPU) could be designed into LSI. This would be as an alternative to the standard calculator architecture. As perceived by Intel, this would be advantageous, as semiconductor memory would be needed to complete the system; ROM to hold the arithmetic routines and RAM for the variables.

In the event, Beecom were not interested in speculative technology and disappeared from the scene. However, Intel decided to go ahead and build this micro CPU with the hope that someone would find an application for the aptly named **microprocessor unit** (MPU). Thus was the 4004 born.

Although the 4004 was primitive, requiring only 2300 transistors for its implementation, interest was sufficiently high to quickly improve the original design. Like the 4004, the 4040 MPU dealt with data four bits at a time, but within a year the 8008 and then the 8080 8-bit equivalents were on the market. The current Intel 8-bit processor, the 8085, is virtually identical to the 8080, but runs off a single power supply and has an integral clock generator. Introduced in the mid 1970s, it formed the basis for the 16 and 32-bit 8086 family, which are the powerhouse of the ubiquitous IBM personal computer.

Many other companies jumped on the bandwagon; notably Motorola who introduced their 6800 MPU in 1974. Their current 8-bit device, the 6809, became available in 1979, around the same time the 16/32-bit 68000-family was announced. The Intel/Motorola-based families with their offsprings and relations account for the majority of microprocessors used at the current time.

The first generation of MPUs were rather simple devices, designed to replace sequential logic circuitry, rather than the computers they set out to ape. However, as their power increased, they eventually took over the role of computer as well, reducing the cost of computing a thousandfold or more. Although they are perhaps better known in their role as computers, the majority of microprocessor applications still lie in implementing sequential logic. As such, they are one solution of the problem of making a complex LSI/VLSI device sufficiently general purpose to ensure commercially viable numbers can be sold.

In essence, the MPU is a highly integrated arithmetic processing unit which executes a series of instructions held in memory. By changing these codes, the personality of the system can be radically altered with little or no change in the peripheral support hardware. Conventional implementations, where the character of the system is only altered by changing the hardware, are known as random logic. The programmable logic implementations introduced in Sections 3.3 and 4.5 are only extensions of this technique, with on-chip wiring alterations. Microprocessor-based systems are a uniquely flexible implementation of this programmable logic ethos.

Although sequential machines of any complexity can be designed using these techniques, systems of a complexity exceeding around 32 states [3] become so complex in practice, that the alternative of using a microprocessor-based circuit is nearly always more satisfactory. The main advantage of state-machine based implementations lies in the domain of high speed, where a nanosecond response to input stimuli is desirable. Microprocessor-based controllers are best for medium-speed complex applications.

Microprocessor-based design involves both hardware and software (programming) techniques. This chapter looks at the MPU through hardware eyes, although it is impossible to disassociate the two strands. Section 6.2 will discuss software in more detail and the problems of software development.

5.1 Stored Program Processing

The architecture of the great majority of general-purpose microprocessors is modelled after the **von Neumann computer** [4]. In essence, the von Neumann architecture comprizes a central processing unit (CPU), a memory and a connecting highway carrying data back and forth. In practice the CPU must communicate with the outside world. Data from or to suitable interface ports are also funnelled through the data highway.

The CPU executes the various machine operations, such as Add, Subtract, AND, OR, which are stored in memory. The sequence of instructions constitutes the program. Data resulting from, or used by, the program is also stored in memory. Under the management of the control unit, program instructions are fetched sequentially from memory, decoded and executed. This fetch and execute cycle constitutes the operating rhythm of the computer and continues indefinitely as long as the system is activated. From this discussion, the CPU may be seen to be an arithmetic logic

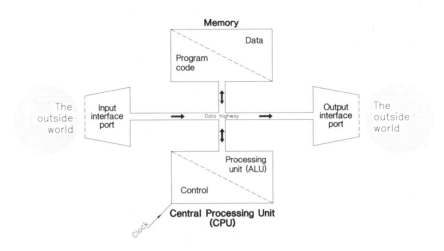

Figure 5.1: An elementary von Neumann computer.

unit (see Section 3.2.3) whose mode is altered by control circuitry acting on the behest of a series of binary codes stored in memory.

The term computer generally is used to denote a complete system of CPU, memory and peripherals (typically a keyboard and VDU). Where the CPU is implemented with a microprocessor, the term microcomputer or personal computer (PC) is sometimes given. Generally, a microprocessor is equivalent to the CPU but integrated on the one chip. Microcomputer units (MCUs) integrate memory and input/output ports to give a complete computer on a chip. MCUs trade the power of the CPU against the additional system integration, but they are still adequate for most embedded control applications. An example of a MCU is given in Section 5.4.

In this section, we will look at a hypothetical von Neumann CPU, which we call BASIC (BAsic All-purpose Stored-Instruction Computer). Because of the close affinity of MPU and CPU, it is not necessary to distinguish between them at this point. However, BASIC's structure has been based, at least partly, on the Motorola 6800 family of MPUs, which are the subject of succeeding sections.

After reading this section you should:

- Appreciate the von Newmann computer structure, with its common data highway.

- Understand the fetch and execute rhythm and its interaction with the CPU's internal registers and mill.

- Comprehend the structure of instructions as an op-code:operand pair with particular reference to the various address modes.

- Understand the role of the microprogram in the operation of the CPU.

- Have an understanding of the basic instruction categories of data movement, arithmetic, and conditional branching.

- Be able to write simple programs in terms of the instruction set of a hypothetical CPU.

5.1.1 The Fetch and Execute Cycle

Consider the functional diagram of Fig. 5.2, which shows the interaction of BASIC's CPU with memory. Each addressable location holds a 8-bit binary number (see Section 4.5) which may be interpreted by a von Neumann CPU either as an instruction or data.

A **computer program** is defined as a string of individual instructions together with any associated data structures. This string begins at a predetermined point; in our example, at location $00000000b$ (or $00h$) – remember from Section 1.1.2, a trailing b indicates binary and h hexadecimal. As instructions are normally stored in sequence, an internal counter in the CPU is used to keep track of the current instruction byte. This sequencer is commonly known as the **Program Counter** (sometimes Instruction Pointer). To fetch an instruction byte, the CPU transfers the contents of the Program Counter (PC) into the Address buffer register. This directly addresses the memory via the **address bus** (see Fig. 4.46). The resulting data is connected to the CPU via the **data bus** and is loaded into the Data buffer register. During this time the $R/\overline{W}$ direction control line is High, to indicate a read cycle. For a write cycle $R/\overline{W}$ is Low and it is the CPU which puts data on the data bus.

For the purpose of our example, we have shown a simple program that implements the statement $Z = Z + 2$. The variable Z is known to reside at location $2Fh$ and is limited in size to $00 - FFh$ (0 to 255) if unsigned or $80 - 7Fh$ (-128 to $+127$) if signed. Three instructions are needed to implement this function. The first brings the variable Z down to the CPU and loads it into the **Accumulator register**. It is known by the mnemonic LDA (LoaD Accumulator). Then the constant two is added, i.e. ADDA #2 (ADD to A the number two). Finally, the augmented variable, still in the Accumulator, is stored back to its location in memory (STA is STore to Accumulator).

Using mnemonics to designate instructions, makes it easier for us humans to write and decipher programs, but the underlying reality are the binary codes in memory. Thus LDA is actually $1001\ 0110b$ ($96h$), ADDA is $1000\ 1011b$ ($8Bh$) and STA is $1001\ 0111b$ ($97h$). The CPU does not want to know about mnemonics or even hexadecimal codes. As we shall see in Section 6.2, computer system programs are used to translate from more human-oriented coding to the fundamental **machine code**.

Each of the instructions used in our Load-Add-Store program have a 2-part structure. The first byte is the **op-code**. This is the code which defines the operation and says something about where the data will be found. All instructions of no matter what length, will be headed with an op-code. The second byte either holds the absolute address of the data; eg. $1001\ 0111 - 0010\ 1111b$ ($97\text{-}2Fh$ is STA Z) or the immediate data itself, eg. $1000\ 1011 - 0000\ 0010b$ ($8B\text{-}02h$ is ADDA #2) The various means of determining the operand location are known as the **address modes**. Thus, so far we have used the absolute and immediate address modes. Some of the bits in the op-code are used to carry address mode information. We will be returning to address modes in succeeding sections.

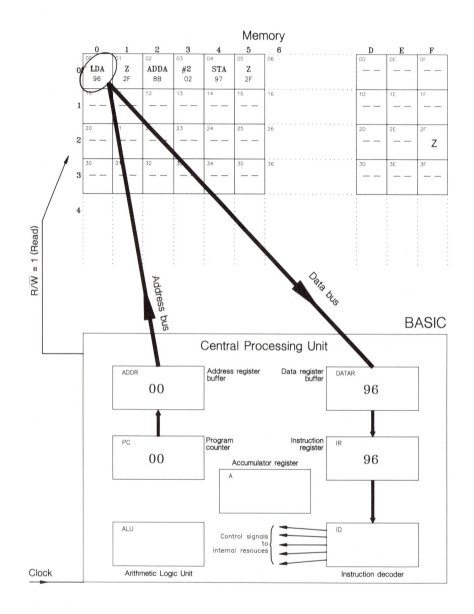

Figure 5.2: The CPU caught in the act of reading the first op-code of the program.

Once an op-code has been moved down into the Data register buffer, it is transferred to and held by the Instruction register as the input to the Instruction decoder. This generates the appropriate sequence of actions; as a consequence of which any subsequent instruction bytes and operand are fetched, and the requested operation executed.

The essence of computer operation is the rhythm of the **fetch and execute cycle**. This is the repetitive fetching of an instruction, interpretation and execution. In terms of our example program and Fig. 5.3 we have:

(a) Fetch I

PC = 00h to Address Buffer register. CPU fetches contents of memory location 00h (the op-code for **LDA**) to the Data Buffer register and thus to the Instruction register. The **PC** is incremented (**PC++**).

II

PC = 01h to **Address Buffer register**. CPU fetches contents of memory location 01h (the address of Z) to the Data Buffer register. **PC++**.

Execute

The operand address 2Fh to Address Buffer register. CPU fetches data in location 2Fh (ie. Z) to the Data Buffer register and *loads* it into the Accumulator.

(b) Fetch I

PC = 02h to Address Buffer register. CPU fetches contents of memory location 02h (the op-code for **ADDA**) to the Data Buffer register and thus to the Instruction register. **PC++**.

II

PC = 03h to Address Buffer register. CPU fetches contents memory location 03h (the constant 02) to the Data Buffer register. **PC++**.

Execute

The ALU is configured to *add* the operands in the Accumulator (Z) and the Data Buffer register (02). The sum is put back in the Accumulator ($Z + 02$).

(c) Fetch I

PC = 04h to Address Buffer register. CPU fetches contents of memory location 04h (the op-code for **STA**) to the Data Buffer register and thus to the Instruction register. **PC++**.

II **PC** = 05h to Address Buffer register. CPU fetches contents of memory location 05h (the address of Z) to the Data Buffer register. **PC++**.

Execute The operand address 2Fh to Address Buffer register. CPU moves the contents of the Accumulator to the Data Buffer register and *stores* it at address 2Fh (updates Z).

Having established the fundamental operating rhythm of the computer, we will now look more closely at the internal architecture of BASIC's CPU.

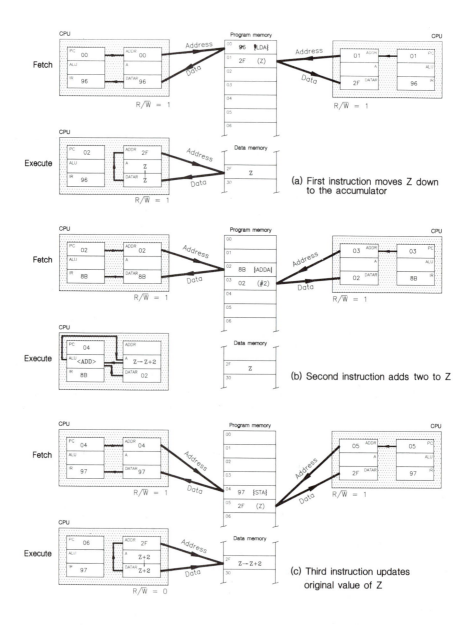

Figure 5.3: A trace of a simple LOAD-ADD-STORE program.

5.1.2 A Simple Central Processing Unit

The CPU configuration shown in Figs. 5.2 and 5.3 is highly simplified, and a somewhat more detailed picture is given in Fig. 5.4. As well as the data and address buses, there are three miscellaneous signals grouped together as the control bus. The $R/\overline{W}$ signal is the conventional **Read/Write** command used to alert the memory to the direction of data flow. **Reset** clears the **Program Counter**, which then points to the first program byte at $00h$. The clock is used to synchronize internal data movements.

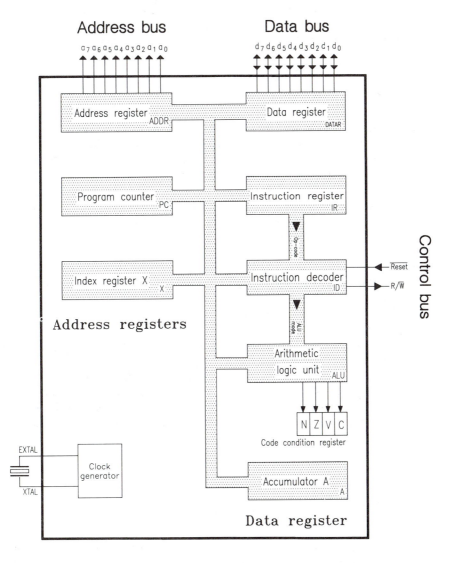

Figure 5.4: Internal arrangement of BASIC's CPU.

Internally the Data and Address register buffers hold information sent or request-ed by the CPU and are capable of driving external circuitry. The ALU provides the arithmetic and logic capabilities of the CPU, whilst the Accumulator holds an operand or result of an operation.

The Program Counter points to the program instruction which is about to be executed and is automatically incremented after each byte is fetched. This register can be thought of as a parallel loading up-counter (see Section 4.2.2), as certain instructions can cause an address to be loaded directly into the PC, overriding the normal increment mode. For example, the operation Jump (JMP-address) loads the specified address into the PC. This results in the instruction at the jump-to address being executed next, and then all following instructions, as the PC proceeds to increment normally. If the instruction at $10{:}11h$ is JMP-1Eh, then the program sequence is

$$0A{:}0B \rightarrow 0C{:}0D \rightarrow 0E{:}0F \rightarrow 10{:}11 \overset{\text{JMP}}{\Longrightarrow} 1E{:}1F \rightarrow 20{:}21 \cdots$$

Like the Program Counter, the Index register ($\mathbf{X}$) holds an address. This address can be used to point to an operand in memory, with the advantage that it can be altered at any time by the program. Before developing this further we must examine the concepts of address mode and effective address.

In general, where an operand is involved, an instruction carries information re-garding its whereabouts. The various techniques used to calculate its exact location, known as its **effective address (EA)**, are known as **address modes**. The address modes used by BASIC's instructions are:

INHERENT or REGISTER DIRECT

Op-code

Inherent instructions usually target an internal register or do not have any operand. Examples of the former are CLeaR ACCUMULATOR (CLRA) or INcREMENT THE INdeX REGISTER (INX), which target the A and X registers respectively. The in-struction No OPeration (NOP) is an example where no operand is involved. In-herent instructions usually have all necessary information encoded in the op-code itself; that is the target location is inherently in the op-code. Thus CLRA is coded as $4Fh$; a single byte.

IMMEDIATE

op code	# data

Immediate instructions have a byte following the op-code, which is the data itself. As this data is part of the program, it is best treated as a constant. Essentially the effective address of the operand is immediately following the op-code. An example is ADDA #70h, coded as 8B-70*h*, which adds 70*h* (112) to the Accumulator.

DIRECT or ABSOLUTE

| op-code | Address |

Absolute instructions have the address of the operand directly following the op-code. Thus ADDA 70h, coded as 9B-70*h*, will add the *contents of* memory location 70*h* to the Accumulator. Although the effective address is fixed as part of the program, the operand data is a variable.

INDEXED or ADDRESS REGISTER INDIRECT

| op-code | unsigned X offset |

Indexed instructions calculate the effective address as the contents of the Index register plus the fixed offset following the op-code. Thus ADDA 10h,X, coded as AB-10*h*, will compute the operand's location as X + 10*h*. Now if the Index register happened to be 60*h* at this time, the EA would be 70*h*, and the nett result would be the addition of the object stored at 70*h* to the Accumulator. Although this seems a roundabout method of pointing to location 70*h*, it does have the advantage that the EA can be changed at any time by altering the state of X. Thus neither the operand nor its location are fixed in this address mode. This is particularly useful when scanning through large blocks of data, as in Examples 5.2 and 5.3.

RELATIVE

| op-code | Signed PC offset |

The Relative address mode computes the EA as the PC plus offset. For example, BRA 06, coded as 20-06*h*, branches forward six places, i.e. six is added to the PC. In BASIC, the Relative address mode is only applicable to the Branch operations. These are used to skip from one part of a program to another; usually conditional on the outcome of some test or action. Thus we can code statements such as:

> IF Z is zero
> > THEN DO this;
> > ELSE DO that;

We will discuss Branch instructions later.

Table 5.1 shows in more detail, the sequence of machine operations required to implement some of BASIC's instructions. Each op-code (steps 1 & 2) causes the CPU to cycle through a unique set of steps or **microinstructions** [5, 6]. Usually these are fixed by the manufacturer, but in certain cases the user can define a personalized set of microprograms. However, this is rare and the programmer normally works from the instruction set provided by the original designers (e.g. see Table 5.2).

The Instruction decoder shown in Fig. 5.4, deciphers the op-code brought down at the beginning of the fetch phase to the Instruction register. Figure 5.5 gives a

Step	Add to Accum (Absolute) ADDA = 9Bh	Add to Accum (Indexed) ADDA = ABh	Add to Accum (Immediate) ADDA = 8Bh	Branch if Equal to Zero (Relative) BEQ = 27h	Jump to (Absolute) JMP = 7Eh	Store Accum (Absolute) STA = 97h
1	PC to addr bus	PC to addr bus	PC to addr bus	PC to addr bus	PC to addr bus	PC to addr bus
2	R/W̄= 1 Data bus to Instruction reg PC++	R/W̄= 1 Data bus to Instruction reg PC++	R/W̄= 1 Data bus to Instruction reg PC++	R/W̄= 1 Data bus to Instruction reg PC++	R/W̄= 1 Data bus to Instruction reg PC++	R/W̄= 1 Data bus to Instruction reg PC++
3	PC to addr bus	PC to addr bus	PC to addr bus	PC to addr bus	PC to addr bus	PC to addr bus
4	R/W̄= 1 data bus to Data buffer reg PC++	R/W̄= 1 data bus to Data buffer reg PC++	R/W̄= 1 data bus to Data buffer reg PC++	R/W̄= 1 data bus to Data buffer reg PC++	R/W̄= 1 data bus to Data buffer reg PC++	R/W̄= 1 data bus to Data buffer reg PC++
5	Operand address to address bus	Gate address offset + [X] to ALU	Immediate operand to ALU	IF Z = 0 THEN return to Step 1 IF Z = 1 THEN gate offset+[PC] to ALU	Put operand address into PC	Put operand address on address bus
6	R/W̄= 1 data bus to ALU	ALU sum to address bus = [X] + offset	ADD command to ALU	ALU sum put into PC [PC]←[PC]+offset	Return to Step 1	R/W̄= 0 Accum to data bus
7	ADD command to ALU	R/W̄= 1 data bus to ALU	Return to Step 1	Return to Step 1	—	Return to Step 1
8	Return to Step 1	ADD command to ALU	—	—	—	—
9	—	Return to Step 1	—	—	—	—

Table 5.1: Showing the microprograms required to implement some of BASIC's instructions.

hypothetical implementation of the Instruction decoder. The 8-bit op-code together with the microcounter, act to address a ROM (or PLA). Each op-code addresses a different region of ROM, and as the microcounter goes through its cycle, the ROM generates the control sequence pertinent to the instruction. The last step of the sequence resets the microcounter, effectively causing a return to step 1; which fetches the next op-code. Usually, the op-code is partitioned to reduce the size of the control ROM. For example, all the LS nybbles of the ADDA instructions in Tables 5.1 and 5.2 are Bh. This can be used directly as the ALU function code for Add (see Fig. 3.50). Bits 5 & 4 define the address mode, with 00h for immediate, 01h for direct and 10h for indexed.

Returning to Fig. 5.4, we still require to explain the function of the **Code Condition register (CCR)** or Status register. This register is normally considered to be an array of separate flip flops used as **flags** or semaphores, to signal information regarding a previous operation carried out by the ALU. For example, if an Add or Subtract operation produces a carry or borrow respectively, then the C flag is set. Similarly the Z flag is set if the result of the operation was zero. The N flag sets whenever the most significant bit of the result is 1. If the operands involved in the operation are being treated as signed numbers, then this indicates a negative result. In the same situation, a sign overflow is signalled by the V flag, as illustrated in Example 2.43.

The state of the flags in the **CCR** are used by the Conditional Branch operations to decide whether the offset specified in the second byte of the instruction is added to the **PC**. This addition forces the program to break its orderly incremental sequence and skip to a different routine.

The Branch operation illustrated in Table 5.2 is a Conditional Branch, as the

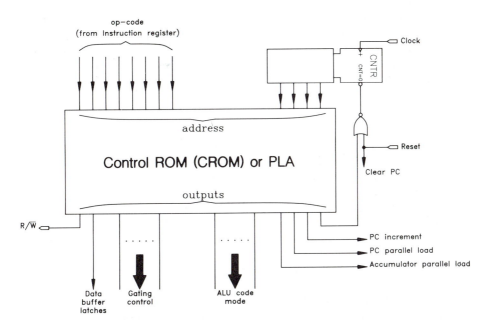

Figure 5.5: Possible implementation of the Instruction decoder (Control Unit).

skip only occurs if the **Z flag** has been set by a previous instruction. For example:

```
               LDA SWITCHES    ;Get the state of the switch bank
               BEQ NO_SWITCH   ;IF all Off THEN skip
        SET:   --- -----       ;Routine if a switch is set
               --- -----
               --- -----
               --- -----
               --- -----
   NO_SWITCH:  --- -----       ;Routine if no switch is set
```

Here the state of a bank of switches is put into the **Accumulator**. The act of loading
sets the **Z flag** if the operand is all zero ($00000000b$). The following BRANCH IF E-
QUAL TO ZERO (**BEQ**) instruction will skip forward to the routine I have labelled
NO_SWITCH, otherwise the sequence simply proceeds on to the routine labelled
SET. I have embellished the program with comments, which are distinguished from
instructions with a leading semicolon. Labels are conventionally differentiated by a
following colon, except when appearing as an operand.

There are two points to note concerning Branch operations. Firstly the **PC**
automatically increments after each byte is fetched (see Table 5.1). Thus the relative
offset is added onto a **PC** which has already gone forward two places. Thus the
instruction **BEQ 06** is a conditional skip forward to eight bytes past the location of
the instruction itself. If you actually wanted to go forward six places, the instruction

BEQ 04 would have to be used.

The second point to note is that a branch backwards is possible. This is because offsets are treated as signed numbers. Thus offsets of 80h and greater are effectively negative numbers (i.e. the sign bit is 1). As an example, let us assume that PC = 32h (00110010b); then the instruction BNE F0h will conditionally branch backwards by 16 (10h) places thus:

$$
\begin{array}{l}
\quad 0011\ 0010 \\
+1111\ 0000 \\
\hline
\cancel{1}\,\overline{0010\ 0010} = 22h
\end{array}
$$

The 2's complement of F0h is of course 10h (16). Remember that the offset will be from two bytes *past* the BNE op-code, as in the forward case.

Conditional Branches are important in that they permit computers to make decisions and take appropriate actions. Thus "if the water level in the tank is too low then open the valve and continue monitoring, otherwise proceed to the next stage". Reacting to external events distinguishes a computer/microprocessor from a simple sequencer.

To complete our discussion, it is instructive to write some programs. To do this we need to have the instruction set listing all operations which can be implemented by our BASIC MPU; which is given in Table 5.2.

Each operation is tabulated with its associated mnemonic in the leftmost column. The several possible op-codes are listed in the appropriate address mode column. In the **CCR** column, the response of the four flags are shown for each instruction. This information is essential when using the Conditional Branch operations.

Usually the manufacturer of the CPU/MPU provides a programming manual describing each operation in detail. However, except for the more intricate instructions, the thumbnail outline of the operation given in the rightmost column of the table is adequate.

The instructions may be grouped as follows:

MOVEMENT OPERATIONS

This covers Loading (incoming) and Storing (outgoing) operations for both the Accumulator and Index register.

ARITHMETIC OPERATIONS

Both addition and subtraction are provided. In both cases the facility of including the carry/borrow from the previous operation is included (ADCA and SBCA respectively).

Also included are incrementation of either the contents of **A**, **X** or data at any read/write memory location. Additionally, the contents of any read/write memory byte may be cleared. Of course incrementing and clearing can be implemented using addition and the appropriate data movement operations respectively, but their inclusion makes for convenience.

Operation/mnemonic		Immd	Direct	Index	Inher	Relat	N	Z	V	C	Operation
				Address Mode					CCR		
Add	ADDA	8B	9B	AB			↕	↕	↕	↕	A + M → A
Add with carry	ADCA	89	99	A9			↕	↕	↕	↕	A + M + C → A
Subtract	SUBA	80	90	A0			↕	↕	↕	↕	A − M → A
Subtract with carry	SBCA	82	92	A2			↕	↕	↕	↕	A − M − C → A
Load Accumulator	LDA	86	96	A6			↕	↕	R	·	M → A
Store Accumulator	STA		97	A7			↕	↕	R	·	A → M
Clear	CLR		7F	6F			R	S	R	R	0000 → M
Clear	CLRA				4F		R	S	R	R	0000 → A
Increment	INC		7C	6C			↕	↕	↕	·	M + 1 → M
Increment	INCA				4C		↕	↕	↕	·	A + 1 → A
Load Index Register	LDX	CE	DE	EE			↕	↕	R	·	M → X
Store Index Register	STX		DF	EF			↕	↕	R	·	X → M
Increment Index Register	INX				08		·	·	·	·	X + 1 → X
Jump	JMP		7E	6E			·	·	·	·	PC → address
Branch if higher	BHI					22	·	·	·	·	Branch if C + Z = 0
Branch if lower or same	BLS					23	·	·	·	·	Branch if C + Z = 1
Branch if not equal zero	BNE					26	·	·	·	·	Branch if Z = 0
Branch if equal zero	BEQ					27	·	·	·	·	Branch if Z = 1

Legend
R   Reset always
S   Set always
↕   Test and set if true, cleared otherwise
·   Not affected
→   transfers into
N   Negative (sign bit)

Z   Zero (byte)
V   Overflow, 2's complement
C   Carry
+   Plus except from BHI/BLS where
    logical OR is implied
A = Contents of Accumulator

PC = Contents of Program Counter
X = Contents of Index Register
CCR = Contents of Code Condition Register
M = Contents of memory

Table 5.2: The instruction set for BASIC's CPU.

PROGRAM COUNTER OPERATIONS

Instructions in this category modify the linear progression of the **PC**. In our instruction set, this is covered by an unconditional Jump and four Conditional Branch instructions. The Branch operations are normally used after a comparison of the contents of the Accumulator and a number m. This comparison is implemented as a subtraction of m from [**A**] (the contents of **A**), which activates the flags in the **CCR** appropriately (see Section 1.2.2). The various outcomes are:

[**A**] EQ	m	**Z** flag set	(Contents of **A** equals m)
[**A**] NEQ	m	**Z** flag clear	(Contents of **A** not equal to m)
[**A**] HI	m	**Z** & **C** clear	(Contents of **A** higher than m)
[**A**] LS	m	**Z** or **C** set	(Contents of **A** lower than or same as m)

Based on these results, the four Conditional Branch decisions are taken.

BEQ (BRANCH IF EQUAL)	Branches if **Z** $= 1$
BNE (BRANCH IF NOT EQUAL)	Branches if **Z** $= 0$
BHI (BRANCH IF HIGHER THAN)	Branches if **C**+**Z** $= 0$ (both clear)
BLS (BRANCH IF LOWER OR SAME)	Branches if **C**+**Z** $= 1$ (any set)

If the test is confirmed, the offset is added to the **PC**, else no alteration is made.

Sometimes the BEQ/BNE pair are used without a testing subtraction, to determine if the contents of a memory location is all zero. This is done by loading the data into the Accumulator, i.e. LDA m. From Table 5.2 we see that LDA sets the **Z** flag if $m = 0$, otherwise it is cleared. How could you check for zero in the Accumulator itself?

The collection of ordered steps or instructions necessary to implement a problem, is known as the **program**. Writing a program is essentially heuristic, but it is possible to identify several steps:

1. Converting the problem to an algorithm amenable to solution by the computer/microprocessor.

2. Listing the program instructions to implement the algorithm in an efficient manner. This form is known as an assembly-level program.

3. Coding the program in the binary form in which the instructions will be stored in memory. This is a machine-language program.

4. Downloading the machine-code listing (sometimes called a hex file) into the target memory and testing the program.

Programs in this section are listed in their mnemonic form, i.e. at assembly level. In addition, the operand address or data may be given in hexadecimal code or referred to by label. The whole program is then translated by hand, using Table 5.2, to hexadecimal. Normally the hardware/software used to load the program into the target memory will accept hexadecimal characters and translate to binary. This hexadecimal **machine-code file** is the only information of relevance in our program listings; labels, mnemonics and comments are decoration for human documentation purposes.

Although it is possible to hand assemble short programs for simple CPU/MPUs, this process is extremely tedious and error prone. For real software and hardware it is unrealistic. Fortunately boring rote tasks like this are ideal for computer implementation, and the **assembler** is one of a range of computer-aided engineering (CAE) programs which simplify the task of coding programs. Essentially an assembler takes a file – prepared using a word processor or editor – comprizing mnemonics and labels, and translates to a hexadecimal file readable by the loading software (perhaps an EPROM programmer). On the way it produces various intermediate files for documentation purposes, similar to the hand generated listings used in this section.

We will use an assembler to produce the program listings from the next section onwards. However, we will defer the discussion of how an assembler operates until Section 6.2.2.

Example 5.1

Write a program to add two 16-bit words P and Q, stored at 70:71h and 72:73h respectively. The sum is to be stored at 7D:7E:7Fh.

Solution

Where numbers of size larger than the memory word size are to be processed, **multiple-precision arithmetic** must be used. In this case, two 16-bit words are to be added, giving a possible 17-bit sum. For example FF:FF + FF:FF = 1:FF:FEh (65,535 + 65,535 = 131,070). This is done by adding the two least significant bytes to give the least significant byte of the sum (steps 40–60); then the two most significant bytes together with the carry from the last addition (steps 80–100).

If there is a carry from this last addition, then this must be put into the most significant sum byte, which can only be 1 or 0. To do this, the Accumulator is zeroed and the carry plus nothing added (ADCA #0). Notice that in step 120 the zeroing

Step	Label	Location	Code	Instruction		Commentary
10				.processor BASIC		
20				.define	P_LOW = 70h, Q_LOW = 71h, P_HIGH = 72h,	
					Q_HIGH = 73h, SUM_LOW = 7Dh,	
					SUM_MID = 7Eh, SUM_HIGH = 7Fh	
30				*;Add two lower bytes of P and Q to give lower byte of sum*		
40	DPADD:	00	96 70	LDA	P_LOW	*;LS byte P to A*
50		02	9B 72	ADDA	Q_LOW	*;LS byte Q added*
60		04	97 7D	STA	SUM_LOW	*;Put away as LS byte of SUM*
70				*;Now add the two higher bytes of P and Q with carry to give the middle byte of SUM*		
80		06	96 71	LDA	P_HIGH	*;MS byte P to A*
90		08	99 73	ADCA	Q_HIGH	*;MS byte Q plus carry added*
100		0A	97 7E	STA	SUM_MID	*;Put away as middle byte of SUM*
110				*;The carry bit from the last addition is the upper byte of the sum*		
120		0C	86 00	LDA	#00	*;Clears A without affecting C flag*
130		0E	89 00	ADCA	#00	*;Effectively adds previous carry only*
140		10	97 7F	STA	SUM_HIGH	*;Put away as the high byte of SUM*
150				.end		

Table 5.3: A double-precision addition.

is done by immediately loading the constant 00h into the Accumulator rather than using the more obvious CLEAR ACCUMULATOR (CLRA) instruction. This is because the latter also clears the C flag, whilst the former does not! Thus are software bugs born! Care must always be taken in using the state of a flag, to ensure that no such side effects are inadvertently missed.

The listing format is headed with a declaration of the processor type and then a list of labels are defined together with their value. The pseudo instructions .processor, .define and .end are not real machine instructions but are ways of passing information to the assembler. They are distinguished by a leading period. Although these programs are hand assembled, we are using this notation in preparation for the following sections.

Example 5.2

Write a program to add two 5-byte length numbers P and Q located at 60 – 64h and 65 – 69h respectively. The 6-byte sum is to be located at 70 – 75h.

Solution

The obvious solution to this problem is to rewrite the program of Example 5.1, but using five additions. However, another approach would be to repeat the addition routine inside a **loop** five times. This is more efficient in program length, as each of the five additions is virtually identical, except that the data locations advance once per word. The loop approach is illustrated in the flow chart of Fig. 5.6. Here the Index register is used as a pointer to the byte number being processed, advancing each loop pass from 0 through 4.

A **flow diagram** for the program is shown in Fig. 5.6. Such a diagram is part of

Step	Label	Location	Code	Instruction		Commentary
10				.processor BASIC		
20				.define	LOOP_CNT = 7Fh, BASE = 60h,	
					SUM_HIGH = 75h	
30	;Initialize loop counter to -5, IX pointed to base address and clear carry					
40	ADD_5:	00	86 FB	LDA	#−5	;Prepare to initialize counter to -5
50		02	97 7F	STA	LOOP_CNT	;which is kept in a spare memory byte
60		04	CE 60	LDX	#BASE	;Point IX to bottom of data array
70		06	4F	CLRA		;Clears the carry flag as a side effect
80	;DO the addition P[x] + Q[x] = SUM[x] WHILE LOOP_CNT is not zero					
90	LOOP:	07	A6 00	LDA	0,X	;Get P[x]
100		09	A9 05	ADCA	5,X	;add to Q[x] with old carry
110		0B	A7 10	STA	10h,X	;and put away as SUM[x]
120		0D	08	INX		;Advance the data pointer
130		0E	7C 7F	INC	LOOP_CNT	;Increment loop counter
140		10	26 F5	BNE	LOOP	;IF not yet zero THEN repeat loop
150	;Only the carry remains as the sum byte					
160		12	86 00	LDA	#00	;Clears A without affecting C flag
170		14	89 00	ADCA	#00	;Add previous carry only
180		16	97 75	STA	SUM_HIGH	;and put away as high byte of SUM
190				.end		

Table 5.4: Using a loop to add two 5-byte numbers.

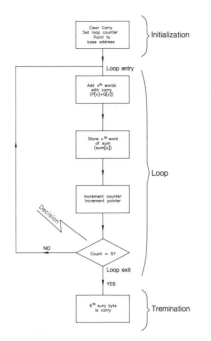

Figure 5.6: A flow diagram illustrating the concept of a program loop.

the process of converting the specification into an algorithm. As well as clarifying the algorithm, flow diagrams provide documentation for debugging and maintenance purposes. In general, boxes are used to indicate any kind of processing function, such as addition. The diamond symbol represents a decision that determines which of a number of alternative paths are followed on the basis of a decision process.

Several points arise from the flow diagram. Firstly, some means of determining the number of times the loop is traversed must be devised in order to eventually get out! With the primitive set of instructions available to us, the only possible approach is to use a memory location as a counter, which must be incremented and tested after each pass through the loop. In this case location 7Fh has been arbitrarily chosen to store **Loop_cnt** and is initially set to -5 (FBh) in step 40. After five passes, **Loop_cnt** becomes zero, which then causes the program execution to pass through the BRANCH IF NOT EQUAL instruction of step 140 and out of the loop. In general for good **structured programming**, there should only be one way into and one way out of a loop. Notice how the use of a label in step 140 clarifies the branching destination. In this case a skip backwards of eleven places is needed, remembering that the **PC** has already gone forward to 12h (-11 is $1,11110101b = $ F5h). An assembler will automatically do this calculation for you if you use a label.

Finally, the resulting carry is moved into the most significant byte of the sum; in the same manner as the previous example.

Although the listing of Table 5.4 is only slightly shorter (23 bytes against 36 bytes), this advantage is increased for longer data arrays; such as in Example 5.3. However, the downside is a much slower execution time. This is because of the various 'book-keeping' instructions (steps 120–140) which must be repeated each loop pass. Also indexed operations are more complex and therefore take longer than their absolute counterparts to execute (see Table 5.1).

Example 5.3

Write a program that will clear all memory locations between 80h and FFh.

Solution

This is a very simple program. Essentially the Index register is pointed to the first memory location, and a zeroed Accumulator sent out. Inside the loop the Index register is progressively advanced, pointing to each memory byte in turn until it wraps around from FFh (1111 1111b) to 00h (00000000b).

The only question arising is, why use the STA 0,X instruction (with the Accumulator cleared outside the loop) instead of the more obvious CLR 0,X. The reason lies with information not given in Table 5.2. The former takes five clock cycles to complete, whilst the latter takes six. As the loop is traversed 128 times, then that number of cycles is saved, against the extra one byte needed to hold STA 0,X.

How many bytes of program did this loop program save over the linear equivalent? If CLRA takes two cycles, LDX # three and STA absolute, INX and BNE all take four cycles, how much longer will the loop equivalent take?

Step	Label	Location	Code	Instruction		Commentary
10				.processor BASIC		
20				.define BASE = 80h		
30				;Initialize by clearing Accumulator & pointing to the base of the array of memory locations		
40		00	CE 80	LDX	#BASE	;Point IX to bottom of data array
50		02	4F	CLRA		;Clears Accumulator
60				;DO the clearing WHILE LOOP_CNT until IX comes around to zero		
70	LOOP:	03	A7 00	STA	0,X	;Clear memory[x]
80		05	08	INX		;Advance the data pointer
90		06	26 FB	BNE	LOOP	;IF not yet zero THEN repeat loop
100				.end		

Table 5.5: Using a loop to clear a bank of memory.

5.2   The 6809 Microprocessor Unit

In 1974 Motorola introduced the 6800 [7] as a direct competitor to the Intel 8080, which at that time was the standard 8-bit microprocessor. The 6800 was perceived to be the easier of the two to use by virtue of its single 5 V supply requirement and a clean internal structure. The 8085 MPU is the current Intel 8-bit device. First produced in 1976, it also runs off a single power supply, with the bonus of an integral clock generator, but has a virtually identical instruction set to the 8080. Soon after, Zilog manufactured its Z80 MPU, which is upwardly compatible with Intel's offering, with a much extended instruction set and additional registers [8]. The 6809 MPU [9, 10, 11], introduced in 1979, was seen as Motorola's answer to the Z80 and these both represent the most powerful general-purpose 8-bit devices currently available.

By the early 1980s, the focus was moving to 16 and 32-bit MPUs and to single-chip microcomputer units (MCUs), and it is unlikely that there will be further significant developments in general-purpose 8-bit devices. Nevertheless, these M-PUs are powerful enough to replace many applications which would use random logic implementations, and at the time of writing, still outsell their newer and more glamorous offspring. The 6809's architecture is relatively straightforward, and for these reasons we have chosen to use this to illustrate microprocessor design techniques. In Section 5.4 we will look at some of the newer developments in this field.

After reading this section you should:

- Know the internal architecture of the 6809 MPU and the function of the various registers.

- Understand the function and the timing interaction of the major 6809 control signals.

- Appreciate the various address modes used to specify the effective address of the operand, especially the versatile indexed schemes.

- Appreciate the structure, utility and mechanism of a subroutine, and its interaction with the stack.

- Be able to write simple subroutines, passing parameters back and forth between the calling program.

- Understand the role of the interrupt and how the microprocessor handles these exceptional events.

5.2.1 Architecture

The internal structure of the 6809 MPU is shown in Fig. 5.7. If it looks suspiciously like BASIC's structure of Fig. 5.4, this is because this hypothetical device was modelled after the 6800 MPU, the 6809's ancestor. The BASIC CPU has one severe failing, the restriction of an 8-bit address bus. This limits the memory to 256 bytes, which has to hold both the program and data. This is clearly inadequate. Increasing the address bus to 16 bits expands the number of possible byte locations to 2^{16} (65,536) or 64 Kbyte (1 K = 2^{10} = 1024).

The 6809 MPU requires only a 40-pin package, which covers the eight data lines, 16 address lines, 14 control signals and the two power pins. Some MPUs have a pin count as low as 16, which is achieved by time sharing some pins. Thus, at the beginning of the clock cycle the data bus may carry part of the address, only reverting to the data part way through. This approach requires external latch circuits to unscramble these signals.

Registers to the left of the diagram are address oriented, and hold a full 16-bit address, except for the Direct Page register. Besides the Address register, Program Counter (PC) and Index register_X, the 6809 has a second Index register_Y and two Stack Pointer registers, Stack Pointer_S and Stack Pointer_U. Stack Pointers aim at an area of read/write memory called the stack, which is used for temporary data

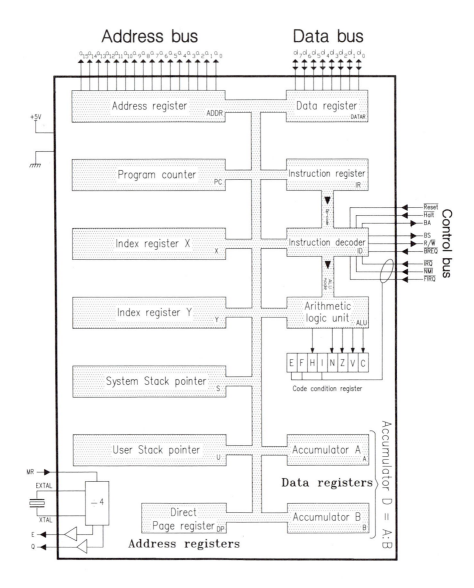

Figure 5.7: The 6809 microprocessor internal structure.

storage. We will look at the structure of a stack in the next two sections. The Direct Page register holds an 8-bit offset for a short form of absolute addressing, which is discussed in the following section.

Registers to the right-hand of the diagram deal with 8-bit data from the data bus. The Instruction register holds the op-code brought down during the fetch phase. The Instruction decoder generates the appropriate internal action including setting up the mode of the Arithmetic Logic Unit (ALU). The ALU can add, subtract, multiply and implement the primary logic operations, as well as shift data left or right. The processing size of the ALU normally defines the size of the MPU, which in this case is 8-bit. The data bus normally matches the ALU size, but in some cases can be smaller, with multiple Move operations being used to build up the data.

The 6809 MPU has two 8-bit Accumulators, classified as Data registers. With one minor exception, all instructions can target either Accumulator; for example ADDA #6 or ADDB #6 adds the constant six to the contents of Accumulator_A or Accumulator_B respectively. A few instructions can combine the two as a single 16-bit register called Accumulator_D (for double). Thus ADDD #1234h effectively adds $34h$ to Accumulator_B and $12h$ plus carry to Accumulator_A in one instruction. However, double instructions require two passes through the 8-bit ALU.

The Code Condition register (CCR) has the four flags previously discussed, i.e. C for carry/borrow, Z for zero, N for bit 7/negative and V for 2's complement overflow. The H flag is the carry between bits 3 and 4, i.e. the half carry between lower and upper nybbles. It is used for BCD arithmetic where these nybbles are BCD decades. We will discuss this in Section 5.2.2. The E flag, I and F masks are used for interrupt handling, which is the subject of Sections 5.2.3 and 5.3.3.

Looking at the external signals in more detail we have:

DATA BUS (D(n))

A single bidirectional 8-bit data bus carries both instruction and operand data to and from the MPU (read and write respectively). When enabled, data lines can drive up to four 74 LS loads and 130 pF without external buffering. Data lines are high impedance (turned Off) when the processor is halted or in a Direct Memory Access (DMA) mode.

ADDRESS BUS (A(n))

Sixteen address lines can be externally decoded to directly activate up to 2^{16} byte locations, the data from which can then be connected to the common data bus. During cycles when the MPU is internally processing, the address bus is set to all ones (FFFFh) and the data bus to Read. When enabled, up to four 74 LS loads and 90 pF can be driven. $\overline{\text{Halt}}$ and $\overline{\text{DMA/BREQ}}$ float this bus.

CONTROL BUS

All MPUs have similar data and address buses, but differ considerably in the miscellany of functions conveniently lumped together as the control bus. These indicate to the outside world the status of the processor, or allow these external circuits control over the processor operation.

Power (V_{CC}, V_{SS})

A single 5 V ±5% supply dissipating a maximum of 1.0 W (200 mA). The analogous Hitachi 6309 CMOS MPU dissipates 60 mW during normal operation and 10 mW in its sleep mode.

Read/$\overline{\text{Write}}$ (R/$\overline{\text{W}}$)

Used to indicate the status of the data bus, High for Read and Low for Write. $\overline{\text{Halt}}$ and $\overline{\text{DMA/BREQ}}$ float this signal.

$\overline{\text{Halt}}$

A Low level here causes the MPU to stop running at the end of the present instruction. Both data and address buses are floated, as is R/$\overline{\text{W}}$. While halted the MPU does not respond to external interrupt requests. The system clocks (E & Q) continue running.

$\overline{\text{DMA/BREQ}}$

This is similar to $\overline{\text{Halt}}$ in that data, address and R/$\overline{\text{W}}$ signals are floated. However, the MPU does not wait until the end of the current instruction execution. This gives a latency (response delay) of $1\frac{1}{2}$ cycles as opposed to a worst-case Halt latency of 21 cycles. The payback is that with the processor clock frozen, the internal dynamic registers will loose data unless periodically refreshed. Thus the MPU automatically pulls out of this mode every 14 clock cycles for an internal refresh before resuming (cycle stealing).

$\overline{\text{Reset}}$

A Low level at this input will reset the MPU. As long as this pin is held Low the vector address FFFEh will be presented on the address bus. On release, the 16-bit data stored at FFFEh and FFFFh will be moved to the Program Counter; thus the Reset vector FFFE:Fh should always hold the restart address.

   $\overline{\text{Reset}}$ should be held Low for not less than 100 ms to permit the clock generator to stabilize after a power-on. As the $\overline{\text{Reset}}$ pin has a Schmitt-trigger input with a threshold (4 V minimum) higher than that of standard TTL-compatible peripherals (2 V maximum), a simple CR network may be used to reset the entire system. This is because the peripheral devices will be out of their reset state before the MPU.

Non-Maskable Interrupt ($\overline{\text{NMI}}$)

A negative *edge* (pulse width one clock cycle minimum) at this pin forces the MPU to complete its current instruction, save all internal registers (except the System Stack Pointer, SP) on the System stack and vector to a program whose start address is held in the NMI vector FFFC:Dh. The E flag in the CCR is set to indicate that the entire set of MPU registers (machine state) has been saved. The I and F mask bits are set to prevent further interrupts from this source. If the NMI program service routine is terminated by the RеTurn from Interrupt (RTI) instruction, the machine state is restored and the interrupted program continues. After Reset, $\overline{\text{NMI}}$ will not be recognized until the **SSP** is set up (e.g. LDS #TOS+1 points the **SSP** to the top of the stack, TOS). More details are given in Section 5.2.3.

Fast Interrupt Request ($\overline{\text{FIRQ}}$)

A Low *level* at this pin causes an interrupt in a similar manner to $\overline{\text{NMI}}$. However, this time the interrupt will be locked out if the F mask in the **CCR** is set (as it is automatically when the MPU is Reset). If **F** is clear then the MPU will vector via FFF6:7h after saving only the **PC** and **CCR** on the System Stack. The F and I masks are set to lock out any further maskable interrupts and the E flag cleared to show that the entire machine state has not been saved. As $\overline{\text{FIRQ}}$ is level sensitive, the source of this signal must go back High before the end of the service routine.

Interrupt Request ($\overline{\text{IRQ}}$)

A Low *level* at this pin causes the MPU to vector via FFF8:9h to the start of the IRQ service routine, provided that the I mask bit is cleared (it is set automatically when the MPU is Reset). The entire machine state is saved on the System stack and I mask set to prevent any further IRQ interrupts (but not FIRQ or NMI). As in $\overline{\text{FIRQ}}$, the $\overline{\text{IRQ}}$ signal must be removed before the end of the service routine. On RTI the machine state will be restored, and as this includes the **CCR**, the I mask will return Low automatically.

Bus Available, Bus Status (BA, BS)

These are status signals which may be decoded for external control purposes. Their four states (BA, BS) are:

      00 : Normally running
      01 : Interrupt or reset in progress
      10 : A software SYNC is in progress (see Section 5.2.3).
      11 : MPU halted or has granted its bus to $\overline{\text{DMA/BREQ}}$

Clock (XTAL, EXTAL)

An on-chip oscillator requires an external parallel-resonant crystal between the X-TAL and EXTAL pins and two small capacitors to ground. The internal oscillator provides a processor clocking rate of one quarter of the crystal resonant frequency. The basic 6809 MPU is a 1 MHz device requiring a 4 MHz crystal, whilst the 68A09 and 68B09 1.5 and 2 MHz versions need 6 and 8 MHz crystals respectively. In all cases there is a lower frequency limit at 100 kHz due to the need to keep the internal dynamic registers constantly refreshed. If desired, an external TTL-level oscillator may be used to drive EXTAL, with XTAL grounded.

Enable, Quadrature (E, Q)

These are buffered clock signals from the internal (or external) clock generator.

They are used to synchronize devices taking data from or putting data on the data bus. We will look at the timing relationship between these signals and the main buses in the following section. E is sometimes labelled ϕ_2 after the second phase clock signal needed for the 6800 MPU, which fulfilled a similar role.

Memory Ready ($\overline{\text{MRDY}}$)

This is a control input to the internal clock oscillator. By activating $\overline{\text{MRDY}}$, a slow external memory or peripheral device can freeze the oscillator until its data is ready. This is subject to a maximum of 10 ms in order to keep the MPU's dynamic registers happy.

A microprocessor monitors and controls external events by sending and receiving information via its data bus through interface circuitry. In order to interface to a MPU it is necessary to understand the interplay between the relevant buses and control signals. These involve sequences of events and are usually presented as timing diagrams.

Consider the execution of the instruction **LDA 6000h**, which moves the contents of location $6000h$ down into Accumulator_A ($[A] \leftarrow [6000]$). This instruction takes

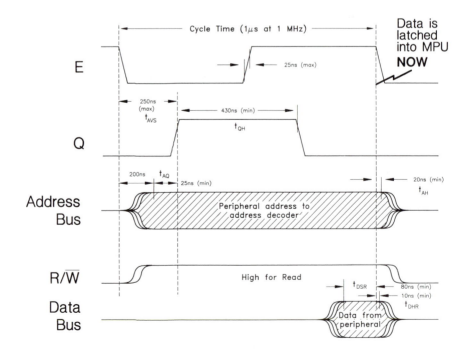

Figure 5.8: A snapshot of the 6809 MPU reading data from a peripheral device. Worst-case worst-case 1 MHz device times are shown.

four clock cycles to implement, three to fetch down the 3-byte instruction (B6-60-
00*h*) and one to send out the peripheral (memory or otherwise) address and put the
resulting data into Accumulator A. Figure 5.8 shows a somewhat simplified state of
affairs during that last cycle, with the assumption of a 1 MHz clock frequency. The
address will be out and stable by not later than 25 ns before Q goes High (t_{AQ}).
The external device (at 6000 hex in our example) must then respond and set up its
data on the bus by no later than 80 ns (t_{DSR}) before the falling edge of E, which
signals the cycle end. Such data must remain held for a least 10 ns (t_{DHR}) to ensure
successful latching into the internal Data register.

Writing data to an external device or memory cell is broadly similar, as illustrated in Fig. 5.9; which shows the waveforms associated with, for example, the last
cycle of a STA 8000h (Store) instruction.

Once again the address and R/$\overline{W}$ signals appear just before the rising edge of Q.
This time it is the MPU which places the data on the bus, which will be stable well
before the falling edge of Q. This data will disappear within 30 ns of the cycle end
(t_{DHW}); the corresponding address hold time t_{AH} is 20 ns.

When doing a Write action, the falling edge of Q signals to the destination
memory or output port that data is valid. In the latter situation, this edge is
typically used to trigger an array of flip flops or disable an array of latches (see the
output port in Fig. 4.14. In the reading situation, the MPU grabs data on the bus
at the falling edge of the E cycle. The rising edge of Q signals that the address is
valid in both reading and writing situations.

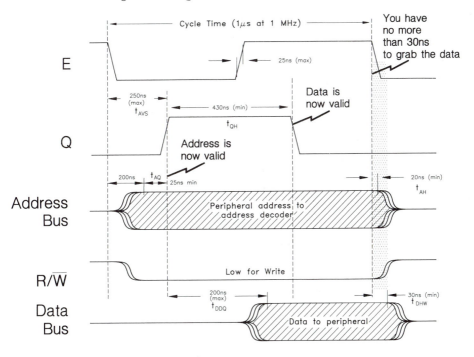

Figure 5.9: Sending data to the outside world.

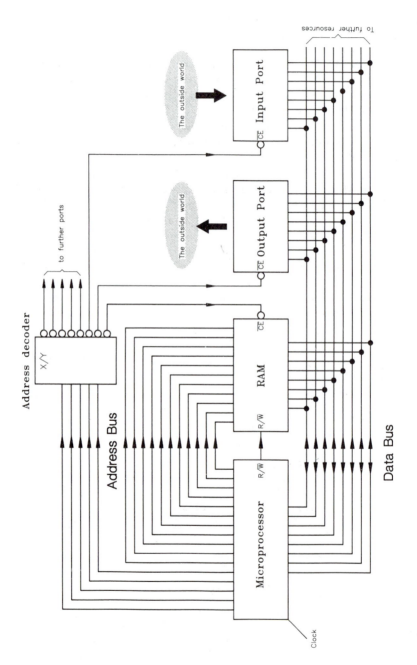

Figure 5.10: The structure of a synchronous common-bus microcomputer.

The basic structure of a synchronous common data bus MPU-based system is shown in Fig. 5.10. The term synchronous is used to denote that normal communication between peripheral device and MPU is open loop, with the latter having no knowledge of whether data is available or will be accepted at the end of a clock cycle. Use of the $\overline{\text{MRDY}}$ input to slow things down is considered an abnormal interchange.

As all external devices communicate to the master through a single data highway, it is necessary to ensure that only one is active on any exchange. All microprocessors use an address bus for this purpose. Taken together with external decoding circuitry, each target can be assigned a specific address and thus enabled uniquely. As depicted in Fig. 5.10, only one central decoder is used, but in a larger system there is likely to be a central decoder dividing the available memory space into zones or pages and local decoders providing the 'fine print'. Memory chips of course are not single devices, but comprise a multitude of addressable cells; they have their secondary decoder on-board (see Fig. 4.44(b)). The 808x MPU family can use a separate address structure for memory and peripheral selection. As well as requiring additional pins on the package, special instructions must be provided to use this scheme.

We will look at address decoding and interfacing in detail in Section 5.3. Meanwhile we will examine the 6809's machine-level software.

5.2.2 Machine-Level Software

The 6809 instruction set comprizes 59 distinct operations. These are listed in Table 5.6, where each operation is tabulated in all its versions with the corresponding op-code listed in the appropriate address-mode column. Thus the Add operation comes in three varieties, ADDA (ADD TO ACCUMULATOR_A), ADDB (ADD TO AC-CUMULATOR_B) and ADDD (ADD TO ACCUMULATOR_D). The former has the op-code 8Bh for the Immediate address mode, 9Bh for Direct, ABh for Indexed and BBh for Extended Direct. As the 6809 can use not only **X**, but **Y, S, U** or **PC** as its Index register, the Index op-code is extended to 16 bits by using a post-byte. Thus ADDA 0,X has the op-code AB-84h and ADDA 0,Y is AB-94h. The use of a post-byte gives the 6809 MPU a total of 1464 op-codes [9].

Each operation requires a set number of clock periods for implementation, as indicated under the $\sim$ symbol. Thus ADDA Immediate takes 2 $\sim$, Direct takes 4 $\sim$ and Extended Direct 5 $\sim$. The Indexed mode is more complex, being listed as 4+ $\sim$. The execution time here depends on the nature of the Index offset, which we will discuss later, but the additional time can be as much as 8 $\sim$. For example ADDA 0,X takes $4 + 0 = 4 \sim$, but ADDA 8000h,X takes $4 + 4 = 8 \sim$. For a 1 MHz clock, $\sim$ translates directly to microseconds.

The # column lists the number of bytes for each situation. Thus ADDA #06 takes two bytes 8B-06h, ADDA 06 coded as 9B-06h is also two bytes long. The extended direct version, which has a 2-byte address, is three bytes; e.g. ADDA 9000h is BB-90-00h. As would be expected, the indexed modes are of variable length. Thus ADDA 0,X is AB-94h (two bytes) whilst ADDA 8000h,X is AB-89-80-00h (four bytes).

Each instruction carries a thumbnail description of the operation or conditional branch test as appropriate. The effects of the operation on each of the core five code condition register flags are also indicated. The three interrupt related masks and flag (**I**, **F** and **E**) are not affected by any software instruction, except `ANDCC` and `ORCC`.

Before looking at the instructions in more detail, we will catalog the address modes available to the 6809 programmer. All the address modes available to the BASIC CPU (see Table 5.2) are provided with the addition of an extended version of direct addressing, which carries a full 16 bit address. As we have already observed, the indexed mode has been considerably enhanced.

In the following catalog, the op-code may be one or two bytes.

Inherent

op-code

All the operand information is contained in the op-code, with no specific address-related bytes following. Most of the 6809 inherent operations are one byte long. An example is `NOP` (NO OPERATION). Motorola also classify most register-direct instructions as inherent, for example `INCA` (INCREMENT A).

Register Direct, $\sum$R

op-code	post-byte

Information concerning the source register(s) and/or destination register(s) are contained in a post-byte. For example `TFR A,B` (TRANSFER THE CONTENTS OF A TO B) is coded as 0001 1111 1000 1001b (1F-89h). The post-byte here is divided into two fields. The left field specifies the source register, and the right the destination. Each register is encoded as a bit in a 4-wide code. Thus 1000b is **A** and 1001b is **B**. A list of codes is given bottom right in Table 5.6(b). The Transfer, Exchange, Push, and Pull operations (see Section 5.2.3) come under this category.

Immediate,   #kk

op-code	constant

8 bit

op-code	constant

16 bit

With immediate addressing, the byte or bytes following the op-code are constant data and not a pointer to data. Some examples are:

```
(8B-30)         ADD   #30h    ;Add the constant 30h
(8E-20-00)      LDX   #2000h  ;Put the constant 2000h in X
(10-8C-21-FF)   CMPY  #21FFh  ;Compare [Y] with the constant 21FFh
```

The pound (hash) symbol # is commonly used to indicate a constant number.

Instruction	Forms	Immediate Op	~	#	Direct Op	~	#	Indexed Op	~	#	Extended Op	~	#	Inherent Op	~	#	Description	H	N	Z	V	C
ABX														3A	3	1	B + X → X (Unsigned)	•	•	•	•	•
ADC	ADCA	89	2	2	99	4	2	A9	4+	2+	B9	5	3				A + M + C → A	↕	↕	↕	↕	↕
	ADCB	C9	2	2	D9	4	2	E9	4+	2+	F9	5	3				B + M + C → B	↕	↕	↕	↕	↕
ADD	ADDA	8B	2	2	9B	4	2	AB	4+	2+	BB	5	3				A + M → A	↕	↕	↕	↕	↕
	ADDB	CB	2	2	DB	4	2	EB	4+	2+	FB	5	3				B + M → B	↕	↕	↕	↕	↕
	ADDD	C3	4	3	D3	6	2	E3	6+	2+	F3	7	3				D + M:M + 1 → D	•	↕	↕	↕	↕
AND	ANDA	84	2	2	94	4	2	A4	4+	2+	B4	5	3				A Λ M → A	•	↕	↕	0	•
	ANDB	C4	2	2	D4	4	2	E4	4+	2+	F4	5	3				B Λ M → B	•	↕	↕	0	•
	ANDCC	1C	3	2													CC Λ IMM → CC					7
ASL	ASLA													48	2	1	A	8	↕	↕	↕	↕
	ASLB													58	2	1	B	8	↕	↕	↕	↕
	ASL				08	6	2	68	6+	2+	78	7	3				M	8	↕	↕	↕	↕
ASR	ASRB													47	2	1	A	8	↕	↕	•	↕
	ASR													57	2	1	B	8	↕	↕	•	↕
	ASR				07	6	2	67	6+	2+	77	7	3				M	8	↕	↕	•	↕
BIT	BITA	85	2	2	95	4	2	A5	4+	2+	B5	5	3				Bit Test A (M Λ A)	•	↕	↕	0	•
	BITB	C5	2	2	D5	4	2	E5	4+	2+	F5	5	3				Bit Test B (M Λ B)	•	↕	↕	0	•
CLR	CLRA													4F	2	1	0 → A	•	0	1	0	0
	CLRB													5F	2	1	0 → B	•	0	1	0	0
	CLR				0F	6	2	6F	6+	2+	7F	7	3				0 → M	•	0	1	0	0
CMP	CMPA	81	2	2	91	4	2	A1	4+	2+	B1	5	3				Compare M from A	8	↕	↕	↕	↕
	CMPB	C1	2	2	D1	4	2	E1	4+	2+	F1	5	3				Compare M from B	8	↕	↕	↕	↕
	CMPD	10 83	5	4	10 93	7	3	10 A3	7+	3+	10 B3	8	4				Compare M:M + 1 from D	•	↕	↕	↕	↕
	CMPS	11 8C	5	4	11 9C	7	3	11 AC	7+	3+	11 BC	8	4				Compare M:M + 1 from S	•	↕	↕	↕	↕
	CMPU	11 83	5	4	11 93	7	3	11 A3	7+	3+	11 B3	8	4				Compare M:M + 1 from U	•	↕	↕	↕	↕
	CMPX	8C	4	3	9C	6	2	AC	6+	2+	BC	7	3				Compare M:M + 1 from X	•	↕	↕	↕	↕
	CMPY	10 8C	5	4	10 9C	7	3	10 AC	7+	3+	10 BC	8	4				Compare M:M + 1 from Y	•	↕	↕	↕	↕
COM	COMA													43	2	1	Ā → A	•	↕	↕	0	1
	COMB													53	2	1	B̄ → B	•	↕	↕	0	1
	COM				03	6	2	63	6+	2+	73	7	3				M̄ → M	•	↕	↕	0	1
CWAI		3C	≥20	2													CC Λ IMM → CC Wait for Interrupt					7
DAA														19	2	1	Decimal Adjust A	•	↕	↕	0	↕
DEC	DECA													4A	2	1	A - 1 → A	•	↕	↕	↕	•
	DECB													5A	2	1	B - 1 → B	•	↕	↕	↕	•
	DEC				0A	6	2	6A	6+	2+	7A	7	3				M - 1 → M	•	↕	↕	↕	•
EOR	EORA	88	2	2	98	4	2	A8	4+	2+	B8	5	3				A ⊻ M → A	•	↕	↕	0	•
	EORB	C8	2	2	D8	4	2	E8	4+	2+	F8	5	3				B ⊻ M → B	•	↕	↕	0	•
EXG	R1, R2	1E	8	2													R1 ↔ R2[2]	•	•	•	•	•
INC	INCA													4C	2	1	A + 1 → A	•	↕	↕	↕	•
	INCB													5C	2	1	B + 1 → B	•	↕	↕	↕	•
	INC				0C	6	2	6C	6+	2+	7C	7	3				M + 1 → M	•	↕	↕	↕	•
JMP					0E	3	2	6E	3+	2+	7E	4	3				EA[3] → PC	•	•	•	•	•
JSR					9D	7	2	AD	7+	2+	BD	8	3				Jump to Subroutine	•	•	•	•	•
LD	LDA	86	2	2	96	4	2	A6	4+	2+	B6	5	3				M → A	•	↕	↕	0	•
	LDB	C6	2	2	D6	4	2	E6	4+	2+	F6	5	3				M → B	•	↕	↕	0	•
	LDD	CC	3	3	DC	5	2	EC	5+	2+	FC	6	3				M:M + 1 → D	•	↕	↕	0	•
	LDS	10 CE	4	4	10 DE	6	3	10 EE	6+	3+	10 FE	7	4				M:M + 1 → S	•	↕	↕	0	•
	LDU	CE	3	3	DE	5	2	EE	5+	2+	FE	6	3				M:M + 1 → U	•	↕	↕	0	•
	LDX	8E	3	3	9E	5	2	AE	5+	2+	BE	6	3				M:M + 1 → X	•	↕	↕	0	•
	LDY	10 8E	4	4	10 9E	6	3	10 AE	6+	3+	10 BE	7	4				M:M + 1 → Y	•	↕	↕	0	•
LEA	LEAS							32	4+	2+							EA[3] → S	•	•	•	•	•
	LEAU							33	4+	2+							EA[3] → U	•	•	•	•	•
	LEAX							30	4+	2+							EA[3] → X	•	•	↕	•	•
	LEAY							31	4+	2+							EA[3] → Y	•	•	↕	•	•

Legend:

OP	Operation Code (Hexadecimal)	M̄	Complement of M	↕	Test and set if true, cleared otherwise
~	Number of MPU Cycles	→	Transfer Into	•	Not Affected
#	Number of Program Bytes	H	Half-carry (from bit 3)	CC	Condition Code Register
+	Arithmetic Plus	N	Negative (sign bit)	:	Concatenation
-	Arithmetic Minus	Z	Zero (Reset)	V	Logical or
•	Multiply	V	Overflow, 2's complement	Λ	Logical and
		C	Carry from ALU	⊻	Logical Exclusive or

Table 5.6: (a) The M6809 instruction set (*continued next page*).

Instruction	Forms	Imm Op	Imm ~	Imm #	Dir Op	Dir ~	Dir #	Idx Op	Idx ~	Idx #	Ext Op	Ext ~	Ext #	Inh Op	Inh ~	Inh #	Description	H	N	Z	V	C
LSL	LSLA													48	2	1	A	•	↕	↕	↕	↕
	LSLB													58	2	1	B	•	↕	↕	↕	↕
	LSL				08	6	2	68	6+	2+	78	7	3				M	•	↕	↕	↕	↕
LSR	LSRA													44	2	1	A	•	0	↕	•	↕
	LSRB													54	2	1	B 0→	•	0	↕	•	↕
	LSR				04	6	2	64	6+	2+	74		3				M	•	0	↕	•	↕
MUL														3D	11	1	A × B → D (Unsigned)	•	•	↕	•	9
NEG	NEGA													40	2	1	Ā + 1 → A	8	↕	↕	↕	↕
	NEGB													50	2	1	B̄ + 1 → B	8	↕	↕	↕	↕
	NEG				00	6	2	60	6+	2+	70	7	3				M̄ + 1 → M	8	↕	↕	↕	↕
NOP														12	2	1	No Operation	•	•	•	•	•
OR	ORA	8A	2	2	9A	4	2	AA	4+	2+	BA	5	3				A V M → A	•	↕	↕	0	•
	ORB	CA	2	2	DA	4	2	EA	4+	2+	FA	5	3				B V M → B	•	↕	↕	0	•
	ORCC	1A	3	2													CC V IMM → CC			7		
PSH	PSHS	34	5+4	2													Push Registers on S Stack	•	•	•	•	•
	PSHU	36	5+4	2													Push Registers on U Stack	•	•	•	•	•
PUL	PULS	35	5+4	2													Pull Registers from S Stack	•	•	•	•	•
	PULU	37	5+4	2													Pull Registers from U Stack	•	•	•	•	•
ROL	ROLA													49	2	1	A	•	↕	↕	↕	↕
	ROLB													59	2	1	B	•	↕	↕	↕	↕
	ROL				09	6	2	69	6+	2+	79	7	3				M	•	↕	↕	↕	↕
ROR	RORA													46	2	1	A	•	↕	↕	•	↕
	RORB													56	2	1	B	•	↕	↕	•	↕
	ROR				06	6	2	66	6+	2+	76	7	3				M	•	↕	↕	•	↕
RTI														3B	6/15	1	Return From Interrupt			7		
RTS														39	5	1	Return from Subroutine	•	•	•	•	•
SBC	SBCA	82	2	2	92	4	2	A2	4+	2+	B2	5	3				A − M − C → A	8	↕	↕	↕	↕
	SBCB	C2	2	2	D2	4	2	E2	4+	2+	F2	5	3				B − M − C → B	8	↕	↕	↕	↕
SEX														1D	2	1	Sign Extend B into A	•	↕	↕	0	•
ST	STA				97	4	2	A7	4+	2+	B7	5	3				A → M	•	↕	↕	0	•
	STB				D7	4	2	E7	4+	2+	F7	5	3				B → M	•	↕	↕	0	•
	STD				DD	5	2	ED	5+	2+	FD	6	3				D → M M+1	•	↕	↕	0	•
	STS				10 DF	6	3	10 EF	6+	3+	10 FF	7	4				S → M M+1	•	↕	↕	0	•
	STU				DF	5	2	EF	5+	2+	FF	6	3				U → M M+1	•	↕	↕	0	•
	STX				9F	5	2	AF	5+	2+	BF	6	3				X → M M+1	•	↕	↕	0	•
	STY				10 9F	6	3	10 AF	6+	3+	10 BF	7	4				Y → M M+1	•	↕	↕	0	•
SUB	SUBA	80	2	2	90	4	2	A0	4+	2+	B0	5	3				A − M → A	8	↕	↕	↕	↕
	SUBB	C0	2	2	D0	4	2	E0	4+	2+	F0	5	3				B − M → B	8	↕	↕	↕	↕
	SUBD	83	4	3	93	6	2	A3	6+	2+	B3	7	3				D − M M+1 → D	•	↕	↕	↕	↕
SWI	SWI[6]													3F	19	1	Software Interrupt 1	•	•	•	•	•
	SWI2[6]													10 3F	20	2	Software Interrupt 2	•	•	•	•	•
	SWI3[6]													11 3F	20	2	Software Interrupt 3	•	•	•	•	•
SYNC														13	≥4	1	Synchronize to Interrupt	•	•	•	•	•
TFR	R1, R2	1F	6	2													R1 → R2[2]	•	•	•	•	•
TST	TSTA													4D	2	1	Test A	•	↕	↕	0	•
	TSTB													5D	2	1	Test B	•	↕	↕	0	•
	TST				0D	6	2	6D	6+	2+	7D	7	3				Test M	•	↕	↕	0	•

Notes:

1. This column gives a base cycle and byte count. To obtain total count, add the values obtained from the INDEXED ADDRESSING MODE table.

2. R1 and R2 may be any pair of 8 bit or any pair of 16 bit registers.
   The 8 bit registers are: A, B, CC, DP
   The 16 bit registers are: X, Y, U, S, D, PC

3. EA is the effective address.

4. The PSH and PUL instructions require 5 cycles plus 1 cycle for each **byte** pushed or pulled.

5. 5(6) means: 5 cycles if branch not taken, 6 cycles if taken (Branch instructions).

6. SWI sets I and F bits. SWI2 and SWI3 do not affect I and F.

7. Conditions Codes set as a direct result of the instruction.

8. Value of half-carry flag is undefined.

9. Special Case — Carry set if b7 is SET.

TRANSFER/EXCHANGE POST BYTE

SOURCE	DESTINATION

REGISTER FIELD

0000	D (A B)	1000 A
0001	X	1001 B
0010	Y	1010 CCR
0011	U	1011 DPR
0100	S	
0101	PC	

Table 5.6: (b) The M6809 instruction set (*continued next page*).

Branch Instructions

Instruction	Forms	OP	~	#	Description	H	N	Z	V	C
BCC	BCC	24	3	2	Branch C=0	•	•	•	•	•
	LBCC	10 5(6) 24		4	Long Branch C=0	•	•	•	•	•
BCS	BCS	25	3	2	Branch C=1	•	•	•	•	•
	LBCS	10 5(6) 25		4	Long Branch C=1	•	•	•	•	•
BEQ	BEQ	27	3	2	Branch Z=1	•	•	•	•	•
	LBEQ	10 5(6) 27		4	Long Branch Z=1	•	•	•	•	•
BGE	BGE	2C	3	2	Branch ≥ Zero	•	•	•	•	•
	LBGE	10 5(6) 2C		4	Long Branch ≥ Zero	•	•	•	•	•
BGT	BGT	2E	3	2	Branch > Zero	•	•	•	•	•
	LBGT	10 5(6) 2E		4	Long Branch > Zero	•	•	•	•	•
BHI	BHI	22	3	2	Branch Higher	•	•	•	•	•
	LBHI	10 5(6) 22		4	Long Branch Higher	•	•	•	•	•
BHS	BHS	24	3	2	Branch Higher or Same	•	•	•	•	•
	LBHS	10 5(6) 24		4	Long Branch Higher or Same	•	•	•	•	•
BLE	BLE	2F	3	2	Branch ≤ Zero	•	•	•	•	•
	LBLE	10 5(6) 2F		4	Long Branch ≤ Zero	•	•	•	•	•
BLO	BLO	25	3	2	Branch lower	•	•	•	•	•
	LBLO	10 5(6) 25		4	Long Branch Lower	•	•	•	•	•

Instruction	Forms	OP	~	#	Description	H	N	Z	V	C
BLS	BLS	23	3	2	Branch Lower or Same	•	•	•	•	•
	LBLS	10 5(6) 23		4	Long Branch Lower or Same	•	•	•	•	•
BLT	BLT	2D	3	2	Branch < Zero	•	•	•	•	•
	LBLT	10 5(6) 2D		4	Long Branch < Zero	•	•	•	•	•
BMI	BMI	2B	3	2	Branch Minus	•	•	•	•	•
	LBMI	10 5(6) 2B		4	Long Branch Minus	•	•	•	•	•
BNE	BNE	26	3	2	Branch Z=0	•	•	•	•	•
	LBNE	10 5(6) 26		4	Long Branch Z≠0	•	•	•	•	•
BPL	BPL	2A	3	2	Branch Plus	•	•	•	•	•
	LBPL	10 5(6) 2A		4	Long Branch Plus	•	•	•	•	•
BRA	BRA	20	3	2	Branch Always	•	•	•	•	•
	LBRA	16	5	3	Long Branch Always	•	•	•	•	•
BRN	BRN	21	3	2	Branch Never	•	•	•	•	•
	LBRN	10 21	5	4	Long Branch Never	•	•	•	•	•
BSR	BSR	8D	7	2	Branch to Subroutine	•	•	•	•	•
	LBSR	17	9	3	Long Branch to Subroutine	•	•	•	•	•
BVC	BVC	28	3	2	Branch V=0	•	•	•	•	•
	LBVC	10 5(6) 28		4	Long Branch V=0	•	•	•	•	•
BVS	BVS	29	3	2	Branch V=1	p	•	•	•	•
	LBVS	10 5(6) 29		4	Long Branch V=1	•	•	•	•	•

SIMPLE BRANCHES

	OP	~	#
BRA	20	3	2
LBRA	16	5	3
BRN	21	3	2
LBRN	1021	5	4
BSR	8D	7	2
LBSR	17	9	3

SIMPLE CONDITIONAL BRANCHES (Notes 1-4)

Test	True	OP	False	OP
N=1	BMI	2B	BPL	2A
Z=1	BEQ	27	BNE	26
V=1	BVS	29	BVC	28
C=1	BCS	25	BCC	24

SIGNED CONDITIONAL BRANCHES (Notes 1-4)

Test	True	OP	False	OP
r>m	BGT	2E	BLE	2F
r≥m	BGE	2C	BLT	2D
r=m	BEQ	27	BNE	26
r≤m	BLE	2F	BGT	2E
r<m	BLT	2D	BGE	2C

UNSIGNED CONDITIONAL BRANCHES (Notes 1-4)

Test	True	OP	False	OP
r>m	BHI	22	BLS	23
r≥m	BHS	24	BLO	25
r=m	BEQ	27	BNE	26
r≤m	BLS	23	BHI	22
r<m	BLO	25	BHS	24

Notes:
1. All conditional branches have both short and long variations.
2. All short branches are 2 bytes and require 3 cycles.
3. All conditional long branches are formed by prefixing the short branch opcode with $10 and using a 16-bit destination offset.
4. All conditional long branches require 4 bytes and 6 cycles if the branch is taken or 5 cycles if the branch is not taken.

Table 5.6: (c) (*continued*). The M6809 instruction set. Reproduced by courtesy of Motorola Semiconductor Products Ltd.

Absolute,   **,M**

| op-code | DP offset |

Short (Direct)

| op-code | Address |

Long (Extended Direct)

In absolute addressing, the address itself — either in whole or part — follows the op-code. In the BASIC CPU, addresses are only eight bits long and we named Absolute addressing, Direct. With the 6809, the equivalent mode carries a 16-bit address and Motorola terms this Extended Direct. There is a short version just called Direct where the effective address (EA) is the concatenation of the **Direct Page register** with the byte following the op-code. Thus if this register is set at, say, 80h, then the instruction LDA 08h, coded as 96-08h, effectively brings down the byte from address *8008h*.

Absolute Indirect,   **[M]**

| op-code | 9Fh | Pointer to address |

Here the op-code is followed by a post-byte 9Fh and then a 16-bit address. This is not the address of the operand but a pointer to where the operand address is stored in memory. Thus, if the locations 2000:2001h hold the address 80-08h, then the instruction: LDA [2000h] — coded as AF-9F-20-00h — effectively fetches the data down from 2000h and then 2001h, puts them together as a 16-bit address and sends this address out on the address bus to fetch the data into Accumulator_A. Although the location in memory of this pointer address is absolute, the pointer residing there can be altered as the program progresses.

As an example, consider the problem of implementing a subroutine (see Section 5.2.3) which will process in some way the contents of an array of data. Rather than passing each element of the array to the subroutine it makes sense to send only the address or pointer to the first element. This can be done by using an absolute address, say 2000:2001h, to store the pointer prior to jumping to the subroutine. The subroutine can then use this pointer as a sort of base address to access any element of the array relative to this location.

Branch Relative

| op-code | offset |

8-bit (Short)

| op-code | offset |

16-bit (Long)

In our BASIC CPU, the 8-bit offset following the op-code was conditionally added to the 8-bit **PC**. Here the **PC** is 16 bits long, but regular (or short) Branches still carry an 8-bit offset. In implementing a skip, this offset is sign extended before addition. Effectively this means that offsets between 80h and FFh are treated as negative. For example the instruction BRA-06 is coded as 20-FAh (FAh is the 2's complement of 06h) when the **PC** is at E108h is implemented as:

$$
\begin{array}{llll}
& 1110 & 0001 & 0000 & 1000 \\
+ & 1111 & 1111 & 1111 & 1010 \\
\hline
1 & 1110 & 0001 & 0000 & 0010
\end{array}
$$

(PC) = E108h
(offset) = $FFFA h = -6$
(E102h, which is E108$h - 0006h$)

If calculating this by hand, it must be remembered that the **PC** is already point-ing to the next instruction; thus the maximum forward point is $(00)7Fh + 2 = 127 + 2 = 129$ bytes from the op-code and $(FF)80h + 2 = -128 + 2 = 126$ bytes back. Long Branches have a 16-bit offset and can range from $+32{,}767$ and $-32{,}768$ bytes from the following op-code, effectively anywhere in the full 64 K address space of memory that the processor can address at one time. Of course Long Branch code is bigger and slower to execute (see Table 5.6(c)).

Indexed

The Absolute address modes are used where operands lie in fixed locations. In many cases, this places an unacceptable restriction on the data structures which can easily be processed. Thus in Example 5.3, a large array of data was cleared by effectively using a variable address. In BASIC's language, the ability to compute an effective address (EA) was limited to a constant positive 8-bit offset to a single Index register; thus LDA 8,X means that if **X** is 8000h at the time of execution, then 8008h is the EA of the data brought down to Accumulator_A, i.e. [A] ← [X]+8. The 6809 has an additional complement of Index registers (**X, Y, S, U** and sometimes the **PC**); as well as an extended repertoiré of offsets. Constant offsets of up to $\pm 2^{15}$ are now possible, and Accumulator_A, _B or _D can act as a variable offset. In addition; automatic increment or decrementation submodes are possible. A level of indirection is also provided for most combinations. Table 5.7 summarizes the submodes, which are coded as an op-code followed by a post-byte. Notice that absolute indirect is part of this table, although strictly it is not indexed.

Constant Offset from Register

| op-code | post-byte | | | 0,R or ,R |

| op-code | post-byte±n | | | ± n,R (5-bit) |

| op-code | post-byte | ±n | | ± n,R (8-bit) |

| op-code | post-byte | ±n | | ± n,R (16-bit) |

Here the effective address is $R \pm n$ where **R** is **X, Y, S** or **U**. The actual machine code produced depends on the size of n, with a single post-byte capable of intregally handling up to ± 15. This complex encoding scheme is worthwhile, as most offsets are small; for example, an analysis has shown that 40% of this type of indexing uses a zero offset [9]. Indirect Constant Offset Index does not have an 8-bit (± 127) offset version, the 16-bit variety being used. Fortunately the task of evaluating the post-byte and following bytes is handled automatically by the assembler.

Type	Forms	Non Indirect				Indirect			
		Assembler Form	Postbyte OP Code	× / ~	+ / #	Assembler Form	Postbyte OP Code	+ / ~	+ / #
Constant Offset From R (twos complement offset)	No Offset	,R	1RR00100	0	0	[,R]	1RR10100	3	0
	5 Bit Offset	n, R	0RRnnnnn	1	0	defaults to 8-bit			
	8 Bit Offset	n, R	1RR01000	1	1	[n, R]	1RR11000	4	1
	16 Bit Offset	n, R	1RR01001	4	2	[n, R]	1RR11001	7	2
Accumulator Offset From R (twos complement offset)	A — Register Offset	A, R	1RR00110	1	0	[A, R]	1RR10110	4	0
	B — Register Offset	B, R	1RR00101	1	0	[B, R]	1RR10101	4	0
	D — Register Offset	D, R	1RR01011	4	0	[D, R]	1RR11011	7	0
Auto Increment/Decrement R	Increment By 1	,R+	1RR00000	2	0	not allowed			
	Increment By 2	,R++	1RR00001	3	0	[,R++]	1RR10001	6	0
	Decrement By 1	,-R	1RR00010	2	0	not allowed			
	Decrement By 2	,--R	1RR00011	3	0	[,--R]	1RR10011	6	0
Constant Offset From PC (twos complement offset)	8 Bit Offset	n, PCR	1XX01100	1	1	[n, PCR]	1XX11100	4	1
	16 Bit Offset	n, PCR	1XX01101	5	2	[n, PCR]	1XX11101	8	2
Extended Indirect	16 Bit Address	—	—	—	—	[n]	10011111	5	2

R = X, Y, U or S   X = 00   Y = 01
X = Don't Care   U = 10   S = 11

+ and + Indicate the number of additional cycles and bytes for the particular variation

Table 5.7: Indexed mode machine-code data. Reproduced by courtesy of Motorola Semiconductor Products Ltd.

Post Auto Increment / Pre Auto Decrement from Register

op-code	post-byte

,R+ / ,R++ / ,-R / ,--R

As we saw in Example 5.3, indexing comes in to its own when stepping through blocks of memory, arrays and related structures. To avoid having to follow (or lead) the use of the Index register with an Increment or Decrement, this mode provides for automatic advance or retard; thus:

```
LDA ,R+    LDA ,-R
LDA ,R++   LDA ,--R
```

where R is X, Y, S or U. Example 5.3 now becomes:

```
       LDX  #BASE    ;Point X to bottom of data array
       CLRA          ;Clears Accumulator_A
LOOP:  STA  0,X+     ;Clear memory[n], increment n
       BNE  LOOP
```

Notice that incrementing is done *after* the Index register is used and decrementing is *before* the Index register is used. Double increment/decrement modes are useful when the arrays contain addresses or other double-byte data. Indirection is only available for this double form, as by its nature addresses are likely being accessed.

Accumulator Offset from Register, A,R / B,R / D,R

op-code	post-byte

As an alternative to a constant offset, any Accumulator can hold a variable offset to an Index register, eg.:

```
LDA   B,X        ;[A] <- [SEX|[B]+[X]]
LDB   A,Y        ;[B] <- [SEX|[A]+[Y]]
LDX   D,U        ;[X] <- [[D]+[U]]:[[D]+[U]+1]]
```

Note that the value of the 8-bit Accumulators are sign extended before the addition, giving a range of $+127$ through -128. Thus if **B** is FEh, then *FFFEh* is added to the X Index register in the first example above to give the effective address. Of course, FFFEh is effectively -2, so the target memory location is actually **X** $- 2$. If this is not desirable, Accumulator_A may be cleared and **D** used as the offset, eg.:

```
CLRA
LDA   D,X        ;[A] <- [00|[B]+[X]]
```

and this allows an offset of up to $+255$ (FFh) in the B Accumulator.

Use of an Accumulator allows the offset to be calculated as the program runs. A typical example is listed below, where we require access to one of a table (array) of ten elements; actually the 7-segment code. The requested element is already in the Accumulator_B (the decimal number 0 – 9), and it is to be replaced with the 7-segment equivalent code on exit. We are assuming that the subroutine starts at E200h.

```
E200:1:2    8E-E2-06              LDX #TABLE_BOT   ;Point X to table
E203:4      E6-85                 LDB B,X          ;Get element [B]
E205        39                    RTS              ;Exit

;Table of 7-segment codes begins here
E206-E20A   01-4F-12-06-4C    TABLE_BOT: .BYTE 1,4Fh,12h,6,4Ch
E20B-E20F   24-20-0F-00-0C               .BYTE 24h,20h,0Fh,0,0Ch
```

The first instruction puts the absolute address of the first table element (E206h) in the X Index register. The effective address calculated in the following instruction is **B** + **X**. If we assume that **B** = 04h on entry, then this gives (00)04 + E206 = E20Ah. The data in here is 4Ch and this is the value loaded into Accumulator_B. Notice the assembler directive .BYTE, which states that the following bytes are pure data and not program instructions.

Constant Offset from Program Counter

op-code	post-byte	$\pm n$		$\pm$ n,PC (8-bit)

op-code	post-byte	$\pm n$		$\pm$ n,PC (16-bit)

One of the major advantages of the Relative address mode is that it produces **position independent code (PIC)**. Thus a Branch is relative to where the program is at the time the decision is taken. If the program is moved to a different part of memory, all the offsets move with it unchanged. This is what differenciates a Branch from a Jump operation. The Program Counter Offset mode extends the PIC capability to any instruction which has an Indexed address mode. This is similar to the Constant Offset from Register mode, but with the **Program Counter** being the Index register. For example in:

```
LDA    200h,PC      ;[A] <- [200+[PC]]
```

the data 200*h* bytes on from where the **PC** is on execution (pointing to the following instruction) is placed in Accumulator_A. This of course is not an absolute address, as only the distance from the instruction is of interest. PIC is especially suitable for use in ROM (i.e. firmware) which can be placed anywhere in the address space. Thus a vendor could sell a ROM-based floating-point package with no à priori knowledge of where the customer will locate the firmware in memory.

As an example of this, consider the 7-segment decoder routine previously discussed. Line 1 of the actual code (shown second column from the left) contained the bytes E2-06*h*, which is the absolute location of the table bottom. If, say, the table of data was to start at C180*h*, then the ROM would have to be reprogrammed to make these two bytes C1-80*h*; the rest of the code remaining unaltered. Here is a PIC version of the same routine:

```
C102:3:4    30-8C-03                 LEAX  3,PC
;Effective address PC+3 is loaded into X, which then points to the table
C105:6      E6-85                     LDB   B,X    ;Get element [B]
C107        39                        RTS

;Table of 7-segment codes begins here
C108-C10C   01-4F-12-06-4C  TABLE_BOT:  .BYTE 1,4Fh,12h,6,4Ch
C10D-C111   24-20-0F-00-0C              .BYTE 24h.20h,0Fh,0,0Ch
```

The only difference between the two programs is in line 1. In the first case, the *absolute* address of the table bottom is put into the X Index register. In the relocatable case, the X Index register is loaded with the contents of the **Program Counter+3**, which is again the address of the bottom of the table; but is the difference between the instruction following step 1 (i.e. C107*h*) and the base of the table. If the program is bodily moved somewhere else, the offset of three bytes to the table remains the same. Thus the address of the table is calculated during each run rather than before (at load time).

As with Branch operations, assemblers save the programmer having to calculate this offset, by permitting the use of an absolute label in this type of address mode; thus assembling:

```
    LEAX  TABLE_BOT,PC
```

still produces the same code 30-8C-03*h*, i.e. the label **TABLE_BOT** is interpreted by the assembler as the *distance* from the following instruction to the absolute address **TABLE_BOT** and not the absolute value C108*h*.

We will discuss the LOAD EFFECTIVE ADDRESS (**LEA**) instruction shortly. Here we observe that an effective address computed by any of the Direct Index address modes, except Post-Increment/Pre-Decrement, can be loaded into one of these four registers. A few examples are:

```
LEAX  +2,X     ;The EA of X+2 is put into X, effectively incrementing X by 2
LEAY  D,X      ;Adds [D] to [X] and puts sum in Y
LEAS  -20,S    ;Moves the Stack Pointer down 20 bytes
```

To complete this section we will examine the various categories of instructions in more detail, where necessary, using illustrative example programs. Although the code for our BASIC CPU was hand assembled (see Tables 5.3 – 5.5), this process is difficult and not recommended for real MPUs. A glance at Table 5.6 will show why! Thus for these example programs and all succeeding programs in this text, a commercial **assembler** has been used. The process of assembly is discussed in detail in Section 6.2.2; here we will simply observe that an editor or word processor is used to type in the **source program** which can then be used as the input to the assembler, which translates to **machine code**. The source code is simply a listing of the instruction mnemonics, labels and comments, together with directives to the assembler.

To illustrate this process, let us go through the process of coding and translating a subroutine to multiply two 256 element byte arrays to give a single 256 element word array.

Example 5.4

Two byte-arrays called **Array_1** and **Array_2** are stored consecutively from $2000h$ onwards are to be multiplied to give a single product array called **Array_3**. The relationship is:

$$\sum_{n=0}^{255} \textbf{Array\_3[n]} = \textbf{Array\_1[n]} \times \textbf{Array\_2[n]}$$

This product array is to be stored from $3000h$ upwards, and each element requires a double-byte location.

Solution

The only really new instruction we will need for this program is MULTIPLY. MUL multiplies the contents of the A and B Accumulators with the 16-bit product overwriting both Accumulators in the order **A:B**, i.e. [D] ← [A] × [B] (**D** becomes **A** times **B**).

As each multiplication is identical, simply advancing up through the array index n, the program structure is obviously going to be a **loop**. This requires three elements:

Initialize

Before entering a loop, all variables must be given their starting value. In this case the address of **Array_1[0]** and **Array_2[0]** are put into Index registers X and Y respectively.

Loop Body

The repetitive element of this segment is the multiplication of the two bytes, **Array_1[n]** and **Array_2[n]**. The latter is always 256 bytes ahead of **Array_1[n]** and allows the use of a single pointer to obtain both, i.e. LDA 256,X gets **Array_2[n]**, and LDB 0,X+ gets **Array_1[n]**. Using the Post-Increment Index address mode, automatically advances the pointer to the next element. In a similar manner the product is consigned to **Array_3[n]** using the Double Post-Increment Index mode (STD ,Y++) to move this array's pointer on twice, to accommodate the double-byte product size.

Loop Exit

Other than for an endless loop, some mechanism must be available to exit the circulation. In this case we quit whenever the X pointer reaches 256 beyond the start of **Array_1**, i.e. CMPX #Array_1+256 : BNE ALOOP. As we shall see, the Compare operation is really a subtraction, and thus the Z flag will only be set when the contents of the X Index register and the operand (**Array_1**+256) (i.e. 2100h) are equal.

```
            .processor m6809
            .define     Array_1 = 2000h, Array_2 = 2100h,
                        Array_3 = 3000h
;Initialize array element n=0 by pointing to the bottom of Array_1 and Array_3
ARRAY_MUL: ldx  #Array_1          ;Point X to bottom of Array_1
           ldy  #Array_3          ;Likewise point Y to product array
;WHILE n not equal to 256 DO Array_1[n] x Array_2[n]
ALOOP:     lda  256,x             ;Get Array_2[n], the multiplicand
           ldb  ,x+               ;Get Array_1[n], the multiplier. Inc n
           mul                    ;Multiply them
           std  ,y++              ;Put 2-byte product away & move on twice
           cmpx #Array_1+256      ;Have we passed the last element yet?
           bne  ALOOP             ;IF not THEN next multiplication
;All done, so finish
           rts                    ;ELSE end of subroutine
           .end
```

Table 5.8: Source code for array multiplication.

The source code for this program, as shown in Table 5.8 uses the pseudo operator .`processor` to name the microprocessor and start the code, which is terminated by

.end. The .define operator enables us to name the variables **Array_1**, **Array_2** and **Array_3**. As in Tables 5.3 – 5.5, comments are prefixed with a semicolon and labels commencing a line are followed by a colon.

As in all computer programs (for example a word processor) the syntax and operating instructions differ between manufacturers, although the end result is similar. Thus if you are using an assembler you must follow your local rules. Fortunately, most assemblers use the MPU manufacturer's mnemonics rather than making up their own, so only the pseudo operators differ. Although I have spaced out the source code of Table 5.8 to clarify the structure of each line, this assembler only requires a space to be left between instruction and operand. Thus the statement:

```
ALOOP:LDX #Array_1;Point X to bottom of Array_1, the multiplicand!
```

is readable by the assembler, but is not very good looking to the human. The line:

```
ALOOP: LDX#Array_1 ;Point X to bottom of Array_1, the multiplicand!
```

is not acceptable to the assembler, as there is no space between instruction and operand.

Once the **source program** has been typed in and stored as a file, typically on magnetic disk, then the assembler can be run. As we shall see in Section 6.2.2, the assembler produces many files based on this source. For now the most important of these is the **listing file**, which is used for documentation purposes. This reproduces the original source material together with the resulting machine code, which is listed alongside.

```
 1                            .processor m6809
 2                            .define    Array_1 = 2000h, Array_2 = 2100h,
 3                                       Array_3 = 3000h
 4       ;Initialize array element n=0 by pointing to the bottom of Array_1 and Array_3
 5 E000 8E2000 ARRAY_MUL: ldx #Array_1      ;Point X to bottom of Array_1
 6 E003 108E3000           ldy #Array_3      ;Likewise point Y to product array
 7       ;WHILE n not equal to 256 DO Array_1[n] x Array_2[n]
 8 E007 A6890100  ALOOP: lda  256,x          ;Get Array_2[n], the multiplicand
 9 E00B E680             ldb  ,x+            ;Get Array_1[n], the multiplier. Inc n
10 E00D 3D              mul                ;Multiply them
11 E00E EDA1            std  ,y++           ;Put 2-byte product away & move on twice
12 E010 8C2100          cmpx #Array_1+256  ;Have we passed the last element yet
13 E013 26F2            bne  ALOOP          ;IF not THEN next multiplication
14       ;All done, so finish
15 E015 39              rts                ;ELSE end of subroutine
16                      .end
```

Table 5.9: The resulting listing file.

The listing shown in Table 5.9 is actually the outcome of a further stage of processing, known as linking (see Fig. 6.10). The **linker** brings together several programs (if there is more than one assembled file), puts them together and locates them in the specified memory area. All the 6809 programs in this text are located beginning at E000*h* up to FFFF*h*. We have assumed a 8K-byte ROM (typically a 2764 EPROM) occupying this space. 6809 code is usually placed at the top of its memory space (0000 – FFFF*h*), as the Reset and Interrupt vectors must be in situe between FFF2 – FFFF*h*. Where appropriate, we will assume RAM from 0000*h*

Move Instructions

Operation		Mnemonic	V	N	Z	C	Description
Exchange							Exchanges two like-sized
	R1↔R2[1]	EXG R1,R2	•	•	•	•	register contents
Eg.		EXG A,B	•	•	•	•	[A]↔[B]
Load							Moves data to register
	to A; to B	LDA; LDB	0	√	√	•	[A]←[M]; [B]←[M]
	to D	LDD	0	√	√	•	[D]←[M:M+1]
	to X; to Y	LDX; LDY	0	√	√	•	[X]←[M:M+1]; [Y]←[M:M+1]
	to S; to U	LDS; LDU	0	√	√	•	[S]←[M:M+1]; [U]←[M:M+1]
Push							Moves registers onto Stack
	to System stack	PSHS regs	•	•	•	•	Listed registers to S stack
	to User stack	PSHU regs	•	•	•	•	Listed registers to U stack
Eg.		PSHS A,B,X	•	•	•	•	A,B & X to S stack
Pull							Moves stack data to registers
	from System stack	PULS regs	•	•	•	•	S stack to listed registers
	from User stack	PULU regs	•	•	•	•	U stack to listed registers
Eg.		PULS A,B,X	•	•	•	•	S stack to A,B & X
Store							Moves data from register
	from A; from B	STA; STB	0	√	√	•	[M]←[A];[M]←[B]
	from D	STD	0	√	√	•	[M:M+1]←[D]
	from X; from Y	STX; STY	0	√	√	•	[M:M+1]←[X]; [M:M+1]←[Y]
	from S; from U	STS; STU	0	√	√	•	[M:M+1]←[S]; [M:M+1]←[U]
Transfer							Transfers two like-sized
	R1↔R2[1]	TFR R1,R2	•	•	•	•	register contents
Eg.		TFR A,DP	•	•	•	•	[DP]←[A]

0   Flag always reset
1   Flag always set
•   Flag not affected
√   Flag operates in the normal way

Note 1 : Register pairs must either be 8-bit A,B,CC,DP or 16-bit X,Y,S,U,PC.

Table 5.10: Move instructions

upwards. The actual locations of the program and RAM memories are relatively unimportant, as the code produced is substantially unaffected by this detail.

Typically around a third of operations at machine-code level involve shuffling data in between registers and out to memory [12], so we will look first of all at data movement instructions, as summarized in Table 5.10.

The Load and Store operations transfer data between memory and register. Both 8- and 16-bit moves are possible, but as the memory is byte-addressable the latter move involves two consecutive transfers. Thus the instruction LDX 0C100h will perform as shown in Fig. 5.11(a). Also shown is the reverse process of storing. Note how in both cases the most significant byte starts or ends up in the least significant memory location; thus the high byte of **X** comes from C100h, whilst the lower from C101h. This reverse order is the standard in Motorola devices, whereas the Intel 808x family use the opposite arrangement.

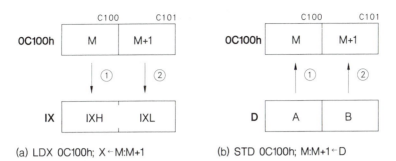

(a) LDX 0C100h; X←M:M+1   (b) STD 0C100h; M:M+1←D

Figure 5.11: Moving 16-bit data at 'one go'.

Notice that no STORE TO DIRECT PAGE REGISTER instruction exists. To set up this register to, say, $80h$ the sequence:

```
LDA    #80h
TFR    A,DP
```

first places the number $80h$ in Accumulator_A (it could be _B) and then transfers this to the DP register. This overhead is justified as the DP register is (or should be) rarely altered. The Transfer instruction can move the contents of any 8-bit register (**A, B ,DP, CC**) to any other; or any 16-bit register contents (**X, Y, U, S, D, PC**) to any other. The four higher bits of the post-byte determine the source register whilst the lower the destination, according to the code:

$$0000 = \textbf{D} \quad 0001 = \textbf{X} \quad 0010 = \textbf{Y} \quad 0011 = \textbf{U} \quad 0100 = \textbf{S}$$
$$0101 = \textbf{PC} \quad 1000 = \textbf{A} \quad 1001 = \textbf{B} \quad 1010 = \textbf{CCR} \quad 1011 = \textbf{DPR}$$

thus TFR A,DP is coded as 1F-8Bh (post-byte 1000 1011b). The Exchange instruction works in a similar way between like-sized registers with the same post-byte construction.

The 6809 implements the normal Add and Subtract operations, with and without carry, targeted on an 8-bit Accumulator. A Accumulator_D-based 16-bit Add and Subtract is also provided, but unfortunately not with a carry. An unsigned addition of Accumulator_B to the 16-bit Index register_X can also be classed as double, but the 8-bit addend is promoted to 16-bit at addition time, by assuming an upper byte of zero; hence the terminology unsigned.

It is possible to **promote** a signed number in the B Accumulator to its 16-bit equivalent in the D Accumulator by using the SIGN EXTENSION instruction. This zeros Accumulator_A if bit 7 of **B** is 0 and fills **A** with ones ([A] ← FFh) otherwise; for example **B** = 10110011b (−83) becomes **D** = *11111111*10110011b (−83). The SIGN EXTENSION (**SEX**) instruction makes the 6809 unique as the only MPU offering sex appeal!

Any 16-bit Index or Stack register can be summed with an 8-bit Accumulator (which is automatically sign extended), Accumulator_D or a constant by means of

Arithmetic Instructions

Operation		Mnemonic	V	N	Z	C	Description
Add							Binary addition
	to A; to B	ADDA; ADDB	√	√	√	√	[A]←[A]+[M]; [B]←[B]+[M]
	to D	ADDD	√	√	√	√	[D]←[D]+[M:M+1]
	B to X	ABX	•	•	•	•	[X]←[X]+[(00)B]
Add with Carry							Includes carry
	to A; to B	ADCA; ADCB	√	√	√	√	[A]←[A]+[M]+C; [B]←[B]+[M]+C
Clear							Destination contents zeroed
	memory	CLR	0	0	1	0	[M]←00
	A; B	CLRA; CLRB	0	0	1	0	[A]←00; [B]←00
Decrement							Subtract one, produce no carry
	memory	DEC	1	√	√	•	[M]←[M]−1
	A; B	DECA; DECB	1	√	√	•	[A]←[A]−1; [B]←[B]−1
Increment							Add one, produce no carry
	memory	INC	2	√	√	•	[M]←[M]+1
	A;B	INCA; INCB	2	√	√	•	[A]←[A]+1; [B]←[B]+1
Load Effective Address							Effective Address to register
	X;Y	LEAX; LEAY	•	•	√	•	[X]←EA; [Y]←EA
	S;U	LEAS; LEAU	•	•	•	•	[S]←EA; [U]←EA
Multiply							Multiplies [A] by [B]
		MUL	•	•	√	3	[D]←[A]× [B]
Negate							Reverses 2's complement sign
	memory	NEG	4	√	√	5	[M]← −[M]
	A;B	NEGA; NEGB	4	√	√	5	[A]← −[A]; [B]← −[B]
Sign Extend							Promotes signed B to signed D
		SEX	•	√	√	•	[D]←(00)[B] or [D]←(FF)[B]
Subtract							Binary subtraction
	from A; from B	SUBA; SUBB	√	√	√	√	[A]←[A]−[M]; [B]←[B]−[M]
	from D	SUBD	√	√	√	√	[D]←[D]−[M:M+1]
Subt with Carry							Includes carry (borrow)
	from A; from B	SBCA; SBCB	√	√	√	√	[A]←[A]−[M]−C; [B]←[B]−[M]−C

Note 1 : Overflow set when passes from 10000000 to 01111111, i.e. an apparent sign change.
Note 2 : Overflow set when passes from 01111111 to 10000000, i.e. an apparent sign change.
Note 3 : Carry set to state of bit 7 product, i.e. MSB of lower byte; for rounding off.
Note 4 : Overflow set if original data is 10000000 (−128), as there is no +128.
Note 5 : Carry set if original data is 00000000; for multiple-byte negation.

Table 5.11: Arithmetic operations

the Load Effective Address (LEA) instruction. This makes use of the arithmetic computation of effective addresses in the various Indexed address modes. We have already used this instruction to illustrate the Program Counter Offset Indexed address mode and position independent code. Consider this further example:

LEAX 1,X   (30-01)

calculates the effective address as $X+1$ and loads it into the X Index register ($[X] \leftarrow [X] + 1$); thus it is the equivalent to an INCREMENT X (INX) instruction; which is missing from the 6809's repertoiré. Much more powerful permutations of LEA exist, thus:

LEAY A,X   (31-96)

promotes a signed number in Accumulator_A to 16-bits, adds this to the contents of the X Index register and puts the result in the Y Index register ($[Y] \leftarrow SEX\|[A] + [X]$)!

The contents of any read-write memory location, or any 8-bit Accumulator can be directly incremented or decremented by using the INC or DEC instruction. As noted, the X, Y, S and U registers can be similarly augmented by using the LEA instruction. Notice that INC and DEC do not set the Carry flag, which makes multiple-byte increment and decrement operations awkward (use ADD #1 and SUB #1 instead). Increment sets the oVerflow flag when the target goes from $0,1111111b$ through to $1,0000000b$ (seemingly from + to −) and Decrement does likewise when going from $1,0000000b$ through to $0,1111111b$ (− to +). INC and DEC on memory are classified as **read-modify-write** operations; as during execution, data is fetched from memory, modified and then sent back. Clearing (CLR) memory strangely works in the same way, although the original value is irrelevant. As we have just seen, it is possible to multiply the two 8-bit Accumulator contents to give a 16-bit product in the D Accumulator. For this purpose the multiplier and multiplicand are treated as unsigned. The Carry flag is set to the state of bit 7 of the product (top of B). This is the bit which should be added to the upper byte of the product if the object is to produce a rounded-off 8-bit result (moving the binary point left eight places makes bit 7 equivalent to $\frac{1}{2}$). Thus the sequence:

```
MUL        ; Multiply (A) & (B)
ADCA #0    ; Add Carry to (A)
```

is equivalent to dividing the product by 256 and adding the $\frac{1}{2}$ bit to the result in Accumulator_A.

One instruction omitted from Table 5.11 because of its limited utility, is DAA. DECIMAL ADJUST ACCUMULATOR_A enables the ADDA binary addition instruction to be used on two 8-bit BCD numbers. Following on from this addition, DAA applies a correction factor as outlined in Example 1.18. This adds six onto the lower nybble (4-bit decade) if the outcome of the nybble addition is more than nine or a carry is passed from bit 3 to bit 4 (the half carry). After this is done, a correction of six is conditionally added to the upper nybble if that outcome is greater than nine or there was a carry out from bit 7. As the H flag is involved in this correction process, DAA can normally only be used after an instruction which affects this flag. A glance at Fig. 5.7 shows that this only applies to ADDA and ADCA. Thus, unlike all other Accumulator-based 6809 instructions, DAA has no counterpart for Accumulator_B.

A common misconception concerning this instruction is that it can be used to
convert from binary to BCD. This is incorrect. DAA can only be used to correct the
binary addition of a 2-decade BCD byte in Accumulator_A with another similarly
formatted number. Thus the program fragment:

```
 LDA    #14h  ; 14h is 0001 0100b, which is BCD for fourteen
 ADDA   #26h  ; Add to it 0010 0110b, which is BCD for twenty six
;The outcome of 14h+26h is 0011 1010b (3Ah). This needs six added
 DAA          ; to give 0100 0000b, which is forty in BCD
```

Although DAA can be used to implement BCD subtraction by first finding the
10's complement and then adding with correction [13], its use in BCD arithmetic is
really rather limited. If input and output data is BCD form, the normal procedure
is to convert from BCD to binary, do the arithmetic and then convert back to BCD.
As our next example we will show how the latter can be accomplished.

Example 5.5

The output process of a system produces an 8-bit natural binary value located in Ac-
cumulator_B. As a prerequisite to displaying in decimal, this is to be converted into 3-
decade BCD located in the Accumulator pair A:B in the form 00|BCD3:BCD2|BCD1.

Solution

The basic process used in the program of Table 5.12 is to repetitively subtract
one from the binary data whilst adding one to the BCD number with a correction
to keep this latter count in BCD. This is rather like having an 8-bit binary down
counter alongside a 3-decade BCD up counter. The latter is cleared before the count
commences (steps 4 & 5) and the process is terminated when the down counter
reaches zero (step 7).

As the Accumulators are used in the body of the routine, two temporary memory
locations are employed to keep the BCD count in the form 00|BCD3-BCD2|BCD1,

```
1                              .processor m6809
2                              .define    MBCD = 0000, LBCD = 0001
3                          ; The binary number is already in Accumulator_B
4  E000 0F01  BIN8_TO_BCD: clr   LBCD         ; Zero all BCD nybbles
5  E002 0F00              clr    MBCD
6                          ; DO subtract one in binary and add one in BCD WHILE binary not zero
7  E004 5D    BLOOP:       tstb                ; Is binary data zero?
8  E005 2710              beq    EXIT          ; IF so THEN finish
9  E007 5A                decb                 ; ELSE one less binary
10 E008 9601              lda    LBCD          ; and one more BCD
11 E00A 8B01              adda   #1
12 E00C 19                daa                  ; Correct to BCD
13 E00D 9701              sta    LBCD
14 E00F 9600              lda    MBCD          ; Any carry over gets added
15 E011 8900              adca   #0            ; to the upper BCD decade
16 E013 9700              sta    MBCD          ; No correction required
17 E015 20ED              bra    BLOOP
18                          ; Return with 00:BCD3 in A and BCD2:BCD1 in B
19 E017 DC00  EXIT:        ldd    MBCD          ; D is A:B, so BCD data transferred
20 E019 39                rts                  ; in one fell swoop
21                              .end
```

Table 5.12: Binary to BCD conversion.

called **MBCD** and **LBCD** respectively. These pairs of bytes are transferred to the Accumulator pair A:B at the end of the program by the single instruction LDD MBCD in line 19. We have used ADDA #1 instead of INCA, as the latter does not affect the H flag. Actually the H flag is never set in this program; can you figure out why? The addition of the carry to the upper decade never needs correction as its maximum value is only two ($11111111b \rightarrow 255$).

This is not really a terribly good algorithm to use for conversion, as it is slow; especially where larger numbers are involved. A quicker method is to repetitively subtract a hundred from the binary number until the residue is below this value. The tally of successful subtractions is the hundreds decade. Similarly for the tens, and the residue is the units decade. For larger numbers the powers of ten can be stored as constants in a table, and successively extracted in a loop to give the n BCD decade counts.

It is of course possible to multiply or divide by powers of two by shifting left or right as appropriate. Also a combination of shift and add or shift and subtract can be used to multiply or divide by any number [14]. Table 5.13 gives the range of shift instructions available. All of these operate on an 8-bit Accumulator or on any read/write memory location through the read-modify-write mechanism.

Shifting Instructions

Operation	Mnemonic	V	N	Z	C	Description
Shift left, arithmetic or logic						Linear shift left into carry
memory	ASL	1	√	√	b7	$C \leftarrow \boxed{} \leftarrow 0$
A;B	ASLA; ASLB	1	√	√	b7	
Shift right, logic						Linear shift right into carry
memory	LSR	•	√	√	b0	$0 \rightarrow \boxed{} \rightarrow C$
A;B	LSRA; LSRB	•	√	√	b0	
Shift right, arithmetic						As above but keeps sign bit
memory	ASR	•	√	√	b0	$b7 \rightarrow \boxed{} \rightarrow C$
A;B	ASRA; ASRB	•	√	√	b0	
Rotate left						Circular shift left into carry
memory	ROL	1	√	√	b7	$C \leftarrow \boxed{} \leftarrow C$
A;B	ROLA; ROLB	1	√	√	b7	
Rotate right						Circular shift right into carry
memory	ROR	•	√	√	b0	$C \rightarrow \boxed{} \rightarrow C$
A;B	RORA; RORB	•	√	√	b0	

Note 1: $V = b_7 \oplus b_6$ before shift.

Table 5.13: Shifting instructions.

Linear arithmetic shifts move the 8-bit operand left or right with the Carry flag catching the emerging bit. In the case of ASR, the sign bit propagates right; thus $1,1110100$ (-12) becomes $1,1111010$ (-6) becomes $1,1111101$ (-3) etc. and $0,0001100$ ($+12$) becomes $0,0000110$ ($+6$) becomes $0,0000011$ ($+3$) etc. The Logic Shift Right equivalent simply shifts in zeros from the left. Logic Shift Left and Arithmetic Shift Left are equivalent, and some assemblers permit the use of the alternative LSL mnemonic.

Circular or Rotate shifts are similar to Add with Carry, in that they can be used for multiple operations. A Rotate takes in a carry from a previous Shift and in turn saves its ejected bit in the C flag. Thus, say, a 24-bit word stored in M:M+1:M+2 can be shifted left once by the sequence [15]:

```
ASL   M
ROL   M+1
ROL   M+2
```

In all types of Left Shifts, the oVerflow flag is set when bits 7 & 6 differ before the shift (i.e. $b_7 \oplus b_6$); this means that the (apparent) sign will change after the Shift.

Shifting operations are frequently used to bitwise examine a word. This is illustrated by the following example.

Example 5.6

Write a program that will determine the highest logic 1 in a data byte in Accumulator_B. For instance, if the pattern is $00101111b$, the outcome — which is to be in Accumulator_A — will be $00000101b$ (bit 5).

Solution

The answer given in Table 5.14 uses Accumulator_A as a counter. The data settings are successively shifted right and the count incremented. As the Logic Shift Left operation brings in logic 0s from the left; eventually the residue will become all zeros, and the process terminated. Thus 00010111 (1) $\rightarrow$ 00001011 (2) $\rightarrow$ 00000101 (3) $\rightarrow$ 00000010 (4) $\rightarrow$ 00000001 (5) $\rightarrow$ 00000000. Why should LSLB be used in preference to ASLB?

The program does not distinguish between no bits set and bit 0 set. How would you modify it to do so?

```
1                              .processor m6809
2                         ; Initialize by clearing the count.  Data is already in B
3 E000 4F       HIGH_BIT:  clra              ; Count is zeroed
4                         ; WHILE data is not zero, shift right and add bit to Count
5 E001 54       HLOOP:     lsrb              ; Shift rightmost bit into Carry
6 E002 2703                beq EXIT          ; IF residue is 00000000 THEN finished
7 E004 4C                  inca             ; ELSE increment shift tally
8 E005 20FA                bra HLOOP         ; and do another shift right
9 E007 39       EXIT:      rts               ; The final count is in A
10                         .end
```

Table 5.14: Shifting to find the highest set bit.

Shifting right pops out the rightmost bit into the C flag. Here its value was ignored, but in many situations this can be used to examine the data on a bit by bit basis. For instance, we could simply modify our program to add all the carry bits to Accumulator_A, thus counting the total number of set bits in the byte.

The logic operations of bitwise AND, OR, EOR and NOT (Complement) are provided, as shown in Table 5.15. The only unusual feature here are the special instructions ANDCC and ORCC, for clearing or setting flags in the Code Condition register. Thus to clear the I mask (see Fig. 5.7) we have:

> ANDCC   #11101111b   (1C-EF)

and to set it:

> ORCC   #00010000b   (1C-10)

This saves having to provide a series of separate instructions, such as the CLI and SEI (CLEAR and SET INTERRUPT MASK), of the 6800 MPU; and also enables more than one flag to be set or cleared in a single instruction.

Logic Instructions

Operation		Mnemonic	V	N	Z	C	Description
AND							Logic bitwise AND
	A;B	ASL	0	√	√	•	$[A] \leftarrow [A]\cdot[M]$; $[B] \leftarrow [B]\cdot[M]$
	CC	ANDCC #nn		Can clear			$[CCR] \leftarrow [CCR]\cdot\#nn$
Complement							Invert (1's complement)
	memory	COM	0	√	√	1	$[M] \leftarrow [\overline{M}]$
	A;B	COMA; COMB	0	√	√	1	$[A] \leftarrow [\overline{A}]$; $[B] \leftarrow [\overline{B}]$
Exclusive-OR							Logic bitwise Exclusive-OR
	A;B	EORA; EORB	0	√	√	•	$[A] \leftarrow [A] \oplus [M]$; $[B] \leftarrow [B] \oplus [M]$
OR							Logic bitwise Inclusive-OR
	A;B	ORA; ORB	0	√	√	•	$[A] \leftarrow [A]+[M]$; $[B] \leftarrow [B]+[M]$
	CC	ORCC #nn		Can set			$[CCR] \leftarrow [CCR]+\#nn$

Table 5.15: Logic instructions.

ANDing with a logic 0 always gives a 0, and hence this operation can be used to clear any bit or bits in an Accumulator or read/write memory location. Thus if B was 10011101b before the instruction ANDB #00001111b, then the resulting data in B would be 0000 1101b. In effect we have separated off the lower nybble from the byte. Similarly ORing with a logic 1 always gives a 1. The same starting data with the instruction ORB #01000000b, results in 11011101b.

EORing with a logic 1 inverts that bit, hence this operation allows us to toggle any bit or bits. Again, starting with the same data, the instruction EORB #11110000b gives [B] ← 01101101b. The EOR operation can also be used to check for changes, as EORing unlike logic levels always gives a logic 1. This is the basis for the following example.

Example 5.7

An array of eight switches situated at address 9000h is to be monitored for a change. Determine where the change occurred and what way the changed switch was thrown; On → Off or Off → On. Assume that On is logic 1. The change data is to be placed in Accumulator_B and the polarity data in Accumulator_A.

Solution

Essentially we wish to go round a loop waiting for someone to throw a switch, and when this happens to leave the routine with information concerning which switch was thrown and which way.

```
1                          .processor m6809
2                          .define    Switch = 9000h, Old = 0000
3 E000 B69000  CHANGE: lda    Switch    ; Initial value of settings
4 E003 9700            sta    Old       ; Put current reading in
5                      ;Continually monitor Switch looking for a change
6 E005 B69000  CLOOP:  lda    Switch    ; Get current settings
7 E008 9800            eora   Old       ; EORing with the old value detects changes
8 E00A 27F9            beq    CLOOP     ; IF no change THEN look again
9                      ; Exit the loop only if a change has occurred
10 E00C 1F89           tfr    a,b       ; Copy the change byte in B
11 E00E 9400           anda   Old       ; Determine the polarity of the changes
12 E010 39             rts              ; Which are recorded in A
13                          .end
```

Table 5.16: Looking for changes.

In the routine of Table 5.16, a temporary memory location called **Old** is used to hold the first sample of the state of the switches, steps 3 & 4. This state is read exactly as if 9000h where a normal memory location, although it is of course read-only data.

The loop continually reads the switch state and EORs this with the old value (steps 6–8). If there has been no change, then all bits will return zero and the Z flag will be set. As soon as a change occurs, the non-zero outcome causes the loop test to fail and the program to exit the loop. Not only is this data non-zero but there will be a logic 1 in each location where a change occurs. For example, if the original settings are 00011100b and switch 7 is turned On, i.e. 10011100b, then the EORing of these gives 10000000b. This change data is copied to Accumulator_B as specified (step 10).

The change byte indicates where the alteration occurred but not which way, 0 → 1 or 1 → 0. This is determined by ANDing the change word with the old data. If the old bit in the changed position was 1 then 1·1 gives a corresponding logic 1 in the like position. In our example, the original setting was Off, thus 0·1 gives a logic 0 in bit 7, i.e. **Old**·change = 00011100·10000000 → 00000000. Of course the principle is the same if more than one switch changes between samples. The subroutine of Example 5.6 can then be used to determine the highest changed bit.

The program of Table 5.16 illustrates a problem with real live situations. What if the switch port fails, maybe because of a dry joint? In this situation the system will hang up in an endless loop looking for a change which will never occur. A more robust approach might be to give up if no change occurs after a fixed time and return an error code if time-out occurs. And how do we handle switch bounce (see Examples 5.30 & 5.31)?

The setting of the **CCR** flags can be used after an operation to deduce, and hence act on, the state of the operand data. Thus, to determine if the value of a port located at, say, 8080h is zero, then:

```
LDA 8080h          (86-80-80)
BEQ SOMEWHERE      (27-xx)
```

will bring its contents into Accumulator_A and set the Z flag if it is zero. The BRANCH IF EQUAL TO ZERO instruction will then cause the program to skip to another place. The N flag is also set if bit 7 is logic 1, and thus a Load can enable us to test the state of this bit. The problem is, Load destroys the old contents of Accumulator_A, and the new data is probably of little interest. A non-destructive equivalent of Load is Test, as shown in Table 5.17. The sequence now becomes:

```
TST 8080h          (7D-80-80)
BEQ SOMEWHERE      (27-xx)
```

but the Accumulator contents are not overwritten. However 16-bit tests must be carried out using a 16-bit Load.

Data Test Instructions

Operation	Mnemonic	V	N	Z	C	Description
Bit Test						Non-destructive AND
A;B	BITA; BITB	0	√	√	•	[A]·[M]; [B]·[M]
Compare						Non-destructive subtract
with A;B	CMPA; CMPB	√	√	√	√	[A]−[M]; [B]−[M]
with D	CMPD	√	√	√	√	[D]−[M:M+1]
with X;Y	CMPX; CMPY	√	√	√	√	[X]−[M:M+1]; [Y]−[M:M+1]
with S;U	CMPS; CMPU	√	√	√	√	[S]−[M:M+1]; [U]−[M:M+1]
Test for Zero or Minus						Non-destructive subtract from zero
memory	TST	0	√	√	•	[M]−00
A;B	TSTA; TSTB	0	√	√	•	[A]−00; [B]−00

Table 5.17: Data testing operations.

Test can only check for all bits zero or the state of bit 7. For data already in an 8-bit Accumulator, ANDing can check the state of any bit; thus:

```
ANDA    #00100000b          (84-20)
```

will set the Z flag if bit 5 is 0, otherwise Z = 0. Once again this is a destructive test, and the equivalent from Table 5.17 is Bit Test; thus:

```
BITA    #00100000b          (85-20)
```

does the same thing, but the contents of Accumulator_A remain unchanged, and more tests can subsequently be carried out without reloading.

Comparison of the magnitude of data in an Accumulator with either a constant or data in memory requires a different approach. Mathematically this can be done by subtracting [M] from [A] (see Section 1.2.2) and checking the state of the flags. Which flags are relevant depend on whether the numbers are to be treated as unsigned (magnitude only) or signed. Taking the former first gives:

[A] *Higher than* [M] : [A]−[M] gives no Carry & non-Zero; C=0, Z=0 ($\overline{C + Z}$=1).
[A] *Equal to*   [M] : [A]−[M] gives Zero;   (Z=1).
[A] *Lower than* [M] : [A]−[M] gives a Carry;   (C=1).

The signed situation is more complex, involving the Negative and oVerflow flags. Where a subtraction occurs and the difference is *positive*, then either bit 7 will be 0 and there will be no overflow (both N and V are 0) or else an overflow will occur with bit 7 a logic 1 (both N and V are 1). Logically, this is detected by the function $\overline{N \oplus V}$. A *negative* difference is signalled whenever there is no overflow and the sign bit is 1 (N is 1 and V is 0) or else an overflow occurs together with a positive sign bit (N is 0 and V is 1). Logically, this is N$\oplus$V. Based on these outcomes we have:

[A] *Greater than* [M] : [A]−[M] $\rightarrow$ non-zero +ve result; ($\overline{N \oplus V} \cdot \overline{Z} = 1$ or N$\oplus$V+Z = 0).
[A] *Equal to*   [M] : [A]−[M] $\rightarrow$ zero;   (Z=1).
[A] *Less than*   [M] : [A]−[M] $\rightarrow$ a negative result;   (N$\oplus$V = 1).

Subtraction is a destructive test operation and Compare is its non-destructive counterpart. It is the most powerful of the Data Testing operations, as it can be applied to both Index and Stack Pointer registers as well as 8- and 16-bit Accumulators.

All Conditional operations in the 6809 take the form of a Branch instruction. These cause the Program Counter to skip n places forward or backwards; usually based on the state of the CCR flags. Excluding BRANCH TO SUBROUTINE (see Section 5.2.3), there are 16 Branches provided, which can be considered as the true or false outcome of eight flag combinations. Thus BRANCH IF CARRY SET (BCS) and BRANCH IF CARRY CLEAR (BCC) are based on the one test (C = ?).

If the test is true, the offset following the Branch op-code is added to the Program Counter. Thus if the Carry flag is zero:

        E100/1   (24-08)   BCC-08

will add $0008h$ to the Program Counter state E102h to give PC = E10Ah. Note that the PC is already pointing to the following instruction when execution occurs, giving an effective destination of ten places on from the Branch location. The Branch offset is sign extended before addition to the Program Counter; thus if flag N = 0:

        E100/1   (24-F8)   BPL-F8

gives PC $\longrightarrow$ E102h + $FFF8h$ = E0FAh, which is eight places back (six places back from the Branch itself). With a single signed-byte offset, the maximum range is +125 and −129 bytes.

Each 6809 Branch has a long equivalent which uses a double-byte offset. Thus the Conditional Branch:

Program Counter Instructions

Operation	Mnemonic	Description
Bcc		cc is the logical condition tested
LBcc		
Always (True)	BRA; LBRA	Always affirmed regardless of flags
Never (False)	BRN; LBRN	Never carried out
Equal	BEQ; LBEQ	Z flag set (Zero result)
not Equal	BNE; LBNE	Z flag clear (Non-zero result)
Carry Set	BCS; LBCS[1]	[Acc] Lower Than (Carry = 1)
Carry Clear	BCC; LBCC[2]	[Acc] Higher or Same as (Carry = 0)
Lower or Same	BLS; LBLS	[Acc] Lower or Same as $(C+Z=1)$
Higher Than	BHI; LBHI	[Acc] Higher Than $(C+Z=0)$
Minus	BMI; LBMI	N flag set (Bit7 = 1)
Plus	BPL; LBPL	N flag clear (Bit7 = 0)
Overflow Set	BVS; LBVS	V flag set
Overflow Clear	BVC; LBVC	V flag clear
Greater Than*	BGT; LBGT	[Acc] Greater Than $(\overline{N \oplus V} \cdot \overline{Z} = 1)$
Less Than or Equal*	BLE; LBLE	[Acc] Less Than or Equal $(N \oplus V \cdot Z = 0)$
Greater Than or Equal*	BGE; LBGE	[Acc] Greater Than or Equal $(N \oplus V = 1)$
Less Than*	BLT; LBLT	[Acc] Less Than $(N \oplus V = 0)$
Jump	JMP	Absolute unconditional goto
No Operation	NOP	Only increments Program Counter

* 2's complement Branch

Note 1 : Some assemblers allow the alternative BLO
Note 2 : Some assemblers allow the alternative BHS

Table 5.18: Operations which affect the Program Counter.

E100/1/2/3 (10-24-10-0F)   BCC-100F

if true forces **PC** to E104h + 100Fh = F113h.

Long Branches can go anywhere in the 64 K memory space, but occupy more room and take longer to execute. A Short Branch requires 3 cycles, whereas a Long Branch takes 6 cycles if carried out and 5 if not. Except for LONG BRANCH ALWAYS (LBRA) the opcode has a 10h byte fronting the normal Short Branch op-code; thus occupying four memory bytes. LBRA has a special op-code of 16h, giving a 3-byte instruction always taking 5 cycles. Using a LONG BRANCH ALWAYS instead of a Jump is useful for position independent code, as by definition, the offset is relative to the **Program Counter**; the absolute destination being irrelevant. A Jump is made to an absolute location which cannot be altered unless the ROM is reprogrammed.

Although Long Branches will cope with all destinations, where possible Short Branches should be used for efficiency. However, it can be difficult sometimes to predict whether a destination is within range. Some assemblers will choose for you at assembly time if advised accordingly, although it is unlikely to choose the Short Branch in all legal situations.

The remaining instruction in Table 5.18 is NO OPERATION. NOP does just this but is one byte long and as a consequence the fetch increments the **Program Counter**; taking 2 cycles to do it. NOPs are normally used in situations where a delay is necessary. BRANCH NEVER (BRN) is a 2-byte NOP with a 3-cycle delay and LBRN takes up four bytes for a 5-cycle delay.

5.2.3   Subroutines, Stacks and Interrupts

A structured approach to hardware design partitions the system into functional modules. Thus, a certain system may be divided into input, output, oscillator, counter and decoder subsystems. These circuits are frequently wired or plugged into a motherboard which carries services, such as power supplies. Each module has a well defined function and may be designed, implemented and tested as a separate entity. This may not produce the smallest and most efficient implementation, but it is likely that the product will come to market earlier and be more maintainable due to its testability.

This top-down modular approach [16] is also recommended for software design. The software analog to the hardware module is called a **subroutine**. A subroutine may be defined as a self-standing sequence of instructions which can be called from anywhere and, having been run, will return control whence it was called. For example, the code for the calculation of $\sin(x)$ may be stored offside the main program. To exercise the function:

$$y = \sin(x)$$

the program must jump out to the beginning of the code (the input), carrying with it the value of x (the input signal). On return, after execution, the outcome y (the output signal) will be found at some prearranged location. These software modules are analogous to their hardware cousins, as they can be inserted into a motherboard (the main program), take input signals and have outcomes. Good programming techniques are used to enforce a single entry and exit point to a subroutine and to ensure a minimum interaction with data areas used by other modules. The main program should do a minimum of processing, merely initializing appropriate parameters and interface registers, calling up subroutines in the appropriate sequence and pass parameters back and forth.

The same subroutine can be called up several times from a program, but with different data. Thus the code for, say, $\sin(x)$ need only appear in memory once. By organizing subroutines in the form of libraries; functions may be reused between projects and bought in from external sources.

In essence, getting to a subroutine involves nothing more than placing the address of its opening instruction in the **PC**, i.e. doing a Jump or Branch. Thus, if we take as an example a subroutine which evokes a fixed delay of 0.1 s (i.e. does nothing for 100 ms) and is located starting at E100h, then JMP 0E100h will transfer control. With an assembler, the subroutine entry point is always identified with a label, which will be evaluated when assembled, eg. JMP DELAY_100; see Table 5.20.

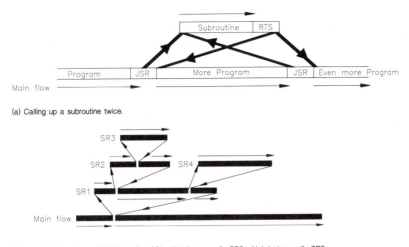

(a) Calling up a subroutine twice.

(b) Nested subroutines with Main calling SR1 which in turn calls SR2 which in turn calls SR3.
    SR1 also calls SR4 later.

Figure 5.12: Subroutine calling.

The problem lies not in getting there but returning afterwards. As can be seen from Fig. 5.12, the jumping-off point can be from anywhere in the main program or indeed from another subroutine (the latter process is known as nesting). Thus the MPU needs to remember the value of the **PC** before its contents are changed (by the Jump).

We could do this by using either a designated memory location or an internal register, eg. **LEAX 0,PC** puts **PC** plus $0000h$ into **X**. This is not very satisfactory for nested subroutines, as the return address for the secondary subroutine will overwrite the return address of the primary caller and the MPU will literally get lost.

To get around this problem, an area of read/write memory is set aside by the programmer for the temporary storage of return addresses. This memory is known as a **stack** and is organized as a last-in first-out (LIFO) store, with the **System Stack Pointer register** pointing to the last data byte pushed out. The System Stack Pointer is automatically decremented *before* a data byte is pushed out (pre-decrement) and conversely an automatic increment is performed *after* a data byte is pulled in from the stack (post-increment). In this respect the stack is like an office spike, with aide-mémoires pushed onto the spike when being stored and lifted off again — when circumstances permit — in the reverse order.

As an example, consider a situation where the System Stack Pointer has been initialized at the start of the main program to $4000h$ (eg. **LDS #4000h**). This procedure assigns memory below $4000h$ for the stack, as shown in Fig. 5.13(a). If we use the instruction JSR (JUMP TO SUBROUTINE) or BSR (BRANCH TO SUBROUTINE) instead of a plain JMP or BRA, then before the **PC** is given its new value, the **System Stack Pointer (SSP)** is moved down two places as the old value is pushed out, see Fig. 5.13(b). This saved value is in fact the location of the following instruction, as the **PC** has been incremented after the fetch phase. A return inward simply

Subroutine Instructions

Operation			Mnemonic	Description
Call				Transfer to subroutine
	Jump to subroutine		JSR ea	Push PC onto Stack, PC←ea
	Branch to subroutine[1]			
		short	BSR offset$_8$	Push PC onto Stack, PC←PC+sex|offset$_8$
		long	LBSR offset$_{16}$	Push PC onto Stack, PC←PC+offset$_{16}$
Return				Transfer back to caller
	from subroutine		RTS	Pull original PC back from Stack

Note 1: Available in signed 8-bit offset ($+127$, -128) & signed 16-bit offset ($+32,767$, $-32,768$) varieties. Most assemblers can choose the appropriate versions automatically.

Table 5.19: Subroutine instructions.

involves the mirror operation of pulling this address back out of the stack into the **PC**, whilst incrementing the **SSP**. This is done by terminating a subroutine with the instruction RTS (RETURN FROM SUBROUTINE), see Fig. 5.13(c). Some MPUs use the mnemonics CALL and RET for these operations.

As each further subroutine is called, its jumping-off point is pushed onto the stack, which grows downwards. As the return sequence from a nested call must be in reverse, the last call out has to be the first return in. This is exactly the structure of the push down LIFO stack. The nesting depth is limited only by the space allocated for the stack.

There is nothing special about the software of a subroutine, except that it must be terminated by RTS. In fact all our previous 6809-based examples were subroutines. For our first example in this section, we will implement a 100 ms delay function.

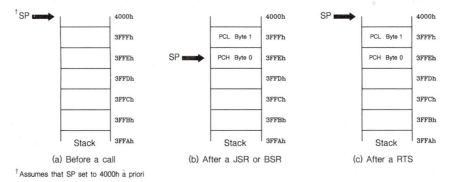

(a) Before a call   (b) After a JSR or BSR   (c) After a RTS

† Assumes that SP set to 4000h à priori

Figure 5.13: The stack before and after.

Example 5.8

Write a subroutine to implement a 100 ms dead time.

Solution

The listing of Table 5.20 simply puts the constant N into the X Index register and decrements until zero. The Decrement and Branch loop takes 8 cycles each pass plus a fixed entry and exit overhead of 8 cycles too. If the processor is clocked at 1 MHz, then a cycle translates directly to 1 μs. Thus in line 7 we evaluate N according to the relationship $8N + 8 = 100,000$; which is 12,499. Notice how the subroutine is documented, with a statement of its function, data entry and any registers altered on exit.

```
1                      .processor     m6809
2              ;************************************************************
3              ;* This subroutine does nothing and takes 0.1s to do it     *
4              ;* ENTRY : Non                                              *
5              ;* EXIT  : X Address register = 0000, CCR destroyed         *
6              ;************************************************************
7                      .define        N =12499
8  E000 8E30D3 DELAY_100 ldx   #N               ;Initial delay factor  , 3~
9  E003 301F  DLOOP:   leax  -1,x              ;Decrement             , Nx5~
10 E005 26FC          bne   DLOOP             ;to zero               , Nx3~
11 E007 39            rts                     ;                      , 5~
12                     .end
```

Table 5.20: A subroutine giving a fixed delay of 100 ms when called.

In our calculation we should strictly account for the delay in calling the subroutine. However, this will depend on which of the three Call instruction/address modes used to evoke this delay. In our case this inaccuracy will be less than one part in 10,000. This will not be the situation where short delays are implemented in this manner. The overhead of calling and returning from a subroutine may cause problems in time-sensitive applications and in such — rare — instances, in-line code may be used.

As well as being the repository of the location of the caller's jumping-off address when a subroutine is evoked, the stack can be used as a general-purpose LIFO store. Two stack-related instructions are provided for this purpose; PuSH and PULL (sometimes known as POP). In the 6809, any combination of registers may be pushed out on the stack, and similarly retrieved. Thus PSHS A,B,X saves the A and B Accumulators and X Index register on the stack, in the process decrementing the System Stack Pointer by four. Sometime later the instruction PULS A,B,X pops the data out again; incrementing the Stack Pointer and restoring this data to its original registers. The programmer must take care that the PuSH and PULL instructions use the same registers and that nothing has moved the System Stack Pointer in between. As the System stack is used automatically by called subroutines and, as we shall see, by interrupts, this is not always straightforward. The 6809 provides a second **User Stack Pointer (USP)** which is recommended for private stack operations. Only the System stack is used for subroutines and interrupts and thus the two functions can be kept separate. The PSHU and PULU instructions target the User stack.

Registers have their ranking order when pushed onto the stack, as shown in Fig. 5.14; with the Program Counter being the first to go and the Code Condition

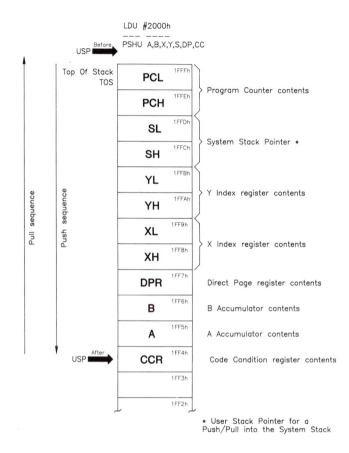

Figure 5.14: Stacking registers into memory. Also applicable to interrupts.

register last. This order is adhered to where the full complement is not specified. Thus PSHU A,B,X first pushes XL|XH, then B and finally A. The order of specifying the registers to the assembler is irrelevant; the same outcome results from the command PSHU B,X,A. At the machine-code level, the byte following the op-code defines which of the eight registers are saved; in this example, this is $00010110b$ for PC:S:Y:X:DPR:B:A:CCR. This gives the code 36-16h for PSHU A,B,X.

Example 5.9

Write a subroutine to give a delay of $M \times 0.1$ s, where M is a byte-sized parameter passed in the B Accumulator. None of the registers are to be altered on return.

Solution

The main difference from the previous example is the necessity for the calling program to pass a parameter to the subroutine. This is done via the **B** Accumulator. Thus the sequence:

```
LDB #100    ;one hundred 0.1 s delays
JSR DELAY   ;is 10 s
```

will call up a 10 s delay.

```
1                        .processor    m6809
2              ;*****************************************************************
3              ;* This subroutine does nothing and takes Mx0.1s to do it       *
4              ;* EXAMPLE : M = 10; delay = 1 second                           *
5              ;* ENTRY   : M passed in Accumulator_B                          *
6              ;* EXIT    : All registers unchanged                            *
7              ;*****************************************************************
8                        .define       N = 12499
9  E000 3415   DELAY:     pshs  b,x,cc           ;Save all used register
10 E002 8E30D3 DELAY_100: ldx   #N               ;100 ms delay loop
11 E005 301F   DLOOP:     leax  -1,x
12 E007 26FC              bne   DLOOP
13 E009 5A                decb                   ;One less M.  IF not yet zero
14 E00A 26F6              bne   DELAY_100         ;THEN another 100 ms
15 E00C 3515              puls  b,x,cc            ;ELSE retrieve used registers
16 E00E 39                rts                     ;and exit
17                        .end
```

Table 5.21: A transparent variable-delay subroutine.

The listing of Table 5.21 uses the basic 100 ms subroutine to delay each decrement of M (i.e. Accumulator_B) down to zero. Thus one hundred passes through this inner loop will result from the caller's sequence above.

The registers **X** and **B** are involved in this process and the flags are altered. The PuSH:PULL sandwich of lines 9 and 15 save and restore the entry values of these registers for exit. A subroutine with the property that none of its registers are altered is known as **transparent**.

What would happen if the delay parameter were zero, and how could you avoid this problem?

Although parameter passing via internal registers is quick and efficient, it is only applicable where a few variables are involved. A more general technique uses the stack to send out parameters [17, 18], as shown in the next example.

Example 5.10

Repeat the previous example, but this time pass the delay parameter M through the User stack.

Solution

In calling up the subroutine of Table 5.22, the delay parameter is pushed onto the User stack. Thus to call up a 10 s delay we have:

```
LDB #100      ;one hundred 0.1 s delays is 10 s
PSHU B        ;Push parameter out
JSR DELAY     ;and call it up
```

In the listing we have decremented this delay in situe in the User stack at step 16 by using the U register in the Indexed address mode. Besides this, the subroutine is similar to that of the previous example, with the addition of step 20. This instruction ensures that on return the U register has been restored to its original value, despite the main program's PUSh. If this were not done, then the User Stack Pointer would grow downwards indefinitely. This compensation could be done in the main program.

```
 1                              .processor      m6809
 2                      ;*********************************************************************
 3                      ;* This subroutine does nothing and takes Mx0.1s to do it          *
 4                      ;* EXAMPLE : M = 10; delay = 1 second                              *
 5                      ;* ENTRY   : M passed in thru the User stack at U                  *
 6                      ;* EXIT    : All registers unchanged                               *
 7                      ;*********************************************************************
 8                              .define         N = 12499
 9 E000 3411   DELAY:          pshs x,cc                       ;Save all used register
10            ;
11 E002 8E30D3 DELAY_100:      ldx  #N                         ;100 ms delay loop
12            ;
13 E005 301F  DLOOP:          leax -1,x                       ;Decrement
14 E007 26FC                  bne  DLOOP                      ;to zero
15            ;
16 E009 6AC4                  dec  0,u                        ;One less M.  IF not yet zero
17 E00B 26F5                  bne  DELAY_100                  ;THEN another 100 ms
18            ;
19 E00D 3511                  puls x,cc                       ;ELSE retrieve used registers
20 E00F 3341                  leau 1,u                        ;Clean up the user stack
21 E011 39                    rts                             ;and exit
22                            .end
```

Table 5.22: Passing a parameter through the stack.

In a simple example such as this, using a stack to pass parameters is inefficient. However, as many parameters as may be necessary can use this procedure without limitation.

A stack can also be used by a subroutine as a private area to store temporary variables which are to be discarded on return. In this case a Stack Pointer is moved down n bytes, and a pointer used to mark the top of this gap or frame. High-level languages frequently use this procedure, and an example is given in Table 6.30.

Our final subroutine here is a slightly more sophisticated example where the System stack is used both to send and return data.

Example 5.11

As part of a piece of medical equipment, where safety is of the utmost importance, the system read/write memory is to be periodically checked. This is to be done

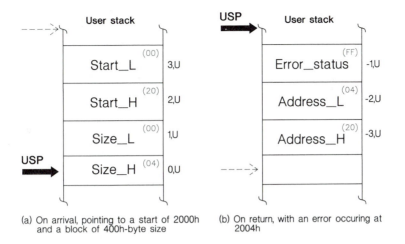

(a) On arrival, pointing to a start of 2000h and a block of 400h-byte size

(b) On return, with an error occuring at 2004h

Figure 5.15: The stack before and after.

by sending the test vector $01010101b$ to each byte in turn and checking for its safe delivery [19]. As this is a destructive test, then the original data must be stored away safely and returned afterwards.

Solution

The subroutine accepts two data words as arguments. The first to be pushed out is the memory-block start address followed by the size of the block. Thus a calling sequence might be:

```
LDD   #2000h
PSHU  D
LDD   #1024
PSHU  D
JSR   MEM_TST
```

for a 1 Kbyte block of memory beginning at $2000h$. After this is done, the User stack looks like Fig. 5.15(a).

At completion an error status byte is returned (NULL $= 00h$ for success and -1 (FFh) for failure) together with the failed-at address. This also uses the User stack, which is shown in Fig. 5.15(b). At this point the **USP** has been moved back to its original position.

The listing shown in Table 5.23 extracts the start and size parameters in steps 11 & 12 using **U** as an Index register. The main test loop simply uses the **X** Index register to advance through the memory block, extracting the original data, sending out the test vector and returning it if successful. If the test fails, the loop exits (line 18) and makes the error status -1 (step 26). The normal exit is when the size parameter (now in **Y**) is decremented to zero. In this case the error status is zeroed. After this, the User stack is cleaned up by adding four to **U** (step 28) and both the error status and the final address placed in the User stack for return, steps 29 – 32.

```
 1                              .processor      m6809
 2                    ;*******************************************************************
 3                    ;* This subroutine does a non destructive test of RAM            *
 4                    ;* beginning at Start for Size bytes.  Returns an error status    *
 5                    ;* of 00 if OK and -1 if a failure occurs.  In the event of the   *
 6                    ;* latter, the failure address is also returned                   *
 7                    ;* ENTRY   : Block size at U:U+1, start address at U+2:U+3         *
 8                    ;* EXIT    : Error status at U-1; last address at U-2:U-3          *
 9                    ;*******************************************************************
10 E000 3437          MEM_TST:   pshs  a,b,x,y,cc           ;Save all used registers
11 E002 AE42                     ldx   2,u                  ;Put start address in X
12 E004 10AEC4                   ldy   0,u                  ;and size of block in Y
13 E007 C655                     ldb   #01010101b           ;and the test vector in B
14                    ; DO the test procedure WHILE no error occurs or all bytes are correct
15 E009 A684          TEST_LOOP: lda   0,x                  ;Get original data
16 E00B E784                     stb   0,x                  ;Put the test vector up
17 E00D E184                     cmpb  0,x                  ;Has it arrived safely
18 E00F 2609                     bne   ERROR                ;IF not THEN exit on a fail
19 E011 A780                     sta   ,x+                  ;Put data back and advance pointer
20 E013 313F                     leay  -1,y                 ;Now decrement byte count
21 E015 26F2                     bne   TEST_LOOP            ;and repeat until zero
22                    ; Leave loop here only if everything is OK
23 E017 5F                       clrb                       ; Error status is 00h for OK
24 E018 2002                     bra   EXIT
25                    ;
26 E01A C6FF          ERROR:     ldb   #-1                  ; -1 (FFh) is the error status
27                    ;
28 E01C 3344          EXIT:      leau  4,u                  ;Clean up user stack
29 E01E E75F                     stb   -1,u                 ;Push out the error status
30 E020 AF5D                     stx   -3,u                 ;and the last address tested
31 E022 3537                     puls  a,b,x,y,cc           ;Retrieve the entry state
32 E024 39                       rts                        ;and return
33                               .end
```

Table 5.23: A non-destructive memory test.

Actually the information carried back on the error status is redundant; examining the address parameter is sufficient. Can you see why?

Using a stack for parameter passing and local storage has the advantage that no absolute address is used. Thus there is no reason why a subroutine should not call itself. This **recursive** attribute can be useful for certain mathematical operations [20].

As we will see, stack-based data also allows a subroutine to be interrupted and then the interrupt service routine to call up the same subroutine. Such code is known as a **re-enterant** subroutine.

Subroutines are predictable events in that they are called up wherever and whenever the program dictates. Real-time situations where the MPU interacts with external physical events are not as simple as this. Very often something happens out there which necessitates immediate action by the MPU. Thus we require a mechanism whereby an external event can force the MPU to go to a subroutine. As this situation is not dictated by the software, in essence such **interrupts** occur at random as far as the MPU is concerned.

A simple example of this scenario is shown in Fig. 5.16, where we wish to measure time in 1 ms 'ticks' between the peaks of an electrocardiograph signal (ECG or heart

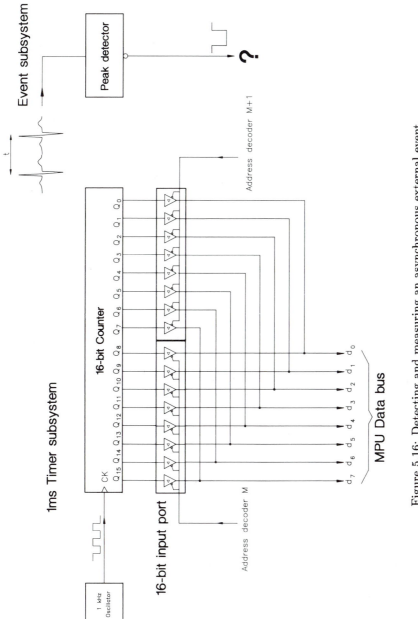

Figure 5.16: Detecting and measuring an asynchronous external event.

wave). A 16-bit counter is incremented at a 1 kHz rate and when the peak occurs
the MPU must be alerted to read this timer within 1 ms of the event. If the
response is longer than this, then the counter will have gone on and the reading will
be incorrect. The mechanism of interfacing the counter to the data bus is covered
in Section 5.3.2, here all we are interested in is how the external event is able to
stop the MPU in its tracks, go to a subroutine which reads the count, and return
it to the background program.

One approach would be to continually monitor the peak detector's output until
an event is detected. This would involve 1000 reads each second, and maybe 999 of
these will be negative. This **polling** approach is fine if there are only a few events
being measured and the background processing task is not too onerous. However,
in this instance we may also be measuring blood pressure, temperature etc. for a
whole ward of patients. In that case the MPU will spend most of its time polling,
leaving little time for processing.

To circumvent this problem all MPUs have at least one input labelled Interrupt.
When this pin is tugged (typically by going Low or on a Low-going edge), the MPU
will temporarily suspend its operation and go to an **interrupt service routine
(ISR)**. This is just a subroutine entered via an interrupt. At the end of the ISR,
control is passed back to the background program. As seen from the point of view
of the MPU, interrupts happen at random. Thus care must be taken that the
machine state (i.e. state of the registers) has not been disrupted when control does
return. Furthermore, there may be many different events, any of which can request
an interrupt. In such cases, some means must be found to distinguish between the
source of the service request and prioritize when more than one peripheral requires
attention.

Although the minutia of the response to an interrupt request varies considerably
from processor to processor, the following phases can usually be identified:

1. Finishing the current instruction.

2. Ignore the request if the appropriate mask (if any) is set.

3. Save, at the very least, the state of the **PC** (which is needed to get back) and
   the **CCR** (which is bound to be altered by the ISR).

4. Enter the appropriate service routine; the foreground program.

5. Execute the defined task.

6. Restore the processor state and return to the point in the background program
   where control was first transferred.

Due to the randomness of interrupts, the system response to such events must
ensure that the interrupted program (the background program) is oblivious to the
fact that the processor has 'gone away for a while' to service an external request.
In some ways this is akin to transparency in subroutines, but is more difficult to
implement due to the indeterminacy of the action.

The 6809 MPU has three interrupt pins, labelled $\overline{\text{NMI}}$, $\overline{\text{IRQ}}$ and $\overline{\text{FIRQ}}$ for Non_Ma-
skable_Interrupt, Interrupt_Request and Fast_Interrupt_Request; see Section 5.2.1. Of
these, the NMI request has the highest priority. When activated by a ⌐_ edge,

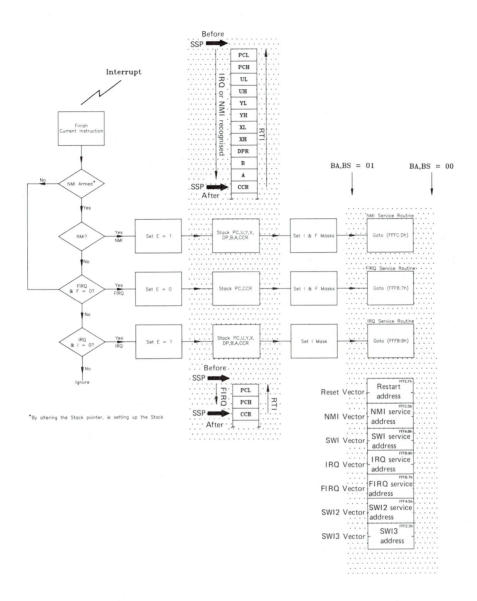

Figure 5.17: How the 6809 responds to an interrupt request.

the MPU responds by automatically pushing every internal register away in the System stack, whilst setting the E flag in the **CCR** to show that the Entire state has been saved. Next, both I and F masks in the **CCR** are set, and this locks out any subsequent IRQ or FIRQ requests. Finally the processor goes to the NMI vector **FFFC:D***h* to get the start address of the NMI ISR. This is signalled by the Bus Status pins **BA BS** going to state 01*b*; which can be used as an acknowledge to the peripheral that its request is receiving attention. Normally the Interrupt and Reset vectors are fixed in ROM.

In order to correctly respond to an interrupt, a System stack must be set up before a request is received. In the case of $\overline{\text{NMI}}$ this is difficult, as there is no way of locking out the MPU's response. To avoid an erroneous reaction to a $\overline{\text{NMI}}$ directly following $\overline{\text{Reset}}$, the 6809 delays its response to such a request until after an instruction altering the state of the System Stack Pointer, e.g. **LDS #07FFh**. This then arms the internal NMI circuitry.

The FIRQ response is similar to NMI, except that this is locked out when the F mask bit is set, as it is by $\overline{\text{NMI}}$ and also on $\overline{\text{Reset}}$. Thus to use $\overline{\text{FIRQ}}$ we must clear this mask bit, e.g. **ANDCC #10111111b**. Conversely **ORCC #01000000b** inhibits $\overline{\text{FIRQ}}$. The FIRQ response only stacks away the **PC** and **CCR**, leaving the ISR to PUSH/PULL any other registers which may be used. This is reflected by its 9-cycle response time as opposed to the 18-cycle latency of the NMI and IRQ responses. The E flag is cleared to indicate that the entire state is not saved, and the start of the ISR is located in FFF6:7*h*.

The lowest priority is accorded to the IRQ response. This is locked out by both the NMI and FIRQ responses, which set the I mask; as does Reset. If both Masks are clear, then all registers are saved, **E** is set and the system vectors via FFF8:9*h* to its ISR.

Both $\overline{\text{IRQ}}$ and $\overline{\text{FIRQ}}$ are Low-level activated. This means that their respective pins *must not still be Low* when the ISR terminates; otherwise another interrupt response will immediately occur. Multiple responses will not happen during an ISR as the I and F masks as appropriate are set before the ISR vector is fetched, see Fig. 5.17. This is not a problem with $\overline{\text{NMI}}$, as it is edge triggered.

As in the case of a subroutine, an interrupt service routine is a normal program but this time terminated by the instruction RTI (RETURN FROM INTERRUPT). RTI restores the registers pushed out on the System stack; it looks at the E flag to determine which of these need to go back. Execution of the background program then recommences at the next instruction following that which was interrupted.

A little thought shows that data cannot be passed to and from an ISR using internal registers. In such cases variables are normally located in known absolute locations, which can be read by the background program and altered by the foreground program (i.e. the ISR). Care must be taken when such global variables are larger than the natural size of the instruction data width. For example, consider a central heating system reading the time in the form hh:mm. If, say, the time is 09:59 and hours are first read (09 hours). If an interrupt then occurs; it may be 10:00 by the time the MPU gets back to reading the minutes. This read will yield 00 (i.e. 00 minutes). The MPU now thinks it is 9.00 am and may take an erroneous action; such as toggling the pump.

Besides RTI, the 6809 has two interrupt-related instructions. These are SYNC and CWAI. The former stops processing and waits for an external interrupt to occur [21].

If this is masked out, or lasts for less than three clock cycles, the program simply continues normal processing. If neither is the case, then the interrupt is serviced in the normal way. Both Data and address buses are turned Off during this wait. CWAI (CLEAR CCR BITS AND WAIT FOR INTERRUPT) ANDs the CCR with an immediate byte, typically to clear the I and F masks, stacks the entire state and waits for an interrupt to happen. For example, CWAI #10101111b clears the F and I masks, stacks everything away and waits ....

The 6809 has three instructions under the category of Software Interrupts, SWI, SWI2 and SWI3. These push the entire state onto the System stack and vector via the appropriate location, shown in Fig. 5.17, to the start of their respective ISR. Software Interrupts are normally used when the user software is running on hardware under the shell of an operating system (OS). An OS is a software package designed to insulate the user's application software from the surrounding hardware. Thus the application software can be moved unchanged to a different hardware environment provided that the OS that comes with it has been adapted. Typical commercial OSs are PCDOS/MSDOS (for IBM PCs) and UNIX (for workstations). Software Interrupts, often called Traps, are used to pass control from the user's software back to this system overlay software. The operating system defines the SWI vectors, and the designer requires no knowledge of the absolute addresses used by this system software. A simple example uses a Software Interrupt as a breakpoint. When the breakpoint is reached (SWI), control is transferred to the OS which then typically prints out the contents of all internal registers (from the System stack) as a debugging aid.

We will look at interrupts again in Section 5.3.3. Here let us finish off by writing an ISR to read the timer of Fig. 5.16 and calculate the difference between the last reading. We will assume that $\overline{\text{NMI}}$ is used, and thus we do not have to worry about removing the interrupt signal on return.

Example 5.12

Write an ISR to calculate δt in the system shown in Fig. 5.16. Two global variables **Old_time** and **Delta_time** are known to both background and foreground routines.

Solution

```
1                       .processor m6809
2         ;***********************************************************************
3         ;* This interrupt service routine calculates the peak-to-peak time variation*
4         ;* ENTRY : Global variables Old_time and Delta_time.  Timer read at 9000:1h *
5         ;* EXIT  : Old_time and Delta_time updated                              *
6         ;***********************************************************************
7                       .define TIMER = 9000h, Old_time = 0000h, Delta_time = 0002h
8  E300 FC9000  TIME:   ldd     TIMER        ; Get current 1ms count
9  E303 3406            pshs    d            ; Put it away for safe keeping
10 E305 9300            subd    Old_time     ; Subtract previous value
11 E307 DD02            std     Delta_time   ; Gives the new difference in ms
12 E309 3506            puls    d            ; Get the current value back
13 E30B DD00            std     Old_time     ; which is now the new previous value
14 E30D 3B              rti                  ; and quit
15                      .end
```

Table 5.24: Evaluating the ECG period.

All we do in Table 5.24 is get the new time and push it out to the System stack for safekeeping. Then we get the previous reading from **Old_time**, subtract the new time (at 0,S on the System stack) and put the difference away at **Delta_time**. Finally the new time is pulled back from the System stack and updates **Old_time**. Note that on return from the ISR the value of the D Accumulator will be restored to its original pre-interrupt value.

5.3   Interfacing

A microprocessor on its own is incapable of doing anything useful. Embedded in the real world, we must find the means of getting information to and from the MPU. Any physical process which can be sensed is a candidate to input data, and likewise the MPU controls the physical environment by outputting data to transducers. For example, in a glasshouse; air, soil and external temperatures, humidity and time may be monitored. The environment may be altered by operating a heater, opening windows and switching water sprinklers.

We have seen from Figs. 5.1 and 5.10 that all such data is funnelled through a data highway. This one bus supports both memory and ports through which the data flows into and out of the system. As the MPU is a digital system, such **ports** are digital in nature. Many physical parameters are analog, for example temperature; and analog/digital conversion stages are required.

As all the system resources share the same data path, some means must be found to select at any time the source or target device, whether it be a memory location or port. At the software level each operand is given an address; thus the instruction LDA 9000h means bring down to Accumulator_A the data to be found at location $9000h$. Externally this translates to the pattern 1001 0000 0000 0000b on the address bus. What actually lives up at $9000h$ is a function of the system hardware. The hardware designer must allocate the system resources to the available address range, and inform the software designer of the resulting memory map. Thus we might have the following situation.

0000h – 07FFh	2k-byte RAM
9000h	Air temperature input port
9001h	Soil temperature input port
9002h	External temperature input port
9003h	Humidity input port
9004h	Heater control output port
9005h	Window position output port
9006h	Sprinkler output port
E000h – FFFFh	4k-byte program ROM

Except for the ROM, which in the 6809 MPU is nearly always at the top of the map to hold the Reset and Interrupt vectors, the position of the other resources is at the whim of the hardware designer.

All this is rather like a telephone system, where each subscriber has a unique number. In order to make the connection, a series of telephone exchanges must decode this subscriber number. In a similar fashion, the address decoder detects the various patterns on the address bus, and contacts the appropriate device; which can then take part in the data interchange. Although this is shown as a single box in Fig. 5.10; in practice this function is often devolved throughout the system. Thus whilst the RAM chip is shown selected as a whole by the primary address decoder, the on-board (secondary) chip decoder uses the lower eleven address lines to home in on one memory cell (see also Fig. 4.46).

In this section we will look at the design of address decoders and input/output ports of various degrees of complexity. At its completion you should be able to:

- Design a simple address decoder and characterize it in terms of image and multiple-selection addresses.

- Use 3-state buffers as a simple input port.

- Use flip flops or latches to implement a simple output port.

- Use the above to construct a pulse-width modulation power controller.

- Interface both an analog input and output signal port to the MPU.

- Interface ports of greater width than the data bus.

- Implement an interface where one or more devices interrupt the microprocessor.

- Use a LSI software configurable device to parallel interface.

- Understand the technique of handshaking in controlling the flow of data between a peripheral device and the microprocessor.

- Understand the principle of asynchronous serial data communication.

- Use a LSI software configurable device as a serial interface.

5.3.1 Address Decoding

From our introductory discussion, the **address decoder** is in essence a circuit detecting ranges of binary patterns. Any of the SSI, MSI or LSI combinational techniques introduced in Chapter 3 would be applicable to this task. As there is nothing new involved in the design of an address decoder, we will restrict ourselves to looking at some typical examples.

Normally a small system uses a decoder to split up the available address space into zones or pages, each of which covers an application, such as read/write memory, read only memory, input/output ports. Any page may be split into smaller ranges or individual addresses by further decoder stages. In this respect a page decoder is rather like the area code telephone exchange, with local exchanges getting down to the subscriber level.

A simple example of this is shown in Fig. 5.18(a). Here a natural 3 to 8-line decoder acts on the three uppermost address lines to give eight address zones. Thus all addresses between 0000 0000 0000 0000b and 0001 1111 1111 1111b (0000h – 1FFFh) will activate the page 0 line. Each page spans a range of 8 kbyte (2^{13}) addresses. Finer pages can of course be decoded using larger decoders which omit

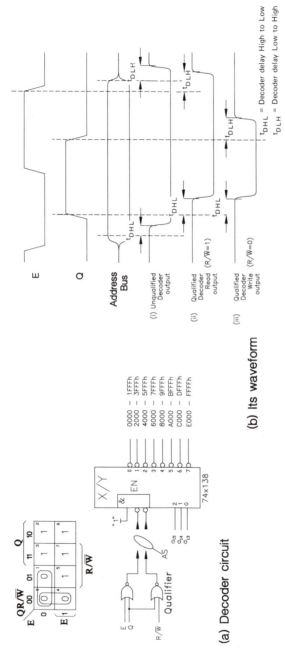

(b) Its waveform

(a) Decoder circuit

Figure 5.18: An elementary page decoder.

less address variables. Thus a 5 to 32-line decoder would give 32 8 Kbyte (2^{11}) pages.

We have already studied the bus waveforms of the 6809 MPU in Figs. 5.8 and 5.9. There we saw that the address signals were synchronized by the E clock; appearing before the cycle was 25% over and being removed shortly after the end of the cycle. When the MPU does a read, the device addressed must place its data on the bus before the end of the cycle, when the MPU grabs it. When doing a write cycle, the MPU places its data on the bus no later than 75% through the cycle and removes it very shortly after the end of the cycle.

The top three waveforms of Fig. 5.18(b) shows the relationship between the E and Q clock signals and address bus. From this we can make the following observations:

1. The address lines have stabilized by the rising edge of Q.

2. The address lines remain stable until the falling edge of E.

Thus we can use the relationship E+Q to enable the decoder as an Address Strobe (AS). The use of AS to qualify the address decoder ensures that no spurious decoding spikes occur before or after the address signals are stable.

One further point remains. From Fig. 5.9 we see that when the MPU does a write, its outgoing data is stable by the falling edge of Q. It is better to use this edge to complete the transfer of the data to the output port or read/write memory cell rather than wait to the end of the E cycle ($\neg\!\!\!\!\sqcup$). This is because this data is only guaranteed stable for no more than 30 ns after the cycle end, and the delay through the decoder can easily exceed this, as shown in Fig. 5.18(b)I. Taking this into account, we have for our Address Strobe:

$$AS = ((E+Q) \cdot R/\overline{W}) + (Q \cdot \overline{R/\overline{W}})$$

Entering this into a K-map and minimizing the zeros gives, after a little manipulation:

$$AS = (E+Q) \cdot (Q + R/\overline{W})$$

Making use of the 74x138's ANDed Enable inputs gives us the qualifier circuit of Fig. 5.18(a) and waveforms of Fig. 5.18(b)II and III (see also Example 2.12).

Many MPUs automatically generate an Address Strobe of this nature. Thus the 6800 MPU has VMA (Valid_Memory_Address), the 68000 family has $\overline{AS}$ and the 808x family has $\overline{ALE}$ (Address_Latch_Enable).

Example 5.13

Given the page decoder of Fig. 5.18, how would you enable a 27256 EPROM which will lie between 8000h and FFFFh?

Solution

The 27256 EPROM is organized as a 32 Kbyte array of 8-bit bytes. As each page only covers 8 K, then the upper four pages can be ORed together using a 4-I/P AND gate (active-Low input/active-Low output OR gate) to generate the EPROM enabling pulse. Actually $a_{15} = 1$ on its own would do the same job!

Example 5.14

Based on the page decoder of Fig. 5.18, design a secondary decoder to select one of six input/output ports between addresses 9000h and 9FFFh.

Solution

The primary decoder feeding our port decoder has no page at 9000h. However, we can qualify page 4 (a_{15} a_{14} a_{13} = 100b) with a_{12} = 1 to get a base address of 9000h. In the simple scheme of Fig. 5.19(a), an AND gate is used to detect the zone 9000h − 9FFFh and to further qualify an array of six NAND gates; each operating on one further address line. Thus output $\overline{\text{Port\_0 EN}}$ goes Low whenever the address is 1001 *XXXX XXXX XXXX*b AND a_0 is 1; i.e. 1001 *XXXX XXXX XXX*1b. The *X*s have their normal don't care meaning and indicate an address variable omitted from the decoder equation. In this case there are eleven variables missing, which means that each output will respond to a total of 2^{11} (2048) addresses in all. The lowest of these addresses, where *X* = 0, is known as the base address, and all others as **image addresses**. In general where n address variables are missing, there are

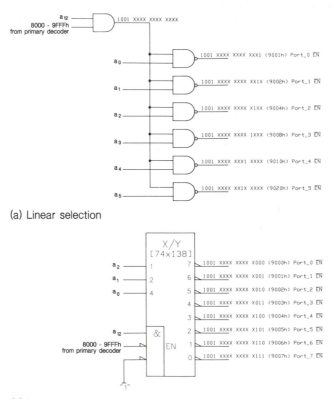

(a) Linear selection

(b) Partial decoding

Figure 5.19: Two simple secondary decoders.

$2^n - 1$ image addresses. Thus in our example, output $\overline{\text{Port\_0 EN}}$ will respond to addresses $9001h$; $9003h$; $9005h$; $9007h \cdots 9FFFh$.

Besides being inefficient, the linear select circuit has a more insidious problem. Certain addresses can cause more than one output to be active at the one time. For example, an instruction such as **LDA 9FFFh** will enable all ports simultaneously; a rather dubious state of affairs. Of course the software engineer will be told which addresses are legitimate, and thus **multiple selection** should never occur. However, this is not robust programming, as there is always the possibility of a software bug; which in rare situations does output an illegal address. This could also occur if the MPU should run berserk due to noise. Software that can potentially damage hardware is not a desirable feature.

The alternative arrangement, shown in Fig. 5.19(b), is much more satisfactory. Here a second 3 to 8-line decoder, as qualified by page 4 and a_{12}, operates on the lower three address lines to give eight Port Enables. Although we still have image addresses ($2^9 - 1 = 511$ this time), there is no multiple-selection problem. The circuit is labelled a partial decoder, as not all address variables are involved. Can you modify the circuit so that no image addresses are produced?

None of the decoding schemes thus far are very flexible, in that considerable rewiring is necessary in order to change address. This is awkward in the case of an expandable system where additional functions can be plugged in. For example, you might wish to purchase additional memory or an analog/digital acquisition card for your personal computer. In such circumstances the address range that your additional function will respond to must be able to be easily tailored to suit the existing system's memory map. Such cards normally come with an array of switches, which can be quickly set as appropriate. This is normally done by using an equality comparator to compare the address lines with the switch settings.

Example 5.15

A certain plug-in expansion card is to have an on-board primary decoder to permit the user to relocate the card to any desired 256-byte location in steps of 256 bytes. Show how this could be done.

Solution

The basis of the decoder shown in Fig. 5.20 is an octal equality detector, such as the 74x688 (see Fig. 3.53). The decoder output is active whenever the bit pattern $a_{15} \cdots a_9$ (**P**) equals that setup by the eight switches (**Q**). With the switches as shown in the diagram, this match occurs at addresses $9000h - 90FFh$. The lower eight address lines can then be further decoded to select up to 256 (2^8) input/output ports within this range. The base address may be altered between $00h$ to FFh by simply changing the switches to the appropriate value. How could you alter this circuit to move the base address in increments of 1024 (1 Kbyte), reserving 1 Kbyte for on-board use?

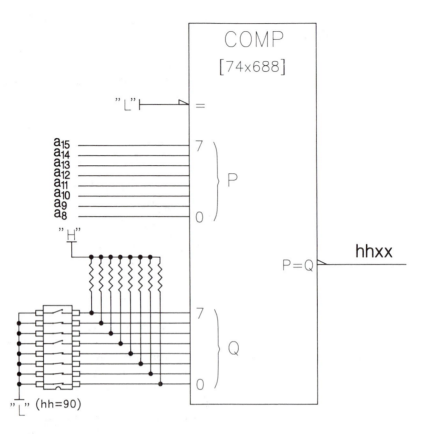

Figure 5.20: A reconfigurable address decoder. Shown set to base 9000h.

5.3.2 Parallel Ports

Data originating or destined to the outside world passes through **ports** attached to the data bus. As this bus is a shared resource, such ports must have the ability to be connected and disconnected as directed by the address decoder.

Ports may be classified as a combination of input, output, serial or parallel. In this section we look at the situation where data is handled in parallel, leaving serial transmission until Section 5.3.4.

As our first example, consider the problem of arranging for the MPU to read an array of eight switches. Interposed between the switches and the data bus is the **input port**. This port must be transparent when enabled by the address decoder and turned Off whenever deselected; exactly the property of the 3-state buffer.

Based on this premise, the input port shown in Fig. 5.21 comprizes eight such buffers interposed between the switches and data lines. Each buffer's Enable is driven in parallel directly by the address decoder's output. Thus when selected, the switches are gated through to the bus; otherwise they are disconnected. Qualifying the Port_Enable by R/$\overline{\text{W}}$ guards against an accidental write to this address. R/$\overline{\text{W}}$ is

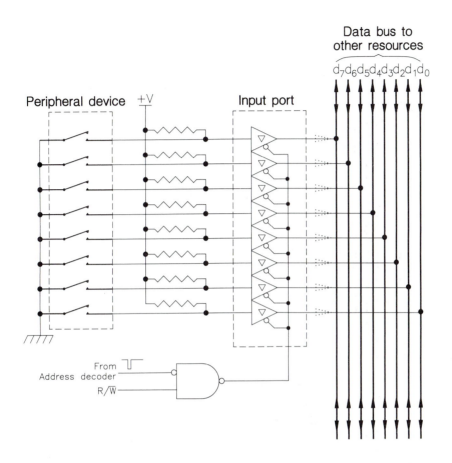

Figure 5.21: A simple 8-bit input port.

often incorporated into the address decoder directly (see page 546) or even ignored. Octal arrays of 3-state buffers with a boosted current output, such as the 74x244, make convenient single-chip input ports, see Fig. 5.23.

At any one time, a selected port is only enabled during the duration of the active address decoder pulse; which as we saw in Fig. 5.18(b), is rather less than 1 μs. However, the response of 74 series 3-state buffers is generally better than 20 ns. Nevertheless, this settling time for long bus lines must be taken into account when high-speed MPUs are used, and the bus lines properly terminated to reduce transmission line reflections [22].

As data on the bus is constantly changing as the MPU transacts its business, an **output port** must be capable of grabbing and holding on to data targeted to it. Typically these memory elements are latches or flip flops.

As an example, consider the problem of actuating eight electromechanical relays. As shown in Fig. 5.22, the relay coils are isolated from the data lines by eight D flip

Data bus to
other resources

$d_7 d_6 d_5 d_4 d_3 d_2 d_1 d_0$

Output port   Peripheral device

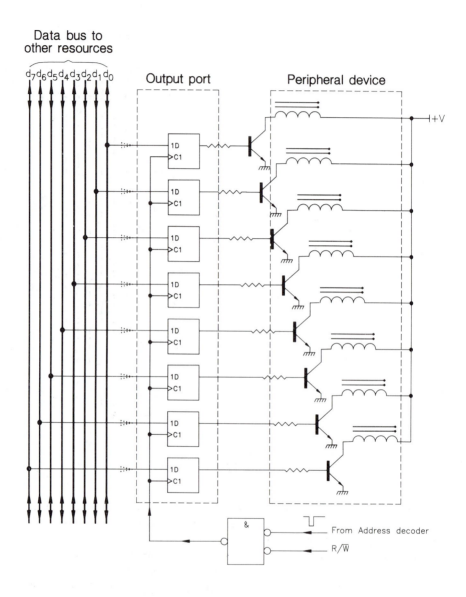

From Address decoder

R/$\overline{W}$

Figure 5.22: Driving eight electromechanical relays.

flops. These are clocked by the rising edge of an address decoder output ANDed by $\overline{\text{R/W}}$ (write). We assume that the address decoder is qualified by Q as in Fig. 5.18, to trigger the flip flops well before the end of the cycle. This avoids the hazardous race indicated in Fig. 5.9 between the propagation delay through the address decoder and the data being removed from the bus. If this is not the case, then the $\overline{\text{R/W}}$ signal may be ANDed with Q to effectively do the same thing. Similar timing considerations hold as for the input port.

Example 5.16

As part of a controlled environment system, a MPU is to alter the thermal input using pulse-width modulation (PWM) switching of a heater. The heating power is to be a function of eight switches, linearly varying from zero with $n = 00h$ to full power with $n = \text{FFh}$. Show how you would interface the switches and PWM output, and write a suitable software loop to implement this function.

Solution

In the implementation of Fig. 5.23, we have used a 74x244 octal 3-state buffer as an input port for the eight switches and a single D flip flop for the 1-line output port. This is cleared when the MPU is Reset and the heater is then Off. It is assumed that the address decoder is qualified by Q in the normal way. The $\overline{\text{R/W}}$ signal could also be used as a qualifier.

The software shown in Table 5.25 splits the On + Off cycle into 256 steps, as recorded by the spare memory location **Count**. At the very beginning of the cycle, the heater is turned On by storing a 1 out at the flip flop. As **Count** is advanced, it eventually equals n, and at that point the heater is turned Off. **Count** continues to be incremented until it wraps around back to zero and the process then repeats. The higher is n, the longer is the heater On as a function of the cycle length. We have already proved on page 278, that the average power is directly a function of n as specified. The complete cycle takes less than 5 ms, and the resulting pulse frequency of 200 Hz is smoothed by the thermal inertia of the heater. How would

```
1                              .processor m6809
2                              .define Switch = 9000h, PWM = 9001h, Count = 0000h
3                      ; Forever increment Count, turning heater On at the beginning and Off
4                      ; at when Count = Switch.
5  E000 B69000  MAIN:      lda    Switch   ;Get n
6  E003 C601               ldb    #01      ;Turn heater On
7  E005 F79001             stb    PWM
8  E008 0F00               clr    Count    ;Zero Count
9  E00A 9100    LOOP:      cmpa   Count    ;Is Count equal Switch settings
10 E00C 2604               bne    CONT     ;IF not THEN continue with the count
11 E00E 5F                 clrb            ;ELSE turn heater Off
12 E00F F79001             stb    PWM
13 E012 0C00    CONT:      inc    Count    ;One more count
14 E014 26F4               bne    LOOP     ;IF not yet complete THEN again
15 E016 20E8               bra    MAIN     ;ELSE repeat complete On-Off cycle
16                         .end
```

Table 5.25: Software pulse-width modulation.

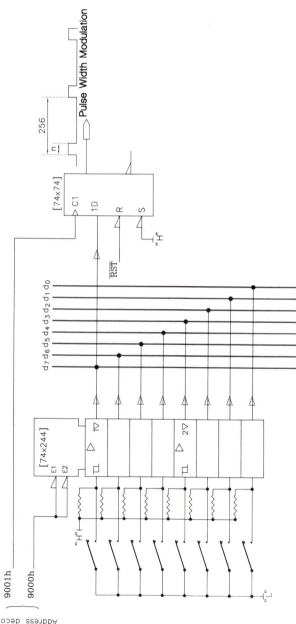

Figure 5.23: Interface for the PWM system.

you alter the routine if the input were two BCD thumbwheel switches with the range 00 – 99?

Although our system works, it is rather useless, as it spends all its time simply marking time. In reality interrupts may be used to make the system multi-task, as discussed in the next Section. Alternatively, PWM hardware controlled by the MPU, as in Example 3.34 may be used to take the processing load off the MPU.

Many devices are available with integral 3-state buffers or latches which are specifically designed to be directly connected to the data bus.

Most ROM devices have 3-state buffers (see Fig. 3.57) so that the selected cell can be gated to the bus without additional buffering. Each cell of a selected RAM cell can be thought of as an I/O device controlled by R/$\overline{W}$, also with integral 3-state buffers, see Fig. 4.46.

Although memory chips are interfaced to the data bus in the normal way, they strictly speaking are not ports as there is no communication with the outside world. As our example of a MPU-compatible device, we will briefly look at two analog $\leftrightarrow$ digital converters. The AD7524, shown in Fig. 5.25, transforms an 8-bit digital byte to an equivalent analog signal. The actual conversion process switches the eight digital levels into a resistor network so that the LSB is worth only $\frac{1}{128}$th of the MSB at the summed output [23]. An integral 8-bit latch array allows direct connection to the data bus. In this manner we can generate an analog voltage $\mathcal{F}_n$, where n is the digital value from 00h to FFh (0 to 255). Thus if the LSB is worth 1 mV, then the analog range is 0 to 2.55 V; directly proportional to n.

The converse process of converting an analog quantity to a digital equivalent is somewhat more complex [24]. The AD7576 8-bit analog to digital (A/D) converter uses a technique known as successive approximation. As we see in Fig. 5.24, the AD7576 contains an integral D/A converter (DAC), analog magnitude comparator (COMP) and a Successive Approximation Register (SAR). The process begins by setting the SAR to 10000000b, which produces an analog voltage, via DAC, of $V_{max}/2$. This is compared with the analog input voltage V_{in}. If $V_{max}/2 < V_{in}$, then SAR bit 7 is retained, otherwise it is cleared. Next the pattern $b_7$1000000b is tried. This produces either $3V_{max}/4$ or $V_{max}/4$ (11000000b or 01000000b) and the comparison process repeated. After eight trials, the SAR holds the binary equivalent.

This is similar to the beam balance method of evaluating an unknown weight n. One by one the known weights are taken out of their box, put on the pan and either left there or returned according to whether the aggregate weight is too heavy or too light. Thus if we have eight weights from 1 gm to 128 gm and the unknown weight is 67.4 gm, we would have:

Test 1	128 gm	=	10000000b	: Too heavy
Test 2	64 gm	=	01000000b	: Too light
Test 3	96 gm	=	01100000b	: Too heavy
Test 4	80 gm	=	01010000b	: Too heavy
Test 5	72 gm	=	01001000b	: Too heavy
Test 6	68 gm	=	01000100b	: Too heavy
Test 7	66 gm	=	01000010b	: Too light
Test 8	67 gm	=	01000011b	: Too light

ANALOG DEVICES

LC²MOS
10μs μP Compatible 8-Bit ADC

AD7576

FEATURES
Single +5V Operation with External Positive
   Reference
Fast Conversion Time: 10μs
No Missed Codes Over Full Temperature Range
Microprocessor Compatible
Low Cost
Low Power (15mW)
100ns Data Access Time

GENERAL DESCRIPTION
The AD7576 is a low cost, low power, microprocessor compatible
8-bit analog-to-digital converter, which uses the successive
approximation technique to achieve a fast conversion time of
10μs. The device is designed to operate with an external reference
of +1.23V (standard bandgap reference) and converts input
signals from 0V to $2V_{REF}$.

The part is designed for ease of microprocessor interface with
three control inputs ($\overline{CS}$, $\overline{RD}$ and MODE) controlling all ADC
operations such as starting conversion and reading data. The
interface logic allows the part to be easily configured as a memory
mapped device. All data outputs use latched, three-state output
buffer circuitry to allow direct connection to a microprocessor
data bus or system input port. The output latches serve to make
the conversion process transparent to the microprocessor.

The part is designed for single +5V operation, has on-board
comparator, interface logic, and internal/external clock option.
This makes the AD7576 ideal for most ADC/μP interface
applications.

The AD7576 is fabricated in an advanced, all ion-implanted
high speed Linear Compatible CMOS (LC²MOS) process and is
packaged in a small, 0.3″ wide, 18-pin DIP.

PRODUCT HIGHLIGHTS
1. Single Supply Operation
   Operation from a single +5V supply with a +1.23V reference
   allows operation of the AD7576 with microprocessor systems
   without any additional power supplies.

2. Low Power
   CMOS fabrication of the AD7576 results in a very low power
   dissipation figure of 15mW typical.
3. Versatile Interface Logic
   The AD7576 can be configured to perform continuous conversions or to convert on command. It can be interfaced as
   SLOW-MEMORY or ROM, allowing versatile interfacing to
   most microprocessors.
4. Fast Conversion Time
   The fabrication of the AD7576 on Analog Devices' Linear
   Compatible CMOS (LC²MOS) process enables fast conversion
   times of 10μs, eliminating the need for expensive Sample-and-
   Holds in many low frequency applications.

AD7576 FUNCTIONAL DIAGRAM

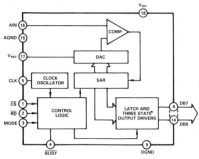

Two Technology Way; Norwood, MA 02062-9106 U.S.A.
Tel: 617/329-4700   **Twx: 710/394-6577**
Telex: 174059   **Cables: ANALOG NORWOODMASS**

Figure 5.24: The AD7576 microprocessor compatible A/D converter. Reproduced
by courtesy of Analog Devices Inc.

giving 67 gm (i.e. 01000011b) as the nearest approximation.

The AD7576 operates in two modes [25]. In the synchronous mode, the comparison process is triggered when Chip_Select ($\overline{\text{CS}}$) is pulsed Low. During conversion the $\overline{\text{BUSY}}$ status line goes Low. When the conversion is complete, the contents of the SAR are dumped into an internal register with 3-state buffered outputs (see also Fig. 4.14). This data may be read by bringing both $\overline{\text{CS}}$ and $\overline{\text{RD}}$ Low, which enables the 3-state buffers (and also starts a new conversion afterwards).

In the asynchronous mode, conversions occur regularly and are not triggered by a pulse on $\overline{\text{CS}}$. Data may be read at any time, due to the latched output. The arrival of the latest sample is announced by the rising edge of $\overline{\text{BUSY}}$.

Whilst all this sounds complicated, the MPU-compatible nature of these devices makes interfacing easy. An example of this is given in Fig. 5.25, where an 8-bit analog input and one 8-bit analog output port are shown. The single address 9000h is used for both input and output, with R/$\overline{\text{W}}$ selecting between them. The $\overline{\text{BUSY}}$ line has been ignored, as the AD7576 can complete its conversion in only 10 μs. Notice the $\cap$ inverted cup symbol used to denote a non-digital signal.

Example 5.17

Using the analog input/output port of Fig. 5.25, write a routine that will square an incoming bipolar analog signal.

Solution

The AD7576 has a unipolar conversion range 0 − 2.46 V. An equivalent bipolar range of ±1.23 V can be accommodated by adding +1.23 V to the incoming signal. This effectively produces the offset code illustrated in Example 1.29. As we saw there, conversion to 2's complement code is accomplished simply by inverting the MSB, as done in step 6 of Table 5.26 by using the EOR operation.

The 6809's MUL instruction is only defined for unsigned operands. Thus based on the state of the N flag after the EORA instruction, we negate a negative outcome. The resulting modulus is then copied to Accumulator_B and multiplied to give the square. This product is of course 16-bit, so only the upper byte is sent out to the digital to analog converter. The MUL instruction sets the C flag if bit 7 of the lower

```
1                          .processor m6809
2                          .define Input = 9000h, Output = 9000h
3       ; This routine endlessly produces the analog square of a bipolar incoming
4       ; analog signal in offset code.
5  E000 B69000 MAIN:     lda   Input       ; Get analog input voltage                        5~
6  E003 8880             eora #10000000b ; Toggle MSB to convert to 2's complement 5~
7  E005 2A01             bpl   CONTINUE    ; IF positive THEN continue                        4~
8  E007 40               nega              ; ELSE make positive
9  E008 1F89  CONTINUE:  tfr   a,b         ; Copy modulus of n into B                         6~
10 E00A 3D               mul               ; Multiply to give n squared                      11~
11 E00B 8900             adca #0           ; Round up by adding Carry to upper byte           2~
12 E00D B79000           sta   Output      ; Send out                                          5~
13 E010 20EE             bra   MAIN        ; and repeat forever                                4~
14                       .end
```

Table 5.26: Analog squaring.

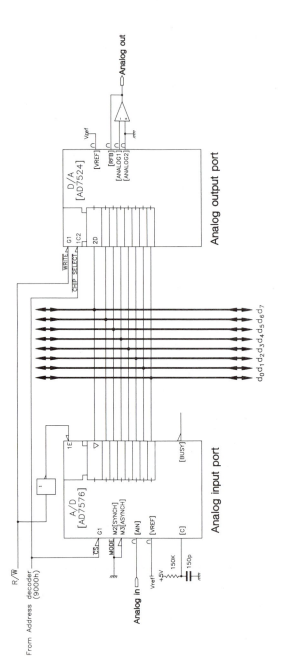

Figure 5.25: An analog I/O port.

product byte is one. Adding this to the upper byte gives us a rounding up process; step 11, see page 465.

The execution time for this process takes 44 cycles. Thus using a 1 MHz clock gives a sampling duration of 44 μs or a rate of 22,727 Hz. From the sampling theorem (see Section 1.1), this gives an upper analog input frequency of 11.37 kHz, if no information is to be lost.

What if we wanted a 12 or 16-bit input or output port; how do we handle this with an 8-bit bus? Well we cannot read or write more than eight bits simultaneously, but we can implement ports of whatever size from the requisite number of separate ports. The data is then communicated as a series of sequential read or writes. Figure 5.16 showed an example of a 16-bit input port comprising two individual 8-bit ports at separate locations.

MPU-compatible A/D and D/A converters having data paths greater than eight bits usually have provision for connection to 8-bit data buses. Generally this is done by having separate 3-state enables for the lower and higher bytes. For example, the AD7572 has a 12-bit data bus D11...D0, which can be directly connected to a 12-bit (or larger) MPU. As an alternative, the control line HBEN (High_Byte_ENable) can be used to multiplex lines D11...D8 onto D3...D0. With HBEN High, output pins 13...16 carry D11...D8 and when Low, D3...D0. Normally HBEN is connected to address line a_0, with the overall $\overline{\text{CS}}$ driven from the address decoder. Thus D7...D0 is read at **Address** and D11...D8 at **Address+1** (assuming that a_0 is omitted from the address decoder).

5.3.3 Interrupt Handling

Back in Section 5.2.3 we discussed the MPU's response to an external signal at its $\overline{\text{NMI}}$, $\overline{\text{IRQ}}$ or $\overline{\text{FIRQ}}$ pins. Essentially signalling an **interrupt** causes the MPU to drop whatever it is doing, push out its internal state into the System stack and go to a special subroutine known as an **interrupt service routine (ISR)**. The starting address for each ISR, one for each type of interrupt, are stored at the top of memory ROM, as shown in Fig. 5.17. These are the internal details of how the MPU responds to an interrupt request. Here we look at some situations where external devices demand service; with special reference to hardware necessary to handle the interrupt signal.

For our first example, consider the problem of keeping a clock so that accurate time markers can be attached to events occurring in real time. One approach already considered, would be to use a delay loop to sound out the seconds (or whatever is the desired resolution). In practice this would be rather useless, as keeping such a clock would be a full time occupation, with no time left over to do anything else of consequence. This is an ideal application for interrupts, as all that is necessary is to use an external precision oscillator to 'kick' the MPU on each tick. The MPU then updates its time count and goes back to its background task. If the oscillator ticks at 100 Hz and the update takes, say, 50 μs, then only 0.5% of the background processing time is lost.

Example 5.18

A certain system needs to keep a record of elapsed time since the MPU was Reset. This information is to be kept in an array of four memory bytes. The format of this array is: **Hour : Min : Sec : Jiffy**; where each element is a BCD representation, and with **Jiffy** holding 0.01 s ticks.

The timing element is to be a precision 100 Hz oscillator. Show how this may be interfaced to the MPU's $\overline{\text{IRQ}}$ input and write an appropriate ISR.

Solution

A first approach to this problem would be to connect the oscillator directly to the $\overline{\text{IRQ}}$ pin. However, if this is attempted, the results will be somewhat spectacular! As $\overline{\text{IRQ}}$ is active on a level, the MPU will be continually interrupted as long as the timing oscillator is Low. Thus instead of incrementing the time array by one jiffy, perhaps a thousand will be added. Therefore we must ensure that by the time the MPU returns from its ISR, the $\overline{\text{IRQ}}$ pin has gone back High.

One solution to this one-shot problem, is to interpose a narrow-pulse generator

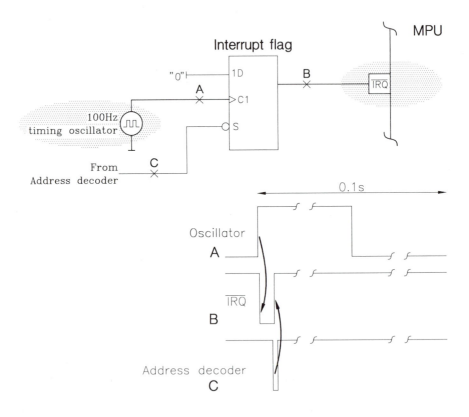

Figure 5.26: Interfacing the oscillator.

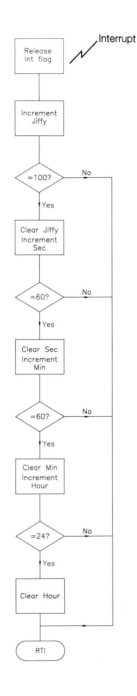

Figure 5.27: Flow chart for the real-time clock.

between oscillator and MPU. Typically comprizing a capacitor-resistor Schmitt-trigger network, the time constant would be set to be not less than the MPU's clock period and not longer than the ISR execution time, say, 20 μs. For reasons that will become apparent later, the synchronous alternative shown in Fig. 5.26 is the preferred approach. Here a D flip flop is clocked by the timing oscillator. With D held permanently 0, then $\overline{\text{IRQ}}$ will go to 0. This **Interrupt flag** will remain in this active state until its asynchronous **Set** (S) is activated. This release mechanism is activated by connecting S to an address decoder output. Thus the Interrupt flag release is memory mapped and activated by a dummy read or write in the ISR itself. For example, if 9007h is connected to S, then the flag can be released by the instruction **STA** 9007h; as shown in waveform C of Fig. 5.26.

```
 1                           .processor m6809
 2           ;****************************************************************************
 3           ;* This interrupt service routine keeps a real-time clock                  *
 4           ;* ENTRY : Global byte variables Hour, Min, Sec, Jiffy                      *
 5           ;* EXIT  : The above variables updated                                      *
 6           ;****************************************************************************
 7                           .define Hour = 0030h, Min = 0031h, Sec = 0032h, Jiffy = 0033h,
 8                                   Flag = 9007h
 9 E300 B79007 CLOCK:   sta     Flag            ; Reset Int flag
10 E303 9633             lda     Jiffy           ; Get .01s count
11 E305 4C               inca                    ; One more jiffy
12 E306 19               daa                     ; in BCD
13 E307 9733             sta     Jiffy           ; updated
14 E309 2624             bne     EXIT            ; Finish if no overflow
15           ; IF Jiffy overflowed from 99h to (1)00h THEN increment seconds count
16 E30B 9632             lda     Sec             ; Get seconds count
17 E30D 4C               inca                    ; One more second
18 E30E 19               daa                     ; in BCD
19 E30F 9732             sta     Sec             ; updated
20 E311 8160             cmpa    #60h            ; Too many seconds?
21 E313 261A             bne     EXIT            ; Finish if not
22           ; IF Sec overflowed to 60h THEN increment minutes count
23 E315 0F32             clr     Sec             ; First reset seconds count
24 E317 9631             lda     Min             ; Get minutes count
25 E319 4C               inca                    ; One more minute
26 E31A 19               daa                     ; in BCD
27 E31B 9731             sta     Min             ; updated
28 E31D 8160             cmpa    #60h            ; Too many minutes?
29 E31F 260E             bne     EXIT            ; Finish if not
30           ; IF Min overflowed to 60h THEN increment hours count
31 E321 0F31             clr     Min             ; First reset minutes count
32 E323 9630             lda     Hour            ; Get hours count
33 E325 4C               inca                    ; One more hour
34 E326 19               daa                     ; in BCD
35 E327 9730             sta     Hour            ; updated
36 E329 8124             cmpa    #24h            ; Too many hours?
37 E32B 2602             bne     EXIT            ; Finish if not
38 E32D 0F30             clr     Hour            ; On hours overflow reset Hour count
39 E32F 3B     EXIT:    rti
40                       .end
```

Table 5.27: A real-time clock program.

With the hardware sorted out, we can turn our attention to the software. As can be seen from the flow chart of Fig. 5.27 this simply involves incrementing the Jiffy byte, testing for overflow (99 → 100) and exiting if none. If there is overflow, then **Jiffy** is zeroed and the Second's count incremented. This process is continued, if necessary, right up to the Hour's count, which we have assumed to be of the 24-hour variety.

Table 5.27 shows a possible coding. After the Interrupt flag is lowered (step 9) the software is divided into four similar sections; one for each of the four time-bytes. They differ only in reflecting the three counting bases, i.e. a hundred for **Jiffy**, sixty for **Min** and **Sec** and 24 for **Hour** (time is the last bastion of the non-metric unit!). Using the instruction **DAA** after each Increment keeps the count in BCD as specified. We assume that during the initialization phase of the background program, all time array bytes are cleared. This would be done before the **ANDCC #11101111b** instruction, which clears the I mask after Reset.

We could of course have used the $\overline{\text{FIRQ}}$ input to create the interrupt. If this were the case, the ISR would have to have a **PSHS A/PULS A** sandwich to ensure that Accumulator A was unchanged on exit, because only **PC** and **CCR** are automatically saved.

As $\overline{\text{NMI}}$ is edge-triggered, the timing oscillator could be directly connected without the necessity of using an external D flip flop. However, the NMI response cannot be masked out, and this is undesirable where the time array is being read by the background program (see Section 5.2.3). For this reason, the use of $\overline{\text{NMI}}$ is normally reserved for top priority emergency situations. Thus, say, a mains failure detector could quickly move vital data to a battery backed-up area of RAM, where it can be retrieved later. Also, as we shall see, the edge-triggered nature of $\overline{\text{NMI}}$ means that only one source of interrupts should normally be connected to this pin.

What if there are lots of external devices which can request an interrupt? Well, if each interrupt signal were generated from an open-collector source, they could be commoned to the one pin, as shown in Fig. 3.17. Most interface devices which are designed to request interrupts, have integral open-collector buffers (see Section 5.3.4); or alternatively, external buffers may be used, as shown in Fig. 5.28.

Example 5.19

The ECG period counter of Fig. 5.16 is to be implemented, but using an internal counter. Both the 1 kHz oscillator and peak detector are to send an interrupt to the MPU. Develop both the necessary hardware to interface these two signals to the one $\overline{\text{IRQ}}$ pin, and to distinguish between them.

Solution

In Fig. 5.28, each source clocks its own private Interrupt flag, which is commoned via an open-collector buffer to the $\overline{\text{IRQ}}$ pin. The state of either flip flop can be interrogated as bit 7 through an individually addressed 3-state buffer; i.e., through one of two 1-bit input ports.

The ISR outlined in Table 5.28, firstly polls each flag in turn (steps 10 – 13). If a raised flag is detected, that flag is lowered and the appropriate action taken. Thus if the Oscillator flag is active, the double-byte **Count** is incremented. Alternatively, if it is the peak detector; the difference between old and new counts is evaluated

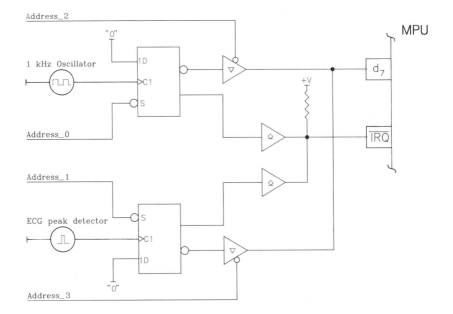

Figure 5.28: Two interrupt sources.

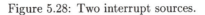

```
 1                            .processor m6809
 2        ;****************************************************************
 3        ;* This interrupt service routine calculates the peak-to-peak time variation*
 4        ;* ENTRY : Global double-byte variables Old_time, Delta_time and Count    *
 5        ;* EXIT  : Old_time, Delta_time and Count updated                          *
 6        ;****************************************************************
 7                            .define Count = 0000h, Old_time = 0002h, Delta_time = 0004h,
 8                                    Osc_flag = 9000h, Peak_flag = 9001h,
 9                                    Osc_status = 9002h, Peak_status = 9003h
10 E300 7D9002 POLL:   tst    Osc_status    ; Bit7 is the oscillator status
11 E303 2B06           bmi    INC_COUNT     ; IF set THEN record a tick
12 E305 7D9003         tst    Peak_status   ; Bit7 is the peak-detector status
13 E308 2B0D           bmi    BEAT          ; IF set THEN a heart beat
14 E30A 3B     EXIT:   rti                  ; ELSE nothing doing; exit
15        ; Increment double-byte Count on an oscillator tick
16 E30B B79000 INC_COUNT:sta  Osc_flag      ; First lower the oscillator flag
17 E30E DC00           ldd    Count         ; Get 1ms count
18 E310 C30001         addd   #1            ; Increment it
19 E313 DD00           std    Count         ; and update it
20 E315 20F3           bra    EXIT          ; and go home
21        ; On a heart beat evaluate beat-to-beat difference and update various times
22 E317 B79001 BEAT:   sta    Peak_flag     ; First lower the oscillator flag
23 E31A DC00           ldd    Count         ; Get current 1ms count
24 E31C 3406           pshs   d             ; Put it away for safe keeping
25 E31E 9302           subd   Old_time      ; Subtract previous value
26 E320 DD04           std    Delta_time    ; Gives the new difference in ms
27 E322 3506           puls   d             ; Get the current value back
28 E324 DD02           std    Old_time      ; which is now the new previous value
29 E326 20E2           bra    EXIT          ; and quit
30                     .end
```

Table 5.28: Software beat-to-beat variation counter.

to give the difference. **Old_time** is then updated and **Count** cleared (see Table 5.24). The three time variables are stored in absolute locations and so are globally known to the background routine or other ISRs.

If both interrupts happen virtually simultaneously, the unserviced request will still be present on return and will then be acted upon. Essentially, the order of polling in software defines the priority accorded to these requests in the event of simultaneous cries for help. In Table 5.28 the oscillator has priority over the peak detector.

Example 5.21 gives another situation whereby two peripheral devices request service via the one Interrupt pin.

The principle of polling n separate status locations looking for the source of the interrupt request is quite general and can be extended to any number. A slight variation clumps the status buffers together in groups of eight, with each group having its own address. Software then can shift these bits out, in the manner of Example 5.6.

Where a large number of interrupting peripherals are involved, polling can take a considerable time. If a fast response is necessary, a Priority encoder can be used in the manner of Fig. 3.38, to directly provide the binary position of the highest priority request. By expanding these Priority encoders, up to 256 requests can be read at one 8-bit input port. Where speed is of the essence, this binary vector can even be put on the data bus when the MPU is fetching down its interrupt vector, rather than the fixed ROM-located addresses [26]. In this manner, one of up to 256 ISRs can be directly entered with no software polling necessary.

5.3.4   LSI Interface Devices

The functions of input, output, interrupt handling and handshaking in general are well enough defined to allow the economic production of special-purpose interface ICs. General-purpose interface devices have to be flexible enough to deal with the myriad of differing applications, and often rival the MPU in complexity. Virtually all such LSI interface devices are software configurable. This engenders flexibility by allowing the MPU to alter the operation of the port by loading specific bit patterns into Control registers. As these Control registers are continually accessible to the MPU, the function of such an interface port may be dynamically changed as the program progresses.

In this Section we will look at two relatively simple devices. The first of these is the Motorola 6821 Peripheral Interface Adapter (PIA) which deals with parallel I/O and the second is the Motorola 6850 Asynchronous Communication Interface Adapter (ACIA) which is a serial device.

The 6821 PIA shown in Fig. 5.29 is a typical parallel software programmable interface circuit. The PIA contains two separate 8-bit ports, either of which may be configured as input or output on a bit by bit basis. As seen by the MPU, each port has two registers; the Control register and the I/O Data/Data Direction register combo. The actual register targeted by the MPU is a function of the Register_Select pins RS0 and RS1. The Register_Select decoder chooses between Ports A and B (RS1 = 0 and 1 respectively). RS0 selects between registers within a port, with

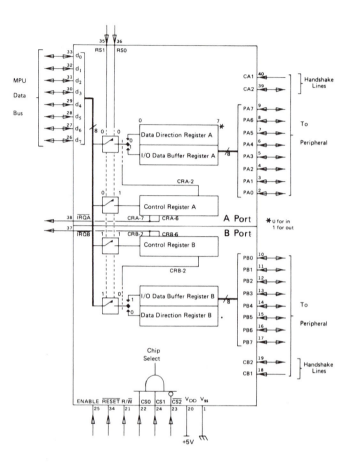

Figure 5.29: The 6821 Peripheral Interface Adapter.

RS0 = 0 giving the I/O Data/Data Direction combo and RS0 = 1 picking the Control register. Normally RS1 RS0 are driven from address lines a_1a_0, so that these registers appear to lie at adjacent addresses (see Fig 5.31).

The central feature of any I/O port is the Data register. In the PIA, this comprizes a flip flop array for storing outgoing data, back-to-back with an octal 3-state buffer for incoming data (see Fig 5.30). The actual status of any port, as either input or output, depends on the state of an associated **Data Direction register** (DDR). Thus to use Port A as an output, we must set DDR_A to $11111111b$; whereas if DDR_A were cleared (as it is on Reset), then Port A will be an input port. As each I/O Data register bit has a corresponding DDR bit, a port can be a mixture of input and output lines. For example, if DDR_A was set up to $11100000b$, then PA0...PA4 are input lines, whilst PA5...PA7 are latched output pins. From the equivalent circuit of Fig. 5.30, we see that when DDR_A bit n is 1, then flip flop n's output

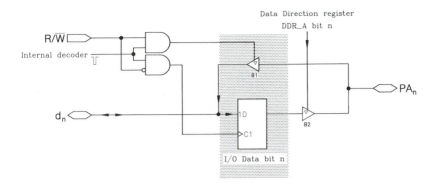

Figure 5.30: Equivalent circuit for bit n of Port A.

directly drives the port pin as an output. Should the MPU read a bit programmed as an output, then the state of the pin will be read through the normal input 3-state buffer B1.

When DDR_A bit n is 0, then the flip flop output is disconnected and the state of the port pin PAn is read in the normal way through B1. However, there is nothing to stop the MPU writing data to the flip flop, but this will have no external effect unless the port bit is subsequently changed to output.

Port B is a little different to Port A, in that additional output buffering is provided. In this case, reading a Port B bit configured as an output gives the state of the flip flop and not the port pin. These may not be the same if the port is sourcing or sinking large currents.

As the Data Direction register is usually only set up at the beginning of the program, it shares the same internal address as the frequently used I/O Data register. This saves having an additional Register_Select pin. They are shown paired in Fig. 5.29 to emphasize this. The actual register accessed at this address depends on bit 2 of the port's Control register. For example, if CRA_2 is 0, then DDR_A is accessed when the PIA is enabled and RS1 RS0 = 00; whereas CRA_2 = 1 enables the I/O Data register under the same conditions.

For our first example, we show how the PIA may be configured as a simple input/output port; leaving our discussion of the handshake facilities until later.

Example 5.20

A certain system is to continually monitor the state of eight switches, and on the basis of this value n, continually count between the limits $0 \leftrightarrow (n-1)$. The count is to be displayed on an array of eight light emitting diodes (LEDs) at a nominal rate of 10 Hz.

Solution

Integrating the PIA into the MPU system is straightforward. The data bus, and R/$\overline{\text{W}}$ are common with the MPU. The PIA is reset from the same source as the

MPU ($\overline{\text{RST}}$), and clears all internal registers. The PIA's Enable input synchronizes internal transfers to the MPU's clock cycle when driven by the E clock. All three Chip_Select inputs, CS0 CS1 $\overline{\text{CS2}}$ have to be active together to enable the PIA. In Fig. 5.31, we have driven $\overline{\text{CS2}}$ from a 9000h address decoder output and tied the other Chip_Select inputs High. As the PIA is directly synchronized by the E clock, the decoder output should *not* be qualified by E or Q. If several PIAs are used, the Chip_Select inputs may be connected to various address lines as a type of linear selection. With address lines a_0 and a_1 being used to drive RS0 and RS1, the address decoder should *not* include these variables. With this arrangement, the four internal register/register pairs are mapped at sequential addresses thus:

I/O Data register_A/Data Direction register_A	9000h
Control register_A	9001h
I/O Data register_B/Data Direction register_B	9002h
Control register_B	9003h

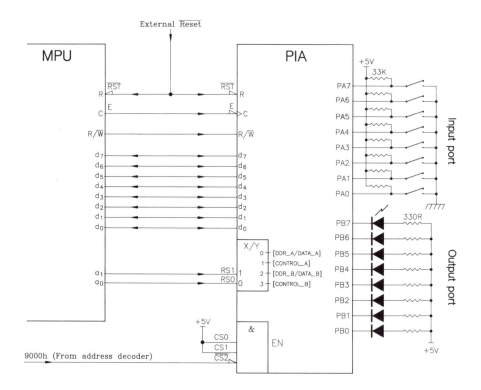

Figure 5.31: The PIA as a simple input/output port.

If the two address lines were interchanged, what would be the memory map and what would you perceive to be the advantage [27]?

With the hardware sorted out we can turn our attention to the software, which is listed in Table 5.29.

```
1                              .processor m6809
2                ;****************************************************************
3                ;* This routine repetitively counts up and down at a 10Hz rate  *
4                ;* between the limits 0 and n-1, where n is the switch setting   *
5                ;* INPUT  : An 8-bit switch array giving n at Port A             *
6                ;* OUTPUT : An 8-wide switch array displaying the count at Port B *
7                ;****************************************************************
8                              .define DATA_A = 9000h, DDR_A = 9000h, CONTROL_A = 9001h,
9                                      DATA_B = 9002h, DDR_B = 9002h, CONTROL_B = 9003h
10                        ;First setup the PIA
11 E000 7F9001 MAIN:    clr     CONTROL_A     ;Clearing Control bit 2 gives
12 E003 7F9003          clr     CONTROL_B     ;access to the Data Direction registers
13 E006 7F9000          clr     DDR_A         ;Make Port A an input for the switches
14 E009 86FF            lda     #11111111b    ;Make Port B an output for the LEDs
15 E00B B79002          sta     DDR_B
16 E00E 8604            lda     #00000100b    ;Now change over from DDRs
17 E010 B79001          sta     CONTROL_A     ;to I/O Data registers by making
18 E013 B79003          sta     CONTROL_B     ;Control bits 2 = "1"
19 E016 4F              clra                  ;Initialize the count
20                      ;Now enter the up loop; incrementing until count = n
21 E017 B19000 ULOOP:   cmpa    DATA_A        ;Compare with switch settings
22 E01A 270B            beq     DLOOP         ;IF at the top THEN go to the down count
23 E01C 1F89            tfr     a,b           ;ELSE prepare to display the count
24 E01E 53              comb                  ;Active-low LEDs
25 E01F F79002          stb     DATA_B        ;Send it out
26 E022 8D11            bsr     DELAY         ;for 100ms
27 E024 4C              inca                  ;Increment count
28 E025 20F0            bra     ULOOP         ;and repeat
29                      ;This is the down count loop
30 E027 4A     DLOOP:   deca                  ;Decrement the count
31 E028 1F89            tfr     a,b           ;Prepare to display the count
32 E02A 53              comb                  ;Active-low LEDs
33 E02B F79002          stb     DATA_B        ;Send it out
34 E02E 8D05            bsr     DELAY         ;for 100ms
35 E030 4D              tsta                  ;Down to zero yet?
36 E031 26F4            bne     DLOOP         ;IF not THEN again
37 E033 20E2            bra     ULOOP         ;ELSE do an up count
38                      ;The 100ms delay subroutine
39 E035 8E2B67 DELAY:   ldx     #11111        ;9x11,111 is 100,000 microseconds
40 E038 301F  DELOOP:   leax    -1,x          ;Decrement X, 5~
41 E03A 26FC            bne     DELOOP        ;to zero, 4~
42 E03C 39              rts
43                      .end
```

Table 5.29: An up-down modulo-n counter.

Steps 11–18 deal with the setting up of the PIA to the appropriate configuration; here with Port A as an input and Port B as an output. Clearing both Control registers makes bit 2 logic 0, giving access to the DDRs. DDR_A is then cleared to make all Port A lines inputs. All three of these actions are actually automatically carried out when the PIA is Reset, so can strictly be omitted. Finally all DDR_B bits are set to 1 to make Port B an output.

Once the port directions are set up, it only remains to load the Control registers with their final bit pattern. In this example we only require to make bits 2 of the

Control registers logic 1, to switch over from the DDRs to I/O Data registers. The other Control register bits which configure the handshake lines, may be left cleared.

The algorithm itself uses Accumulator_A as the counter and a 0.1 s delay subroutine to give the counting rate. The only problem is that the LEDs, as shown in Fig. 5.31, light on a Low. To get around this, on display (steps 23 – 25) the count is transferred to Accumulator_B, and then complemented before being sent out to Port B.

The up-count loop is exited when the count equals n (steps 21 & 22). On entry to the down-count loop, the decrement is implemented first; thus the last displayed state is $(n-1)$. With the down-count test (step 35) occurring after the display, a simple test for zero is sufficient to exit back to the up-count loop after a display of state 0. What would happen if the switches were all set Low and what could you do about it?

In Section 5.3.3, we saw that an interrupt-handling facility is important to interfacing peripheral devices. Each of the 6821's ports has two **handshake lines**, (see page 323), to enable a peripheral to request access to the MPU and for the MPU to acknowledge this request. Lines CA1 and CB1 are input lines only, whilst the CA2 and CB2 lines can be programmed as input or output according to the setting of the appropriate Control register's bit 5.

Initially we will look at our options when the handshake lines are used as inputs (CR_5 = 0), which are summarized at the top of Fig. 5.32. There are only two possibilities to choose from. Firstly, we can define which edge is active. Thus, setting bit CRA_1 to 1 makes the ⌐ -edge of line CA1 the active event. Similarly, if CRA_4 were 0, then the ⌐_ -edge of CA2 is the active event. When an active event occurs, either bit CR_7 or CR_6 are set, corresponding to handshake line 1 or 2 respectively. Thus the top two bits of the Control register are actually status bits rather than control bits. They are *read-only*, and are cleared only when the MPU reads the appropriate Data register.

The second option determines whether an active edge sends an interrupt to the MPU. This is done via the PIA's interrupt output lines $\overline{\text{IRQA}}$ and $\overline{\text{IRQB}}$ for Port A and B respectively. Thus, for example, a logic 1 in Control bit CRA_1 will enable an active event on handshake line CA1 to bring $\overline{\text{IRQA}}$ Low. Likewise, if CRA_3 is logic 1, $\overline{\text{IRQA}}$ will be brought Low by an active event on line CA2. Both sources can be enabled to generate an interrupt; as the MPU can determine which was the source by examining Control bits CR_6 and CR_7. The PIA's $\overline{\text{IRQ}}$ lines are open-collector, which means that the two lines can be connected together with other open-collector interrupt request lines, as shown in Fig. 3.17. The MPU can then poll the Control bits of the various peripherals, in order to determine the origin of the request. In any event, when found, the relevant Control bits must be cleared to remove the interrupt request; in the same manner as the interrupt flag in Fig. 5.26.

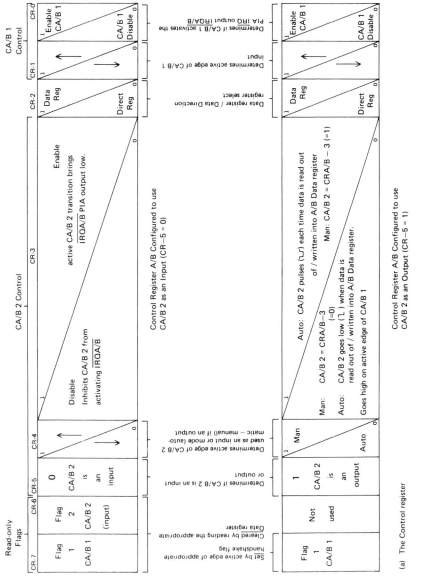

(a) The Control register

Figure 5.32: Configuring the PIA using the Control register.

Example 5.21

One recurring problem in electronic engineering is that of transmitting remotely acquired data long distances. Suppose you are building a factory automation system that must measure humidity in a mill located several thousands of meters away. Sending the raw analog signal so far would be disastrous, as noise would swamp the signal. Obviously the analog parameter must be digitized as close to the sensor as possible. This data could then be sent in series over, say, a radio channel, copper or fiber-optic cable, to the main computer.

This solution will require a MPU at the sensor's site to digitize, serialize (see later) and transmit the data. Where many sensors are remotely dispersed, this may be too expensive; will require multiple clean power supplies, and in very harsh environments may prove unreliable. When measuring slowly changing parameters, an alternative technique is to use a voltage-controlled oscillator (VCO) to replace all this circuitry. The VCO produces a pulse rate proportional to input voltage; which in turn is provided by the sensor. As well as simplicity and low cost, the power requirements are reduced to such an extent, that it may be provided along the same conductors carrying the data [28]. So to our example!

A certain remote sensor/VCO measures temperature between 0°C and 100°C, generating corresponding pulse frequencies between 500 and 2500 Hz. At the control MPU-based system, a 10 Hz oscillator is to be used to gate this input. Both VCO and gate oscillators are to generate interrupts, and the resulting pulse count converted to temperature, which is to be presented in binary at a PIA port. Describe the hardware and software necessary to accomplish this conversion.

Solution

The hardware configuration of our system is similar to that of the previous example, in addition with $\overline{\text{IRQA}}$ and $\overline{\text{IRQB}}$ tied together and connected to the MPU's $\overline{\text{IRQ}}$ pull-up node. The 10 Hz gate oscillator is connected to handshake line CA1, whilst the received (and cleaned up) VCO signal drives CA2. Port B is again used as an output port.

The software of Table 5.30 is presented as two listings, showing the background main routine and the interrupt service routine foreground code. Generally the PIA and similar programmable interface devices are set up in the background program, as are any global variables and the System Stack pointer, before the Interrupt mask is cleared. Then the main routines commence.

In steps 11 & 12, Control register_A is set up as follows:

CRA_0 = 1 Enables an interrupt to be generated from CA1.
CRA_1 = 1 On a ⌐‾ (polarity irrelevant in this example).
CRA_2 = 1 I/O Data register_A connected rather than DDR_A.
CRA_3 = 1 Enables an interrupt to be generated from CA2.
CRA_4 = 1 On a ⌐‾ (polarity irrelevant in this example).
CRA_5 = 0 CA2 configured as an input.
CRA_6   The Interrupt flag for CA2.
CRA_7   The Interrupt flag for CA1.

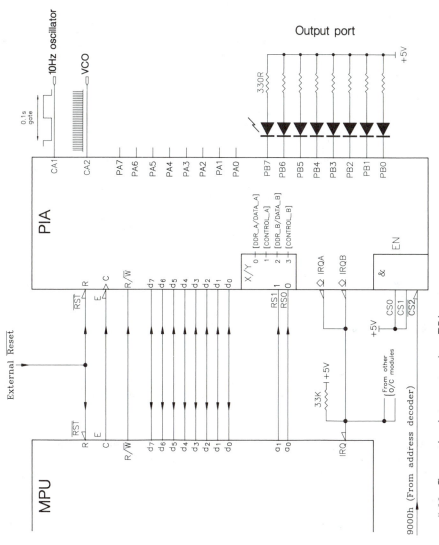

Figure 5.33: Generating interrupts via a PIA.

```
 1                                   .processor m6809
 2                                   .define DATA_A = 9000h, DDR_A = 9000h, CONTROL_A = 9001h,
 3                                           DATA_B = 9002h, DDR_B = 9002h, CONTROL_B = 9003h
 4                          ;Sets up PIA
 5 E000 10CE2000 MAIN:     lds    #2000h      ;Top of stack
 6 E004 7F9003             clr    CONTROL_B  ;Access to Port B's DDR
 7 E007 86FF               lda    #11111111b ;Make this port all output
 8 E009 B79002             sta    DDR_B
 9 E00C 8604               lda    #00000100b ;Changeover to Port B's I/O Data register
10 E00E B79002             sta    DDR_B
11 E011 861F               lda    #00011111b ;CA1 enabled to make an int on +ve edge
12 E013 B79001             sta    CONTROL_A  ;CA2 set to i/p & to make int on +ve edge
13 E016 1C2F               andcc  #00101111b ;Clearing I mask lets MPU react to IRQ
14                         ;Main program continues here
15
16
```

(a): The main background program

```
 1              ;************************************************************
 2              ;* ISR to determine the temperature from a VCO input       *
 3              ;* ranging from 500 Hz @ 0 C to 2,500 Hz at 100 C          *
 4              ;* INPUT : 0.1s gate pulse at CA1 and VCO at CA2           *
 5              ;* OUTPUT: Temperature displayed at Port B                 *
 6              ;************************************************************
 7              ;First determine which of the two sources sent the request
 8                         .define Count = 0030h
 9 E300 B69001 TEMPERATURE:lda   CONTROL_A   ;Examine interrupt flags
10 E303 F69000             ldb    DATA_A     ;Dummy read of Port a clears int flags
11 E306 2B07               bmi    GATE       ;IF bit 7 set THEN a gate event
12 E308 48                 asla              ;Shift to examine bit 6
13 E309 2A0F               bpl    EXIT       ;IF not set THEN exit
             ;Land here if a VCO event
14 E30B 0C30               inc    Count      ;One more blip recorded
15 E30D 200B               bra    EXIT       ;and finished
             ;Land here if a gate event
16 E30F 9630  GATE:        lda    Count      ;Get blip count
17 E311 0F30               clr    Count      ;Reset it for next go
18 E313 8032               suba   #50        ;Take away the offset
19 E315 44                 lsra              ;Divide by two to give deg C
20 E316 43                 coma              ;LEDs are active-low, so complement
21 E317 B79002             sta    DATA_B     ;output to Port B
22 E31A 3B    EXIT:        rti               ;One exit point
                           .end
```

(b): The interrupt service routine

Table 5.30: Using a VCO to determine long-range temperature.

The ISR itself begins by examining the two Interrupt flag bits, after which they are cleared by doing an (irrelevant) read of I/O Data register_A (step 10). If CRA_7 is set, then it is the gate oscillator. If CRA_6 is set, then it is the VCO. If neither is set, then we show an exit, but in practice the ISR would continue by looking at other devices.

A VCO interrupt is serviced by simply incrementing a count kept in absolute memory. A register cannot be used for this purpose, as these are lost on the RETURN FROM INTERRUPT (although a register could be used in conjunction with $\overline{\text{FIRQ}}$, this is not considered good practice, as it is too easy for the background program to use a register resource and thus inadvertently destroy data). As the gate width is 100 ms, this count should lie between 50 and 250, and thus can be accommodated in a single byte. Although not done here, robust programming should check for over or underflow, perhaps due to noise, and set an error code as appropriate.

A gate event is more complex. Firstly **Count** must be read and converted to temperature according to the relationship:

$$°C = (\textbf{Count} - 50)/2$$

as is done in steps 18 & 19, and then cleared for the next gate. Once again, robust programming would apply a filtering technique to the temperature readings (perhaps setting a maximum slew rate as twice the average rate of change of the last 16 readings) and ignoring readings where an error flag is set. The LEDs display this binary data after complementation to reflect their active-Low nature.

Handshake lines CA2 and CB2 can be configured as outputs by setting Control bit CR_5 to logic 1. In this situation, Control bits CR_3 and CR_4 act in a different fashion; as shown in the lower half of Fig. 5.32. The simplest mode of operation is known as Manual, and is chosen by setting Control bit CR_4 = 1. Here CA2/CB2 will simply follow the state of Control bit CR_3. Thus to bring line CA2 Low and then subsequently High, we have:

```
        LDB    CONTROL_A         ;Get settings
        ANDB   #11110111b        ;Clear bit 3, leave others alone
        STB    CONTROL_A         ;Bring CA2 Low
```

; Sometime later

```
        LDB    CONTROL_A         ;Get settings
        ORB    #00001000b        ;Set bit 3, leave others alone
        STB    CONTROL_A         ;Bring CA2 High
```

Alternatively the EOR instruction can be used in the same manner, to toggle a bit, but this is not so robust (why?).

As an alternative to this Manual mode, it is possible to have handshake lines 2 pulse automatically in response to a certain sequence of events. As set up by CR_4 = 0, there are two submodes to Automatic. If CRA_3 is logic 1, CA2 will pulse Low each time data is read from I/O Data register_A, as shown in Fig. 5.34(a). This can be used to tell the peripheral device that data has been accepted ($\overline{DAC}$, see Fig. 4.23). The duration of this pulse is that of the MPU's clock cycle; 1 µs with a 1 MHz clock.

The other Automatic mode is similar, but this time CA2 stays Low indefinitely until the peripheral responds by activating the CA1 line in response, as shown in Fig. 5.34(b). This can be used to tell the MPU that new data has been read.

Although both the PIA's ports are virtually identical, there is a slight bias towards Port B being used as an output port. This is physically reflected in the beefed up output buffers in side B, which guarantee a minimum of 1 mA into the base of a Darlington-connected transistor. As we have already observed, reading Port B configured as an output is unaffected by what electrically is going on at the actual pins; unlike Port A. This bias is further reflected in the action of Port B's CB2 line configured as an output in the Automatic mode. Here the line is brought Low after a *write* to I/O Data register_B, as opposed to a read. Also, for some obscure reason, it is synchronized by the rising edge of E.

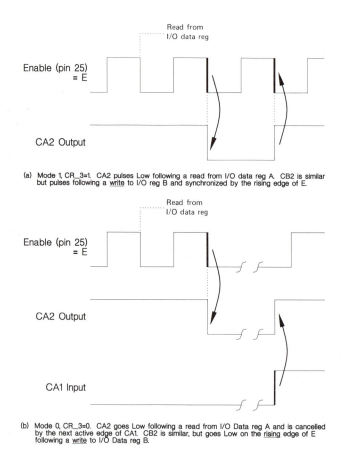

(a) Mode 1, CR_3=1. CA2 pulses Low following a read from I/O data reg A. CB2 is similar
      but pulses following a write to I/O reg B and synchronized by the rising edge of E.

(b) Mode 0, CR_3=0. CA2 goes Low following a read from I/O Data reg A and is cancelled
      by the next active edge of CA1. CB2 is similar, but goes Low on the rising edge of E
      following a write to I/O Data reg B.

Figure 5.34: Automatic handshake modes, $CR\_5/CR\_4 = 10$.

Example 5.22

A certain 8-bit analog to digital (A/D) converter is controlled by a $\overline{\text{Start\_Convert}}$ ($\overline{\text{SC}}$) input and its status reflected by the $\overline{\text{Busy}}$ line. It is to be used as part of a data logging scheme, with the sampling frequency determined by an external oscillator. Each time a sample is requested, the MPU is to be interrupted and the A/D coaxed into giving its digital equivalent of the analog signal.

It has been suggested that a PIA be used as the interface. Show how this could be done, and give a possible coding describing in what way the Control registers might be set up, and write a driver routine that puts the data in an absolute location called **Data**, and sets another location called **Flag** to a non-zero value.

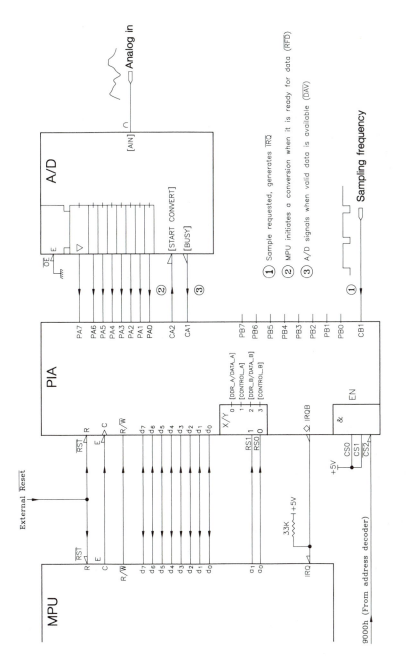

Figure 5.35: Periodically sampling an analog quantity.

Solution

In Fig. 5.35 we have used Port A to read the data. Handshake line CA2 is configured as an Automatic mode output to pulse $\overline{SC}$ and start the conversion; with the rising edge of $\overline{Busy}$ being used via CA1 to signal completion. The sample oscillator employs CB1 to interrupt the MPU, which then enters the ISR.

The settings of the two Control registers are:

> CRA_0 = 0 No interrupt generated by CA1
> CRA_1 = 1 Active on rising edge of $\overline{Busy}$
> CRA_2 = 1 Switch from DDR_A to I/O Data register_A selected.
> CRA_3 = 1 Automatic pulse mode.
> CRA_4 = 0 Auto mode.
> CRA_5 = 1 CA2 is an output line.
> CRB_0 = 1 Interrupt generated by CB1
> CRB_1 = 0 Active on falling edge (irrelevant)

all other bits being immaterial.

```
 1                                  .processor m6809
 2                  ; Main background routine sets up the PIA
 3                               .define DATA_A = 9000h, DDR_A = 9000h, CONTROL_A = 9001h,
 4                                       DATA_B = 9002h, DDR_B = 9002h, CONTROL_B = 9003h,
 5                                       Data = 0030h, Flag = 0031h
 6                  ; Sets up PIA
 7 E000 10CE2000 MAIN:     lds    #2000h        ; Top of stack
 8 E004 7F9001             clr    CONTROL_A     ; Access to Port A's DDR
 9 E007 7F9000             clr    DDR_A         ; Make Port A an input
10 E00A 862E               lda    #00101110b    ; Setup handshake CA2 autopulse to SC
11 E00C B79001             sta    CONTROL_A     ; CA1 positive-edge action from BUSY
12 E00F 8605               lda    #00000101b    ; Set up handshake CB1 as a -ve-trigger
13 E011 B79003             sta    CONTROL_B     ; from sampling oscillator
14 E014 1C2F               andcc  #00101111b    ; Clr I mask, to allow MPU to react to IRQ
15                  ; Main program continues here
16                  ;
```

(a) The main background program

```
 1 E300 B69000 A_D_DRIVER: lda    DATA_A        ; Dummy read starts the conversion
 2 E303 0F31               clr    Flag          ; Error flag cleared
 3 E305 8E03E8             ldx    #1000         ; Try for DAV no more than 1000 times
 4                  ; This is the sampling loop looking for new data with a timeout
 5 E308 301F     LOOP:     leax   -1,x          ; Decrement time-out; equals zero yet?
 6 E30A 270C               beq    QUIT          ; IF so THEN exit without data
 7 E30C 7D9001             tst    CONTROL_A     ; ELSE has new data arrived, Busy gone Hi?
 8 E30F 26F7               bne    LOOP          ; IF not yet THEN try again
 9                  ; Reach here if data has become available
10 E311 B69000             lda    DATA_A        ; Get data and clear CRA_7
11 E314 9730               sta    Data          ; Put it away as requested
12 E316 0C31               inc    Flag          ; Signal a successful acquisition
13 E318 B69002  QUIT:      lda    DATA_B        ; Dummy read cancels interrupt flag CRB_7
14 E31B 3B                 rti                  ; and return
15                         .end
```

(b) Foreground interrupt service routine

Table 5.31: The A/D handler.

The ISR driver routine simply does a dummy read of Port A to pulse $\overline{SC}$; monitors the flag CRA_7, which is set when $\overline{Busy}$ goes back High, (i.e. conversion complete). I limited this wait and see exercise to 1000 tries, in case a hardware fault should cause hang-up. In practice an error code should be returned in the event of a time-out. If the CRA_7 flag is set before time-out, the A/D's data is read (which also clears CRA_7) and put into **Data. Flag** is set to non-zero to indicate a successful acquisition.

On exit, a dummy read of Port B is made to clear the Interrupt flag bit CRB_7; which of course is set by the sampling oscillator. We have assumed that only one source of interrupt request exists; otherwise an initial search must be carried out when the ISR is entered.

Two final points. If a MPU-compatible A/D is used (as is likely) the integral 3-state buffers must be permanently enabled, as shown in the diagram, where $\overline{\text{Output\_Enable}}$ ($\overline{\text{OE}}$) is connected to ground. This is because the PIA acts as the interface to the bus. Also, we have assumed that the CA2 pulse is sufficiently long to successfully activate the A/D's $\overline{\text{SC}}$ input. If, say, this were specified as 5 μs minimum, then the Manual mode should be used instead. Perhaps $\overline{\text{SC}}$ is $\overline{}\diagdown\underline{}$ triggered. Then Auto mode 0 could be used with the end of $\overline{\text{Busy}}$ cancelling $\overline{\text{SC}}$. Care must be taken to read the appropriate data sheets!

Most data transmission between remote locations is made using a **serial format**. This involves sending data words bit by bit in sequence using a single communications link. This considerably reduces the channel cost as compared to a multipath connection. Transmission media, such as telephone or radio, are naturally adapted to single channel working. The pay-off is the relative slowness of the technique. Basically there are two ways of serial working. Synchronous transmission sends large blocks of data sandwiched by a synchronizing signature, for example $1010101010b$. This is the most efficient method, but both the remote transmitter and receiver timing clocks must remain accurately synchronized over a relatively long time period. The alternative, discussed below, is to synchronize each word.

One of the features of early computer development was the extensive use of existing technology. An essential adjunct of any computer-oriented installation is a data terminal. At that time the communications industry made considerable use of the teletypewriter (literally a 'typewriter from afar'; Greek, tele = far). These TTYs were used for the Telex service, whereby alphanumeric characters are sent over telephone and radio links in a serial manner. Data is converted between serial and parallel formats in the terminal itself.

Until the early 1980s, TTYs were electromechanical machines, driven by a synchronous electric motor. This meant that synchronization between remote terminals could only be guaranteed for short periods. To get around this problem, each word transmitted was proceeded by a start bit and followed by a stop bit. A typical example is shown in Fig. 5.36. While the line is idling, a logic 1 (break level) is transmitted. A logic 0 signals the start of a word. After the word has been sent, a logic 1 terminates the sequence. Electro-mechanical terminals typically print ten characters per second, and require a minimum of two stop bits. This requires a transmission rate of 110 bits per second, or 110 **baud**. Faster rates utilized in purely electronic systems require only one stop bit, and are typically used in multiples of 300 baud. Thus an IBM PC can transmit at rates up to 19,200 baud (1920 characters per second).

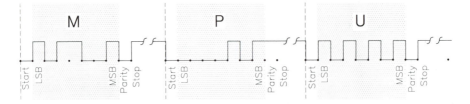

Figure 5.36: Transmitting the message string "MPU" in the asynchronous serial mode, with even one's parity and a minimum of one stop bit.

Although not the most efficient of techniques, the asynchronous protocol outlined here has the major advantage of being an international standard. There are slight differences in the format, some of which are outlined in Fig. 5.37. Thus the word can be eight or nine bits long and may have an odd or even parity (see Fig. 2.22), but these permutations are limited.

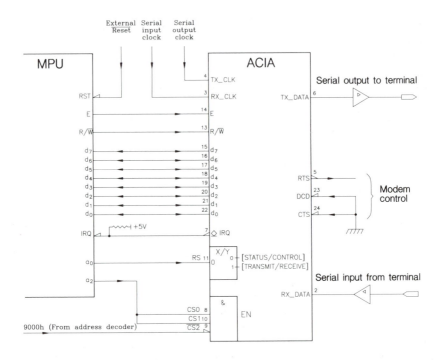

Figure 5.37: A typical interconnection between a serial terminal and MPU using the 6850 ACIA.

Given that it is necessary for a MPU to interface in a serial manner with a peripheral, we have the problem of converting an outgoing byte of parallel information on the data bus to a serial format, and sandwiching it with start and stop bits. Similarly, incoming serial data must be captured and synchronized and made available to be read by the MPU. This can be done using a 1-bit input and output port and using software to do the serialization and other tasks. Although this approach is occasionally used (for example the Apple II microcomputer), it ties up the processor for an inordinate amount of time.

The serial interface problem is sufficiently well defined to enable standard LSI devices to be manufactured for this specific task. These are generally known as the **Universal Asynchronous Receiver Transmitter (UART)**. A UART may be read from or written to by the controller and is timed by a crystal oscillator. The baud rate may be set by changing this crystal frequency or by altering a frequency dividing circuit. The latter may be external and set by switches or internal and configured by bit patterns in a Control register. UARTs are available as stand-alone devices [29], or MPU compatible ready to hang onto the data bus.

The 6850 **Asynchronous Communication Interface Adapter (ACIA)** shown in Fig. 5.37 is an example of a software configurable MPU-compatible UART [30, 31]. To the MPU, the ACIA looks like two memory locations, targeted by Register Select (RS), which is shown driven by a_0. The other connections are the standard data bus, R/$\overline{\text{W}}$, E and $\overline{\text{IRQ}}$. Like the PIA, three Chip-Selects are provided. In Fig. 5.37, CS0/CS1 are connected to a_2, which in conjunction with the address decoder's $9000h$ driving $\overline{\text{CS2}}$, maps the ACIA to $9004h/9005h$. As in the PIA, this should not be qualified by the MPU's clock signals, as the ACIA is designed to be directly qualified by E.

The serialized output and input to the 6850 are the normal logic TTL levels. These are not recommended for transmission over $\approx$30 cm (one foot). Typically the serialized signals are buffered to higher voltage levels. The RS-232 standard is extensively used, and a range of 15 m (50′) at a rate of 2400 baud is easily achieved by mapping logic 0 to +12 V and logic 1 to −12 V (nominal) [32]. The RS-423 standard also shown in Fig. 5.38 is similar, but can manage up to 1 km at 110 baud.

Both RS-232 and RS-423 standards are single-ended schemes, where the receiver measures the potential between signal line and ground reference. Even though the transmitter and receiver grounds are connected through the transmission line return, the impedance over a long distance connection may support a significant difference in the two ground potentials, which will degrade the performance.

The RS-422 standard, shown in Fig. 5.38(c), employs differential transmission. Here the signal is represented as the difference in potential across two balanced lines. Thus logic 0 may be represented by +5 V/0 V and logic 1 by 0 V/+5 V. The receiver detects differences down to ±200 mV across its differential input. Signal lines can have common voltages up to ±7 V from local earth without degradation of performance. Furthermore, the output impedance of RS-422 drivers matches the characteristic impedance of 100 Ω twisted-pair line. Data sent at 9600 baud can be sent up to 1 km without using line repeaters.

Very long distances can be accommodated using existing telephone or radio links. Now, a standard telephone channel has a bandwidth of 300 – 3400 Hz; thus it is not possible to impress the digital signals directly on the lines. Instead, these baseband signals are typically used to modulate a tone. This Frequency Shift Keying (FSK) modulation technique can utilize a telephone line to support either one simultaneous bi-directional (duplex) communications channel at up to 300 baud or a single (simplex) 1200 baud channel. The former uses a low band with 1070 Hz

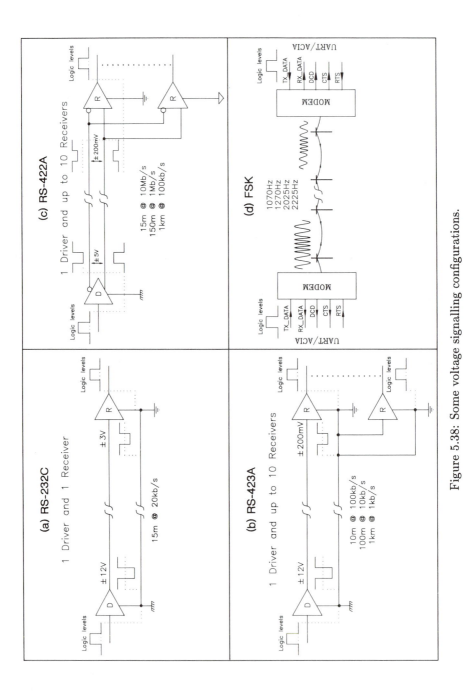

Figure 5.38: Some voltage signalling configurations.

for logic 0 (space) and 1270 Hz for logic 1 (mark) [32]. The high band uses 2025 and 2225 Hz respectively. Larger capacity systems are usually based on varying the phase of a carrier wave, known as Phase Shift Keying (PSK).

Relatively complex circuitry is necessary both to modulate and demodulate the carrier. This modem will also generate status signals indicating the readiness of the channel to participate in the communication link [31]. Typically this will include Incoming_Data_Carrier_Detect ($\overline{\text{DCD}}$) and Clear_To_Send_out ($\overline{\text{CTS}}$). Most UARTs, including the 6850 ACIA, have $\overline{\text{DCD}}$ and $\overline{\text{CTS}}$ control inputs and a Request_To_Send ($\overline{\text{RTS}}$) output to the modem. In Fig. 5.37 we have grounded the $\overline{\text{DCD}}$ and $\overline{\text{CTS}}$ inputs to simulate a ready modem.

In the 6850 ACIA, the transmit and receive rates are governed by separate external oscillators, driving the TX_CLK and RX_CLK inputs respectively. The ACIA is normally configured so that the bit rate is $\frac{1}{16}$ of this frequency. Thus for a 19,200 baud rate link, both oscillators should be set at 307,200 Hz. Typically a 2.4576 MHz crystal is used in conjunction with a Baud-Rate Generator IC to provide the standard frequencies associated with multiples of 300 baud. In this case a $\div 8$ would be selected.

Internally the ACIA appears as two register pairs, as depicted in Fig. 5.39. Each pair lies at the same address, as selected by RS, but one register is read-only and one is write-only. The Data register pair comprises the Transmit Data register and Receive Data register. Outgoing data may be written into the former, whence it is internally transferred to the Transmit Shift register (TSR), for packaging and serialization (TX_DATA). Should the previous byte still be in the process of transmission, this transfer will be delayed until the TSR is empty. The status of this double buffered activity is reported by bit S1 of the Status register. As the TDR is write-only, the MPU cannot read data which has been previously put into this register. This prohibits operations on this data which involves bringing data into the MPU, processing it (for example shifting) and putting the data back; i.e. read-modify-write. The same restriction applied to the read-only Receive Data register.

Reading the same address accesses incoming data from the Receive Data register (RDR). Serial data from the terminal is shifted into the Receive Shift register at a rate determined by the receive clock RX_CLK. After a complete word is shifted in, it is automatically transferred to the RDR, unless the MPU did not read the data which had been previously put into this register. When a new word has been loaded into the RDR, bit S0 of the Status register is set. If the load is inhibited due to this overrun condition, then bit S5 is set.

When RS is Low, the read-only Status register may be examined or the write-only Control register altered. The Status register enables the MPU to test for:

Bit 0: Receive_Data_Register_Full (RDRF)

This is set when a new word has been received and passed to the RDR. It is automatically cleared when the RDR is read. It is inhibited if the $\overline{\text{DCD}}$ input is High (see S2).

Bit 1: Transmit_Data_Register_Empty (TDRE)

This is set when a word has been passed from the TDR to the Transmit Shift register and signifies that the way is clear to send another word. It is cleared

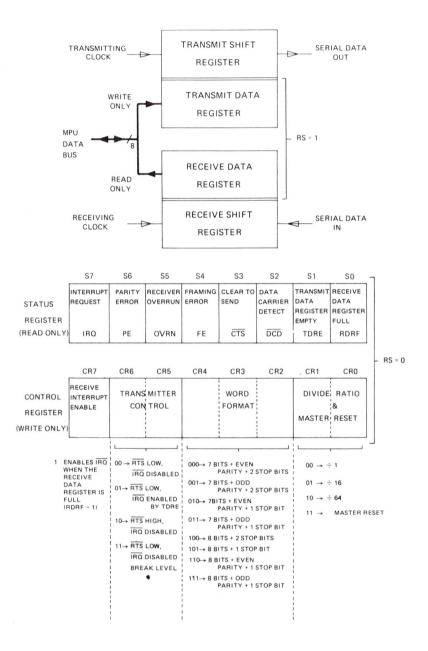

Figure 5.39: The register structure of the 6850 ACIA.

when the next word is sent before the last word is shifted out. It is inhibited when the $\overline{\text{CTS}}$ input is High (see S3).

Bit 2: Data_Carrier_Detect (DCD)

This is set when the $\overline{\text{DCD}}$ input is High (the modem fails to find a carrier). If this is the case, the RDRF status bit (S0) is inhibited. It is cleared when $\overline{\text{DCD}}$ goes Low and the Status register followed by the RDR are read or a Master Reset occurs. If the $\overline{\text{DCD}}$ remains High after the Status register then RDR are read or when a Master Reset occurs, then this bit simply follows the state of the $\overline{\text{DCD}}$ input for subsequent changes.

Bit 3: Clear_To_Send (CTS)

This follows the state of the $\overline{\text{CTS}}$ input. If High, it indicates that the modem is unable to accept data for transmission. In this case the TDRE bit (S1) will be inhibited.

Bit 4: Framing_Error (FE)

A 1 in this position indicates that a stop bit was not received, implying loss of synchronization.

Bit 5: Receiver_Overrun (OVRN)

When set, OVRN indicates that one or more word has been received and lost since the MPU last read the RDR.

Bit 6: Parity_Error (PE)

When set, this indicates an erroneous parity check outcome in the word held in the RDR.

Bit 7: Interrupt_Request (IRQ)

As configured by the Control register, this can be set when RDR is full, the TDR is empty or there is a loss of the modem's receive carrier. IRQ is cleared by reading or writing as appropriate to the pertinent Data register.

The Control register is addressed at the same location as the Status register, but is enabled when the MPU writes. The setting of this register provides software control over the word format, clock rate and interrupt options.

Bits 0 and 1: Divide Ratio and Master Reset

The 6850 ACIA has no hardware Reset pin, although it will detect a power-on situation and clear the Status register bits (except $\overline{\text{DCD}}$ and $\overline{\text{CTS}}$). To release this state, bits 0 and 1 must subsequently be set to 11. After this first store, the $\overline{\text{RTS}}$ line can optionally be used to wake up the modem by manipulating Control register bits 5 and 6.

It is unusual to use Receive_Clock to directly shift in received data (00 = ÷1), as this would require synchronization to the data pulse train at RX_DATA. Ideally the ACIA should sample around the mid-point of each incoming data bit. Taking mode 01 (÷16) as an example, Receive_Clock should be set to sixteen times the baud frequency. The ACIA then synchronizes the incoming bit pattern by sampling on positive-going transitions of Receive_Clock. If the input remains Low for nine consecutive samples, a valid start bit is assumed to have been found. Furthermore, the approximate mid-point has been located, and each subsequent sixteen receive ___/‾ clock edges will find the centerpoint of the following bits. Mode 10 ($\div 64$) is similar, but 33 samples are used to confirm the center of the start bit. The division rate also applies to Transmit_Clock.

Bits 2, 3 and 4: Word Format

Eight word formats are listed in Fig. 5.39. When a 7-bit plus parity format is used, the parity bit is replaced in the Receive Data register by bit $7 = 0$.

Bits 5 and 6: Transmit Control

This permits the ACIA to interrupt the MPU when the **TDR** is empty (mode 01). It is also used to wiggle the $\overline{\text{RTS}}$ modem control output. Initially $\overline{\text{RTS}}$ should be brought Low and IRQ disabled. Then when the modem awakes, it should activate $\overline{\text{CTS}}$ and the ACIA can then continue. A break level (mode 11) is the continuous transmission of a logic 0.

Bit 7: Receive Interrupt Enable

This permits the ACIA to interrupt the MPU when there is a new word waiting in the **RDR**. It is also possible to generate an interrupt where there is a loss of modem carrier, $\overline{\text{DCD}}$.

Finally, a simple example will tie some of these concepts together.

Example 5.23

Write a transparent subroutine called **OUTCH** (for OUTput CHaracter) that will use an 6850 ACIA based at $9004h$ to send out one ASCII-coded character, pre-loaded in Accumulator_A by the caller, to a terminal which is set up to recognize words of format eight bits and no parity. A $\div 16$ ratio is to be chosen.

The subroutine is to return an error code in Accumulator_B as follows:

Error code = $00h$ for a successful transmission.
Error code = $01h$ if the $\overline{\text{CTS}}$ input is High, i.e. the terminal is not ready.
Error code = FFh if the Transmit Data register remains full after an attempt
                to send lasting around one second.

Solution

The solution shown in Table 5.32 is in two parts. The ACIA is set up at the beginning of the main routine, first to software reset it (Control bits 1:0 = 11) and then as follows:

CR_1:0   =   01 Divide by 16 mode

CR_4:3:2 = 101 8 bits + 1 stop but with no parity

CR_6:5   =   00 Interrupt on transmit disabled, and $\overline{\text{RTS}}$ = Low (i.e. ready)

The subroutine itself firstly saves any registers used in its body and then fetches the Status register contents.

The initial test is of bit 3, which reflects the state of the $\overline{\text{CTS}}$ pin. If this is High, the terminal or modem is unready (perhaps a printer out of paper) and the subroutine exited with the error status 01h in Accumulator_B.

If the terminal is ready, then a polling loop is entered. This repetitively checks Status bit 1, by shifting right twice into the C flag. There are two ways out of this loop. If TDRE is 1, then the Transmit Shift register is empty and the data can be

```
1                           .processor m6809
2                           .define    ACIA_SR  = 9004h, ACIA_CR  = 9004h,
3                                      ACIA_RDR = 9005h, ACIA_TDR = 9005h
4  E000 8603     MAIN:       lda  000000011b ;ACIA's master reset code
5  E002 B79004               sta  ACIA_CR    ;to Control register
6  E005 8615                 lda  #00010101b ;8-bit, no parity, div by 16, RTS = 0
7  E007 B79004               sta  ACIA_CR    ;to Control register
8                        ; Set up other peripherals followed by main background code
```

(a) Setting up the ACIA

```
12            ;************************************************************************
13            ;* FUNCTION: Transmits one character, prestored in Acc.A               *
14            ;* ENTRY   : Acc.A holds byte (typically an ASCII character) to be o/p *
15            ;* EXIT    : Acc.B is 00h for successful, 01h if CTS is High,           *
16            ;* EXIT    : and FFh if TDRE is stuck Low                               *
17            ;************************************************************************
18 E00A 3411   OUTCH:    pshs cc,x         ;Save all used registers
19 E00C F69004           ldb  ACIA_SR      ;Check Status register to see if TX ready
20 E00F C508             bitb #00001000b   ;Looking at Clear To Send (CTS)
21 E011 2615             bne  CTS_ERROR    ;IF so THEN go to error handler
22            ;
23 E013 8EFFFF           ldx  #0FFFFh      ;ELSE load up the time-out constant
24 E016 F69004 OUTCH_L:  ldb  ACIA_SR      ;Get Status again
25 E019 301F             leax -1,x         ;Decrement time-out for one more try
26 E01B 54               lsrb              ;Looking for TDRE = 1
27 E01C 54               lsrb              ;which tells us we can go ahead and TX
28 E01D 250D             bcs  OUT          ;IF yes THEN go ahead and output character
29 E01F 8C0000           cmpx #0           ;ELSE check if timeout down to zero
30 E022 26F2             bne  OUTCH_L      ;IF not THEN go try again for set TDRE flag
31            ; Land here if timed out and the ACIA is still not ready to transmit
32 E024 C6FF             ldb  #-1          ;Error status for time out
33 E026 2008             bra  EXIT
34            ; Land here if the modem has not asserted CTS, ie, not clear to send
35 E028 C601   CTS_ERROR: ldb #01h         ;Clear To Send error status byte
36 E02A 2004             bra  EXIT
37            ; Land here if OK to send byte
38 E02C B79005 OUT:      sta  ACIA_TDR     ;All clear, so send it out
39 E02F 5F               clrb              ;Code for a successful transmission
40            ; Always exit thru here
41 E030 3511   EXIT:     puls cc,x         ;Restore used registers
42 E032 39               rts
43                       .end
```

(b) The subroutine itself

Table 5.32: Sending out a serialized byte.

stored in the **TDR**. The subroutine is then exited with an error status of 00*h*. If
Index register_X decrements to zero before **TDRE** becomes 1, then a time-out error
is recorded and the subroutine quit. This time-out takes just over 1.6 s, but can be
shortened by lowering the initial setting of **X** in step 23.

5.4 Third Generation Microprocessors

The 6809 MPU used as the illustrative example for the previous sections, represented the state of the art at the end of the 1970s. Implemented with 15,000 transistors,
it is around three times more complex than the first generation of 8-bit MPUs. In
the intervening decade, advances in fabrication techniques have permitted devices
of well over one million transistors to be successfully manufactured. How has this
hundredfold increase in circuitry been reflected in MPU technology?

There are several ways in which this potential has been exploited. The obvious
way is more of the same, with bigger address and data paths coupled with corresponding increases in the size and number of internal registers. The range and
complexity of machine instructions, both at the operational and address-mode level, can similarly be enhanced. Newer MPUs typically incorporate integral floating-
point hardware, in order to directly implement a range of floating-point arithmetic
operations. Even when this is not the case, most current MPUs are designed to
work in tandem with an external floating-point co-processor chip.

As we have seen, MPUs operate in a serial manner and are at the slow end
of the processing speed spectrum. Newer technologies and the smaller physical
size of the integrated active devices, have permitted an increase in operation rate
to better than 30 million instructions per second (30 MIPS). As well as upping
the clock speed, the increase in processing throughput has been aided by caching.
An instruction cache is an area of program memory which is integral to the MPU.
Instead of waiting for an instruction to be completed before fetching the next down,
instructions are continually being fetched into this internal memory, while the MPU
is doing internal operations which do not use the external buses. Rather than using
a dumb fetch mechanism, the hit rate (i.e. where an instruction is in place in the
cache) is considerably improved if Branches are recognized and program code from
the branch-to point is loaded, in case the test is affirmative at execution time.
Integrating both the cache and cache-handling into the MPU is a common feature
in current devices.

As an example, Fig. 5.40 illustrates the internal structure of the 68000 16/32-bit
family of MPUs [33]. This was introduced around the same time as the 6809 MPU
and really is not much more powerful, but it represents the start of a dynasty rather
than the end of the line. The latest member of this family at the time of writing
is the 68040 MPU. This is software compatible with the 68000, but has a 32-bit
ALU. The 68000 MPU (1979) was fabricated in 3.5 micron (μm) technology (the
resolution of the smallest object in silicon) and contains 68,000 — coincidentally —
transistors. It is capable of around 2 MIPS. The 68040 MPU, introduced in 1989,
uses 0.7 micron geometry and packs in 1.2 million transistors. Up to 30 MIPS or six
million floating-point operations (6 MFLOPS) can be delivered, with the help of its
integrated floating-point unit (FPU) and 4 Kbyte instruction and data caches. It is
predicted that by 1994 the 68060? MPU will be fabricated in 0.5 micron technology

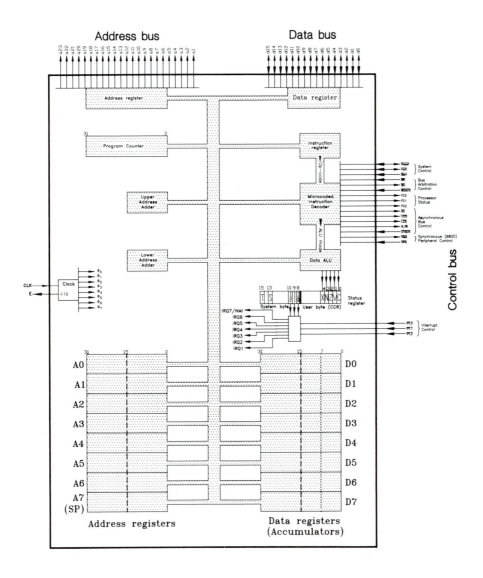

Figure 5.40: The 68000 microprocessor.

and will be implemented using four million transistors!

Internally, the 68000 family has eight 32-bit Data registers (Accumulators) and eight 32-bit Address registers. With the exception of **A7**, which is used by the MPU as its System Stack Pointer, the registers are general purpose. Thus a instruction targeting a Data register operates identically irrespective of which register is specified, eg.:

```
ADD.L #60,D0        ; Add 60 to D0 in 32-bit resolution
........
........
........
ADD.L #60,D7        ; Add 60 to D7 in 32-bit resolution
```

Most instructions can treat a Data register as an 8-bit, 16-bit or 32-bit object. Thus:

```
ADD.B #60,D1        ; Add 60 to lower 8-bit byte
ADD.W #60,D1        ; Add 60 to lower 16-bit word
ADD.L #60,D1        ; Add 60 to 32-bit long word
```

Address registers are targeted by a restricted number of instructions, and they can be treated as sign-extended 16-bit or full 32-bit pointers. For example, if the contents of **A0** where 0000C000h, then the instruction ADD.B 6(A0.W),D0 adds to the lower eight bits of **D0** the contents of address $FFFFC000 + 6h$. The instruction ADD.B 6(A0.L),D0 will add to the lower eight bits of **D0** the contents of address 0000C000 + $6h$. Address-specific instructions can target any of the eight Address registers in an identical manner.

The 24-bit address bus means that addresses above $00FFFFFFh$ are not reflected outside the chip. Nevertheless, 2^{24} (16,777,216) supports 16 Mbytes of address space. Family members from the 68020 upwards use a full 32-bit address bus, giving 4 Gbytes of address space. The 16-bit data bus supports 32-bit long-word transfers from adjacent words (rather like the 16-bit double operations in the 6809 MPU were implemented as two 8-bit transfers). Once again, later family devices use the full 32-bit bus.

Strictly a 16-bit data bus should be supported by an address structure expressed in 16-bit words rather than 8-bit bytes. However, the 68000 can deal with bytes as its smallest object and so its address bus is considered to carry a byte address. Thus the instruction MOVE.B 0C000h,D0 will move the data byte in the location C000h down to the lower eight bits of Data register_D0. The 68000 does not have an a$_0$ pin; instead the Upper_Data_Strobe (UDS) pulses when an even-byte address is used. The Lower_Data_Strobe (LDS) similarly pulses whenever an odd-byte address is accessed, e.g. MOVE.B 0C001h,D0. Word data causes both UDS and LDS to pulse, eg. MOVE.W 0C000h,D0. In this case, the byte at C000h appears on data lines d$_{15}$...d$_7$ as enabled by UDS and C001h on lines d$_7$...d$_0$ as enabled by LDS. Typically, two 8-bit memory banks are used to feed both halves of the data bus, as enabled by the appropriate Data strobe [34]. Address_Strobe (AS) acts as a general enable for the address decoder, indicating a stable address on the bus.

Although the principle of interfacing with a common data bus and address decoder is the same as for the 6809 MPU, the 68000 family handle this in a different way. Rather than assume the peripheral interface or memory is available at the end of the clock cycle, the addressed device is required to send a signal back to the MPU's $\overline{\text{DTACK}}$ ($\overline{\text{DaTa\_ACKnowledge}}$) whenever it is ready. If this has not been sent back on time, the MPU goes into a wait state. This asynchronous approach is especially valuable for the faster processors dealing with slower interface devices. In this situation, the clock rate does not have to be adjusted to suit the lowest common denominator.

When the 68000 was introduced, most interface circuitry (like the 6821 PIA) was designed with the synchronous interface scheme of the 6800/9 family in mind. Thus the 68000 can be switched into this 6800 mode if $\overline{\text{VPA}}$ ($\overline{\text{Valid\_Peripheral\_Address}}$) is used instead of $\overline{\text{DTACK}}$. In this situation, the E clock is used for synchronization (no Q clock) and VMA (Valid_Memory_Address, an address strobe from the original 6800 MPU). An external oscillator must be used to clock the MPU, and rates of up to 12 MHz (three internal cycles per μs) are possible. Clock rates of up to 50 MHz are used for the newer family members.

The 68000 supports seven hardware interrupts, as requested by a 3-bit code sent to $\overline{\text{IPL0 IPL1 IPL2}}$ ($\overline{\text{Interrupt\_Level\_0}} \ldots \overline{2}$). This code defines one of seven levels. Thus if a peripheral sends the pattern 100b (active-Low 3), it is requesting a level-3 interrupt. Typically, the several requesting peripherals generating this code via a 74x148 Priority encoder (see Fig. 3.40). The $\overline{\text{Bus\_ERRor}}$ ($\overline{\text{BERR}}$) input also generates a type of interrupt (interrupt-like responses are known as exceptions in the 68000 family). External circuitry is used to detect a problem, such as a peripheral interface not returning a $\overline{\text{DTACK}}$, and signal this via $\overline{\text{BERR}}$.

Although the 68000's software is of little concern in this review, we will conclude with a simple example.

Example 5.24

Design the 68000-coding for a subroutine which will convert an 8-bit binary quantity in the lower byte of Data register_D0 to a string of three ASCII-coded decimal digits. Thus if **D0.L** is 00100011b (67), then we require the string $'0''6''7'$, coded as 30h-36h-37h.

Solution

The direct approach simply repetitively subtracts hundreds from the binary value, incrementing the hundreds count for each successful go. Then tens are repetitively subtracted; this time incrementing the tens count. The residue is the units. This is the technique illustrated by the flow chart in Fig. 5.41.

The implementation of this is shown in Table 5.33. As the ASCII code for the numbers 0... 9 is 30h... 39h, a direct translation is possible by initializing the three memory locations **Hunds**, **Tens** and **Units** to 30h, which is ASCII for zero (see Table 1.4), steps 11–13.

In both the hundreds and tens modules, a Compare operation is made to see if a successful subtraction can be made. If the source constant is larger than the destination operand, then the **Carry flag** will be set when the virtual subtraction Destination − Source is made. In this situation, the BCS instruction of steps 16 & 22 are equivalent to BLO (BRANCH IF LOwER THAN). If the C flag is not set, then

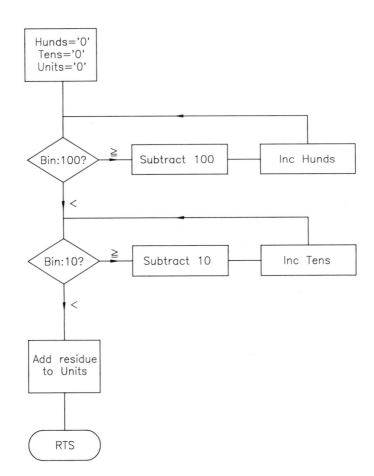

Figure 5.41: Conversion algorithm for 8-bit binary to 3-digit ASCII-coded decimal.

the constant is subtracted and one added to the appropriate count. The 68000 has
no Increment operation, instead the ADDQ (ADD Quick) instruction can be used for
small constants (1 to 8).

Whatever is left after the last ten is subtracted is the units. The instruction
ADD.B D0,Unit adds this directly to the contents of memory as the destination
without having to do this addition internally and then send the result out; as would
be the case with the 6809 MPU.

This algorithm could simply be extended to binary values up to $2^{32} - 1$ (4,294,-
967,295), by using Long (.L) instructions. However, this would require nine Com-
pare:Subtract:Increment routines; all virtually identical. A better approach would
be to store the constants 1 billion down to ten in the form of a look-up table (see
page 457) and use one of the Address registers as an advancing index.

```
1                                 .processor m68000
2       ;*******************************************************************
3       ;* FUNCTION: Converts 8-bit binary to 3-digit ASCII-coded decimal    *
4       ;* EXAMPLE : [D0.B]=FFh -> [Hunds]=32h ('2'), [Tens]=35h ('5'),      *
5       ;*           [Units]=35h ('5'), i.e. decimal 255                     *
6       ;* ENTRY   : Hundred's digit in C012h, ten's in C013h, unit's in C014h *
7       ;* EXIT    : [D0.B]=Units, CCR altered                               *
8       ;*******************************************************************
9                                 .define Hunds=0C012h, Tens=0C013h, Units=0C014h
10          ; Initialization
11 000400 13FC00300000C012  BIN_2_BCD: move.b #30h,Hunds   ;30h is ASCII for zero
12 000408 13FC00300000C013             move.b #30h,Tens    ;Put into Hundreds
13 000410 13FC00300000C014             move.b #30h,Units   ;Tens and Units
14                  ;Now see how many hundreds there are
15 000418 0C000064          HUN: cmp.b  #100,D0            ;Is binary less than 100?
16 00041C 650C                   bcs    TEN                ;IF yes THEN go try tens
17 00041E 04000064               sub.b  #100,D0            ;ELSE subtract 100
18 000422 52390000C012           addq.b #1,Hunds           ;One more hundred
19 000428 60EE                   bra    HUN                ;and repeat
20                  ; See how many tens there are
21 00042A 0C00000A          TEN: cmp.b  #10,D0             ;Is binary less than 10
22 00042E 650C                   bcs    UNIT               ;IF yes THEN go to units
23 000430 0400000A               sub.b  #10,D0             ;ELSE subtract 10
24 000434 52390000C013           addq.b #1,Tens            ;One more ten
25 00043A 60EE                   bra    TEN                ;and repeat
26                  ; What's left is the units
27 00043C D1390000043C      UNIT: add.b  D0,Unit           ; Add residue to Units
28 000442 4E75                   rts                       ; and return
29                                 .end
```

Table 5.33: Binary to decimal code.

Building CPUs of ever greater complexity is not the only way to use the extra silicon available due to more sophisticated fabrication technologies. The alternative approach adds memory and peripheral interface devices to a more basic CPU. The outcome of this process is a simple computer on a chip, called a **MicroComputer Unit (MCU)** or microcontroller.

MCUs are generally used in embedded control applications, hidden from view. For example, they are typically embedded in your TV controller, vending machines, microwave oven and automobile; as well as sophisticated products like robotics and telecommunications. Ordinary MPUs are of course used as embedded controllers, and indeed their volume sales from this source far exceeds their more visible role in small computers. Generally MCUs are used for less powerful applications, where typically their ability to reduce the size of the electronics is most important. More powerful systems often use multiple MCUs working in tandem; each controlling one specific task, under the aegis of a more potent conventional microprocessor. Thus a robot may use a MCU to control each of its joints, with the whole working under the conductorship of, say, a 68040 32-bit MPU.

The first concrete expression of this approach led to the Texas Instruments TMS1000 family of 4-bit MCUs. This was followed in 1976 by Intel's 8048 MCU, which put an 8-bit CPU, RAM and ROM memory and interface on the one chip. Eight-bit MCUs are now the best selling category, only recently overhauling the 4-bit types. Sixteen and 32-bit devices began to appear in the mid 1980s, for example the Motorola 68300 series (based on the 68000 family), enhancing the CPU power as well as system integration.

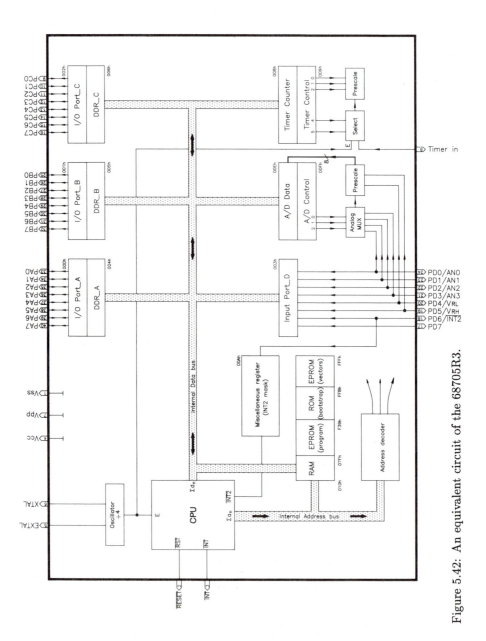

Figure 5.42: An equivalent circuit of the 68705R3.

Our example for this section is the 68705R3 MCU, which is illustrated in Fig. 5.42 [35] The 68705R3 comprises an 8-bit CPU together with three parallel 8-bit programmable I/O ports, a single 8-bit output port shared with a 4-channel analog to digital converter and a second interrupt request input, $\overline{\text{INT2}}$. Also provided is an 8-bit timer counter, which can be clocked from outside (pin 8) or from the system clock E; both of which can be prescaled by up to $\div 128$.

On-board read-only memory of just under 4 Kbytes is provided, most of which is EPROM programmable by the user. A small ROM holds the self-programming code. The bottom 128 bytes are occupied by RAM, of which locations 000 – 00Fh hold the various peripheral control data, such as the port Data Direction registers. The remaining 112 bytes can be used as a stack and for storage of variables.

With the memory map only extending to FFFh, the Program Counter need only be 12 bits wide. The similarly sized address bus is not accessible to the outside world, with all address decoding being internally implemented.

The CPU itself is a rather cut-down version of the 6800-family architecture. There is only one Accumulator, and the Code Condition register does not have a 2's complement oVerflow flag (V flag). The ALU can neither multiply nor do 2's complement arithmetic, but does feature the full range of logic operations. Although the Index register is only eight bit wide, the offset for the Indexed address mode can be up to 16 bits.

The Stack Pointer reflects the limited capacity of the internal RAM. Although it is twelve bits wide, the top seven bits are permanently fixed at 0000011b. The instruction RSP (RESET STACK POINTER) sets the SP to $000001111111b$ (7Fh), as does a hardware Reset. The bottom of the stack is then $000001100000b$ (60h), giving a maximum stack size of 32 bytes. Although this is small; up to 16 nested subroutines may be called, or 13 levels and one interrupt. No PUSH/PULL instructions are provided.

Rather than give a purely software example, we will conclude this section by showing how the 68705R3 can be used as a simple digital voltmeter.

Example 5.25

It is proposed to use a 68705R3-based system as a digital voltmeter. The voltage is to be read out on a 2-digit 7-segment display to indicate values between 00 and 99 V. The scaling of the input amplifiers are such that this translates to the binary range 00000000b – 11000110b (00 – 198). This analog input is fed to the system via Channel_0. The overall circuit diagram is shown in Fig. 5.44.

Solution

There are three parts to the software. The input routine gets the output of the analog to digital converter and scales it to the appropriate range. The binary to BCD routine converts this value to the 2-digit BCD equivalent, which is taken by the output routine and sent to the two output display devices.

Before looking at the software, we need to examine the peripheral hardware and analog port in a little more detail. A simplified equivalent of the 6805's analog port is shown in Fig. 5.45. One of eight inputs is fed to the A/D converter through an analog multiplexer, as addressed from the lower three bits of the A/D Control

Internal Address bus   Internal Data bus

$a_{11} a_{10} a_9 a_8 a_7 a_6 a_5 a_4 a_3 a_2 a_1 a_0$ $d_7 d_6 d_5 d_4 d_3 d_2 d_1 d_0$

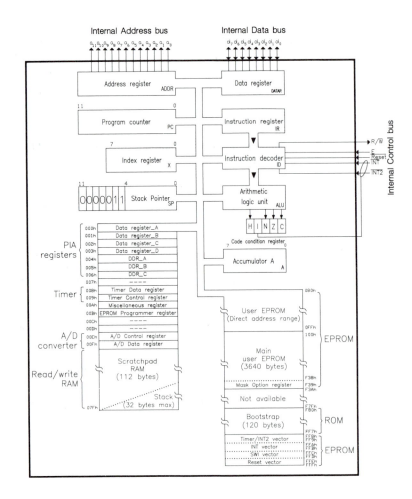

Figure 5.43: The 68705R3 CPU and memory map.

register at address 00Eh. Four of these inputs are externally accessible, whilst the others are internal voltages derived from an external precision voltage reference, and can be used for calibration purposes. The A/D conversion process gives a digital equivalent as a fraction of V_{ref}, with FFh for $V_{in} = V_{ref}$.

Once selected, the analog input is sampled for a period of five processor cycles (5 μs for a 4 MHz crystal) and then held constant for the duration of the conversion; another 25 cycles.

The A/D converter continually cycles, and at the completion of each conversion, dumps its data into the A/D Result register. Thus, the digitized data can be read at any time at 00Fh. Altering the A/D Control register, for example changing the channel number, automatically aborts the conversion in progress and starts a new conversion. If bit 7, the End_Of_Conversion status bit is cleared, then the completion

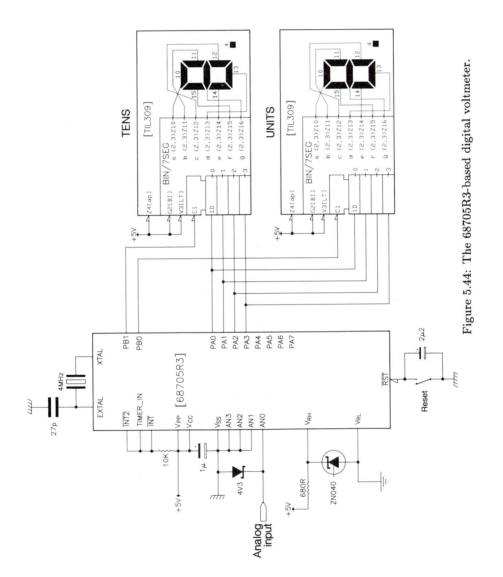

Figure 5.44: The 68705R3-based digital voltmeter.

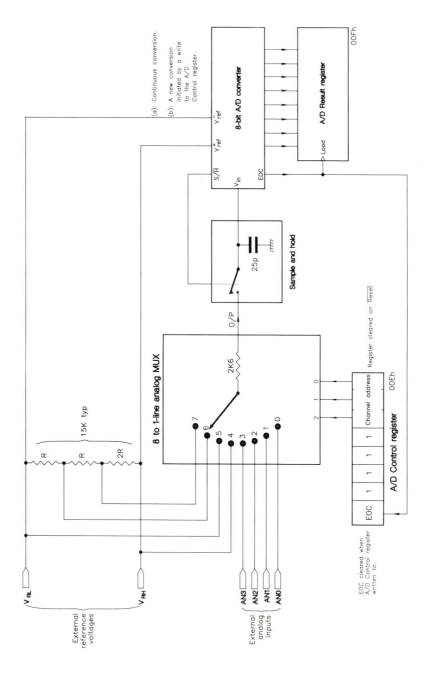

Figure 5.45: The 6805's analog port.

of this conversion can be determined by the state of this bit.

As we are only using Channel_0 in this example, the A/D subsystem is simply initialized by clearing the A/D Control register (step 13). Indeed, this is done when the MCU is Reset.

The output is displayed using two intelligent 7-segment displays. The TIL309 has an internal 4-bit latch fronting a 7-segment decoder, which drives an integral 7-segment plus decimal point display. The decoder features Lamp_Test (LT) and Blanking_Input (BI) inputs, both of which are unused and consequently tied High in Fig. 5.44. The decimal point is also unused and thus dp is additionally tied Low.

Both displays are connected to the same four port lines (PA3 – PA0). They are distinguished by using either PB0 or PB1 to pulse the appropriate TIL309's latch according to the data presented in the lower nybble in Port A.

Initializing the 68705's peripherals is simply a matter of setting bits in the Data Direction registers controlling Port A & B and clearing the A/D Control register to switch to Channel_0; steps 10 – 13 in Table 5.34.

The voltage is read directly from the A/D Result register. Shifting this byte right once divides by two, as required by the analog scaling factor. Conversion to BCD follows the technique of Table 5.32, except that only tens and units are involved; steps 18 – 23.

```
1              .processor m6805
2              ;*****************************************************************
3              ; Routine to use a 68705R3 as a digital voltmeter               *
4              ; INPUT : 0 - 99V dc                                            *
5              ; OUTPUT: Two-digit 7-segment display                          *
6              ;*****************************************************************
7              .define PORT_A=000, DDR_A=004, PORT_B=001, DDR_B=005,
8                      A_D_CONTROL=00Eh, A_D_RESULT=00Fh, Tens=012h
9              ; Initialize registers
10 0080 A6 FF      MAIN: lda  #11111111b  ; Prepare to make ports A&B outputs
11 0082 B7 04            sta  DDR_A
12 0084 B7 05            sta  DDR_B
13 0086 3F 0E            clr  A_D_CONTROL ; Switch to channel 0
14              ; Acquire temperature
15 0088 B6 0F      LOOP: lda  A_D_RESULT  ; Read the analog data
16 008A 44               lsra             ; Divide by 2 gives temperature
17              ; Now convert to 2-digit BCD
18 008B 3F 12            clr  Tens        ; Zero ten's count
19 008D A1 0A  TEN_LOOP: cmp  #10         ; Is binary less than ten
20 008F 25 06            bcs  OUTPUT      ; IF yes THEN finish
21 0091 A0 0A            sub  #10         ; ELSE take away ten
22 0093 3C 12            inc  Tens        ; and one more ten count
23 0095 20 F6            bra  TEN_LOOP    ; Go again
24              ; The residue in the Accumulator is the units
25 0097 B7 00    OUTPUT: sta  PORT_A      ; Send out units
26 0099 11 01            bclr 0,PORT_B    ; Pulse units display
27 009B 10 01            bset 0,PORT_B
28 009D B6 12            lda  Tens        ; Get tens digit
29 009F B7 00            sta  PORT_A      ; Send it out
30 00A1 13 01            bclr 1,PORT_B    ; Pulse tens display
31 00A3 12 01            bset 1,PORT_B
32 00A5 20 E1            bra  LOOP        ; and repeat
33                       .end
```

Table 5.34: The software circuit for the voltmeter.

Finally, each BCD nybble is sent to Port A in turn and either PB0 or PB1 pulsed. This is accomplished by bringing the appropriate bit Low and then High. This uses the 6805 family instructions BCLR (BIT CLEAR) and BSET (BIT SET), steps 26 & 27 and 30 & 31. These allow programmers to either clear or set any one bit at a read/write memory location (in a similar vein, the 6805 has a BRCLR n and BRSET n instruction which cause a Branch if a bit n at any memory location is clear or set respectively.

Our solution is of course only a skeleton of a working implementation. For example, a filtering algorithm could be incorporated into the input routine to reduce the effect of noise on the display. Over-range should also be detected (numbers above 198) and indicated, perhaps by flashing 99. In a realistic system, the input signal would be fronted by a variable-gain amplifier. The MCU would determine what amplification to use, for example $\times 1$, $\times 10$, $\times 100$ and use the decimal point to indicate the true value. The number of display digits would be increased appropriately. Using four Port A lines to drive a dual 2 to 4-line decoder would be capable of accommodating four digits and selecting any one of four decimal points and hence spanning four $\times 10$ ranges.

5.5   Examples

5.5.1   Worked Examples

Example 5.26

A MPU-based test rig is to be designed to check out 8-core cable sections during manufacture, for open and short circuit. The cable is connected as shown in Fig. 5.46. Each conductor is to be tested in turn by storing a single logic 1 at the output port (eg. 00001000b for conductor 3). The result of this test vector is available at the input port. Three types of fault are possible. Type 1 is a simple

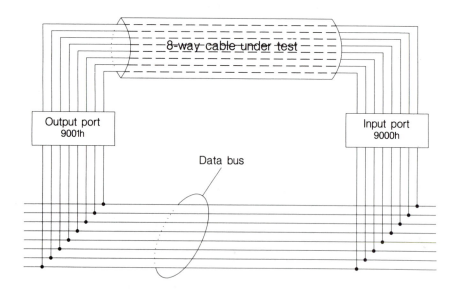

Figure 5.46: Testing cable.

open circuit, eg. 00001000*b* → 00000000*b*. Type 2 is a short circuit, eg. 00001000*b* → 11001000*b*. Type 3 is a compound short circuit/open circuit, eg. 00001000*b* → 11000000*b*.

You are asked to design software to the following specification:

1. The test subroutine should return a status indicator which is zero if no fault, otherwise 1, 2 or 3 according to the fault type.

2. If a fault, the test vector causing failure should also be returned.

Solution

The test procedure algorithm involves the following phases:

1. Initialize relevant variables.

2. For $n = 0$ to 7.

3. Send out test vector n.

4. If outcome is satisfactory and $n < 8$, then go to step 2.

5. If $n = 8$, then exit with no fault.

```
1                            .processor      m6809
2               ;*****************************************************************
3               ;* Subroutine checks the status of 8-core cable lengths          *
4               ;* Locates three types of faults                                 *
5               ;* Fault 1 indicates an open circuit                             *
6               ;* Fault 2 indicates a short circuit between two wires           *
7               ;* Fault 3 indicates a mixture of open and short circuit         *
8               ;* ENTRY : None                                                  *
9               ;* EXIT  : Last test vector in A                                 *
10              ;* EXIT  : Error type 0, 1, 2, 3 in B; 0 indicates no fault      *
11              ;*****************************************************************
12                           .define Cable_in = 9000h, Cable_out = 9001h, Error = 0000h
13  E000 0F00   TEST:   clr     Error       ; Initial error type is 0
14  E002 8601           lda     #00000001b  ; The initial test loop
15              ; For n=0 to 7, send out test vector and check.  Exit if error
16  E004 B79000 T_LOOP: sta     Cable_in    ; Send out test vector
17  E007 8E07D0         ldx     #2000       ; Wait for a while to settle
18  E00A 301F   D_LOOP: leax    -1,x
19  E00C 26FC           bne     D_LOOP
20  E00E 1F89           tfr     a,b         ; Then copy test vector across to B
21  E010 F89001         eorb    Cable_out   ; and compare with outcome
22  E013 2605           bne     FAULT       ; IF not the same THEN do error handling
23  E015 48             lsla                ; The next vector
24  E016 2514           bcs     EXIT        ; unless a one pops out!
25  E018 20EA           bra     T_LOOP      ; Repeat test
26              ; Land here if an error has occurred
27  E01A 0C00   FAULT:  inc     Error       ; First check for an open-circuit fault
28  E01C 7D9001         tst     Cable_out   ; as indicated by an all zeros return
29  E01F 270B           beq     EXIT        ; IF true THEN error type 1
30  E021 0C00           inc     Error       ; ELSE try for a short-circuit fault by
31  E023 1F89           tfr     a,b         ; ANDing test vector
32  E025 F49001         andb    Cable_out   ; with received pattern
33  E028 2602           bne     EXIT        ; IF test bit still there THEN a short
34  E02A 0C00           inc     Error       ; ELSE a mixed open- and short-circuit
35              ; Return with test vector in A; error type in B
36  E02C D600   EXIT:   ldb     Error
37  E02E 39             rts
39                      .end
```

Table 5.35: A cable-test subroutine

6. Otherwise check for an all-zero outcome. If true, then exit with a type 1 fault (simple open circuit).

7. Otherwise must be a short circuit type fault. Check to see if the original logic 1 has come through. If it has, we have a type 2 (simple short circuit) fault, otherwise type 3 (both open and short circuit). Return with type number.

The listing itself, as presented in Table 5.35, follows this procedure closely. Memory location **Error** is used to temporarily hold the error number, initialized to 0; whilst internal registers hold the other variables. The eight test vectors from $00000001b$ through $10000000b$ are generated by shifting the initial pattern once left each time around the main loop, steps 16–25. Each vector is sent out to the cable, and after a short delay to allow any transients to die down, the outcome is compared with the excitation pattern, step 21. If they are the same for all eight tests, then the subroutine is exited with an error number of 0 (no error).

If the comparison fails, then the outcome checked for an all-zeros situation, steps 28 & 29. If this is the case, then the tested wire has an open circuit and this is a type 1 error, as indicated by the previous increment of **Error** (step 27).

Where this test also fails, then some type of short circuit must have occurred. We can distinguish between the situation where there is also an open circuit of the tested wire by ANDing the test vector with the received pattern from the cable. If there was no open circuit, then we should get a single 1 at position n; which is the tested location (eg. $00001000 \cdot 10101000 = 00001000$, where there is a short circuit between conductors 3, 5 and 7). This represents a type 2 error; steps 30 – 33. Otherwise a type 3 error exists (eg. $00001000 \cdot 10100000 = 00000000$, where conductor 3 is open circuit and shorted to 5 & 7); which is signalled by the extra increment of step 34.

In practice considerable attention would have to be made to the analog interfaces to the cable, as long lengths of conductor are efficient gatherers of noise, and false alarms are likely to be expensive!

Example 5.27

A certain TV panel game has eight contestants, who will answer questions posed by the umpire. Each contestant has a single push switch which is logic 1 when pressed, and a light at his/her desk. There is a single communal buzzer.

You are asked to design a suitable interface located in the range $6000h – 60FFh$.

Solution

The implementation adopted in Fig. 5.47 uses an octal 3-state buffer as the input port for the switches and octal D flip flop array to drive the accompanying indicator lamps. The buzzer is interfaced to d_0 with a single D flip flop used as a 1-bit output port.

The address decoder is based on a partial decoding scheme. A front-end 74x10 NAND gate enables a 74x138 decoder whenever $a_{15}\,a_{14}\,a_{13}\,a_{12}\,a_{11}\,a_{10}\,a_9 = 0110000b$. The 74x138 also requires a_8 and $(R/\overline{W} + Q)$ to complete its enabling. The latter cuts the transaction short by Q whenever the MPU is doing a write $(R/\overline{W} = 0)$ to avoid the write-to hazard (See Fig. 5.18). There are $2^6 - 1 = 63$ images.

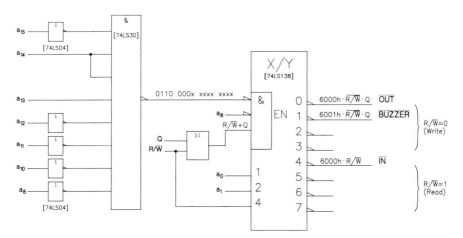

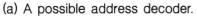

(a) A possible address decoder.

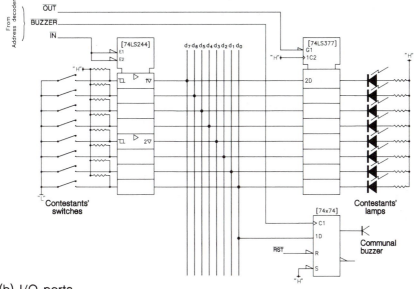

(b) I/O ports.

Figure 5.47: Panel game interface.

The R/$\overline{\text{W}}$ control is also used as one of the 74x138's address select inputs. This effectively gives two co-incident address ranges $6000h - 6003h$; one for a writing action ($Y_0 - Y_3$) and one for a reading action ($Y_4 - Y_7$). Thus the switch port and lamp ports share the same address $6000h$, but the former is activated when reading and the latter when writing.

Example 5.28

Construct a suitable software circuit to drive the panel-game hardware of Fig. 5.47. This routine is to sound the buzzer for a brief period when any switch is pressed; light the appropriate lamp indicating the first contestant who responds to the question, and lock out any further switch activity for around twenty seconds.

Solution

A task analysis of this problem indicates the following procedures:

1. Wait for someone to press a switch.

2. Determine which switch (or one switch, if several simultaneous presses) is set.

```
 1                              .processor    m6809
 2                   ;**********************************************************
 3                   ;* Routine implements the panel game strategy            *
 4                   ;* INPUTS : Eight switches at 9000h                       *
 5                   ;* OUTPUTS: Eight lamps at 9000h and a single buffer at 9001h  *
 6                   ;**********************************************************
 7                              .define Switches = 9000h, Lamps = 9000h, Buzzer = 9001h
 8                   ; DO Task 1: Wait for someone to press a switch
 9 E000 7D9000 MAIN:           tst     Switches   ; Wait for inspiration!
10 E003 27FB                   beq     MAIN
11                   ; DO Task 2, Determine which switch (or one switch)
12 E005 8680                   lda     #10000000b ; First test vector
13 E007 B59000 WHICH_ONE: bita  Switches   ; Look for highest set switch
14 E00A 2605                   bne     DISPLAY    ; IF found THEN display it
15 E00C 44                     lsra               ; ELSE next test vector
16 E00D 24F8                   bcc     WHICH_ONE
17 E00F 20EF                   bra     MAIN       ; Unless none is found
18                   ; DO Task 3: Activate lamp
19 E011 43     DISPLAY:        coma               ; Lamps are active Low
20 E012 B79000                 sta     Lamps
21                   ; DO Task 4: Turn on buzzer
22 E015 4F                     clra
23 E016 B79001                 sta     Buzzer     ; Turned On by Low
24 E019 8EFFFF                 ldx     #0ffffh    ; for around 0.5s
25 E01C 301F   BUZ_LOOP:       leax    -1,x
26 E01E 26FC                   bne     BUZ_LOOP
27 E020 4A                     deca               ; Turned Off by High
28 E021 B79001                 sta     Buzzer
29                   ; DO Task 5: Go dead for 20 seconds
30 E024 8628                   lda     #40        ; Time out after 40 0.5s
31 E026 8EFFFF D_LOOP1:        ldx     #0ffffh
32 E029 301F   D_LOOP2:        leax    -1,x       ; Time out the half seconds
33 E02B 26FC                   bne     D_LOOP2
34 E02D 4A                     deca               ; One less half second
35 E02E 26F9                   bne     D_LOOP2
36                   ; DO Task 6: Clear lamps and repeat
37 E030 4A                     deca               ; Makes A = 11111111b
38 E031 B79000                 sta     Lamps      ; Turns lamps all Off
39 E034 20CA                   bra     MAIN       ; Go again
40                              .end
```

Table 5.36: Listing for the panel game.

3. Activate the relevant lamp.

4. Activate the buzzer for a short time.

5. Go dead for twenty seconds.

6. Clear the lamps and go to step 1.

The listing given in Table 5.36 follows this procedure closely. The only thing of note is task 2, which determines who was quickest. In reality the chances of more than one request being sent within the few μs between program lines 9 and 13 are minimal, but to ensure no possible argument, a moving mask with a single 1 is ANDed with the switch settings until the first set bit is found. Thus if the switch pattern is 01000100b, then the mask 01000000b when ANDed (line 13) will produce a non-zero outcome. The mask is then inverted (the lamps are active-Low) and used to activate the lamp array. Of course this produces a certain bias, as any lower request is ignored. As a fail safe, if no switch is set when read (perhaps due to switch bounce) execution is returned to task 1.

Example 5.29

The principle of operation of the stepper motor is illustrated in Fig. 5.48. By activating the appropriate armature coils, a magnetic field can be set up in one of several directions. The rotor will align itself with this field in order to keep the magnetic path's reluctance to a minimum [36]. Thus if we energize coils A & B, we generate a field going to the north east. If A is then switched Off and C energized, then the field switches to the south east, and the rotor swings around accordingly one 90° step. Assuming that logic 1 energizes the attached coil, we have:

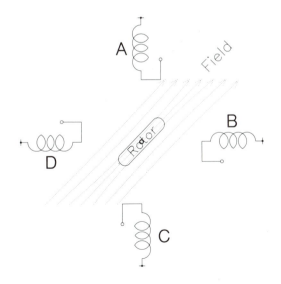

Figure 5.48: The stepper motor

D	C	B	A		Position
0	0	1	1	↗↗	0
0	1	1	0	↘↘	1
1	1	0	0	↙↙	2
1	0	0	1	↖↖	3

Can you see the relationship between these patterns?

Write a driver routine that will cause such a stepper motor connected to a 4-bit output port to rotate one step clockwise when called. You may assume that the current field number $(0 - 3)$ is stored as the global variable **Position**.

Solution

The approach given in Table 5.37 uses a look-up table to store the four coil energization patterns. The **X Index register** is used as a pointer to the bottom of this table and the variable **Position** as an offset to the nth entry; step 16. Incrementing **Position** must be modulo-4; i.e. fold over every four increments. This is done in step 13 by ANDing with $00000011b$, effectively zeroing the upper six bits.

The scheme described here is known as the full-step mode, where each step is 90 electrical degrees. The armature coils are usually repeated around the frame of the motor; so mechanical degrees are normally an integral fraction of electrical degrees. An alternative approach energizes both single and two coils in sequence to give $45°$ steps. The disadvantage of this half-step mode is that the field strength varies by $\sqrt{2}$ between single and dual energization steps. Can you repeat this example for this mode, and introduce a global variable to control the direction of rotation?


```
 1                          .processor m6809
 2            ;*****************************************************************
 3            ;* Driver routine rotates stepper motor one step clockwise    *
 4            ;* ENTRY: Location set at current position                    *
 5            ;* EXIT : Position incremented.  No registers altered         *
 6            ;*****************************************************************
 7                          .define Position = 0000, Output = 9000h
 8 E000 3417   STEP:        pshs    a,b,x,cc    ; Save all used registers
 9 E002 8EE016              ldx     #STEP_TABLE ; Point X to bottom of code table
10 E005 9600               lda     Position    ; Get current position
11 E007 1F89               tfr     a,b         ; Copy into Acc.B
12 E009 5C                 incb                ; Move on one
13 E00A C403               andb    #00000011b  ; modulo-4
14 E00C D700               stb     Position    ; The new position
15            ; Now do the deed
16 E00E A686               lda     a,x         ; Get relevant pattern from table
17 E010 B79000             sta     Output      ; Send it to the motor
18 E013 3517               puls    a,b,x,cc    ; Get old register contents back
19 E015 39                 rts                 ; and return
20            ;
21            ; This is the table of stepper codes
22 E016 0306C009
             STEP_TABLE: .byte   0011b, 0110b, 1100b, 1001b
23                          .end
```

Table 5.37: The stepper driver.

Example 5.30

In a canning factory, tins of peas on a conveyer belt continually pass through a tunnel oven, where the peas are cooked and sterilized; as shown in the diagram. Photocell/light beam detectors are used to sense tins, both entering and leaving the oven. The output of these sensors are logic 1 when the beam is broken.

You are asked to design an interrupt-driven interface suitable for this system. A buzzer is to be sounded if the number of tins in the oven exceeds four, indicating that a spillage has occurred.

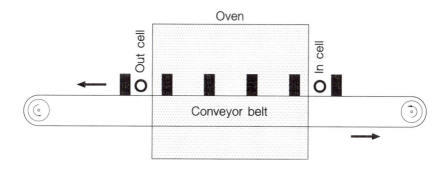

Figure 5.49: The pea-canning system.

Solution

Two D flip flops are provided, each acting as an interrupt flag for the photocells. Open-collector buffers driven by these flags give a composite interrupt signal activating the MPU's $\overline{\text{IRQ}}$ pin. When the MPU responds and enters the interrupt service routine (ISR), it can determine which cell sent the request by reading the state of these interrupt flags through the conventional 2-bit input port, B1 B2.

The buzzer could be activated through a 1-bit output port, as in Fig. 5.47. However, the RS latch, shown here, is a viable alternative; requiring two decoder lines, one to turn the buzzer On and the other for Off. The data on the bus is irrelevant for the buzzer operation.

The software detailed in Table 5.38 is split into four routines. The background routine simply sets up a stack area (we have assumed RAM from 0000h–1FFFh), turns the buzzer Off and clears the global variable **Count**. After this the MPU waits for an interrupt, which can either come from an in-going or out-going can. On return from the interrupt service routine, the can count is checked to see if it is over four. Depending on the outcome of this test, the buzzer is either turned On or Off. The main routine then returns to again wait for an interrupt. In practice this simple loop would be replaced by other more productive tasks. After all, a major reason for using interrupts is that the processor is too busy doing other things to poll interfaces. In this case, the overrange test and alarm routine would be implemented in the ISR itself.

The ISR reads the input port and determines which bit is set. There are three possible scenarios. If bit 7 is High, then the in-cell requested service. Bit 6 signals

```
 1                          .processor m6809
 2                  ;*****************************************************************
 3                  ;* Oven safety routine alarms when number of cans in oven >=4  *
 4                  ;* Uses IRQ to sense cans going into and out of the oven        *
 5                  ;*****************************************************************
 6                          .define Cell_state = 9000h, Buzz_on   = 9001h,
 7                                  Buzz_off  = 9002h, Cancel_in = 9003h,
 8                                  Cancel_out = 9004h, Count = 0000h
 9                  ; Main (background) routine
10 E000 10CE2000MAIN:      lds     #2000h        ; Set up System stack
11 E004 B69002            lda     Buzz_off      ; On Reset turn buzzer off
12 E007 0F00              clr     Count         ; and zero can count
13 E009 3CEF    MLOOP:    cwai    #1110111      ; Clear I mask and wait for interrupt
14                  ; When a can passes a sensor go to interrupt service routine
15                  ; On return, check for overrange
16 E00B 9600              lda     Count         ; Get can count
17 E00D 8105              cmpa    #5            ; Test for less than 5
18 E00F 2405              bcc     ALARM         ; IF yes THEN sound the alarm
19 E011 B69002            lda     Buzz_off      ; ELSE turn buzzer Off
20 E014 20F3              bra     MLOOP         ; and wait for next can to pass
21 E016 B69001  ALARM:    lda     Buzz_on       ; Sounding the alarm
22 E019 20EE              bra     MLOOP         ; and wait for next can to pass
23                  ;*****************************************************************
24                  ;* Foreground interrupt service routine                        *
25                  ;*****************************************************************
26 E01B B69000  CAN:      lda     Cell_state    ; First find out if In or Out
27 E01E 2B0C              bmi     IN            ; Bit 7 is connected to the In cell
28 E020 48                lsla                  ; IF not set THEN check the Out cell
29 E021 2A10              bpl     CAN_EXIT      ; IF not set THEN a false alarm
30                  ; Service Out can
31 E023 0A00    OUT:      dec     Count         ; One more can out
32 E025 8D0D              bsr     DELAY         ; Delay awhile
33 E027 B69004            lda     Cancel_out    ; Lift In interrupt flag
34 E02A 2007              bra     CAN_EXIT      ; and exit
35                  ; Service In can
36 E02C 0C00    IN:       inc     Count         ; One more can in
37 E02E 8D04              bsr     DELAY         ; Delay awhile
38 E030 B69003            lda     Cancel_in     ; Lift Out interrupt flag
39                  ; The exit
40 E033 3B      CAN_EXIT: rti
41                  ;*****************************************************************
42                  ;* Delay for around 0.6s to avoid possible flicker from the    *
43                  ;* photocells (rather like switch bounce) causing xple events  *
44                  ;*****************************************************************
45 E034 8EFFFF  DELAY:    ldx     #0ffffh
46 E037 301F    D_LOOP:   leax    -1,x          ; Decrement
47 E039 26FC              bne     D_LOOP        ; to zero
48 E03B 39                rts
49                  ;*****************************************************************
50                  ;* This is the 6809's vector table                             *
51                  ;*****************************************************************
52                  VECTOR:  .org   MAIN+1ff8h   ; 1FF8h on from 0E000h is FFF8h
53 FFF8 E01B              .word   CAN           ; Put address CAN in the IRQ vector
54 FFFA 00000000          .word   [2]           ; Go on to FFFEh, the Reset vector
55 FFFE E000              .word   MAIN          ; Put in the address MAIN for Restart
56                          .end
57
```

Table 5.38: Pea-canning software.

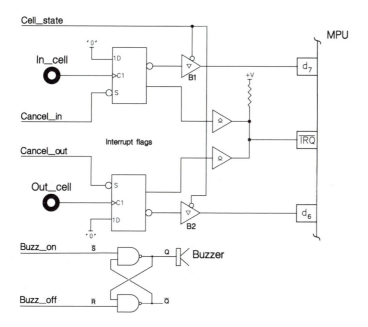

Figure 5.50: Oven safety hardware.

a request from the out-cell, and neither signals a false alarm (in a real situation there is likely to be other sources of interrupt). Rather than immediately clearing the appropriate interrupt flag, we have chosen to delay for a short time to reduce the possibility of a noisy signal retriggering. This is most likely at the edge of the shadow, especially where 50/60 Hz artificial illumination may contaminate the light beam. An out-going can decrements the variable **Count**, whilst an in-going can increments.

The delay subroutine is a simple decrement to zero loop called up by the ISR. As the value of the registers are restored at the end of the ISR, the **X register** (and any other registers) can be used with impunity.

Finally the IRQ and Reset vectors are set up using the command .org MAIN + 1FF8h and .word directive. The former moves the origin (org) to the address **MAIN** (E000h here) plus 1FF8h, i.e. FFF8h. The starting address of the ISR is the label **CAN** (E01Bh in the listing) and the pseudo instruction .word CAN puts this value into FFF8:9h (.word is a double .byte). Skipping two words takes us up to FFFEh. To ensure a Reset to the start of the background program, the address **MAIN** is inserted here at FFFE:Fh. We assume here a ROM between E000h–FFFFh; typically a 2764 EPROM.

In a practical system there probably would be a numerical display showing the aggregate of cans (four was a ridiculous value, chosen for illustrative purposes only) in the oven; some means of resetting to a non-zero value after a jam, and some signal in the (unlikely) event of a sub-zero count being computed.

Example 5.31

The intelligence of the letter sorter of Fig. 3.34 is to be implemented using a MPU. Show how the four photocells and four solenoids could be interfaced and design a suitable software circuit.

Solution

Based on the specification, we can use a single PIA port as our interface, with four lines programmed as inputs and four as outputs. This gives the configuration shown in Fig. 5.51(a).

The software algorithm is described in Fig. 5.51(b). Essentially, after the rising edge of the object detector cell **A**, one of four actions occur, depending on the state of the size-sensing cells **B C D**. The loop is not completed until the object completely passes cell **A**, giving a falling edge.

```
 1                               .processor m6809
 2                 ;*********************************************************
 3                 ;* Letter sorting routine, using a PIA to interface      *
 4                 ;* the four photocells and four size-solenoids           *
 5                 ;*********************************************************
 6                         .define DATA_A = 9000h, DDR_A = 9000h, CONTROL_A = 9001h
 7                 ; First setup the PIA
 8 E000 7F9001 MAIN:     clr      CONTROL_A  ; Make CR_2 to access DDR_A
 9 E003 860F             lda      #00001111b ; Make Port_A I I I I O O O O
10 E005 B79000           sta      DDR_A
11 E008 8604             lda      #00000100b ; Now change over from DDR_A
12 E00A B79001           sta      CONTROL_A  ; to I/O Data register_A
13                 ; DO forever
14                 ; Wait for envelope to activate cell A
15 E00D 7D9000 WAIT_4_1: tst      DATA_A     ; Look for a logic 1
16 E010 2AFB             bpl      WAIT_4_1   ; from cell A
17 E012 8D24             bsr      DELAY      ; When it comes DO a debounce delay
18 E014 B69000           lda      DATA_A     ; before reading cells A-D
19 E017 2AF4             bpl      WAIT_4_1   ; Check that cell A still logic 1
20                 ; IF cell B set, THEN must be extra long envelope
21 E019 C608             ldb      #00001000b ; Make solenoid pattern for extra-long
22 E01B 48               lsla                ; Shift cell pattern over once
23 E01C 2B09             bmi      OUTPUT     ; IF cell B THEN output solenoid pattern
24                 ; ELSE IF cell C active, THEN must be long envelope
25 E01E 54               lsrb                ; Create solenoid pattern for long
26 E01F 48               lsla                ; Shift cell pattern over once again
27 E020 2B05             bmi      OUTPUT     ; IF cell C THEN output solenoid pattern
28                 ; ELSE IF cell D active, THEN must be medium envelope
29 E022 54               lsrb                ; Create solenoid vector for medium
30 E023 48               lsla                ; Shift cell pattern over once again
31 E024 2B01             bmi      OUTPUT     ; IF cell D THEN output solenoid pattern
32                 ; ELSE must be short envelope
33 E026 54               lsrb                ; Create solenoid pattern for short
34 E027 F79000 OUTPUT:   stb      DATA_A     ; Activate solenoid
35                 ; Wait for envelope to pass cell A
36 E02A 7D9000 WAIT_4_0: tst      DATA_A     ; Look for a logic 0
37 E02D 2BFB             bmi      WAIT_4_0   ; from cell A
38 E02F 8D07             bsr      DELAY      ; When it comes DO a debounce delay
39 E031 7D9000           tst      DATA_A     ; IF cell A is still logic 0
40 E034 2AD7             bpl      WAIT_4_1   ; THEN wait for the next envelope
41 E036 20F2             bra      WAIT_4_0   ; ELSE try again for cell A = 0
42                 ; This is the short delay subroutine
43 E038 8E3000 DELAY:    ldx      #3000h     ; Delay parameter gives approx 0.1s delay
44 E03B 301F  DLOOP:     leax     -1,x       ; Decrement
45 E03D 26FC             bne      DLOOP      ; until zero
46 E03F 39               rts
47                        .end
```

Table 5.39: Software to sort envelopes by size.

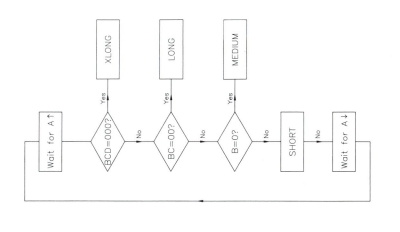

(b) Software algorithm

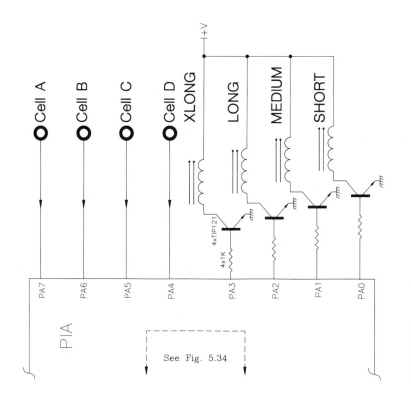

(a) PIA-based hardware

Figure 5.51: Letter sorting.

The listing of Table 5.39 firstly initializes the PIA by sending the pattern 00001111b to Data Direction register_A, making the upper four lines inputs and the lower four outputs.

Monitoring bit 7 is accomplished using the TST instruction. TeST IF MINUS OR ZERO sets the N flag if this bit is logic 1; causing the Conditional Branch of step 16 to fail and operation to pass into the main body of the loop. A short delay at this point helps avoid any false triggering if the light-beam break is not clean, in an analogous way to switch bounce (see Example 4.27). If cell **A** is still set, then a series of three tests are now made by progressively shifting the bits representing the cells **B**, **C** and **D** into the MSB, where the Conditional Branch BMI can redirect processing to the output routine. At the same time the solenoid activation vector, which is a single 1, is moved in sequence from 00001000b (solenoid XLONG) → 00000100b (LONG) → 00000010b (MEDIUM) → 00000001b (SHORT). Which of these vectors is sent to the solenoids depends on the outcome of this series of bit tests.

Finally we must wait until the envelope sense cell returns to zero, before repeating the loop. This is done in a similar manner to the logic 1 transition in steps 36–40. A short delay is once again used to avoid any false triggering.

We have assumed that the MPU has nothing else to do except monitor this process. If this is not the case, cell **A** can be used to activate a PIA handshake input, which will set bit 6 or 7 of the Control register. This in turn can be used to send an interrupt to the MPU.

Example 5.32

A certain dentist's surgery has two treatment rooms, **A** and **B**. Each room has a call switch (SW1A and SW1B in Fig. 5.52(a)) linked to a control box in the receptionist's office. This contains a 6809 MPU-based circuit interfaced to these remote call switches, two local cancel switches on the box (labelled SW2A and SW2B), two different colored lamps (LA and LB) and one common buzzer.

The operating specification is as follows:

1. Any dentist may press his/her switch to alert the receptionist. At the office the appropriate lamp will light and the common buzzer will sound for nominally one second.

2. The receptionist's lamp will remain lit until the appropriate local cancel switch is pressed.

Solution

The hardware interface for this project is relatively straightforward. The four switches are directly connected to the handshake lines as shown in the diagram. Three Port B lines are used as outputs to drive the two lamps and one buzzer.

Some thought needs to be taken with the software. The algorithm shown in Fig. 5.52(b) keeps the responses to the two dentists completely separate. Isolating the paths reduces the chance of interaction between the two sequences.

The PIA is configured in lines 4–10 to recognize negative-going edges on the four handshake lines, with CA2 and CB2 as inputs. On this basis, the initial wait loop simply repetitively tests bit 7 of the two Control registers until one of the dentists

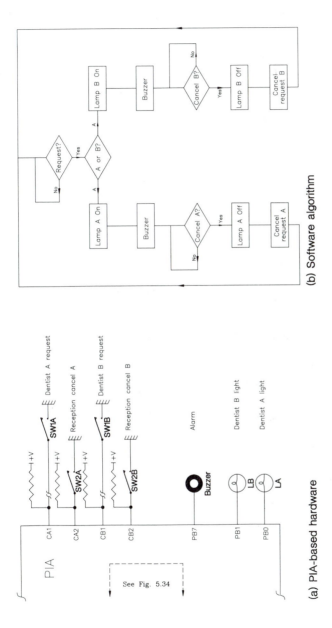

(a) PIA-based hardware

(b) Software algorithm

Figure 5.52: The dentists' annunciator.

requests the next patient. In this case, the corresponding bit 7 goes to logic 1.
When tested (step 12), this appears as a negative and the loop is exited either to
path A or path B as requested.

Both paths are similar. Three Port B lines have been programmed as outputs
and are used to turn the buzzer on (active-Low) and the appropriate lamp. After
entering a nominal 1-second delay subroutine, the buzzer is turned Off and the
software enters a polling loop waiting for the receptionist to respond and cancel the
call. There is no simple test for bits other than 7 (i.e. TST), so the contents of the
entire Control register_A are fetched and all bits ANDed out except bit 6. If the
result is zero, then the process is repeated until the receptionist hits the button and
brings bit 6 to 1. The lamp is then turned Off.

```
 1                            .processor m6809
 2                            .define DATA_A = 9000h, CONTROL_A = 9001h, DDR_B = 9002h,
 3                                    DATA_B = 9002h, CONTROL_B = 9003h
 4 E000 8604    MAIN:     lda  #00000100b   ; CA1 & CA2 set to be -ve edge triggered
 5 E002 B79001            sta  CONTROL_A
 6 E005 7F9003            clr  CONTROL_B     ; Access into DDR_B
 7 E008 8683             lda  #10000011b    ; to make lines PB7, PB1 & PB0 outputs
 8 E00A B79002            sta  DDR_B
 9 E00D 8604             lda  #00000100b    ; CB1 & CB2 set to be -ve edge triggered
10 E00F B79003            sta  CONTROL_B
11                   ; Now monitor SW1A and SW1B for a request for the next patient
12 E012 7D9001 WAIT_LOOP: tst  CONTROL_A   ; Bit7 of CONTROL_A set
13 E015 2B22             bmi  DENTIST_A     ; IF yes THEN dentist A requesting
14 E017 7D9003            tst  CONTROL_B    ; ELSE try dentist B
15 E01A 2AF6             bpl  WAIT_LOOP     ; IF not THEN repeat the poll loop
16                   ; Dentist B's code
17 E01C 867D   DENTIST_B: lda  #01111101b  ; First turn on the buzzer and lamp
18 E01E B79002            sta  DATA_B
19 E021 8D33             bsr  DELAY         ; Hang around for a second
20 E023 86FD             lda  #11111101b    ; and turn the buzzer Off
21 E025 B79002            sta  DATA_B
22 E028 B69003 BLOOP:    lda  CONTROL_B     ; Now interrogate the receptionist's
23 E02B 8440             anda #01000000b    ; cancel switch, ie bit6
24 E02D 27F9             beq  BLOOP         ; IF not yet pressed THEN try again
25 E02F 86FF             lda  #11111111b    ; ELSE turn Off lamp
26 E031 B79002            sta  DATA_B
27 E034 B69002            lda  DATA_B       ; Reset request B by doing a dummy read
28 E037 20D9             bra  WAIT_LOOP     ; and go back to start
29                   ; Dentist A's code
30 E039 867E   DENTIST_A: lda  #01111110b  ; First turn on the buzzer and lamp A
31 E03B B79002            sta  DATA_B
32 E03E 8D16             bsr  DELAY         ; Hang around for a second
33 E040 86FE             lda  #11111110b    ; and turn the buzzer Off
34 E042 B79002            sta  DATA_B
35 E045 B69001 ALOOP:    lda  CONTROL_A     ; Now interrogate the receptionist's
36 E048 8440             anda #01000000b    ; cancel switch, ie bit6
37 E04A 27F9             beq  ALOOP         ; IF not yet pressed THEN try again
38 E04C 86FF             lda  #11111111b    ; ELSE turn Off lamp
39 E04E B79002            sta  DATA_B
40 E051 B69000            lda  DATA_A       ; Reset request A by doing a dummy read
41 E054 20BC             bra  WAIT_LOOP     ; and go back to start
42                   ; This is the delay for a nominal second subroutine
43 E056 8EFFFF DELAY:    ldx  #0ffffh       ; Delay loop repeats 65,535
44 E059 301F   DLOOP:    leax -1,x          ; Decrement              5~
45 E05B 12               nop                ;                        2~
46 E05C 12               nop                ;                        2~
47 E05D 12               nop                ;                        2~
48 E05E 12               nop                ;                        2~
49 E05F 26F8             bne  DLOOP         ; until zero             4~
50 E061 39               rts
51                            .end
```

Table 5.40: Software for the annunciator.

Before returning, the pertinent Data register is read in order to cancel the o-riginal request, steps 27 and 40. Leaving the cancellation to the end reduces the chances of the dentists' switches bouncing on release and resetting the flag.

Although the separate path approach means that coincident requests are barred, when the system returns to its wait loop, the neglected request will be immediately processed. Connecting each dentists' switches to separate sides of the PIA means that a dummy read of a Control register only cancels flags due to that dentist alone. This would not be the case if, say, the request switches were connected to CA1 and CA2.

Example 5.33

A certain disco display is to be controlled by a microprocessor. The output display is a group of four differently colored lamps and the input is a microphone feeding an analog to digital converter. The objective of the system is to sequentially light each bulb, so that the repetitive rate is nominally proportional to the amplitude of the sound.

You are asked to design the interface and software which will:

1. Read the sound level from the microphone.

2. Use this data to create a variable delay.

3. Output the required pattern to the lamps.

Pertinent details are:

1. The microphone amplifier produces a voltage from 0 V for dead quiet to 2.55 V for ear-splitting shriek.

2. The A/D converter provides a conversion byte of 00h to FFh $(0 - 255)$ over an input voltage range 0 V to 2.55 V.

3. A lamp is turned On by a logic 0.

4. The minimum On time is to be 100 ms, with the maximum being 25.5 s (dead quiet).

Solution

The interface hardware is shown in Fig 5.53. It is similar to that described back in Fig. 5.35, but the sampling rate is software controlled. Four Port B lines are used to drive the lamps.

At the software level, a task analysis yields three phases:

1. A subroutine to read the sound level, say, 256 times and then to average the sum of the readings. This procedure smooths the sound level.

2. A subroutine to give a delay between 100 ms and 25.6 s over the full range of input parameter derived from task 1.

3. A main routine calling tasks 1 & 2 and generating the lamp pattern.

```
 1                              .processor m6809
 2                              .define DATA_A = 9000h, DDR_A  = 9000h, CONTROL_A = 9001h,
 3                                      DDR_B  = 9002h, DATA_B = 9002h, CONTROL_B = 9003h,
 4                                      Pattern= 0000h
 5                           ; First setup PIA
 6 E000 7F9001    DISCO: clr       CONTROL_A  ; Get into DDR_A
 7 E003 7F9000           clr       DDR_A      ; Make A/D port all inputs
 8 E006 862C             lda       #00101100b ; Set CA2 as output, auto pulse for SC
 9 E008 B79001           sta       CONTROL_A  ; CA1 triggers of -ve edge of BUSY
10 E00B 7F9003           clr       CONTROL_B  ; Access into DDR_B
11 E00E 860F             lda       #00001111b ; to make lines PB3-PB0 outputs
12 E010 B79002           sta       DDR_B
13 E013 8604             lda       #00000100b ; Change over from DDR_B to DATA_B
14 E015 B79003           sta       CONTROL_B
15                           ; This is the main routine, which repeats forever
16 E018 10CE2000   MAIN: lds       #2000h     ; Set up a stack for the subroutines
17 E01C 86EE      BEGIN: lda       #11101110b ; The initial pattern of the lamps
18 E01E 9700             sta       Pattern    ; Put it away for safekeeping
19 E020 BDE033           jsr       GET_IT     ; Get the averaged level n, back in A
20 E023 BDE04A   MLOOP: jsr       DELAY      ; Delay nx0.1 s
21 E026 9600             lda       Pattern    ; Get the current lamp pattern
22 E028 B79002           sta       DATA_B     ; Activate the lamps
23 E02B 1A01             orcc      #00000001b ; Set C flag
24 E02D 0900             rol       PATTERN    ; Shift pattern left with a 1 coming in
25 E02F 25F2             bcs       MLOOP      ; Repeat unless a 0 pops out
26 E031 20E9             bra       BEGIN      ; in which case initialize the pattern
27 ; *******************************************************************************
28 ; Subroutine getting the analog data.  Called by MAIN, returns with data in Acc.A*
29 ; *******************************************************************************
30 E033 5F       GET_IT: clrb                 ; Acc.B holds the loop count, set at 256
31 E034 8E0000           ldx       #0         ; Index_X holds the sum of k samples
32 E037 B69001 READ_LOOP: lda     CONTROL_A  ; A dummy read causes CA2 (SC) to pulse
33 E03A 7D9001 WAIT_LOOP: tst      CONTROL_A  ; Bit7 set yet by BUSY
34 E03D 2AFB             bpl       WAIT_LOOP  ; IF not yet THEN try again
35 E03F B69000           lda       DATA_A     ; ELSE go and get it
36                           ; Having got the data add it to the 16-bit partial sum
37 E042 3086             leax      a,x        ; A plus X to X, level + sum <- sum
38                           ; Check for 256 samples yet
39 E044 5C               incb                 ; One more sample
40 E045 26F0             bne       READ_LOOP  ; IF not wrapped around to 0 THEN sample
41 E047 1F10             tfr       x,d        ; ELSE move 16-bit data down to ACC.D
42 E049 39               rts                  ; which returns upper 8-bits in ACC.A
43 ; *******************************************************************************
44 ; Subroutine giving a delay = [A] times 100 ms                                 *
45 ; *******************************************************************************
46                           ; Do nothing for 100 ms while [A] > 00
47 E04A 8E2B67   DELAY: ldx       #11111d    ; The delay constant
48 E04D 301F     DLOOP: leax      -1,x       ; Decrement                 5~
49 E04F 26FC             bne       DLOOP      ; down to zero              4~
50 E051 4D               tsta                 ; 100 ms count down to zero
51 E052 2701             beq       DEXIT      ; IF yes THEN finished
52 E054 4A               deca                 ; ELSE another go
53 E055 39       DEXIT: rts
54                           ; Reset vector assuming a 2764 EPROM
55                              .org      DISCO+1FFEh; Takes us up to FFFEh
56 FFFE E000                   .word     DISCO      ; Puts in the 16-bit address DISCO
57                              .end
```

Table 5.41: Disco software.

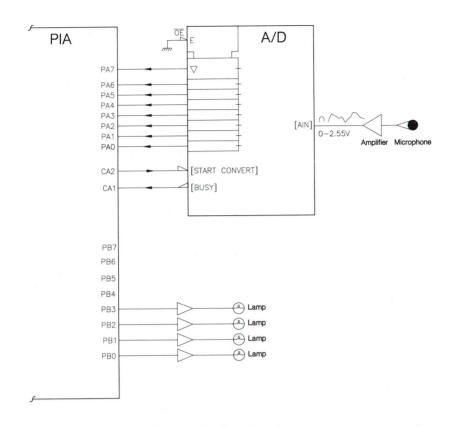

Figure 5.53: The disco display.

In the listing shown in Table 5.41, task 3 is given first. The PIA is configured in the appropriate manner so that the A/D's $\overline{\text{Start\_Convert}}$ is pulsed automatically whenever Data register_A is read. The A/D signals end of conversion by bringing $\overline{\text{Busy}}$ Low, and thus CA1 is set up to be ‾_ triggered. A stack is set up in step 16 to facilitate the subroutines.

The main routine proper, which repeats forever, simply calls up subroutines implementing task 1 and then task 2. A pattern is kept in a known RAM location and is shifted left once each pass through the loop. As only the lower four bits are of consequence, a trace bit is planted in bit 4, i.e. 11101110 in step 17. After four shifts, the marker 0 is shifted out and signals the end of the sequence. Setting the C flag and using the Rotate operation ensures that 1s are shifted in (lamp Off) rather than 0s (steps 23 and 24).

Task 1 is implemented by the subroutine **GET_IT**. This fetches the data 256 times, adding the 8-bit values to a 16-bit running total, held in Index register_X. On exit, this 16-bit grand total is transferred to the double Accumulator_D, with the upper eight in Accumulator_A. Effectively using this as the return value is equivalent to dividing by 256 (hence the choice of this constant!).

The final task is implemented by a simple parametized delay subroutine, as described in Example 5.9. The inner loop takes nine cycles, which at a 1 MHz clock rate is 9 μs. Going around 11,111 times gives just less than 100 ms, as desired. The delay parameter is passed in Accumulator_A, and varies from 00 to FFh (0 – 255). As this is tested *after* the inner loop (step 50), then there will be a corresponding 1 – 256 times 0.1 s delay before return.

Example 5.34

A MPU-based system is to be designed to act as a depth sounder for a boat. The MPU is to activate an ultrasonic sounder; sense the arrival of the echo and determine the distance between the hull of the boat and river bottom.

You are required to design the interface and software which will:

1. Activate the ultrasonic sounder and zero the time count.

2. Read the count when the echo comes back.

3. Hence determine the distance in meters.

4. Display the data as two 7-segment digits.

5. Sound an alarm buzzer if the distance is less than five meters.

6. Repeat 1 – 5 forever.

Details of the hardware are:

1. The ultrasonic sounder is pulsed by a ⌐_ edge and has a hull to sea-bottom range limited to a maximum of 99 meters.

2. The receiver gives a logic 0 when the echo is sensed.

3. The speed of sound in water is 366 meters/second.

4. The buzzer is active-Low.

5. A 183 Hz oscillator is available for timing purposes.

Solution

A possible hardware configuration is shown in Fig. 5.54. All four handshake lines are used. CA2 is configured as an output to activate the sounder whilst CB2 is likewise configured to operate the warning buzzer. The microphone/buffer state is sensed by CA1, set to respond to a ⌐_ . The timing oscillator uses CB1 to send an interrupt at a rate of 183 times per second; in essence recording the distance in 2-meter units between the ship's hull, river bottom and back again. This is equivalent to measuring the hull-bottom distance in meters, and obviates the need to divide by two if the more obvious 366 Hz timer were used.

As we have set up CA2 in the Automatic mode, reading Port A in step 18 pulses the sounder. We assume that the resulting 1 μs (at a 1 MHz clock rate) pulse is sufficiently long in the absence of any information to the contrary. At the same time we clear the count and error memory bytes.

When the echo returns, as sensed by CA1, the flag CRA_7 will be set. Thus we need only wait around in a loop polling for this event. But what if an echo never comes back, perhaps because a shoal of fish scatter and weaken the ultrasonic sound pulse? Then the system will lock up, forever waiting the return and never again pulsing the sounder. Thus the polling loop of steps 22 – 27 include a time-out down count, which restricts the number of unsuccessful tries to 5000. If the loop is exited via this mechanism, the variable **Error** is incremented to carry this fact back to the display routine.

While all this is going on in the background, the MPU is being interrupted at a rate of 183 times each second; each interrupt signalling a hull-bottom distance of one meter. The ISR servicing this interrupt, steps 60 – 66, (which we assume initiated

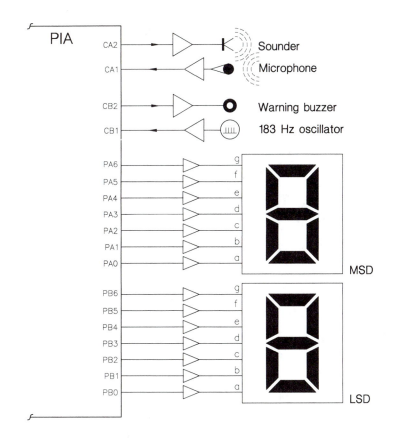

Figure 5.54: Depth sounding hardware.

via the $\overline{\text{IRQ}}$ input) simply increments the variable **Count**; which will subsequently be displayed by the background program after the echo returns. Two points need to be brought out. Firstly the count is kept in BCD, using the instruction **DAA** to facilitate the display format. A single byte can hold a 2-digit BCD number from 00 to 99. Secondly there is the possibility that the distance will exceed 99 meters. In that case the **Carry flag** will be set whenever one is added to 99 (giving 9Ah) and **DAA**ed. In this situation the variable **Error** is incremented to indicate a problem.

The display routine firstly checks **Error**, and if this is non-zero, diverts processing to the error handing routine. This simply blanks out both digits, steps 54 – 57. If there is no error, then **Count** is fetched and each BCD nybble converted to active-Low 7-segment code (steps 68 – 72) before being dispatched to the appropriate port. The subroutine **SVNSEG** is based on the code developed in Table 1.3.

```
 1                                .processor m6809
 2                                .define DATA_A = 9000h, DDR_A = 9000h, CONTROL_A = 9001h,
 3                                        DATA_B = 9002h, DDR_B = 9002h, CONTROL_B = 9003h,
 4                                        Count = 0000h, Error = 0001h
 5                        ; Initialization of PIA, global variables and interrupt system
 6  E000 7F9001 MAIN:           clr  CONTROL_A     ; Prepare to make Port A output
 7  E003 C6FF                   ldb  #11111111b
 8  E005 B79000                 sta  DDR_A
 9  E008 862C                   lda  #00101100b    ; CA2 Auto, pulses sounder on read
10  E00A B79001                 sta  CONTROL_A     ; CA1 -ve edge trig, no interrupt
11  E00D 7F9003                 clr  CONTROL_B     ; Access into DDR_B
12  E010 F79002                 stb  DDR_B         ; making Port_B all outputs
13  E013 863F                   lda  #00111111b    ; CB1 i/p from receiver setting IRQ,
14  E015 B79003                 sta  CONTROL_B     ; CB2 Man control of warning buzzer
15  E018 10CE2000               lds  #2000h        ; Set up stack for sub & interrupts
16  E01C 1A10                   orcc #00010000b    ; Clear I mask
17                        ; and so begin by pulsing the sounder
18  E01E B69000 START:          lda  DATA_A        ; Dummy read pulses snder, clr flags
19  E021 0F00                   clr  Count         ; Reset the duo-meter count
20  E023 0F01                   clr  Error         ; and error parameter
21                        ; Wait for the echo to come back
22  E025 8E1388                 ldx  #5000         ; Time-out parameter
23  E028 7D9001 ECHO_LOOP:      tst  CONTROL_A     ; Has the echo arrived back
24  E02B 2B06                   bmi  DISPLAY       ; IF yes THEN display distance
25  E02D 301F                   leax -1,x         ; ELSE one off time-out
26  E02F 26F7                   bne  ECHO_LOOP     ; IF time-out not ended THEN again
27  E031 0C01                   inc  Error         ; ELSE signal an error
28                        ; IF echo has come back THEN display Count unless Error indicated
29  E033 0D01 DISPLAY:          tst  Error         ; Check for an error
30  E035 2630                   bne  ERROR_HANDLER ; IF so THEN do not display
31  E037 9600                   lda  Count         ; ELSE get Count, distance to bottom
32  E039 1F89                   tfr  a,b           ; Copy into Acc.B
33  E03B 840F                   anda #00001111b    ; Blank out MSD
34  E03D BDE07D                 jsr  SVNSEG        ; Convert to 7-segment code
35  E040 B79002                 sta  DATA_B        ; and display it
36  E043 1F98                   tfr  b,a           ; Get Count again
37  E045 44                     lsra               ; Move MSD into lower four bits
38  E046 44                     lsra
39  E047 44                     lsra
40  E048 44                     lsra
41  E049 BDE07D                 jsr  SVNSEG        ; Convert to 7-segment code
42  E04C B79000                 sta  DATA_A        ; and display it
43  E04F C106                   cmpb #06h          ; Check for less than five meters
44  E051 250A                   bcs  WARNING_ON    ; IF yes THEN warning On!
45  E053 B69003                 lda  CONTROL_B     ; ELSE turn buzzer Off
46  E056 8A08                   ora  #00001000b    ; by sending a 1 to it
47  E058 B79003                 sta  CONTROL_B
48  E05B 20C1                   bra  START
49  E05D B69003 WARNING_ON:     lda  CONTROL_B     ; ELSE turn buzzer On
50  E060 84F7                   anda #11110111b    ; by sending a 0 to it
51  E062 B79003                 sta  CONTROL_B
52  E065 20B7                   bra  START
```

```
53                      ; Go here if an error has occurred
54 E067 86FF   ERROR_HANDLER:  lda  #11111111b    ; Error is tru, so blank out display
55 E069 B79000                 sta  DDR_A
56 E06C B79002                 sta  DDR_B
57 E06F 20AD                   bra  START         ; and repeat
58                      ; Now the foreground program which increments Count in BCD
59                      ; and signals an error if a carry is generated
60 E071 9600   DISTANCE:       lda  Count
61 E073 8B01                   adda #1             ; One more meter
62 E075 19                     daa                 ; in BCD
63 E076 2402                   bcc  NEXT           ; IF not 99 -> 100 THEN no error
64 E078 0C01                   inc  Error          ; ELSE signal an error
65 E07A 9700   NEXT:           sta  Count          ; Restore new Count
66 E07C 3B                     rti                 ; and return
67                      ; Now the 7-segment decoder, n sent in Acc.A, code returned likewise
68 E07D 8EE083 SVNSEG:         ldx  #TABLE         ; Point X to the base of the table
69 E080 A686                   lda  a,x            ; Get down the 7-segment equivalent
70 E082 39                     rts                 ; and return with it in Acc.A
71 E083 40     TABLE:          .byte 01000000b, 01111001b, 00100100b, 00110000b,
72                                   00011001b, 00010010b, 00000010b, 01111000b,
73                                   00000000b, 00011000b
74                      ; Finally the vectors
75                             .org  MAIN+1FF8h    ; The IRQ vector
76 FFF8 E071                   .word DISTANCE      ; Label DISTANCE is the ISR start
77 FFFA 00000000                .word [2]           ; Skip two unused vectors
78 FFFE E000                   .word MAIN          ; Start address of background prog
79                             .end
```

Table 5.42: Coding for the depth sounder.

5.5.2 Self Assessment Examples

SAE 5.1

Based on the table of Fig. 4.71(c), devise a subroutine that will continuously cycle through a 7-bit pseudo-random binary-number sequence; sending these numbers to a D/A converter located at address $9020h$. How would you modify your subroutine to return a single pseudo random digit in response to a 'seed' number passed to it?

SAE 5.2

Write a subroutine which will convert an 8-bit Gray-coded byte to its equivalent binary byte. Accumulator_A is to be used both to send and return the data. Hint: Use the Toggle algorithm illustrated in Example 4.28. How could you extend this process for words of greater than eight bits?

SAE 5.3

With the same analog conditions as outlined in Example 5.17, write a routine to continually read an incoming full-range sinusoid and output a full-wave rectified equivalent of maximum amplitude.

SAE 5.4

A hex keypad is connected to a PIA, as shown in Fig. 5.55. Write a subroutine that will scan the keyboard and return with the appropriate 4-bit code n in Accumulator_B *after* key n is pressed and then released. Your software should include code to eliminate keybounce both on closure and opening. Hint: Keep the row lines Low and monitor the column lines for a Low. Check which column is active and then scan the rows looking for the Y co-ordinate. Each X-line is worth four and Y-line is one.

What would happen with your code if two keys were simultaneously pressed; known as roll-over? How could you extend the concept to an 8 × 8 keyboard? What additional logic would be necessary to interrupt the MPU whenever a key was pressed, rather than polling waiting for activity?

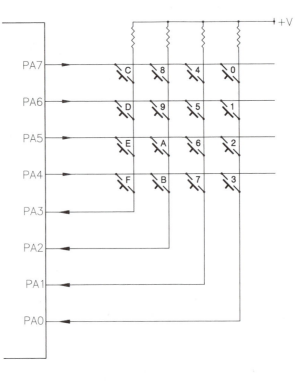

Figure 5.55: Interfacing a keypad to a MPU.

SAE 5.5

Keyboard encoding is a standard task, and as such specific hardware peripheral interface devices are available to take the processing load off the MPU. The 74C922 keypad encoder shown in Fig. 5.56 is typical of these. It incorporates all the logic to encode an array of 16 switches into natural 4-bit binary code. The switches are normally arranged in a 4 × 4 matrix, and sequentially scanned in the manner described in SAE 5.4. Internal pull-up resistors are provided on key inputs. The circuit automatically debounces the switch by delaying decoding according to the value of C_1. The scanning rate is determined by C_2 on an internal oscillator. Note the symbology used to indicate these non-logic connections —✕— .

A Data_AVailable (DAV) output signals a keyboard entry, and returns Low only when the key is released; even if another switch has been closed in the meantime.

In this case DAV will return High to indicate acceptance of this second key, giving 2-key roll-over. Internal latches store the last entry made, even after the key has been released.

The outputs are tri-state; allowing direct connection to the data bus of a microprocessor. Show how you could interface the 74C922 to the 6809 MPU using $\overline{\text{OE}}$ to enable the device and DAV to poll for a keypress. Based on your configuration, write an equivalent subroutine to that of SAE 5.4.

A better approach to keyboard handling is obtained if the 74C922 is used to generate an interrupt when a key is closed. Show how you would use DAV to do this and write a suitable interrupt service routine. What would be the advantages using this technique?

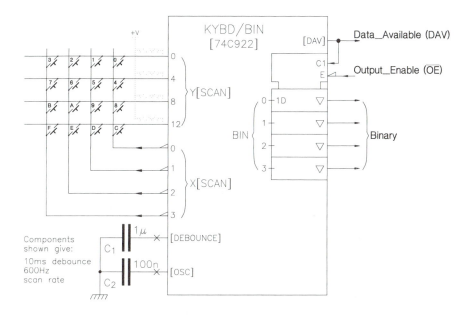

Figure 5.56: The 74C922 16-keypad encoder.

SAE 5.6

Interfacing digital electronics to the analog world invariably introduces noise into the signal, even if there was none there before. One of the simplest filtering algorithms to enhance the signal to noise ratio is digital smoothing. This technique involves generating a composite value in which each point is replaced by an average of itself with its nearest neighbours, i.e. post samples.

The waveform shown to the left of Fig. 5.57 has a noise blip situated at its 5th sample ($n = 5$). The smoothed version is the equivalent with each point generated according to the formula:

$$\mathcal{F}(n) = (0.25)A_{n-2} + (0.5)A_{n-1} + (0.25)A_n$$

Write a subroutine reading one sample from a A/D converter and returning with the composite value. Remember that the last two samples will have to be stored somewhere and updated each time the subroutine terminates.

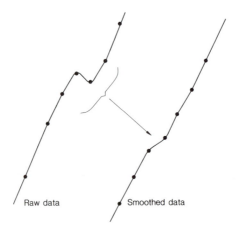

Figure 5.57: Three-point smoothing.

SAE 5.7

Based on the subroutine developed in Example 5.26, write a routine that will rotate the stepper-motor rotor through one complete 360° circle. The motor has a 9° mechanical step and maximum stepping rate of 200 steps per second.

SAE 5.8

It is quite feasible to use a parallel port as a serial input or output, by using a suitable delay routine between bit changes. For example the early Apple computers used a PIA rather than a UART.

Using a 6821 PIA handshake line 1, write a subroutine to serially transmit an 8-bit byte passed in Accumulator_A. The data is to be transmitted preceded by a Low start bit, LSB first, and terminated by a High stop bit. The transmit rate is 300 baud.

SAE 5.9

A certain photocopier has a replicate facility whereby up to 256 originals placed in hopper A are copied on blank paper held in hopper B. The number is entered by the operator on a keypad, with keys labelled 0 – 9 and Start, Reset. You may assume the latter are simply re-labelled keys E and F in Fig. 5.55. The user enters the number from 1 to 256 and presses Start. If a mistake is made, the Reset key enables another entry to be made and also acts as an abort command if copying is actually in progress.

The copying involves turning On the motor which extracts paper from hopper A, labelled Blank_load and waiting for the blank paper to actuate a microswitch when it gets to a predetermined point called Blank_loaded_point. The motor is then turned Off and the Original_load motor turned On. When the original arrives at its commencing point, it triggers the Original_load_point microswitch and the relevant motor turned Off.

With both sheets of paper in their correct position, two separate conveyer motors called Copy_A and Copy_B are switched On and the copy action commences. When the copy process is complete, the original and copy sheets will be found in their appropriate output bins, triggering their respective microswitches Copy_A_over and Copy_B_over on their trailing edge. Before the cycle is repeated the machine must delay for 10 ms.

Show how you might interface these handshake signals and keyboard to a microprocessor and write a routine to sequence the four motors in the appropriate manner. What additional facility might you expect to be incorporated in a practical machine?

SAE 5.10

A cassette tape recorder is interfaced to a MPU-controlled system via a PIA connected as follows:

Inputs			Outputs		
PA0	$\cdots$	Write_Enable	PB0	$\cdots$	Record
PA1	$\cdots$	Left_end_stop	PB1	$\cdots$	Rewind
PA2	$\cdots$	Right_end_stop	PB2	$\cdots$	Fast Forward
PA3	$\cdots$	Cassette_present	PB3	$\cdots$	Play
PA7	$\cdots$	Data_in	PB4	$\cdots$	Stop
			PB7	$\cdots$	Data_Out

All signals are active-High and have their normal meaning; however, there are a few points to note. PA0 will be true if the write-protect tab is left on the cassette. PA1 will be High if the tape has been wound to its left extremity and PA2 likewise to its right. Note that the motor will still run until turned Off (PB4).

Data leaving the PIA from PB7 is modulated so that it can be recorded onto tape. The converse is also true, so that data can be read off the tape and presented in its baseband binary form directly readable at PA7.

1. Write a subroutine which will rewind the tape to its start when a cassette is loaded, and leave with all motors stopped.

2. Write a subroutine which will advance the tape for ten seconds, to ensure that the tape leader has passed the recording/playback head. Exit this subroutine with all motors stopped.

3. Write a subroutine which will transmit all data stored in a tape data buffer at memory locations 2000h − 2FFFh in series out through the PIA to the tape recorder. You may assume a subroutine **OUTCH** as in Example 5.23, which sends this data in asynchronous serial mode at 300 baud.

4. Write a main routine to initialize the PIA and then call up the above subroutines so that the tape is rewound, then wound past the leader and make the recording. The tape is then rewound. How long would it take to complete this exercise?

SAE 5.11

A MPU-based system is to control a shortwave radio receiver. This receiver has a voltage-controlled oscillator which has a linear frequency span of $3.5 - 3.755$ MHz for a voltage range of $0 - 1$ volt. You are asked to design the interface and software which will perform the control and display functions.

The 4-digit 7-segment display will show the frequency to a resolution of 1 kHz from 3500 through 3755, and will allow the operator to scan up and down the frequency scale. The scanning operation is controlled via two button switches, marked **UP** and **DOWN**. The frequency will change in steps of 1 kHz each 100 ms as long as the appropriate button is depressed.

SAE 5.12

Light-controlled pedestrian crossings in the UK (Pelican crossings) obey the following mode of operation (see Examples 3.12 & 4.33):

1. The sequence of lights is initiated when a Cross_request signal has been received and at least nominally two minutes has elapsed since the last cycle. Any request arriving before the end of this period is stored and processed after this time.

2. After the request has been granted, the lights operate according to the sequence:

GREEN   (standby)
AMBER   (3 seconds)
RED   (15 seconds)
FLASHING AMBER   (10 seconds - five flashes)
GREEN   (back to standby)

Design a suitable hardware and software circuit. You may assume a 1 μs machine cycle.

References

[1] Noyce, R.N.; A History of Microprocessor Development at Intel, *IEEE MICRO*, **1**, no. 1, Feb. 1981, pp.8–21.

[2] Garetz, M.; Evolution of the Microprocessor, *BYTE*, **10**, no. 9, Sept. 1985, pp.209–215.

[3] Comer, D.J.; Digital System Design: State Machine versus Microprocessor Controller, *IEEE Transactions on Education*, **E-30**, no. 2, May 1987, pp.102–106.

[4] von Neumann, J. et al.; Preliminary Discussions of the Logical Design of an Electronic Computing Instrument, *US Army Ordinance Department Report*, 1946. Reprinted in Bell, C.G. and Newell, A. (eds.), *Computer Structures: Readings and Examples*, McGraw-Hill, 1971, pp.92–119.

[5] Lewis, D.R.; Microprogramming, *Electronic Design*, **21**, no. 17, 16th Aug. 1973, pp.58–63.

[6] Hedges, T.M.; Replacing Hardwire Logic with Microcode, *Electronics*, **51**, no. 23, 9th Nov. 1978, pp.125–129.

[7] Cahill, S.J.; *Designing Microprocessor-Based Digital Circuits*, Prentice-Hall, 1985.

[8] Fraser, D.A. et al.; *Introduction to Microprocessor Engineering*, Ellis Horwood, 1985, Chapter 3.

[9] Ritter, T and Boney, J.; A Microprocessor for the Revolution: The 6809, *BYTE*, **4**, part 1, no. 1, Jan. 1979, pp.14–42; part 2, no. 2, Feb. 1979, pp.32–42; part 3, no. 3, Mar. 1979, pp.46–52.

[10] Waklerly, J.F.; *Microcomputer Architecture and Programming: The 68000 Family*, Wiley, 1989, Chapter 16.

[11] Loveday, G.C. and Brighouse, B.D.; *Microprocessors in Engineering Systems*, Pitman, 1987.

[12] van de Goor, A.J.; *Computer Architecture and Design*, Addison-Wesley, 1989, Section 4.1.

[13] Cahill, S.J.; *Digital and Microprocessor Engineering*, Ellis Horwood, 1st ed., 1981, Section 5.2.

[14] Bartee, T.C.; *Digital Computer Fundamentals*, 5th ed., McGraw-Hill, 1981, Section 6.16.

[15] Cahill, S.J.; *The Single Chip Microcomputer*, Prentice-Hall, 1987, Section 1.2.

[16] Yourdon, E.; *Techniques of Program Structure and Design*, Prentice-Hall, 1975, Section 3.4.

[17] Maurer, W.D.; Subroutine Parameters, *BYTE*, **4**, no. 7, July 1979, pp.226–230.

[18] Kilian, M.; Highs and Lows of Parameter Passing, *BYTE*, **10**, no. 11, Nov. 1985, pp.151–158.

[19] Gilmour, P.S.; Caveat Tester, *Embedded Systems Programming*, **4**, no. 7, July 1991, pp.58–65.

[20] Waklerly, J.F.; *Microcomputer Architecture and Programming: The 68000 Family*, Wiley, 1989, Section 9.4.2.

[21] Motorola application note AN-865; *The MC6809/MC6809E SYNC Instruction*.

[22] Catt, I. et al.; *Digital Hardware Design*, MacMillan, 1979, Chapter 4.

[23] Hoeschele, D.F. Jr.; *Analog-to-Digital/Digital-to-Analog Conversion Techniques*, Wiley, 1968, Section 5.2.

[24] Clayton, G.G.; *Data Converters*, MacMillan, 1982, Sections 3.4–3.7.

[25] Cahill, S.J.; *C for the Microprocessor Engineer*, Prentice-Hall, 1994, Section 12.3.

[26] Motorola application note AN-866; *Vectoring by Device using Interrupt Sync Acknowledge with the MC6809/MC6809E*.

[27] Gilmore, J. and Huntington, R.; Designing with the 6820 Peripheral Interface Adapter, *Electronics*, **49**, no. 26, 23rd Dec. 1976, pp.85–86.

[28] Ganssle, J.G; VCO-based Sensors, *Embedded Systems Programming*, **4**, no. 6, June 1991, pp.77-80.

[29] Cahill, S.J.; *Digital and Microprocessor Engineering*, Ellis Horwood, 1st ed., 1981, Section 5.3.

[30] Fronheiser, K.; *Device Operation and System Implementation of the Asynchronous Commumication Interface Adapter*, Motorola Applications Note AN-754.

[31] Lenk, J.D.; *Handbook of Data Communications*, Prentice-Hall, Chapter 3, 1984.

[32] Lenk, J.D.; *Handbook of Data Communications*, Prentice-Hall, Chapter 1, 1984.

[33] Starnes, T.W.; Design Philosophy Behind Motorola's MC68000; Part 1: A 16-bit Processor with Multiple 32-bit Registers; Part 2: Data Movement, Arithmetic, and Logic Instructions; Part 3: Advanced Instructions, *BYTE*, **8**, no. 4, April 1983, pp.70–92; no. 5, May 1983, pp.342–367; no. 6, June 1983, pp.339–349.

[34] Cahill, S.J.; *C for the Microprocessor Engineer*, Prentice-Hall, 1994, Section 3.2.

[35] Cahill, S.J.; *The Single Chip Microcomputer*, Prentice-Hall, 1987.

[36] Giacomo, P.; A Stepping Motor Primer; Part 1: Theory of Operation; Part 2: Interfacing and Other Considerations, *BYTE*, **4**, no. 2, Feb. 1979, pp.90–105; no. 3, March 1979, pp.142–149.

Chapter 6

110

Computer-Aided
Engineering

Within a few years following the introduction of the first commercial electronic computers, programs were being used to aid in the development of applications software packages. This reduced the tedium and error rate in coding routines in the native machine code of the target hardware. High-level symbolic languages, themselves a software package, insulated the programmer from the underlying hardware structure, and rapidly led to large and highly sophisticated software structures.

This 'bootstrap' process, whereby software tools beget better software tools, was paralleled by a growth in computer power, storage capacity and dramatic fall in the cost of computing. Coupling this newly available computing power with graphics terminals led to the extensive use of **computer-aided design (CAD)** packages in the 1960s, particularly in the aerospace industry. Computer-based techniques specifically targeted to solving engineering problems, as opposed to, say, generating patterns for the textile industry, are often known as **computer-aided engineering (CAE)**. Both expressions are in common use.

Even restricted to the electronics industry, the scope of CAE is huge. From aiding the engineers ingenuity (the terms engineer and ingenious share the same Latin root *ingenium* — as one who begets ingenious contrivances), through project scheduling, electronic design, PCB and ASIC layout, testing, manufacture, quality control, goods inward, and documentation. The abbreviation **CADMAT** for computer-aided design manufacturing and testing, is sometimes used to describe this gamut of CAE packages.

Within the limited objectives of this text, we will pick two areas which relate to topics involving the design of digital systems, both of which have been covered in previous chapters. The first of these involves the conversion of a combinational or sequential specification to a programmable logic device (PLD), typically a PAL or PLE/ROM. The second of these is the use of software aids in producing code for a microprocessor-based system. We have already made use of an assembler package in Chapter 5 to translate from mnemonics to machine code without looking at the process in any depth. Here we look at just what an assembler does, and other tools that generate, test and program code for this significant area of digital technology.

Before beginning this material, it should be noted that CAE packages are commercial products, and as such all have their own driving rules. Rather than use abstract examples, I have utilized real-world packages. This of course involves a certain amount of discussion which is only relevant to that particular product. I have used these examples to illustrate the principles and typical features available for the various processes, but you will have to adapt the source code to suit the syntax of the actual package you will be using yourself.

6.1   Programmable Logic

The process of personalizing a blank PLD to implement a logic specification has been covered in Sections 3.3 & 4.5. The objective there was to examine the various architectures and manually deduce the fuse pattern that would generate the correct input/output relationship. The end point was either a stylized diagram showing the location of intact fuses (eg. see Fig. 3.65) or a tabular representation giving essentially the same information (eg. see Fig. 3.69).

For a project of any size, manual generation of the fuse pattern is tedious and error prone. A slight change in specification may require an extensive rework. However, the fun really starts when the fuses are actually blown; observing that one device may require feeding several thousand identification numbers without error into the PLD programmer! Clearly this is not an attractive proposition and is a prime candidate for automation.

The overall objective of this section is to examine the role of CAE in PLD design. Before going into the details we need to outline the process of going from concept to programmed device. The key phases in this transformation are:

1. Transfer the design out of the engineer's head into a form which can be manipulated by CAE tools. This will require defining the logic in the form of Boolean equations, truth tables or state tables; using the appropriate syntax.

2. Generate AND-OR equations that will fit into the appropriate PLD architecture.

3. Check that the outcome will truly implement the specified behavior.

4. Map equations to a fuse plot in a form that will be recognized by the PLD programmer.

5. Blow device and verify that the requisite fuse states have been altered.

This progression is shown in Fig. 6.1. Starting at the right of the diagram, the designer enters the strategy into the computer using a text editor/word processor. In some cases a schematic capture program is used instead to enter the logic in the form of a circuit diagram, although this is only really useful where an existing design is to be retrofitted into a PLD. The resulting file is known as a **source file**.

The source file is the input to the CAE program. On this basis, the appropriate equations and implementing fuse patterns will be deduced. The output is a file containing the list of fuse states, 0 or 1, in a format understood by the PLD

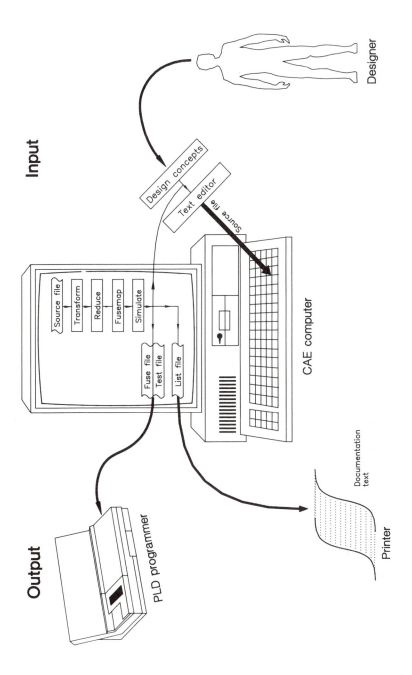

Figure 6.1: The PLD design process.

programmer (top right). This file will usually contain test vectors, allowing the programmer to check the device once it is programmed. A second file shown is the **listing file**, used for documentation purposes only. It normally gives the original source code, resulting equations, fuse plot, fuse file and test vectors.

Before a device is programmed, most CAE PLD packages allow the designer to reverse engineer the resulting equations. A sequence of test patterns can be entered and the resulting response monitored for adherence to the original specification. This stimulation process really checks out the designer's ability to transcribe his or her thoughts into the form and syntax demanded by the CAE PLD package, rather than the correctness of the translation.

We will explore the various input formats available on a typical CAE PLD package in Section 6.1.1, using a series of combinational and sequentially-based examples. Here we are particularly interested in the outcome in the form of equations and fuse plot. In Section 6.1.2, we will examine the simulation and programming facilities in more detail.

After reading this section you will:

- Appreciate the overall transformation from source code to fuse file.

- Have seen the equation, table, stream, map and state transition table techniques of source entry.

- Understand the role of simulation in the CAE process.

- Understand the JEDEC file syntax, including test vectors.

6.1.1 PLD Software

CAE software of whatever origin requires the designer to symbolize the various Boolean and arithmetic operators. As the input device is invariably a standard computer keyboard, these symbols are likely to be somewhat stylized. Unfortunately they also differ from package to package. For example PALASM (for PAL ASeMbler, see page 238) uses *, + and / for AND, OR and NOT respectively [1]. Thus before looking at an actual example it will be useful to summarize the main symbols used in the OrCAD/PLD compiler[1] The OrCAD/PLD program which is utilized for the examples in Section 6.1, is one of a suite of packages allowing schematic capture of electronic diagrams (OrCAD/SDT), their use to layout printed circuit boards (OrCAD/PCB), to simulate the electrical behavior of these circuits (OrCAD/VST) and of course to program PLDs. The OrCAD/PLD package can be used on its own without a schematic front-end, which is the the manner of its usage here.

The left-hand column of Table 6.1 allows a simple ASCII keyboard to be used as an input device. Thus the expression $\mathcal{F} = \text{A}\cdot\text{B}+\overline{\text{C}}$ can be entered as F = A <and> B <or> C<not>. However, a standard keyboard allows the use of the shorter symbols shown in the next column. Now our expression can be entered as F = A&B#C' or F = A&B#!C. Some operations have alternative shorthand symbols. Thus we can use a suffix apostrophe for <not> or a prefix ! for <notp>. These alternatives are given to the right of Table 6.1. However, even where the alternatives are used in the

---

[1]OrCAD Corp., 3175 N.W. Aloclek Drive, Hillsboro, Oregon 97124, U.S.A. and ARS Microsystems Ltd. Herriad Business Centre, Alton Road, Basingstoke, Hants, RG25 2PN, U.K.

source file, the resulting documentation file invariably reverts back to the preferred symbols.

`<and>`	`&`	AND	eg. `A&B`
`<or>`	`#`	OR	eg. `A#B`
`<not>`	`'`	NOT	eg. `A'`; also prefix `!`, eg. `!A`
`<xor>`	`##`	EOR	eg. `A##B`; also `$`
`<nand>`	`&'`	NAND	eg. `A&'B` or `A!&B`, also `(A&B)'` or `!(A&B)`
`<nor>`	`#'`	NOR	eg. `A#'B` or `A!#B`, also `(A#B)'` or `!(A#B)`
`<enor>`	`##'`	ENOR	eg. `A##'B`; also `A!$B`
`<asgn>`	`=`	Assigns an expression to an output signal, eg. `f = A#B`	
`<eq>`	`==`	Is equivalent to, i.e. $\equiv$, eg. IF `A==1` THEN DO something	
`<ne>`	`/=`	Is not equivalent to, i.e. $\neq$; also `!=` or `<>`	
`<le>`	`<=`	Is less than or equivalent to, i.e. $\leq$, eg. IF `A<=B` THEN DO something	
`<lt>`	`<`	Is less than, eg. IF `A<B` THEN DO something	
`<leq>`	`>=`	Is greater than or equal to, i.e. $\geq$, eg. IF `A>= B` THEN DO something	
`<lt>`	`>`	Is greater than, eg. IF `A<B` THEN DO something	
`<add>`	`+`	Addition	eg. `F=A+B`
`<sub>`	`-`	Subtraction	eg. `F=A-B`
`<mult>`	`*`	Multiplication	eg. `F=A*B`
`<div>`	`/`	Divide	eg. `F=A/B`
`<mod>`	`\`	Modulus	eg. `n=(n+1)\10`
`<RightArrow>`	`->`	Maps to	eg. `DCBA -> WXYZ`
`<Tristate>`	`??`	3-state	eg. `F=(A&B)??W`
	`~`	Range	eg. `A[5~0]`; also `..`, eg. `A[5..0]`

Table 6.1: Common operators.

Most of the operations are self evident. The `<mod>` operator constrains the range of a variable or expression to a base. Thus if we have a 4-bit variable n which is being incremented, then it will cycle $0,1,2,\ldots,14,15,0,1,\ldots$; i.e. modulus 16. If, say, we require a modulus 10 count, then the count will be $0,1,2,\ldots,7,8,9,0,1,\ldots$. The expression for this modulus 10 incrementation would be `n = (n+1)\10`. The `<Tristate>` operator allows logic to enable a PLD output 3-state buffer. If the internal AND-OR logic is represented by W, and this has to be gated to the output pin F whenever both the variables A and B are 1, then we have the expression `F = (A&B)??W`.

Finally there is some confusion between the assignment operator `=` and equivalence operator `==`. The former *changes* the value of the left-hand variable to that of the right-hand expression. Thus `H = A+6` will assign the value of H to that of the current value of A plus six. The equivalence function `H == A+6` is true if the current value of H is the same as that of six more than A, otherwise false. False is defined as 0 and true as 1. Thus, the rather weird expression `n = (n+1) + (n==12)` means that the new value of n is the original value of n plus 1 plus an extra one if the original value happened to be 12. Thus a count would go $0,1,2,\ldots,11,12,14,15$.

Now for some examples.

Example 6.1

For our first case study we will rework the simple logic of the automobile warning
and hazard lights, first introduced in Example 2.6, to fit into a 16L8 PAL.

Solution

The designer's source file for this problem is reproduced in Table 6.2. Each active
line is preceded by a |, which if omitted is treated as a comment. Comments can
be added to an active line following a second |, as in lines 9&10. Keywords such as
in:, out: and Active-high: are always suffixed by a full colon. We will describe
the syntax of this file using a line by line analysis:

```
| PAL16L8       in:(H,R,L,F), out:(R_Lights, L_Lights)
|
| Title: "Car hazard lights"
        "S.J. Cahill V.20/08/92"
|
| Active-high: H,R,L,F
| Active-low:  R_Lights, L_Lights
|
| R_Lights = (!H&R&!L&F)#(H&!R&!L&F)#(H&!R&L&F)#(H&R&!L&F) | Right lights are p5,9,11,13
| L_Lights = (!H&!R&L&F)#(H&!R&!L&F)#(H&!R&L&F)#(H&R&!L&F) | Left  lights are p3,9,11,13
```

Table 6.2: Source code for the automobile hazard warning logic.

Line 1 The label PAL16L8 identifies a library component describing the features of
    this device, such as pin numbers, type of output etc., to the compiler. The
    keyword in: lists the parenthesized input variables, as does out: for the
    output variables. These variables will automatically be assigned pins, begin-
    ning, for this device, at pin 1 and working up to pin 11 (see Fig. 3.65). If the
    designer wishes to manually assign, then instead of using in: and out:, then
    each pin number is followed by the variable name; as shown in Example 6.2.
    The 16L8 has six input/output lines, and if these are to be utilized, then the
    keyword io: should be used.

Line 3 An optional formal title is given here using the keyword title:. This is
    followed by one or more phrases in quotation marks. This title will appear
    automatically in all files subsequently generated by the compiler.

Lines 6&7 All signals must be assigned as active-High or active-Low using the
    keywords Active-high: and Active-low: respectively. If only one of these
    keywords are used, then any omitted literals are assumed to be the opposite.
    With variables allocated in this way, inversion should not be used in any
    defining equations. Thus, an output Z that is to go Low whenever A is High,
    B and C are Low, i.e. $\overline{Z} = A \cdot \overline{B} \cdot \overline{C}$, should be defined as Active-Low: and
    subsequently entered as Z = A & B' & C'.

Lines 9&10 These are the defining equations. They are extracted in the normal
    way from the truth table in Fig. 2.9(b).

With the source text complete, it is saved as a file: in this case TABLE 6_1.PLD, and can be used at any time as the input file to the compiler. As can be seen from Fig. 6.1, after the compiler digests the source file it produces several output files. The fuse and test files will be discussed in the next section. The listing file is purely for documentation purposes. This file TABLE 6_1.LST which is produced by our example source file of Table 6.2 is reproduced verbatim in Table 6.3.

There are five sections to this file. The first of these, lines 1–10, is simply a reproduction of the original source file. More interesting are lines 11–16. These are the reduced equations that are to be actually implemented by the PAL:

$$R\_Lights \;=\; (H \cdot \overline{R} \cdot F) + (R \cdot \overline{L} \cdot F)$$
$$L\_Lights \;=\; (H \cdot \overline{L} \cdot F) + (\overline{R} \cdot L \cdot F)$$

Each output has two product terms ORed together. These are listed attached to the output signal name and are prefixed with the row number of the logic diagram of Fig. 3.65. Thus R_Lights is generated by rows 1 & 2, and L_Lights by rows 57 & 58.

The SIGNAL ASSIGNMENT section gives the pin numbers assigned to each signal and the column connected to each input (see Fig. 3.65). Each output lists the

```
OrCAD/PLD COMPILER  V1.20E 5/31/90  (Source file TABLE6_1)
| PAL16L8        in:(H,R,L,F), out:(R_Lights, L_Lights)
|
| Title: "Car hazard lights"
|
| Active-high: H,R,L,F
| Active-low:  R_Lights, L_Lights
|
| R_Lights = (!H&R&!L&F)#(H&!R&!L&F)#(H&!R&L&F)#(H&R&!L&F) | Right lights are p5,9,11,13
| L_Lights = (!H&!R&L&F)#(H&!R&!L&F)#(H&!R&L&F)#(H&R&!L&F) | Left  lights are p3,9,11,13
RESOLVED EXPRESSIONS (Reduction 2)
Signal name      Row   Sum-of-product terms
R_Lights          1    H  R' F
                  2    R  L' F
L_Lights         57    H  L' F
                 58    R' L  F
SIGNAL ASSIGNMENT
                                       Rows
 Pin    Signal name   Column    --------------   Activity
                                Beg Avail Used
  1.    H                2       -    -    -      High
  2.    R                0       -    -    -      High
  3.    L                4       -    -    -      High
  4.    F                8       -    -    -      High
  5.    -               12       -    -    -
  6.    -               16       -    -    -
  7.    -               20       -    -    -
  8.    -               24       -    -    -
  9.    -               28       -    -    -
 11.    -               30       -    -    -
 12.    L_Lights         -       56   8    2      Low    (Three-state)
 13.    -               26       48   8    0             (Three-state)
 14.    -               22       40   8    0             (Three-state)
 15.    -               18       32   8    0             (Three-state)
 16.    -               14       24   8    0             (Three-state)
 17.    -               10       16   8    0             (Three-state)
 18.    -                6        8   8    0             (Three-state)
 19.    R_Lights         -        0   8    2      Low    (Three-state)
                                    ----  ----
                                     64    4   (6%)
I200  No fatal errors found in source code.
I201  No warnings.
```

Table 6.3: The resulting listing file (*continued next page*).

```
FUSE MAP FOR PAL16L8
      0  2  4  6  8 10 12 14 16 18 20 22 24 26 28 30
   0  -- -- -- -- -- -- -- -- -- -- -- -- -- -- -- --
  32  -x x- -- -- x- -- -- -- -- -- -- -- -- -- -- --
  64  x- -- -x -- x- -- -- -- -- -- -- -- -- -- -- --
  96  xx xx xx xx xx xx xx xx xx xx xx xx xx xx xx xx
 128  xx xx xx xx xx xx xx xx xx xx xx xx xx xx xx xx
 160  xx xx xx xx xx xx xx xx xx xx xx xx xx xx xx xx
 192  xx xx xx xx xx xx xx xx xx xx xx xx xx xx xx xx
 224  xx xx xx xx xx xx xx xx xx xx xx xx xx xx xx xx
 256  xx xx xx xx xx xx xx xx xx xx xx xx xx xx xx xx
 288  xx xx xx xx xx xx xx xx xx xx xx xx xx xx xx xx
 320  xx xx xx xx xx xx xx xx xx xx xx xx xx xx xx xx
 352  xx xx xx xx xx xx xx xx xx xx xx xx xx xx xx xx
 384  xx xx xx xx xx xx xx xx xx xx xx xx xx xx xx xx
 416  xx xx xx xx xx xx xx xx xx xx xx xx xx xx xx xx
 448  xx xx xx xx xx xx xx xx xx xx xx xx xx xx xx xx
 480  xx xx xx xx xx xx xx xx xx xx xx xx xx xx xx xx
 512  xx xx xx xx xx xx xx xx xx xx xx xx xx xx xx xx
 544  xx xx xx xx xx xx xx xx xx xx xx xx xx xx xx xx
 576  xx xx xx xx xx xx xx xx xx xx xx xx xx xx xx xx
 608  xx xx xx xx xx xx xx xx xx xx xx xx xx xx xx xx
 640  xx xx xx xx xx xx xx xx xx xx xx xx xx xx xx xx
 672  xx xx xx xx xx xx xx xx xx xx xx xx xx xx xx xx
 704  xx xx xx xx xx xx xx xx xx xx xx xx xx xx xx xx
 736  xx xx xx xx xx xx xx xx xx xx xx xx xx xx xx xx
 768  xx xx xx xx xx xx xx xx xx xx xx xx xx xx xx xx
 800  xx xx xx xx xx xx xx xx xx xx xx xx xx xx xx xx
 832  xx xx xx xx xx xx xx xx xx xx xx xx xx xx xx xx
 864  xx xx xx xx xx xx xx xx xx xx xx xx xx xx xx xx
 896  xx xx xx xx xx xx xx xx xx xx xx xx xx xx xx xx
 928  xx xx xx xx xx xx xx xx xx xx xx xx xx xx xx xx
 960  xx xx xx xx xx xx xx xx xx xx xx xx xx xx xx xx
 992  xx xx xx xx xx xx xx xx xx xx xx xx xx xx xx xx
1024  xx xx xx xx xx xx xx xx xx xx xx xx xx xx xx xx
1056  xx xx xx xx xx xx xx xx xx xx xx xx xx xx xx xx
1088  xx xx xx xx xx xx xx xx xx xx xx xx xx xx xx xx
1120  xx xx xx xx xx xx xx xx xx xx xx xx xx xx xx xx
1152  xx xx xx xx xx xx xx xx xx xx xx xx xx xx xx xx
1184  xx xx xx xx xx xx xx xx xx xx xx xx xx xx xx xx
1216  xx xx xx xx xx xx xx xx xx xx xx xx xx xx xx xx
1248  xx xx xx xx xx xx xx xx xx xx xx xx xx xx xx xx
1280  xx xx xx xx xx xx xx xx xx xx xx xx xx xx xx xx
1312  xx xx xx xx xx xx xx xx xx xx xx xx xx xx xx xx
1344  xx xx xx xx xx xx xx xx xx xx xx xx xx xx xx xx
1376  xx xx xx xx xx xx xx xx xx xx xx xx xx xx xx xx
1408  xx xx xx xx xx xx xx xx xx xx xx xx xx xx xx xx
1440  xx xx xx xx xx xx xx xx xx xx xx xx xx xx xx xx
1472  xx xx xx xx xx xx xx xx xx xx xx xx xx xx xx xx
1504  xx xx xx xx xx xx xx xx xx xx xx xx xx xx xx xx
1536  xx xx xx xx xx xx xx xx xx xx xx xx xx xx xx xx
1568  xx xx xx xx xx xx xx xx xx xx xx xx xx xx xx xx
1600  xx xx xx xx xx xx xx xx xx xx xx xx xx xx xx xx
1632  xx xx xx xx xx xx xx xx xx xx xx xx xx xx xx xx
1664  xx xx xx xx xx xx xx xx xx xx xx xx xx xx xx xx
1696  xx xx xx xx xx xx xx xx xx xx xx xx xx xx xx xx
1728  xx xx xx xx xx xx xx xx xx xx xx xx xx xx xx xx
1760  xx xx xx xx xx xx xx xx xx xx xx xx xx xx xx xx
1792  -- -- -- -- -- -- -- -- -- -- -- -- -- -- -- --
1824  -- x- -x -- x- -- -- -- -- -- -- -- -- -- -- --
1856  -x -- x- -- x- -- -- -- -- -- -- -- -- -- -- --
1888  xx xx xx xx xx xx xx xx xx xx xx xx xx xx xx xx
1920  xx xx xx xx xx xx xx xx xx xx xx xx xx xx xx xx
1952  xx xx xx xx xx xx xx xx xx xx xx xx xx xx xx xx
1984  xx xx xx xx xx xx xx xx xx xx xx xx xx xx xx xx
2016  xx xx xx xx xx xx xx xx xx xx xx xx xx xx xx xx
      Legend:  x fuse intact
               - fuse open
      180 fuses open of 2048 total.
OrCAD/PLD
Type:      PAL16L8
Title:     Car hazard lights
*
QP20* QF2048* QV1024*
F0*
L0000  11 11 11 11 11 11 11 11 11 11 11 11 11 11 11 11 *
L0032  10 01 11 11 01 11 11 11 11 11 11 11 11 11 11 11 *
L0064  01 11 10 11 01 11 11 11 11 11 11 11 11 11 11 11 *
L1792  11 11 11 11 11 11 11 11 11 11 11 11 11 11 11 11 *
L1824  11 01 10 11 01 11 11 11 11 11 11 11 11 11 11 11 *
L1856  10 11 01 11 01 11 11 11 11 11 11 11 11 11 11 11 *
C1787*
I202  8/20/92  1:02 pm  (Thursday)
I203  Memory utilization 960/24171 (4%)
I204  Elapsed time 22 seconds
```

Table 6.3: (*continued*). The resulting listing file.

starting row number, how many rows are available and how many are used. Thus the L_Lights OR gate is driven by product rows from 56 up to 63, of which 2 out of 8 are used. Pins 13–18 are input/output, and have both columns and rows listed. In all there are 64 product rows available in the PAL16L8, with four used. A total of 4% of the fuses are reported blown.

The fuse map is a representation of the logic diagram of Fig. 3.65, showing the state of each of the 2048 fuses in the form of 64 rows. This is purely diagrammatic. Notice that the fuse rows 0 and 1792 are completely blown. These are the enable product terms for the output 3-state buffers; on by default.

The final section is a version of the fuse map understood by the PLD programmer. This JEDEC file is discussed in more detail in the next section. Here it can be seen that it comprizes rows corresponding to used product lines. A altered fuse is represented by a logic 1, and a logic 0 represents intact. Rows with all fuses intact are not included, as no programming is necessary. Six rows are shown; the four output product terms and the two 3-state buffers.

All this is finally reported as taking 22 seconds to compile (on a rather slow 16 MHz 80386-based personal computer)!

Finally before leaving this example; what if we required active-High outputs? All we need do is replace lines 6 & 7 by the statement: `Active-high: "all"` (or even omit all references to activity). The compiler then produces the equations:

```
RESOLVED EXPRESSIONS (Reduction 1)

Signal name      Row    Sum-of-product terms

R_Lights'          1    H' R'
                   2    H' L
                   3    R  L
                   4    F'

L_Lights'         57    H' R
                  58    H' L'
                  59    R  L
                  60    F'
```

where the apostrophe suffix to the output signals indicates an active-Low generation by the AND-OR matrix; which will be cancelled by the inverting output buffers. In PALs with polarity selection, such as the 18P8 or 16V8 devices, the `Active-high:`/`Active-low:` directives simply alter the polarity fuse. The compiler will automatically try the inverted equations (with the appropriate polarity setting) if the first try does not fit the device.

Example 6.2

A certain 6809 MPU-based system has the following memory map [2]:

RAM   (60L256), 32 K-byte $0000h - 7FFFh$

PIA0	(6821),	digital I/O	$8000h - 8003h$
PIA1	(6821),	digital I/O	$8008h - 800Bh$
ACIA0	(6551),	serial I/O	$8010h - 8013h$
ACIA1	(6551),	serial I/O	$8018h - 801Bh$
PIT	(6840),	timer	$8020h - 8027h$
A/D	(ZN439),	analog input	$8028h$
D/A0	(ZN558),	analog output	$8080h$
D/A1	(ZN558),	analog output	$8081h$
ROM	(27256),	32K EPROM	$9000h - FFFFh$

The circuit has already been laid out, and is shown in Fig. 6.2. Determine a suitable set of AND-OR equations to implement this specification and to fit the 16L8 PAL.

Solution

The circuit illustrated in Fig. 6.2, uses the PAL to act as a primary decoder, distinguishing between RAM, EPROM, I/O range $8000h - 8028h$ and the two analog output devices. The PAL also generates a $\overline{R/W}$ signal which is used to disable the RAM's output buffers when doing a Write as well as for other unspecified purposes.

In the previous example we allowed the compiler to automatically assign pins to the signal list using the keywords in: and out:. Here the pins have been determined in advance by the circuit board. In this situation we force an assignment by following each pin number by the signal, as shown in lines 3–5. Thus 11: RW obliges the compiler to treat the signal R/W as input to the matrix at pin 11. Notice that the operator ~ can be used to mark out a range of pins, eg. 1~9: means assign pins 1 up to 9 in order to the following signals. The outcome of this explicit assignment

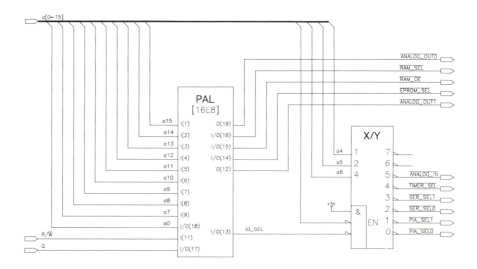

Figure 6.2: The PAL-based address decoder.

```
OrCAD/PLD COMPILER  V1.20E 5/31/90   (Source file TABLE6_3)
|PAL16L8   1~9:A[15~7],      12:ANALOG_OUT1, 13:IO_SEL,
|          14: EPROM_SEL, 15:RAM_OE,  16:RAM_SEL,    17:Q,
|          18: A0,          19:ANALOG_OUT0
|          Active-high:  A[15~7], A0, Q, RW
|          Active-low:   IO_SEL, EPROM_SEL, RAM_OE, RAM_SEL, ANALOG_OUT0, ANALOG_OUT1
|          Title:        "Address decoder"
|
|ANALOG_OUT0 = (A[15~7]   == 10000000100b) & (A0==0) & RW' & Q
|ANALOG_OUT1 = (A[15~7]   == 10000000100b) & (A0==1) & RW' & Q
|IO_SEL      = (A[15~12] ==   8h)                         | Address range 8XXXh
|EPROM_SEL   = ((A[15~12]== 1001b) # (A[15~13] == 101b) # (A[15~14] == 11b)) & RW'
|RAM_OE      = RW
|RAM_SEL     = (RW' & Q & A15') # (RW & A15')             | write or read
RESOLVED EXPRESSIONS (Reduction 1)
Signal name      Row    Sum-of-product terms
ANALOG_OUT0       1     A15' A14' A13' A12' A11' A10' A9  A8' A7' RW' Q  A0'
ANALOG_OUT1      57     A15' A14' A13' A12' A11' A10' A9  A8' A7' RW' Q  A0
IO_SEL           49     A15  A14' A13' A12'
EPROM_SEL        41     A15  A14  RW'
                 42     A15  A13  RW'
                 43     A15  A12  RW'
RAM_OE           33     RW
RAM_SEL          25     A15' RW
                 26     A15' Q
SIGNAL ASSIGNMENT
                                        Rows
  Pin   Signal name   Column    ---------------     Activity
                                Beg Avail Used
   1.    A15            2        -    -    -         High
   2.    A14            0        -    -    -         High
   3.    A13            4        -    -    -         High
   4.    A12            8        -    -    -         High
   5.    A11           12        -    -    -         High
   6.    A10           16        -    -    -         High
   7.    A9            20        -    -    -         High
   8.    A8            24        -    -    -         High
   9.    A7            28        -    -    -         High
  11.    RW            30        -    -    -         High
  12.    ANALOG_OUT1    -       56    8    1         Low      (Three-state)
  13.    IO_SEL        27       48    8    1         Low      (Three-state)
  14.    EPROM_SEL     23       40    8    3         Low      (Three-state)
  15.    RAM_OE        19       32    8    1         Low      (Three-state)
  16.    RAM_SEL       15       24    8    2         Low      (Three-state)
  17.    Q             10       16    8    0         High     (Three-state)
  18.    A0             6        8    8    0         High     (Three-state)
  19.    ANALOG_OUT0    -        0    8    1         Low      (Three-state)
                                ---- ----
                                 64    9   (14%)
```

Table 6.4: A PAL-based microprocessor address decoder.

is seen under the heading of SIGNAL ASSIGNMENT in Table 6.4.

The source equations implementing this specification are listed in lines 10–15. Unlike the purely Boolean relationships used in Example 6.1, these equations use a mixture of Boolean operators, the equality comparison operator == and the range operator ~. Indeed, any of the operators listed in Table 6.1 can be mixed in a defining equation. For example, line 9 states that ANALOG_OUT0 is active whenever the variables A_{15} – A_7 have the value $10000000100b$ AND A_0 is logic 0 AND R/$\overline{W}$ is logic 0 AND Q is logic 1. The only difficult equation here is that for the EPROM. The 27256 IC specified here would potentially cover the address range $8000h$ – $FFFFh$. However, we have to inhibit the range $8000h$ – $8FFFh$ to allow co-existence with the various I/O devices. Thus EPROM_OE is selected whenever $A_{15} A_{14} A_{13} A_{12}$ = $1001b$ ($9000h$ – $9FFFh$) or whenever $A_{15} A_{14} A_{13}$ = $101b$ ($A000h$ –$BFFFh$) or else when $A_{15} A_{14} = 11b$ (C000h – FFFFh). The whole is enabled whenever $R/\overline{W}$ is Low. An alternative statement is to say enable the EPROM whenever A_{15} is 1 and $A_{15} A_{14} A_{13} A_{12}$ is not equal to $1000b$, i.e. :

```
|EPROM_SEL = ((A15 == 1) & (A[15~12] == 1000b)') & RW'
```

The resolved pure Boolean AND-OR equations are shown in the normal way in the RESOLVED EXPRESSIONS section. The source equations could of course be entered in a similar manner at the start, but clarity of expression is an important attribute leading to a more dependable outcome, and better documentation. Good documentation is essential for software maintainability. The term maintainability is used in this context as the ability to update or adapt the software at some future date.

The first PLD packages simply converted (or assembled) source Boolean equations into analogous AND-OR equations in a form suitable for implementation by the target device. Such forms usually bear little resemblance to the original problem. For example, a counter is more naturally defined with a counting sequence, rather than entering equations, such as on page 331.

Using high-level entry forms closer to the problem specification, and thus further away from the underlying AND-OR structure, demands more from the CAE software. High-level PLD packages with this type of capability are known as **compilers** as opposed to PLD assemblers. This apes the terminology of microprocessor language translators, where assemblers give a 1:1 correspondence between source code and the underlying machine code, and compilers allow the use of abstract high-level language, see Section 6.2.

In combinational logic the most natural way of expressing the specified transfer function is the truth table. Most of our examples in previous chapters have begun with this construction. The OrCAD/PLD compiler uses two entry formats based on this approach; the Table: and Stream: constructs.

Example 6.3

Design a π generator to the specification of Example 2.38, using a 16V8 PAL.

Solution

The source code for our problem is reproduced in lines 1–26 of Table 6.5, which is part of the listing file. The 16V8 does not have dedicated output lines, so the output signals are assigned pins using the io: (input/output) keyword. Lines 8–26 are the defining truth table. The keyword Table: is followed by the list of input variables, the maps-to symbol and the output signals, i.e. Table: D,C,B,A -> W,X,Y,Z. The table itself is enclosed in braces and lists each input combination mapping to the required output. Thus line 25 states 15 -> 0011b, which says that the output response to an input $D\,C\,B\,A = 1111b$ (p_{15}) is $W\,X\,Y\,Z = 0011b$. Any base can be used for the input or output groups; I used decimal for the input (i.e. p-number) and binary (suffix b) for the output group. In this case an all-decimal notation would have been clearer, eg. line 25 becomes 15 -> 3.

The resulting equations are given in lines 29–44 in the normal way. A comparison with Fig. 2.49 shows that the equations are identical to those evaluated by hand using K-maps!

```
OrCAD/PLD COMPILER  V1.20E 5/31/90  (Source file TABLE6_2)
| PAL16V8        in:(D,C,B,A), io:(W,X,Y,Z)
|
| Title: " Pi generator to 15 decimal points"
|
| Active-high: "All"
|
| Table: D,C,B,A -> W,X,Y,Z  | Binary -> pi
| {
|          0  -> 0011b
|          1  -> 0001b
|          2  -> 0100b
|          3  -> 0001b
|          4  -> 0101b
|          5  -> 1001b
|          6  -> 0010b
|          7  -> 0110b
|          8  -> 0101b
|          9  -> 0011b
|         10  -> 0101b
|         11  -> 1000b
|         12  -> 1001b
|         13  -> 0111b
|         14  -> 1001b
|         15  -> 0011b
| }
I289  Complex GAL architecture selected.
RESOLVED EXPRESSIONS (Reduction 2)
Signal name      Row     Sum-of-product terms
W                  1      D'  C   B'  A
                   2      D   C'  B   A
                   3      D   C   A'
X                  9      D'  C   B'  A'
                  10      D'  C   B   A
                  11      D   C   B'  A
                  12      D   C'  A'
                  13      C'  B   A'
Y                 17      D'  C'  B'  A'
                  18      D'  C   B
                  19      D   B'  A
                  20      C   B   A
Z                 25      D'  C'  A
                  26      D   C
                  27      D   A'
                  28      B'
SIGNAL ASSIGNMENT
                                      Rows
  Pin    Signal name   Column   --------------   Activity
                                Beg Avail Used

  1.       -              2      -    -    -              (Clock)
  2.       D              0      -    -    -      High
  3.       C              4      -    -    -      High
  4.       B              8      -    -    -      High
  5.       A             12      -    -    -      High
  6.       -             16      -    -    -
  7.       -             20      -    -    -
  8.       -             24      -    -    -
  9.       -             28      -    -    -
 11.       -             30      -    -    -              (Enable)
 12.       -              -      56   8    0              (Three-state)
 13.       -             26      48   8    0              (Three-state)
 14.       -             22      40   8    0              (Three-state)
 15.       -             18      32   8    0              (Three-state)
 16.       Z             14      24   8    4      High    (Three-state)
 17.       Y             10      16   8    4      High    (Three-state)
 18.       X              6       8   8    5      High    (Three-state)
 19.       W              0       0   8    3      High    (Three-state)
                                     ----  ----
                                      64   16   (25%)
```

Table 6.5: Specifying the constant π using the table construction.

It can be quite laborious for long truth tables listing every possible input and its corresponding output, especially considering that in most cases the input is simply a count from 0 to 2^n. For these cases the OrCAD/PLD compiler provides a modified table construct called Stream.

Example 6.4

Repeat Example 6.3, but using a PLE5P8 PROM/PLE. This time the constant is to be generated to 31 decimal places, and an active-High output is to activate a right-hand decimal point.

Solution

The constant π to 31 decimal places is given as:

$$\pi = 3.141\ 592\ 653\ 589\ 793\ 238\ 462\ 643\ 383\ 279\ 5$$

and this is simply listed in lines 11 & 12 of Table 6.6. The **Stream:** construction, like **Table:**, has a header giving all n input variables mapped to output variables,

```
OrCAD/PLD COMPILER  V1.20E 5/31/90  (Source file TABLE6_5)
| PROM32B8     in:(E,D,C,B,A), out:(dp,W,X,Y,Z)
|
| Title: " Pi generator to 31 decimal points using a PLE5P8"
|
| Active-high: "All"
|
| Stream: E,D,C,B,A -> dp,W,X,Y,Z  | Binary -> pi
| {
|       10011b,1,4,1,5,9,2,6,5,3,5,8,9,7,9,3,
|          2 ,3,8,4,6,2,6,4,3,3,8,3,2,7,9,5
| }
SIGNAL ASSIGNMENT
 Pin     Signal name    Address   Data    Activity
                          bit      bit
  2.       E              4        -        High
  3.       D              3        -        High
  4.       C              2        -        High
  5.       B              1        -        High
  6.       A              0        -        High
 16.       -              -        0
 17.       -              -        1
 18.       -              -        2
 19.       Z              -        3        High
 20.       Y              -        4        High
 21.       X              -        5        High
 22.       W              -        6        High
 23.       dp             -        7        High
HEXADECIMAL OBJECT FILE
Addr   0  1  2  3  4  5  6  7  8  9  A  B  C  D  E  F
0000  98 08 20 08 28 48 10 30 28 18 28 40 48 38 48 18
0010  10 18 40 20 30 10 30 20 18 18 40 18 10 38 48 28
I202  8/30/92  9:06 pm  (Sunday)
I203  Memory utilization 455/25377 (2%)
I204  Elapsed time 20 seconds
```

Table 6.6: Illustrating the Stream construction.

with the data following inside braces. This data is simply a list of all possible 2^n output values.

In our example, the dp output is active at the same time as the initial 3, and I have listed this data point in binary (*1.0011b*, dp $= 1$ and W X Y Z $= 3$) to clarify the value given, and to show that number bases can be mixed. The decimal equivalent is 19.

Notice the library part number in line 3 is PROM32B8. This means that the target is a 32×8-bit word PROM, which is shown in the address (input) and data (output) pin allocation. This is followed by a listing of the entire contents of the programmed PROM/PLE, under the heading HEXADECIMAL OBJECT FILE. The periphery is the address (two rows of 16), with the stored data at the intersection of row/column. Thus the contents of, say, address 001Dh is 38h. Each of these data values is $\times 8$ those in the like stream position, as the 5-bit output has been assigned to $D_7 \ldots D_3$ with $D_2 D_1 D_0$ being 000b. Hence 38h is 56, which is stream data 7 (second digit from the end).

Specifying the behavior of sequential logic is more difficult than for combinational logic. In essence our descriptions in Chapter 4 involved state diagrams or state tables. These tabulated the response of the system in each of its states to all possible programmable inputs (i.e. stimuli). The simplest of these machines was the synchronous counter, which in its elementary form has no programmable inputs and thus has only one response in each state. We will use counters to begin our discussion here.

In using CAE software to configure our target PLD, we could of course derive the setting equations in the classical manner, following the path outlined in Section 4.3. These equations are then input in the same manner as in Example 6.1. However, most PLD packages are capable of deriving these equations on the basis of a state behavorial description, eg. a state table. Each package of course has its own way of doing this. The OrCAD/PLD product uses a map construction for counter-like machines, and a sophisticated procedural language for the more complex cases.

A **map** construction gives the relationship between the present state and the next (after clocking) state. This uses the keyword Map: with the relationships inside braces. For a standard 4-bit natural 8-4-2-1 synchronous counter the relationship is written as:

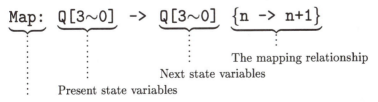

The mapping relationship

Next state variables

Present state variables

The identifying keyword

Following the Map: keyword are listed the input (present state) and output (next state) signals separated by the map arrow ->. In most cases the input and output variables $Q_3 Q_2 Q_1 Q_0$ (Q[3~0]) are the same. The actual relationship in braces says that any state n will become one more after the clock. The range of n is $0 \ldots 15$, as defined by the four state variables Q[3~0]. If we had wanted an 8-bit counter, then the state variables would have been Q[7~0] and n would have spanned the range $0 \ldots 255$ automatically. n will overflow back to zero, eg. $15 \rightarrow 0$ or $255 \rightarrow 0$, as appropriate to the modulo-16 or modulo-256 range. The variable character n must be used for map descriptions.

The map relationship can be rather more complex than simple incrementation (or decrementation), with conditional statements being attached. For example, a BCD counter could be described as:

```
Map: Q[3~0] -> Q[3~0] {
                        n -> n+1, n< 9
                        n -> 0,   n>=9
                      }
```

which states that the count should be incremented IF its state has not reached 9, ELSE go to state 0. Each IF statement is indicated by a comma and each ELSE as a new line (or space). This specification also covers the illegal states 10–15. The mapping relationship {n ->(n+1)\10} is similar using the modulus operator. The resulting count will still be $0 \ldots 9$ and repeat, but the illegal state response will be different. Can you deduce how?

This conditional facility allows information concerning programmable inputs to be entered. For example the following statement gives a 6-bit up/down counter with reset and parallel load facilities:

```
Map: Q[5~0] -> Q[5~0]
     {
       n->n+1,     Reset'& Load'& Up
       n->n-1,     Reset'& Load'& Up'
       n->0,       Reset & Up
       n->63,      Reset & Down
       n->D[5~0],  Reset'& Load
     }
```

which states that:

1. Increment IF both **Reset** AND **Load** are inactive and **Up** is active.

2. Decrement IF both **Reset** AND **Load** are inactive and **Up** is inactive.

3. If the count direction is up and **Reset** is active, then clear the count irrespective of the state of **Load**.

4. If the count direction is down and **Reset** is active, then preset the count to $1111111b$ irrespective of **Load**.

5. If **Load** is active and **Reset** is not, then make the counter state equal to the 6-bit parallel data $D_5D_4D_3D_2D_1D_0$, irrespective of the count direction.

Of course both reset and load facilities are synchronized by the clock.

```
OrCAD/PLD COMPILER  V1.20E 5/31/90  (Source file TABLE6_6)
| PAL16R4          in:(Reset, Up), out:Q[3~0], clock:Count
|                  Register:Q[3~0]
|
|                  Active-high: Up
|                  Active-low:  Reset, Q[3~0]
|                  Title:       "An elevator counter"
|
| Map: Q[3~0] -> Q[3~0]
| {
  * Up conditions
|                  n -> n+1, Reset' & Up & n/=12
  Increment if going up and not Reset and if not on the 12th floor
|                  n -> n+2, Reset' & Up & n==12
  Else skip the 13th floor
|
  * Down conditions
|                  n -> n-1, Reset' & Up' & n/=14
  Decrement if going down and not Reset and if not on 14th floor
|                  n -> n-2, Reset' & Up' & n==14
  Else skip 13th floor
|
  * Reset condition
|                  n -> 1, Reset
  If Reset active
| }
RESOLVED EXPRESSIONS (Reduction 1)
Signal name      Row   Sum-of-product terms
Q3                16   Reset' Up' Q3' Q2' Q1' Q0'
                  17   Reset' Up  Q3' Q2  Q1  Q0
                  18   Reset' Up' Q3  Q2
                  19   Reset' Up' Q3  Q0
                  20   Reset' Up  Q3  Q2'
                  21   Reset' Up  Q3  Q0'
                  22   Reset' Q3  Q2' Q1
                  23   Reset' Q3  Q1' Q0
Q2                24   Reset' Up' Q2' Q1' Q0'
                  25   Reset' Up  Q2' Q1  Q0
                  26   Reset' Up' Q2  Q1
                  27   Reset' Up' Q2  Q0
                  28   Reset' Up  Q2  Q0'
                  29   Reset' Q2  Q1' Q0
                  30   Reset' Q2  Q1  Q0'
Q1                32   Reset' Q3  Q2  Q1' Q0'
                  33   Reset' Up' Q1' Q0'
                  34   Reset' Up' Q1  Q0
                  35   Reset' Up  Q1' Q0
                  36   Reset' Up  Q1  Q0'
Q0                40   Up' Q1' Q0'
                  41   Up  Q1  Q0'
                  42   Q3' Q0'
                  43   Q2' Q0'
                  44   Reset
SIGNAL ASSIGNMENT
                                         Rows
 Pin    Signal name   Column        --------------    Activity
                                    Beg Avail Used
  1.     Count          -            -    -    -        High     (Clock)
  2.     Reset          1            -    -    -        Low
  3.     Up             4            -    -    -        High
  4.     -              8            -    -    -
  5.     -              12           -    -    -
  6.     -              16           -    -    -
  7.     -              20           -    -    -
  8.     -              24           -    -    -
  9.     -              28           -    -    -
 12.     -              30           56   8    0                 (Three-state)
 13.     -              26           48   8    0                 (Three-state)
 14.     Q0             23           40   8    5        Low      (Registered)
 15.     Q1             19           32   8    5        Low      (Registered)
 16.     Q2             15           24   8    7        Low      (Registered)
 17.     Q3             11           16   8    8        Low      (Registered)
 18.     -              6            8    8    0                 (Three-state)
 19.     -              2            0    8    0                 (Three-state)
                                         ---- ----
                                          64   25  (39%)
```

Table 6.7: The hotel elevator skip counter.

Example 6.5

A 14-storey hotel has floors labelled 1...12 & 14,15. No one likes staying in a room on the 13th floor! You are asked to design an up/down counter for the elevator that will skip state $1101b$ when going in either direction. A reset signal is generated when the elevator is at rest on the ground floor, and sensors midway between floors are used to clock this skip counter.

Solution

The mapping function shown in Table 6.7 states that:

1. The count is to be up if **Reset** is inactive, **Up** is active and the elevator is not coming from the 12th floor.

2. If the elevator is coming up from the 12th floor, then add two to skip 13.

3. If the elevator is going down, **Reset** is inactive and it is not coming from the 14th floor, then decrement the count.

4. Otherwise subtract two to skip the 13th floor.

5. If **Reset** is active, then reset the count to the 1st floor irrespective of all other conditions.

Adding an automatic reset facility means that any noise-induced malfunction will not be cumulative, and correct operation will be resumed each time the car reaches ground.

In the listing we have specified a 16R4 PAL as the target device. I have followed the `in:` and `out:` declarations by the keyword `Register:`, which tells the compiler that the signals `Q[3~0]` are the outputs of flip flops rather than combinational. I have also named the clock input **Count** by using the `clock:` keyword. The resulting equations directly follow the logic of the mapping function and fit comfortably into the PAL, using 39% of available rows (product terms). However, I did specify that `Q[3~0]` was active-Low to fit the output inverting buffers (see Fig. 4.52). The compiler was unable to derive equations for an active-High outcome. If this is desired, then a 16V8 device could be used with the same equations. Alternatively, for this specific example it would be possible to generate both active-Low and active-High outputs. How could this be done? Note that a mixture of entry formats, eg. equations and maps, can be used to facilitate this type of problem.

The map method of data entry can be used for sequential machines in general, but is best suited for counters, which by definition have the same relationship applying to the transition from all (or at least most) states; eg. increment, decrement, reset. A general sequential machine needs to be specified on a state-by-state basis. To facilitate this level of detail, all PLD compilers have a generalized textual state diagram entry format. In the OrCAD/PLD compiler this is called a **Procedure**.

To illustrate the syntax of a Procedure, consider the flow diagram of Fig. 4.56(b); which defines a sequential machine acting as a magnitude comparator on two streams of data X_1X_2. This could be described as follows:

```
|     Procedure: Reset, Q[1~0]
|     {
|         EQUAL.      Z1 = 1                        |Z1 active for equal
|                     X1 &X2'? -> GREATER           |IF X1 active THEN go to greater
|                     X1'&X2 ? -> LESS              |IF X2 active THEN go to less
|                              -> EQUAL             |ELSE still equal
|         GREATER.    Z2 = 1                        |Z2 active for greater
|                              -> GREATER           |Dead end until Reset
|         LESS.       Z3 = 1                        |Z3 active for less
|                              -> LESS              |Dead end until Reset
|     }
```

Following the keyword **Procedure:**, the first variable is always the reset signal (however named) and this is followed by the state variable range. The state transitions and outputs are then tabulated inside braces.

The left column lists the current state, with their names suffixed by a period. The compiler will automatically make a state assignment, with the first state listed always being made zero. Alternatively a manual assignment can be made by using state numbers in place of names (or names assigned using the **States:** keyword).

Following the state name or number is an optional condition for the indicated transition. Thus the statement X1&X2'? means IF X1=1 AND X2=0 THEN.... This condition is always suffixed by a ?. An alternative to this statement would be X[1~2]==10b?.

The transition itself uses the map symbol -> followed by the new (i.e. destination) state name. In this case -> GREATER — this state name does not have an appended period. Comments can be added in the normal way following a second |.

This example is a Moore machine, which by definition has an output simply as a function of the state. Any active output is simply listed in a line covered by the present state, usually in the same line as the state first appears; eg. LESS. Z3=1 means if in state LESS then make the Z_3 output active irrespective of the value of the stimuli inputs X_1X_2. The alternative to be used for a Mealy description is given in the next example.

Example 6.6

Repeat Example 4.32, but incorporating all logic in a single GAL16V8.

Solution

From the flow diagram of Fig. 4.66 we see that the car-park monitor has three states, called REST, IN and OUT; two stimuli inputs X_1 and X_2 (representing the two sensors), and two output variables Z_1 (for out) and Z_2 (for in). These are listed in the normal way at the top of Table 6.8 using the **in:**, **io:** and **Register:** keywords. In addition an input is utilized as Reset, and the Clock and Enable inputs named as CK and EN. Both Reset and EN inputs are declared active-Low, with the remainder being active-High by default.

The Procedure itself lists the three present states REST., IN. and OUT., followed by all possible transition paths; as shown in Fig. 4.66(b). This flow diagram describes a Moore machine, in which the outputs depend both on the present state

```
OrCAD/PLD COMPILER  V1.20E 5/31/90  (Source file TABLE6_7)
| GAL16V8        in:(X[1~2], Reset), io:(Q[1~0], Z[1~2]), clock:CK, enable:EN
|                Register: Q[1~0]
|                Active-low: Reset,EN
|
|                Title:       "A car-park monitor"
|
| Procedure: Reset, Q[1~0]
| {
|        REST. X1?                 -> IN  | Possible incoming car
|              X2?                 -> OUT | Possible outgoing car
|                                  -> REST| ELSE remain in this state
|
|        IN.   X1'&X2'?            -> REST| Both beams unbroken
|              X1 &X2'?            -> IN  | Intermediate case
|              X1'&X2 ?            -> IN  | Intermediate case
|              X1 &X2 ?(Z1=1 -> IN )| Signal ingoing car
|
|        OUT.  X1'&X2'?            -> REST| Both beams unbroken
|              X1 &X2'?            -> OUT | Intermediate state
|              X1'&X2 ?            -> OUT | Intermediate state
|              X1 &X2 ?(Z2=1 -> OUT)| Signal outgoing car
| }
STATE TABLE FOR Q
```

State Label	State Number		
	Decimal	Binary	Level
REST	0	00	LL
IN	1	01	LH
OUT	2	10	HL
(Alphabetical)			
IN	1	01	LH
OUT	2	10	HL
REST	0	00	LL

RESOLVED EXPRESSIONS (Reduction 3)

Signal name	Row	Sum-of-product terms
Q0	8	X2 Reset' Q1' Q0
	9	X1 Reset' Q1'
Q1	0	X1' X2 Reset' Q0'
	1	X1 Reset' Q1 Q0'
Z1	17	X1 X2 Reset' Q1' Q0
Z2	25	X1 X2 Reset' Q1 Q0'

SIGNAL ASSIGNMENT

Pin	Signal name	Column	Rows			Activity	
			Beg	Avail	Used		
1.	CK	-	-	-	-	High	(Clock)
2.	X1	0	-	-	-	High	
3.	X2	4	-	-	-	High	
4.	Reset	9	-	-	-	Low	
5.	-	12	-	-	-		
6.	-	16	-	-	-		
7.	-	20	-	-	-		
8.	-	24	-	-	-		
9.	-	28	-	-	-		
11.	EN	-	-	-	-	Low	(Enable)
12.	-	30	56	8	0		(Three-state)
13.	-	26	48	8	0		(Three-state)
14.	-	22	40	8	0		(Three-state)
15.	-	18	32	8	0		(Three-state)
16.	Z2	14	24	8	1	High	(Three-state)
17.	Z1	10	16	8	1	High	(Three-state)
18.	Q0	6	8	8	2	High	(Registered)
19.	Q1	2	0	8	2	High	(Registered)
			64	6	(9%)		

Table 6.8: Describing the car-park monitor using a procedure.

and on the stimuli (programmable) inputs X_1X_2. This is shown in our procedure by bracketing the appropriate transition with the corresponding output. Thus the line:

```
|   X1 & X2?      (Z1=1 -> IN)
```

means that IF both X_1 and X_2 are active when in state IN., THEN make Z_1 active and the next state still will be IN. This is shown in Fig. 4.66(b) by the notation alongside the sling at state 1, 11/10. In this way any transition may show an output activity depending both on an input condition and a present state. Inactive outputs need not be shown, eg. (Z1=1 Z2=0 -> IN), as this is assumed as default.

With this procedure as input, the compiler lists the state assignment (REST = 00b, IN = 01b and OUT = 10b). This is followed in the normal way by the computed Boolean equations and the signal assignment table. The resulting fuse map is not shown in the table.

6.1.2 Testing and Programming

With the completion of a successful compilation, a fuse file is produced (see Fig. 6.1). This can subsequently be downloaded into the programmer and the PLD blasted. However, a 'successful' compilation, as defined by a reported "no errors", such as shown in Table 6.3, really only means that the syntax of the source file has the correct syntax. It does not mean that the programmed device will do as the designer expects. This could be because the system was initially incorrectly described or entered into the source file. Whatever the reason, it makes sense to verify the design *before* proceeding to the programming phase. All PLD compilers support **simulation**. This is a type of back substitution, whereby the behavior of the resulting equations is checked against the expected responses. Normally the designer specifies a series of test patterns, or vectors, in the original source file. After the source code has been compiled, these test vectors are back substituted by the simulator, enabling the designer to validate the logical behavior of the PLD.

The syntax of these **test vectors** are very much compiler dependent. The simulator description structure of the OrCAD/PLD compiler is headed by the keyword **Vectors:**, with the simulation commands enclosed in braces in the usual manner. When the compiler is run, it produces a separate file (a .VEC file) with information concerning the signals and test patterns. If there are no syntax errors, then the program **vectors** can be executed. This then produces a display of the appropriate signals. Thus, if we had an original source file TABLE6_8.PLD, then a typical run would be:

```
        pld table6_8     Invokes the compiler on TABLE6_8.PLD
    vectors table6_8     Invokes the simulator on TABLE6_8.VEC
```

Some examples will elucidate.

Example 6.7

To repeat the hazard warning lights logic of Example 6.1, but including a simulation description structure and a simulation run.

Solution

The source code shown in Table 6.9 is identical to that in Table 6.2, with three additional simulation instructions appearing at the end within the `Vectors:` environment. These are:

Display

> This tells the simulator what variables to display. In this case H, R, L, F, "->", L, R means list inputs H, R, L and F, followed by the verbatim text in quotes, ->, and the resulting outputs L and R.

Test

> This specifies which inputs are to be exercised, in our case all four inputs. The `Test` command can have a following list of numeric values to give a range of input test values instead of all possible combinations. Thus `Test H, R, L, F = 1xxxb` would only check the response of the system to input patterns with H permanently 1. This is useful where large numbers of input variables are involved.

End

> This closes the session and saves the test vectors in the JEDEC file, shown in Table 6.13.

Running the simulator after a successful compilation gives the truth table of Table 6.10. This shows the two outputs for all 16 combinations of the four inputs. Comparing this to the original specification of Fig. 2.9 shows complete agreement between the expected and actual outcome.

Both `Display` and `Test` are considerably more sophisticated than demonstrated in this simple example. For instance, data can be displayed in binary, octal, decimal,

```
| PAL16L8        in:(H,R,L,F), out:(R_Lights, L_Lights)
|
| Title: "Car hazard lights"
|        "S.J. Cahill V.20/08/92"
|
| Active-high: H,R,L,F
| Active-low:  R_Lights, L_Lights
|
| R_Lights = (!H&R&!L&F)#(H&!R&!L&F)#(H&!R&L&F)#(H&R&!L&F)  | Right lights are p5,9,11,13
| L_Lights = (!H&!R&L&F)#(H&!R&!L&F)#(H&!R&L&F)#(H&R&!L&F)  | Left  lights are p3,9,11,13
|
| Vectors:
|         {
|         Display H, R, L, F, " -> ", L, R
|         Test    H, R, L, F
|         End
|         }
```

Table 6.9: Source code for the hazard warning logic, including a simulation description.

```
OrCAD TEST VECTOR GENERATOR  V1.20E 6/6/90
-
|         {
|           Display H, R, L, F, " -> ", L, R
-|          Test    H, R, L, F
0 0 0 0 -> 0 0
0 0 0 1 -> 0 0
0 0 1 0 -> 1 0
0 0 1 1 -> 1 0
0 1 0 0 -> 0 1
0 1 0 1 -> 0 1
0 1 1 0 -> 1 1
0 1 1 1 -> 1 1
1 0 0 0 -> 0 0
1 0 0 1 -> 0 0
1 0 1 0 -> 1 0
1 0 1 1 -> 1 0
1 1 0 0 -> 0 1
1 1 0 1 -> 0 1
1 1 1 0 -> 1 1
1 1 1 1 -> 1 1
-|          End
```

Table 6.10: The resulting simulation output.

hexadecimal, levels (H and L) and as a chart-like pseudo waveform. Our next example illustrates some of these facilities, in looking at the more difficult task of simulating sequential machines.

Example 6.8

To check out the logic developed for the elevator counter of Example 6.5.

Solution

The fundamental difference between a sequential and combinational circuit is that the state of the former depends not only on the input, but on the history of input changes. Simulating such a circuit causes difficulties, in that at the beginning of a simulation session, the state is unknown. This cannot be determined simply as a function of the inputs; Reset and Up in our case. Thus the first simulation line in Table 6.12 has an output listed as UU UU UU UU, i.e. undefined.

In situations such as this, the first step in a simulation script must be to place the system in a known state. This is normally done by activating the system Reset or similar override signal, such as Preset. This is the function of the command Test Reset=1; Count=0,1,0 in the vector script of Table 6.11. This 'clocks' the circuit with the sequence $0 \rightarrow 1 \rightarrow 0$ (＿／＼＿) with Reset active. The outcome is displayed in line 8 of Table 6.12, where the machine is shown in state $001b$, or decimal 01 (floor 1).

The two following Test commands exercise the counter with Reset inactive. The first of these is:

Test   Reset = 0; Up = 1; Count = 13(0,1),0

which states that 'with Reset inactive and with Up active; then exercise Count by doing 13 times 0 and 1, with a final 0'. The outcome of this is the up count

```
| Vectors:
| {
|   Display (Count)c, Reset, Up, (Q[3~0])c, "   (",(Q[3~0])d,")"
|   Test    Reset=1; Count=0,1,0            | Define known state
|   Test    Reset=0; Up=1; Count = 13(0,1),0 | Try 13 up pulses
|   Test    Reset=0; Up=0; Count = 13(0,1),0 | Try 13 down pulses
|   End
| }
```

Table 6.11: Simulation script for the elevator counter.

illustrated in lines 10–36 of Table 6.12. Beginning from the left, this shows that the Count signal in chart form ((Count)c in the Display statement), Reset and Up in binary, Q_3, Q_2, Q_1, Q_0 in both chart form and decimal. The skip over state 13 is clearly seen from this latter decimal form ((Q[3~0])d in the Display statement)

The final test run is similar, but this time with the elevator going down from floor 15 to 1. Once again the outcome in lines 38–64 shows the skip over the phantom floor 13.

Although this session has verified the basic operation of the design, it is by no means an exhaustive test. To thoroughly test the circuit, we should make sure that changes in both Reset and Up work from each of the fourteen legal and two illegal states. For a n bit up/down counter, this requires $2(2^n - 1)(2^{n-1} + 1)$ clock cycles. In this case 270 cycles are required. However, a 12-bit counter needs over 16 million cycles for an exhaustive trial! This calculation warns that most sequential machines with a useful level of complexity can never be completely tested. Rather, we must be satisfied with a judicious chosen subset of test sequences. This choice demands considerable skill of the designer, even though there are software packages which will aid in the generation of suitable test vectors.

———————

Once the designer is satisfied that the circuit logic is correct, he/she can proceed to programming the actual chip. Most PLD programmers allow the operator to manually enter the fuse numbers that are to be altered from the keyboard. Although this list will often be held in memory and can subsequently be edited to correct erroneous inputs, this is not to be recommended. Normally the PLD compiler generates this list in a form that the PLD programmer can understand. This **fuse file** can be downloaded from the computer to the programmer at any time, as shown in the photograph of Fig. 6.3. Initially, every PLD programmer manufacturer specified its own fuse file format. However, to avoid a proliferation of such proprietary efforts, the Joint Electron Device Engineering Council (JEDEC) released a standard file format [3] which has been adopted by virtually all PLD related commercial equipment.

The **JEDEC file** produced by Example 6.7 is reproduced in Table 6.13, with comments added on the right of each line. The file must start with the ASCII character STX (START_OF_TEXT = $02h$, see Table 1.4) and end with an ETX (END_OF_TEXT = $03h$). Comments can be added before the first asterisk (*). After this, each field commences with an identifier letter and ends with a *.

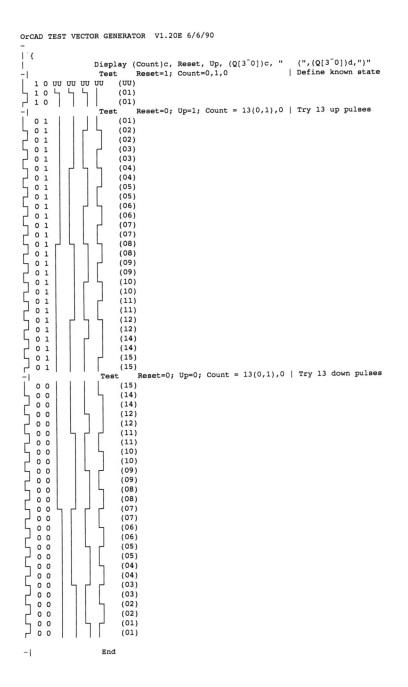

```
OrCAD TEST VECTOR GENERATOR   V1.20E 6/6/90
-
| `{
|                    Display (Count)c, Reset, Up, (Q[3~0])c, "   (",(Q[3~0])d,")"
-|                   Test    Reset=1; Count=0,1,0              | Define known state
  1 0 UU UU UU UU    (UU)
  1 0              | (01)
  1 0              | (01)
-|                   Test    Reset=0; Up=1; Count = 13(0,1),0 | Try 13 up pulses
  0 1                (01)
  0 1                (02)
  0 1                (02)
  0 1                (03)
  0 1                (03)
  0 1                (04)
  0 1                (04)
  0 1                (05)
  0 1                (05)
  0 1                (06)
  0 1                (06)
  0 1                (07)
  0 1                (07)
  0 1                (08)
  0 1                (08)
  0 1                (09)
  0 1                (09)
  0 1                (10)
  0 1                (10)
  0 1                (11)
  0 1                (11)
  0 1                (12)
  0 1                (12)
  0 1                (14)
  0 1                (14)
  0 1                (15)
  0 1                (15)
-|                   Test    Reset=0; Up=0; Count = 13(0,1),0 | Try 13 down pulses
  0 0                (15)
  0 0                (14)
  0 0                (14)
  0 0                (12)
  0 0                (12)
  0 0                (11)
  0 0                (11)
  0 0                (10)
  0 0                (10)
  0 0                (09)
  0 0                (09)
  0 0                (08)
  0 0                (08)
  0 0                (07)
  0 0                (07)
  0 0                (06)
  0 0                (06)
  0 0                (05)
  0 0                (05)
  0 0                (04)
  0 0                (04)
  0 0                (03)
  0 0                (03)
  0 0                (02)
  0 0                (02)
  0 0                (01)
  0 0                (01)

-|                   End
```

Table 6.12: Simulation run for the elevator counter.

The file proper of Table 6.13 begins with three Quality fields. The QP field gives the number of pins in the device (20 pins for the PAL16L8); QF is the number of fuses and QV the maximum number of test vectors allowed in the file. The F field gives the default fuse state (0 means connection made).

The programming information proper is given by the List (L) fields. These give a starting fuse number in decimal, followed by a row of fuse values, 1 meaning program and 0 for leave in default state (in this listing, given by the F0* statement). Each L row usually corresponds to a physical row (product line) in the device, see Fig. 3.65. Any rows that are to be left in their complete virgin state are omitted. This information is terminated by a C field, which is the checksum of all fuses (see page 623).

When we ran the simulator in Example 6.7, this made a copy of the test vectors in the JEDEC file. Each vector is headed by a V identifier, followed by a decimal test vector number. This is then followed on by the test condition for the various device pins. These include 0 to apply a logic 0 to that input pin, 1 for logic 1, N for no test (eg. power supplies at pins 10 & 20), H to expect a High level at the output pin and L to expect an output Low level.

```
Test vector no. 16                    GND (not tested)
    ⋮                                   ⋮   L_Lights          R_Lights
    ⋮        H R L F                    ⋮   ⋮                 ⋮ V_CC (not tested)
    ⋮        ⋮ ⋮ ⋮ ⋮                    ⋮   ⋮                 ⋮ ⋮
 V00016      1 1 1 1 0 0 0 0 0 N 0 H 0 0 0 0 0 0 H N *
             ⋮ ⋮ ⋮ ⋮ ⋮ ⋮ ⋮ ⋮ ⋮ ⋮  ⋮  ⋮  ⋮  ⋮  ⋮  ⋮  ⋮  ⋮  ⋮  ⋮
             1 2 3 4 5 6 7 8 9 10 11 12 13 14 15 16 17 18 19 20   (pins)
```

```
<02h>                                              <- STX (Start of TeXt)
OrCAD/PLD                                          <- Comments
Type:        PAL16L8                               <-  ...
Title:       Active-High Car hazard lights         <-  ...
*                                                  <- down to first *
QP20* QF2048* QV1024*                              <- Quantity fields
F0*                                                <- Default Fuse state
L0000 11 11 11 11 11 11 11 11 11 11 11 11 11 11 11 11 * <- Fuse List
L0032 10 01 11 11 01 11 11 11 11 11 11 11 11 11 11 11 * <- One for each row
L0064 01 11 10 11 01 11 11 11 11 11 11 11 11 11 11 11 * <- with programmed fuses
L1792 11 11 11 11 11 11 11 11 11 11 11 11 11 11 11 11 * <- Intact rows are omitted
L1824 11 01 10 11 01 11 11 11 11 11 11 11 11 11 11 11 * <- Each row begins with
L1856 10 11 01 11 11 11 11 11 11 11 11 11 11 11 11 11 * <- the JEDEC fuse number
C1787*                                             <- Fuse checksum
V00001 000000000N0H000000HN*                       <- Test vectors
V00002 000100000N0H000000HN*                       <- to be executed
V00003 001000000N0H000000HN*                       <- by the fuse
V00004 001100000N0L000000HN*                       <- programmer
V00005 010000000N0H000000HN*                       <-  ...
V00006 010100000N0H000000LN*                       <-  ...
V00007 011000000N0H000000HN*                       <-  ...
V00008 011100000N0H000000HN*                       <-  ...
V00009 100000000N0H000000HN*                       <-  ...
V00010 100100000N0L000000LN*                       <-  ...
V00011 101000000N0H000000HN*                       <-  ...
V00012 101100000N0L000000HN*                       <-  ...
V00013 110000000N0H000000HN*                       <-  ...
V00014 110100000N0L000000LN*                       <-  ...
V00015 111000000N0H000000HN*                       <-  ...
V00016 111100000N0H000000HN*                       <-  ...
<03h>                                              <- ETX (End of TeXt)
AF12                                               <- Checksum of whole file
```

Table 6.13: An annotated JEDEC file.

Figure 6.3: Showing a PLD programmer in action.

The line above shows vector 16 in detail, illustrating the signals associated with each pin. As in the original simulation of Fig. 6.10, there are 16 vectors in all.

The final character following EXT is the checksum of the entire file. This allows the programmers downloading routine to verify the overall correctness of the transaction.

Once the PLD is programmed, the programmer can use the JEDEC test vectors to check that the fuses have indeed been blown to satisfy these requirements. This fuse verify can only check the fuses, not the PLD logic circuitry, eg. gates, buffers. Thus it does not guarantee that the PLD is bound to operate correctly.

Most PLDs use special on-chip circuitry during the programming phase. This circuitry is also used by the PLD programmer to verify the fuses after programming. In newer devices it is possible to disable this, now redundant, circuitry by blowing a security fuse. Once blown, the verification circuitry is disabled and this makes it more difficult for unauthorized personnel to determine the fuse pattern.

6.2 Designing Microprocessor-Based Circuitry

Designing and manufacturing a successful MPU-based contraption involves more than just writing the code and wiring together the requisite chips. From the conceptual specification to the final boxed product rolling down the production conveyer belt, is a multi-task operation. Many of these myriad tasks, whether technical, commercial or production, benefit from computer-based assistance. Here we look at some of these techniques as applied to the software development and hardware testing phases of the operation.

After reading this section, you should:

- Be aware of the advantages and disadvantages of the commercial microcomputer, single-board computer and chip-level based implementation strategies involved in developing MPU-based products.

- Understand the role of the microprocessor development system (MDS), and in particular the in-circuit emulator (ICE), in developing a MPU-based circuit.

- Appreciate the advantages of designing circuits with in-built testability.

- Know the difference between machine code, assembly-level and high-level languages.

- Understand the absolute and relative assembly processes, including translation and linkage.

- Appreciate the use of simulators to debug software at both machine and high-levels.

- Understand the advantages and disadvantages of both assemblers and compilers in generating embedded code.

6.2.1   The System Design

At the starting line, the customer will specify the system in a global sense; essentially what goes in and what comes out. The 'black box' implementing this transfer function is likely to be mentioned, if at all, *en passant*. Of course, there will be technical constraints imposed by this specification, such as size, speed and power supply, but these will often do no more than point the finger towards a likely implementation strategy. The final hardware and software (if applicable) will be dictated by a large number of considerations including financial targets, marketing, available development equipment and procurable expertize.

There are several critical steps between agreeing a specification and actually getting down to the nitty gritty of hardware/software design. One of the more important of these involves the selection of the system transducers, since these form the interface between the electronics and the real world. These will be chosen on the basis of an analysis of the parameters involved, together with their measurement and interconversion to an analogous electrical quality.

The choice of transducer is not unduly influenced by the technology which will be used for the central processing electronics. However, their selection at this time, coupled with a system task analysis, will permit a rough block diagram to be made of the system. In Fig. 6.4, this is indicated under the heading of System formulation.

With a functional draft of the system now selected, some thought can be given to the technology of the central electronics. At the macro level, this will involve a partition between the analog and digital processes. For example; should an input

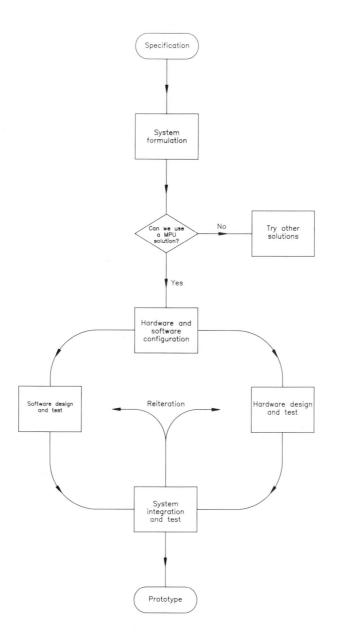

Figure 6.4: A broad outline of system development

analog signal be filtered before conversion to digital (analog filter) or after (a digital software filter)? Most implementations rely on a mixture of both hardware and software types of processing.

At the hardware digital end of things, the choice essentially lies between random logic (i.e. hard-wired combinational and sequential circuitry) and microprocessor-based configurations. Conventional logic is usually best for for small systems with few functions, which are unlikely to require expansion. In larger systems, this type of logic may appear in the guise of application specific integrated circuits, where numbers warrant.

In general MPUs do everything sequentially, one thing at a time, while random logic can process in parallel. Thus, where nanosecond speed is important, conventional logic is indicated — but note that analog techniques can often implement a task in an even shorter time. It is possible to run many microprocessor chips in parallel to increase the throughput, but frequently a mixed logic approach is applied where a MPU is used in a supervisory role to control the action of a supporting cast of ordinary logic and analog circuitry.

Assuming that a MPU-based solution is decided upon, the processing tasks must be partitioned between hardware and software. If we take an alphanumeric readout as a simple example; then the choice is between an expensive intelligent display incorporating an integral decoder latch — such as the TIL309 of Fig. 5.44 —, or a cheaper dumb display where the segment patterns are picked out by software. The former will cost more on a unit basis, but the latter will require money before the product is launched, to design the software-driver package. This of course is at a fairly trivial level, but in general, hardware is available off the shelf and therefore has a low initial design cost and takes some load off the central processor. Software is rarely obtainable off the shelf and requires initial investment in a (highly paid) software engineer, but is usually more flexible than a hardware-only solution. Thus, when technically feasible, a software-oriented solution is indicated for large production runs, where the initial investment is amortized by a lower unit cost.

With the tasks allocated between hardware and software, what choices has the designer in implementing the hardware? There are three main approaches to the problem.

In situations where the ratio of design cost to production numbers is poor, a system implementation should be considered. This entails using a commercial microcomputer — such as an IBM PC — as the processor. Such instruments are normally sold with a keyboard, VDU, disk and sufficient memory to handle most tasks. Ruggedized rack mounting industrial and portable versions are also available. Generally, the hardware engineer will be concerned only to customize the system, by designing specialist supporting hardware and interface circuitry. The software engineer will create a software package based on this computer to drive the hardware. Frequently the computer will support commercially-available software development tools, such as editors, assemblers, compilers and debug packages; which facilitates the software design process at low cost.

Tailoring a general-purpose machine to a **semi-dedicated** role requires a relatively low 'up-front' investment and low production costs. Furthermore, documentation and the provision of service facilities are eased, as a pre-existing commercial product is used. Technically this type of implementation is bulky, but where facilities such as a disk drive and VDU are needed, the size and unit cost are not necessarily greater than a custom-designed equivalent. Sometimes the customer may already have a suitable microcomputer; the vendor simply selling the hardware plug-in interface and software package. For the end user, this can be an attractive proposition. In particular, the problem of servicing at a remote site is considerably eased.

Thus a system-level implementation is indicated when low-to-medium production runs are in prospect and the system complexity is high, eg. computerized laboratory equipment. For one-offs, this approach is the only economically viable proposition, provided that such a system will fit into the technical boundary constraints. For example, it would be obviously ridiculous (but technically flexible) to employ this technique for a washing machine controller.

At the middle range of complexity, a system may be constructed using a bought in **single-board computer** (SBC). Sometimes several modules are used (eg. MPU, memory, interface), and these are plugged into a mother-board carrying a bus structure. If necessary these may be augmented with in-house designed cards to complete the configuration.

Although the cost of these bought-in cards is many times that of the material cost of self-produced equivalents, they are likely to be competitive in production runs of up to around a thousand. Like system-implemented configurations, they considerably reduce the up-front hardware expenses and do not require elaborate production and test facilities. By shortening the design time, the product can be marketed earlier, and subsequently the economics improved by substitution of in-house boards. Whilst more expensive than a system based on a commercial microcomputer, a board-level implementation gives greater flexibility to configure the hardware to the specific product needs. Furthermore, in a multiple-card configuration, at least some of the standard modules can be used for more than one product (eg. a memory card) thus gaining the cost benefits of larger-purchase volumes. Reference [4] gives an example of this approach.

Neither system or board-level implementations provide an economical means of production for volumes much in excess of a thousand, with the exception of high-complexity/value products. In many cases, technical demands, such as size and speed, preclude these techniques, even for small production runs. In such situations, a fundamental chip-level design, as outlined in Fig. 6.5, is indicated.

Chip-level involves implementation at the integrated circuit level. In this situation, the circuit is fabricated from scratch; giving a configuration **dedicated** to the specific application. Given that the designers require an intimate knowledge of, for example, a spectrum of integrated circuits, CAE techniques for PCB and ASIC design, software techniques, and must keep an eye on the eventual production process; the cost of developing, testing and production of such systems is large. Furthermore, the up-front expenses are high and may cause cash flow problems. However, the materials cost is low, and this approach is often the best technical solution to the problem.

Software implementation for most dedicated MPU-based systems, irrespective of the hardware implementation category, is developed in an analogous way to chip-level design. This is emphasized in Fig 6.5, by the two parallel tracks. Other than monitors and operating systems, there is little in the way of off-the-shelf ROM-resident (firmware) packages. There is however, a considerable body of high-level routines published; which can be adapted and compiled down to the chosen target.

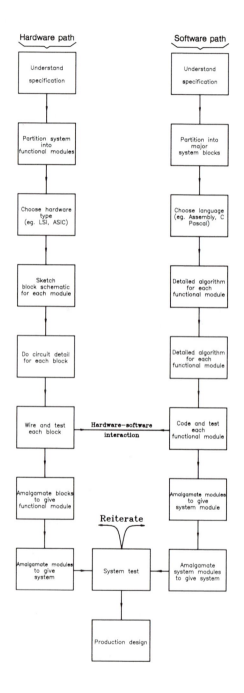

Figure 6.5: Fundamental-level design.

Nevertheless, in general software design is an expensive proposition, and is difficult to amortize in small production runs.

Standard microprocessor-based circuitry uses a MPU chip, together with individual ICs for memory and I/O interface. address decoding and other support logic (glue logic) will likely be implemented using programmable logic devices to reduce the chip count (see Example 6.2). Higher production runs may economically utilize single-chip microcontroller units [5]. A typical example is shown in Fig. 5.42.

It is possible to integrate the fabrication pattern of some MPUs onto your own custom IC. These are held as standard cells in the library of the appropriate CAE package. Provided that memory and other cell patterns are available, in principle a custom MPU-based system can be integrated onto one silicon chip. However, this approach is really only applicable to very large scale production runs and requires considerable skill. Custom hard-disk controllers are typical of products which use this technique.

In general MPU-based hardware designs are fairly similar; comprizing a microprocessor, ROM, RAM, address decoder and peripheral circuits to communicate with the outside world. Thus the main thrust is going to be in the fields of software, integration of the hardware and software, together with testing and debugging. Equipment aimed at providing these facilities is known as a **microprocessor development system (MDS)** [6].

Historically the MDS was introduced in the 1970's by the semiconductor houses

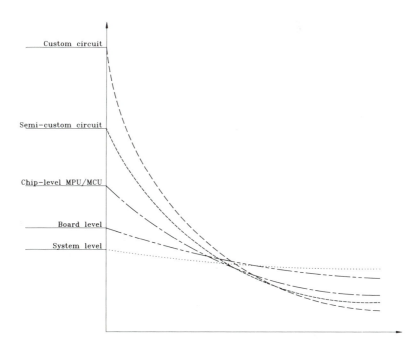

Figure 6.6: A cost versus production comparison.

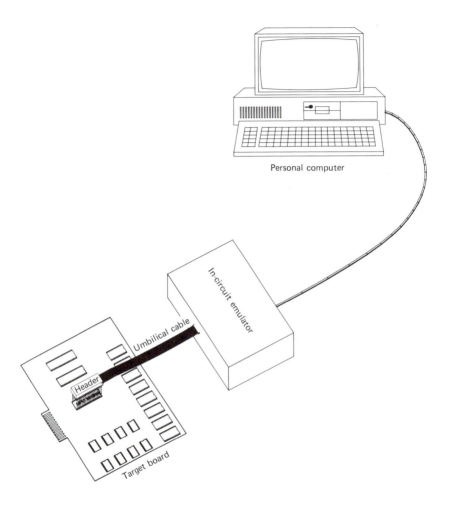

Figure 6.7: A PC-based in-circuit emulator.

as a development aid, in order to promote sales of their particular line of micro-processors. These were essentially small dedicated microcomputers, hosting soft-ware tools and supporting hardware facilities such as EPROM programmers and in-circuit emulators. Later, general equipment manufacturers introduced universal MDS, which could be adapted to work with any of a wide range of devices [7].

A dedicated MDS is very expensive, typically costing from $20,000 upwards. A somewhat more affordable solution is based on the use of a personal computer (PC) as the computing engine [8]. The appropriate software tools, such as assembler, run from disk in the normal way. Hardware components either plug into the PC's expansion bus or communicate via a serial link. We will look at some of the software tools in the next two sections; here we will examine the role of the in-circuit emulator as the connection between the target hardware and the software in the MDS's computer.

The **in-circuit emulator (ICE)** is a hardware device which allows the development system to take over the running of the hardware prototype. Without such a facility the designer would have to take the output from the assembler or compiler (see Table 6.23(b)) and program an EPROM. This firmware would then have to be physically carried across and plugged into the target system, which would then be powered up and monitored using the normal hardware tools. The designer has little influence on how the system performs in this situation, which makes debugging virtually impossible. A variation of this technique uses a ROMulator. This is a RAM pack with a flying lead and DIL plug masquerading as an EPROM. Machine code can be downloaded into the ROMulator in-situ in the target EPROM socket. Such software is easier to change as compared to firmware, and some limited monitoring of the target execution path is possible.

Figure 6.7 shows a typical configuration, with the ICE being plugged into the MPU's socket in a target board. Here the ICE replaces the target microprocessor via an umbilical cable and plug. The ICE itself hosts the same processor as the target, sometimes piggybacked onto the umbilical plug (or pod), to be as close to the target as possible. This is the arrangement shown in the photograph of Fig. 6.8. This slave microprocessor is controlled by the ICE master microprocessor, which also communicates with a computer via a serial link [9]. Generally, changing the target processor only involves changing the pod and PC software.

Although many stand-alone ICEs will operate with a dumb terminal host, the internal ROM-based ICE commands are very elementary. Using an intelligent terminal, such as a PC, allows a much more powerful and user-friendly software interface to insulate the user from the complexities of the ICE itself. Aids, such as menus and helpful prompts, are useful to novice users. As with other software packages discussed in this text, the protocols and commands available are very product dependent; doubly so here, as both hardware and software are manufacturer specific. The following examples are based on the Noral SDT ICE running under the Prism package,[2] but the facilities available are similar to most products [9].

All ICEs permit shadowing of the target's memory. Thus memory is available to the slave emulator MPU on-board the ICE itself as well as down on the target system. As seen by this slave, its memory map can be set in chunks between either local (known as overlay memory) or target memory. As an example, consider a target with ROM between E000h–FFFFh, RAM between 0000h–1FFFh and peripheral circuits in the range 9000h–9FFFh. Normally on powerup, all memory is mapped to the target as read/write. To 'move' the peripheral circuits and ROM into ICE memory, use the MMO (MEMORY MAP OVERLAY) commands thus:

```
MMO     9000h,  9FFFh
MMO     0E000h, 0FFFFh, P
```

where P stands for WRITE PROTECTED — an error will be printed if software attempts to write to any of this overlay memory — i.e. simulating ROM.

After this is done, the memory map is displayed, as in Table 6.14, by entering the command MM. Sixteen blocks can be allocated in this manner, in minimum

---

[2]Noral Microelectronics, Logic House, Gate St., Blackburn, Lancs, BB1 3AQ, UK.

Figure 6.8: Emulating a target board.

increments of 4 Kbytes. Also shown in the listing is a memory test of RAM on the target board using the MT (MEMORY TEST) command. This particular test (type 1) writes 01010101b and then 10101010b into all specified locations. More sophisticated tests are available. The M (for MEMORY) command displays a range of memory locations. The contents of any read/write location can also be changed from the keyboard using this command.

Using this overlay memory technique, resources may be gradually switched from the ICE to the prototype system. Thus the peripherals can be initially mapped to overlay RAM locations and used to test the software. The real peripherals can then be exercised by switching from the overlay environment to the target.

Typical facilities provided by an ICE are:

1: File Handling

Downloading machine-code and symbol files into memory. The LD command in Table 6.14 is an example.

2: Memory

Enables us to examine and optionally change any read/write memory location. The command M 0000,16 in Table 6.14 displays a block of 16 bytes of memory starting at 0000h.

```
> mmo 09000h,09fffh                                    Memory Map to overlay
> mmo 0e000h,0ffffh                                    Memory Map to overlay
> mm                                                    Show Mapping
Ref   Type        Start Addr  End Addr  Mapping attribute

2     Target      0000        8FFF      Read / Write          Target
3     Overlay     9000        9FFF      Overlay Read / Write  In ICE
4     Target      A000        DFFF      Read / Write          Target
5     Overlay     E000        FFFF      Overlay Read / Write  In ICE
Free overlay RAM = 116K bytes    Mapping resolution = 4K bytes
> mt 0000,1fffh,1                                       Test target RAM
Memory test complete (8192 tests) : 0 failure(s)
> m 0000,16                                             Look at memory
Address      0  1  2  3  4  5  6  7  8  9  A  B  C  D  E  F

0000        AA AA AA AA AA AA AA AA AA AA AA AA AA AA AA AA   ................
0010        AA AA AA AA AA AA AA AA AA AA AA AA AA AA AA AA   ................

> ld a:table534.nor inthex                              Load in machine code
> $s                                                    Examine symbols

*** Module Symbols for : TABLE5_34
0000   Error
9000   Cable_in
9001   Cable_out
E000   TEST
E004   T_LOOP
E00A   D_LOOP
E01A   FAULT
E02C   EXIT
> rw sp 2000h                                           Change SP to 2000h
> r                                                     Examine registers
  A B     X      Y     DP  USP    PC    SP      EFHINZVC
D=0401  0000   0000   00  0000   E000  2000   CCR=11010000
>
```

Table 6.14: Memory mapping and testing.

3: Register, examine and change

To examine and change any internal register. Thus RW SP 2000h writes the value $2000h$ into the System Stack Pointer.

4: Step execution

To execute the directed software in the target environment step by step, usually displaying registers and other information after each step.

5: Breakpoints

Insertion of conditions, which may be software or/and external signals, to halt execution.

6: Execute

Full speed execution until a breakpoint is reached.

7: Trace analysis

This can be either a software or real-time trace. In the case of the latter, the system runs to a breakpoint. At this juncture, the contents of a display buffer can be read both before and after this event. The state of various external signals can be displayed, as well as address, data and control bus signals. Unlike a software trace, this data is acquired in real time and only displayed when execution has terminated.

To illustrate some of these points, consider the cable testing system of Example 5.34. This program is shown in the central debugging window of Table 6.15 below. The smaller window above this allows us to monitor selected memory locations or blocks as we step through the program. The MONM (MONitor MEMORY) commands setting this up is shown in the command area at the bottom of the page. The register window at the top right shows the state of all the MPU's registers. Notice how the System Stack Pointer is set to 2000h in Table 6.14 using the RW (REGISTER WRITE) command. Below this the state of the two stacks (S and U) are shown. This is useful when parameters are passed to and from subroutines through the stack (For example, see Table 6.29).

In Table 6.15 the program has been stepped through until the third test vector has been sent out — item 1 in the monitor window. The return value is shown in item 2 in the monitor window as 00000000b, indicating an open-circuit. On stepping

```
┌═Data Monitor═══════════════════════════════════════╗      ╔═Regs════════════╗♦┐
│ 1. 9000 B = 00000100                                │      │  PC = E02E         │
│ 2. 9001 B = 00000000                                │      │  A : B             │
│ 3. 0000 d = 1                                       │      │  04 01             │
│ 4.                                                  │      │   X = 0000         │
│ 5.                                                  │      │   Y = 0000         │
│ 6.                                                  │      │  DP = 00           │
│ 7.                                                  │      │ USP = 0000         │
│ 8.                                                  │      │  SP = 2000         │
│ 9.                                                  │      │    EFHINZVC        │
│10.                                                  │      │ CCR=11010000       │
│11.                                                  │      ╠═Stack═══════════╣  │
│12.                                                  │      │+1E F2    +1E 80 │  │
│13.                                                  │      │+1D F2    +1D 80 │  │
│14.                                                  │      │+1C F2    +1C 80 │  │
├─[ MODE ]: ASM, MODULE: TABLE5_34───────────────────┤      │+1B F2    +1B 80 │  │
│TEST:                                                │      │+1A F2    +1A 80 │  │
│ E000 0F00      CLR     <0H {Error}                  │      │+19 F2    +19 80 │  │
│ E002 8601      LDA     #1H                          │      │+18 F2    +18 80 │  │
│T_LOOP:                                              │      │+17 F2    +17 80 │  │
│ E004 B79000    STA     9000H {Cable_in}             │      │+16 F2    +16 80 │  │
│ E007 8E07D0    LDX     #7D0H                         │     │+15 F2    +15 80 │  │
│D_LOOP:                                              │      │+14 F2    +14 80 │  │
│ E00A 301F      LEAX    -1H,X                         │     │+13 F2    +13 80 │  │
│ E00C 26FC      BNE     0E00AH {D_LOOP}              │      │+12 F2    +12 80 │  │
│ E00E 1F89      TFR     A,B                           │     │+11 F2    +11 80 │  │
│ E010 F89001    EORB    9001H {Cable_out}            │      │+10 F2    +10 80 │  │
│ E013 2605      BNE     0E01AH {FAULT}               │      │+0F F2    +0F 80 │  │
│ E015 48        ASLA                                 │      │+0E F2    +0E 80 │  │
│ E016 2514      BCS     0E02CH {EXIT}                │      │+0D F2    +0D 80 │  │
│ E018 20EA      BRA     0E004H {T_LOOP}              │      │+0C F2    +0C 80 │  │
│FAULT:                                               │      │+0B F2    +0B 80 │  │
│ E01A 0C00      INC     <0H {Error}                  │      │+0A F2    +0A 80 │  │
│ E01C 7D9001    TST     9001H {Cable_out}            │      │+09 F2    +09 80 │  │
│ E01F 270B      BEQ     0E02CH {EXIT}                │      │+08 F2    +08 80 │  │
│ E021 0C00      INC     <0H {Error}                  │      │+07 F2    +07 80 │  │
│ E023 1F89      TFR     A,B                           │     │+06 F2    +06 80 │  │
│ E025 F49001    ANDB    9001H {Cable_out}            │      │+05 F2    +05 80 │  │
│ E028 2602      BNE     0E02CH {EXIT}                │      │+04 F2    +04 80 │  │
│ E02A 0C00      INC     <0H {Error}                  │      │+03 F2    +03 80 │  │
│EXIT:                                                │      │+02 F2    +02 80 │  │
│ E02C D600      LDB     <0H {Error}                  │      │+01 F2    +01 80 │  │
│ E02E 39        RTS                                  │      │SP→F2    USP→01  │  │
└↕↑♦↓═|READY|════[ S ]=[ SO ]=[ GO ]=[ BRK ]═════════╧═════════════════════════╧─┘

> cmon
> monm Cable_in b
> monm Cable_out b
> monm Error d
>
```

Table 6.15: Executing the Cable-Test program.

on to the end of the program, the state of **Error** (memory location 0000h) is seen
to be decimal 1, indicating a type-1 fault, which is returned in Accumulator_B.
Accumulator_A returns the test vector 04h. The register values are shown in the top
right box, and are highlighted when they change. The instruction being executed
is also highlighted on the screen. A mouse is clicked on the [S] or [GO] boxes to
STEP or GO AND EXECUTE as appropriate.

In-circuit emulators can be used both for the design phases of a new project or
for servicing existing equipment. However, they are expensive, relatively bulky and
fragile. Thus it makes sense to design for testability with simple equipment at the
onset, especially where in-the-field servicing is contemplated, and leave the ICE for
'tough nut' cases which can be returned to base.

A simple hardware approach to this problem provides a free-run facility, whereby
the MPU can be set to repetitively cycle through its entire memory space. The
actual details vary somewhat with device. The circuit appropriate to the 6809 MPU
is shown in Fig. 6.9. Here a header is inserted in series with the data bus. Removing
this header isolates the data bus, which is then set to logic 1 via the high-valued
pull-up resistors. Closing the free-run switch forces d_7 and d_5 to logic 0, giving a
permanent data bus signature of 01011111b, or 5Fh. The diodes prevent interaction
between d_7 and d_5 when the switch is open. They can be eliminated by using a
double-pole switch instead of the single-pole variety shown.

With the data bus highjacked, as shown in Fig. 6.9(b), the MPU can then be
reset. The MPU will then attempt to read its start-up address at FFFE:Fh. It will
of course read 5F5Fh. Putting this in the **PC**, it will then proceed to read its first
op-code, which will be $\cdots$ 5Fh! Now 5Fh is **CLRB**, a single-byte inherent instruction.
After clearing **B**, the next instruction at 5F60h will be read; and will be $\cdots$ **CLRB**.
Thus the address bus will continually increment, acting as a 16-bit counter. As this

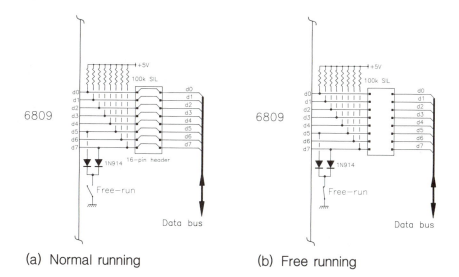

(a) Normal running   (b) Free running

Figure 6.9: Free-running the 6809 MPU.

instruction takes two cycles to implement, the total time for an address count for a
1 MHz clock is $2 \times 65,536 = 0.131072$ s.

A cycling address bus permits the address decoder and the various Chip Enables
to be checked with an oscilloscope or even logic probe. An oscilloscope can even
be used to check simple input ports when enabled (as R/$\overline{\text{W}}$ will always be High
for CLRB). Free-running also checks out the MPU itself, clock circuits and various
status lines. Open-circuited data bus lines can also be detected. Changing from
free-run to normal-run modes takes only a few seconds.

A software approach to in-field testability can be used in addition or instead
of hardware testing. Here a suite of test routines can be run to exercise various
parts of the system. For example, in a system with analog output ports, continuous
ramps may be generated to check out the A/D converters. An input D/A converter
may be tested by continually sampling it and routing the digitized word through
to an output port. RAM operation can be verified by placing test patterns in
each location, much as described earlier with the ICE [10]. The contents of ROM
locations can be summed together to create a test signature, or checksum. This is
compared with the à priori known correct value for verification.

In an embedded system the diagnostic routines may be resident in ROM with
the normal software, or (less conveniently) may be plugged in as an alternative.
It may even be run under the control of an ICE. In either case, diagnostic ports
such as switch inputs (to select which diagnostic routine is to be run) and LED
or numerical outputs, will need to be incorporated in the hardware at the outset,
if existing facilities are not suitable [11, 12]. In systems with a disk drive, such
diagnostics may be introduced on a floppy disk. The VDU output of a PC makes an
ideal reporter for diagnostic purposes. When a PC is switched on, it automatically
checks out the integrity of the system RAM, disk drives and keyboard as a matter
of course.

6.2.2 Assembly-Level Software

Consider the fragment of code below. To a 68000-family MPU this makes perfect
sense. Indeed a series of binary bits, typically represented by nominal 0 V and
5 V potentials stored in memory, is the only code that a MPU or any other type
of computer can understand. To the software engineer, interpreting programs in
pure **machine code** is virtually impossible. Writing code in this form is torturous;
involving at the very least working out each operation code by hand, together with
bits representing source, destination and any applicable data; evaluating relative
offsets and keeping tally of where data is stored.

```
0001000000111000 0001001000110100
0101110000000000
0001111000000000 000100100110101
```

Even with a program written in such a form, some means of putting or loading
in the code to its final place in memory must be found. Very early computers did
not use electronic memory at all; the code being configured by wire links. Using
switches to set up each memory address and its corresponding data, in effect a kind
of direct memory access, was still used up to the 1960s to enter a short start-up

program. This program was known as bootstrap; as once in and executed, a paper-tape reader could be controlled. Programs could then be read in from this source, i.e. the computer was able to pick itself up by its own bootstraps.

Using the computer to aid in translating code from more user-friendly forms to machine code and loading this into memory began in the late 1940s. At the very least it permitted the use of higher order number bases such as octal and hexadecimal. Using the latter, our code fragment becomes:

```
1038  1234
5C00
1E00  1235
```

A hexadecimal loader will translate this to binary and put the code in designated addresses. Hexadecimal coding has little to commend it, except that the number of keystrokes is reduced (but there are more keys!) and it is slightly easier to spot certain types of errors. Nevertheless, this technique was extensively used in the early 1970s for microprocessor software generation and is still occasionally used in education as an introduction to programming simple MPUs.

At the very least, a symbolic translator or **assembler** is required for serious programming. This allows the use of mnemonics for the instructions and internal registers, with names for constants, variables and addresses. We now have:

```
        .define  CONSTANT = 6
        MOVE.B   NUM1,D0        ; Get the first number
        ADDQ.B   #CONSTANT,D0   ; Add the constant to it
        MOVE.B   D0,NUM2        ; to give the second number
        ......   ............
        .ORG     1234h          ; This is the data area
NUM1:   .BYTE    [1]            ; NUM1 lives at 1234h
NUM2:   .BYTE    [1]            ; and NUM2 at 1235h
```

Giving names to addresses and constants is especially valuable for long programs. Together with the use of comments, this makes code written in assembly level easier to maintain. Furthermore, programs can be written as separate modules, with symbols defined in only one module and a linker program used to put them together with their actual values. This assembly of modules into one program gave the name **assembly level** to this type of language [13]. Of course assemblers/linkers and their ancillary programs are much more complex than simple hexadecimal loaders. Thus they demand more of the computer running them; especially in the area of memory and backup store. Because of this, their use in small MPU-based projects was limited until the early 1980s, when powerful personal computers (made possible by MPUs) appeared. Prior to this, either mainframe and minicomputers or target-specific microprocessor development systems were required. Any of these solution were expensive.

We used assemblers at some length in Chapter 5, to present a more palatable interface to the reader of the (binary) software aspects of several MPUs. Without going into any detail, we have seen that a symbolic assembler program (or assembler for short) allows us to use pre-defined symbols for the instructions and various processor registers, and to define names for constants, variables and memory locations.

They take the drudgery out of calculating relative offsets and converting number bases. Comments, which are ignored at translation time, make maintenance easier than raw code. The use of a convenient editor allows alteration to be easily made to the source code; which can then be quickly retranslated with the updated symbolic and offset values [13, 14].

Assemblers are one of a class of translator programs and are available from a wide range of originators for most target processors. Although some attempt has been made to standardize syntax [15, 16], normally each package has its own rules. Generally the MPU manufacturer's recommended mnemonics are adhered to reasonably closely. Directives, or pseudo operators, used to pass information to the assembler program, do differ considerably.

As in the programs introduced in the first part of this chapter, the programmer must prepare the source form of the code in the appropriate format and syntax. This preparation involves the use of an editor program or word processor. The actual one used is irrelevant, provided that the text is stored in a form which can be read by the translating program. Most operating systems come with a basic editor, eg. MSDOS's EDLIN and UNIX's ED.

Assemblers can be broadly classified as absolute or relocatable, according to the type of code they produce. An **absolute assembler** normally generates a file with the machine code and its absolute location ready to be loaded into memory. This machine code file is a finished entity, to which no further alterations need be or should be made before loading. The output of a **relocatable assembler** is not yet complete, as it usually does not contain information regarding the eventual location of the machine code in memory. Furthermore, symbols may be used in the source code which are not defined at this juncture and which are assumed to be in modules coming from elsewhere. It will be the job of a **linker program** to satisfy these unrequited references and to define code addresses.

Absolute assemblers tend to be simpler to use, as the path between source and machine code is more direct; as can be seen in Fig. 6.10. Despite their simplicity, they are rarely used in major projects due to their lack of flexibility.

As a demonstration, consider the absolute source code shown in Table 6.16. This uses the same syntax as the listings presented in Chapter 5, except for the new directive .ORG. As this source is to be processed by an absolute assembler, the programmer must specify the start address or origin (i.e. .ORG) of each section of code or data. The .ORG directive may be used as many times as required to locate the various sectors; thus, if necessary, each subroutine may be located at a specific start address.

The absolute assembler in translating this source code input, produces four kinds of output. Should there be a problem with the syntax of the source text, an **error file** will be produced, giving the line in which it occurred and usually a curt description. Sometimes a syntax error in one line can lead to problems in several other places. Table 6.17 is an example of such a file: it was generated by replacing the instruction DECB in line 14 of our source by the illegal mnemonic DEB and the referenced label **SLOOP** in line 13 by **LOOP**.

If all goes well, zero errors will be produced. This does not of course guarantee that the program will work, only that there are no syntax errors! In this situation a **listing file** will be generated. This shows the original source code together with addresses and the translated code. Other information may be provided as well.

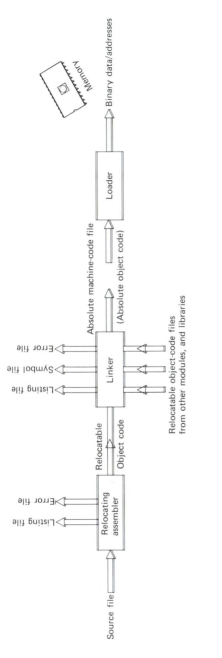

Figure 6.10: Assembly-level machine code translation.

```
                    .processor m6809
;**********************************************************
;* FUNCTION : Sums all unsigned integers up to n (max 255) *
;* ENTRY    : n is passed in Accumulator B                 *
;* EXIT     : Sum is returned in Accumulator D             *
;* EXIT     : No other register contents disturbed         *
;**********************************************************
;
                    .org    0c000h       ; Program starts at 0C000h
; While n>0, sum=sum+n, decrement n
SUM_OF_INT:         pshs    x,cc         ; Save X and CCR on stack
                    ldx     #0           ; Clear sum
SLOOP:              abx                  ; Add n (in B) to sum
                    decb                 ; Decrement n
                    bne     SLOOP        ; IF n>0 THEN repeat
; Put all variables in their correct place
                    tfr     x,d          ; Sum returned in D
                    puls    x,cc         ; Retrieve all used registers
EXIT:               rts
                    .end
```

Table 6.16: Source code for an absolute assembler.

```
x6809 (1):

a:tab6_2_3.s 14: unknown op-code deb
a:tab6_2_3.s 14: deb not defined in file or include
a:tab6_2_3.s 15: LOOP not defined in file or include
a:tab6_2_3.s: 3 errors detected
```

Table 6.17: An error report if Table 6.16 is altered by replacing **DECB** by **DEB** and the label **SLOOP** by **LOOP**. The source file is named TAB6_2_3.S.

Listing files of this nature are for documentation only, and have no executable role.

```
 1                          .processor m6809
 2                  ;**********************************************************
 3                  ;* FUNCTION : Sums all unsigned integers up to n (max 255) *
 4                  ;* ENTRY    : n is passed in Accumulator B                 *
 5                  ;* EXIT     : Sum is returned in Accumulator D             *
 6                  ;* EXIT     : No other register contents disturbed         *
 7                  ;**********************************************************
 8                  ;
 9                              .org  0c000h     ; Program starts at 0C000h
10                  ; While n>0, sum=sum+n, decrement n
11 C000  3411       SUM_OF_INT: pshs  x,cc       ; Save X and CCR on stack
12 C002  8E0000                 ldx   #0         ; Clear sum
13 C005  3A         SLOOP:      abx              ; Add n (in B) to sum
14 C006  5A                     decb             ; Decrement n
15 C007  26FC                   bne   SLOOP      ; IF n>0 THEN repeat
16                  ; Put all variables in their correct place
17 C009  1F10                   tfr   x,d        ; Sum returned in D
18 C00B  3511                   puls  x,cc       ; Retrieve all used registers
19 C00D  39         EXIT:       rts
20                              .end
```

Table 6.18: Listing file produced from the source code of Table 6.16.

Symbol files list all symbols which occur in the program, giving name, location and sometimes other information. In Table 6.19, three labels are implicitly identified; **SUM_OF_INT** is located at C000h (the 0X prefix is the hexadecimal indicator used in the C language), **SLOOP** at C005h, and **EXIT** at C00Dh. The suffix t indicates text, which means appearing as part of the program. The suffix a is used to indicate an absolute symbol, i.e. one that has been defined using the .define directive (see page 461).

```
0xC000t SUM_OF_INT
0xC005t SLOOP
0xC00Dt EXIT
```

Table 6.19: Symbol file produced from the absolute source of Table 6.16.

Symbol files are commonly used by simulator and in-circuit emulator software to replace addresses by their symbolic equivalents, to aid in the debug process (see Table 6.15). They are also useful as a documentation aid.

All the program examples illustrated in the last chapter where assembled using a **relocating assembler** followed by a linker; as shown in the lower path of Fig. 6.10. These programs were rather trivial, and thus the linker was simply used to place the code to its absolute location. A long program is best implemented by breaking it up into a number of functionally distinct modules, which can be developed separately. Each module will likely cross-reference variables from other modules and possibly with a library of standard functions. Full details of these will not be known at the time these modules are designed. Thus there will be a need for a task builder to bring all these bits together, filling in these external symbols to give a single composite executable program. This task builder is called a linkage-editor or simply **linker** [17, 18].

The most important difference between an absolute and relocatable assembler is in the treatment of symbols. We will use a slightly modified listing of Table 5.35 to illustrate these concepts. Symbols explicitly allocated constant values by the programmer, such as **Cable_in** and **Cable_out** in line 13 of Table 6.20, are absolute and require no further processing by the linker. This is reasonable, as they refer to absolute physical locations of hardware ports, and should not be altered.

Symbols defined implicitly by attaching a label to an instruction are relocatable, since their value is only known relative to the start of the module; the location of which will be determined by the linker. The label **T_LOOP** in line 17 of Table 6.20 is relocatable five bytes after the start of the module. This is clearly shown in Table 6.21 which is produced by the assembler before the code is processed by the linker (see Fig. 6.10). Even more vague are symbols referred to but not defined in a module. Such symbols are assumed to be defined in some other module and should be declared so by using the .external directive. The linker will do its best to find a matching symbol in another module or library. There are no external symbols in Table 6.20.

Besides being tagged Absolute, Relocatable or External; symbols have the attributes of being global (public) or local. By default, local symbols cannot be referenced from an outside module, for example **T_LOOP** in line 17. If a symbol is

```
                        .processor       m6809
;******************************************************************
;* Subroutine checks the status of 8-core cable lengths           *
;* Locates three types of faults                                  *
;* Fault 1 indicates an open circuit                              *
;* Fault 2 indicates a short circuit between two wires            *
;* Fault 3 indicates a mixture of open and short circuit          *
;* ENTRY : None                                                   *
;* EXIT  : Last test vector in A                                  *
;* EXIT  : Error type 0, 1, 2, 3 in B; 0 indicates no fault       *
;******************************************************************
                        .psect   _text          ; Text stream (program in ROM)
                        .define Cable_in = 9000h, Cable_out = 9001h
TEST:                   clr      Error           ; Initial error type is 0
                        lda      #00000001b      ; The initial test loop
; For n=0 to 7, send out test vector and check.  Exit if error
T_LOOP:                 sta      Cable_in        ; Send out test vector
                        ldx      #2000           ; Wait for a while to settle
D_LOOP:                 leax     -1,x
                        bne      D_LOOP
                        tfr      a,b             ; Then copy test vector across to B
                        eorb     Cable_out       ; and compare with outcome
                        bne      FAULT           ; IF not the same THEN do error handling
                        lsla                     ; The next vector
                        bcs      EXIT            ; unless a one pops out!
                        bra      T_LOOP          ; Repeat test
; Land here if an error has occurred
FAULT:                  inc      Error           ; First check for an open-circuit fault
                        tst      Cable_out       ; as indicated by an all zeros return
                        beq      EXIT            ; IF true THEN error type 1
                        inc      Error           ; ELSE try for a short-circuit fault by
                        tfr      a,b             ; ANDing test vector
                        andb     Cable_out       ; with received pattern
                        bne      EXIT            ; IF test bit still there THEN a short circuit
                        inc      Error           ; ELSE a mixed open- and short-circuit
; Return with test vector in A; error type in B
EXIT:                   ldb      Error
                        rts
;
                        .psect   _data          ; Data stream (RAM)
ERROR:                  .byte    [1]            ; Reserve one byte called ERROR
;
                        .public TEST, T_LOOP, D_LOOP, FAULT, EXIT, ERROR
                        .end
```

Table 6.20: Relocatable source for the cable-test module of Table 5.35.

to be globally known, then it must be declared as such. In line 43 **TEST**, **FAULT**, **EXIT** and **Error** are declared public by using the directive `.public`. Being able to use local labels, not known to external programs, is convenient. Thus if two modules had used the label **LOOP**, then the linker would be unable to resolve the duplication unless they were local to their own module. The assembler must pass on the symbol names, tags and attributes to the linker together with the machine code in its output relocatable **object code** file.

Machine code is passed to the linker in streams. The RTS[3] assemblers used in this text, fundamentally identify two streams, one for program code and the other for data. The listing of Table 6.20 uses the directives `.psect _text` for the former and `.psect _data` for the latter, where `.psect` stands for program section. Most embedded microprocessor systems will require text (which includes tables of constants) in ROM and use RAM for variable data. The linker will start each section at a user-specified address, and as the modules are put together, the two streams

---

[3]Real Time Systems, M & G House, Head Road, Douglas, Isle of Man and Intermetrics Microsystems Software, Inc., 733 Concord Avenue, Cambridge MA 02138, U.S.A.

are concatenated from this point. In our example program the object **Error** was put in the _data stream by the declaration of line 40. Assigning absolute locations for such variables, as was done in the original listing of Table 5.35 is not recommended in modular software, as the same locations may be used by several programmers. Better let the linker allocate addresses. The .byte [1] directive in line 41 simply says to the linker "reserve one byte in the _data space and call it **Error**".

The code emerging from the assembler is shown in Table 6.21. This lists both the _text and _data sections starting from 0000*h*, as their final value is unknown until linked. If there were external variables, they would be given the temporary value of zero also.

The linker program has several tasks to perform:

1. To concatenate code from the various input modules in the specified order to give one contiguous machine-code file.

2. To resolve any inter-module and library external symbolic references.

```
1                        .processor    m6809
2             ;************************************************************
3             ;* Subroutine checks the status of 8-core cable lengths     *
4             ;* Locates three types of faults                            *
5             ;* Fault 1 indicates an open circuit                        *
6             ;* Fault 2 indicates a short circuit between two wires       *
7             ;* Fault 3 indicates a mixture of open and short circuit     *
8             ;* ENTRY : None                                             *
9             ;* EXIT  : Last test vector in A                            *
10            ;* EXIT  : Error type 0, 1, 2, 3 in B; 0 indicates no fault *
11            ;************************************************************
12                        .psect   _text      ; Text stream (program in ROM)
13                        .define Cable_in = 9000h, Cable_out = 9001h
14 0000 7F0034 TEST:  clr     Error      ; Initial error type is 0
15 0003 8601          lda     #00000001b ; The initial test loop
16            ; For n=0 to 7, send out test vector and check. Exit if error
17 0005 B79000 T_LOOP: sta     Cable_in   ; Send out test vector
18 0008 8E07D0        ldx     #2000      ; Wait for a while to settle
19 000B 301F   D_LOOP: leax    -1,x
20 000D 26FC          bne     D_LOOP
21 000F 1F89          tfr     a,b        ; Then copy test vector across to B
22 0011 F89001        eorb    Cable_out  ; and compare with outcome
23 0014 2605          bne     FAULT      ; IF not the same THEN do error handling
24 0016 48            lsla               ; The next vector
25 0017 2517          bcs     EXIT       ; unless a one pops out!
26 0019 20EA          bra     T_LOOP     ; Repeat test
27            ; Land here if an error has occurred
28 001B 7C0034 FAULT: inc     Error      ; First check for an open-circuit fault
29 001E 7D9001        tst     Cable_out  ; as indicated by an all zeros return
30 0021 270D          beq     EXIT       ; IF true THEN error type 1
31 0023 7C0034        inc     Error      ; ELSE try for a short-circuit fault by
32 0026 1F89          tfr     a,b        ; ANDing test vector
33 0028 F49001        andb    Cable_out  ; with received pattern
34 002B 2603          bne     EXIT       ; IF test bit still there THEN a short
35 002D 7C0034        inc     Error      ; ELSE a mixed open- and short-circuit
36            ; Return with test vector in A; error type in B
37 0030 F60034 EXIT:  ldb     Error
38 0033 39            rts
39                    ;
40                        .psect   _data      ; Data stream (RAM)
41 0000 00     ERROR: .byte   [1]        ; Reserve one byte called ERROR
42                    ;
43                        .public TEST, FAULT, EXIT, Error
44                        .end
```

Table 6.21: What the code looks like after assembling but before linking.

3. To extract code from libraries into the output machine code.

4. To generate the machine-code file, together with any symbol, listing and link-
   time error files.

As an example, imagine that our software comprizes of three separately assembled modules. Module MAIN.S repetitively calls up the module CABLE_TEST.S,
placing the resulting error value in an array for later analysis. A final module,
called VECTOR.S places the Reset vector up at the top of ROM. If these are
assembled, then the process will produce three object code files, typically called
MAIN.O, CABLE_TEST.O and VECTOR.O. Let us assume that we wish to
locate _text in module MAIN beginning at E000h, followed by _text from module
CABLE_TEST. Then put _text in module VECTOR beginning at FFFEh. All
_data from these modules are to be concatenated in the module order given, com-
mencing at 0000h. Then if the linker program is called LINKX, we might invoke
the process with the command:

```
LINKX -db 0000 -tb 0xe000 main.o cable_test.o -tb 0xfffe vector.o
-o cable.xeq
```

The command line is; reading from left to right:

```
-db   0000    Start data bias at zero
-tb 0xe000    Start text bias at E000h (note the use of the prefix 0x for hex)
main.o        Scan object module main.o
cable_test.o  then object module cable_test.o
-tb 0xfffe    Any further text begins at FFFEh
vector.o      Scan object module vector.o
-o cable.xeq  Name the resulting output file cable.xeq
```

The action of these commands can clearly be seen by looking at the addresses in
the listing file produced after linking, Table 6.22. The module MAIN has its _text
located between E000–E00Ah. The following module CABLE_TEST then begins
at E00Bh and continues on to E03Eh. The final module commences at FFFEh. This
places the address **MAIN** in the word location FFFE:Fh, using the directive .word.
The .external address **MAIN** is known to VECTOR through the linker, as module
MAIN declared the label **MAIN** as .public in line 13. Module MAIN reserves 500
bytes for an array placed in the _data stream. This is located by the linker between
0000–01F3h, placing the byte **ERROR** in module CABLE_TEST at the following
location 01F4h.

While code is being passed through the linker from the various input object files,
a composite symbol table is built up. For our example, this combined symbol table
is shown in Table 6.23(a), which gives the final location of all the public symbols.
If any symbols remain unresolved at this point, then they are indicated as errors.
However, if the format of the linker's output object code is the same relocatable
mode as the input, the the resulting file can be linked later with other object files.

The final objective of all these processes is the absolute **machine-code file**.
This gives addresses and their contents, ready to loaded into memory and run.
In the microprocessor world there are several different formats in common use.
Although these de facto standards are manufacturer specific, in the main they can

```
1                        .processor m6809
2                        .psect      _text
3                        .external  TEST  ; Linker, you'll find MAIN in another module!
4                      ;
5  E000 108E0000 MAIN:  ldy #ERROR_ARRAY ; Point Y to start of this run's error array
6  E004 BDE00B   LOOP:  jsr TEST        ; Go test the cable
7  E007 E7A0            stb ,y+         ; Store error code away and advance one
8  E009 20F9            bra LOOP        ; Next test
9                      ;
10                       .psect _data
11 0000      ERROR_ARRAY: .byte [500]   ; Hold 500 bytes in the data stream for array
12                      ;
13                       .public MAIN  ; Make MAIN known to the linker
14                       .end
1                        .processor      m6809
2                      ;*************************************************************
3                      ;* Subroutine checks the status of 8-core cable lengths      *
4                      ;* Locates three types of faults                             *
5                      ;* Fault 1 indicates an open circuit                         *
6                      ;* Fault 2 indicates a short circuit between two wires        *
7                      ;* Fault 3 indicates a mixture of open and short circuit      *
8                      ;* ENTRY : None                                              *
9                      ;* EXIT  : Last test vector in A                             *
10                     ;* EXIT  : Error type 0, 1, 2, 3 in B; 0 indicates no fault  *
11                     ;*************************************************************
12                       .psect _text       ; Text stream (program in ROM)
13                       .define Cable_in = 9000h, Cable_out = 9001h
14 E00B 7F01F4   TEST:  clr    Error     ; Initial error type is 0
15 E00E 8601            lda    #00000001b; The initial test loop
16                     ; For n=0 to 7, send out test vector and check.  Exit if error
17 E010 B79000  T_LOOP: sta    Cable_in  ; Send out test vector
18 E013 8E07D0          ldx    #2000     ; Wait for a while to settle
19 E016 301F   D_LOOP:  leax   -1,x
20 E018 26FC            bne    D_LOOP
21 E01A 1F89            tfr    a,b       ; Then copy test vector across to B
22 E01C F89001          eorb   Cable_out ; and compare with outcome
23 E01F 2605            bne    FAULT     ; IF not the same THEN do error handling
24 E021 48              lsla             ; The next vector
25 E022 2517            bcs    EXIT      ; unless a one pops out!
26 E024 20EA            bra    T_LOOP    ; Repeat test
27                     ; Land here if an error has occurred
28 E026 7C01F4  FAULT:  inc    Error     ; First check for an open-circuit fault
29 E029 7D9001          tst    Cable_out ; as indicated by an all zeros return
30 E02C 270D            beq    EXIT      ; IF true THEN error type 1
31 E02E 7C01F4          inc    Error     ; ELSE try for a short-circuit fault by
32 E031 1F89            tfr    a,b       ; ANDing test vector
33 E033 F49001          andb   Cable_out ; with received pattern
34 E036 2603            bne    EXIT      ; IF test bit still there THEN a short cct
35 E038 7C01F4          inc    Error     ; ELSE a mixed open- and short-circuit
36                     ; Return with test vector in A; error type in B
37 E03B F601F4  EXIT:   ldb    Error
38 E03E 39              rts
39                     ;
40                       .psect _data       ; Data stream (RAM)
41 01F4 00      ERROR:  .byte  [1]        ; Reserve one byte called ERROR
42                     ;
43                       .public TEST, FAULT, EXIT, Error
44                       .end
1                        .processor m6809
2                        .psect _text
3                        .external MAIN  ; Linker, you'll find MAIN in another module
4  FFFE E000   RESET:  .word  MAIN     ; Put the 16-bit start address in here
5                        .end
```

Table 6.22: Linking three modules together.

be used interchangeable for any brand of MPU. The machine-code file shown in Table 6.23(b) is the Intel hexadecimal object format, originally designed for the 8080 MPU. Each code record line contains a starting full colon marker followed by a byte giving the number of code bytes in that line. The record is terminated by a checksum byte; defined as the 2's complement of the modulo-256 (8-bit) sum of all the preceding bytes (two hexadecimal digits). As a check, the loader program sums all bytes plus the checksum for each line and accepts the veracity of the data if the result is zero.

As an example, expanding the first line of the code gives:

:	Start of line
20	Number of code bytes (32)
E000	Address of the first byte
00	Record type (00 = code, 01 = end of record)
108E0000BDE00BE7A0......C1F89F8900126	Machine code
AB	Checksum

Sometimes the symbol and machine-code information is combined into a composite symbolized file.

```
0xe016T D_LOOP
0xe03bT EXIT
0x01f4D Error
0xe026T FAULT
0xe000T MAIN
0xe00bT TEST
0xe010T T_LOOP
```

(a): Composite symbol table after linking.

```
:20E00000108E0000BDE00BE7A020F97F01F48601B790008E07D0301F26FC1F89F8900126AB
:20E020000548251720EA7C01F47D9001270D7C01F41F89F4900126037C01F4F601F439003E
:20FFE0000000000000000000000000000000000000000000000000000000000000E00021
:00E000011F
```

(b): The absolute machine-code file.

Table 6.23: Output from the linker.

Absolute files are accepted by most PROM programmers, giving the final link in the chain of Fig. 6.10. The software in the PROM programmer that accepts, checks and interprets the data in these absolute machine-code files is called a **loader**. In some cases the target system is a computer-like system, such as a microprocessor development system, with a resident operating system and user program running in RAM. In such instances the loader program will be part of the operating system. Sometimes the machine-code file format is not absolute, and it is left to the relocating loader program to decide in what part of memory the program is to reside in. This is the case in the MSDOS operating system, where the machine-code files reside on disk as .EXE files and are relocated at run time by the loader. Machine code files of this type can be generated by any software package targeted to a PROM/PLE device. For example Table 6.24 shows the output from the PLD compiler for the PLE5P8 of Example 6.4.

:1000000098082008284810302818284048384818F0
:10001000101840203010302018184018103848288
:00000001FF

Table 6.24: Machine-code file for the π generator PLE5P8.

The actual mechanism of the translation process used by the assembler is of little importance to us here. Most assemblers are described as 2-pass, as historically all but the simplest read the source code — which was originally on paper tape or punched cards — twice through from beginning to end. During the first pass a location counter keeps track of where each instruction is to be placed relative to the beginning of the code. As each operation mnemonic is encountered, the location counter is incremented by the appropriate number; thus LDY #0000 causes the location counter to advance by four. As labels are encountered, their name and the state of the location counter are stored in the symbol table, which is built up during the first pass. Labels which are explicitly defined, using the .define directive are of course added to the symbol table without a translation being necessary. It is necessary to build up a symbol table in pass 1 to cope with forward references; thus an instruction BRA NEXT, where **NEXT** is further on down the source file, cannot be fully translated until **NEXT** has been reached and given a value. Some assemblers may save any translated machine code to speed up the second pass.

During the second pass, the translation is repeated, but this time any references to symbolic names are replaced by the values extracted from the symbol table. With the translation complete, an object file is created to pass to the linker, with external symbols being marked but left blank.

Given that a program has been written and assembled, how is it to be checked? If the target hardware has been built (or bought in) and tested, then an EPROM can be programmed with the code; plugged in, and power applied. However, if a software malfunction occurs, we have no means of monitoring such a naked target. We could of course use an in-circuit emulator as described earlier in the last section, but the ICE is an expensive piece of equipment and as such may be a shared resource between several products and thus not always available. As such, using an ICE simply to check out a software algorithm is akin to using a sledge hammer to crack a nut.

An alternative approach is to use a computer with a suitable software package to simulate the target microprocessor [19]. This package is known as a **cross simulator** or sometimes as a low-level symbolic debugger. One major advantage of the use of a simulator is that no target hardware is involved. This means that the hardware and software design stages can stay apart longer. Thus the ICE can be used for the hardware/software interaction phases and to investigate obscure problems, final testing and in-field trouble-shooting. Typical facilities offered by a simulator are:

• **Disassembly** To display the contents of simulated target memory in instruction mnemonics — a sort of reverse assembler.

- **Register and memory examine/change**

    To examine any internal register(s) or memory location(s) and make any necessary changes.

- **Step execution**

    To execute the target program one or more instructions at a time, usually displaying registers after each one.

- **Trace execution**

    Similar to Step, but as fast as can be displayed.

- **Breakpoints**

    Insertion of conditions, such as reaching a certain address, which causes execution to pause or stop.

- **Execute**

    Similar to Trace, but as fast as the simulator can operate with no screen output. Normally stops when a breakpoint is encountered.

As an example we will use the COSMIC/Intermetrics[4] Mimic simulator to simulate a slightly modified version of the Sum Of Integer program of Table 6.16.

Table 6.25 is a log of a typical simulation session to which I have added comments. After loading the file generated by the linker into the simulator, the process was:

1. Disassemble program mnemonics from code loaded into simulated memory, that is memory in the PC (e 0xe000, 0xe00f).

2. Change the System Stack Pointer to 400h, the top of the simulated System stack ($s=0x400).

3. Change Accumulator_B to 4, thereby simulating a calling program sending out the integer four ($b=4).

4. Put in a breakpoint at the end of the program at the RTS instruction (b=EXIT).

5. Trace through the program from beginning to the breakpoint giving a line-by-line record of the state of the registers (t 0xe000).

The progress of the program can be clearly seen from the trace. Accumulator_B is decremented with each pass through the loop, whilst at the same time **X** is augmented. The final value of 000Ah or decimal 10 (4+3+2+1) is transferred to **D** for return, and the old value of **X** and the Code Condition register pulled out from the System stack. Notice how the System Stack pointer is decremented to 03FDh after the PSHS instruction and restored again by the PULS instruction.

Whilst the session in Table 6.25 may superficially resemble the equivalent process using an ICE, remember that this result was obtained from a run on a personal computer powered by an Intel 80386 MPU; with not a 6809 in sight!

---

[4]COSMIC SARL, 33 Rue Le Corbusier, Europarc Creteil, 94035 Creteil Cedex, France; Real Time Systems, M & G House, Head Road, Douglas, Isle of Man and Intermetrics Microsystems Software, Inc., 733 Concord Avenue, Cambridge MA 02138, U.S.A.

```
e 0xe000, 0xe00f                        ; Disassemble program as seen by Mimic

    0xe000          SUM_OF_IN:
    0xe000 3411          pshs  cc,x
    0xe002 8e0000        ldx   #0x0000
    0xe005          SLOOP:
    0xe005 3a            abx
    0xe006 5a            decb
    0xe007 26fc          bne   SLOOP
    0xe009 1f10          tfr   x,d
    0xe00b 3511          puls  cc,x
    0xe00d          EXIT:
--> 0xe00d 39            rts

$s=0x400                                ; Make SP = 400h
$b=4                                    ; Make Acc.B = 04h

b=EXIT                                  ; Break at EXIT (ie E00Dh)

t 0xe000                                ; Trace from the beginning to break point

cc:........ dp:00 a:00 b:04 x:0000 y:0000 u:0000 s:0400 pc:e000 pshs  cc,x
cc:........ dp:00 a:00 b:04 x:0000 y:0000 u:0000 s:03fd pc:e002 ldx   #0000
cc:.....Z.. dp:00 a:00 b:04 x:0000 y:0000 u:0000 s:03fd pc:e005 abx
cc:.....Z.. dp:00 a:00 b:04 x:0004 y:0000 u:0000 s:03fd pc:e006 decb
cc:........ dp:00 a:00 b:03 x:0004 y:0000 u:0000 s:03fd pc:e007 bne   SLOOP
cc:........ dp:00 a:00 b:03 x:0004 y:0000 u:0000 s:03fd pc:e005 abx
cc:........ dp:00 a:00 b:03 x:0007 y:0000 u:0000 s:03fd pc:e006 decb
cc:........ dp:00 a:00 b:02 x:0007 y:0000 u:0000 s:03fd pc:e007 bne   SLOOP
cc:........ dp:00 a:00 b:02 x:0007 y:0000 u:0000 s:03fd pc:e005 abx
cc:........ dp:00 a:00 b:02 x:0009 y:0000 u:0000 s:03fd pc:e006 decb
cc:........ dp:00 a:00 b:01 x:0009 y:0000 u:0000 s:03fd pc:e007 bne   SLOOP
cc:........ dp:00 a:00 b:01 x:0009 y:0000 u:0000 s:03fd pc:e005 abx
cc:........ dp:00 a:00 b:01 x:000a y:0000 u:0000 s:03fd pc:e006 decb
cc:.....Z.. dp:00 a:00 b:00 x:000a y:0000 u:0000 s:03fd pc:e007 bne   SLOOP
cc:.....Z.. dp:00 a:00 b:00 x:000a y:0000 u:0000 s:03fd pc:e009 tfr   x,d
cc:.....Z.. dp:00 a:00 b:0a x:000a y:0000 u:0000 s:03fd pc:e00b puls  cc,x
cc:........ dp:00 a:00 b:0a x:0000 y:0000 u:0000 s:0400 pc:e00d (rts   )
```

Table 6.25: Simulating the Sum Of Integers program.

6.2.3   High-Level Languages

Assembly-level language is machine-oriented, with generally a one-to-one correspondence to the machine instructions. As such, code written at this level bears little relationship to the problem being implemented. The use of a **high-level language** permits a description of the problem in an algorithmically-oriented terminology. In the language **C** the code fragment introducing the last section becomes:

```
#define    CONSTANT = 6
unsigned char X,Y;       /* Define X and Y as unsigned bytes */
{Y=X+CONSTANT;}          /* The process                      */
```

Now we no longer need to keep track of exactly where **X** and **Y** have to be stored. Also we have a large repertoiré of mathematical and text-handling functions, which do not have a one-to-one machine-level counterpart. Notice that our program did not indicate which processor's machine code would eventually be produced; the target might just as well be a Z80 or a 68000.

Of course there are problems in using high level languages, especially when the target is an embedded MPU-based system. In general the further away the level is from the machine code, the more isolated the programmer is from the raw hardware.

The idea of a high-level language being defined as a function of the 'distance' it is removed from the ultimate machine code is illustrated in Fig. 6.11. At the highest level we have human thought defining the specification and problem algorithm. A high-level language expresses this algorithm in a concise and analytical manner.

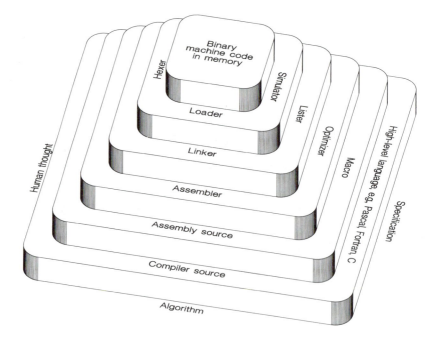

Figure 6.11: Onion skin view of the steps leading to an executable program.

The greater the language level the closer it is to human thought and hence is more closely modelled to the problem. There is a large spectrum of languages spanning the range between human thought and assembly level. Assemblers model the underlying machine code, with no correlation in any way with the original problem. Macroassemblers allow the programmer to define sequences of machine-level instructions and give these formulations names. Macro instructions can then be used as a kind of simple high-level language.

The one-to-one correspondence between assembly-level code and machine code makes the task of the assembler relatively easy. The equivalent high-level to machine code translation is much more onerous. The translation package operating on high-level source code is known as a **compiler**. The closer a computer language is to human language, the more difficult is the compiler's task. Because of the complexity, a compiler demands much more of the host computing engine, and is corresponding more expensive than an assembler. For these reasons, the use of compilers to generate machine code for embedded MPU circuitry is relatively new, although high-level languages have been extensively used for large computers since the 1950s.

Historically, the high-level language Fortran (FORmula TRANslation) was introduced in the 1950s to insulate the programmer from the nasty realities of the underlying hardware. Given the large resources provided, even then, by mainframe computers and the standardization of input and output terminals, this was a desirable route to follow. Fortran was quickly followed by a raft of alternative languages, such as COBOL (COmmon Business Oriented Language), Algol (ALGOrithmic Language), Pascal, Modulo-2, Ada, PL/M (Programming Language for Microprocessors), and Occam. Each language was claimed by its originators to fill some as yet uncovered niche. Thus, Fortran was targeted to the scientific community, COBOL for business interests, Pascal and Modulo-2 for education, Occam for multiprocessing networks and BASIC (Beginners All-purpose Symbolic Instruction Code) for everyone. Such is the proliferation of different languages that one (faintly humorous) definition of a computer scientist [20] is one who, when presented with a problem to solve, invents a new programming language instead!

The main advantages of the use of a high-level code over assembly level, is insulation of the program writer from the hardware and the consequential ease of moving the program to a different computer. Portability has obvious financial benefits. If the same package, with relatively minor alterations, can run on any computer, the the huge cost of writing, debugging and maintaining a program is amortized over a much larger customer base. In addition, a programmer's expertize can be recycled over many projects involving different processors, instead of having to learn a plethora of assembly languages and hardware quirks. As it takes approximately the same time to write and debug a line of code in any language,........ and as a high-level instruction will, by definition, do much more than a single machine instruction; then the advantages of these algorithmic languages seem overwhelming. Not so obvious are the attributes of structure, reliability, maintainability and documentation.

We saw in Fig. 6.5 that the software design path involved a systematic decomposition of the system down to small functional modules. This approach is known as **top-down design** [21]. An example of this is shown in Fig. 6.12. The major system blocks are usually readily identified from the system specification. Generally

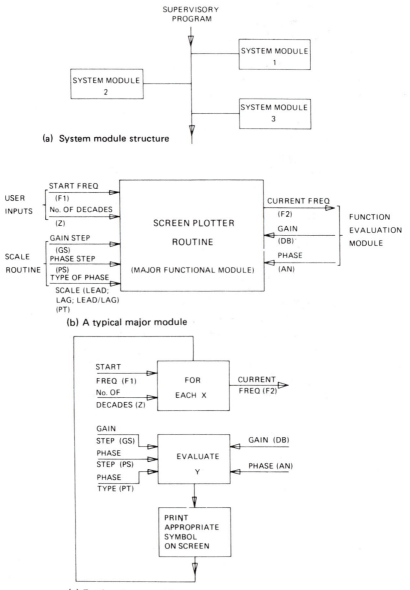

(a) System module structure

(b) A typical major module

(c) Further decomposition

Figure 6.12: System software decomposition

these blocks are linked by the main supervisory routine acting as a central spine, as shown in Fig. 6.12(a). This serves to sequence the major functions in the requisite manner, usually depending on information from the outside world. One possibility is to develop the supervisory program first, with as yet ungenerated modules replaced by stubs. These stubs return test data to the supervisory program on demand, simulating the absent module. No matter what order of development is followed in this modular approach, modules should not overlap by sharing routines, although well-defined common subroutines are permitted. This stand-alone property enables modules to be altered, updated and debugged without interacting with other system modules.

The system modules must in turn be partitioned into a series of major functional modules, each of which carry out a clearly identified task. The interface between the various functional modules making up the system module must be clearly identified, as shown in Fig. 6.12(b). This is analogous to indicating signal lines and functions in a logic circuit. In the software documentation, the name and form of each of these variables must be listed, together with their originating point and format.

Frequently major functional modules are too large for successful algorithm development. In such cases the process of decomposition may be continued, as shown in Fig. 6.12(c), until the complexity is such that the algorithm strategy is straightforward.

Algorithm development is essentially personalized, in that each designer has his or her own approach. Nevertheless, the adoption of an orderly approach to the construction of software not only aids in the synthesis process, but also facilitates documentation, and hence future maintenance. Where only a limited set of software structures is used to realize the algorithm, the process is known as **structured programming**. There are three standard structures commonly used in structured programs, as shown in Fig. 6.13. However several versions exist of each kind, and seven configurations have been identified [22]. The use of a non-standard structure does not invalidate the procedure, but all structures must have only one entry and exit point. This reduces and clarifies the interaction between programming elements, thus easing debugging.

The simplest structure involves a simple process, or list of processes. As can be seen from Fig. 6.13(a), there are no alternative paths within this structure.

Except for the most trivial of programs, some element of decision must be made in order to allow the system to react to outside conditions. The most common of these constructions is shown in Fig. 6.13(b). Depending on the outcome of the test, either process A or process B is carried out. In some cases the test may be implied, with the decision being based on a flag set by a previous process. As an example, consider a variable **Vin** read from an analog port. The variable **Vout** is to be made equal to this value but clipped to no more than a constant **max**. In the language **C**, this could be stated as:

```
if (Vin > max)
        {Vout = max;}
else {Vout = Vin;}
```

Any of the processes in the IF-THEN-ELSE structure can in turn be another decision strategy, giving a tree structure. The C function is designed to return the factorial of **n** over the range 0–12:

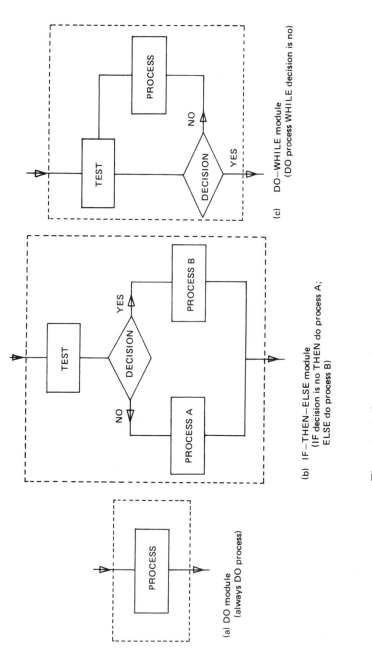

Figure 6.13: Structured programming building blocks

```
unsigned long  factor(int n)
{
        unsigned long factorial;
        if(n==0||n==1)   {factorial=1;}
        else if(n==2)    {factorial=2;}
        else if(n==3)    {factorial=6;}
        else if(n==4)    {factorial=24;}
        else if(n==5)    {factorial=120;}
        else if(n==6)    {factorial=720;}
        else if(n==7)    {factorial=5040;}
        else if(n==8)    {factorial=40320;}
        else if(n==9)    {factorial=362880;}
        else if(n==10)   {factorial=3628800;}
        else if(n==11)   {factorial=39916800;}
        else if(n==12)   {factorial=479001600;}
        else             {factorial=0;}  /* Error condition */
        return(factorial);

}
```

Without going into the syntax of this example in detail, the function **factor()** is defined to accept an *integer* **n** (16-bits) and return an *unsigned long* integer (32-bits). The unsigned long int variable **factorial** is assigned a value depending on the outcome of thirteen comparison decisions using an **if-else** tree. Notice the use of the == operator to mean 'equivalent to'. The first decision also uses the || operator as logic OR; thus the statement reads 'if **n** is equivalent to 0 or to 1 then make **factorial** equal to 1'. The { } pair enclose a process, called a statement in **C**, i.e., **begin** and **begin:end**. Once a decision is true, the THEN process is carried out and control passes to the end of the tree structure. Why do you think the value of **n** is limited to 12?

The basic loop construction is shown in Fig. 6.13(c). Here the process continually executes until a decision is made to exit the loop. This DO-WHILE structure is illustrated in the following program fragment, which implements the factorial function above, but using repetitive multiplication.

```
unsigned long  factor(int n)
    {
    unsigned long factorial;
    factorial=1;                         /* Initial value    */
    if(n>12)          {factorial=0;}     /* Error condition */
    else                                 /* Begin else       */
        {
        while(n>1)                       /* Repetitively     */
            {
            factorial=factorial*n;  /* xply by n        */
            n=n-1;                  /* decrementing n  */
            }                       /* down to one      */
        }
    return(factorial);
    }
```

If **n** is less than 2 on entry to the WHILE loop loop, the process is never carried out. Where the process must be carried out at least once, an equivalent structure with the test at the end of the process can be used. This is sometimes known as a REPEAT-UNTIL structure.

In all cases the process box may in turn contain structures of its own, as the designer decomposes from the system flowchart down to the finer details. For example, the process in Fig. 6.13(c) may be another DO-WHILE loop, giving a construction known as a nested loop.

Irrespective of the structures adopted, it can be seen that only one entry and one exit point is allowed. If another module entered process A directly in Fig. 6.13(b), then this would be an example of unstructured coding. Process A would have to be repeated separately for the other module. However, writing process A as a subroutine will allow its use by more than one module. Because of the restrictions imposed on the software designer by structured programming, the final code is likely to be both longer and slower. Nevertheless, in most cases the resulting clarity of design will give better results in the long term. More details are given in references [23, 24].

Although these paradigms can be, and are, implemented at assembly level; there is little to encourage the programmer to resist the temptation to write 'spaghetti code'.

Example 6.9

Design a subroutine which will produce the 2's complement of an n-byte number stored in consecutive ascending memory locations. The calling program points Index register_X to the lowest byte, and Accumulator_B holds the byte count n.

Solution

As discussed in Section 1.2.2, the 2's complement of a number can be created by straight inversion plus one. Thus the byte $00001001b$ becomes $11110110b + 1 = 11110111b$. The instruction **neg** performs this operation for most MPUs. Hence a byte up in memory at, say, $0020h$ is 2's complemented by the instruction **neg 0020h**.

A moments thought shows that if the original number is composed of several bytes, then negating each byte in turn will not produce the desired multibyte 2's complement. This is because the $+1$ is a one-off operation which should be added to the overall conglomerate: eg. the 2-byte word $\boxed{00000000}\boxed{01010101} \rightarrow \boxed{11111111}\boxed{10101010} + 1 = \boxed{11111111}\boxed{10101011}$. Normally this can be implemented by 2's complementing the lowest byte and 1's complementing i.e. inverting the rest. The exception to this is if the 2's complemented byte overflows, i.e. $00000000 \Rightarrow 11111111 + 1 = 00000000$ carry 1. This carry indicates that the next higher byte must have a one added after complementation. Thus for example we have: $\boxed{01010101}\boxed{00000000} \rightarrow \boxed{10101011}\boxed{00000000}$. This result has been produced by negating both bytes, rather than negating the lower byte and inverting the upper byte.

The 6809's NEG instruction sets the C flag whenever there is an overflow, which only occurs if the original byte is $00000000b$. Furthermore the instruction COM, which does a straight complement or inversion, always clears the C flag. As a consequence

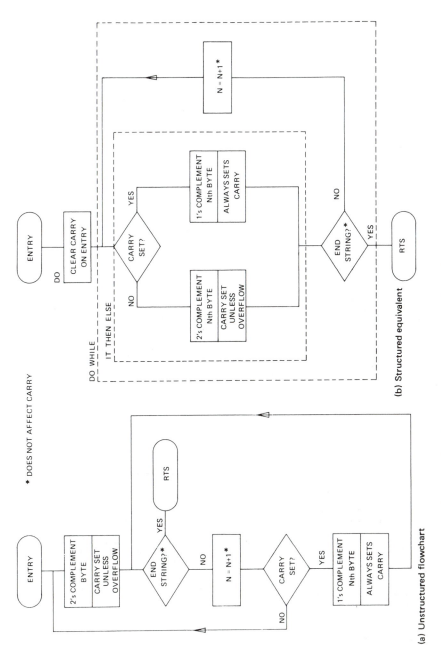

Figure 6.14: Two algorithms for multibyte 2's complementations.

of this, a simple task analysis for multibyte 2's complementation would be:

1. $i = 0$, $C = 0$

2. WHILE $(I < n)$ DO

3. BEGIN WHILE

4. IF $(C = 0)$ THEN {2's complement byte i and IF (the outcome is zero) THEN $\{C = 1\}$ }

5. ELSE {1's complement byte i}

6. Increment i

7. END WHILE

```
 1                              .processor m6809
 2              ;****************************************************************
 3              ;* Produces the 2's complement of an n-byte string              *
 4              ;* ENTRY: N-byte number is stored in consecutive RAM locations  *
 5              ;* ENTRY: X points to LSB data, B holds the number of bytes N    *
 6              ;* EXIT : X points to MSB data, B is zero                        *
 7              ;****************************************************************
 8 E000 6080   COMP2:      neg    ,x+     ; 2's comp data byte pointed to by X, inc X
 9 E002 5A     COMP1:      decb           ; One less byte (doesn't affect carry flag)
10 E003 2601               bne    CONTINUE ; IF count not down to zero THEN next byte
11 E005 39                 rts            ; ELSE finished
12              ; The rest of the data bytes only need normal inversion unless
13              ; the last neg was 00000000 -> 11111111+1 = 00000000 with C=0
14              ; In this case do another neg and repeat
15 E006 24F8   CONTINUE:   bcc    COMP2   ; IF neg made C=1 THEN 2's comp next byte
16 E008 6380               com    ,x+     ; ELSE do an ordinary inversion.
17 E00A 20F6               bra    COMP1   ; As C=1 after com, continue for all bytes
18                         .end
19
20
```

(a): Unstructured code.

```
 1                              .processor m6809
 2              ;****************************************************************
 3              ;* Produces the 2's complement of an n-byte string              *
 4              ;* ENTRY: N-byte number is stored in consecutive RAM locations  *
 5              ;* ENTRY: X points to LSB data, B holds the number of bytes N    *
 6              ;* EXIT : X points to MSB data, B is zero                        *
 7              ;****************************************************************
 8 E000 1CFE   COMP2:      andcc #11111110b ; Clear C flag
 9 E002 2504   COM_LOOP:   bcs    ONES_COMP ; IF YES THEN DO 1's complement
10 E004 6080               neg    ,x+      ; ELSE BEGIN 2's comp; clear C on overflow
11 E006 2002               bra    END_STRING ; END DO 2's complement
12 E008 6380   ONES_COMP:  com    ,x+      ; DO 1's complement and always set C flag
13              ; Check for end of data string
14 E00A 5A     END_STRING: decb            ; DO WHILE n>0
15 E00B 26F5               bne    COM_LOOP
16 E00D 39                 rts
17                         .end
```

(b): Structured code.

Table 6.26: Two assembly-level coding strategies implementing a multi-byte 2's complement subroutine.

A flow chart implementing this process is shown in Fig. 6.14. Because of the relatively complex interrelationship of the component routines, it is not possible to isolate modules with one entry and one exit point. The coding of this algorithm, given in Table 6.26(a) 2's complements the LSbyte in step 8, as pointed to by **X**. By using the Post-Increment address mode, this Index register then automatically points to the next higher byte. This is equivalent to incrementing i in the task analysis. Steps 9 & 10 simply increments a loop counter to permit an exit after n iterations. The **C** flag is not affected by these intervening instructions, allowing step 15 to test for overflow from step 8. As long as the **C** flag is clear, a Branch back to step 8 ensures a string of 2's complement operations. When the chain is broken, any further operations are 1's complements (step 16). Remember that COM always sets **C**, irrespective of the outcome.

The alternative solution of Table. 6.26(b) closely mirrors the structured flowchart of Fig. 6.14. Here the **C** flag is cleared on entry to the routine and before the IF-THEN-ELSE structure. Step 9 implements the THEN/ELSE decision, giving either a 2's complement or 1's complement operation as directed by the state of **C**. As in the previous coding, the **X** register is used to point to the target byte, and is automatically incremented. Accumulator_B acts as a loop counter for the DO-WHILE outer module to force an exit when the conversion is complete.

The software engineer gets little help in writing such code at assembly level as there are no structures embedded in the language as *per se*. To illustrate the difference we will repeat this exercise using the **C** language.

Example 6.10

To write an equivalent multi-byte 2's complement function coded in the language **C**. Two parameters are to be passed to the function (function is the **C** equivalent to assembly's subroutine. The variable **address** is to point to the lower byte of the data string, and **n** is the number of bytes in the string. The function does not return a value as such, so is prefixed with the descriptor void.

Solution

The coding of Table 6.27 has been written to mirror the task analysis above. The name of the function is multibyte_2s_comp and is defined in line 1 to expect the two variables. The first of these is typed as unsigned char *address. The * operator used in this context denotes 'contents of' (and rather confusingly, is also used for multiplication). Thus this declaration reads that the first variable passed is called **address** and it points to an object of type unsigned char. In C'eze, an object of size char is usually an 8-bit byte (big enough to hold an alphanumeric *character*, see Table 1.4. The unsigned variety then has a range from 00–FFh or 0–255. Thus **address** is a pointer variable to a byte (i.e. a byte address). Similarly **n** is a byte-sized object passed to the function.

Two variables are used in the body of the function; **i** and **c** are declared to be unsigned byte objects, and are also initialized in line 3 to zero. Variable **i** is the loop variable used by the DO-WHILE loop to decide when to exit and **c** mimics the Carry

```
void  multibyte_2s_comp(unsigned char *address, unsigned char n)
        {
        unsigned char i=0, c=0;
        while(i<n)
                {
                if(c==0)                          /* IF C is equivalent to zero   */
                        {                          /* THEN                          */
                        *address = - *address;    /* DO a 2's complement           */
                        if(*address=0) {c=1;}     /* IF an overflow occurs THEN set c */
                        }
                else {*address = ! *address;}     /* ELSE DO a 1's complement       */
                i++; address++;                    /* On to the next index and address */
                }                                  /* Only pass here when i==n       */
        }
```

Table 6.27: A high-level direct equivalent to our multi-byte 2's complement algorithm.

flag as used by the IF-THEN-ELSE structure to decide which path to take. From
Fig. 6.13(b) we have to either 2's complement or 1's complement on the state of **c**. In
the first instance this variable is zero, and thus the first IF's argument c==0 will be
true and the THEN path is taken. Line 8 reads *address = - *address;, which says
"the contents of the byte pointed to by **address** are replaced by the negative of what
it originally was". Assuming that the compiler uses 2's complement arithmetic,
then the - operator will give the 2's complement of the operand. Now we have
already seen that overflow occurs when the outcome of this exercise is 00000000b.
Thus the following line is a nested IF which makes **c** non zero in this situation, and
breaks the chain. After this THEN path has been completed, control jumps over the
ELSE path to line 12. Once **c** has been set to 1, this 2's complement path will never
be re-entered, as the 1's complement ELSE path does not alter **c**. The **C** operator
! performs simple inversion, i.e. 1's complement, in line 11. Finally the operator
++ is used to increment the loop variable and pointer to repeat the iteration. The
++ operator could be incorporated into another statement, rather than being used
in a stand-alone mode; eg. while(i++<n). Using the ++ after the variable means
'increment after usage', whilst a prefix means 'increment before usage'.

   All this syntax may be confusing at a first reading, but the object of this demonstration is not to teach the reader how to program in **C** but to show how a high-
level language can naturally mirror the structured processes. The interested reader
should refer to [25, 26, 27, 28] for further details in the **C** language.

────────────

   The advantages of using of high-level languages to produce code for embedded MPU targets is not so obvious. Isolation of the software from the underlying
hardware is a distinct drawback for such targets. What is required is a sort of
midi-level language having the ability of seeing down into the hardware, for example to manipulate addresses and to examine single bit, but keeping many of the
general advantages of a higher-level code. The first higher-level language for MPUs
was PL/M (a Programming Language for Microprocessors), which was developed
by Intel in the middle 1970s for the 8080 series of devices. PL/M provides block
structure and flow control statements – DO-WHILE, IF-THEN-ELSE etc. However, although it represented an improvement over assembler language, it still had features

which related strongly to the 8080 family processor, and thus was not easy to use for other types of MPU.

At the present time **C** (and its derivative **C++**) is the most popular high-level language for embedded MPU systems. Historically **C** was developed as a language for writing operating systems. In the early 1970s, Ken Thompson — an employee at Bell Labs — developed the first version of the UNIX operating system. This was written in assembly language for the PDP7 minicomputer. At its simplest level, an operating system is a program which makes the detailed operation of the computer terminals, such as keyboard and disk organization, invisible to the operator. The writer of an operating system program must be able to poke around the various registers and memory locations of the target machine. As such, assembly language was mandatory at that time, giving intimate machine contact and tight, fast code. However, the sheer size of such a project means that it is likely to be a team effort, with all the difficulties in integrating the code, and foibles, of several people. A great deal of self discipline and skill is demanded of such personnel, as is attention to documentation. Even with this, the final result cannot be easily used in machines with other processors — needs a nearly complete rewrite – and hard to maintain.

In the beginning there was CPL (Combined Programming Language), a language developed jointly by Cambridge and London universities in the mid 1960s. BCPL (Basic CPL) was a somewhat less complex but more efficient variant designed as a compiler-writing tool in the late 1960's [29]. At around that time, Bell System Laboratories were working on the UNIX operating system for their DEC PDP series of mini-computers. Early versions of UNIX were written in assembly language [30]. In an attempt to promote the spread of this operating system to different hardware environments, some work was done with the aim of rewriting UNIX in a portable language. The language B [31], which was essentially BCPL with a different syntax (and was named for the first letter of that language), was developed for that purpose in 1970 [32]; initially targeted to the PDP-11 mini-computer.

Both BCPL and B only used one type of object, the natural size machine word (16 bits for the PDP-11). This typeless structure led to difficulties in dealing with individual bytes and floating-point computation. **C** (the second letter of BCPL) was developed in 1972 to address this problem; by creating a range of objects of both integer and floating-point types (see Fig. 1.6). This enhanced its portability and flexibility. UNIX was reworked in **C** during the summer of 1973, comprizing around 10,000 lines of high-level code and 1000 lines at assembly level [33]. It occupied some 30% more storage than the original version.

Although **C** has been closely associated with UNIX; over the intervening years it has escaped to appear in compilers running under virtually every known operating system, and targeted to mainframe CPUs down to single chip microcontrollers. Furthermore, although originally a systems programming language, it is now used to write applications programs ranging from CAD down to the intelligence behind smart egg-timers!

For over ten years, the official definition of **C** was the first edition of *The C Programming Language*; written by the language's originators, Brian W. Kernighan and Dennis M. Ritchie. It is a tribute to the power and simplicity of the language, that over the years it has survived virtually intact; resisting the tendency to split into dialects and new versions. In 1983 the American National Standards Institute (ANSI) established the X3J11 committee to provide a modern and comprehensive definition of **C** to reflect the enhanced role of this language. The resulting definition, known as Standard or ANSII **C**, was approved in 1991.

Even with the availability of languages such as **C**, until relatively recently assembly language was the preferred choice for MPU-based digital circuitry. There are many reasons behind this. The main goal of embedded MPU software was seen as producing tight (compact) and fast code. This is the bailiwick of assembly language. As the cost of memory decreases and MPU power increases, this does not have the same primacy as it once did. Furthermore, many high-level languages permit assembler-generated modules to be linked in with compiler produced code. Thus time-critical sections of code can be written at low-level.

Another problem is the compiler itself. Compilers are by definition rather more sophisticated than an equivalent assembler. This arduous task demands more computing power to run the compiler and means that the compiler is relatively expensive. Also debugging programs running on an embedded MPU system written in a high-level language is a difficult task. This is mainly because the actual code run by the MPU is at machine/assembly level even though the source is high-level language. This is rather like debugging code produced by someone else, which can be a nightmare.

High-level simulators and in-circuit emulator software packages are now appearing which allow monitoring at both high-level source level and at assembly level. Powerful PCs and workstations to run these tools and the compilers are now readily available and affordable. Compilers are also getting more efficient, and the gap between assembly and compiler-originated code is acceptable in many cases. The trade off between the two approaches is between reliability, portability and the cost of writing code. In general large projects are difficult and expensive to code reliably at assembly level, but where resources are limited, typically in a MCU, or time is critical, then assembly-level code still has the edge.

As our final example of the section we will repeat the sum of integers subroutine illustrated at assembler level in Table 6.18.

Example 6.11

Write a function in **C** to evaluate the sum of all unsigned byte-sized integers up to n. The Value of n is to be passed to the function, and an unsigned word-sized outcome returned as the function value.

Solution

The algorithm implemented in Table 6.28 is the same as the original assembly-level listing, namely continually adding **n** to the initially cleared **sum**, as **n** is decremented to zero. Let us dissect it line by line.

Line 1 This line names the function **sum_of_n**, declares that it returns an **unsigned short int** (16-bit unsigned object), and expects an **unsigned char** (8-bit byte) to be passed to it called **n**.

Line 2 A left brace thus { means **begin**. All **begin**s must be matched with an **end**, which is denoted by a right brace }. It is good programming practice to indent right each **begin** from the column of the immediately preceding lines(s) and to ensure that **begin** and **end** braces line up. In this case line 10 is the corresponding **end** brace. Between lines 2 and 10 is the body of the function **sum_of_n**.

Line 3 There is only one variable which is local to our function. Its name and type are defined here. Thus **sum** is of type **unsigned short** (16-bit word). In **C**, all variables must be defined before they are used (unless they are declared as external). A definition tells the compiler what properties the named variable has, eg. size, so that it can allocate suitable storage. By prefixing this definition by the keyword **static**, I am telling the compiler that **sum** is to be stored at an absolute address in RAM rather than on the stack, which is the default. This will make the assembly code emitted by the compiler easier to follow (Table 6.29). This line is terminated by a semicolon ; as are all statements in **C**.

Line 4 Here we assign (=) the value 0 to the variable **sum**. A definition and an initializing assignment can frequently be combined. Thus:

```
static unsigned short sum = 0;
```

is a legitimate statement combining lines 3 and 4.

Line 5 In evaluating **sum** we require to repeat the same process for as long as **n** is greater than zero. This is the purpose of the **while** construction introduced in this line. The body of the loop, that is the statement which appears between the following left and right braces of lines 6 and 8, is continually executed for as long as the expression in the parentheses evaluates to non zero (true in **C**). This test is done *before* each pass through the body. Thus in our example, on entry the expression n > 0 is evaluated. If true, then **n** is added to sum, **n** decremented (all in line 7), and the loop test repeated. Eventually **n** reaches zero. Then the expression n > 0 evaluates to false (zero), and the statement following the closing brace is entered (line 9).

An alternative is simply **while(n)**, which will also terminate when **n** reaches zero (false). This is similar to the difference at assembly level between the Test and Compare operations.

```
unsigned short sum_of_n(unsigned char n)
    {
    static unsigned short sum;
    sum=0;
    while(n>0)
        {
        sum=sum+n--;
        }
    return(sum);
    }
```

Table 6.28: Definition of function sum_of_n()

Line 6 The opening brace defining the `while` body. Notice, that for style it is indented.

Line 7 The right expression to the assignment is evaluated as `sum+n` and the resulting value given to the left variable `sum`. After this, the value of `n` as used in this evaluation is decremented; as commanded by the suffix Decrement operator `--`. This saves using a separate statement, such as in line 11 of Table 6.27. Alternatively the Post-Decrement operation could be incorporated into the `while` operand thus: `while(n-- >0)`.

> This expression uses mixed-sizes of operands, i.e. adding a `char` to a `short` object. In cases of this sort, the compiler will extend all objects to the size of the largest of the two. Thus in Table 6.29, line 22, `n` is unsigned extended to 16 bits before being added to the 16-bit `sum`.

> An alternative to line 6 is `sum+=n--;`, which reads augment `sum` by `n` and then decrement `n`.

Line 8 The `end while` brace. Notice the style with the opening and closing braces in line. The compiler does not give a hoot about style, style is for human readability, and to reduce the possibility of errors. Braces are used to surround compound statements, i.e. sequences of single statements. Such blocks can be treated in exactly the way a single statement is. Except where they surround a body of a function, braces may be omitted when the block has only one statement. In our example lines 5–8 could be replaced by the single line:

```
while(n)   sum+=sum--;
```

which reads, while `n` is non zero, add `n` to `sum` and decrement `n`. **C** can be written in terse style like this, but the result can be difficult to read.

Line 9 Only one value can be returned from a **C** function, and the `return` instruction specifies which parameter. The compiler will check that the size of this parameter matches the prefix of the function declared in line 1. The value of the function is the value of this variable. Thus, if we had a function that returned the square root of a constant passed to it, then the expression in the calling function:

```
x = sqr_root(y);
```

would assign the returned value of `sqr_root(y)` to `x`.

Line 10 The closing brace for function sum_of_n().

Passing this source code through the Intermetrics/COSMIC cross C compiler to 6809 code gives the assembly-level listing of Table 6.29. This listing shows each of the original ten high-level source lines as comments, together with the resulting assembly-level code. Thus the statement `sum=0;`, which is line C4, produces the code:

```
clra
clrb
std       L3_sum
```

which clears the 16-bit Accumulator_D (remember this is made up of the two 8-bit Accumulators concatenated, and there is no CLRD instruction) and puts zero in the absolute memory bytes (at 0001:2h, reserved by the compiler for the object L3_sum. This latter is the assembly-level equivalent name for the high-level object sum. I have added my own comments into the listing, as indicated by the ;### sequence. The compiler is not bright enough to understand the code it produces!

Whilst most of the code is straightforward, a few points need to be elucidated. This compiler passes the char-sized parameter n to the subroutine through Accumulator_B. In line 8 this is pushed out onto the System stack, along with the value of the U register. The following line sets up the User Stack register to point to the byte just above n. Thus, at any time n can be retrieved by using the effective address -1,u; for example in lines 17 and 21. Whilst this may seem rather a rigmarole, where several variables are passed, accessing them in this manner using the one pointer is effective. In this role the U register is known as a Frame pointer. By default, the compiler will also use the stack in this manner to store variables internal to the function. However, in this case I have declared sum to be static, and the compiler reserved two bytes in absolute memory in program segment .psect _bss.

```
 1                            ; Compilateur C pour MC6809 (COSMIC-France)
 2                                    .list  +
 3                                    .psect _bss
 4     0001               L3_sum: .byte   [2]     ;### Reserve one word in RAM at 0001:2
 5                            ;   1   unsigned short sum_of_n(unsigned char n)
 6                            ;   2     {
 7                                    .psect _text
 8     E000  3444      _sum_of_n:    pshs    u,b       ;### Push n, passed thru B, on Stack
 9     E002  3361                    leau    1,s       ;### Point USP to just above n
10                            ;   3       static unsigned short sum;
11                            ;   4       sum=0;
12     E004  4F                       clra              ;### Make double-byte sum = 0000h
13     E005  5F                       clrb
14     E006  FD0001                   std     L3_sum
15                            L1:     ; line 5
16                            ;   5       while(n>0)
17     E009  E65F                     ldb     -1,u      ;### Get n out of the stack
18     E00B  270B                     beq     L11       ;### IF zero THEN exit WHILE loop
19                            ;   6         {
20                            ;   7         sum=sum+n--;
21     E00D  6A5F                     dec     -1,u      ;### ELSE decrement n in situe
22     E00F  4F                       clra              ;### Extend n to unsigned 16 bits
23     E010  F30001                   addd    L3_sum ;### Add 16-bit sum to it
24     E013  FD0001                   std     L3_sum ;### and update sum as sum+n
25                            ;   8         }
26     E016  20F1                     bra     L1        ;### Repeat WHILE loop
27                            L11:    ; line 8
28                            ;   9       return(sum);
29     E018  FC0001                   ldd     L3_sum ;### Sum is returned in D accumulator
30     E01B  32C4                     leas    ,u        ;### Restore SSP to just above n
31     E01D  35C0                     puls    u,pc      ;### Get back old value of U and PC
32                            ;  10     }                ### Same as puls u : rts!
33                                    .public _sum_of_n
34                                    .end
```

Table 6.29: 6809-assembly-level code produced by the compiler, assembler, linker chain.

This program section is similar to the `.psect _data` used in the assembly programs of Section 6.2.2.

At the conclusion of the function, the old value of the Frame pointer is retrieved from the stack, with the same instruction being used to retrieve the caller's **PC**, a surreptitious way of doing a `rts`. The actual `return()` is done by moving the value of **L3_sum** into Accumulator_D in line 29.

Once the compiler has produced machine-level, as exemplified by this listing, it can be passed through the linker, as described in Fig. 6.10, to produce the machine-code file for downloading to the target memory. The linker will bring together code from the various libraries provided with the compiler and other modules compiled or assembled separately. Most **C** compilers produce code which goes through an intermediate assembly-level stage in this manner. This gives the flexibility of linking in code from languages other than **C** and even going in and tweaking the assembly-level code before the linker; but this is not recommended!

Finally, to emphasize the portability aspects of using a high-level language, Table 6.30 shows the resulting assembly-level code produced by passing the identical source code through the Intermetrics/COSMIC compiler for the 68000 MPU. The

```
~~1COSMIC 3.32 as68k
 1                                          .bss
 2                                          .even
 3 0E000 T                    L3_sum:       .=.+2                        *## Reserve word for sum
 4                                   *       1  unsigned short sum_of_n(unsigned char n)
 5                                   *       2    {
 6                                          .text
 7                                          .even
 8 00400 T   4e56 0000        _sum_of_n: link      a6,#0      *## A6 is Frame pointer
 9                                   *       3    static unsigned short sum;
10                                   *       4    sum=0;
11 00404 T   4279 0000E000 G             clr.w   L3_sum    *## Clear sum
12 0040a T                   L1:  *line    5,       words     5
13                                   *       5    while(n>0)
14 0040a T   4a2e 000b                    tst.b   11(a6)    *## n is passed thru Stack
15 0040e T   67 16                        beq.s   L11       *## IF n==0 THEN exit WHILE
16                                   *       6      {
17                                   *       7      sum=sum+n--;
18 00410 T   1e2e 000b                    move.b  11(a6),d7 *## ELSE copy n into D7.B
19 00414 T   532e 000b                    subq.b  #1,11(a6) *## Decrement it in situe
20 00418 T   0287 000000ff                and.l   #255,d7   *## extended to word size
21 0041e T   df79 0000E000 G             add.w   d7,L3_sum *## Add n to sum
22                                   *       8      }
23 00424 T   60 e4                        bra.s   L1        *## REPEAT WHILE
24 00426 T                   L11:  *line   8,       words     19
25                                   *       9    return(sum);
26 00426 T   7e00                         moveq.l  #0,d7     *## Return sum thru D7
27 00428 T   3e39 0000E000 G             move.w  L3_sum,d7 *## Extended to 32 bits
28 0042e T   4e5e                         unlk    a6        *## Restore old value of A6
29 00430 T   4e75                         rts               *## End of subroutine
30                                 *fnsize=25
31                                          .globl  _sum_of_n
32                                   *      10    }
              no assembler errors
              code segment size = 50
              data segment size = 0
Information extracted from tab6_214.xeq
SOURCE FILE : tab6_214.c
  FUNCTION : extern unsigned short sum_of_n() lines 1 to 10 at 0x400-0x432
    VARIABLES:
      argument unsigned char n at 0xb from frame pointer
      static unsigned short sum  at 0xe000
```

Table 6.30: Cross compilation to another microprocessor.

listing is presented without any further comment, simply to illustrate the principle.

We have previously mentioned that one of the major problems in writing code in a high-level language which is targeted to an embedded circuit, is that of debugging. We can of course use a simulator or in-circuit emulator to trace the progress of the compiler emitted assembly-level code. A painful process at best, akin to debugging someone else's poorly documented program. This is because we have understood and written the program in high-level code, and it is the compiler's code that actually runs on the hardware. Ideally, the person who is debugging a program needs to view the logical flow of events at the level of abstraction at which he or she conceived them. This usually means at the source level [34].

Figure 6.15 shows a screen dump of the Intermetrics/Cosmic CXDB09 source-level simulator operating on the **C** program of Table. 6.28. In the central window we see the original source code, together with the corresponding assembly code (see Table 6.29). The program is being single stepped and is at source line 7 when this snapshot was taken. As well as highlighting line 7, the corresponding assembly code lines are also likewise emphasized. The top left window is used to monitor source variables, in this case **n** and **sum**. Source objects can be changed by the operator at any time, and the command window at the bottom shows **n** being set to 5. The top right window shows the current function, together with previous calling functions (non in this simple example), and their passed values. Other data can be accessed, such as a listing of all variables, their type and where they are stored, the MPU's registers and the state of the stack.

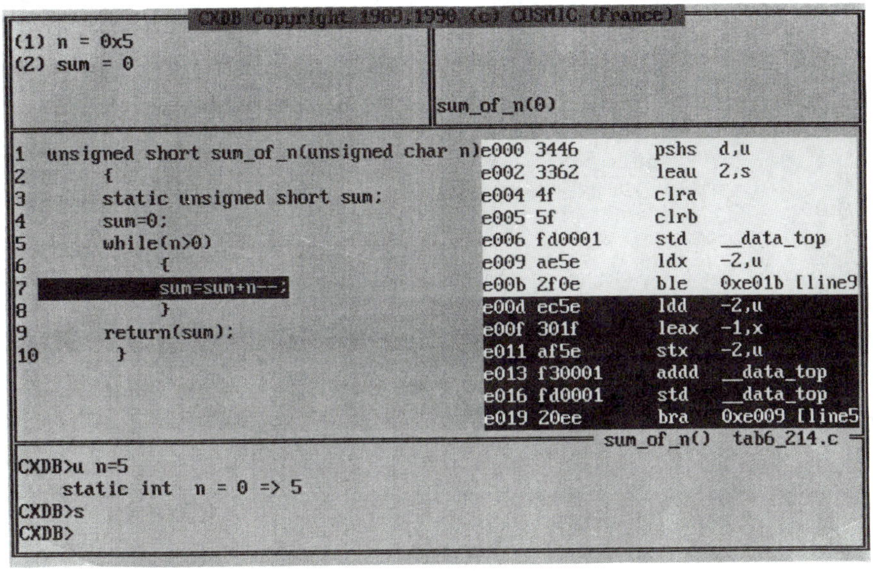

```
CXDB Copyright 1989,1990 (c) COSMIC (France)
(1) n = 0x5
(2) sum = 0

                                      sum_of_n(0)

1   unsigned short sum_of_n(unsigned char n)e000 3446      pshs   d,u
2       {                                  e002 3362      leau   2,s
3       static unsigned short sum;         e004 4f        clra
4       sum=0;                             e005 5f        clrb
5       while(n>0)                         e006 fd0001    std    __data_top
6           {                              e009 ae5e      ldx    -2,u
7           sum=sum+n--;                   e00b 2f0e      ble    0xe01b [line9
8           }                              e00d ec5e      ldd    -2,u
9       return(sum);                       e00f 301f      leax   -1,x
10      }                                  e011 af5e      stx    -2,u
                                           e013 f30001    addd   __data_top
                                           e016 fd0001    std    __data_top
                                           e019 20ee      bra    0xe009 [line5
                                      sum_of_n()     tab6_214.c
CXDB>u n=5
     static int   n = 0 => 5
CXDB>s
CXDB>
```

Figure 6.15: High-level simulation.

The CXDB simulator a front layer over a assembly-level simulator, actually pretending that the computer is a 6809 MPU. Actually it is the MIMIC simulator illustrated in the previous section. Other products are available which operate using an in-circuit emulator to execute the target code. Facilities are similar, but real hardware is being exercised, and the software is running in its actual environment.

References

[1] Schmitz, N. and Greiner, J.; Software Aids in PAL Circuit Design, Simulation and Verification, *Electronic Design*, **32**, no. 12, May 31st, 1984, pp.243–249.

[2] Cahill, S.J. et al.; Acquisition and Analysis of Heart Rate Variability Signals, *Automedica*, **13**, 1991, pp.121–139.

[3] JEDEC Solid State Products Engineering Council, Standard 3A, *Standard Data Transfer Format Between Data Preparation System and Programmable Logic Device Programmer*, May 1986. Electronic Industries Association. Standards Sales Office, 2001 Eye Street, N.W. Washington, D.C. 20006, U.S.A.

[4] Blasewitz, R.M. and Stern, F.; *Microcomputer Systems*, Hayden, 1982, Section 9.5.

[5] Cahill, S.J.; *The Single Chip Microcomputer*, Prentice-Hall, 1987, Part 2.

[6] McCann, T. and Findlay, D.; Microprocessor Product Design: The role of the Development System, *The Radio and Electronic Engineer*, **52**, no. 2, Feb. 1982, pp.67–84.

[7] Ferguson, J.; *Microprocessor Systems Design*, Addison-Wesley, 1985, Chapter 5.1.

[8] Ferguson, J.; *Microprocessor Systems Design*, Addison-Wesley, 1985, Chapter 5.2.

[9] Ferguson, J.; In-Circuit Emulation, *Electronic & Wireless World*, **90**, June 1984, pp.53–55.

[10] Gilmour, P.P.; Caveat Tester, *Embedded Systems*, **4**, no. 7, July 1991, pp.59–65.

[11] Cahill, S.J.; *C for the Microprocessor Engineer*, Prentice-Hall, 1994, Chapter 15.

[12] Mittag l.; Debugging with Hardware, *Embedded Systems*, **4**, no. 10, Oct. 1991, pp.43–47.

[13] Barron, D.W.; *Assemblers and Loaders*, MacDonald and Janes, 3rd ed., 1978, Chapters 1–4.

[14] Calingaert, P.; *Assemblers, Compilers and Program Translation*, Computer Science Press, Springer-Verlag, 1979, Chapter 2.

[15] Fischer, W.P.; Microprocessor Assembly Language Draft Standard, *Computer*, **12**, no. 12, Dec. 1979, pp.96–109.

[16] American National Standards Institute; *Standard for Microprocessor Assembly Language*, 694-1985.

[17] Barron, D.W.; *Assemblers and Loaders*, MacDonald and Janes, 3rd ed., 1978, Chapter 5.

[18] Calingaert, P.; *Assemblers, Compilers and Program Translation*, Computer Science Press, Springer-Verlag, 1979, Chapter 8.

[19] Alty, J.; Development without Development Systems, from *Microprocessor Development and Development Systems*, ed. Tseng, V., Granada, 1982, Chapter 8.

[20] Davies, A.C.; Features of High-Level Languages for Microprocessors, *Microprocessors and Microsystems*, **11**, no. 2, March 1987, pp.77–87.

[21] Ulrickson, R.W.; Solve Software Problems Step by Step, *Electronic Design*, **25**, no. 2, Jan. 18th, 1977, pp.54–58.

[22] Ulrickson, R.W.; Software Modules are the Building Blocks, *Electronic Design*, **25**, no. 3, Feb. 1st, 1977. pp.62–66.

[23] Yourdon, E.; *Techniques of Program Structure and Design*, Prentice-Hall, 1975, Chapter 4.

[24] Walker, G.; Towards a Structured 6809 Assembly Language, *BYTE*, **6**, no. 11, Nov. 1981, pp.370–382.

[25] Cahill, S.J.; *C and the Microprocessor Engineer*, Prentice-Hall, 1994.

[26] Kernighan, B. and Ritchie, B.W.; *The C Programming Language*, Prentice-Hall, 2nd ed., 1988.

[27] Banahan, M.; *The C Book*, Addison-Wesley, 1988.

[28] Pohl, I. and Kelly A.L.; *A Book on C*, Benjamin/Cummings, 2nd ed., 1990.

[29] Richards, M.; BCPL: A Tool for Compiler Writing and Systems Programming, *Proc. AFIPS SJCC*, **34**, 1969, pp.557–566.

[30] Ritchie, D.M. and Thompson, K.; The UNIX Time-Sharing System, *Bell System Technical Journal*, **57**, no. 6, part 2, July–Aug. 1978, pp.1905–1929.

[31] Johnson, S.C. and Kernighan, B.W.; The Programming Language B, *Comp. Sci. Tech. Rep. no. 8*, Bell Laboratories, Jan. 1973.

[32] Ritchie, D.M. et. al.; The C Programming Language, *Bell System Technical Journal*, **57**, no. 6, part 2, July–Aug. 1978, pp.1991–2019.

[33] Thompson, K.; UNIX Implementation, *Bell System Technical Journal*, **57**, no. 6, part 2, July–Aug. 1978, pp.1931–1946.

[34] Williams, T.; Cross-Development Tools Expand their Horizons, *Computer Design*, **29**, no. 3, 1st Feb. 1990, pp.63 – 70.

Appendix A

Explanation of Logic Symbols

by F.A. Mann

Reproduced by courtesy of Texas Instruments Ltd

TABLE OF CONTENTS

LIST OF TABLES

If you have questions on this Explanation
of Logic Symbols, please contact:

IEEE Standards may be purchased from:

F.A. Mann MS 49
Texas Instruments Incorporated
P.O. Box 225012
Dallas, Texas 75265
Telephone (214) 995-2867

Institute of Electrical and Electronics Engineers, Inc
345 East 47th Street
New York, N.Y. 10017

International Electrotechnical Commission (IEC)
publications may be purchased from:

American National Standards Institute, Inc.
1430 Broadway
New York, N.Y. 10018

Texas Instruments

EXPLANATION OF LOGIC SYMBOLS

───

by F. A. Mann

1   INTRODUCTION

The International Electrotechnical Commission (IEC) has been developing a very powerful symbolic language that can show the relationship of each input of a digital logic circuit to each output without showing explicitly the internal logic. At the heart of the system is dependency notation, which will be explained in Section 4.

The system was introduced in the USA in a rudimentary form in IEEE/ANSI Standard Y32.14-1973. Lacking at that time a complete development of dependency notation, it offered little more than a substitution of rectangular shapes for the familiar distinctive shapes for representing the basic functions of AND, OR, negation, etc. This is no longer the case.

Internationally, Working Group 2 of IEC Technical Committee TC-3 is preparing a new document (Publication 617-12) that will consolidate the original work started in the mid 1960's and published in 1972 (Publication 117-15) and the amendments and supplements that have followed. Similarly for the USA, IEEE Committee SCC 11.9 is revising the publication IEEE Std 91/ANSI Y32.14. Texas Instruments is participating in the work of both organizations and this Data Book introduces new logic symbols in anticipation of the new standards. When changes are made as the standards develop, future editions will take those changes into account.

The following explanation of the new symbolic language is necessarily brief and greatly condensed from what the standards publications will finally contain. This is not intended to be sufficient for those people who will be developing symbols for new devices. It is primarily intended to make possible the understanding of the symbols used in this book; comparing the symbols with functional block diagrams and/or function tables will further help that understanding.

2   SYMBOL COMPOSITION

A symbol comprises an outline or a combination of outlines together with one or more qualifying symbols. The shape of the symbols is not significant. As shown in Figure 1, general qualifying symbols are used to tell exactly what logical operation is performed by the elements. Table I shows the general qualifying symbols used in this data book. Input lines are placed on the left and output lines are placed on the right. When an exception is made to that convention, the direction of signal flow is indicated by an arrow as shown in Figure 11.

All outputs of a single, unsubdivided element always have identical internal logic states determined by the function of the element except when otherwise indicated by an associated qualifying symbol or label inside the element.

───

TEXAS INSTRUMENTS

EXPLANATION OF LOGIC SYMBOLS

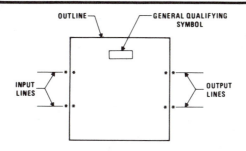

*Possible positions for qualifying symbols relating to inputs and outputs

FIGURE 1 – SYMBOL COMPOSITION

The outlines of elements may be abutted or embedded in which case the following conventions apply. There is no logic connection between the elements when the line common to their outlines is in the direction of signal flow. There is at least one logic connection between the elements when the line common to their outlines is perpendicular to the direction of signal flow. The number of logic connections between elements will be clarified by the use of qualifying symbols and this is discussed further under that topic. If no indications are shown on either side of the common line, it is assumed there is only one connection.

When a circuit has one or more inputs that are common to more than one element of the circuit, the common-control block may be used. This is the only distinctively shaped outline used in the IEC system. Figure 2 shows that unless otherwise qualified by dependency notation, an input to the common-control block is an input to each of the elements below the common-control block.

COMMON-CONTROL BLOCK

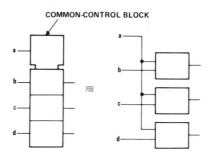

FIGURE 2 – ILLUSTRATION OF COMMON- CONTROL BLOCK

TEXAS INSTRUMENTS

EXPLANATION OF LOGIC SYMBOLS

A common output depending on all elements of the array can be shown as the output of a common-output element. Its distinctive visual feature is the double line at its top. In addition the common-output element may have other inputs as shown in Figure 3. The function of the common-output element must be shown by use of a general qualifying symbol.

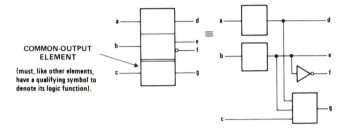

COMMON-OUTPUT
ELEMENT

(must, like other elements, have a qualifying symbol to denote its logic function).

FIGURE 3 – ILLUSTRATION OF COMMON-OUTPUT ELEMENT

3   QUALIFYING SYMBOLS

3.1 General Qualifying Symbols

Table I shows the general qualifying symbols used in this data book. These characters are placed near the top center or the geometric center of a symbol or symbol element to define the basic function of the device represented by the symbol or of the element.

3.2 Qualifying Symbols for Inputs and Outputs

Qualifying symbols for inputs and outputs are shown in Table II and will be familiar to most users with the possible exception of the logic polarity and analog signal indicators. The older logic negation indicator means that the external 0 state produces the internal 1 state. The internal 1 state means the active state. Logic negation may be used in pure logic diagrams; in order to tie the external 1 and 0 logic states to the levels H (high) and L (low), a statement of whether positive logic (1 = H, 0 = L) or negative logic (1 = L, 0 = H) is being used is required or must be assumed. Logic polarity indicators eliminate the need for calling out the logic convention and are used in this data book in the symbology for actual devices. The presence of the triangular polarity indicator indicates that the L logic level will produce the internal 1 state (the active state) or that, in the case of an output, the internal 1 state will produce the external L level. Note how the active direction of transition for a dynamic input is indicated in positive logic, negative logic, and with polarity indication.

EXPLANATION OF LOGIC SYMBOLS

TABLE I – GENERAL QUALIFYING SYMBOLS

SYMBOL	DESCRIPTION	EXAMPLE
&	AND gate or function.	'HC00
>1	OR gate or function. The symbol was chosen to indicate that at least one active input is needed to activate the output.	'HC02
=1	Exclusive OR. One and only one input must be active to activate the output.	'HC86
=	Logic identity. All inputs must stand at same state.	'HC86
2k	An even number of inputs must be active.	'HC280
2k+1	An odd number of inputs must be active.	'HC86
1	The one input must be active.	'HC04
▷ or ◁	A buffer or element with more than usual output capability (symbol is oriented in the direction of signal flow).	'HC240
⎍	Schmitt trigger; element with hysteresis.	'HC132
X/Y	Coder, code converter (DEC/BCD, BIN/OUT, BIN/7-SEG, etc.).	'HC42
MUX	Multiplexer/data selector.	'HC151
DMUX or DX	Demultiplexer.	'HC138
Σ	Adder.	*
P−Q	Subtracter.	*
CPG	Look-ahead carry generator.	*
π	Multiplier.	*
COMP	Magnitude comparator.	'HC85
ALU	Arithmetic logic unit.	*
⊓	Retriggerable monostable.	'HC123
1⊓	Non-retriggerable monostable (one-shot).	'HC221
G⎍⎍	Astable element. Showing waveform is optional.	*
!G⎍⎍	Synchronously starting astable.	*
G!⎍⎍	Astable element that stops with a completed pulse.	*
SRGm	Shift register. m = number of bits.	'HC164
CTRm	Counter. m = number of bits; cycle length = 2^m.	'HC590
CTR DIVm	Counter with cycle length = m.	'HC160
RCTRm	Asynchronous (ripple-carry) counter; cycle length = 2^m.	'HC4020
ROM	Read-only memory.	*
RAM	Random-access read/write memory.	'HC189
FIFO	First-in, first-out memory.	*
I=0	Element powers up cleared to 0 state.	*
Φ	Highly complex function; "gray box" symbol with limited detail shown under special rules.	*

*Not all of the general qualifying symbols have been used in this book, but they are included here for the sake of completeness.

Texas Instruments

EXPLANATION OF LOGIC SYMBOLS

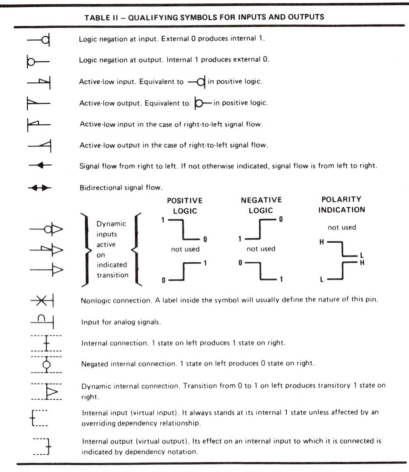

TABLE II – QUALIFYING SYMBOLS FOR INPUTS AND OUTPUTS

Logic negation at input. External 0 produces internal 1.

Logic negation at output. Internal 1 produces external 0.

Active-low input. Equivalent to —d in positive logic.

Active-low output. Equivalent to ▷— in positive logic.

Active-low input in the case of right-to-left signal flow.

Active-low output in the case of right-to-left signal flow.

Signal flow from right to left. If not otherwise indicated, signal flow is from left to right.

Bidirectional signal flow.

Dynamic inputs active on indicated transition

	POSITIVE LOGIC	NEGATIVE LOGIC	POLARITY INDICATION
	1 ⌐_0	⌐_0 1	not used
	not used	not used	H ⌐_L
	0 ⌐_1	0 ⌐_1	L ⌐_H

Nonlogic connection. A label inside the symbol will usually define the nature of this pin.

Input for analog signals.

Internal connection. 1 state on left produces 1 state on right.

Negated internal connection. 1 state on left produces 0 state on right.

Dynamic internal connection. Transition from 0 to 1 on left produces transitory 1 state on right.

Internal input (virtual input). It always stands at its internal 1 state unless affected by an overriding dependency relationship.

Internal output (virtual output). Its effect on an internal input to which it is connected is indicated by dependency notation.

The internal connections between logic elements abutted together in a symbol may be indicated by the symbols shown. Each logic connection may be shown by the presence of qualifying symbols at one or both sides of the common line and if confusion can arise about the numbers of connections, use can be made of one of the internal connection symbols.

The internal (virtual) input is an input originating somewhere else in the circuit and is not connected directly to a terminal. The internal (virtual) output is likewise not connected directly to a terminal.

TEXAS INSTRUMENTS

EXPLANATION OF LOGIC SYMBOLS

TABLE III – SYMBOLS INSIDE THE OUTLINE

	Postponed output (of a pulse-triggered flip-flop). The output changes when input initiating change (e.g., a C input) returns to its initial external state or level. See § 5.
	Bi-threshold input (input with hysteresis)
	Open-drain or similar output that can supply a relatively low-impedance L level when not turned off. Requires external pull-up. Capable of positive-logic wired-AND connection.
	Passive-pull-up output is similar to open-drain output but is suplemented with a built-in passive pull-up.
	Open-source or similar output that can supply a relatively low-impedance H level when not turned off. Requires external pull-down. Capable of positive-logic wired-OR connection.
	Passive-pull-down output is similar to open-source output but is supplemented with a built-in passive pull-down.
	3-state output
	Output with more than usual output capability (symbol is oriented in the direction of signal flow).
EN	Enable input When at its internal 1-state, all outputs are enabled. When at its internal 0-state, open-drain and open-source outputs are off, three-state outputs are at normally defined internal logic states and at external high-impedance state, and all other outputs (e.g., totem-poles) are at the internal 0-state.
J, K, R, S, T	Usual meanings associated with flip-flops (e.g., R = reset, T = toggle)
D	Data input to a storage element equivalent to:
→m ←m	Shift right (left) inputs, m = 1, 2, 3 etc. If m = 1, it is usually not shown.
+m −m	Counting up (down) inputs, m = 1, 2, 3 etc. If m = 1, it is usually not shown.
	Binary grouping. m is highest power of 2.
CT = 15	The contents-setting input, when active, causes the content of a register to take on the indicated value.
CT = 9	The content output is active if the content of the register is as indicated.
	Input line grouping . . . . indicates two or more terminals used to implement a single logic input. e.g., The paired expander inputs of SN7450.
"1"	Fixed-state output always stands at its internal 1 state. For example, see SN74185.

TEXAS INSTRUMENTS

EXPLANATION OF LOGIC SYMBOLS

The application of internal inputs and outputs requires an understanding of dependency notation, which is explained in Section 4.

In an array of elements, if the same general qualifying symbol and the same qualifying symbols associated with inputs and outputs would appear inside each of the elements of the array, these qualifying symbols are usually shown only in the first element. This is done to reduce clutter and to save time in recognition. Similarly, large identical elements that are subdivided into smaller elements may each be represented by an unsubdivided outline. The SN54HC242 symbol illustrates this principle.

3.3 Symbols Inside the Outline

Table III shows some symbols used inside the outline. Note particularly that open-collector, open-emitter, and three-state outputs have distinctive symbols. Also note that an EN input affects all of the outputs of the circuit and has no effect on inputs. When an enable input affects only certain outputs and/or affects one or more inputs, a form of dependency notation will indicate this (see 4.9). The effects of the EN input on the various types of outputs are shown.

It is particularly important to note that a D input is always the data input of a storage element. At its internal 1 state, the D input sets the storage element to its 1 state, and at its internal 0 state it resets the storage element to its 0 state.

The binary grouping symbol will be explained more fully in Section 8. Binary-weighted inputs are arranged in order and the binary weights of the least-significant and the most-significant lines are indicated by numbers. In this data book weights of input and output lines will be represented by powers of two usually only when the binary grouping symbol is used, otherwise, decimal numbers will be used. The grouped inputs generate an internal number on which a mathematical function can be performed or that can be an identifying number for dependency notation. See Figure 28. A frequent use is in addresses for memories.

Reversed in direction, the binary grouping symbol can be used with outputs. The concept is analogous to that for the inputs and the weighted outputs will indicate the internal number assumed to be developed within the circuit.

Other symbols are used inside the outlines in this data book in accordance with the IEC/IEEE standards but are not shown here. Generally these are associated with arithmetic operations and are self-explanatory.

When nonstandardized information is shown inside an outline, it is usually enclosed in square brackets [like these] .

TEXAS INSTRUMENTS

EXPLANATION OF LOGIC SYMBOLS

4   DEPENDENCY NOTATION

4.1 General Explanation

Dependency notation is the powerful tool that sets the IEC symbols apart from previous systems and makes compact, meaningful, symbols possible. It provides the means of denoting the relationship between inputs, outputs, or inputs and outputs without actually showing all the elements and inter-connections involved. The information provided by dependency notation supplements that provided by the qualifying symbols for an element's function.

In the convention for the dependency notation, use will be made of the terms "affecting" and "affected". In cases where it is not evident which inputs must be considered as being the affecting or the affected ones (e.g., if they stand in an AND relationship), the choice may be made in any convenient way.

So far, ten types of dependency have been defined and all of these are used in this data book. They are listed below in the order in which they are presented and are summarized in Table IV following 4.11.

Section	Dependency Type or Other Subject
4.2	G, AND
4.3	General rules for dependency notation
4.4	V, OR
4.5	N, Negate, (Exclusive OR)
4.6	Z, Interconnection
4.7	C, Control
4.8	S, Set and R, Reset
4.9	EN, Enable
4.10	M, Mode
4.11	A, Address

4.2 G (AND) Dependency

A common relationship between two signals is to have them ANDed together. This has traditionally been shown by explicitly drawing an AND gate with the signals connected to the inputs of the gate. The 1972 IEC publication and the 1973 IEEE/ANSI standard showed several ways to show this AND relationship using dependency notation. While nine other forms of dependency have since been defined, the ways to invoke AND dependency are now reduced to one.

TEXAS INSTRUMENTS

EXPLANATION OF LOGIC SYMBOLS

In Figure 4 input **b** is ANDed with input a and the complement of **b** is ANDed with c. The letter G has been chosen to indicate AND relationships and is placed at input **b**, inside the symbol. A number considered appropriate by the symbol designer (1 has been used here) is placed after the letter G and also at each affected input. Note the bar over the 1 at input **c**.

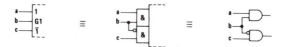

FIGURE 4 – G DEPENDENCY BETWEEN INPUTS

In Figure 5, output **b** affects input **a** with an AND relationship. The lower example shows that it is the internal logic state of **b**, unaffected by the negation sign, that is ANDed. Figure 6 shows input **a** to be ANDed with a dynamic input **b**.

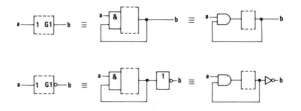

FIGURE 5 – G DEPENDENCY BETWEEN OUTPUTS AND INPUTS

FIGURE 6 – G DEPENDENCY WITH A DYNAMIC INPUT

The rules for G dependency can be summarized thus:

When a Gm input or output (m is a number) stands at its internal 1 state, all inputs and outputs affected by Gm stand at their normally defined internal logic states. When the Gm input or output stands at its 0 state, all inputs and outputs affected by Gm stand at their internal 0 states.

EXPLANATION OF LOGIC SYMBOLS

4.3 Conventions for the Application of Dependency Notation in General

The rules for applying dependency relationships in general follow the same pattern as was illustrated for G dependency.

Application of dependency notation is accomplished by:

1) labeling the input (or output) *affecting* other inputs or outputs with the letter symbol indicating the relationship involved (e.g., G for AND) followed by an identifying number, appropriately chosen; and

2) labeling each input or output *affected* by that affecting input (or output) with that same number.

If it is the complement of the internal logic state of the affecting input or output that does the affecting, then a bar is placed over the identifying numbers at the affected inputs or outputs. See Figure 4.

If two affecting inputs or outputs have the same letter and same identifying number, they stand in an OR relationship to each other. See Figure 7.

FIGURE 7 – OR'ED AFFECTING INPUTS

If the affected input or output requires a label to denote its function (e.g., "D"), this label will be *prefixed* by the identifying number of the affecting input. See Figure 12.

If an input or output is affected by more than one affecting input, the identifying numbers of each of the affecting inputs will appear in the label of the affected one, separated by commas. The normal reading order of these numbers is the same as the sequence of the affecting relationships. See Figure 12.

If the labels denoting the functions of affected inputs or outputs must be numbers, (e.g., outputs of a coder), the identifying numbers to be associated with both affecting inputs and affected inputs or outputs will be replaced by another character selected to avoid ambiguity, e.g., Greek letters. See Figure 8.

TEXAS INSTRUMENTS

EXPLANATION OF LOGIC SYMBOLS

FIGURE 8 – SUBSTITUTION FOR NUMBERS

4.4 V (OR) Dependency

The symbol denoting OR dependency is the letter V. See Figure 9.

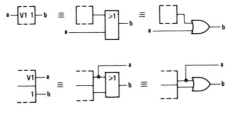

FIGURE 9 – V (OR) DEPENDENCY

When a Vm input or output stands at its internal 1 state, all inputs and outputs affected by Vm stand at their internal 1 states. When the Vm input or output stands at its internal 0 state, all inputs and outputs affected by Vm stand at their normally defined internal logic states.

4.5 N (Negate) (X-OR) Dependency

The symbol denoting negate dependency is the letter N. See Figure 10. Each input or output affected by an Nm input or output stands in an exclusive-OR relationship with the Nm input or output.

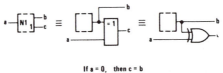

If a = 0, then c = b
If a = 1, then c = b

FIGURE 10 – N (NEGATE) (X-OR) DEPENDENCY

TEXAS INSTRUMENTS

EXPLANATION OF LOGIC SYMBOLS

When an Nm input or output stands at its internal 1 state, the internal logic state of each input and each output affected by Nm is the complement of what it would otherwise be. When an Nm input or output stands at its internal 0 state, all inputs and outputs affected by Nm stand at their normally defined internal logic states.

4.6 Z (Interconnection) Dependency

The symbol denoting interconnection dependency is the letter Z.

Interconnection dependency is used to indicate the existence of internal logic connections between inputs, outputs, internal inputs, and/or internal outputs.

The internal logic state of an input or output affected by a Zm input or output will be the same as the internal logic state of the Zm input or output, unless modified by additional dependency notation. See Figure 11.

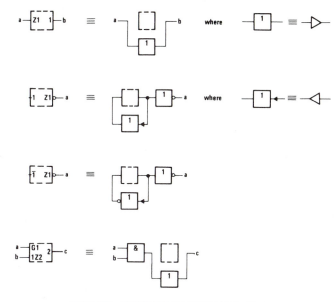

FIGURE 11 – Z (INTERCONNECTION) DEPENDENCY

TEXAS INSTRUMENTS

EXPLANATION OF LOGIC SYMBOLS

4.7 C (Control) Dependency

The symbol denoting control dependency is the letter C.

Control inputs are usually used to enable or disable the data (D, J, K, R, or S) inputs of storage elements. They may take on their internal 1 states (be active) either statically or dynamically. In the latter case the dynamic input symbol is used as shown in the third example of Figure 12.

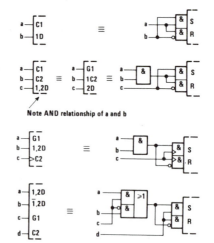

Note AND relationship of a and b

Input c selects which of a or b is stored when d goes low.

FIGURE 12 – C (CONTROL) DEPENDENCY

When a Cm input or output stands at its internal 1 state, the inputs affected by Cm have their normally defined effect on the function of the element, i.e., these inputs are enabled. When a Cm input or output stands at its internal 0 state, the inputs affected by Cm are disabled and have no effect on the function of the element.

4.8 S (Set) and R (Reset) Dependencies

The symbol denoting set dependency is the letter S. The symbol denoting reset dependency is the letter R.

TEXAS INSTRUMENTS

EXPLANATION OF LOGIC SYMBOLS

Set and reset dependencies are used if it is necessary to specify the effect of the combination R=S=1 on a bistable element. Case 1 in Figure 13 does not use S or R dependency.

When an S*m* input is at its internal 1 state, outputs affected by the Sm input will react, regardless of the state of an R input, as they normally would react to the combination S=1, R=0. See cases 2, 4, and 5 in Figure 13.

When an R*m* input is at its internal 1 state, outputs affected by the Rm input will react, regardless of the state of an S input, as they normally would react to the combination S=0, R=1. See cases 3, 4, and 5 in Figure 13.

When an S*m* or R*m* input is at its internal 0 state, it has no effect.

Note that the noncomplementary output patterns in cases 4 and 5 are only pseudo stable. The simultaneous return of the inputs to S=R=0 produces an unforeseeable stable and complementary output pattern.

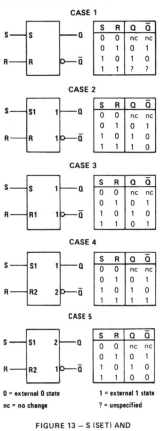

CASE 1

S	R	Q	Q̄
0	0	nc	nc
0	1	0	1
1	0	1	0
1	1	?	?

CASE 2

S	R	Q	Q̄
0	0	nc	nc
0	1	0	1
1	0	1	0
1	1	1	0

CASE 3

S	R	Q	Q̄
0	0	nc	nc
0	1	0	1
1	0	1	0
1	1	0	1

CASE 4

S	R	Q	Q̄
0	0	nc	nc
0	1	0	1
1	0	1	0
1	1	1	1

CASE 5

S	R	Q	Q̄
0	0	nc	nc
0	1	0	1
1	0	1	0
1	1	0	0

0 = external 0 state   1 = external 1 state

nc = no change   ? = unspecified

FIGURE 13 — S (SET) AND
R (RESET) DEPENDENCIES

4.9 EN (Enable) Dependency

The symbol denoting enable dependency is the combination of letters EN.

An EN*m* input has the same effect on outputs as an EN input, see 3.1, but it effects only those outputs labeled with the identifying number *m*. It also affects those inputs labeled with the identifying number *m*. By contrast, an EN input affects all outputs and no inputs. The effect of an EN*m* input on an affected input is identical to that of a C*m* input. See Figure 14.

TEXAS INSTRUMENTS

EXPLANATION OF LOGIC SYMBOLS

When an EN*m* input stands at its internal 1 state, the inputs affected by EN*m* have their normally defined effect on the function of the element and the outputs affected by this input stand at their normally defined internal logic states, i.e., these inputs and outputs are enabled.

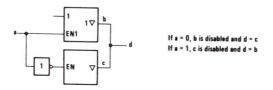

If a = 0, b is disabled and d = c
If a = 1, c is disabled and d = b

FIGURE 14 – EN (ENABLE) DEPENDENCY

When an EN*m* input stands at its internal 0 state, the inputs affected by EN*m* are disabled and have no effect on the function of the element, and the outputs affected by EN*m* are also disabled. Open-collector outputs are turned off, three-state outputs stand at their normally defined internal logic states but externally exhibit high impedance, and all other outputs (e.g., totem-pole outputs) stand at their internal 0 states.

4.10   M (Mode) Dependency

The symbol denoting mode dependency is the letter M.

Mode dependency is used to indicate that the effects of particular inputs and outputs of an element depend on the mode in which the element is operating.

If an input or output has the same effect in different modes of operation, the identifying numbers of the relevant affecting M*m* inputs will appear in the label of that affected input or output between parentheses and separated by solidi. See Figure 19.

4.10.1   M Dependency Affecting Inputs

M dependency affects inputs the same as C dependency. When an M*m* input or M*m* output stands at its internal 1 state, the inputs affected by this M*m* input or M*m* output have their normally defined effect on the function of the element, i.e., the inputs are enabled.

When an M*m* input or M*m* output stands at its internal 0 state, the inputs affected by this M*m* input or M*m* output have no effect on the function of the element. When an affected input has several sets of labels separated by solidi (e.g., C4/2→/3+), any set in which the identifying number of the M*m* input or M*m* output appears has no effect and is to be ignored. This represents disabling of some of the functions of a multifunction input.

EXPLANATION OF LOGIC SYMBOLS

The circuit in Figure 15 has two inputs, **b** and **c**, that control which one of four modes (0, 1, 2, or 3) will exist at any time. Inputs **d**, **e**, and **f** are D inputs subject to dynamic control (clocking) by the **a** input. The numbers 1 and 2 are in the series chosen to indicate the modes so inputs **e** and **f** are only enabled in mode 1 (for parallel loading) and input **d** is only enabled in mode 2 (for serial loading). Note that input **a** has three functions. It is the clock for entering data. In mode 2, it causes right shifting of data, which means a shift away from the control block. In mode 3, it causes the contents of the register to be incremented by one count.

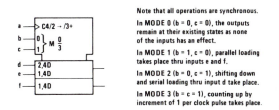

Note that all operations are synchronous.

In MODE 0 (b = 0, c = 0), the outputs remain at their existing states as none of the inputs has an effect.

In MODE 1 (b = 1, c = 0), parallel loading takes place thru inputs e and f.

In MODE 2 (b = 0, c = 1), shifting down and serial loading thru input d take place.

In MODE 3 (b = c = 1), counting up by increment of 1 per clock pulse takes place.

FIGURE 15 — M (MODE) DEPENDENCY AFFECTING INPUTS

4.10.2   M Dependency Affecting Outputs

When an M*m* input or M*m* output stands at its internal 1 state, the affected outputs stand at their normally defined internal logic states, i.e., the outputs are enabled.

When an M*m* input or M*m* output stands at its internal 0 state, at each affected output any set of labels containing the identifying number of that M*m* input or M*m* output has no effect and is to be ignored. When an output has several different sets of labels separated by solidi (e.g., 2,4/3,5), only those sets in which the identifying number of this M*m* input or M*m* output appears are to be ignored.

In Figure 16, mode 1 exists when the **a** input stands at its internal 1 state. The delayed output symbol is effective only in mode 1 (when input **a** = 1) in which case the device functions as a pulse-triggered flip-flop. See Section 5. When input **a** = 0, the device is not in mode 1 so the delayed output symbol has no effect and the device functions as a transparent latch.

FIGURE 16 — TYPE OF FLIP-FLOP DETERMINED BY MODE

TEXAS INSTRUMENTS

EXPLANATION OF LOGIC SYMBOLS

In Figure 17, if input **a** stands at its internal 1 state establishing mode 1, output **b** will stand at its internal 1 state only when the content of the register equals 9. Since output **b** is located in the common-control block with no defined function outside of mode 1, the state of this output outside of mode 1 is not defined by the symbol.

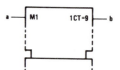

FIGURE 17 – DISABLING AN OUTPUT OF THE
COMMON-CONTROL BLOCK

In Figure 18, if input **a** stands at its internal 1 state establishing mode 1, output **b** will stand at its internal 1 state only when the content of the register equals 15. If input **a** stands at its internal 0 state, output **b** will stand at its internal 1 state only when the content of the register equals 0.

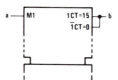

FIGURE 18 – DETERMINING AN OUTPUT'S
FUNCTION

In Figure 19 inputs **a** and **b** are binary weighted to generate the numbers 0, 1, 2, or 3. This determines which one of the four modes exists.

At output **e** the label set causing negation (if **c** = 1) is effective only in modes 2 and 3. In modes 0 and 1 this output stands at its normally defined state as if it had no labels. At output **f** the label set has effect when the mode is not 0 so output **e** is negated (if

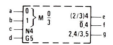

FIGURE 19 – DEPENDENT RELATIONSHIPS
AFFECTED BY MODE

c = 1) in modes 1, 2, and 3. In mode 0 the label set has no effect so the output stands at its normally defined state. In this example 0,4 is equivalent to (1/2/3)4. At output **g** there are two label sets. The first set, causing negation (if **c** = 1), is effective only in mode 2. The second set, subjecting **g** to AND dependency on **d**, has effect only in mode 3.

Note that in mode 0 none of the dependency relationships has any effect on the outputs, so **e**, **f**, and **g** will all stand at the same state.

4.11   A (Address) Dependency

The symbol denoting address dependency is the letter A.

EXPLANATION OF LOGIC SYMBOLS

Address dependency provides a clear representation of those elements, particularly memories, that use address control inputs to select specified sections of a multidimensional array. Such a section of a memory array is usually called a word. The purpose of address dependency is to allow a symbolic presentation of the entire array. An input of the array shown at a particular element of this general section is common to the corresponding elements of all selected sections of the array. An output of the array shown at a particular element of this general section is the result of the OR function of the outputs of the corresponding elements of selected sections. If the label of an output of the array shown at a particular element of this general section indicates that this output is an open-circuit output or a three-state output, then this indication refers to the output of the array and not to those of the sections of the array.

Inputs that are not affected by any affecting address input have their normally defined effect on all sections of the array, whereas inputs affected by an address input have their normally defined effect only on the section selected by that address input.

An affecting address input is labelled with the letter A followed by an identifying number that corresponds with the address of the particular section of the array selected by this input. Within the general section presented by the symbol, inputs and outputs affected by an Am input are labelled with the letter A, which stands for the identifying numbers, i.e., the addresses, of the particular sections.

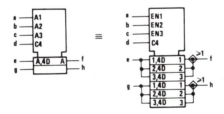

FIGURE 20 — A (ADDRESS) DEPENDENCY

Figure 20 shows a 3-word by 2-bit memory having a separate address line for each word and uses EN dependency to explain the operation. To select word 1, input **a** is taken to its 1 state, which establishes mode 1. Data can now be clocked into the inputs marked "1,4D". Unless words 2 and 3 are also selected, data cannot be clocked in at the inputs marked "2,4D" and "3,4D". The outputs will be the OR functions of the selected outputs, i.e., only those enabled by the active EN functions.

The identifying numbers of affecting address inputs correspond with the addresses of the sections selected by these inputs. They need not necessarily differ from those of other affecting dependency inputs (e.g., G, V, N, . . .), because in the general section presented by the symbol they are replaced by the letter A.

TEXAS INSTRUMENTS

EXPLANATION OF LOGIC SYMBOLS

If there are several sets of affecting Am inputs for the purpose of independent and possibly simultaneous access to sections of the array, then the letter A is modified to 1A, 2A, . . . Because they have access to the same sections of the array, these sets of A inputs may have the same identifying numbers.

Figure 21 is another illustration of the concept.

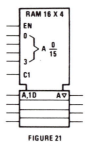

FIGURE 21

FIGURE 21 – ARRAY OF 16 SECTIONS OF FOUR TRANSPARENT LATCHES WITH 3-STATE OUTPUTS
COMPRISING A 16-WORD X 4-BIT RANDOM-ACCESS MEMORY

TABLE IV – SUMMARY OF DEPENDENCY NOTATION

TYPE OF DEPENDENCY	LETTER SYMBOL*	AFFECTING INPUT AT ITS 1-STATE	AFFECTING INPUT AT ITS 0-STATE
Address	A	Permits action (address selected)	Prevents action (address not selected)
Control	C	Permits action	Prevents action
Enable	EN	Permits action	Prevents action of inputs. ◇ outputs off. ▽ outputs at external high impedance, no change in internal logic state. Other outputs at internal 0 state.
AND	G	Permits action	Imposes 0 state
Mode	M	Permits action (mode selected)	Prevents action (mode not selected)
Negate (X-OR)	N	Complements state	No effect
RESET	R	Affected output reacts as it would to S = 0, R = 1	No effect
SET	S	Affected output reacts as it would to S = 1, R = 0	No effect
OR	V	Imposes 1 state	Permits action
Interconnection	Z	Imposes 1 state	Imposes 0 state

* These letter symbols appear at the AFFECTING input (or output) and are followed by a number. Each input (or output) AFFECTED by that input is labeled with that same number. When the labels EN, R, and S appear at inputs without the following numbers, the descriptions above do not apply. The action of these inputs is described under "Symbols Inside The Outline", see 3.1.

TEXAS INSTRUMENTS

EXPLANATION OF LOGIC SYMBOLS

BISTABLE ELEMENTS

The dynamic input symbol, the postponed output symbol, and dependency notation provide the tools to differentiate four main types of bistable elements and make synchronous and asynchronous inputs easily recognizable. See Figure 22. The first column shows the essential distinguishing features; the other columns show examples.

Transparent latches have a level-operated control input. The D input is active as long as the C input is at its internal 1 state. The outputs respond immediately. Edge-triggered elements accept data from D, J, K, R, or S inputs on the active transition of C. Pulse-triggered elements require the setup of data before the start of the control pulse; the C input is considered static since the data must be maintained as long as C is at its 1 state. The output is postponed until C returns to its 0 state. The data-lock-out element is similar to the pulse-triggered version except that the C input is considered dynamic in that shortly after C goes through its active transition, the data inputs are disabled and data does not have to be held. However, the output is still postponed until the C input returns to its initial external level.

Notice that synchronous inputs can be readily recognized by their dependency labels (1D, 1J, 1K, 1S, 1R) compared to the asynchronous inputs (S, R), which are not dependent on the C inputs.

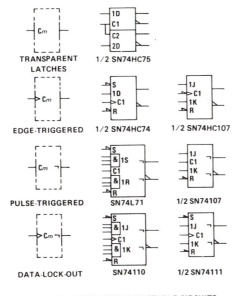

FIGURE 22 – FOUR TYPES OF BISTABLE CIRCUITS

TEXAS INSTRUMENTS

EXPLANATION OF LOGIC SYMBOLS

6   CODERS

The general symbol for a coder or code converter is shown in Figure 23. X and Y may be replaced by appropriate indications of the code used to represent the information at the inputs and at the outputs, respectively.

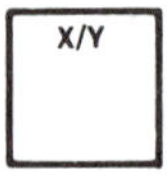

FIGURE 23 – CODER GENERAL SYMBOL

Indication of code conversion is based on the following rule:

> Depending on the input code, the internal logic states of the inputs determine an internal value. This value is reproduced by the internal logic states of the outputs, depending on the output code.

The indication of the relationships between the internal logic states of the inputs and the internal value is accomplished by:

1) labelling the inputs with numbers. In this case the internal value equals the sum of the weights associated with those inputs that stand at their internal 1-state, or by
2) replacing X by an appropriate indication of the input code and labelling the inputs with characters that refer to this code.

The relationships between the internal value and the internal logic states of the outputs are indicated by:

1) labelling each output with a list of numbers representing those internal values that lead to the internal 1-state of that output. These numbers shall be separated by solidi as in Figure 24. This labelling may also be applied when Y is replaced by a letter denoting a type of dependency (see Section 7). If a continuous range of internal values produces the internal 1 state of an output, this can be indicated by two numbers that are inclusively the beginning and the end of the range, with these two numbers separated by three dots, e.g., 4 . . . 9 = 4/5/6/7/8/9, or by
2) replacing Y by an appropriate indication of the output code and labelling the outputs with characters that refer to this code as in Figure 25.

Alternatively, the general symbol may be used together with an appropriate reference to a table in which the relationship between the inputs and outputs is indicated. This is a recommended way to symbolize a PROM after it has been programmed.

EXPLANATION OF LOGIC SYMBOLS

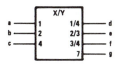

FUNCTION TABLE

INPUTS			OUTPUTS			
c	b	a	g	f	e	d
0	0	0	0	0	0	0
0	0	1	0	0	0	1
0	1	0	0	0	1	0
0	1	1	0	1	1	0
1	0	0	0	1	0	1
1	0	1	0	0	0	0
1	1	0	0	0	0	0
1	1	1	1	0	0	0

FIGURE 24 – AN X/Y CODE CONVERTER

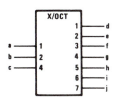

FUNCTION TABLE

INPUTS			OUTPUTS						
c	b	a	j	i	h	g	f	e	d
0	0	0	0	0	0	0	0	0	0
0	0	1	0	0	0	0	0	0	1
0	1	0	0	0	0	0	0	1	0
0	1	1	0	0	0	0	1	0	0
1	0	0	0	0	0	1	0	0	0
1	0	1	0	0	1	0	0	0	0
1	1	0	0	1	0	0	0	0	0
1	1	1	1	0	0	0	0	0	0

FIGURE 25 – AN X/OCTAL CODE CONVERTER

7   USE OF A CODER TO PRODUCE AFFECTING INPUTS

It often occurs that a set of affecting inputs for dependency notation is produced by decoding the signals on certain inputs to an element. In such a case use can be made of the symbol for a coder as an embedded symbol. See Figure 26.

FIGURE 26 – PRODUCING VARIOUS TYPES OF DEPENDENCIES

If all affecting inputs produced by a coder are of the same type and their identifying numbers correspond with the numbers shown at the outputs of the coder, Y (in the qualifying symbol X/Y) may be replaced by the letter denoting the type of dependency. The indications of the affecting inputs should then be omitted. See Figure 27.

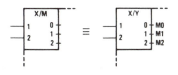

FIGURE 27 – PRODUCING ONE TYPE OF DEPENDENCY

T E X A S   I N S T R U M E N T S

EXPLANATION OF LOGIC SYMBOLS

8   USE OF BINARY GROUPING TO PRODUCE AFFECTING INPUTS

If all affecting inputs produced by a coder are of the same type and have consecutive identifying numbers not necessarily corresponding with the numbers that would have been shown at the outputs of the coder, use can be made of the binary grouping symbol (see 3.1). k external lines effectively generate 2^k internal inputs. The bracket is followed by the letter denoting the type of dependency followed by $\frac{m1}{m2}$. The m1 is to be replaced by the smallest identifying number and the m2 by the largest one, as shown in Figure 28.

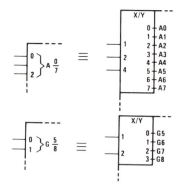

FIGURE 28 – USE OF THE BINARY GROUPING SYMBOL

9   SEQUENCE OF INPUT LABELS

If an input having a single functional effect is affected by other inputs, the qualifying symbol (if there is any) for that functional effect is preceded by the labels corresponding to the affecting inputs. The left-to-right order of these preceding labels is the order in which the effects or modifications must be applied. The affected input has no functional effect on the element if the logic state of any one of the affecting inputs, considered separately, would cause the affected input to have no effect, regardless of the logic states of other affecting inputs.

If an input has several different functional effects or has several different sets of affecting inputs, depending on the mode of action, the input may be shown as often as required. However, there are cases in which this method of presentation is not advantageous. In those cases the input may be shown once with the different sets of labels separated by solidi. See Figure 29. No meaning is attached to the order of these sets of labels. If one of the functional effects of an input is that of an unlabelled input of the element, a solidus will precede the first set of labels shown.

TEXAS INSTRUMENTS

EXPLANATION OF LOGIC SYMBOLS

If all inputs of a combinational element are disabled (caused to have no effect on the function of the element), the internal logic states of the outputs of the element are not specified by the symbol. If all inputs of a sequential element are disabled, the content of this element is not changed and the outputs remain at their existing internal logic states.

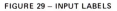

FIGURE 29 – INPUT LABELS

Labels may be factored using algebraic techniques.

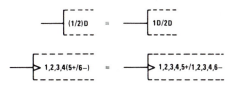

FIGURE 30 – FACTORING INPUT LABELS

10 SEQUENCE OF OUTPUT LABELS

If an output has a number of different labels, regardless of whether they are identifying numbers of affecting inputs or outputs or not, these labels are shown in the following order:

1) if the postponed output symbol has to be shown, this comes first, if necessary preceded by the indications of the inputs to which it must be applied;

2) followed by the labels indicating modifications of the internal logic state of the output, such that the left-to-right order of these labels corresponds with the order in which their effects must be applied;

3) followed by the label indicating the effect of the output on inputs and other outputs of the element.

EXPLANATION OF LOGIC SYMBOLS

Symbols for open-circuit or three-state outputs, where applicable, are placed just inside the outside boundary of the symbol adjacent to the output line. See Figure 31.

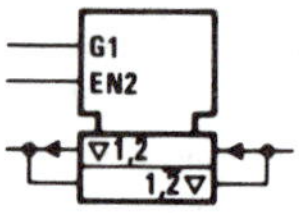

FIGURE 31 – PLACEMENT OF 3-STATE SYMBOLS

If an output needs several different sets of labels that represent alternative functions (e.g., depending on the mode of action), these sets may be shown on different output lines that must be connected outside the outline. However, there are cases in which this method of presentation is not advantageous. In those cases the output may be shown once with the different sets of labels separated by solidi. See Figure 32.

Two adjacent identifying numbers of affecting inputs in a set of labels that are not already separated by a nonnumeric character should be separated by a comma.

If a set of labels of an output not containing a solidus contains the identifying number of an affecting Mm input standing at its internal 0 state, this set of labels has no effect on that output.

Labels may be factored using algebraic techniques.

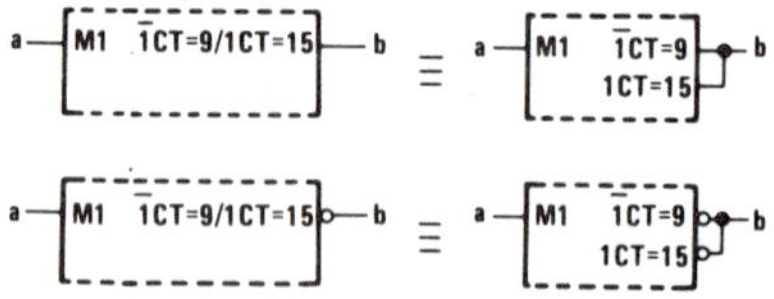

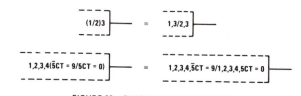

FIGURE 32 – OUTPUT LABELS

FIGURE 33 – FACTORING OUTPUT LABELS

If you have questions on this Explanation of Logic Symbols, please contact:

F.A. Mann MS 49
Texas Instruments Incorporated
P.O. Box 225012
Dallas, Texas 75265
Telephone (214) 995-2867

IEEE Standards may be purchased from:

Institute of Electrical and Electronics Engineers, Inc.
345 East 47th Street
New York, N.Y. 10017

International Electrotechnical Commission (IEC) publications may be purchased from:

American National Standards Institute, Inc.
1430 Broadway
New York, N.Y. 10018

TEXAS INSTRUMENTS

Appendix B

Acronyms and Abbreviations

A	Accumulator (A)
ACIA	Asynchronous Communication Interface Adapter
A/D	Analog to Digital converter
ALU	Arithmetic Logic Unit
ASCII	American Standard Code for Information Interchange
ASIC	Application Specific IC
B	Accumulator B
BCD	Binary Coded Decimal
CAE	Computer Aided Engineering
CCR	Code Condition Register
CD	Compact disk
CPU	Central Processor Unit
D	Double accumulator
D/A	Digital to Analog converter
DDR	Data Direction register (in PIA)
EA	Effective Address
EEPROM	Electrically Erasable PROM
EPROM	Erasable Programmable Read-Only Memory
FSK	Frequency Shift Keying
G	4,294,967,296 (2^{32})
GAL	Generic Array Logic PAL device
IBM	International Business Machines company
IC	Integrated Circuit
ICE	In-Circuit Emulator
ISR	Interrupt Service Routine
JEDEC	Joint Electron Device Engineering Council
K	1024 (2^{10})
LED	Light Emitting Diode
LIFO	Last-In First-Out
LSB	Least Significant Bit

LSI	Large Scale Integration
MCU	MicroController Unit
MDS	Microprocessor Development System
MFLOPS	Million FLoating point Operations Per Second
MIPS	Million Instructions Per Second
M	1,048,576 (2^{20})
MPU	MicroProcessor Unit
MSB	Most Significant Bit
MSD	Most Significant Digit
MCU	MicroComputer Unit
MSI	Medium Scale Integration
NRE	Non-Recurring Expenses
OS	Operating system
OTP	One Time Programmable
PAL	Programmable Array Logic device
PC	Personal Computer
PC	Program counter
PCB	Printed Circuit Board
PCM	Pulse Code Modulation
PIA	Peripheral Interface Adapter
PLA	Programmable Logic Array
PLE	Programmable Logic Element
PROM	Programmable Read-Only Memory
PSK	Phase Shift Keying
PWM	Pulse Width Modulation
SOP	Sum of Product (function)
S/N	Signal to Noise ratio
S	System Stack Pointer
SP	Stack Pointer
SPDT	Single-pole double-throw (switch)
SSI	Small Scale Integration
TTY	TeleTypeWriter
U	User Stack Pointer
UART	Universal Asynchronous Receiver Transmitter
VDU	Visual Display Unit
ULM	Universal Logic Module
VCO	Voltage-Controlled Oscillator
VLSI	Very Large Scale Integration
X	Index register (X)
Y	Y Index register

Index